# The Perfect War

## *Technowar in Vietnam*

by JAMES WILLIAM GIBSON

THE ATLANTIC MONTHLY PRESS

*New York*

*Published simultaneously in Canada*
*Printed in the United States of America*

FIRST PAPERBACK EDITION

For acknowledgments, please see page 524.

Library of Congress Cataloging-in-Publication Data

Gibson, James William.
The perfect war.
Bibliography: p.
Includes index.
I. Vietnamese Conflict, 1961–1975.   I. Title.
DS557.7.G53 1986      959.704'3      86–14144
ISBN 0–87113–799–2 (pbk.)

Atlantic Monthly Press
841 Broadway
New York, NY 10003

00 01 02 03   10 9 8 7 6 5 4 3 2

# Contents

# Tables

# Preface

Have you seen the light? The white light? The great
light? The Guiding Light? Do you have the vision?
—Marine Drill Instructor in Gustov
Hasford's *Short-Timers*

METAPHORS of light and darkness abound in Vietnam War literature. For years American war-managers talked about finding the
"light at the end of the tunnel," a way to victory and an end to the war. The
years of research and writing were my darkness; this book stands as what
light I could generate from the fragmented ruins of American defeat.

Helpful comments on various drafts of the manuscript came from Pro-
fessor Wendell Bell of Yale University, Professor Kurt Wolff of Brandeis,
Professor Jeffrey Alexander of UCLA, Professor Douglas Kellner of the
University of Texas at Austin, and Mr. John Stockwell, formerly with the
CIA and now an author.

Special thanks to Ms. Carol Lynn Mithers for careful editing of early drafts,
substantial help in writing clearly, and great emotional support. Ms. Joyce
Johnson of the Atlantic Monthly Press did an excellent job with the final
manuscript. Ms. Roberta Pryor, my literary representative, served me well.

Ms. Carol Bernstein Ferry and Mr. W. H. Ferry helped me at one point
with a grant. Professor Robert Horwitz of the University of California at
San Diego and Mr. John Earl Frazier also helped me financially at crucial
times. And my parents, Mr. and Mrs. James W. Gibson, gave the most.

Let me end with a word or two on the names of countries. The Ameri-
canized spelling of Viet Nam — Vietnam — is used throughout the book
except when quotations use the original name. Other American names,
such as "North Vietnam" for the People's Democratic Republic of Viet
Nam, and "South Vietnam" for the Republic of Viet Nam, are used interchangeably with the full names. Such usage is not intended to signify
political positions, to affirm or contest the legitimacy of any government.
The political connotations of "North" and "South" are discussed where
appropriate. Finally, all emphases in quotations come from me, not the
original authors.

# Introduction to the 2000 Edition

Iᴺ the fall of 1986, when *The Perfect War* was first published, Ronald Reagan's campaign to overcome the crisis of American defeat in Vietnam was running full blast. From 1981 through 1988 the administration spent over two trillion dollars on the military, an amount equal to that spent from 1946 through 1980 — a thirty-four-year period encompassing both the Korean and Vietnam Wars.[1] Translated into more comprehensible terms, for every $100 spent on machinery, buildings, and other fixed capital in the civilian economy, the United States was spending $87 on the military. The Cold War of the 1980s was sucking up nearly half the nation's new wealth.

White House and CIA officials also resurrected the kinds of covert actions and interventions discredited by the Vietnam War. On October 5, 1986, their extensive clandestine war against the socialist Sandinista government in Nicaragua started to surface and publicly unravel when the Sandinistas successfully shot down a C-123 cargo plane. Eugene Hosenfus, the sole survivor of the crash, told his captors that he thought he was working on a CIA operation, just as he had over a decade before in Laos. After all, he was flying in the very same type of aircraft and was working with many of the same men. Back in Washington, D.C., the White House case officer in charge of the operation, Marine Lt. Col. Oliver North, began shredding documents. North, as his friend (and presidential speech writer) Patrick Buchanan recalled, worried that after yet another U.S. defeat, this time in Central America, "I may one day be leading young Marines into battle at Gila Bend [Arizona]."[2]

However absurd Oliver North's fantasies might appear today, film produceers and mass-market magazine and book publishers created hundreds of war stories during the 1980s. We won them all; the stigma of defeat in Vietnam was vanquished. Never had World War III looked so appealing as in Tom Clancy's bestseller *Red Storm Rising* (1986), an epic of high-tech conventional combat against the Soviet Union. Our ships, planes, and tanks were all the best, our senior commanders sagacious father figures who treated their soldiers as adopted sons.[3] A larger paramilitary movement, though, saw the military as being hopelessly constrained by corrupt and cowardly political elites who were afraid to unleash America's full martial powers and who would thus repeat the failures of Vietnam. Sylvester Stallone's John Rambo character, the former Green Beret, is recruited by the CIA in the 1985 classic *Rambo: First Blood, Part* 2 to conduct a covert reconnaissance mission in Laos in search of American POWs. He asks: "Do we get to win this time?" Only if individuals or small groups of American warriors fought their own private wars outside the establishment could the country's enemies be defeated and America restored to its pre-Vietnam, pre–civil rights, and pre-feminist golden age. (Paramilitary culture became the subject of my second book, *Warrior Dreams: Paramilitary Culture in Post-Vietnam America,* 1994.)

*The Perfect War* thus met a hostile political and cultural environment. Its argument, that the United States could not have defeated Vietnam even by further escalation because of fundamental flaws in its concept of war as a kind of high-technology, capital-intensive production process, challenged Americans' common-sense notions about what counted in the "real" world. The book argued against the conservative thesis that victory was denied the military by what the Joint Chiefs of Staff called "self-imposed restraints" from civilian leaders.

But *The Perfect War* offered liberals no solace either. It rejected their frequently stated thesis that the history of U.S. involvement in Vietnam should be understood primarily as a series of mistakes or errors in judgment by political elites and their high-level advisers. To the contrary, the book argues that both Republican and Democratic leaders of the Vietnam era shared a deeply mechanical worldview. In this bipartisan paradigm of power and knowledge, communism was a monolithic entity, and political power was to be measured in an accountant's ledger where economic wealth and technologically advanced weapons were the only realities that counted. Within this mechanistic conceptual universe, American escalation made perfect sense; whatever political and military victories the Vietnamese Communists achieved could always be reversed at the next level of military escalation. *The Perfect War* argues that American conduct during the Vietnam War should be understood in terms of its fundamental concepts, its structure of operations, and its system for generating reports and knowledge about the war.

Since 1986, some of *The Perfect War*'s breakthrough contributions have made their way into mainstream scholarship and debate. Whereas previously many critics argued that the United States lacked a clear military objective because its forces did not occupy and retain territories after battles, that argument faded away after my book appeared. By its extensive focus on General William Westmoreland's strategy of reaching the "crossover point," defined as when enemy casualties exceeded replacements, *The Perfect War* demonstrated the war managers' logic in not having U.S. soldiers occupy land, but instead moving them relentlessly around the country in helicopter and mechanized search-and-destroy operations in order to kill Vietnamese opponents as quickly as possible. *The Perfect War,* through its extensive use of documents from the often ignored *Pentagon Papers,* also made it clear that Technowar's bombing campaign against North Vietnam — even if radically escalated — could not have stopped the relatively small amounts of supplies (twenty-five tons a day in 1967 — a load readily handled by a few dozen pickup trucks) our enemies needed to support the war in the South.

But in other respects, both the theoretical ideas and historical scholarship in *The Perfect War* have proven to be too hot, too threatening for the contemporary neoliberal-neoconservative academy to handle. For example, although it is now commonly recognized that General Westmoreland and other high-level war managers sought to determine the productivity of search-and-destroy operations through body counts and kill ratios measuring how many Vietnamese were killed for each U.S. casualty, the consequences of this approach for both the Vietnamese and Americans have often been ignored.

"If it's dead and it's Vietnamese, it's VC" was one common saying — also known as the "Mere Gook Rule." Any dead Vietnamese could be added to the body count. The very language of the war managers, the concepts of body counts and kill ratios, helped expand the already considerable social distance between U.S. forces and the Vietnamese, making killing easier. Similarly, the abstract idea that the war could be won by reaching the crossover point made such practices as large-scale bombing and artillery shelling of the countryside acceptable on the grounds that if the population fled the countryside in terror, the Vietcong could not readily replace casualties via recruitment. *The Perfect War* insists that atrocities against Vietnamese routinely resulted from the production logic in which the war was conceptualized and fought. While the 1969 My Lai massacre was a particularly well-organized assault on a village, it was by no means an isolated case.

Nor were the Vietnamese the only casualties of Technowar. In order to kill Vietnamese with their technologically superior air and artillery support, U.S. ground forces had to first find them. In practice this meant that infantry soldiers were often used as "bait," and frequently suffered from ambushes during search-and-destroy operations. After the 1968 Tet Offensive, when it became clear that U.S. strategy had failed and that we would eventually leave Vietnam, American ground forces increasingly found their use as expendable bait — in order to rack up body counts required for their officers' promotions — an unacceptable sacrifice of their lives. Discipline broke down from 1969 through 1971; search-and-avoid began to replace search-and-destroy. Grenade attacks (called "fraggings") and other actions against aggressive officers by their own troops brought the U.S. ground war to a halt. Political and military leaders had no choice but to withdraw an army that would no longer obey orders.

It is a long way from this kind of analysis to the contemporary mainstream debate on the Vietnam War. In 1999, Robert S. McNamara, the former U.S. Secretary of Defense in the Kennedy and Johnson administrations (1961–1968), and several coauthors published *Argument Without End: In Search of Answers to the Vietnam Tragedy*.[4] Funded by the Council on Foreign Relations, McNamara and his associates sponsored six invitation-only conferences on the Vietnam War with Vietnamese political-military leaders from 1995 through 1999. The goal of the conferences, McNamara said to Vietnamese general Vo Nguyen Giap, was to "examine our mind-sets, and to look at specific instances where we — Hanoi and Washington — may have been mistaken, have misunderstood each other."[5] The book features transcriptions of these meetings and commentaries by McNamara and his four coauthors.

McNamara's conceptual limits became clear immediately when he urged conference participants to begin discussion of the war starting in January 1961, when the Kennedy administration came to power. The Vietnamese immediately disagreed, arguing that they fought an anticolonial war against France from 1946 through 1954, signed an agreement in Geneva guaranteeing national elections in two years, and then had to suffer years of violent repression from the Diem regime — financed by the United States — before initiating armed guerrilla resistance in 1960. McNamara's entourage wasn't too interested, noting that the major policymakers from that era were all dead. Retired Foreign Minister Nguyen Co Thach subsequently turned to Vietnamese scholar Luu Doan Huynh and asked, "Excuse me, Huynh, are you dead? You're not dead, are you?" Assured that he was not, Thach continued, "You see, he is not dead. And I am not dead, either. Many of us on this side of the table are not dead. We would be happy to discuss the significance of the Geneva Conference with anyone you send to Hanoi who is not dead."[6]

One U.S. foreign-policy official from that era, Chester L. Cooper, asked, "What was it that made you think in this period [1954–1956] that the United States was your enemy? Was it propaganda from the Soviets and the Chinese?"[7] Cooper insisted on American virtue and innocence, that the United States was not really hostile, and wasn't really seeking to destroy the movement to reunify Vietnam. To which Luu Doan Huynh responded, "But really, your bullets are the killers of our people. We see that this is America's gift to Vietnam — allowing the French to kill our people. This is the most convincing evidence we have of America's loyalties in this affair. So how can we conclude that you are not our enemy?"[8]

Finally, the conference discussion moved into the early 1960s, when McNamara's reign began. McNamara was a graduate of Harvard Business School, and his commentary recalls the importance of Harvard professor Thomas Schelling's 1960 book, *Strategy of Conflict,* to Kennedy administration officials. Using game theory (in which both sides share fundamental assumptions), Schelling stressed the ways in which the threat of force and exercise of force communicated intent. "The objective," McNamara wrote, "is to bend an opponent's will via the threat to continue on up the ladder of escalation."[9]

In the 1960s Cambridge defense intellectuals lamented that Ho Chi Minh had never been offered a fellowship by Harvard, where he could have studied Schelling's conflict theory and Henry Kissinger's theory of limited war! McNamara scoffs at the fantasy and recognizes that Schelling's theory failed utterly when applied to Vietnam. But still, the idea that the Vietnamese simply did not understand American war managers had a deep hold on him and his entourage. Later on McNamara dismissed the covert operations (called 34-A) off the North Vietnamese coast that led to the Gulf of Tonkin incident and the first U.S. air strikes against the North. The Vietnamese overreacted, McNamara said, when a local commander ordered torpedo boats to attack a U.S. destroyer in August 1964: "First, covert operations almost always convey to those on the receiving end more hostile intent or capability than is meant or available. . . . If Hanoi had only known that *we* [italics in original] attributed virtually zero military significance to the 34-A program."[10] Similarly, Col. Herbert Schandler, a military historian and contributor to the book, says that the Vietnamese Communist leaders just did not properly interpret the significance of U.S. search-and-destroy operations, bombardment and chemical defoliation of the countryside, and sustained bombing against the North — which killed 50,000 civilians a year, according to McNamara's own analysis in *The Pentagon Papers*. "We had no burning desire even to harm North Vietnam in any way," the colonel insisted. "We just wanted to demonstrate to you that you could not win militarily in the South."[11]

If only the Vietnamese were like us, the foreign-policy elite sighs. Then they would have understood what good guys we were, how limited were our martial ambitions, the ways in which our military deployments were but signifying messages. The Vietnam War was just a tragic misunderstanding, a series of mistakes and miscommunications. To their credit, the Vietnamese representatives at the conference never once played the game by agreeing to the notion that the war was a tragedy caused by mistakes on both sides. As Tran Quang Co, a former Vietnamese foreign-policy official, concluded at the end of one session, "We understand better now that the U.S. understands very little about Vietnam."[12]

Thus, twenty-five years after the fall or liberation of Saigon, the United States still refuses to recognize its culpability in the destruction of Vietnam and other parts of Southeast Asia, the vast carnage inflicted, and the losses incurred by its own soldiers and their families as well. *The Perfect War* was written to counter the limited liberal-conservative discourse about Vietnam that makes such grand obfuscation possible.

In the absence of a broad, far-ranging national discussion, defeat in Vietnam led to the rebuilding and redeployment of Technowar. The 1991 war against Iraq at first seemed like a complete validation of Technowar — images of advanced technological weapons in action dominated reporting. U.S. television news repeatedly broadcast footage from the Department of Defense taken from video cameras inside the noses of precision-guided bombs — the footage showed each bomb zooming in on an Iraqi bunker and then exploding. Patriot antimissile missiles were reported to have blown apart the dreaded Iraqi Scud missiles in midflight before the Scuds reached their targets. And surely the Iraqi soldiers died by the hundreds of thousands in their bunkers as bombs rained down from B-52 bombings.

But as the years have gone by, the glow of reported victories has tarnished. Subsequent studies found that neither the precision-guided bombs nor the Patriot antimissile missiles worked as first reported by the military and the news media. Most of Saddam Hussein's missile launchers survived repeated air assaults — his decoys worked — while the Scud warheads got through after all. And of course, Saddam Hussein and his regime survived. Technowar did indeed kill Iraqi troops by the thousands, and bombing destroyed the industrial infrastructure of Iraq. But the Iraqi political and military regime remained intact. Since the war, much of the Iraqi population, while remaining critical of Saddam Hussein, has turned against the United States and Western Europe because of material deprivations and an estimated 1.5 million civilian deaths attributed to lack of food and medicine caused by war damage and the postwar embargo. The 1991 war does not qualify as a long-term political victory for the United States.

Two years later, in the summer and fall of 1993, U.S. military forces conducted a more limited incursion in Somalia. U.S. Army Delta Force commandos and other special operations operatives, accompanied by men from a Ranger infantry-assault battalion, conducted a series of raids from helicopters to capture Somalian leaders from the Habr Gidr clan in the nation's capital city, Mogadishu. United States commanders in Somalia wanted to bring these clan leaders to trial for an attack they supposedly ordered against United Nations soldiers involved in peace-keeping and famine relief. From the American perspective, a trial would be part of "nation building" in Somalia.

But as the raids progressed, the military showed thoughtless contempt for the local citizenry, and the people of Mogadishu became alienated. Journalist Mark Bowden described the decline of the popular goodwill that had first accompanied United Nations relief efforts: "They all despised the Rangers, and the Black Hawks [transport helicopters], which seemed now to be over the city continually. They flew in groups, at all hours of the day and night, swooping down so low they destroyed whole neighborhoods, blew down market stalls, and terrorized cattle. Women walking down the streets would have their colorful robes blown off. Some had infants torn from their arms by the powerful updraft. . . . Mogadishu felt brutalized and harassed."[13] To many Somalians, the United States had simply chosen to back one clan and attack another in the country's long civil war.

On October 3 another helicopter assault landed about one hundred Delta commandos and Rangers in the heart of the Habr Gidr clan's district in Mogadishu. The finely choreographed raid soon fell apart. Veterans from the war against the Russians in Afghanistan had taught Somalians how to fight helicopters with rocket-propelled grenades. And while few Mogadishu citizens had extensive training, many had military rifles and grenades, and were willing to die. Thousands upon thousands of men, women, and children poured into the neighborhood to fight. They shot down two Black Hawk transports, crippled two others, and pinned down troops. With no organized relief forces prepared to come to their assistance, the Delta commandos and Rangers lost eighteen killed and dozens of wounded before a United Nations armored column rescued them the next day. Although U.S. helicopter gunships and commandos killed no less than an estimated five hundred Somalians and wounded one thousand others, the Battle of the Black Sea, or what the Somalians call *Ma-alinti Rangers* (The Day of the Rangers), brought U.S. military involvement in that country to an end. Once again, the United States badly underestimated the ability and willingness of a Third World people armed with low-tech weapons to resist intervention and national humiliation.

The air war over Serbia and Kosovo in the spring and summer of 1999 represents the most recent deployment of U.S. high-technology warfare. Serbia's industrial infrastructure was devastated in many places; normal life will not resume there for years, perhaps decades, but the bombing did not politically destabilize the Milosevic regime. Serbian army units in Kosovo also remained functional during the bombardment. Serbian forces executed an estimated 11,000 ethnic Albanians and drove several hundred thousand more into exile while American and NATO jets flew their missions. As was the case with the war against Iraq, the air strikes against Serbian forces and industrial infrastructure did not produce a long-term political victory.

It should be amply clear that Technowar has the capacity to destroy, but it cannot persuade political leaders and entire societies to simply give up and submit to American will. And yet, U.S. political and military leaders remain completely entranced in a mechanistic paradigm: the jets, the helicopters, the advanced command, control, and communication systems with their computers and video screens all appear as absolute realities, as unquestionable indices of American superiority. The idea that political power and national identity involve social and cultural processes not reducible to technology remains unthinkable.

Thus our country enters the millennium still in the grip of this mechanistic logic and technocratic approach to foreign policy. While it is a sad commentary on American politics and intellectual life that the mainstream of scholarship and public commentary on Vietnam remains framed by works such as McNamara's, *The Perfect War* is again ready to take up the challenge.

JWG
Los Angeles
August 1999

## Notes

1. *The Perfect War: Technowar in Vietnam* (1982), p. 452. The original citation says: "Taken from Seymour Melman's address to the Socialist Scholars Conference of April 1–2, 1983, in New York City as reproduced by Alexander Cockburn and James Ridgway, "Annals of the Age of Reagan," *Village Voice,* April 25, 1983, p. 20."

2. James William Gibson, *Warrior Dreams: Paramilitary Culture in Post-Vietnam America* (1994), New York (Hill and Wang, 1994), pp. 283–285.

3. J. William Gibson, "Redeeming Vietnam: Technothriller Novels of the 1980s," *Cultural Critique,* No. 19 (Fall 1988): pp. 179–202.

4. Robert S. McNamara, James Blight, Robert Brigham, Thomas Biersteker, and Colonel Herbert Schandler (U.S. Army, Ret.), *Argument Without End: In Search of Answers to the Vietnam Tragedy* (New York: Public Affairs, 1999).

5. *Ibid.,* p. 23.
6. *Ibid.,* p. 62.
7. *Ibid.,* p. 85.
8. *Ibid.,* p. 87.
9. *Ibid.,* p. 160.
10. *Ibid.,* p. 215.
11. *Ibid.,* p. 191.
12. *Ibid.,* p. 254

13. Mark Bowden, *Black Hawk Down: A Story of Modern War* (New York: Alantic Monthly Press, 1999), p. 75.

# PART I
# In Search of War

## CHAPTER 1

# Trailing the Beast

IN 1973 the Vietnam War moved from front-page news into a rapidly fading historical memory. U.S. troops came home, a peace treaty was signed, American POWs returned, and the war vanished. Two years later network television news showed us the fall of Saigon. Our sensibilities were stunned by incredible pictures of evacuation helicopters being pushed off aircraft carrier flight decks or ordered to crash in the South China Sea because there was no more room for them on American ships. It was as if an imaginary Western had turned into a horror show — the cavalry was shooting its horses after being chased by the Indians back to the fort. President Gerald Ford said that the "book was closed" on American involvement in Indochina.

The nightmare was officially over. But there was no springtime bliss in late April and early May of 1975, no celebration of war's end. Something felt deeply wrong. Something had changed forever.

During the mid- and late 1970s no one wanted to talk about the war. For a while it seemed that Hollywood might come to the rescue, bringing the war to the surface in a way that could conceivably help people understand what had happened. *The Boys in Company C, Coming Home, The Deer Hunter, Go Tell the Spartans,* and *Who'll Stop the Rain?* all appeared in 1977–1978; *Apocalypse Now* came the next year. After the apocalypse, the Hollywood war ended, too. Sometimes veterans made the evening news broadcasts or were characters in television dramas. Either in real life or as fictional characters, they were presented as freaked-out men who replayed Vietnam by committing violence against others or themselves. Veterans were time bombs waiting to go off, a new genre of bogeymen.

Somehow, though, even in news reports about Vietnam veterans, the war itself was never revisited. Debates around the dioxin Agent Orange and post-Vietnam stress-disorder cases made their official appearances in claims for medical benefits or for special consideration in legal contexts. The war thus disappeared as a topic for study and political consideration and instead became dispersed and institutionalized in the complex of medical, psychiatric, and legal discourses. It was as if a new series of medical and judicial problems with no traceable origin had appeared in American society. Or rather, although it was acknowledged that Vietnam was the origin, once the word "Vietnam" was mentioned, the war itself was dismissed and discussion moved on to how an institution could solve the problem.

A similar displacement occurred in the reception of books by Vietnam veterans and journalists. Literally hundreds of memoirs, commentaries, and novels were published from the mid-1960s through the 1970s, but most fell into an abyss of silence: few or no reviews, limited distribution and sales, a quick passage to the discounted "remainder" category. Only a handful of Vietnam authors achieved some fame — Gloria Emerson for *Winners and Losers,* Tim O'Brien for *Going After Cacciato,* Frances FitzGerald for *Fire in the Lake,* and Michael Herr for *Dispatches.* The *New York Times* review of *Dispatches* read in part (my emphases): *"If you think you don't want to read any more about Vietnam,* you are wrong. *Dispatches* is beyond politics, beyond rhetoric. . . . It is as if Dante had gone to hell with a cassette recording of Jimi Hendrix and a pocketful of pills: our *first* rock-and-roll war. Stunning."[1]

According to the reviewer, *Dispatches* was a book about Vietnam that one could read without thinking about Vietnam — the book for someone who doesn't "want to read any more about Vietnam." A new *Inferno?* Forget that Jimi Hendrix was a Vietnam veteran of the 101st Airborne Division. Forget that the pocketful of uppers and downers (amphetamines and barbiturates) belonged to a man on long-range reconnaissance patrol duty who used them to see the jungle at night. Our *"first* rock-and-roll war,*"* the reviewer said. It sounded as if he was expecting a series and *Dispatches* was the best way for the spectators to get ready for the show.

O'Brien's work met a similar response. A quote from a review in the *Philadelphia Inquirer* found its way to the back cover of the paperback version: "Every war has its chroniclers of fear and flight, its Stephen Cranes and Joseph Hellers. Tim O'Brien joins their number." Or read the *New York Times Book Review:* "To call *Going After Cacciato* a novel about war is like calling *Moby Dick* a novel about whales."[2] Take your pick; either way the reviews see the work as literature and view a work of literature as a text without reference to anything other than literature. Somehow O'Brien's story about a soldier who leaves his unit and walks from Vietnam to Paris to attend the peace negotiations does not register in the reviewer's mind as a commentary on the war.

It is not easy to displace war in films about war; it is not easy to avoid war in all news media coverage of Vietnam veterans and their problems; it is not easy for a culture to avoid a very specific war even though book after book is written about it. Nevertheless, the more that was said and written and filmed, the more distant the war itself became.

During the 1970s various liberal interpretations of what happened in Vietnam were considered definitive. Some claimed the great lesson to be learned concerned "the limits of power." The United States had expended too many men and too much money fighting in a country that wasn't so important after all. Other liberals viewed the war as a tragic drama fueled by hubris. Our political leadership, the best and brightest of the land, made a series of "small decisions," each decision being "reasonably regarded at the time as the last that would be necessary." But Fate intervened and lo and behold we found ourselves "entrapped in that nightmare of American strategists, a land war in Asia." It was a sad, sad story, says Arthur M. Schlesinger, Jr., a "tragedy without villains." [3]

Curiously enough, the views of the conservatives were not so different. They offered another way of "getting over Vietnam" without ever searching for the war. In November 1980, President-elect Ronald Reagan declared that Vietnam had been a "noble cause." The war had been lost only because of American "self-imposed restraints." We had not been sufficiently "tough," but no longer would we be weak or timid. Reagan promised to "rebuild" our "defense" capabilities. He announced a new plan for spending $750 billion for the military. A new Rapid Deployment Force was created for quick transport to the Third World. We were ready to go to war again. For months the news media talked and wrote about how the United States had finally gotten over the "Vietnam Syndrome." [4] Never was the question raised about just what it was we were over. The Vietnam part of the "Vietnam Syndrome" was left blank. Perhaps the war was just a normal part of growing up for a young nation, a childhood disease like chicken pox, which leaves behind some small scars but builds character.

In this way a strange consensus developed: it was okay to use the war

as a point of departure for almost any discussion — whether on literature or Greek tragedy or foreign policy — but only as long as you didn't
talk about the war itself. In this way the Vietnam War was abolished
during the 1970s and early 1980s. In this way the war became progressively displaced and repressed at the same time it was written about.

Then during 1983–1984 the Vietnam War became a major cultural
topic. It was as if a legendary monster or unholy beast had finally been
captured and was now on a nationwide tour. The tour began in November 1982, with the dedication and opening of the Vietnam veterans memorial in Washington, D.C. In February 1983 the University of Southern
California sponsored "Vietnam Reconsidered: Lessons From a War,"
the first major academic conference on Vietnam.[5] That fall PBS affili-
ates around the country showed a thirteen-episode series, *Vietnam: A
Television History*. Chain bookstores used the series as a lead-in for
thematic displays offering a new round of war novels, memoirs, and
histories. The *New York Times* signed on with two major cover stories:
the Sunday magazine featured a lengthy story on college courses about
Vietnam and the Sunday book review had a long essay comparing Vietnam War novels to previous war literature.[6] Important court trials made
the news for months. Vietnam veterans filed a class-action suit against
several chemical firms that manufactured the herbicide Agent Orange.
General William Westmoreland sued CBS for libeling him in its 1982
documentary "The Uncounted Enemy: A Vietnam Deception."[7] And
finally a special service was held on Memorial Day 1984, when the
"unidentified" remains of an American soldier killed in Vietnam were
put into the Tomb of the Unknown Soldier at Arlington National Cem-
etery.

All through this period, questions of responsibility for American involvement were assiduously avoided. Although the PBS series had some
excellent footage, it echoed every lie told by administration officials of
the Eisenhower, Kennedy, Johnson, Nixon, and Ford governments. The
series showed Vietnam as a war of good men with honorable intentions
fighting another set of good men with honorable intentions. Thirty years
of warfare appeared as a mythic tragedy dictated by the gods, with the
U.S. government merely a passive partner.[8] Stanley Karnow, a senior
producer of the PBS series, released a companion volume, *Vietnam: A
History* at the same time. Although Karnow had subtitled his book "The
First Complete Account of Vietnam at War," he evidently didn't think
responsibility and causality were important questions: "In human terms

at least, the war in Vietnam was a war nobody won — a struggle between victims. Its origins were complex, its lessons learned, its legacy
to be assessed by future generations. But whether a valid venture or
misguided endeavor, it was a tragedy of epic dimensions." [9]

Myra MacPherson, author of *Long Time Passing: Vietnam and the
Haunted Generation,* published in the spring of 1984, sought "neither
to prove the rightness or wrongness of the war nor to refight old ideological battles but to illuminate the effect of the war as it was on the
generation asked to fight it." [10] How these effects were to be determined
without investigating what the structure of warfare was, who was responsible for that structure, and what American political objectives were
is truly mysterious.

The *New York Times* daily reviewer, Michiko Kakutani, chastised
novels by Vietnam veterans for paying too close attention to warfare
and not enough attention to the problems of literature: "A flaw shared
by many Vietnam novels, in fact, is that they do not become works of
the imagination; rather they retain the predictable shape and close-up,
grainy texture of personal history. . . . This need to testify to what one
has witnessed and somehow to make sense of it through words, however, would have often been better served by a memoir." In her view,
memoir is obviously suitable for personal catharsis, but not much else.
In any case neither memoir nor realist fictional narrative can help us
understand an event beyond rational understanding: "At the same time,
the Vietnam war — which so defies reason and the rules of causality —
also resists such traditional prerogatives of fiction as interpretation." [11]
If the war is beyond rational understanding, then it becomes the occasion for pure literature, texts with referents only in the literary canon,
not the real world of power struggles.

Even Vietnam-related "events" have studiously avoided the war.
Westmoreland dropped his libel charges against CBS before the case
went to the jury. Some of his former aides and other military men had
testified against him with compelling accounts of official deception. But
instead of letting the jury vindicate them, CBS issued a statement testifying to Westmoreland's honor. Thus nothing was really resolved.

Similarly, lawyers for the Vietnam veterans accepted a $180 million
settlement for health damages the day before the trial was to begin. This
out-of-court settlement of the veterans' case against the chemical companies who made Agent Orange meant that the companies successfully
avoided a lengthy public investigation of what they knew about dioxin

contamination and what the government knew. Many veterans were against the settlement for that reason; they suspected the military and chemical manufacturers knew the potential dangers of exposure to dioxins.

Even the memorial ceremony at the Tomb of the Unknown Soldier backed away from the war. Read carefully the *New York Times* account of the ceremonies held for the entombment of the body:

> The Pentagon, which waived its informal rule that 80 percent of a body must be recovered for it to be designated an Unknown, has now *intentionally destroyed all identification records related to the Unknown* to prevent inadvertent disclosure of information that might provide clues to the identity of the man intended to be a universal symbol of Vietnam battle dead.[12]

In other words, the Pentagon had remains that might someday have been identifiable. The military destroyed this man's records in order to stage a symbolic patriotic ritual and thus gain support for future battles. At the same time, the Pentagon did not allow Vietnam veterans to march in the funeral procession. These men did not fit into the choreographed spectacle. They were not dressed in regulation military uniforms, but instead wore "combat fatigues and jeans," topped by the "floppy bush caps they wore in Vietnam's steamy jungles." Three hundred veterans marched anyway.

For the most part, the 1985 media retrospectives on Vietnam followed the patterns formed earlier. Newsmagazines and television vacillated between the liberal Vietnam-as-mistake position and the conservative criticism of self-imposed restraints. Hollywood in particular embraced the latter position with a series of films in which Vietnam veteran characters become warriors again and defeat demonic enemies by disregarding restraints imposed upon them by commanding officers and politicians. The resurgence of Vietnam in the news, in literature and history, and in film was a continuation of the old effort to push the real war with all its political implications farther and farther away. The power structure is obviously deeply afraid of what might happen if the war was really explored.

It was the longest war in American history. It was the longest counting from 1945, when the United States equipped a British expeditionary force to occupy Vietnam before France could send troops to secure its colony. It was the longest counting from 1950, when the United States began paying 80 percent of France's cost in its war against Vietnamese insurgents, the Vietminh. It was the longest counting from 1960, when President Kennedy began increasing U.S. military advisers from several hundred to several thousand. And it was the longest war counting from 1965, when the first American ground combat divisions together with their support units began arriving.

Talking about Vietnam as a "limited war" is misleading. At its peak in 1969, over 550,000 soldiers were stationed in Vietnam. This count excludes thousands of air force personnel in Thailand and thousands of other air force people in Manila and Guam supporting bomber missions. Indeed, the 550,000 count excludes all those people involved in logistical efforts outside Vietnam. An inclusive figure would easily add another 100,000 to 200,000 troops. Viewed as a percentage of total American combat capability, the Vietnam War at its peak involved 40 percent of all United States Army combat-ready divisions, more than half of all Marine Corps divisions, one-third of U.S. naval forces, roughly half the fighter-bombers, and between one-quarter and one-half of all B-52 bombers in the U.S. Air Force Strategic Air Command.

In 1984 American casualty figures hovered around 58,800. (The exact number changes from year to year as some of the 800 soldiers listed as missing in action are reclassified as dead.) Over 300,000 men were wounded; of these, some 150,000 required hospitalization. How many Vietnam veterans have later died from medical conditions connected to the war is not known, but surely the number must be in the thousands.

Americans are not the only ones who died. The South Korean government lost 4,407 soldiers. Australia and New Zealand lost 469, and Thailand suffered 351 dead.[13] Counting casualties among Vietnamese, Laotians, and Cambodians becomes more difficult. The United States government counts South Vietnamese military casualties beginning in 1965 and ends in 1974. For this period it announces a figure of 220,357. Such a precise number seems solid, but it isn't; 1965 marks only the introduction of American combat forces in large numbers, not the beginning of the war. The United States established the Diem regime in 1954 and completely financed its civil and military activities throughout the 1950s and early 1960s. Surely those who died in those years should be counted. Saigon "fell" in 1975. The casualties of that debacle should also be counted.

In Laos it is even harder to count. It was public knowledge that the United States was fighting a war in Vietnam. But despite the few news reports that surfaced from time to time, it never seemed to sink home that a major war was also being fought in Laos. This war was organized

and directed by the Central Intelligence Agency, using tribespeople living in the Laotian mountains. A large number of those people died.
Their deaths should be added, too, but there is no official tabulation
since the war in Laos did not officially exist.

Making a count in Cambodia (now named Kampuchea) presents a
similar problem. For a long time Cambodia managed to stay out of the
Indochina war. However, the United States did not like the "extreme
neutralism" practiced by its ruler, Prince Norodom Sihanouk. Sihanouk
had not approved of North Vietnamese and Vietcong use of Cambodia
as a staging area, but he wanted to avoid open warfare. In 1970 the
United States supported his overthrow. War subsequently came; the
Cambodian army fought and suffered casualties. American fighter-bombers
and B-52s dropped hundreds of thousands of tons of bombs. Much
bombing went unobserved; no one even bothered to watch where the
bombs fell. Cambodia's dead were never counted.

Trying to count "enemy" dead and civilian casualties is even harder.
The official American military statistics for the 1965–1974 period claim
950,765 Vietcong and North Vietnamese regulars killed.[14] Other government estimates say this figure is inflated by one-third. Even disregarding the time frame for counting, these figures are questionable.
Artillery barrages and air strikes were often conducted virtually at random. There is no way of really knowing how many people were killed.
The roll call of the dead, the wounded, refugees, and all those driven
insane by decades of war will never be completed.

If nothing definitive can really be said about the massive destruction,
if one cannot readily find the basic parameters of a war, then how can
one talk about it? Perhaps Vietnam really was a "tragedy without villains," an unfortunate compendium of "small decisions" that just turned
out very badly. The United States should be more alert next time it
becomes militarily involved. There are limits to the power of even the
most powerful country. Or perhaps, as the conservatives say, the United
States should learn to hit harder, faster. Do away with all "self-imposed
restraints," no more fighting with one hand tied behind our back. Avoid
the folly of political negotiations.

Perhaps it is also true that Vietnam veterans suffer only from problems of adjustment to civilian life. Their problems can be explained by
the various intellectual disciplines of adjustment — psychiatry, psychology, social welfare, the law. Here as well, the objective is to adjust to
the present; it is useless to dwell in the past because nothing can really
be learned there. The search for war ends at its beginnings. It finds

nothing. The conventional paths are all small circles. There is no exit from the tunnel. There is only darkness, no light at all.

If you are setting up an ambush, you must first pick a place where men are likely to walk. A well-trodden path is an excellent choice since most Americans are averse to slower, more difficult movement in a dimly lit jungle. Having selected a frequently used trail, you then position your mines and grenades and automatic weapons to achieve overlapping or intersecting "fields of fire." The area where the fields of fire are the most dense is known as the "killing zone."

Search-and-destroy sent many Americans down the trail to the killing zone. Over 80 percent of the firefights were initiated by the enemy.[15] Although high command eventually came to know this, military practice never changed. The old trails continued to be used. "There it is," as the grunts used to say.

Similarly, conventional paths in search of war lead only to destruction of serious intellectual inquiry. War as mistake, war as failure of nerve, war as collection of dates and statistics that are somehow supposed to make it rational and compact enough to readily talk about — none of these definitions can account for the paradox of the ambush that is known lurking, but rarely avoided.

It must be recognized that knowledge neither falls from heaven nor grows on trees, but is instead created in specific social contexts involving political and economic power. Politically and economically powerful people make decisions on the basis of studies produced by professional economists, systems analysts, and political scientists, and they utilize more informal kinds of knowledge, such as the reports created by bureaucracies. It is best, then, not to think of a political and economic power structure making decisions about Vietnam and intellectual knowledge about the war as two separate categories, but instead to approach the search for war in terms of how power and knowledge operate together at a deep structural level of logic. As the French philosopher and historian Michel Foucault indicated, the study of modern societies is best approached as a study of "regimes" of power and knowledge, since the two can no longer be thought separate.[16]

In thinking about Vietnam, two specific relationships must be considered immediately. First, the United States *lost*. The tendency to displace Vietnam into political or literary contexts that never really confront the war represents a flight from recognizing the final outcome. American defeat seems "unreal" to Americans; thus the war itself becomes "unreal." Since previous knowledge about Vietnam provided neither the conceptual frameworks nor the information necessary to comprehend the defeat of the power structure, the war has remained invisible. Displacement hides intellectual bankruptcy. Displacement hides the political and military failure of the power structure.

Second, much primary knowledge about the war was produced by military and other governmental bureaucracies. Bureaucracies produce knowledge for utilization by bureaucracies. Military bureaucracies have no interest, for example, in estimating civilian casualties caused by bombing and air strikes. Civilian casualties detract from their efficiency as military units, and military units are rewarded for efficiency. High civilian casualties also make the actions of military commanders *illegitimate* to the public. There are many other absences of knowledge. Some are simply blank spaces; others indicate places where knowledge about the war was discounted and ignored for various reasons. Such absences constitute problems only if one takes current structures of power and knowledge to be sacrosanct, as having a monopoly on defining reality. Ultimately, though, questioning the definition of reality provided by the United States leads the way out of the tunnel.

The search for war begins in this country, at a time when defeat anywhere appeared *unthinkable* — the end of World War II. The United States emerged from that war as the only true victor, by far the greatest power in world history. Although the other Allies also won, their victories were much different. Great Britain's industrial strength was damaged and its empire was in disarray. France had been defeated and occupied by Nazi Germany. Much French industry had either been bombed by Britain and the United States or looted by Germany. The Soviet Union "won," but over twenty million of its people were killed and millions more wounded. Many of its cities and large areas of countryside were nothing but ruins. China "won," but despite American funding, the warlord Chiang Kai-shek and his subordinate warlords lost to the peasant Communist revolution led by Mao Tse-tung. Even before Chiang Kai-shek's defeat, post–World War II China was largely a wasteland, suffering from famine and civil war. In other words, the United States won World War II and everyone else lost.

It is important to comprehend the changes that occurred *within* the United States that made its success overseas possible. Before World War II, both the world economy and the American economy had been in severe crisis. Unemployment was extremely high. Many factories and other businesses closed; those that remained open had underutilized production capabilities. Compared to 1986, the economy was decentralized. Even as late as 1940, some 175,000 companies produced 70 percent of all manufactured goods, while the hundred largest companies produced 30 percent.

Relationships between the economy and the state changed during the Depression. The United States had long practiced "free-market" capitalism. Franklin Roosevelt and the Democratic-controlled Congress attempted to regulate capitalism in their "New Deal" program. Some endeavors, such as the minimum wage, Social Security, and laws making it easier for labor unions to organize, had impact and became enduring features of advanced capitalism. Federal efforts to organize the economy, however, did not succeed. The Supreme Court declared the National Recovery Act to be unconstitutional; the Court in effect ruled that state powers to regulate and organize the economy were limited. In any case, the New Deal did not succeed in its economic revitalization program. Unemployment levels in 1940 were close to what they had been in 1932, when Roosevelt was first elected.

Then came Pearl Harbor and the Second World War. Phenomenal changes occurred within a few short years. By 1944, the hundred largest manufacturing firms produced 70 percent of the nation's manufactured goods, while all the rest produced only 30 percent.[17] Economic mobilization for war necessitated radical state intervention in the economy. State war-managers favored awarding huge contracts to the largest industrial firms. These administrators thought that only the largest firms had truly "scientific" production lines and that only the largest firms had managerial expertise to produce huge quantities of goods. By the end of the war leading manufacturers had received billions of dollars from the state. Contracts were awarded on a "cost-plus" basis, meaning that the state financed machinery and other production facilities, as well as the costs of labor, and beyond that guaranteed specific profit rates. The federal government thus violated the customary operations of the "free market" and created a state-organized and -financed, highly centralized form of capitalism in which a few firms dominated the economy. The gross national product increased from $91 billion in 1939 to $166 billion in 1945. Such tremendous economic expansion was unprecedented in world history.

Science had always been involved in the production process; you can't produce steel without detailed knowledge of physics, chemistry, metallurgy, and so forth. But in some ways, during the prewar period, science was not fully integrated into the economy. During World War II, however, thousands of scientists were hired by the government and large corporations. As Gerald Piel, a former editor of *Scientific American,* says, "The universities transformed themselves into vast weapons laboratories. Theoretical physicists became engineers, and engineers forced solutions at the frontiers of knowledge." [18] Science was enlisted in the economic production process and military destruction process to an unprecedented degree.

So-called managerial science also was incorporated into the war effort. The original master of "scientific management," Frederick Taylor, had won many adherents among businessmen in the 1920s and 1930s, especially among larger industrial firms confronted by massive unionization. For workers, scientific management meant progressive dissolution of their control over work processes. [19] By the 1940s, management had become a more esoteric discipline. For example, during World War II, Professor Robert McNamara of the Harvard University Business School developed statistical techniques of systems analysis for the War Department as management tools in controlling large organizations. McNamara became famous for organizing flight patterns of bombers and fighters in the air war against Germany. After the war, in the 1950s, he served as general manager and vice president of Ford Motor Company. In 1960, President Kennedy chose him as secretary of defense. Advanced "scientific" methods thus took root in both government and business.

This radical shift from a capitalist economy organized around small to medium-sized firms to an advanced capitalist economy organized around relatively few firms with high-technology production thus occurred through federal government intervention and was directed toward war production. Politics, economics, and science were now united in a new way. Just as the state changed capitalism and changed the practice of science, so too did the now vastly expanded economy and scientific apparatus change the nature and practice of politics, particularly the conduct of foreign policy. As the possessor of an advanced technological system of war production, the United States began to view political relationships with other countries in terms of concepts that have their origin in physical science, economics, and management. A deeply mechanistic world view emerged among the political and economic elite and their intellectual advisers.

The writings of Dr. Henry Kissinger provide a good introduction to modern power and knowledge relationships as they shaped American

foreign policy in the post–World War II era. Kissinger was national
security adviser to President Richard Nixon from 1969 through 1972
and was later secretary of state under Nixon and then Gerald Ford from
1973 through 1976. Before his ascension to formal political power, he
was an important adviser to Nelson Rockefeller and a key intellectual
in the foreign-policy establishment. His books and essays were held in
great esteem.

Kissinger writes that since 1945, American foreign policy has been
based "on the assumption that *technology plus managerial skills* gave
us the ability to reshape the international system and to bring domestic
transformations in 'emerging countries.' "[20] He indicates that there are
virtually no limits to this technical intervention in the world: "A scientific revolution has, for all practical purposes, removed technical limits
from the exercise of power in foreign policy."[21] Power thus becomes
measured solely in technical terms: political power becomes physically
embedded in the United States' large, efficient economy, its war production system capable of creating advanced war machines, and its
economic-managerial science for administering these production systems. By this standard the United States has virtually unlimited power
to control the world.

Moreover, since these physical means of power were created in large
part through science, the United States also maintains a highly privileged position of *knowledge*. The United States knows more about
"reality" itself, reality being defined in terms of physical science. Power
and knowledge thus go together. Knowing "reality" is also "hard work."
The West, in Kissinger's view, had been committed to this hard epistemological work since Sir Isaac Newton first formulated his laws of
physics. Although Kissinger never speaks of "virtues" in connection
with the hard work of the West, such connotations are implicit in his
writings — Max Weber's *Protestant Ethic and the Spirit of Capitalism*
is tacitly enlisted in his program.[22] Power, knowledge, and virtue all
accrue to the United States. Its foreign-policy endeavors are thus blessed.
From this perspective Kissinger discusses the differences between the
Third World and the West. Ultimately, he claims that the West knows
reality and the underdeveloped countries live only in their own delusions:

> As for the difference in philosophical perspective, it may reflect the
> divergence of the two lines of thought which since the Renaissance
> have distinguished the West from the part of the world now called

underdeveloped (with Russia occupying an intermediate position). The West is deeply committed to the notion that the real world is external to the observer, that knowledge consists of recording and classifying data — the more accurately the better. Cultures which have escaped the early impact of Newtonian thinking have retained the essentially pre-Newtonian view that the real world is almost entirely internal to the observer.

Although this attitude was a liability for centuries — because it prevented the development of the technology and consumer goods which the West enjoyed — it offers great flexibility with respect to the contemporary revolutionary turmoil. It enables the societies which do not share our cultural mode to alter reality by influencing the perspective of the observer — a process which we are largely unprepared to handle or even perceive. And this can be accomplished under contemporary conditions without sacrificing technological progress. Technology comes as a gift; acquiring it in its advanced form does not presuppose the philosophical commitment that discovering it imposed on the West. Empirical reality has a much different significance for many of the new countries because in a certain sense they never went through the process of discovering it (with Russia again occupying an intermediate position).[23]

By this theory, American intervention in the Third World not only brings technology and consumer goods into play but also brings *reality* to the Third World. In claiming the West's radical monopoly on knowing reality, the Third World becomes *unreal*. Those who live there and have retained "the essentially pre-Newtonian view that the real world is almost entirely internal to the observer" are therefore totally unlike the West and its leading country. Those who are totally unlike us and live in their own delusions are conceptualized as foreign Others. The foreign Other can be known only within the conceptual framework of technological development and production systems. For instance, the Other may have bicycles. Bicycles can be readily comprehended by the West as a form of "underdeveloped" transportation, as opposed to the trucks and automobiles found in the "developed" West. Bicycles are "less" than cars by definition. In this sense the Other can be known. Insofar as he is like us he is far down on the scale of power and knowledge; insofar as he is not like us, he remains the foreign Other living his self-delusions in an unreal land.

Who defeated the most powerful nation in world history? Who defeated several hundred thousand troops equipped with the most advanced weaponry that the most technologically sophisticated nation had to offer? Who defeated a war budget more than one trillion dollars? For the most part, peasants of underdeveloped agricultural economies defeated the United States. The insurgents of what was called "South Vietnam" were peasants. What was called "North Vietnam" was also a relatively primitive, agricultural economy with little industrial base.

How could a nation of peasants with bicycles defeat the United States? By Kissinger's theory such a defeat is *unthinkable*. Kissinger's claim to a monopoly of true knowledge for the West turns into its opposite. Classifying nations and peoples purely on the basis of their possession, or lack, of technologically advanced production and warfare systems leads only to radical reduction of what can be considered as valid knowledge about the world. This regime of power and knowledge thus creates a world that is "almost entirely internal to the observer." Kissinger writes that "the West is deeply committed to the notion that the real world is external to the observer, that knowledge consists of recording and classifying data — the more accurately the better." He calls this the "Newtonian" view of the world, after the eighteenth-century theoretical physicist Sir Isaac Newton.

However, Newtonian mechanics is a theory about nature. It says nothing about society, about human social relationships. Newtonian mechanics says nothing about societies where millions of peasants are dominated by a few hundred landlords; it says nothing about countries where the population may be yellow or brown or black in skin color, but their rulers have white skins and come from distant lands. It says nothing about social conflict, about social relationships of domination and subordination; and in particular, Newtonian mechanics says nothing about social revolution.

Instead, the deeply mechanistic view of the world can see bicycles of the Third World only as compared to the cars of the West. Bicycles cannot "beat" cars and trucks and planes and railroads. But in 1954, the Vietnamese beat the French in a battle at Dien Bien Phu. Thousands of peasants cut trails through jungles and across mountains; thousands more dug tunnels close to French fortifications; thousands more walked alongside bicycles loaded with supplies for the Vietminh army. Social relationships between the Vietminh soldiers and the peasantry were such that thousands of peasants could be mobilized for the war effort. Social relationships that are rendered invisible by the modern regime of power and knowledge can defeat a system of power that conceives the world only in terms of technological-production systems. At the time, the French were amazed at their loss. The Americans were similarly amazed years later. They did not learn from the French because they thought that the French simply did not have enough tools of war; the United States had many more.

What is at issue concerns conceptually mapping "nature" onto society, of rendering the social world invisible. This false scientific project has historical precedent in the theory of capitalism, the famous nature-like "laws of supply and demand" that govern the market. Adam Smith, eighteenth-century author of *The Wealth of Nations,* is usually awarded credit for positing capitalism as economic nature, the true discovery of the actual order of things, the social organization that imitates nature best. Viewing capitalism as nature, this theory of immutable laws of supply and demand, was later criticized by Karl Marx.

Marx contended that the production process constituted a social relationship between those who owned the means of production (the capitalist) and those who were employed by capitalists as laborers (the working class). The working class collectively produced all wealth, but received only a fraction back as wages; the rest went to the capitalists. Capitalism was based on a specific kind of class domination, not a "natural" order. However, structural relationships of class domination are rendered invisible by the phenomenal form of capitalist production, the commodity. Everything *appears* as a commodity to be bought and sold, even the workers. A loaf of bread appears as an object to be eaten, which is sold in a store for a price. No relationships of class structure are written on the package cover. "The commodity is a mysterious thing," wrote Marx. "In it definite social relationships among men assume the fantastic form of relationships among things." Marx called this project of mapping nature onto society "commodity fetishism."[24]

Ironically, Marx thought that the phenomenal force of commodity fetishism would be attenuated when *science* became a *"direct force of production,* integral to the operation of all basic industry."[25] Science to Marx represented the collective knowledge of society. Although individual bits of knowledge could be privately owned — as in patents — basic scientific advancement resulted from social "poolings" of thousands of individual efforts to know the world. Thus, when science became a "direct force of production, integral to the operation of all basic industry," the relationship of knowledge to the production process would make the social character of production more evident.

Men and women would more readily see that since knowledge was a collective product of the human species, then the goods produced by privately owned industry (using scientific knowledge in the production process) rightfully belonged to society as a whole, not only to the capitalist class. People would see both the moral right and logical necessity for collective ownership and control of the society. Because people would be organizing economic activity together, the goods produced would not appear as independent entities obeying naturelike laws of supply and demand. Collective social organization and decision-making about social development and resource allocation replaces the market. No longer do "definite social relationships among men assume the fantastic form of relationships among things." With the transition to socialism, commodity fetishism and other forms of falsely mapping a model of nature onto society would end. Scientific rationalization of capitalist production was thus a crucial stage in Marx's theory of the transition from capitalism toward socialism.

This prediction for radical social change in advanced capitalist countries did not come true. Instead, a new kind of fetishism came into existence in the post–World War II period. The scientific rationalization and expansion of the production process occurred during wartime; it was directed by the state toward the *production of war*. The largest industrial firms became quantum levels larger, and their owners and top executives entered into new relationships with the government. Privately owned production facilities still dominated the economy, but these firms were state financed to a considerable degree and their products were used by the state to wage war and conduct foreign policy. C. Wright Mills called this new social organization rule by "the power elite." [26] Seymour Melman has used the term "the permanent war-economy." [27] Both men have written works of great merit, but neither fully conveys the transformations of power and knowledge that mark American foreign policy since World War II.

Whereas Marx saw the locus of fetishism and naturalization as structurally situated in the system of commodity production, this new fetishism involved rationalized capitalist production as it was organized for war production. Political and social power became conceptualized and practiced solely in terms of how high societies ranked in their ability to produce high-technology warfare. To those in command of the system, the world's international political and economic relationships appeared as a series of technical or physical problems to be solved by the correct, scientifically determined administration of force: how much war production or threat of war production was necessary to achieve American policy objectives in other nations.

This new fetishism is thus a kind of social physics, a metaphorical transposition of Sir Isaac Newton's world of physical forces and mechanical interactions onto the social world. War-production systems become the units of this social physics. To appropriate Marx's phrasing, in this new fetishism definite social relationships among men assume the fantastic form of relationships among high-technology production systems for producing warfare. And when relationships appear as warfare systems, then social relationships disappear from view just as they do with the system of simple commodity production. For example, how can complex social revolutions be understood by war-managers, when for them the highest form of political power is an atomic bomb that could literally vaporize the revolution? At best, war-managers can only translate social revolution into their own fetishized, technical categories of control and production. How many weapons does the revolution have? What is its structure of command, control, and communication? How do enemy war-managers instrumentally manipulate their people? In this way, Kissinger's claim that the West in general and the United States in particular have an epistemological monopoly on "the notion that the real world is external to the observer" turns back on itself. The question must be asked, who is the foreign Other for whom "the real world is almost entirely internal to the observer"?

The Other is the man mesmerized by his own system of production, his own system for the production of destruction, his own "technology plus managerial skills," which creates the possibility of bringing "domestic transformations in 'emerging countries.' " The Other is the man who writes, "A scientific revolution has, for all practical purposes, removed technical limits from the exercise of power in foreign policy." The history of modern foreign policy is the history of this power and knowledge regime. It is the history of a system totally enclosed upon itself, the history of a regime whose basic assumptions of knowledge are never questioned by those in power. At the same time, these men legitimate their decisions and subsequent actions in terms of a radical monopoly of knowledge: they have a scientific right to intervene in the Third World.

Kissinger is but one man. He has been cited both because of his position and fame and because his writings are so clearly concerned with the questions at hand. Still, he is not solely responsible for the modern regime of power and knowledge. To the contrary, the basic assumptions about power and knowledge articulated by Kissinger were shared by thousands of academics and policymakers. Much of the literature on international relations and development or "modernization" of the Third World shares these same mechanistic assumptions. Fetishism is not an individual problem; it is a characteristic of particular social structures and how those social structures are conceived by members of the society.

In the 1950s, there was one contradiction in the regime of power and knowledge that worried political elites and defense intellectuals. The problem had to do with using the atomic bomb, especially the difficult situation created when both the United States and the Soviet Union had the bomb. Using the atomic bomb became more dangerous to the United States, because the Soviet Union could retaliate in kind. In this event, the vast systems of production on both sides would be destroyed. During the 1950s, this projected scenario was called mutually assured destruction. The scenario placed limits on American ability to intervene militarily in the world. Much effort was expended in attempting to solve this contradiction of virtually limitless technical power that now seemed highly limited.

The most renowned scholar who helped solve this problem was, again, Dr. Henry Kissinger. His book on the subject was entitled *Nuclear Weapons and Foreign Policy* (1957). Kissinger was opposed to all-out nuclear war because such war destroyed the American advantage: "We have seen . . . that the power of modern weapons reduces the importance of our industrial potential in an all-out war because each side can destroy the industrial plant of its opponent with its forces-in-being at the very outset. With modern weapons [atomic weapons], industrial potential can be significant only in a war in which it is not itself the target."[28] From the necessity to preserve American industrial potential, Kissinger derives a strategic doctrine in which this potential can be best used. By virtue of its technological production system, the United States can achieve its foreign-policy objectives by *limited wars* fought as *wars of attrition:*

As a result, limited war has become the form of conflict which enables us to derive the greatest strategic advantage from our industrial potential. It is the best means for achieving a continuous drain of our opponent's resources without exhausting both sides. The prerequisite for deriving a strategic advantage from industrial potential is a weapons system sufficiently complex to require a substantial production effort, but not so destructive as to deprive the victor of any effective margin of superiority. Thus the argument that limited war may turn into a contest of attrition is in fact an argument in favor of a strategy of limited war. A war of attrition is the one war the Soviet bloc could not win.[29]

Kissinger even said that the purpose of limited war was to demonstrate the capacity for destruction by our advanced war-production system, not literally to destroy an enemy: "Strategic doctrine must never lose sight that its purpose is to affect the will of the enemy, not to destroy him, and that we can be limited only by presenting the enemy with an unfavorable calculus of risks."[30] In another formulation of the same theoretical point, Kissinger wrote: "In a limited war the problem is to apply graduated amounts of destruction for limited objectives and also to permit the necessary breathing spaces for political contacts."[31]

All that remained necessary was to reorganize the American military so that it could fight limited wars of attrition. Kissinger gave great priority to preparing the military for this new kind of warfare: "One of the most urgent tasks of American military policy is to create a military capability which can redress the balance in limited wars and which can translate our technological advantage into local superiority."[32]

For the army these were golden words. When preparing for nuclear war during the 1950s, the air force had received most of the money allocated to the Department of Defense; the navy came second and the army got what was left. Prospects for a new mission involving a capital-intensive, technologically sophisticated army were exciting! Now the army, too, could speed up its transformation in organization and doctrine to fit smoothly into modern warfare. This transition had started in the Second World War with Chief of Staff George C. Marshall's decision to adopt the corporate model of organization as a means of managing military logistics. Corporatization of the military continued in the fifties. Close association with business and science in preparing new weapons systems accentuated the trend.

However, the full implications of this transformation go far beyond matters of management and weaponry considered as just *parts* of the American military. The same "fetishism" of technological production systems found in foreign policy similarly occurs within the military. The *social relationships* within the military disappear and all that remain are technological-production systems and ways of managing them. In the early 1950s, Morris Janowitz, a military sociologist, detected conflict between the traditional idea of the officer corps as being composed of "heroic" combat leaders or "gladiators," and the emerging career path of the "military manager."[33] Combat leaders inspire troops to fight in dangerous battle; social relationships of loyalty from top to bottom and bottom to top are crucial. Managers allocate resources. As two other military sociologists, Richard Gabriel and Paul Savage, say, "no one expects anyone to die for IBM or General Motors."[34]

Second, in a world where only technology and production count, the enemy begins to be seen *only* in those terms. The bicycle example in Vietnam was no joke. Limited war fought as a war of attrition means that only information about technological-production systems will count as valid knowledge about the enemy. For the military as well as civilian policymakers, the enemy becomes a mirror image of ourselves, only "less" so. Military strategy becomes a one-factor question about technical forces; success or failure is measured quantitatively. Machine-system meets machine-system and the largest, fastest, most technologically advanced system will win. Any other outcome becomes *unthinkable*. Such is the logic of *Technowar*.

The search for war now leads to the enemy. The enemy, of course, is communism. Although it is self-evident that Communist countries, particularly the Soviet Union, have been the enemy of American foreign policy in the post–World War II era, this same self-evidence tends to obscure just *how* this Communist enemy is conceptualized. Much debate could well ensue: the merits of "private property" capitalism versus "state-planning" of the economy; "representative democracy" versus "democratic centralism" in the Communist party; a privately owned "free press" versus a state-owned and state-censored press. All of these issues are worthy of great scrutiny, research, and debate. Only one subject will be considered here, though, and that is the question of Communist "expansion."

By the end of World War II, the Soviet Union's army occupied Eastern Europe. In most countries except Yugoslavia and Czechoslovakia, the preexisting *internal* Communist movements were relatively weak.

The invading Red Army with its accompanying Communist party political officers proceeded to establish a series of "puppet" or "satellite" governments, all under relatively firm control by the Soviet Union. In Yugoslavia, a large Communist movement, led by Marshal Tito, had fought a guerrilla war against the Nazis and had much popular support. Yugoslavia consequently did not become a "puppet" regime of the Soviet Union. Czechoslovakia did not retain its independence.

The original American concept of Communist expansion comes from Soviet occupation and control of Eastern Europe. Expansion meant "foreign" Communists occupying a country and ruling it without any consent of the native population. This original concept of Communist expansion thus had great historical truth. But historical truth is sometimes detached from its historical context. Communism as the ultimate foreign Other had a theoretical position already prepared for it by the capitalist West.

Capitalists, both the old variant called "laissez-faire" and the new capitalist order coming into existence during the war, understood themselves as being modeled on *nature*. If capitalism was nature, then communism by definition had to be *antinature*. By logical extension, if capitalism represented the natural economic structure of all nations, then by definition a Communist movement could only be *foreign;* it had to come from the *outside* because nature itself occupied the *inside*. In this way the historical truth of the Soviet conquest of Eastern Europe moved into a theoretical position of communism as the inevitable foreign Other.

This fetishized concept of communism as foreign Other, antinature itself, did not permit the United States to comprehend the Chinese revolution in 1949. Parts of China had long been occupied by the capitalist West. Its sovereignty as a nation had been diminished by imperialist conquest. Where the West did not rule, feudal landlord-warlords governed. The United States had special "trade agreements" with China, and sent troops and gunboats to maintain its economic position. Communist-led peasant revolution began in the 1920s in this milieu. Peasants wanted land for themselves and sovereignty from foreign governments.

Japan displaced Western powers in 1939 when it invaded China; the country now became subject to Japanese imperialism. When the United States entered World War II, it supported those Chinese political factions that had benefited from previous business arrangements with the West. These forces, led by Chiang Kai-shek, were known in the United

States as the *Nationalist Chinese*. The very semantic construction of the phrase meant that the Communists were "unnational," and therefore "foreign," not a real Chinese movement by any means. Consequently, the internal social dynamics of the Chinese revolution disappeared. When the Communist-led peasant revolution won in 1949, it appeared to the United States not as an internal social revolution, but as another instance of external Communist expansion ultimately controlled by the Soviet Union. Ironically, the Chinese Communist party had long been in severe conflict with the Soviet Union. Joseph Stalin had not supported the revolution during the war because it conflicted with his own policy of a "united front" with the West against fascism! Some members of the United States State Department knew about the internal dynamics of the Chinese revolution, but they were purged during the 1950s because they were held responsible for the "loss of China" to communism.

In 1950, war began in Korea. The country had been provisionally divided into a Communist northern region and a right-wing military regime in the south. After a long period of military probes by both sides along the provisional boundary, North Korea invaded South Korea. The Korean War will not be explored in depth here; it is sufficient to say that the Korean War consolidated the notion that all Communist movements inevitably come from outside a country's borders and are ultimately controlled by Moscow. Subsequently the United States began massive funding to the French to help them retain their colony, Vietnam, against internal national and social revolution led by Communists. When the French were defeated in 1954, the United States announced a doctrine which would make Vietnam contested grounds for decades.

The domino theory has been much discussed, but rarely scrutinized. "Domino" is a metaphor, but the *nature* of that metaphor has not been seen. On April 7, 1954, the original dominoes — the nations of Southeast Asia — stood up to be counted. President Dwight D. Eisenhower said: "You have a row of dominoes set up, and you knock over the first one, and what will happen to the last one is the certainty that it will go over very quickly, so you could have the beginning of a disintegration that would have the most profound influences." [35]

The falling dominoes were soon joined by a *popping cork*. On April 26, Eisenhower said that Indochina resembled "a sort of cork in the bottle, the bottle being the great area that includes Indonesia, Burma, Thailand, all the surrounding areas of Asia." Secretary of State Dulles added his verse a few days later in an address to a Senate and House Committee: "If Indochina should be lost, there would be a *chain reaction* throughout the Far East and Southeast Asia." [36]

"Falling dominoes," "cork in the bottle," "chain reaction" — what theory is being proposed here? According to one radical historian, Gabriel Kolko, the domino theory constitutes a theory of modern history: "Translated into concrete terms, the domino theory was a counterrevolutionary doctrine which defined modern history as a movement of Third World and dependent nations — those with strategic value to the United States or its capitalist associates — away from colonialism or capitalism and toward national revolution and forms of socialism." [37]

The failure of Kolko's analysis concerns *translation*. He has translated the domino theory into the Marxist theory of society, a theory in which concreteness, history, national revolution, and forms of socialism — emphasis on the plurality — exist as elements of a conceptual framework for understanding the social world. However, in the domino theory, none of these concepts exists: the domino theory effectively abolishes the possibility of history, national revolution, and forms of socialism. The conceptual order it elaborates is entirely different.

"Falling dominoes," "cork in the bottle," "chain reaction" — these terms find their theoretical reference not in the social world of history, where men live and die, but in the lifeless world of Newtonian mechanics. The foreign Other, Communist antinature, invades and destroys the natural order of Vietnam (capitalism). If Vietnam "falls" to communism, then the rest of Asia will surely follow, each fall from grace faster than its predecessor — an inevitable, inexorable mechanical process. Countries no longer have real histories, cultures, and social structures. The names of Asian countries become just that — names marking undifferentiated objects. And these names are inscribed upon a vast ledger, debit or credit, Communist or anti-Communist.

It is now time to name this ledger, to tie together constituent elements of the domino theory and other ideas that conceptualize the social world in terms of nature. The universe of post–World War II American foreign policy will be called *mechanistic anticommunism*. The demonic machine that lives outside of the natural capitalist order is the *foreign Other*. *Technowar* or the *production model of war* designates the military mode of strategy and organization in which war is conceptualized and organized as a high-technology, capital-intensive production process. The military and civilian executives who command the foreign policy and military apparatus are *war-managers*. History for them becomes a series of static points, each point measuring the balance of technological forces between the United States and the foreign Other. Some countries belong on the "credit" or capitalist side of the ledger; other countries belong to the "debit" or socialist side of the ledger. And still other countries, particularly Third World countries, become abstract sites for confrontation. No movement of a Third World country into the "debit" column is ever permanent: the ledger can be transformed by the introduction of more forces. To the war-managers, the policy of mechanistic anticommunism and Technowar against the foreign Other will ultimately produce victory. Since the United States has the most technologically advanced economy and warfare production system, then defeat by a nationalist social revolution in a peasant society becomes *unthinkable*.

There were no "mistakes" made during the Vietnam War. Nor was there a failure of will; the "self-imposed restraints" were only on official paper, not in Technowar practice. Instead, the Vietnam War should be understood in terms of the deep structural logic of how it was conceptualized and fought by American war-managers. Vietnam represents the perfect functioning of this closed, self-referential universe. Vietnam was *The Perfect War*.

# CHAPTER 2

# Legacies of Resistance: Vietnamese Nationalism against the Chinese and French

> The Vietnamese are indeed not a reliable people. An occupation does not last very long before they raise their arms against us from their country. The history of past dynasties has proved this fact.[1]
> — eighteenth-century Chinese emperor

As a distinct ethnicity and culture, the Vietnamese have a long history dating back well over two millennia. As a nation, though, political independence has occurred only in relatively brief historical periods. Chinese rule over Vietnam extended from 111 B.C. to A.D. 43, from 44 to 543, from 603 to 938, and a last brief reign from 1407 to 1427. Originally the Chinese called it "Nam-Viet," meaning "South[ern country of the] Viet." Later the Chinese referred to the middle region as "An-Nam," meaning "pacified South." For centuries the area was known as Annam. Even long after the country became independent from China, it was Chinese political recognition of a new, self-appointed emperor, Gia Long, that provided the occasion for renaming. Gia Long named the country "Viet-Nam" in 1802.

Chinese rule influenced Vietnamese economic, political, and cultural development. China's political system posited an emperor as the mediator between earth and heaven. To administer the empire, the emperor called upon a class of scholars known as "mandarins." To become a mandarin, a man had to pass a series of competitive examinations based on the traditional Confucian Four Books and Five Classics, as well as other traditional Chinese literature. The lengthy preparations tended to favor the wealthier students who could be financed by their families. However, in principle, any *man* could take the exams. Mandarinism provided a system of limited upward mobility, yet because it was based on mastering valued knowledge, the system provided great legitimacy to the emperor.

Confucianism was a political and social philosophy of correct alignment, a way of life, or *Tao* as it was called. By assiduous attention to the past, the correct way of life or *Tao* could be ascertained. Virtually all social and political relationships, such as those within the family and those social relationships outside the family, such as the relationships of mandarin to village, of mandarin to emperor, and emperor to heaven, were informed by the complex system of practical-moral precepts found in Confucianism.

Vietnam adopted this system; it, too, sought the *Tao*. One Vietnamese emperor proclaimed to his court: "We have little virtue; we have transgressed the order of Heaven, and upset the natural course of events; last year the spring was blighted by a long rain; this year there is a long series of drought. . . . Let the mandarins examine my past acts in order to discover any errors or faults, so that they may be remedied." [2]

Through examination, true order would be determined. Confucius said, "I for my part am not one of those who have innate knowledge. I am simply one who loves the past and is diligent in investigating it." [3] The Confucian veneration of the past was important in Vietnamese culture. For Vietnam, the very center of its political culture concerned legends and stories of resistance to the Chinese.

Foremost among the legendary figures are the Trung sisters. Trung Trac was the wife of a feudal lord who was killed by the Chinese in A.D. 39. Rather than mourn and bemoan her fate, Trung Trac joined with her sister Trung Nhi to raise an army. The two sisters defeated the Chinese and secured Vietnamese independence for the first time in over a century and a half. China soon reconquered Vietnam and the two Trung sisters committed suicide. Their failure to maintain Vietnamese independence became in legend insignificant compared to the larger effort of trying to become independent.

Later Vietnamese heroes left more developed archival remains — poems, essays, proclamations, and so forth — for historical study by the Vietnamese mandarins. Nguyen Trai published a famous poem in 1428, a year after the Vietnamese gained their final independence from China:

> Although we have been at times strong,
> at times weak,
> We have at no time lacked heroes. [4]

Other quotations reinforce the cultural prediliction toward the remembrance of heroism. The Vietnamese hero who led the armies that defeated Kublai Khan and the Mongolians (1284–1287) is named Tran Hung Dao. His speech to his troops is famous in Vietnamese history:

> We have all grown up in difficult times. We have seen the enemy's ambassadors stroll about in our streets with conceit, using the owls' and crows' tongues to abuse our courts, flexing their goats' and dogs' bodies to threaten our ministers. Simulating the orders of Khubilai, they have demanded precious stones and embroidered silks to satisfy their boundless appetite. Using the title from the Prince of Chen-an, they have extracted silver and gold from our limited treasures. It is really not different from bringing meat to feed hungry tigers; how should we avoid catastrophe in later times?[5]

Tran Hung Dao goes on to threaten his lieutenants, to admonish them to give up their leisure and instead prepare for war:

> Should the Mongol army invade our country, the cock spur shall not pierce the enemy's armor, nor can the gambler's artifice substitute for military tactics. Then, though you possess many gardens and rice-fields, you will not be rich enough to pay the ransom for your life in thousands of [pieces of] gold. Furthermore, of what usefulness will you be in military matters when you are pushed around by your wife and dragged hither and thither by your children? Your wealth, even when abundant, will not bury the enemy's head. Your hunting dogs, though they are very strong, cannot chase the enemy. It is neither possible for good wine to intoxicate the enemy to death nor for melodious songs to mellow him.
>
> At that time, you and I will be made prisoners. How painful it will be! Not only will my fief go, but your salaries too will be in the hands of others. Not only will my family be dispersed, but yours also will be enslaved by others. Not only will my ancestors' altars be discarded, but your parents' tombs will be evacuated. Not only will I be humiliated in this life, not only will my name be tarnished forever, but you too will not be spared the shame of defeated generals. Will you then be able to enjoy your life according to your desires?[6]

Tran Hung Dao's attempts to shame his troops and motivate them for battle against the Mongols succeeded. The Vietnamese stopped the invasion, and their heroism was "registered in the books of history" as he predicted. This political culture of resistance to foreign invasion has one other element that should be noted. The Vietnamese vilify collaborationists among their own people. One example taken from the era when the Chinese Ming dynasty ruled Vietnam with the help of many Vietnamese mandarins reads: "The mad Ming, steadily awaiting every opportunity, took advantage of the situation to pour poison onto our population, at the same time that a group of scoundrels who longed for treason prepared to sell out our country."[7]

Unfortunately for Vietnam, however, strong resistance to foreign domination did not result in stable Vietnamese governments; royal governments often had great difficulty in ruling effectively. Local and regional warlords frequently usurped the monarch, reducing his role to ritual and ceremonial functions. The most famous governmental rupture lasted over three centuries, from the late fifteenth to the early nineteenth century. In the north, first the Mac and then the Trinh families claimed to be protectors of the Le dynasty. In the south the Nguyen warlords ruled. During the 1630s, the Nguyen constructed two massive walls to divide the country. Ironically, the walls were constructed a few miles north of the seventeenth parallel, which in 1954 would become the "provisional military demarcation line."

Not until 1802, with the victory of Gia Long over Tay-Son, was the country reunited. Gia Long represented the heir to the Nguyen of the south; Tay-Son had defeated the Trinh in the north. His loss to Gia Long meant victory of south over north in some respects. However, understanding Gia Long in terms of political geography does not accurately convey what was important about his government. First, Gia Long founded a *dynasty*. In traditional Confucianism, however, a sovereign rules by the "Mandate of Heaven." The concept is much like the *Tao* or correct way of life, except that the Mandate of Heaven additionally signifies that the people accept the terms of the sovereign's rule as legitimate. For someone to claim the Mandate of Heaven is thus not the same as having the mandate by establishing legitimacy among the people. Loyalty to the monarchy was conceived in terms of believing in the principle of the monarchy. Should any monarch engage in activities that were seen as oppressive by the people, he could be legitimately overthrown in the name of a principled loyalty to the institution of the monarchy and the desire to see the nation in alignment with the "true" Mandate of Heaven. One Vietnamese historian explains the concept as follows: "If the sovereign oppressed the people, he no longer deserved to be treated as the sovereign. His person was no longer sacred, and to kill him was no longer a crime. Revolt against such tyranny not only was reasonable but was a meritorious act and conferred upon its author the right to take over the powers of the sovereign.''[8]

In Gia Long's case, possession of the Mandate of Heaven was problematic. His victory over Tay-Son in the north did not come from a political coalition involving mass mobilization of different social strata, but instead was produced by possession of Western military armaments and battlefield techniques. French missionaries had been active in Vietnam since the early 1600s, and many Vietnamese converted to Catholicism. In the late eighteenth century, one ambitious missionary, Monsignor Pigneau de Bahaine, had raised a small army of some three hundred Frenchmen to serve as advisers to Prince Nguyen Anh, as Gia Long was then named. These advisers were able to help the South Vietnamese to make superior cannons and other modern weapons.

Minh Mang succeeded Gia Long to the throne in 1821. For the next twenty years local revolts occurred both in the north and in the far south. Matters became worse for the two succeeding Nguyen kings, Thieu Tri (1841–1847) and Tu Duc (1847–1883). Local uprisings and tax protests continued. The dike system in the Red River delta was breached several times because of government failure to maintain the system properly. Natural disasters such as drought and locusts and a smallpox epidemic hurt social stability. Even Tu Duc's right to succession was not certain. He killed his elder brother in 1854, and in 1866 killed most of his brother's family. One scholar reviewed this compendium of revolt, disaster, and intrigue and summarized by saying, ''Unlike the Le, however, there is reason to believe that the Nguyen dynasty never really succeeded in establishing its legitimate writ at the village level.''[9] The Mandate of Heaven was thus uncertain.

By the mid-nineteenth century, China, the Celestial Empire herself, had lost her independence to the British, French, and other European powers. In this era of dynastic weakness, French colonialism came to Vietnam. In 1847 a French fleet destroyed several Vietnamese ships in Danang harbor to secure the release of a French missionary held captive. Eleven years later, the French returned with a much larger force and Danang was once again shelled. By 1863 the French had captured six Vietnamese provinces. In 1867 they won more major victories at Vinh Long, Chau Doc, and Ha Tien. During the next decade the French concentrated on the north, securing from King Tu Duc the Treaty of 1874 granting France considerable political and economic privileges.

Tu Duc's attempts to make peace with the French did not succeed. What little remaining popular support the dynasty had from the people dissipated. Most mandarins subsequently moved closer to the French and attempted to govern the population for them. In 1882 another French fleet captured Hanoi. In 1885 Tu Duc's heir, Ham Nghi, fled Hue for the mountains and issued a "Loyalty to the King Edict" calling for renewed national resistance. The French placed his brother, Dong Khanh, on the throne and proceeded to rule Vietnam as a colony.

To begin, the French *abolished* Vietnam! The northern part of Vietnam became known as "'Tonkin" and was incorporated into the French empire as a "protectorate." Hue, the former capital of Vietnam, and the middle region of the colony became "Annam." It, too, was administratively considered a protectorate. Saigon and all territory to the south became "Cochinchina." This new land was taken as a direct colony of the French empire. Since Laos and Cambodia also fell, the entire area was renamed "Indochina," and was ruled by one "governor-general."

The French came to think of their administrative divisions not as a system of domination imposed by them, but instead as simply reflecting three different "essences" of three different peoples. Historian David Marr explains:

> The French would dwell lovingly, for example, on the supposed quaint backwardness, the natural simplicity of the "Annamite" as contrasted with the suave sophistication of the Saigonese or the oxlike toughness of the Tonkinese. Such myths of differentiation became increasingly important as native political challenges to colonial rule intensified in the twentieth century. They were a prime rationale for sustained French presence, for the job of "mediating" regional differences, of providing the necessary order among implicitly divisive native principalities.[10]

In believing their own myths of differentiation, the French made their conquest, rule, and abolition of Vietnam legitimate to themselves, to other Western countries, and, indeed, to some Vietnamese. However, in attempting to grind colonial rule so deeply into Vietnamese culture, the French aroused resistance. Colonialism ruled Vietnam, but at the same time it created contradictions that weakened it.

The economy was transformed for French benefit. Those who fought against the French during the initial colonial wars returned to their native provinces only to find that their land now belonged to either the French or to Vietnamese collaborators. The public or communal property belonging to Vietnamese villages was also redistributed for private ownership to those with either white skins or highly collaborationist tendencies. In the south, much land was directly granted to Frenchmen to establish tea, rubber, and rice plantations. These plantations grew mostly export crops, utilizing a landless peasantry as the labor force.

Two other French policies helped create a landless peasantry besides the direct land appropriations. Tax policy played an important role; taxes were high and payment in *money* was required. Traditionally, taxes had been payable in rice. France controlled the money supply and established government monopolies on salt and other necessities; this change to a money economy resulted in thousands upon thousands of peasants having to sell their land to pay taxes and buy essential items. They subsequently became tenant farmers, turning over their yearly crop to a new landlord class.

The other French policy concerned opium. Immediately after France annexed Saigon in 1862, it began importing opium from India and taxed it at 10 percent of its value. Chinese merchants sold the drug. Much revenue was generated; within six months, the colony was financially self-supporting. As French control progressed, the opium industry quickly followed. One French governor-general, Paul Doumer, achieved great renown for consolidating five separate opium agencies operating in Indochina into one grand opium monopoly. A new refinery was constructed in Saigon and a special quick-burning opium formula was concocted to encourage increased consumption. Poppies came from China rather than India to reduce cost and make opium more readily consumable by the poor. Revenues went up 50 percent in a few years. The colonies now paid for all their official government expenses; trade revenue was pure profit.

Although the French did not tabulate how many Vietnamese peasants lost their land from opium addiction, an estimated 2 percent of the population were addicts by the early twentieth century. A great proportion of Vietnamese plantation workers, tin and coal miners, and urban laborers are reported to have been addicts. By 1918 the administration proudly reported that there were 1,512 licensed opium dens and 3,098 retail shops in Indochina. Collaborationist mandarins occupying administrative positions within the colonies had the highest addiction rate of any social class, a figure estimated at nearly 20 percent.[11]

French colonialism also brought many new jobs to Vietnam. Roads were constructed, hospitals built and staffed, even some French schools entered the area. But at no time was there any doubt who was on top. A Vietnamese might hold the same job as a Frenchman at the low and middle levels of some administrative hierarchy, but the Frenchman always received two to three times the salary.

It is against this background that the revolt of a segment of the scholar-gentry or mandarin class should be understood. During the late nineteenth and early twentieth centuries, at least one part of the mandarin class neither succumbed to opium nor provided the French with literate services and an aura of traditional legitimacy. Instead, this class faction reached back into antiquity to invoke the traditional political culture of resistance to foreign occupation and at the same time reached forward toward the West in attempts to use new knowledge as a means of creating a national resistance movement.

One of the most important beliefs of the Can Vuong movement, the first wave of scholar-gentry resistance against the French, had to do with fighting to the death. In 1883 their writings contained such slogans as:

> We possess our life, but we must know how to give it up.

> Shall we remain silent and thereby earn the reputation of cowards?

> As long as there exist people on this earth, we shall exist.

> As long as there is water, we must bail it out.

> We must read the Proclamation on the victory over the Wu.

> We shall follow the example of those who exterminated the Mongols.[12]

One famous resistance fighter, Phan Dinh Phung, whose brother was captured by the French, was told that only by surrendering could his brother, his family's sacred tombs, and the village be saved. Phan told his officers why he refused to surrender:

> From the time I joined with you in the Can Vuong movement, I determined to forget questions of family and village. Now I have but one tomb, a very large one, that must be defended: the land of Vietnam. I have only one brother, very important, that is in danger: more than twenty million countrymen. If I worry about my own tombs, who will worry about defending the tombs of the rest of the country? If I save my own brother, who will save all the other brothers of our country? There is only one way for me to die now.[13]

In 1894, the French destroyed his family tombs and jailed all his relatives. Hoang Cao Khai, a mandarin serving the French, wrote Phan a letter promising leniency if he surrendered. Phan replied with a tirade against collaborators:

> If our region has suffered to such an extent, it was not only from the misfortunes of war. You must realize that wherever the French go, there flock around them groups of petty men who offer plans and tricks to gain the enemy's confidence. These persons create every kind of enmity; they incriminate innocent persons, blaming one one day, punishing another the next. They use every expedient to squeeze the people out of their possessions. That is how hundreds of misdeeds, thousands of offenses have been perpetrated.[14]

Some time later, he died from dysentery, a common disease among resistance fighters living in the mountains and swamps.

Nguyen Quang Bich was also tempted by the French, who first attempted to buy him and then, failing in that, imprisoned his mother. A portion of his reply is given below:

> You [Frenchmen] came to look our country over, displaying good techniques, clever skills and a well-trained army. And on this basis it seems that more than half of our people have left brightness and righteousness in order to follow you. This land of long civilization, of countless mandarins and proper ceremony has just about become French property. This being the case, you may consider us extremely foolish for not having measured our strength realistically, instead courting disaster by gathering some hundreds of scholar-gentry and several thousand exhausted soldiers to oppose you. But we think repeatedly of the tie between monarch and subject in this world, not shirking temporal responsibilities that are as clearly defined as the waters of the Ching and the Wei rivers and we do not dare forget our obligations. It is simply this tie that we must live up to. . . . Better to endure punishment from you than ever think of punishment from our monarch. Better to be sentenced once than be sentenced for eternity.[15]

The Can Vuong movement stressed struggle over generations. One maxim said, "If we fail, hope shifts to our sons."[16] Setting an example for future generations was far more important than personal survival.

The Can Vuong movement envisioned success in terms of restoration, of a return to a Vietnam ruled by an emperor at the pinnacle of the celestial-social hierarchy, supported by diligent mandarins. Its conception of the world remained feudal — it had little reference to the transformations in social structure wrought by the French that linked the country to a larger capitalist world economy.

The leading scholar-gentry figure who acted to move the Can Vuong forward was Phan Boi Chau. He still retained the idea of restoring the monarchy and even found a descendant of Gia Long to sit upon the throne, but his most serious contribution concerned his journey to Japan. There he wrote *Viet-Nam Vong Su* (History of the Loss of Vietnam). By 1905 the work was smuggled into Vietnam and was successfully received. It included a list of revolutionary heroes, a chronicle and account of French exploitation, and a call for mass resistance:

> Ten thousand Vietnamese can at least kill one hundred Frenchmen,
>
> One thousand Vietnamese can kill ten Frenchmen,
>
> One hundred Vietnamese can kill one Frenchman.
>
> In this way four to five hundred thousand Vietnamese can wipe out four to five thousand Frenchmen!
>
> Those grey-eyed, heavily bearded people cannot live if Vietnam is to live![17]

Phan Boi Chau endorsed Vietnamese participation in the modern world economy in an essay entitled *Tan Viet-Nam*. Subtitles included "No Natural Resource That Is Not Developed," "No Industry That Is Not Begun," and "No Commerce That Is Not Flourishing." Together, these sections broke with previous conceptions of national resistance. The past was invoked, but not emulated or made sacred. Another essay by Phan Boi Chau attempted to bring citizen's government to Vietnam by way of reference to the past: "Listen! The Nation is every citizen's property. Common ownership requires that the people be of one heart, one strength, in common struggle. The world is being swept to its eight points by the wind and rain of the Westerners. But who are we, as a people? The land of Hong-Lac must be renewed, to be again a thing of beauty."[18]

Other scholar-gentry attacked the whole mandarin system and argued for reforming education. Roman script for Vietnamese had been introduced by French priests in the early seventeenth century, but Chinese pictographs prevailed until the "Quoc-ngu" movement of the late nineteenth century. The *quoc-ngu* sought to bring new ideas to Vietnam and disseminate them more widely in Roman script than had been possible with the pictograph system of characters, which took years of study to master. One poem went:

> *Quoc-ngu* is the [saving] spirit in our country,
> We must take it out among our people.
> Books from other countries, books from China,
> Each word, each meaning must be translated clearly.[19]

But the anticolonial movement lead by the scholar-gentry class did
not succeed. In 1908 tax protests occurred throughout Vietnam. The
French retaliated severely. Many peasants who participated in the demonstrations were killed. After the confrontations had been crushed, the
French jailed most of the anticolonial leaders, closed *quoc-ngu* schools,
and attempted to halt publication and circulation of all nationalist books,
pamphlets, and papers. The traditional call for the next generation to
renew the struggle was heard again. One author urged widowed mothers
of men who died in the 1908 revolts to instruct their children: "You
children should remember that it was the French colonial authorities that
killed your father. Today is the anniversary of your father's death. You
must never forget that when you grow up you also may have the same
fate as your father."[20]

One who listened was a boy named Nguyen Tat Thanh. When he was
nine, he heard Phan Boi Chau reciting his anticolonial verses. His father
was a low-level mandarin who hated both the French and the mandarin
system: "Being a mandarin is the ultimate form of slavery."[21] He did
not want his son to follow Confucian studies. Instead, he sent Nguyen
Tat Thanh to Hue to study a western curriculum at the famous Quoc
Hoc academy. As a fifteen-year-old, he participated in the 1908 demonstrations and witnessed their repression. Three years later he quit school
and got a job as a mess boy on a French ocean liner that traveled between France and Vietnam. Later he shipped out on cargo ships throughout
the Mediterranean and the ports of Africa. These expeditions gave Nguyen
Tat Thanh rudimentary insights into the international system of colonial
imperialism.

In 1914 he left the seas to work in London. There he joined the
Overseas Workers Association of Orientals living abroad, met many Fa-
bian socialists, and studied the revolt of Ireland against England. Three
years later he moved to Paris to become more deeply involved in the
Vietnamese community.

By the early twentieth century, Vietnamese students could obtain
scholarships for university study in France. The French hoped to instill
a feeling of French identity in the young Vietnamese, but the results of
their largess were often the opposite. Confronted with the intellectual

and political tradition of the French Revolution, with its ideals of liberty, equality, and fraternity, and having had the direct personal experience of being treated as equals, many Vietnamese students were inspired to become more politically active against colonialism. Other Vietnamese were also in France. During World War I, for example, the French imported some 50,000 to 100,000 Indochinese to serve in labor brigades.

It was on French soil that Nguyen Tat Thanh became a political activist and changed his name to Nguyen Ai-Quoc. "Ai" is a prefix meaning alliance; "Quoc" means "country." Roughly translated his new name meant "Nguyen," as in the old dynasty, "the patriot." [22]

Nguyen Ai-Quoc soon became the premier Vietnamese activist. In 1919 he went to the Versailles Peace Conference to petition for the rights of Vietnam. He based his petition on President Woodrow Wilson's Fourteen Points. Nguyen Ai-Quoc's resolution did not even call for complete Vietnamese independence. Instead, he asked for Vietnamese representation in the French parliament, freedom of the press and the right to assemble, release of all political prisoners, and equality of rights between Vietnamese and French. He called upon the American delegation and was rebuffed. A year later he became the "Indochinese Delegation" to the socialist conference in Tours. There he addressed the fate of Indochina:

> You have all known that French imperialism entered Indochina half a century ago. In its selfish interests, it conquered our country with bayonets. Since then we have not only been oppressed and exploited shamelessly, but also tortured and poisoned pitilessly. Plainly speaking, we have been poisoned with opium, alcohol, etc. I cannot, in some minutes, reveal all the atrocities that the predatory capitalists have inflicted on Indochina. [23]

Although socialists applauded his speech, no concrete actions followed. French socialists wanted to keep the colonies under French rule, but with "better" administration. Someone gave Nguyen Ai-Quoc Lenin's essay "Thesis on the National and Colonial Questions," and directed him to the newly formed Communist Third International. Ironically, he later referred to Lenin in Confucian terms:

> There is a legend in our country as well as in China, on the miraculous "Book of the Wise." When facing great difficulties one opens it and finds a way out. Leninism is not only a miraculous "book of

the wise,'' a compass for us Vietnamese revolutionaries and people: it is also the radiant sun illuminating our path to final victory, to Socialism and Communism.[24]

By 1924 Nguyen Ai-Quoc had found his way to the Soviet Union, participating in the Fifth Congress of the Communist International. He offered severe criticisms of the Communist party: ''We shall establish facts that are beyond imagining and that tempt one to believe that our party is systematically ignoring all matters relating to the colonies.''[25] As opposed to the traditional Marxist emphasis on the industrial working class as the agent for social change, Nguyen Ai-Quoc emphasized organizing the peasantry for revolution: ''The revolt of the colonial peasants is imminent. They have already risen in several colonies, but each time their rebellions have been drowned in blood. If they now seem resigned, that is solely for lack of organization and leadership. It is the duty of the Communist International to work toward their union. . . .''[26]

His criticism of the Communist party should be kept in mind; he would later be regarded by Americans as a complete ''Communist stooge'' under control by Moscow. In December 1924, he left Moscow for Canton, China. His adventures in China and Southeast Asia over the next twenty years were so astounding that one biographer referred to the period as ''some of the most amazing episodes in a life story which at times reads like a tale from *Arabian Nights*.''[27] Foremost among them concerns the founding of the Vietnamese Communist party in February 1930. The new party was immediately torn into several different factions; Nguyen Ai-Quoc's personal intervention rectified the divisions and called for renaming the party as ''Indochinese.'' The Indochinese Communist party had a ten-point manifesto:

1. To overthrow French imperialism, feudalism and the reactionary Vietnamese capitalist class.

2. To make Indochina completely independent.

3. To establish a government composed of workers, peasants, and soldiers.

4. To confiscate the banks and other enterprises belonging to the imperialists and put them under the control of the government.

5. To confiscate the whole of the plantations and property belonging to the imperialists and the Vietnamese reactionary capitalist class and distribute them to poor peasants.

6. To implement the eight-hour working day.

7. To abolish public loans and poll tax. To waive unjust taxes hitting the poor people.

8. To bring back all freedoms to the masses.

9. To carry out universal education.

10. To implement equality between man and woman.[28]

Activism had increased during the 1920s and 1930s among Vietnam's working class — estimated by the late 1920s as 220,000 in number. In February 1928, workers at the Indochinese Brewery and Icehouse in Saigon went on strike. Within a year there were strikes by petroleum workers in Haiphong, rubber plantation workers, rickshaw drivers in Hanoi, textile and railroad workers.[29] In 1930, peasants began hunger marches.

By the mid-1930s, the French tried to contain social revolt by enlarging the democratic process. In 1935, two Communists were elected to the municipal council in Saigon. Two years later, three were elected. In 1938, thousands of Communists and socialists, both Vietnamese and French, demonstrated in Hanoi. The crackdown came in 1939. Previous forms of legal resistance became illegal; the movement went underground and many activists went to China.

In particular, two men went to China in 1940 to find a third man called "Vuong." They were Pham Van Dong and Vo Nguyen Giap, two history teachers from Hue. In his wallet Giap carried a photo of Nguyen Ai-Quoc at the Versailles Peace Conference. Years later he spoke of meeting Vuong:

> A man of mature years stepped toward us, wearing European clothes and a soft felt hat. Compared with the famous photograph, now twenty years old, he looked livelier, more alert. He had let his beard grow. I found myself confronted by a man of shining simplicity. This was the first time I had set eyes on him, yet already we were conscious of deep bonds of friendship. . . . He spoke with the accent of central Vietnam. I would never have believed it possible for him to retain the local accent after so long abroad.[30]

Vuong was, of course, Nguyen Ai-Quoc. The next year, 1941, he called for the convention of the eighth plenum of the Central Committee of the Indochinese Communist party. It was decided to dissolve the party as a separate organization and instead form "a broad National Front uniting not only the workers, peasants, the petit bourgeois and the bourgeois, but also a number of patriotic landowners."[31] This new organization was called "The League for Vietnamese Independence," or "Vietminh." Its charter dedicated the organization to "uniting all patriots, without distinction of wealth, age, sex, religion or political outlook so that they may work together for the liberation of our people and the salvation of our nation."[32] By 1941, World War II had started and the Japanese had overwhelmed the French in Indochina. Consequently, the immediate priority concerned defeating the Japanese: "After the overthrow of the Japanese fascists and French imperialists, a revolutionary government of the Democratic Republic of Vietnam will be set up in the spirit of the new democracy; its emblem will be the red flag with a gold star."[33] Later, on June 6, 1941, the Vietminh issued a proclamation. Entitled "Letter from Abroad," the manifesto read:

Elders!
Prominent personalities!
Some hundreds of years ago, when our country was endangered by the Mongolian invasion, our elders under the Tran dynasty rose up indignantly and called on their sons and daughters throughout the country to rise as one in order to kill the enemy. . . . The elders and prominent personalities of our country should follow the example set by our forefathers in the glorious task of national salvation.
Rich people, soldiers, workers, peasants, intellectuals, employees, traders, youth, and women who warmly love your country! At the present time national liberation is the most important problem. Let us unite together! As one in mind and strength we shall overthrow the Japanese and French and their jackals in order to save people from the situation between boiling water and burning heat. . . .
Revolutionary fighters!
The hour has struck! Raise aloft the insurrectionary banner and guide the people throughout the country to overthrow the Japanese and French! The sacred call of the fatherland is resounding in your ears. . . .
Victory to Vietnam's Revolution!
Victory to the world's Revolution![34]

The program begins with a call to remember the traditional political culture of resistance to foreign domination. It ends with a far different call, a call for Vietnamese revolution as one aspect of world revolution against capitalism. The past is a cultural heritage to be reconceptualized in terms of a free Vietnam existing in an international system of free states. The past is thereby transformed, yet preserved. Such conceptual and practical efforts are known as "dialectics," and this particular dialectic should be remembered. A year after the Vietminh formed, Nguyen Ai-Quoc took yet another name. During his China missions he had been known as "Ho Quang." In 1942, another alias was created: he became Ho Chi Minh, he "Who Enlightens." This name stuck. There is one slight variation, the familial term "Uncle Ho." As his biographers and commentators have noted, Ho Chi Minh played uncle with consummate skill, even making it a habit to give children candy. Ho Chi Minh was fifty-two years old when he took this name. Pham Van Dong, Vo Nguyen Giap, and the other new leaders were all from a different generation, a younger generation. The continuity of Vietnamese political and cultural tradition against foreign occupation had been preserved. Ho Chi Minh was imprisoned by Chiang Kai-shek in 1942. The American Office of Strategic Services secured his release in spring 1943. While in prison, Ho Chi Minh wrote poetry, later published as *Prison Notebook*. It was not written in *quoc-ngu,* but instead in classical Chinese pictographs.

> The poems of our day must be clad in steel.
> Poets too must know how to fight.[35]

CHAPTER 3

# The Permanent War Begins: 1940–1954

FRANCE's control over her Indochinese colonies eroded with the coming of World War II. By late June of 1940 the German army defeated metropolitan France: on June 25 an armistice was signed. A new French government was formed to collaborate with the Germans. Known as the "Vichy" regime, it was headed by an aging French general from the First World War, Marshal Pétain. Since Germany was allied with Japan, the Vichy regime subsequently entered into negotiations with Japan concerning French concessions to the Japanese in Indochina. The initial agreement, signed on August 30, 1940, conceded Japan's "preeminent position" in the Far East and called for more detailed negotiations on Indochina, which would lead to Japan's use of the area for transporting troops and supplies.

On July 29, 1941, Japan acquired control of all ports and airfields. A few months later, on the night of December 7, 1941, Japanese troops surrounded French military garrisons and threatened massive attacks unless the colonial economy met Japan's needs. Admiral Decoux agreed to cooperate. Indochina's products would now go to Japan rather than the world market. Apparently, Japan offered slightly lower prices. As one Frenchman said, "The only thing I really object to is that the Japanese have diminished our profits."[1] The French thus retained *ownership* of their properties. French civil administration and military garrisons remained intact. France continued to rule the Vietnamese, but the French administrators were ruled by the Japanese.

This shift in rule had three major effects. First, Japanese victory weakened the myth of white superiority promulgated by the French. Second, Vietnamese nationalists resisted Japanese occupation; guerrilla operations against the Japanese became their new priority. Third, Japanese conquest of the area had much to do with American entry into the war.

The United States reversed its policy on avoiding confrontation during the summer of 1941, when it became evident the Japanese would take full control of Indochina. On July 26, 1941, President Franklin Roosevelt ordered the seizure or "freezing" of Japanese assets in the United States, together with an embargo of sales and shipments of all petroleum products to Japan. During the negotiations that followed, the United States proposed that Indochina become a completely neutral territory. In return for Japanese agreement on neutralization, Japan would be guaranteed "right of acquisition . . . of supplies and raw materials therefrom on a basis of equality." [2] The oil cut-off pushed the Japanese navy to insist on rapid invasion to obtain Indonesian oil. Negotiations between the United States and Japan failed. Japan bombed Pearl Harbor on December 7, 1941.

Roosevelt subsequently held French colonialism as partly responsible for World War II. On January 22, 1943, he spoke to his son Elliot about what should be done with Indochina after the war: "Don't think for a moment, Elliot, that Americans would be dying in the Pacific tonight if it hadn't been for the shortsighted greed of the French and the British and the Dutch. Shall we allow them to do it all, all over again? . . . The United Nations — when they're organized — they could take over the colonies, couldn't they? Under a mandate, or as trustee — for a certain number of years." [3]

On January 24, 1944, he told Lord Halifax, the British ambassador to the United States, of his displeasure with French colonialism: "France has had [Indochina] — thirty million inhabitants — for nearly one hundred years, and the people are worse off than they were at the beginning. . . . France has milked it for one hundred years. The people of Indochina are entitled to something better than that." [4] Cordell Hull, secretary of state during the war, also noted Roosevelt's interest: "From time to time the President had stated forthrightly to me and to others his view that French Indo-China should be placed under international trusteeship shortly after the end of the war, with a view to its receiving full independence as soon as possible." [5]

Roosevelt's liberalism should be remembered for later discussion of U.S. global foreign policy.

On June 13, 1942, the President signed an executive order creating the Office of Strategic Services, an intelligence agency with several diverse missions. One area had to do with placing agents covertly among the enemy to gather information and recruiting double agents to supply more information and tell lies to the enemy. Another area concerned propaganda — the dissemination of leaflets, the establishment of covert radio stations, and so forth. A third major effort concentrated on the preparation of economic, political, social, and psychological reports on countries, movements, and political leaders. The last mission concerned paramilitary actions and working with partisan guerrilla groups. Stories about OSS men parachuting into Europe have become almost legendary since World War II. OSS activities in Indochina, particularly American contacts with Ho Chi Minh and the Vietnamese, are less well known.

In 1944, Archimedes L. A. Patti, later the author of *Why Vietnam: Prelude to America's Albatross,* was assigned to the "Indochina Desk" of the OSS in Washington. In his research Patti found several references to Ho Chi Minh and the Vietminh. Some concerned Vietnamese efforts to have Ho released from a Chinese prison. Other memos noted that Ho worked part-time for the Office of War Information — the American propaganda agency — and also had contacts with the OSS and the separate Air Ground Aid Section, an organization helping shot-down pilots get back to American bases in southern China. The most interesting file noted that a spokesman for the Vietminh named Pham Viet Tu, had met the U.S. ambassador to China, William R. Langdon, on September 8, 1944. Pham Viet Tu had told Langdon that he was "calling to enlist the sympathy . . . of the United States." Langdon in turn had said: "[It was] quite right for them to make known to American representatives the views and aspirations of the Annamite people, inasmuch as the highest spokesmen of the American Government had in numerous declarations given assurances of the interest of their government in the political welfare and advancement of oppressed peoples in the Orient, among whom the Annamite people might believe themselves to be included." [6]

In his memo to his superiors, the ambassador went on to say that he told the Vietminh he did not think the United States would "undermine" the French empire. At the time, the fall of 1944, Roosevelt had told Secretary of State Cordell Hull to "do nothing in regard to resistance groups or in any other way in relation to Indochina." [7] As Patti understood it, this policy put a limit on American political and military relationships with the Vietminh.

In March 1945, political dynamics in Vietnam changed. The Japanese realized they were losing the war and did not want Indochina returned to the French. On March 9, 1945, they surrounded and captured most French military and police units. Ho Chi Minh and the Vietminh benefited from this abrupt curtailment of French authority. At the time of the attack, General Mordant had positioned his troops to attack them and destroy "a handful of traitorous Annamites." [8] Ironically, the only French troops to escape Japanese attack were this force. The Vietminh led the surviving French troops to refuge in China. Meanwhile, the Permanent Committee of the Vietminh decided to increase its own activities against the Japanese. Japanese fascism was declared to be "the sole enemy of the Vietnamese revolution."

> In consequence, the Vietnamese revolutionaries must make contact with any French group sincerely desirous of fighting the Japanese fascists. The committee has decided to stage a series of local uprisings before launching the general insurrection. A directive from the committee indicates the line to be followed and the courses of action best suited to this preinsurrectional period: the formation of further units of the army of liberation, all over the country, together with military committees, committees of liberation and people's revolutionary committees. But the situation does not yet favor a general insurrection. [9]

After the Japanese coup on March 9, most French, British, Chinese, and American intelligence networks were closed down. Information was needed. American policy subsequently shifted to allow more extensive cooperation: "all groups will be dealt with impartially and irrespective of any particular governmental or political affiliations." [10] Major Patti started searching for Ho Chi Minh. His first contact was with Vuong Minh Phong. The Vietnamese explained the organization of the Indochinese Communist party and the Vietminh and talked of establishing an "independent Indochinese democratic republic." [11] Vietminh would participate in commando raids against the Japanese and help fliers get back to China. In return, the Vietminh wanted official recognition from the United States as the sole legitimate political representative of the Vietnamese people.

Patti and Ho met in southern China soon thereafter. Discussion concerned recent devastations in northern and central Vietnam, where between one and a half and two million people had died from starvation and diseases. A horrible typhoon season had started the disaster, but it had been multiplied by poor French maintenance of the dikes, which caused floods, and the failure of the Decoux government to supply relief. Huge stores of rice in the south were left intact rather than redistributed. The Vietminh stole rice for redistribution, but their efforts could not end the famine. Ho offered Patti an "album of photographic evidence" and a detailed narrative entitled "The Black Book," to pass on to Patti's superiors. [12]

Politically, Ho spoke similarly to Vuong: "We are making preparations for an independent democratic government, to be run by the Vietnamese for the Vietnamese."[13] However, he did not ask for political
recognition from the United States. Patti reports that, unlike most partisan leaders, Ho admitted his forces had some captured weapons and
did not ask for money. Patti remarks: "Ho had revealed his weapons,
such as they were, and had not asked for any funding. OSS was accustomed to paying for intelligence. My conclusion was that much good
would come of that night's meeting."[14] Within the next few months
intelligence reports from the Vietminh found their way to the OSS. Accompanying one report was a request by Ho to forward several documents and letters to the first United Nations conference in San Francisco.

By July 1945, a provisional government organized by the Vietminh
ran six provinces in northern Vietnam. Their troop strength had also
increased; the previous month Ho notified Patti that he had more than
1,000 guerrillas for use against the Japanese. A decision was made to
parachute an OSS team code-named "Deer" into Vietminh headquarters
and begin training their troops with modern weapons and techniques.
The drop was made on July 16, 1945. Major Thomas, the OSS officer
in charge, began his first report with an account of the party held in the
Americans' honor upon their arrival:

> I was then escorted to Mr. Ho, one of the big leaders of the VML
> [Viet Minh League] Party. He speaks excellent English but is very
> weak physically as he recently walked from Tsingsi [Ch'ing-Hsi]. He
> received us most cordially. We were then shown our quarters. They
> had built for us a special bamboo shelter, consisting of a bamboo floor
> a few feet off the ground and a roof of palm leaves. We then had
> supper consisting of beer [recently captured], rice, bamboo sprouts
> and barbecued steaks. They freshly slaughtered a cow in our honor.[15]

Military training started soon thereafter. Both Vo Nguyen Giap and
Chu Van Tan, later to become commanding generals of the Democratic
Republic of Vietnam Army, received instruction from the OSS team.
Second, although the French lieutenant who accompanied the OSS mis-
sion was escorted back to China, the Vietminh requested that OSS radio
facilities be used to convey messages to the French to begin negotia-
tions. On July 25, Ho requested that a five-point plan be carried to the
French.

> We the V.M.L. request the following points be made public by the
> French and incorporated into future policy of French Indo-China.

1. That there be universal suffrage to elect a parliament for the governing of the country, that there be a French Governor-General as President until such time as independence be granted us, that he choose a cabinet or group of advisors acceptable to that parliament. Exact powers of all these officers may be discussed in the future.

2. That independence be given this country in not less than five years and not more than ten.

3. That natural resources of the country be returned to the people of the country by just payment to the present owners, and that France be granted economic concessions.

4. That all freedoms outlined by the United Nations will be granted to the Indochinese.

5. That the sale of opium be prohibited.

We hope that these conditions may be acceptable to the French government.[16]

It is a moderate proposal — independence coming only after a five- to ten-year transition period ruled by a *French* governor-general; no expropriations of French property without payment; and adherence to the United Nations charter of rights, plus the elimination of the opium trade. Patti reports that although the OSS forwarded reports to the French, "Insofar as I could determine, Ho's messages went unanswered and unacknowledged."[17]

On August 6, the United States dropped the atomic bomb on Hiroshima; three days later another bomb destroyed Nagasaki. Ho Chi Mihn soon called for convocations of both the Indochinese Communist party and the People's National Congress of the Vietminh. The ICP began its session on August 13. That night a National Insurrection Committee formed and immediately issued Military Order Number 1, the final call for general insurrection. On the sixteenth, the People's National Congress convened. It was a much broader coalition than the ICP, but its political and ethnic factions concurred in calling for insurrection. The congress elected a provisional government until national elections could be held.

Ho Chi Minh became president of the Viet Nam Committee for National Liberation. Ho's plan called for the Vietminh "to wrest power from the hands of the Japanese and the puppet government before the arrival of the Allied troops in Indochina, so that we, as masters of the country, would welcome these troops coming to disarm the Japanese."[18] In this way the Vietminh hoped to increase their powers in any negotiations with the Allies to achieve Vietnamese independence. But only a massive effort could secure this end. Ho Chi Minh thus appealed to the people:

> The decisive hour for the fate of our nation has struck. Let the people of the whole country rise up, using our own force to liberate ourselves. Many oppressed peoples in the world are emulating each other to advance and win independence. We cannot lag behind.
> Forward! Forward! Under the banner of the Viet Minh, let our people bravely march forward![19]

In late August the Vietminh tried to establish more solid relationships with the United States. Major Thomas and his OSS "Deer" team accompanied the Vietminh as observers to Hanoi, but these were low-ranking American officers, not high-level policymakers. At one point the Vietminh asked that their country be placed under "protectorate" status. They deeply feared occupation by Chiang Kai-shek's troops. They also feared the French. Portions of the Vietminh proposal are given below:

> Should the French attempt to return to Indochina with the intention of governing the country and to act once more as oppressors, the Indo-chinese people are prepared to fight to the end against such reoccupation. On the other hand, if they come as friends to establish commerce, industry, and without aspirations to rule, they will be welcomed the same as any other power.
> The Central Committee wishes to make known to the United States Government that the Indo-Chinese people desire first of all the independence of Indochina, and are hoping that the United States, as a champion of democracy, will assist her in securing this independence in the following manner;
> 1. Prohibiting or by not assisting the French from re-entering Indo-China by force.
> 2. Keeping the Chinese under control, in order that looting and pillaging will be kept to a minimum.
> 3. Sending technical advisors to assist Indo-Chinese to export [sic (exploit)] the resources of the land.

4. Develop[ing] those few industries that Indo-China is capable of supporting.

In conclusion, the Indo-Chinese would like to be placed on the same status as the Philippines for an undetermined period.[20]

Patti comments: "This was the first semiofficial communication addressed to the United States, and I felt it was of sufficient import to forward to General Donovan, to whom it was dispatched by Helliwell on 18 August."[21] (Donovan was the head of the OSS; Helliwell was Patti's commanding officer.) There is no published account of what happened to the Vietminh request.

On August 22, 1945 Major Patti, along with an OSS staff, landed in Hanoi to care for Allied prisoners in Japanese hands and to smooth the way for occupation by Allied forces. Hanoi had been liberated by the Vietminh on August 19. On August 23, more than one hundred thousand people demonstrated in Hue in support of the Vietminh; they called for the abdication of Emperor Bao Dai, who had been installed by the Japanese. The next day Bao Dai told the National Liberation Committee in Hanoi that he would abdicate the throne "so as not to stand in the way of national liberation and the independence of my people."[22] On the twenty-fifth, over half a million people demonstrated in Saigon in support of the Vietminh. The Communists called for renaming Saigon "City of Ho Chi Minh."

Back in Hanoi, preparations were made for declaring national independence. Patti was invited to an important session in drafting the final document. Here is his account of advising the Vietminh on the American Declaration of Independence:

The translator was reading some very familiar words, remarkably similar to our Declaration. The next sentence was, "This immortal statement was made in the Declaration of Independence of the United States of America in 1776."

I stopped him and turned to Ho in amazement and asked if he really intended to use it in his declaration. I don't know why it nettled me — perhaps a feeling of proprietary right, or something equally inane. Nonetheless, I asked. Ho sat back in his chair, his palms together with fingertips touching his lips ever so lightly, as though meditating. Then, with a gentle smile he asked softly, "Should I not use it?" I felt sheepish and embarrassed. Of course, I answered, why should he not? Recovering, I suggested the translator read the passage again

from the beginning. He read, "All men are created equal; they are
endowed by their Creator with certain inalienable rights; among these
are liberty, life, and the pursuit of happiness." Straining to remember, I detected the transposition of words and noted the difference in
the order of "liberty" and "life." Ho snapped to the point, "Why,
of course, there is no liberty without life, and no happiness without
liberty." He entered the correction himself and then pressed me for
more, but I pleaded ignorance, which was the truth. I could not remember the wording of our Declaration.[23]

There are two other accounts of Vietminh agents in search of the
Declaration of Independence. One comes from a lieutenant on the "Deer"
mission into Vietminh headquarters:

> He kept asking me if I could remember the language of our Dec-
> laration, [the lieutenant recalls]. I was a normal American, I couldn't,
> I could have wired up to Kunming and had a copy dropped to me, of
> course, but all he really wanted was the flavor of the thing. The more
> we discussed it, the more he actually seemed to know more about it
> than I did.[24]

The second story comes from William J. Lederer. In 1940 Lederer
was a lieutenant serving on the gunboat *Tutuila* on the Yangtze River
near Chungking, Chiang Kai-shek's headquarters. Lederer was caught
in a Japanese air raid. In the air raid shelter he met some men connected
with Vietnam.

> Father Pierre turned to me and said, "Do you, by any chance have
> a copy of the Declaration of Independence on your ship?"
> "Yes, we do."
> "Nguyen wants to know if we may make a copy of your Declara-
> tion of Independence."
> "Of course."
> Father Pierre came closer to me and said, in a low voice, "Nguyen
> is writing the Declaration of Independence for Indochina."
> "Independence from France?"
> "It will come sooner than you think. The Japanese have broken the
> backs of the French. In a few years Indochina will be able to free
> itself."[25]

Once back on the ship, Father Pierre interpreted Nguyen's remarks
as he transcribed the American Declaration of Independence: "Ah, yes,

that preamble we must use . . . right after that, in here, we will state our complaints and reasons for independence . . . no, that does not apply to us . . . ah, this we must use exactly as the Americans wrote it."[26]

Lederer reports that Father Pierre was later executed as a spy by the Japanese; it is unclear whether or not Nguyen ever made it back to Vietminh headquarters with his copy. Nevertheless, on September 2, 1945, Ho Chi Minh began his independence speech in a very familiar way:

> All men are created equal. The Creator has given us certain inviolable Rights; the right to Life, the right to be Free, and the right to achieve Happiness. These immortal words are taken from the Declaration of Independence of the United States of America in 1776. In a larger sense, this means that: All the people on earth are born equal; All the people have the right to live, to be happy, to be free.[27]

After Ho finished his speech, Vo Nguyen Giap made his. Patti says that he "never bothered to get a verbatim transcript of Giap's speech, but the next morning the Hanoi press quoted Giap as saying the 'United States of America paid the greatest contribution' to the Vietnamese cause for independence and fought with its people 'against fascist Japan, and so the Great American Republic is our good ally.' " Patti sent a complete translation to OSS headquarters. Comments by Ho pertained to the crime of *dividing* Vietnam: "[The French had] imposed inhuman laws . . . set up three different political regimes in the north, the center, and the south of Viet Nam to wreck our national unity and preclude the union of our people."[28] Other attacks concerned prisons and police, the sale of opium and alcohol, French appropriation of Vietnamese land, and the imposition of a horrible tax structure. Patti's memo enclosed Ho's final remarks:

> Summing up the state of affairs in Viet Nam, Ho declared: "The French have fled, the Japanese have capitulated, Emperor Bao Dai has abdicated. Our people have broken the chains which for nearly a century have fettered them and have won independence for the nation. Our people at the same time have overthrown the monarchic regime that has reigned supreme for dozens of centuries. In its place has been established the present Democratic Republic."
>
> Then, addressing his remarks to the world powers, [he said,] "For these reasons, we, members of the Provisional Government, repre-

senting the whole of the Vietnamese people, declare that from now on we break off all relations of a colonial character with France; we repeal all international obligations that France has so far subscribed to on our behalf; and we abolish all the special rights the French have unlawfully acquired in our territory.''

Ho concluded his address with an appeal to the United Nations and, indirectly, to the United States. ''We are convinced that the Allied nations which at Teheren and San Francisco acknowledged the principles of self-determination and equality of nations, will not refuse to acknowledge the independence of Viet Nam. For these reasons, we, members of the Provisional Government of the Democratic Republic of Viet Nam, solemnly declare to the world that Viet Nam has the right to be a free and independent country — and in fact it is so already. The entire Vietnamese people are determined to mobilize all their spiritual and material forces, to sacrifice their lives and property, in order to safeguard their right to liberty and independence.''[29]

Roosevelt's repeated pledges to create a more humane world in which national independence and human rights could be expected had been taken seriously. What happened to those words? At the Yalta Conference in February 1945, President Roosevelt asked Chiang Kai-shek if he wanted Indochina as a province of China. Chiang replied, ''It is no help to us. We don't want it. They are not Chinese.''[30] Chiang had previously tried to coopt the Vietminh and failed. Roosevelt then abandoned any concept of Indochina becoming a trusteeship oriented toward eventual independence unless the French consented. The State Department memo to Ambassador Patrick J. Hurley in China wryly remarked that such consent ''seems unlikely.'' It went on to say it was ''the President's intention at some appropriate time to ask that the French Government give some positive indication of its intentions in regard to the establishment of civil liberties and increasing measures of self-government in Indochina before formulating further declarations of policy in this respect.''[31] Given the wording of the memo, it seems fair to conclude that Roosevelt implicitly consented to French rule. Roosevelt died on April 12.

On July 16, the Potsdam Conference began. There the United States, Britain, China, and the Soviet Union agreed to Chiang Kai-shek's forces' occupying Vietnam north of the sixteenth parallel; British troops were to enter into the south and move north to the sixteenth parallel. Britain had long resisted Roosevelt's early statements on liberating colonies. They were a strong French ally in this respect. On August 28, the Chinese army crossed the border and began its march to Hanoi; by mid-September 200,000 Chinese troops were in place. Around the same time the British commander, Major General Douglas D. Gracey, arrived in Saigon with advance detachments of Indian troops.

On the twenty-second, Gracey released and rearmed over 1,500 French troops who had been prisoners of the Japanese. That night they attacked important municipal facilities and offices of the Vietminh's Provisional Government. Control of the city returned to the French. French soldiers and French residents of Saigon began a general assault of beatings, rapes, and lootings of Vietnamese. The Vietminh counterattack started on the twenty-fourth. OSS Lieutenant Colonel Peter A. Dewey was killed during the fighting that day. His last message to OSS command read: "Cochinchina is burning, the French and the British are finished here, and we [the Americans] ought to clear out of Southeast Asia."[32] Fighting continued through September. On October 2, 1945, a truce was arranged. Gracey's Indian division increased from under 2,000 to over 10,000. Marshal Jacques Philippe Leclerc arrived with the first French combat detachment of 1,000 men, all armed and equipped with new American weapons. The truce broke on October 10 when the Vietminh finally realized that the talks were simply a way for the French and the British to increase their forces. In the days that followed, the French and British troops rearmed the Japanese for attack against the Vietminh. On October 16, the Vietminh gave up Saigon and moved into the countryside.

When Gracey made his first moves against the Vietminh in late September, Ho Chi Minh decided to bring the matter to the attention of President Truman. The OSS relayed the message to Ambassador Hurley in China; Patti feels confident it was transmitted to Washington from there:

From the President of Provisional Government, Vietnam Republic
To the President of the U.S.A., Washington
We beg to inform Your Excellency of following measures taken by
Commander in Chief, British Forces in south Vietnam:
Primo, suppression of the press;
Secundo, release of arms and ammunition to French people;
Tertio, disarmament of Vietnamese police forces.

These measures constitute obvious violations of Vietnamese natural rights, direct menace to internal security, and factors disturbing stability and peace in Southeast Asia.

The Provisional Government, Republic Vietnam, therefore lodges most emphatic protest and requests through your intervention the British authorities concerned cancel those measures.

> Respectfully yours,
> Ho Chi Minh[33]

There was no response to Ho's effort. Patti was scheduled to leave Hanoi and return to the United States on October 1, 1945. Ho Chi Minh invited him to dinner for the evening of September 30. At first the conversation concerned current events. Later he reflected upon his own past, particularly his relationship to communism. Ho and Patti had discussed this before, but once again the subject was brought up. Patti's account reads:

> At the Eighteenth Congress of the French Socialist Party at Tours in December 1920, Ho along with the left-wing element of the party voted to form the French Communist Party and to seek its admission into the Third International (Comintern). Ho commented to me that there were really so few people in the political ambient interested in the colonial problem that he saw no choice. He also reflected aloud how wrong he had been to believe that the French, British, or Russian communists would concern themselves with the Vietnamese problem. "In all the years that followed, no one of the so-called liberal elements have come to the aid of colonials. I place more reliance on the United States to support Viet Nam's independence, before I could expect help from the USSR."
>
> Ho said that the Americans considered him a "Moscow puppet," an "international communist," because he had been to Moscow and had spent many years abroad. But, in fact, he said, he was not a communist in the American sense; he owed only his training to Moscow and, for that, he had repaid Moscow with fifteen years of party work. He had no other commitment. He considered himself a free agent. The *Americans* have given him more material support than the USSR.[34]

At this point Patti remarks that it was late in the evening. Ho stopped his departure with a final message:

Ho asked me to carry back to the United States a message of warm friendship and admiration for the American people. He wanted Americans to know that the people of Viet Nam would long remember the United States as a friend and ally. They would always be grateful for the material help received. But most of all for the example the struggle the history of the United States had set for Viet Nam in its struggle for independence.[35]

It was clear to the French envoy, Jean Sainteny, and the French military commander, General Leclerc, that their strength was not adequate for war. The Chinese in the north had to be removed and the estimated 500,000 troops that would be needed to fight the Vietminh successfully were not available in 1946. In this context the French tried to negotiate a settlement in which their economic privileges would be retained while the Vietnamese would be granted only minimal rights within the newly created French Union, an association composed of France's colonial territories.

In March of 1946, Ho Chi Minh and his associates reluctantly agreed to the French terms — an agreement that was ill received in Vietnam. In order to get the Chinese out, Ho was willing to delay full independence and run the risk that the French would establish some kind of pseudo-independent Vietnamese administration in the far south of Vietnam — Cochinchina, in French terms. During the occupation, the Chinese had looted extensively: industry north of the sixteenth parallel was disassembled and removed to China; large quantities of rice and retail goods had been seized. Ho said: "It is better to sniff the French dung for a while than to eat China's all our lives."[36]

On June 1, 1946, when the Vietnamese delegation was in transit to France for additional negotiations, the French suddenly declared the old emperor, Bao Dai, to be the head of Cochinchina — a new nation separate from the rest of Vietnam. The French were already beginning to subvert the agreement they signed in March; subsequent negotiations on how to implement the March agreement did not include French recognition of the Democratic Republic of Vietnam.

By October it seemed likely that French and the Vietminh would fight a war for control of Vietnam. The next month a French patrol boat in Haiphong Harbor stopped a boat to search for contraband. Vietminh troops rejected the French action as an intrusion on DRV sovereignty and jailed the three French sailors. The French prime minister, Georges

Bidault, authorized a full attack to drive the Vietminh from Haiphong. On November 23, the French cruiser *Suffren* opened fire; over 6,000 Vietnamese were killed and many more wounded that day. The French-Indochina War had begun. It continued for eight years.

Ironically, Ho Chi Minh had tried to avert war by attempting to attract intervention by the United States. Patti reports:

> From mid-November 1945 to March 1946 copies of several telegrams and letters from Ho Chi Minh to the President, the Secretary of State, the Chairman of the Senate Committee on Foreign Relations, and the United Nations reached my desk. They were earnest appeals for intervention in Viet Nam on the basis of the principles embodied in the Atlantic Charter and on humanitarian grounds. In the main they asked for political support in the Vietnamese quest for independence, citing the example of the United States in the Philippines and expressing the hope that the French would follow the American example.[37]

Patti made inquiries in the bureaucracy but found no one listening: "Ho was desperately trying to align his newborn nation with the West and he wanted to put to rest the French charges that he and his Viet Minh were tools of Moscow, but we took no notice of his signal."[38] What signals were the Americans listening to, then? What kind of communication did the State Department listen to? As Patti says, "By the summer of 1946 the word had reached Washington, and all official references to Ho were prefixed 'communist.' "[39] Ho Chi Minh and Democratic Republic of Vietnam had become the foreign Other. Secretary of State Dean Acheson remarked to his subordinates, "Keep in mind Ho's clear record as agent international communism. . . ."[40] At the time the Soviet Union neither recognized the Democratic Republic of Vietnam nor gave it assistance. In 1947 the Truman administration granted financial credits of $160 million to equip French forces for war in Indochina. The Soviet Union had no comment on the American aid program. As Ho said in 1946, "We apparently stand quite alone; we shall have to depend on ourselves."[41]

By transforming Vietnam into a series of messages in which "all official references to Ho were prefixed 'communist,' " a vast reduction of knowledge occurred. To see only the foreign Other through the conceptual grid of mechanistic anticommunism is to see virtually nothing. Vietnamese resistance to Chinese occupation is erased. Gone are the legendary heroes of revolts and rebellions. Gone are the poems, songs, and other accounts that comprise the center of Vietnam's political culture. French colonialism is erased. Gone are the opium dens, the appropriation of land, the high taxes, the jails. Vietnamese resistance to French colonialism is erased. Gone are the memories of the nineteenth-century scholar-gentry with their constant summons for the next generation to take their places. Vietnamese resistance to the Japanese is erased. Gone are the accounts of Vietminh cooperation with the OSS — and, in particular, Ho Chi Minh's efforts to secure recognition and support from the United States.

It is not that the real historical past is literally destroyed, but rather that knowledge of the social-historical world does not *count*. Ho's name had been written in the debit column of the ledger at an early date; he was "Communist" Ho Chi Minh, and that was all that counted. Having been entered into the ledger, the Vietminh could then be treated as opponents within the categories of Technowar — a technological apparatus to be defeated by a larger, more sophisticated technological apparatus.

The $160 million grant from the United States to France in 1947 did not buy victory. Most roads in Cochinchina were held by the French, but they never won the allegiance of the peasantry. Major French offenses failed. Bernard B. Fall reports that by fall 1950 the French were defeated. In one major battle Marshal Leclerc lost 6,000 men out of 40,000. However, in 1950 the Korean War began and mechanistic anticommunism became more firmly established. The Soviet Union and the People's Republic of China finally gave diplomatic recognition to the Democratic Republic of Vietnam. Secretary of State Dean Acheson announced that the recognitions should "remove any illusions as to the 'nationalist' nature of Ho Chi Minh's aims and reveals Ho in his true colors as the mortal enemy of native independence in Indochina."[42]

From 1950 through 1954 French colonial war progressively became an American war against communism utilizing French troops. The United States provided most of the funding and American generals and senior officials reviewed major strategic plans conceived by French high command. In 1950, U.S. financial aid totaled $150 million; the next year it increased threefold to nearly $450 million — 40 percent of the total cost. By 1953, $785 million was allocated. The French became instruments of American foreign policy, and their troops, mercenaries for hire. Although no public official, neither French nor American, would so phrase the relationship, some French officers saw the exchange of blood for money. Bernard B. Fall provides the "contract," as once told him by a French colonel:

> "This is not a military war in the old sense. It is not even a political war. What we're facing here is a social war, a class war. As long as we don't destroy the mandarin class, abolish excessive tenancy rates and do fail to give every farmer his own plot of land, this country'll go communist as soon as we turn our backs.
>
> "As long as we don't give the Vietnamese the only program they could really be expected to fight for, we're doomed to fight this war without any hopes for success and die here like mercenaries. I'm getting close to a thousand dollars a month in pay and allowances for fighting in the rice paddies, and my sector killed one thousand commies last month; that makes it one dollar per commie on my pay."

Fall asked the colonel whether his view was shared by junior officers.

> "Oh, well," said the colonel, puffing at his Gauloise, "they believe they're doing the right thing and that's the way it's got to be. If they knew they were dying uselessly here, it would be like shooting them in the belly and kicking them in the behind at the same time. And when my aide eventually fries in his tank, I want him to believe that he's frying for the good of the country. That's the least I can do for him."
>
> Wainwright [another French colonel] sat there, nodding. This view of the war seemed to be pretty much a consensus. "The Americans," he said, "have been paying an increasing share of the war costs since 1952, with us expending the francs here and their dollars going into our Treasury at home. At least we have the consolation of paying for the prosperity of Frenchmen at home, even though they don't know it. We're getting to the point of Rumania under *Bismarck,* when Bismarck said: 'To be a Bohemian is not a nationality. It is a profession.' "[43]

American military aid for the Indochina War was but a portion of total military aid to France of $2,956,000,000 from 1950 to 1953. Still, money and technology were not by themselves adequate. Technowar conceives the foreign Other as structurally analogous to itself. Social relationships do not *count* in the calculus of military strategy. But as the colonel indicated, the war involved important elements of social structure and culture. It is important to understand how the contradictions of Technowar ultimately led to French-American defeat.

In 1950, American aid began arriving in Vietnam in large amounts. Nineteen fifty was also the year when a new French commander came to Indochina convinced that within fifteen months he could defeat the Vietminh and "save it [Indochina] from Peking and Moscow."[44] General Jean de Lattre Tassigny's military strategy was designed to keep the Vietminh *out*. Under his command thousands of forts were constructed throughout the country, each fort manned by troops numbering from a dozen or so in small forts to several hundred in large ones. Bernard B. Fall describes these forts:

> And there were now the French forts, some downright ridiculous in their exact imitation of the North African "Beau Geste" type (you would almost expect Gary Cooper and Marlene Dietrich to stand atop one of the crenelated towers in a tender embrace while soldiers with gold epaulets and caps with flowing neckguards would steadfastly look the other way), others of the squattish, ugly looking, deeply-dug-in modern bunker type.
>
> In fact the forts not only became standardized, but they were actually assigned model numbers, just like automobiles, such as "FTSV-52" (Ground Forces, South Vietnam, 1952) so that the *afficionados* would immediately know what you were talking about.[45]

Built along roads at regular intervals, these forts represent the technological transformation of war into an abstract space, a space punctuated at regular intervals by the mass-produced consumer durables — the forts. Because each fort represents a point that can be bypassed by the Vietminh, it calls for the construction of another fort a few kilometers away, and that fort in turn calls for another fort. Each new fort needs more troops and weapons. Each destroyed fort calls for study to design a newer, better model for production and distribution. Each new model renders the old model obsolete, which means constant modification of the older forts. The production, distribution, and maintenance of the forts became the end goal as well as the means of war.

General Vo Nguyen Giap discussed the "de Lattre Line" in terms of the contradictions of colonialism: "The ultimate goal of the French colonialists was to grab our land. Faced with our opposition, they had to scatter their forces and set up thousands of military posts, big and small, to protect what they had seized. Thus, the war of aggression undertaken by the French Expeditionary Corps was a process of constant scattering of that army. And the more it was scattered the better conditions we had to destroy it part by part."[46] The foreign Other cannot be kept "out" when the Other lives there. In pursuing "territorial" defense, the French army was broken up into small units, which allowed the Vietminh to concentrate their forces and destroy forts one by one. The Vietminh may well have been the "weaker" force in weapons and machines that count in Technowar, but the distribution of these weapons to defend colonial social structure took away this disadvantage.

By 1953, even the French could see the futility of their construction project. Of 500,000 troops committed to the war, 350,000 were either confined to forts or performing noncombat functions. In the north an estimated 30,000 Vietminh regulars and guerrillas operated behind the de Lattre Line, even though the area was defended by 80,000 French troops in 900 forts. The Vietnamese did not rally to the French. Once a fort was attacked, no local Vietnamese would approach. The French program of "Vietnamization," a project to "feed war by war, to use the Vietnamese troops to fight the Vietnamese," did not succeed very well either.[47] While there were many Vietnamese units, the French had to use both their own troops and troops raised in other French colonies such as Algeria, Morocco, and Senegal. Colonials themselves at home, these troops became Frenchmen when fighting other colonials; it was the one mark of brilliance in an otherwise grim situation.

To reorganize the war, a new general came to Vietnam. General Henri Navarre called for a radical redistribution of military forces, one that concentrated thousands of small forts into a few large ones known as "hedgehogs," and redeployed remaining forces in mechanized battalions and regiments, the famous *Groupes Mobile*. Paratroopers would be used as strategic reserve forces. The Navarre Plan had full American approval. Lieutenant General John W. O'Daniel, responsible for distributing American military supplies in Indochina, loved it, and it was approved by the Joint Chiefs of Staff as well as Secretary of State John Foster Dulles.[48]

Whereas the de Lattre Line approach recognized that a colonial war was at issue by its attempts to separate the people from the Vietminh with an infinite number of forts, each point on the line theoretically responsible for restraining local guerrillas, the Navarre Plan *breaks* with any conception of people's war. Instead, the new plan tacitly reconceptualizes the Vietminh in the image of the French. Theoretically, the very technological force and size of the fortresses and mechanized units would have required the Vietminh to attack in large units, to become like the French. However, since the Vietminh did not possess tanks, airplanes, and the other technological means of war production, they would inevitably be defeated: the more mechanized war machine would surely destroy the primitive one by virtue of the technological superiority of one "machine" over another.

By reformulating war as a struggle between machines, the French theoretically abolished guerrilla war: how could a company of guerrillas attack a large machine? Similarly, the Vietnamese people in this conception of war disappeared as a people whose political allegiance was at issue and reappeared as bodies to be counted. As the French lieutenant said: "What is a Vietminh — A Viet Minh? He is a dead Vietnamese. . . ."[49] Vietminh equals Vietnamese signifies the end of pacification efforts.

No armored column confined to roads could surprise Vietminh forces. Even discounting the fact that Vietminh intelligence networks penetrated many commands, the sheer size, noise, and routinized patterns gave the French away. Bernard B. Fall describes the immense theater signifying a mechanized operation was in progress:

> Like clockwork, each such mop-up operation begins by an aerial reconnaissance, which only puts the commies on notice that something is afoot; then this is followed up by long columns of trucks carrying the troops necessary for the operation. And, as if this weren't sufficient to wake up the whole neighborhood, there generally came along a few tanks to provide for artillery support, I suppose, whose clanking can be heard five miles away.[50]

Consequently, although the French mobile forces were strategically designed to be on the offensive, at the tactical level, the operational level, they were grinding their way into *ambushes*. Entire battle groups were decimated in ambushes, and relief forces sent to rescue them often met another ambush. Mines also hurt French mobile forces. From 1952 to 1954, nearly 400 of 500 armored vehicles destroyed were casualties to mines and booby traps.[51] French forces were superior only in the abstract space of machine versus machine theory. In the concrete space of Vietnam, the Vietminh used French rationalized operations to their advantage, and the theoretically nonexistent guerrillas destroyed tanks with mines, *one by one*.

Hedgehog fortresses fared no better. In the winter of 1953 General Navarre decided to make a camp in northwestern Laos, Dien Bien Phu, the center of his spring campaign. The camp consisted of fortified positions equipped with artillery, mortars, machine guns, and infantry.

Each position could fire on each other's position, and thus protect one another. Sixteen thousand troops defended the camp. Resupply came by air. Dien Bien Phu was both "bait" and "trap," the place where the technologically superior machine would defeat the primitive.

Hedgehog among hedgehogs, the camp's defensibility assumed that the Vietminh could not emplace artillery and ammunition in mountains surrounding the valley fortress. On March 13, 1954, shelling from the mountains began. The French artillery commander committed suicide that night; he saw the end inscribed in the beginning. The subfortress defending the airstrip received the first major ground assault. Once it was gone, only limited supplies could be parachuted down and the wounded could not be removed. Vietminh anti-aircraft guns made even this limited effort difficult. French air forces attempted to destroy enemy artillery and anti-aircraft guns, but they were emplaced deep in the mountains: pushed forward to fire a few rounds, then pulled back to safety, such guns were almost impossible to destroy. On May 8, Dien Bien Phu surrendered. Fifteen hundred men had been killed, 3,000 to 4,000 wounded; the remaining 10,000 were either taken prisoner or were missing in action.[52]

The United States came close to militarily intervening at Dien Bien Phu. In March the French asked for additional B-26 light bombers and a promise of direct American air strikes if the Chinese air force appeared. In response, the chairman of the Joint Chiefs of Staff, Admiral Arthur Redford, proposed Operation Vulture: 60 B-29 heavy bombers stationed in the Philippines and 150 fighter planes flying from carriers in the Gulf of Tonkin would bomb hills surrounding the hedgehog fortress. Secretary of State Dulles thought that Congress would have to approve such strikes, and on April 3 President Eisenhower arranged a conference with congressional power brokers. Discussion revealed that the army thought that ground troops would also have to be committed and that this intervention was not desirable. Congressmen told Dulles and Eisenhower that direct intervention in Indochina would have to be a multinational effort with Great Britain included. Winston Churchill rejected the joint venture proposal on April 27, saying no action was appropriate until the Geneva peace negotiations had been given time to mature.

No thought was given to *how the unthinkable had happened:* how the technologically inferior Vietminh could defeat the French-American war machine. What the Vietminh had lacked in techno-capital they made up for by mobilizing people. Secret roads were constructed; transport con-

# The Military Situation in May 1954

C H I N A

Black R

Red R

Munan Pass

Dien Bien Phu

HANOI

Haiphong

A Long Bay

Thanh Hoa

GULF OF TONKIN

HAINAN

Luang Prabang

V I E T N A M

Vinh

Ha Tinh

CAPE RON

Mekong River

Vientiane

Dong Hoi

L A O S

Savannaket

Hue

Danang

N

S O U T H   C H I N A

THAILAND

Pakse

Quang Ngai

Pleiku

Qui Nhon

S E A

C A M B O D I A

CAPE VARELLA

Cam Ranh Bay

CAPE PADARAN

GULF OF SIAM

Dung River

SAIGON

CAPE ST. JACQUES

| | Areas controlled by the Vietminh |
| | Areas of Vietminh guerrilla activity |

miles   0   50   100   150   200
km   0   50   100 150 200

G.W.WARD

102°

106°

110°

20°

16°

12°

sisted of a mobilized populace pushing loaded bicycles. Artillery pieces were disassembled for the mountain journey and then reassembled in secret caves. Even a mountain river was rechanneled so that when the summer rains came the valley would be flooded. As Giap says of Navarre: "His greater mistake was that with the conception of a bourgeois strategist, he could not visualize the immense possibilities of a people's army and the entire people who were fighting for independence and peace."[53]

Although only 5 percent of the French Union combat forces were destroyed at Dien Bien Phu, the battle closed the war. The Geneva Conference had started April 26, and the fall of Dien Bien Phu pushed the French toward a settlement. Pierre Mendès-France, the new premier-designate, came to Geneva in early June and set a thirty-day limit for successful negotiations. Major world powers had their representatives at the conference (China, Russia, Britain, France, and the United States). The Democratic Republic of Vietnam (the Vietminh) and the Republic of Vietnam also had representatives. This latter country had been formed by France, with former emperor Bao Dai back on the throne.

Both the French and the Vietminh had territories widely dispersed. Some observers have referred to the situation as looking like a "checkerboard" in that the two sides crisscrossed. (See Philippe Devillers and Jean Lacouture's map from their book on the 1954 negotiations, *End of a War* [1969].)

Pham Van Dong, head of the DRV delegation, suggested that the scattered territorial holdings of the Vietminh and the French be exchanged into large blocks, "so that each side would acquire zones representing a single holding that would be relatively large and would facilitate economic activity and administrative control in each respective area."[54] These zones would be established upon a north-south axis, with the Vietminh getting territory in the north and Bao Dai's government getting territory in the south.

The idea was to establish a *provisional boundary*. This line did not signify two sovereign states; it was not intended to be a permanent division of Vietnam into two separate countries. The first article of the Geneva Agreement reads: "A provisional military demarcation line shall be fixed, on either side of which the forces of the two parties shall be grouped after their withdrawal." Another section reads, "The military demarcation line is provisional and should not in any way be interpreted as constituting a political or territorial boundary."[55] This provisional line would hold only until 1956, when *general elections throughout*

*Vietnam* were to be held to decide on a single government for a unified Vietnamese nation.

Vietminh representatives thought the line should be established at the thirteenth or fourteenth parallel. They had recently defeated a major French force at An Tuc near the fourteenth parallel, and Vietminh guerrilla forces had been highly active in the south. Some French officers also agreed with the Vietminh assessment *privately*.[56] However, neither the Chinese delegation, headed by Chou En-lai, nor the Soviet delegation, headed by Molotov, would press the Vietminh position. Both China and the Soviet Union were attempting to establish global détente with the West. When the French offered the eighteenth parallel, Dong was forced into countering with the sixteenth; a compromise established the line at the seventeenth parallel. The Vietminh were not happy with this compromise, but they were confident they would win the 1956 general elections. Other provisions explicitly prohibited introducing additional troops or munitions. Nor could any foreign country establish a military base.

Approximately 95,000 French Union forces — French, Algerians, Moroccans, Senegalese, Vietnamese, Laotians, and Cambodians — had been killed in eight years of war. Wounded numbered in the hundreds of thousands. Eleven billion dollars had been spent. Moreover, the war brought yet another colonial revolution to the French empire: many Algerians who fought in Vietnam returned home to fight for their own independence.

In January, the National Security Council and President Eisenhower directed American diplomats to tell France that any political settlement based on a coalition government was not acceptable. The memo said: "A nominally noncommunist coalition regime would eventually turn the country over to Ho [Chi Minh] with no opportunity for the replacement of the French by the United States or the United Kingdom."[57]

The United States neither signed nor initialed the final conference agreements at Geneva. Eisenhower publicly stated that the accords were simply the "best . . . under the circumstances, in no way binding the future actions of the United States." April and May of 1954 were the great months for the complete articulation of the domino theory. When Dulles first arrived in Geneva, he said, "We hope to find that the aggressors come here in a mood to *purge* themselves of their aggression."[58] These are words directed to demonic nature, nature fallen. Having no natural place within nature, the Communists could be nothing other than foreign aggressors.

With the establishment of the provisional military demarcation line, another transformation of history into the static, mechanical world of anticommunism and Technowar took place. This provisional line created two countries, two separate countries conventionally known as North Vietnam and South Vietnam, the south within nature, the north outside it as the foreign Other battling to get in.

## CHAPTER 4

# America Comes to Vietnam:
# Installing the Mechanisms, 1954–1964

W ITH the French defeat, the United States could no longer support anticommunism in Vietnam at a distance. At first it was a question of finding an anti-Communist leader and establishing an administration that would retain the area for the West without prolonged combat. The United States would soon fill the space vacated by France with a man named Ngo Dinh Diem. Diem came from an upper-class, Catholic family in central Vietnam with a long history of political activism. Emperor Bao Dai had appointed Diem as minister of the interior in 1933, but Diem had resigned within a few months and accused Bao Dai of being "nothing but an instrument in the hands of the French authorities."[1] In 1949, Bao Dai offered him the premiership, but again Diem refused because the position entailed too much subservience to France. Instead, he created a small political party called the Phong Trao Quoc-Gia Qua Kich, or National Extremist Movement, which declared itself to be against both the French and the Vietminh.

Two years later Diem abandoned politics within Vietnam for an extended journey abroad and contact with Vietnamese exiles. After traveling first to Japan and Europe, Diem and his brother, a Catholic bishop named Monsignor Thuc, arrived in the United States. There they made contact with the Maryknoll Fathers and Cardinal Francis Spellman. Cardinal Spellman had great political influence; Diem was soon able to meet Congressmen Mike Mansfield and John F. Kennedy, Henry Luce (the publisher of *Time* and *Life* magazines), Secretary of State John Foster Dulles, congressional Asia expert and conservative leader Dr. Walter H. Judd, and other influential men. Most became highly enthusiastic about Diem and subsequently "sponsored" him.[2]

On June 16, 1954, Bao Dai once again offered the premiership to

Diem. Diem did not immediately accept, but instead held out for three days to secure full civilian and military powers — the powers of an absolute dictator. He succeeded in obtaining the sought-after concessions from Bao Dai. On June 26, 1954, he arrived in Saigon.

Edward Lansdale, the principal agent of the Central Intelligence Agency in Vietnam, was highly impressed with him and soon succeeded in persuading the agency to support Diem and contribute money to bribe Diem's non-Communist opposition into acquiescence. Although the United States spoke of a state-to-state relationship with the new Republic of Vietnam, in reality Diem's presence was contingent upon massive American support. The Republic of Vietnam was a legal fiction; only a weak administrative structure with little popular following existed. The United States was setting up a regime to serve as a relay for anti-Communist efforts.

American intelligence operatives soon helped create a special constituency to support Diem. They began a rumor campaign directed toward Catholics living in the north. The Catholics were told that the Vietminh would close down their churches, that the Virgin Mary had been seen leaving the north and would appear only in the south, and that those Catholics who stayed would be in grave danger, spiritually as well as physically. An estimated 860,000 people, mostly Catholics, were moved south by the United States Navy 7th Fleet.[3] This new population, resettled in central Vietnam on appropriated land and given good financial support, constituted Diem's social base. Both Diem's officer corps and his high-ranking administrative personnel were selected from these Catholics. Since most Vietnamese practice Buddhism, Diem in effect established a severe social division between his government and the Vietnamese people by relying upon a Catholic power base.

Diem's land reform policies further divided the Vietnamese. Vietnam was an agricultural country in which a small landholding class owned most of the land while most of the rural populace owned very little land or no land at all. It was a quasi-feudal social structure characterized by a paternalistic relationship between landlord and tenant. One landlord described the relationship as follows:

> *In the past,* the relationship between the landlord and his tenants was paternalistic. The landlord considered the tenant as an inferior member of his extended family. When the tenant's father died, it was the duty of the landlord to give money to the tenant for the funeral; if his wife was pregnant, the landlord gave money for the birth; if he was in financial ruin, the landlord gave assistance; therefore, the ten-

ant had to behave as an inferior member of the extended family. The landlord enjoyed great prestige vis-a-vis the tenant.[4]

Landlords had also received 40 to 60 percent of the tenants' annual crops as rent. During the war against colonialism, which had also been a class war, Vietminh forces drove most large landowners into the cities. They subsequently undertook various projects to help the peasants. According to one estimate, 500,000 hectares (1 hectare equals 2.47 acres) were distributed to the peasantry.[5] In other areas the Vietminh ended rent payment to landlords or established much lower rents in the 5 to 10 percent range.[6]

Diem *reversed* these gains. Wherever his military forces established themselves, landlords regained their land. Many landlords demanded years of back rent that they had not collected during the war.

Some efforts were made to ameliorate landlord-peasant relationships, but for the most part they were not successful. In 1955, "Ordinance Two" established 25 percent of the crop as maximum rent. In practice this ordinance was rarely enforced; tenant payments often went far beyond this figure.

In 1956, "Ordinance Fifty-seven" declared that the maximum land a family could own was 100 hectares, plus an additional 15 hectares for ancestor worship and another 30 hectares if the owner actually farmed. This law made 30 percent of the cropland in Vietnam available for redistribution; the other 70 percent was owned in parcels of less than 100 hectares and thus was not affected.[7] Peasants were required to *purchase* land available for redistribution. Few tenant farmers could afford such purchases. Of those who could afford a purchase, fewer still succeeded in having their applications approved and processed by Saigon officials. At most, 10 percent of the landless peasantry could take advantage of land reform. Only a small number of peasants benefited by the regime's ascension to power; most lost land and had to pay higher rents. Landlords whose land was redistributed received in compensation shares in industrial enterprises operated by the Diem family.

Appropriation of the nation's wealth in favor of the upper class was accompanied by political dictatorship. A 1955 referendum asking whether Bao Dai should return as monarch or Diem stay as premier of the republic found Diem with 98 percent of the vote. In Saigon he received more votes than registered voters — 98 percent of 605,025 votes cast when there were only approximately 450,000 registered voters. Vote fraud was commented upon in *Life* magazine. An article noted that Diem's

American advisers had contended that a 60 percent margin of victory actually looked better than 98 percent, but Diem "insisted on 98 percent."[8] This small "problem" was downplayed in the article. In 1956, Diem abolished the village councils. These local governing bodies were formed by popular elections in some villages while landlords completely determined their decisions in other villages, but either way, the councils had not been under firm control by Diem. With their demise, the entire governmental apparatus, from military appointments to province and district officials, functioned solely on the basis of responsiveness to Diem and his family. There was no accountability to the people.

In effect, Ngo Dinh Diem saw himself as a modern-day emperor. In his words, "A sacred respect is due to the person of the sovereign. He is the mediator between the people and heaven as he celebrates the national cult." In one interview concerning his religious faith, Diem said, "You know, I consider myself rather as a Spanish Catholic," an index of his extreme conservatism and intolerance. In other interviews he responded to questions concerning his policies with the reply: "I know what is best for my people."[9] From Diem's perspective, the consolidation of a top-down hierarchy made his regime more legitimate to the people, rather than less so.

To dissipate the possibility of resistance, the regime destroyed Vietminh political organizations. Although the Geneva Agreements explicitly had forbidden any retaliation against members of either side who did not withdraw to their respective zones, this provision (Article 14c) had no impact. By 1956, the official estimate for political prisoners in jail or special camps was 20,000, but the actual figure was far higher.[10] In one district with a population of 180,000, some 7,000 people were known to be in jail and another 13,000 were missing.[11] Another report asserted that by the summer of 1956, approximately 90 percent of Communist party cells in one province had been demolished.[12] In 1959, Diem announced Law 10/59, an official anti-Communist act that allowed the government to jail any opposition under the allegation of Communist activity.

Diem's regime appeared successful by the late 1950s. Throughout the decade South Vietnam received huge amounts of foreign aid; only Laos and Korea received more on a per capita basis. American advisers reconstructed military and civilian government structures along advanced, "modern" lines. Lieutenant General John ("Iron Mike") O'Daniel became the first commander of the United States Military Advisory Group in Vietnam in 1954. According to Bernard B. Fall, O'Daniel had previously "acquired an excellent reputation in Korea for setting up divisional training camps that turned out Korean Army divisions in almost *assembly-line* fashion."[13] Later in the fifties, Lieutenant General Samuel Williams took over. He insisted that the developing South Vietnamese army be reorganized into larger units and trained to resist a conventional military invasion from the *north*.

Militarization was also conceived as a way of establishing South Vietnam as a nation. Originally the Joint Chiefs of Staff thought it was "hopeless to expect a U.S. military training mission to achieve success unless the nation is able effectively to perform those governmental functions essential to the successful raising and maintenance of armed forces." However, John Foster Dulles insisted on military involvement "to bolster the government by strengthening the army which supports it."[14]

The United States Operations Mission assisted economic development. Dr. Wesley Fishel of Michigan State University led a team of social scientists to Vietnam to reorganize civil administration and police according to the principles of American public administration. Whenever a department of Diem's government ran out of money, the United States made up the deficit. From the American point of view, the ability of the regime to exist without visible resistance satisfied its one essential function as anti-Communist. That this exchange process required a massive outlay of money to sustain it, that the regime had little popular backing, that dictatorship did not equal democracy — all these "debits" meant little to the single credit of sustained anticommunism.

Although these debits did not theoretically exist as significant factors on the balance sheet of mechanistic anticommunism, they existed as political realities in Vietnam. Ho Chi Minh and other leaders had agreed to the provisional demarcation line at the seventeenth parallel because they were sure they would win reunification elections scheduled for 1956. Some troops were hidden deep in the Mekong Delta and along the Cambodian border but were forbidden to take armed action. The party chose to sustain losses inflicted by the regime and to persist in international efforts to secure elections. According to the Central Committee's 1956 analysis, "The Path of Revolution in the South," repression indicated the social weakness of the regime and prepared people for political action when the time was "ripe."

Yet, with their clumsy fascist policy of violence, can the Americans and Diem create a powerful force to suppress the revolutionary movement?

Assuredly not, because their regime is not founded on any significant political force. On the contrary, almost all segments of the population are opposed to them. For this reason the regime of the Americans
and Diem is not strong. Rather, it is just a cruel and cowardly regime,
which not only has no foundation in the masses but is also being
isolated internationally. Its vicious nature certainly cannot shake the
revolutionary movement, and certainly it cannot long survive.[15]

The strategy of waiting for "ripeness" persisted too long, however.
By late 1958 and early 1959, ethnic tribes in central Vietnam, tribes
formerly allied with the Vietminh against the French, could no longer
countenance delay and struck the South Vietnamese army. Soon former
Vietminh in the same area attacked to take pressure off the tribes.[16]
Cadres throughout the country dug up their old weapons and began to
attack, while agitating within the party for a joint military-political approach.

At the Fifteenth Conference of the Party Central Committee in May
1959, the party decided the situation was "ripe." Party structure was
soon reorganized to facilitate struggle by elevating the southern branch
from a subordinate section to a division of the Central Committee — as
had been in the case in the war against the French. In late 1960 the
National Liberation Front (NLF) was formed to organize all those non-
Communist elements that opposed Diem into a more united organization. Some southerners who had left the south in 1954 began the long
trek home.

By the end of 1959, an estimated 2,500 hamlets were outside of the
regime's control, and two-thirds of them even had an open NLF political structure. Fatalistic resignation to the relationship between landlord
and tenant had been broken by the land redistribution program conducted by the Vietminh years before. Beginning in 1960, Vietcong began to appear in villages to renew the struggle against landlords. Large
landowners were threatened; small landowners were told to reduce their
rents below 25 percent; and tenants were told not to leave their villages
to pay rent, but instead to make landlords come into the countryside and
thus face the Vietcong.[17]

This threefold policy soon led to *militarization* of the landlord-tenant
relationship. Landlords contracted with province and district officials of
the GVN (Republic of Vietnam) to collect rents, for 30 percent of the
take. Government officials in turn contracted with ARVN (Army, Republic of Vietnam) officers to provide troops to force payment. The

government official would get 10 percent of the collected rents, the army officer another 10 percent, and the officer's troops the final 10 percent.[18] Vietnamese peasants were confronted with both the civil administration and the army acting as *direct agents* of landlords.

The Diem regime's alignment with the landlords inevitably brought forth armed response from the peasants. As one National Liberation Front official explained: "Only by sending their sons into the army [NLF forces] and paying taxes [to the NLF] could the war be won, and only by winning the war could they keep their own land. Thus land is a life and death issue, inextricably tied to their own interests."[19]

Land in Vietnam was not just one commodity among others, one way of making a living as opposed to others. Robert L. Samson, an economist, interviewed hundreds of peasants on their farming practices. One question he routinely asked concerned the price of land: "Inquiries regarding the price of land brought puzzled expressions, an occasional reserved smile or chuckle, but usually no reply."[20] From these responses he learned that *there was no price for land;* land was *priceless.*

Mao Tse-tung's revolution had achieved victory years before on this same principle of land for peasants. As Mao says:

> Everything arose out of a specified situation; we organized peasant revolt, we did not instigate it. Revolution is a drama of passion; we did not win the people over by appealing to reason, but by developing hope, trust, and fraternity. In the face of famine, the will to equality takes on a religious force. Then, in the struggle for rice, land, and the rights brought by agrarian reform, the peasants had the conviction that they were fighting for their lives and those of their children. . . .[21]

Revolution in China had been subsumed by American policymakers under the category of expanding monolithic communism. In the same way developing revolution in Vietnam could be seen only as "Chinese communist expansion." However, the growing military strength of the National Liberation Front — from 5,000 in 1960 to 15,000 armed guerrillas in 1961 — represented a developing *internal social revolution.*

For American anti-Communist leaders, Vietnam was a special site, the place where the United States still had time for intervention. Communism could only be stopped *before* Vietnam fell; according to the domino theory, the fast chain reaction of subsequent falling countries (the dominoes) would not leave the United States time for appropriate intervention against Communist expansion. Given the world-determining status accorded Vietnam by U.S. leaders, it should not be surprising that developments in Vietnam could be influenced by world events that had a symbolic connection with the domino theory.

The particular historical event in question was the CIA-sponsored Bay of Pigs invasion of Cuba in April 1961. Although the invasion plan falsely assumed that Fidel Castro had little popular support and that consequently the island's population would support the invading exiles, the failure of the invasion was taken by President Kennedy as an occasion to *reaffirm* the domino theory:

> For we are opposed around the world by a *monolithic* and ruthless conspiracy that relies primarily on covert means for expanding its sphere of influence — on infiltration instead of invasion, on subversion instead of elections, on intimidation instead of free choice, on guerrillas by night instead of armies by day. It is a system which has conscripted vast human and material resources into the building of a tightly knit, highly efficient machine. . . .
>
> We intend to profit from this lesson. We intend to re-examine and re-orient our forces of all kinds — our tactics and our institutions here in this community. We intend to intensify our efforts for a struggle in many ways more difficult than war.[22]

Note the metaphors — monolithic machine, turning the debit into a profitable ledger. Most importantly, though, the failure of the invasion is posed as a *tactical* failure. A new machine, a new *technology of warfare,* would be needed to defeat the machine of the foreign Other. This new machine would be called "counterinsurgency."

Within the Kennedy administration, "counterinsurgency" became the slogan for war mobilization. An interagency task force entitled "Special Group (Counterinsurgency)" led the effort. Robert Kennedy served as the President's personal representative. General Maxwell Taylor came back from retirement to head the committee. (Taylor had previously resigned from the army because of his disagreement with the dominant military strategy of massive nuclear retaliation. His book, *The Uncertain Trumpet* [1960], explicitly called for the military "to play a good game" of limited war.)[23] At the State Department, a new six-week course in counterinsurgency became a career necessity for foreign service officers. The Central Intelligence Agency, the Agency for International Development, and the United States Information Agency similarly began counterinsurgency preparation.

United States Army Special Forces prepared a demonstration for President Kennedy to persuade him that they were the appropriate instrument for limited warfare. Former Special Forces sergeant Donald Duncan describes the preparations made for President Kennedy's review:

> Every enlisted man and officer on Smoke Bomb Hill was affected: men were detailed to build floats, the Psychological Warfare Battalion cranked out millions of leaflets and painted huge posters and backdrops, engineers were detailed to drive huge logs into the mud of McKellar's Lake and support them with cables. Strange equipment appeared. Mock submarines were knocked together. Speeches were written and rehearsed, rewritten and rehearsed again. Sky divers practiced jumping into the lake. Mock battles, complete with ambushes, were rehearsed. A team with a "Rube Goldberg" rocket belt appeared. Hundreds of NCO's [noncommissioned officers] spent countless man-hours picking up bits of paper along the road leading to the lake. Then it was mass rehearsals from morning to night — talkthroughs, walkthroughs, and finally, dress rehearsals. This had to be a real Cecil B. De Mille spectacular. President Kennedy was coming!

The show itself was a great extravaganza:

> A LARK (a small amphibious lighter) lumbered into the lake, carrying a man wearing a rocket contraption — jets roaring, he flew across the water and landed in front of the President. Scuba divers swam to shore from the dummy submarine; skydivers trailing colored smoke tracked in from fifteen thousand feet and hit the water as planned; an expert judo team brutally displayed skills; another group climbed the tall poles and made thrilling rides on a "slide-for-life" into the water. The ambush went off without a hitch — low-level passes were made with L-19s, Caribous, Mohawks, and helicopters; on cue over a thousand men who had been hiding in the brush across the lake stood and removed fatigue shirts, and in their white T-shirts, shooting off hand flares, ran screaming and yelling to the water's edge. They represented the number of guerrillas the twelve-man team can organize and direct. Hundreds of men from the Seventh appeared elsewhere on the lake — all wearing the forbidden beret. The message is clear; these are the skills that every Special Forces man has. We are ready to go. We are yours. Use us. Then millions of leaflets drop over the area — they are printed with the President's picture.

Counterinsurgency was thus presented as the use of unconventional *techniques,* rather than as social and political mobilization. Duncan re-

marks on the hardware and technical performance: "Much of the equipment shown, including the rocket, had never been seen before and
probably would never be seen again, and much of it had no application
to Special Forces anyway." Nonetheless, technology was the only form
of power and technical knowledge was the only form of knowledge that
counted in the war-managers' universe.

President Kennedy authorized Special Forces to wear the green beret
after it had long been forbidden by the military hierarchy. The green
beret would be "a mark of distinction and a badge of courage." More
important, the United States Army Center for Special Warfare received
additional resources and, in Duncan's words, "direct lines to the main
man." [24]

The lesson was not lost upon the rest of the military. The air force
formed Air Commando squadrons for limited warfare. The navy created
the "SEALs" — Sea-Air-Land commandos — for use along coasts and
riverine waterways. The mainstream army increased its tests for large-
scale helicopter warfare. Research on new war technology proliferated;
one Joint Chiefs of Staff memo in 1962 listed 322 items in research and
development.

Research and development for Technowar necessarily implies deployment for testing. Vietnam became coded with another layer of abstrac-
tion, the vocabulary of scientific testing. Maxwell Taylor describes
Vietnam:

> Here we have a going laboratory where we see subversive insur-
> gency, the Ho Chi Minh doctrine, being applied in all its forms. This
> has been a challenge not just for the armed services, but for several
> of the agencies of Government, as many of them are involved in one
> way or another in South Vietnam. On the military side, however, we
> have recognized the importance of the area as a laboratory. We have
> had teams out there looking at the equipment requirements of this kind
> of guerrilla warfare. We have rotated senior officers through there,
> spending several weeks just to talk to people and get the feel of the
> operation, so even though not regularly assigned to Vietnam, they are
> carrying their experience back to their own organizations. [25]

Vietnam also represented a laboratory in social science. Daniel Ellsberg was but one of hundreds who journeyed to Vietnam in the name
of counterinsurgency. Walt Rostow, a trained economist, served as a
presidential adviser. In 1960 Rostow published *The Stages of Economic
Growth: A Non-Communist Manifesto*. In the next to the last chapter he

describes the benefits of colonialism: "Colonies were often established initially not to execute a major objective of national policy, nor even to exclude a rival economic power, but to fill a vacuum; that is, to organize a traditional society incapable of self-organization (or unwilling to organize itself) for modern import and export activity, including production for export." [26] For Rostow, modernization ultimately meant "The Age of High Mass-Consumption," with the United States as the paradigmatic case for others to emulate. Communism was "best understood as a *disease* of the transition to modernization." Rostow does not say that diseases are "foreign" germs, but he does call Communists "scavengers," whose inevitably *external* interventions represent a "crude act of international vandalism." [27] For the United States, war posed the question of "how to conduct wars with just enough violence to be good sports — and to accelerate capital depreciation — without blowing up the planet?" [28]

Rostow's macroeconomic theory of world development was only one component of the economic rationalization of the state. With the appointment of Robert S. McNamara as secretary of defense in 1961, the "managerial" approach to warfare soon permeated the entire military apparatus. In essence, this approach constituted an idea of highly controlled, "manageable," warfare that could be rationally administered for highly specific ends. Three basic steps were involved in this economic rationalization process. First, warfare is approached as a problem of organizing *quantities*. Transforming the world into discrete quantities is therefore a necessary first step in all reasoning about warfare. McNamara comes close to identifying quantification as the most advanced form of human reasoning: "It is true enough that not every conceivable complex human situation can be fully reduced to lines on a graph, or to percentage points on a chart or figures on a balance sheet. But all reality can be reasoned about, and not to quantify what can be quantified is only to be content with something less than the full range of reason." [29]

Having first transformed the elements of warfare into quantities, the managerial approach secondly constructs various models for the *production of warfare*. Using the model of the individual business firm in a capitalist economy, the defense managers tried to find "profit maximization" in warfare. For the individual firm, profit maximization is that point on a production curve where the additional revenue derived from producing one more unit is equal to the cost of producing that unit. To continue production beyond that point the firm would "lose money." Different combinations of ships, planes, and ground troops could be tried out in computer simulations to find the most "cost-effective" victory. The new war-managers recognized that the theory of microeconomics for understanding the behavior of a firm was not exactly identical to warfare, but they did think it was a good analogy. Alain C. Enthoven, head of the Systems Analysis Office in the Department of Defense, noted the slight difference as follows: "We have no equivalent to the point at which marginal costs equals marginal revenue. A complex judgment still has to be made. But data of this kind [marginal costs and marginal products] contribute a great deal to making that judgment an informed one."[30]

A third step was necessary to complete the managerial approach: the foreign Other was conceptualized to act according to the *same* logic of "profit" maximization. The intellectual operation here is called "game theory" and the idea is to simulate a conflict given certain parameters concerning what is a "rational" response by the opposition. Enthoven describes the "breakthrough" or "trick" in his approach as opposed to conventional military practice:

> In the case about uncertainties about enemy behavior, we have often found it useful to play a simple two-person game in which the enemy is permitted to adjust to variations in our posture, in order to evaluate our own alternatives. Of course, thinking through the enemy's counter-move is a time-honored part of military procedure. The trick, in the long-range planning business, is to apply realistic technical, budgetary, lead-time, bureaucratic, and other constraints to the enemy's hypothesized freedom to re-act. A frequent error here is to allow him too much freedom to adjust, the consequences are those of overestimating the opponent. . . .[31]

"Technical, budgetary, lead-time, bureaucratic, and other constraints" are Technowar categories. By definition, the Communist Other, with less resources and more problems than the capitalist West, is "inefficient."

By adopting microeconomics, game theory, systems analysis, and other managerial techniques, the Kennedy administration advanced "limited war" to greater specificity, making it seem much more controllable, manageable, and therefore *desirable* as foreign policy.

Vietnam as the laboratory for weapons development and military science, Vietnam as the laboratory for "social systems engineering," Vietnam as the laboratory for economic modernization: the country had become completely abstracted into the universal space of positive science. It was *the* "test case," and that scientific status subsequently became mapped onto the political world. Maxwell Taylor testifies once again:

> In a broader sense, the failure of our programs in South Vietnam would have heavy influence on the judgments of Burma, India, Indonesia, Malaysia, Japan, Taiwan, the Republic of Korea, and the Republic of the Philippines with respect to U.S. durability, resolution, and trustworthiness. Finally, this being the first *real test* of our determination to defeat the communist wars of national liberation formula, it is not unreasonable to conclude that there would be a corresponding unfavorable effect upon our image in Africa and Latin America.[32]

Multiple, yet analogous, logics of political, economic, military, and scientific "tests" would thus justify increasing American military forces. When Kennedy was elected in 1960, the United States Military Advisory Group in Vietnam numbered around 700. By the end of 1961 this figure increased to 3,200. The next year 11,300 military advisers served, and by 1963 that number had increased to 16,700. Larger, more advanced Technowar equipped with a couple of hundred helicopters and planes, night-seeing devices, lightweight rifles, and millions of dollars in economic aid would surely win.

The same logic that saw only the "credit" of the Diem regime repeated itself in counterinsurgency war. To begin, the Diem regime was a construction by the United States, but it was treated as if it were a sovereign state, an independent, "standing" domino. The discrepancy between the logic of the sovereignty paradigm and the actual absence of a popularly supported state proved fatal. A few Americans glimpsed the truth. George W. Ball, a U.S. State Department official, said, "In a very real sense, South Vietnam is a country with an army and no government."[33] An army with no government is a private army. In 1957 Diem had required that province chiefs, extremely important positions, could no longer be civilians, but instead must be field grade military officers. Increasing concentration of power within the military politicized the army, but at the same time politicization had no end other than private gain.

American officials and scholars saw South Vietnamese corruption as a problem to be solved with proper management: "The widespread corruption within all levels of the GVN was another *problem* which did not receive timely effective attention."[34] Writing the above in hindsight, political scientist Guenter Lewy still did not see that corruption was not a problem to be solved, but an essential structural feature of the relationship between the United States and South Vietnam. Systematic private appropriations of public funds depended on the provision of those funds by the United States to a regime they could not control because such control would violate the appearance of GVN sovereignty.

The Vietnamese people, however, saw the relationship clearly enough to question American claims to altruistic charity. As one farmer said, "After all, if the Americans really wanted to help the people, really wanted the people to benefit, why would they give all the money to the corrupt officials to be stolen?" [35]

Assistant Secretary of State U. Alexis Johnson saw the impossibility of significant reform: "In some cases only radical reforms will obtain the necessary results. Yet the measures we advocate may strike at the very foundations of those aspects of a country's social structure and domestic economy on which rests the basis of a government's control." [36] Although U.S. officials constantly implored Diem and his subordinates to reform, no real institutional pressure, such as a shift from a U.S. advisory program to a "combined" U.S. governmental-military structure, was ever applied. As General Westmoreland later wrote, such a command structure "also might have given credence to the enemy's absurd claim that the United States was no more than a colonial power." [37]

Thus incapable of institutionalizing reform in the south, the United States sought to eliminate an armed revolutionary movement through management techniques and military technology. Two programs were selected as central instruments. Vietnamese were removed from their villages and forced to reside in barbed-wire camps called Strategic Hamlets. This program was conducted principally by the Vietnamese military. The second program concerned tribal people, or Montagnards, living in the mountainous regions. These people were organized into paramilitary forces known as Civilian Irregular Defense Groups. They were trained by United States Army Special Forces troops in conjunction with Vietnamese forces.

Sir Robert Thompson, head of the British Advisory Mission to Diem, first suggested Strategic Hamlets. Thompson had been a leading British official in Malaysia during the Communist insurgency of the fifties. There he had designed and implemented a plan for fortifying villages. In Malaysia the villagers were ethnic Malays while the insurgents were mostly ethnic Chinese who lived in Malaysia, but not in the same areas as the Malay. There were only 8,000 Chinese insurgents against 300,000 ethnic Malayan villagers. [38]

In Vietnam the Strategic Hamlet program faced much different conditions. There, Vietnamese villages would be "protecting" themselves against other Vietnamese who had grown up in the same hamlets and villages. The numbers were also vastly different. Whereas in Malaysia the guerrillas were few compared to government forces, in Vietnam the Vietminh previously had outnumbered the French, and the Vietcong were estimated to outnumber government forces. The proportions of the population to be moved into Strategic Hamlets were also vastly different between Malaysia and Vietnam. Whereas 6 percent were moved in Malaysia, the Strategic Hamlets in Vietnam were to house everyone except a small percentage living in cities!

Strategic Hamlets represented an attempt by a weak government to control physically people it did not understand because of antagonistic class and religious differences. Rural people often lived in small villages or built their homes widely dispersed along canals and other waterways. The land they owned or worked was nearby. Moreover, most people practiced Confucianism (in addition to Buddhism), a religion in which attendance to the ancestors' shrine on the land is an important ritual. The construction of Strategic Hamlets was thus a threefold disruption of peasant life: first, in order to build the hamlets, work in the fields, a necessity for survival, had to stop; second, the distance between forts and fields, in conjunction with dusk-to-dawn curfews, made farming difficult for all and impossible for some; and finally, movement away from home into the hamlets meant that religious practices were halted.

Peasants resisted the program. In some areas, fences and other fortifications were slowly dug by day as the authorities commanded, but were quickly destroyed at night or whenever the Saigon officials and soldiers left. In other areas, even when forts were completed, people balked at further cooperation. One villager, a member of the village self-defense force, explains the importance of common class background to Vietnamese peasants:

> You want to know how the communists got into our strategic hamlet? All of us in the Combat Youth were poor people. We asked ourselves, why should we be carrying rifles and risking our lives when Xoai's son doesn't have to? His family is rich and has used its power to get him out of it. When the communists come in, they never bother us — they go to the homes of those who got rich by taking them from others. Are we so stupid as to protect them?[39]

Yet the program was *represented* as a success in Saigon and Washington. The vast social distance between "top" and "bottom" allowed failure at the "bottom" to be represented as success at the "top." Those in command knew the "bottom" only as a distribution of numbers. Officials had strong motivations to falsify the number of villages they controlled. David Halberstam presents a conversation between Colonel Dong and Mr. Cao, a district administrator with twenty-four villages in his district:

> "How many do you control?" the colonel asked.
>
> "Eight." the chief replied.
>
> Then the colonel smiled and then asked, "And how many did you report that you controlled?"
>
> The chief said sheepishly, "Twenty-four."
>
> Mr. Diem always got a false report. Mr. Cao liked his job; and he and Mr. Dam [local military commander] always reported that ninety-eight percent of the population was with Mr. Diem. And so Mr. Dam did not make any operations, because if he had casualties, Mr. Diem would ask him why there were any, when all the people were with him, and then Mr. Cao and Mr. Dam would lose their good jobs.[40]

Ngo Dinh Nhu, Diem's brother and an extremely powerful man in the regime, personally took charge of Strategic Hamlets when he heard that the Americans were interested. Nhu's plan to fortify two-thirds of the country's sixteen thousand hamlets within fourteen months did not succeed, but the quota method of measuring progress numerically took hold. Regime officials were either rewarded or dismissed according to the number of hamlets they reported pacified. American aid to a province varied according to the number of fortified hamlets reported. Consequently, falsification of reports increased. Some hamlets were divided into two for reporting purposes in order to receive twice the aid, assets which could then be privately appropriated. One American adviser joked, "If you stand still long enough down here, they'll throw a piece of barbed wire around you and call you a strategic hamlet."[41]

One of those who believed in numbers was Admiral Harry D. Felt, commander of all American forces in the Pacific. On January 30, 1963, Admiral Felt announced that the "South Vietnamese should achieve victory in three years." He then defined victory "as the situation wherein the South Vietnamese controlled 90 percent of the rural population." Admiral Felt contended that the Diem government "now controls about 51 percent of the rural population, the Viet-Cong about 8 percent, and the remainder were still uncommitted.''[42] Bernard B. Fall noted Admiral Felt's words endorsing Strategic Hamlets and the Diem regime. He commented:

> One must marvel at the ability to define the loyalty of villagers in percentages (in a country where no census has been taken in thirty years), but this creates an illusion of victory, since in American business or electoral terms, 51 percent of the stock or the vote constitutes a "controlling interest." Unfortunately, it must be feared that the results of a struggle for the allegiance of an underdeveloped country cannot be as easily calculated.[43]

Admiral Felt saw the world in conventional American terms, the debits and credits of Technowar and mechanistic anticommunism. The world was only a matter of numbers correctly inscribed in their appropriate ledgers.

In'reality, though, the contradiction between the spectacle of inflated numbers and the actual situation provided the space for the National Liberation Front's victory. By December 1962, the NLF had won popular allegiance in the overwhelming majority of the nation's hamlets. That such a massive victory could be concealed from those at the top was a function both of social distance and a belief in numerical representation as the scientific mode of representation. Regime officials also followed the French Technowar strategy of maintaining isolated forts to control an area in conjunction with the Strategic Hamlet program. One NLF official pointed out the fallacy of representation isolated from social reality: "If you looked at the military maps, you could see posts everywhere but in fact the surrounding territory was liberated, in the hands of the people. It was the posts that were encircled, not the people. Over vast areas, where the enemy insisted on staying in the countryside, he was forced to live integrated with us, on our terms."[44]

One projected benefit of Strategic Hamlets included creating "free-fire zones." Once a fortified hamlet had been constructed, the surrounding area became a virtually unrestricted target zone for American helicopter gunships and fighter-bombers during daylight, and random, "harassment and interdiction" artillery barrages at night. However, the government's claim to represent the people constituted the political space in which the populace of an area could legitimately protest the bombings, ground operations, and artillery fire. The NLF often led these protests: "You represent the government. Your job is to protect us. Why have you sent planes and artillery to destroy our village? We demand

compensation for every house and tree destroyed." Such was a typical
protest to a district or province official. As the president of the NLF
said, "The pretense that the Saigon regime is a national government
opens up vast possibilities for coordinating military with political struggle."[45]

Army Special Forces fared no better than the Strategic Hamlet program. They recruited Montagnards who lived in the mountains. Montagnards were ethnically distinct from Vietnamese and had a different culture
and language. They were organized into different tribes and practiced a
seminomadic life where villages were moved every few years to open
up new territory for "slash and burn" agriculture. The army hoped to
organize some of the estimated 200,000 tribespeople into paramilitary
units called Civilian Irregular Defense Groups. In theory these groups
would both resist the Vietcong and provide intelligence on Vietcong
movements.

Originally American Special Forces were only supposed to *advise*
Vietnamese Special Forces, called Lac Luong Dac Biet. The Vietnamese in turn were supposed to train and command the Montagnards. Herein
lay the social conflict that destroyed the program. The Vietnamese and
Montagnards had fought each other for centuries. Two great attractions
offered tribespeople for joining CIDGs concerned money and guns. Colonel Francis J. Kelley explains:

> Part of the project's popularity undoubtedly stemmed from the fact
> that the Montagnards could have their weapons back. In the late 1950s
> all the weapons, including the crossbow, had been denied to them by
> the government as a reprisal for Viet Cong depredations and only
> bamboo spears were allowed until the second week in December, 1961
> when the government finally gave permission to train and arm the
> village defenders and strike forces.[46]

If Vietnamese did not want to arm Montagnards in the first place,
then training of the Civilian Irregular Defense Groups by Vietnamese
was a dubious project. Colonel Kelley writes about Vietnamese hostility
and indifference:

> The indifference of the Vietnamese to the needs and feelings of the
> tribesmen grew directly out of their attitude toward the Montagnards,
> whom the Vietnamese had traditionally regarded as an inferior people,
> calling them "moi," or savages, and begrudging them their tribal

lands. This attitude on the part of the Vietnamese plagued the Civilian Irregular Defense Group program from the beginning.[47]

In September 1964, Montagnard troops revolted against their Vietnamese commanders, killing many and taking others prisoners. They demanded virtual autonomy from the Vietnamese regime. Retention of tribal lands with secure titles, representation in the National Assembly, Montagnard courts, schools, participation in the officer corps, and other demands were made upon the Vietnamese. Social and political conflicts thus superseded the technical expertise of American Special Forces.

By the fall of 1963, the unofficial slogan of American officials, "Sink or swim with Ngo Dinh Diem," no longer accurately satirized policy. That May, Ngo Dinh Thuc, Diem's brother and bishop of Hue, had banned religious flags for Buddha's birthday. Three weeks earlier Catholic flags had been displayed for Easter. Banning led to a Buddhist demonstration during which nine people were killed and fourteen injured. On June 11, the monk Thich Quang Duc burned himself to death in protest; his self-immolation was followed by others. By late August, college and high school students protested, only to be beaten and jailed. With the sons and daughters of the upper class — Diem's class base for support — going to jail, the military began to consider a coup.

Henry Cabot Lodge became ambassador to Vietnam in late August; he arrived with power from President Kennedy to decide whom the United States should back. Lodge soon decided that Diem and family must go; he removed U.S. officials favorable to Diem — such as CIA station chief John Richardson — and began negotiations with Vietnamese generals on how and when a coup would proceed. After one false start, the army successfully overthrew the regime on November 1, 1963. Diem and his brother were captured and later killed. American officials had not planned on the killings, but Lieutenant Colonel Lucien Conein still gave $42,000 to Vietnamese generals the next morning to pay their troops.[48]

By American reasoning, the absence of Diem, his brother Nhu, Madame Nhu, and the rest, would have ended the private government and created the possibility for reform; the sovereign state would emerge once corrupt individuals were gone. However, corruption constituted an inherent structural aspect of the American relationship to Vietnam. What was at issue now was a redistribution of goods among various military factions. Nineteen sixty-four saw a succession of coups: Diem was replaced by Duong Van Minh; Minh by Nguyen Kahn; Kahn by Nguyen Cao Ky — the names and politics are not important here. Rather, the rapid succession of personal names signifies both the continuity of a *privatized* regime and the discontinuity of any lasting personal alignments within the apparatus. Within a privatized regime, personal continuity could be the only basis of strength, since all connections in the hierarchy depended on personal ties. With Diem gone, the hierarchy necessary for minimal functioning collapsed. An NLF official describes benefits of the coups:

> They were gifts from heaven for us. Our enemy has been seriously weakened from all points of view, military, political and administrative. Their armed forces have suffered heavy losses on the battlefield and from desertions. The special shock troops which were an essential support for the Diem regime have been eliminated. The military command has been turned upside down and weakened by purges.
>
> For the same reasons, the coercive apparatus, set up over the years with great care by Diem, is utterly shattered, especially at the base. The principal chiefs of security and the secret police, on which mainly depended the protection of the regime and the repression of the revolutionary movement, have been eliminated, purged.
>
> Troops, officers and officials of the army and administration are completely lost; they have no more confidence in their chiefs and have no idea to whom they should be loyal. Their morale, already shattered even before these events because of the repeated victories of the patriotic forces, has fallen to a new low.[49]

By mid-1964 the United States found itself defeated. Strategic Hamlets had failed. Special Forces' Civilian Irregular Defense Groups were in conflict with their Vietnamese commanders and close to revolt. The South Vietnamese regime was incapable of winning the peasantry because of its class base among landlords. Indeed, there was no longer a "regime" in the sense of a relatively stable political alliance and functioning bureaucracy. Instead, civil government and military operations had virtually ceased. The National Liberation Front had made great progress and was close to declaring provisional revolutionary governments in large areas. It should have been a time for the United States to withdraw and reflect upon its failed operations.

However, the logic of Technowar and mechanistic anticommunism was in effect. The concept of rationally managing a limited war, particularly the "advances" that could be made with microeconomics and game theory, offered an alternative to defeat: increase the inputs and the output might well be victory.

At midnight, July 30, 1964, CIA-directed South Vietnamese PT boats raided islands off the North Vietnamese coast, part of a covert action called "34A." Their objective was to trigger North Vietnamese radar posts whose electronic scans could then be codified and pinpointed by American destroyers engaged in "DeSoto" patrols farther up the coast. On August 2, the destroyer *Maddox* reached its northern patrol limit, reversed course, and later in the day was attacked by North Vietnamese PT boats. According to the *Pentagon Papers,* North Vietnamese mistook the ships for the escort vessels of the South Vietnamese raiders. The *Maddox* sank one PT boat; planes from a carrier damaged two others.[50]

Additional South Vietnamese raids occurred during the night of August 3. The next night the *Maddox* reported "continuous torpedo attack," but its fire-control radar could find no target except the *C. Turner Joy,* which it came close to firing upon. The *C. Turner Joy* did not hear any torpedoes, nor could its radar find a target, but it fired anyway. Later that night the captain of the *Maddox* and the commander of the task force both concluded that the "torpedoes" were actually sounds of the *Maddox*'s own propellers and so reported to Washington.[51]

The assumption of an attack by the North Vietnamese took precedence over further questioning: the logic of mechanistic anticommunism appeared confirmed at the precise historical moment its contradictions had brought failure in South Vietnam. That internal failure could now be projected upon the presence of the foreign Other. The State Department had prepared a draft of the Gulf of Tonkin Resolution months before; only events and dates needed inscription. Lyndon Johnson announced that American planes had "retaliated" on the night of August 4; he also called for immediate congressional approval of the Gulf of Tonkin Resolution. The next day the Senate voted 98 to 2 while the House of Representatives voted 441 to 0. Johnson, as commander in chief, now had authority "to take all necessary measures to repel any armed attack against the forces of the United States and to prevent any further aggression."[52] Blood and money, money and blood, the currencies of war were about to increase circulation.

# PART II
# The Green Machine

# CHAPTER 5

# Technowar at Ground Level:
# Search-and-Destroy as Assembly Line

FULL-FLEDGED warfare had been discussed within the Kennedy administration. After Walt Rostow and Maxwell Taylor visited Saigon in the fall of 1961, Taylor declared that sending 10,000 troops there immediately was "an essential action if we are to reverse the current downward trend of events. In fact, I do not believe that our program in South Vietnam will succeed without it." He also stated the consequences of this troop commitment: "If the first contingent is not enough to accomplish the necessary results, it will be difficult to resist the pressure to reinforce. If the ultimate result sought is the closing of the frontiers and the clean-up of the insurgents within SVN, there is no limit to our possible commitment (unless we attack the source in Hanoi)." [1] Fortunately, in Taylor's estimation, North Vietnam was "extremely vulnerable to conventional bombing, a weakness which should be exploited diplomatically in convincing Hanoi to lay off SVN." [2]

Taylor's call for attacking North Vietnam had to wait until his prophecy of counterinsurgency failure became a reality. By late 1964 failure was evident to the war-managers, and in December, U.S. planes began bombing Laos in Operation Barrel Roll — practice for the move north. In February 1965, the National Liberation Front mortared and sabotaged an American air base at Pleiku. Several B-57 bombers were destroyed; eight Americans died and many more were wounded. Soon thereafter began sustained bombing against North Vietnam, Operation Rolling Thunder. McGeorge Bundy, a presidential adviser in Vietnam at the time, claimed to have been deeply affected by his visit to Americans wounded in the attack and wrote a memo advocating "A Policy of Sustained Reprisal." [3] Later, though, he indicated that the call for sustained air attacks had been premeditated. "Pleikus are [like] streetcars," he said, implying that one came along every few minutes.[4] Like the Gulf of Tonkin episode, Pleiku was but a pretext for a "text" already written.

In early March, 3,500 Marines arrived to defend Danang air base. Later in the month the Joint Chiefs of Staff called for a full combat division to be sent to Vietnam and a change in policy to permit troops to engage in offensive combat operations rather than simply guarding the base. President Johnson agreed in April, and announced that 82,000 American troops would be stationed in Vietnam by December. Simultaneously, the public was prepared for further escalations. In Johnson's famous address at Johns Hopkins University in April 1965, an old demon was mentioned: "The confused nature of this conflict cannot mask the fact that it is the new face of an old enemy. Over this war — and all Asia — is another reality: the deepening shadow of Communist China. . . ."[5]

In June, General William Westmoreland, commander of all United States forces in Vietnam, requested an additional 100,000 troops, which would give him forty-four "maneuver battalions" for use against the enemy. Westmoreland added that this troop level was just the beginning: "Instinctively, we believe that there may be substantial additional U.S. force requirements."[6] By late spring of 1965, South Vietnamese government and military apparatuses were crumbling; the long line of coups had not subsided. Battlefield defeats destroyed many ARVN troops. Desertion reached mass proportions; thousands of soldiers vanished each month. By July, American intelligence estimates predicted that the National Liberation Front was ready to form a Provisional Revolutionary Zone in the six northern provinces of South Vietnam and force South Vietnamese troops back into cities and large towns.

Lyndon Johnson made the decision. Vietnam would be preserved. "The battle would be renewed in one country and then in another country, bringing with it perhaps even larger war and crueler conflict as we have learned from the lessons of history."[7] This speech came on July 28, 1965, along with the announcement that the First Cavalry Division (Airmobile) would be sent to Vietnam, bringing the official figure to 125,000. Johnson added that "Additional forces will be needed later, and they will be sent as requested." Not all of Westmoreland's subsequent requests were granted, but additional soldiers were sent:[8]

These figures do not include American soldiers stationed in Thailand and elsewhere in Southeast Asia, nor do they include Koreans, Australians, New Zealanders, or Thai soldiers. It is important to understand that American escalation in Vietnam *did not surprise* political and mil-

Table 5.1
UNITED STATES
MILITARY FORCES
IN VIETNAM

| | |
|---|---|
| 1965 | 184,000 |
| 1966 | 389,000 |
| 1967 | 463,000 |
| 1968 | 495,000 |
| 1969 | 541,000 |

itary managers of Technowar. According to the *Pentagon Papers*, in his original troop request Westmoreland made the following assessment:

The overall concept was based on three assumptions:

(1) That the VC would fight until convinced that military victory was impossible and then would not be willing to endure further punishment.

(2) That the CHICOM's [Chinese Communists] would not intervene except to provide aid and advice.

(3) That friendly forces would maintain control of the air over RVN.

The concept visualized a three-phase operation:

Phase I — The commitment of US/FWMA [Free World Military Assistance] forces during the first half of 1966 in high priority areas necessary to halt the losing trend by the end of 1965.

Phase II — The resumption of the offensive by US/FWMA forces during the first half of 1966 in high priority areas necessary to destroy enemy forces, and reinstitution of rural construction [pacification] activities.

Phase III — If the enemy persisted, a period of a year to a year and a half following Phase II would be required for the defeat and destruction of the remaining enemy forces and base areas.[9]

Westmoreland thought that at least 175,000 troops were required simply to "halt the losing trend." To begin and sustain the offensive (Phase II) required at least another 100,000 and probably more. In November 1965, Secretary of Defense McNamara visited Saigon to talk with Westmoreland and other commanders. Even at this early date, it seemed clear to him that estimates for troops needed to be revised upward. Westmoreland had found a new problem in the input-output matrix of Technowar. American war-managers counted *one* U.S. battalion as the "battalion equivalent" of *three* Vietcong or People's Army of North Vietnamese battalions. The assumption was that the Other is like us, but has less technology at work. However, even when counting one U.S. unit as the equivalent of three enemy units, the *quarterly reports* in late 1965 showed that Technowar could not maintain the quantitative ratio of superiority thought necessary for victory. Military Assistance Command Vietnam describes a descending curve:

> The VC/PAVN buildup rate is predicted to be double that of U.S. Phase II forces. Whereas we will add an average of seven battalions per quarter the enemy will add fifteen. This development has already reduced the November battalion equivalent ratio from an anticipated 3.2 to 1, to 2.8 to 1, and it will be further reduced to 2.5 to 1 by the end of the year. If the trend continues, the December 1966 battalion equivalent ratio, even with the addition of Phase II, will be 2.1 to 1.[10]

McNamara subsequently reported this impending production problem to President Johnson in a memo:

> To meet this possible — and in my view likely — Communist buildup, the presently contemplated Phase I forces will not be enough (approx. 220,000 Americans, almost all in place by the end of 1965). Bearing in mind the nature of the war, the expected weighted combat force ratio of less than 2-to-1 will not be good enough. Nor will the originally contemplated Phase II addition of 28 more U.S. battalions (112,000 men) be enough; the combat force ratio, even with 32 new SVNese battalions, would still be little better than 2-to-1 at the end of 1966.[11]

More troops would have to be sent. The original 1966 figure calling for 275,000 men was upped to approximately 400,000. Nor would this be the end: "And it should be understood that further deployments (perhaps exceeding 200,000) may be needed in 1967." Recall that McNamara was writing in November 1965. He did not think that 600,000 troops in 1967 would ensure transition to Phase III victory: "We should be aware that deployments of the kind I have recommended will not guarantee success. U.S. killed-in-action can be expected to reach 1,000 a month, and the odds are even that we will be faced in early 1967 with a 'no-decision' at an even higher level."[12] Johnson heard only a slightly more favorable projection from General Earle Wheeler, chairman of the Joint Chiefs of Staff. According to David Halberstam, Johnson asked

Wheeler, "Bus, what do you think it will take to do the job?" Wheeler replied that to defeat the Communists in the conventional sense of the term, that is, to completely destroy them militarily and pacify Vietnam, would take an estimated *700,000* to *one million* American troops fighting for *seven years*. [13]

But conventional definitions of victory and defeat were not used by the war-managers. John McNaughton, an assistant secretary of defense, had the following definition of victory: "With respect to the word 'win,' this I think means that we succeed in *demonstrating to the VC that they cannot win*." [14] Similarly, General Westmoreland thought U.S. ground troops and airpower served to *"convince the enemy he would be unable to win."* [15] Victory thus became defined as *persuading* the enemy that he would lose, rather than completely destroying his forces.

United States commanders and military analysts assumed the Vietnamese would give up when they recognized that the Americans were really going to fight and that the United States had vastly superior war technology. For the Americans, the question became one of estimating when the foreign Other would recognize U.S. technological superiority and consequently give up all hopes of victory. From the war-manager perspective, each U.S. act of escalation could possibly persuade the foreign Other to negotiate. The debate on bombing North Vietnam clearly indicates that leading officials saw Technowar as a form of communication:

> If you lay the whole country to waste, it is quite likely that you will induce a mood of fatalism in the Viet Cong. Also, there will be nobody left in North Vietnam on whom to put pressure. . . . What we are interested in here is not destroying Ho Chi Minh (as his successor would probably be worse than he is), but getting him to change his behavior.
> — Ambassador Henry Cabot Lodge, 1964[16]

> Although there presumably is a point at which one more turn of the screw would crack the enemy resistance to negotiations, past experience indicates that we are unlikely to have clear evidence when that point has been reached.
> — CIA analyst, 1966[17]

The North Vietnamese were not the only ones to whom bombing messages were directed. Lodge thought that bombing would create South Vietnamese patriotism and unity: ". . . if we bombed Tchepone [in

Laos] or attacked the [PT] boats and the Vietnamese people knew about it, this would tend to stimulate their morale, unify their efforts and reduce their quarreling.''[18] McGeorge Bundy also wanted to bomb primarily to communicate to the South Vietnamese; reaching Ho Chi Minh by bomb-o-gram was ''an important but longer-range purpose.''[19] Most important, though, Bundy thought that bombing carried a crucial political message to both United States citizens and the world at large. Bombing provided a shield against any accusations of ''losing'' Vietnam because the administration failed to try hard enough. ''What we can say is that even if it fails, the policy will be worth it. At a minimum it will dampen down the charge that we did not do all that we could have done, and this charge will be important in many countries, including our own.''[20]

To the war-managers, the very same bombs thus conveyed different messages to different audiences. They assumed that both their opponents and the rest of the world shared their assumptions on the primacy of mechanical power. Years after the war had been lost by the United States, former Assistant Secretary of State Paul Warnke said, ''The trouble with our policy in Vietnam has been that we guessed wrong with respect to what the North Vietnamese reaction would be. We anticipated that they would respond like reasonable people.''[21] All ''reasonable people'' think within the logic of Technowar; reason itself is identical to weighing debit and credit scales to determine the ''price'' the foreign Other would pay.

This deep belief in technology characterizes the war-managers' approaches to virtually all questions. Ambassador Lodge once thought that the war could be won by announcing that the U.S. war machine was on its way: ''In truth we do not need to define 'victory' and then go ahead and achieve it 100%. If it becomes generally believed that we are sure to win (just as it is now generally believed that we cannot lose) all else would be mopping up. If there is 'the smell of victory' we will be coasting.''[22] This is nothing other than the logic of advertising, where the appearance of some commodity signifies the accessibility of some social goal far beyond the commodity, be it a job promotion by using deodorant or sexual fulfillment by buying a car. The difference is that here the advertiser believes his own advertisement. For the war-managers, the presence of the vast American war machine in comparison to the relatively underdeveloped Vietcong and NVA forces constituted such a fundamental disjuncture in the scales of mechanical power that, as Lodge said — ''just as it is now generally believed that we cannot lose''

— defeat became *unthinkable*. In turn, if to the war-managers defeat is logically impossible, then Technowar must *inevitably* produce *victory*.

Technowar thus constitutes a closed conceptual system; its assumptions and theories about the world were never doubted or tested by the war-managers. If victory would be inevitably produced through technological warfare, then even learning about Vietnamese history, culture, and social structure did not seem worthwhile to the war-managers.

In his memoir, *A Soldier Reports*, Westmoreland commented revealingly on his bedside reading list:

> Beside my bed at home I kept pictures of Kitsy and the children and several books: a Bible, a French grammar; Mao Tse-tung's little red book on theories of guerrilla warfare; a novel, *The Centurians*, about the French fight with the Viet Minh; and several works by Dr. Bernard Fall, who wrote authoritatively on the French experience in Indochina and provided insight into the enemy's thinking and methods. I was usually too tired in late evening to give the books more than occasional attention.[23]

Jean Larteguy published *The Centurians* in 1961; the work concerns French *defeat* in Vietnam by guerrillas.[24] Bernard Fall's books have been quoted from many times; Westmoreland might have learned much from them. And what of the "little red book" by Mao Tse-tung? What could the general have learned from *Quotations from Chairman Mao Tse-tung?*

II. Classes and Class Struggle

The ruthless economic exploitation and political oppression of the peasants by the landlord class forced them into numerous uprisings against its rule. . . . It was the class struggles of the peasants, the peasant uprisings and peasant wars that constituted the real motive force of historical development in Chinese society.[25]

VI. Imperialism and All Reactionaries Are Paper Tigers

The peasants can only plough the land plot by plot. The same is even true of eating a meal. Strategically, we take the eating of a meal lightly — we know we can finish it. But actually we eat it mouthful by mouthful. It is impossible to swallow an entire banquet in one gulp. This is known as the piecemeal solution. In military parlance, it is called wiping out the enemy forces one by one.[26]

VIII. People's War

Considering the revolutionary war as a whole, the operations of the people's guerrillas and those of the main forces of the Red Army complement each other like a man's right arm and left arm, and if we had only the main forces of the Red Army without the people's guerrillas we would be like a warrior with only one arm. In concrete terms, and especially with regard to military operations, when we talk of the people in the base area as a factor, we mean that we have an armed people. This is the main reason the enemy is afraid to approach our base area.[27]

XIV. Relations Between the Army and the People

The army must become one with the people so that they see it as their own army. Such an army will be invincible. . . .[28]

Many other quotations would have been relevant. If Westmoreland had read carefully, he might have found his way to *On Protracted War,* Mao's opus on the theory of revolutionary war. Having gotten that far, the next logical step would have been the books and essays by the Vietnamese military strategist General Vo Nguyen Giap. Both Chinese and Vietnamese Communist publications were available in English. Westmoreland's failure to read was not an individual failure, but a systematic characteristic of U.S. leaders. There was nothing to be learned from the less technologically developed Chinese and Vietnamese social theorists, because they had nothing to say about what really counted.

After the war Westmoreland reflected upon what books were being read among the managerial elite: "Popular reading at that time in the military circles included Henry Kissinger's book *Nuclear Weapons and Foreign Policy* and later General Maxwell D. Taylor's *Uncertain Trumpet.* . . . Such idealistic and theoretical concepts were on the minds of policy makers when I arrived in Vietnam in late January 1964."[29]

Westmoreland said that after his wife and children left Vietnam, his two roommates were his personal physician and a chemical physicist named Dr. William D. McMillan. Dr. McMillan was Westmoreland's principal adviser on war technology. Westmoreland, a graduate of West Point (where the curriculum is oriented toward math and technology), believed in technology: "Since I believed strongly in innovations, in trying anything that might ease the task, I wanted to exploit any technology the scientists might help to develop."[30] He tells how excited he was when the first American tanks arrived in Vietnam and what he expected of them: "While their use among rice paddies and mountainous jungle would be limited, their *firepower* and *psychological impact* elsewhere would be reason enough to employ them."[31] With such logic the entire ground war would be fought.

Westmoreland consequently deployed his forces to places where he could best display advanced technology to the North Vietnamese: "Superior American firepower would be most advantageously employed against the big units, and using it in remote regions would mean fewer civilian casualties and less damage to built up areas."[32] From the beginning of large-scale escalation, major ground forces were stationed primarily along the demilitarized zone in the northern region, in the Central Highlands (a mountainous area bordering southern Laos and northern Cambodia), and in other areas far from the populated coastal plain and Mekong Delta. In this strategy, United States forces did not occupy territory permanently but instead roamed over large areas engaged in search-and-destroy missions against the enemy's main force units, or "bully boys" as Westmoreland called them.

Although he basically followed French strategists in conceiving the North Vietnamese as a technobureaucratic force analogous to his own, Westmoreland still considered guerrillas a serious concern. Stopping infiltration by the foreign Other was the most important problem, but behind this "shield" another war would be fought. The Army of the Republic of Vietnam would fight "termites," the "political subversives and guerrillas" who were "persistently eating away at the structural members of a building, analogously, the structure of the South Vietnamese government."[33] This division of labor between big-unit war fought by Americans and pacification war conducted by ARVN was officially ratified at the Honolulu Conference in October 1966.

At the same time, the policy of assigning ARVN the task of "pacifying" the Vietnamese populace and fighting guerrilla warfare ignored the history of the Diem regime and its successors — a history of failure necessitating the introduction of massive American ground, sea, and air forces! By introducing more forces — in this case both more American ground troops and an enlarged ARVN — the previous "debit" of failure was erased. To the war-managers the prospect of generating internal support for the GVN was highly abstract in comparison to the concrete problem of keeping the foreign Other out. Frontal zones of all American wars in the twentieth century were invoked: World War I had a 455-mile front covered by nearly six million men; World War II had a 570-mile front in western Europe occupied by an Allied army of four and a half million men; Korea had a 123-mile front with nearly one million men. Vietnam, in contrast, had over 900 miles of land borders. According to Westmoreland, it would have required millions of troops to defend their borders in the conventional sense of permanently occupying territory. Similarly, the general did not have enough men to occupy permanently every Vietnamese province and district and keep the "termites," or Vietcong, out.

> Had I at my disposal virtually unlimited manpower, I could have stationed troops permanently in every district or province and thus provided an alternative strategy. That would have enabled the troops to get to know the people intimately, facilitating the task of identifying the subversives and protecting the others against intimidation. Yet to have done that would have required literally millions of men, and I still would have had to maintain a reserve to counter big-unit threats.[34]

This alternative strategy replaces the South Vietnamese government and its army with American ground troops: the division of labor ratified at the Honolulu Conference is theoretically rescinded. But Westmoreland could not secure sufficient troops for this strategy in any case. It was not really an alternative strategy. To replace Vietnamese with Americans is simply a way to create a more-efficient war machine, not a recognition of the social and political dynamics of revolutionary warfare. Instead, the alternative strategy of a purely American war marks adherence to the idea of "pure" mechanistic Technowar against which all variants are second-choice derivatives.

The definition of victory as dependent upon the foreign Other's understanding of his inferiority was thus determined not only by complete confidence in high technology, but by recognition that no other victory was possible. The Vietcong and NVA must understand, because only understanding could ensure American victory. Consequently, to achieve "communication," Westmoreland deployed his maneuver battalions on search-and-destroy missions on the borders and in the Central Highlands. Under this strategy, the United States would fight a war of attrition against the foreign Other by aggressively hunting for enemy base areas in the countryside and achieve the "cross-over point" of killing the enemy faster than he could replace troops.

Search-and-destroy was a continuous process of Technowar production. Lieutenant General Julian J. Ewell (one of Westmoreland's principal generals) later wrote a book summarizing his own efforts to rationalize ground warfare according to management principles. Entitled

*Sharpening the Combat Edge: The Use of Analysis to Reinforce Military Judgment,* Ewell saw ground war as an assembly line: "In Vietnam, with all its ambiguities, one was dealing with a highly repetitive operation. It was comparable to an *assembly line,* whereas one could visualize a 'western war' as an episodic or climactic affair with periods of low activity. It would appear that this type of conflict might require a different approach from an analytical point of view."

In Ewell's terms, "once one decided to apply maximum force, the problem became a technical one of doing it efficiently with the resources available."[35] As with any assembly line, the resources available were labor and capital. Labor consisted of ground troops available for combat operations; the means of production were high-technology, capital-intensive weapons such as planes and artillery. According to Robert McNamara, search-and-destroy valued its labor force: "The thing we value most deeply is not money, but men. We have multiplied the capability of our men [with firepower]. *It's expensive in dollars, but cheap in life.*"[36]

To economize on American lives, commanders were encouraged to use their ground troops only as a reconnaissance. Colonel Sidney S. Berry, Jr.'s 1967 essay on combat tactics was endorsed by the army chief of staff and widely disseminated within the military. A prudent brigade commander "uses his soldiers to find the enemy and supporting firepower to destroy the enemy. He *spends firepower* as if he is a millionaire and husbands lives as if he is a pauper . . . during search and destroy operations, commanders should look upon infantry as the principal combat reconnaissance force and supporting fires as the principal destructive force."[37] Many other commanders echoed this basic logic of infantry search and technological destruction. For example, Army Brigadier General Glenn D. Walker said to reporters, "You don't fight this fellow rifle to rifle. You locate him and back away. Blow the hell out of him and then police up."[38]

This strategy attempted to make the Vietnamese fight according to U.S. preferences. As General Dave Richard Palmer said, "If the United States was unable to match Asian opponents in manpower, the Asians could by *no stretch of the imagination* compete with American technology."[39] If the revolutionary forces could not compete, then American victory was thus both inevitable and "inexpensive" in American lives. But Vietcong and NVA military and political leaders did not accept their spot within the technological universe. Instead, they sought out every flaw in the American war machine; the contradictions of Technowar provided the spaces for the foreign Other to emerge and fight the war on his terms.

To begin, both the noises of war machines — planes, helicopters, and armored vehicles — and the highly routinized pattern of most search-and-destroy missions meant that the Vietnamese knew where American forces were. Even before the first helicopters landed, artillery preparations of landing zones gave ample notice that U.S. forces were preparing for battle. Before artillery could cover a helicopter advance, it had to be "sighted-in" or "registered" on the target. Lieutenant Colonel James R. Ray notes that this procedure created high visibility for American forces: "This registration begins with a high smoke streamer or smoke round, both of which are easily recognizable in the jungle. Should the enemy be in the vicinity of the LZ [landing zone — a cleared area], he immediately knows that we are likely to enter the area. He then has a choice of disappearing into the jungle or defending the LZ."[40] Usually the first wave of helicopters brought in men to secure the landing zone. The second wave brought in additional artillery to provide firepower superiority for subsequent infantry searches of an area. Artillery told the Vietnamese where Americans would conduct their ground searches. Cincinnatus, an historian in the army reserve who seeks anonymity, describes the important significations of artillery in the forward-support base (FSB):

> If the enemy had not located a proposed LZ prior to the beginning of a mission, observations of choppers as they brought in men and material to erect an FSB clearly revealed its location. VC and NVA troops could watch 105mm howitzers being lifted into an LZ from miles away. A minimum of actual ground reconnaissance then led them to the perimeter of the new LZ. Without making contact, an experienced NVA commander could deduce the area through which U.S. troops would conduct their sweep. He could determine how far out from the FSB the GIs would move, for he knew that such units inevitably stayed within supporting range of their 105mm howitzers. *By drawing a 10,000-meter-radius circle* around the location of an FSB, he could plot where the noisy, jangling, littering American troops would be conducting operations.[41]

The Vietnamese also knew where American soldiers were and how many were there by observing helicopter flight patterns. "Airmobile" warfare had developed in the 1950s as a possible solution for U.S. Army survival on the "atomic battlefield." By the early 1960s helicopters were sent in large numbers to develop counterinsurgency. The weakness of dependency upon helicopters was obvious then. *New York Times* correspondent Malcolm Browne found one U.S. military adviser who commented: "After all, when you come to think of it, the use of helicopters is a tacit admission that we don't control the ground. And in the long run, it's control of the ground that wins or loses war." [42] The famous historian and analyst of battles, retired general S. L. A. Marshall, also reports that during his 1962 trip to Vietnam he sternly admonished commanding general Paul Harkins on the contradictions of helicopter counterinsurgency.

> To begin, we were briefed on the military situation by General Paul D. Harkins, who explained how the choppers would be used to field the ARVN companies from one fire flashpoint to another.
>
> But when he had finished briefing, I said, "You know it will not work. Right now Charley [the National Liberation Front or Vietcong] is making himself furtive and hard to find. But once he sees what we intend, he will conform and make himself obvious. There are too few spots approximate to their base camps where choppers can be put down. So they will draw in the ARVN to a preset defense where the birds will be shot up and the soldiers dispersed before they can deploy. Ambush will follow ambush."
>
> Harkins replied: "I can see it coming, but what can be done about it?" And to that, there was not an answer. [43]

Both Marshall and Hawkins saw the inevitable failure, but offered no alternative. In this sense they thought within the horizons of Technowar: the war was a matter of correctly managing a series of technical variables; some could be managed while others could be accepted as a "constant" hazard factor to be included in rational calculations. One famous analyst, Sir Robert Thompson, the British plenipotentiary in Malaysia during the Communist insurgency in the 1950s, thought that helicopters "exaggerated the two great weaknesses of the American character — impatience and aggressiveness." He says that "It is probable that without the helicopter 'search and destroy' would not have been possible and in this sense the helicopter was one of the major contributions to the failure of strategy." [44] Note how in this formulation an entire world-view and system of warfare became reduced to one technological artifact, the helicopter.

Helicopter warfare suited the needs of war-managers. With helicopters, commanding officers could simultaneously be close to the battlefields and at the same time safe from combat hazards as long as they stayed above 1,500 feet, the range of enemy heavy machine guns. General Lewis W. Walt, a former commandant of the Marine Corps and commander of all marines in Vietnam, thought that the helicopter removed field commanders from their bunkers and exposed them to warfare. Walt had nothing but praise for helicopter mobility: "The helicopter ended this dismal restriction. Like the horse a century earlier, it lifted the commander above the tumult and let him speed from place to place with comparative ease and safety." [45]

For most infantry units, the highest officer on the ground during combat operations was the company commander, a man holding the rank of captain or first lieutenant and commanding 100 to 200 troops. Cincinnatus interviewed many former company and platoon commanders who complained of all their battalion, brigade, division, and corps commanders hovering overhead demanding that they be informed by radio on what was happening in a firefight below:

> We always had a horror that one day things would come to a standstill. Overhead would be circling our battalion commander. Above him would be his brigade commander. Higher than both would be the division commander and hovering over him would be his corps commander. All circling in their "charlie-charlie" [command and control] choppers, all demanding to know what was going on down on the ground. So much command and control would be present that those with their "ass in the grass" would no longer be able to function at all. It never happened, but it came close. [46]

By spring 1967 it was evident to army researchers that too much radio traffic from command was undercutting officers in the field. S. L. A. Marshall and Colonel David Hackworth warn of the dangers in their pamphlet, *Vietnam Primer: Lessons Learned:* "Each [military commander] has some reason for being here. But their presence does put an unprecedented strain on the leader at the fighting level, and also on his radios, as everyone 'comes up' on the engaged unit's frequency to give advice. . . . *A rule that must be followed* is that except for rare and unusual circumstances all commanders should follow well established radio procedures and not 'come up' on the radio of the next subordinate unit." [47] But military commanders were incapable of maintaining radio discipline. Consequently, the enemy listened to detailed conversations among senior officers. One soldier explained:

When you updated your commander, you updated everybody, since both the Vietcong and NVA monitored our frequencies. It was very convenient for everyone except for the grunts on the ground. For example, when a helicopter pilot would ask you to mark your location with smoke you couldn't tell him what color you would use. If you did, identically colored smokes would appear in three or four places. Instead you would simply say, "I pop smoke now." He would call back and say, for example, "I identify green." And as soon as the identification of color was heard, you could count on having two or three other green smokes pop in the vicinity, within a grid square [1,000 meters by 1,000 meters] of you. That's how well we were monitored.[48]

Technowar thus squandered its technological advantage by management's proliferating communications. As Major General George Keegan said after the war, "The enemy knew everything there was to know about us. They knew when we were going to strike, where we were going to strike, under what conditions — ground, air, or naval. That permitted him to make do with but a fraction of the assets and resources we required to operate with. This kind of information permitted the enemy to achieve results out of all proportion to relative commitment of firepower."[49]

Moreover, war-managers circling in helicopters lost touch with realities faced by ground troops. Commanders issued orders that were extremely dangerous and often impossible to follow. Army Lieutenant William L. Calley provides an example:

Our colonel would look for VC suspects from — oh, ten thousand feet, and play platoon leader with us. "Oh, Charlie One? I spotted a VC suspect. A few minutes from you." Of course, the colonel could go a kilometer in thirty seconds and I was in the damn foliage: it might take me a lifetime. "Go where the purple smoke is, Charlie One." Of course, there was a fifty-meter hill in between us.
"Negative on the purple smoke."
"You don't see it? Sonofabitch. I'll throw another purple smoke."
"Negative on the purple smoke."
"You sonofabitch! It's right on the other side of the little hill!"
I just got a little fed up. He had that goddam chopper there, he should land and capture the VC suspect himself. Or shoot him: I had to walk there, as if I couldn't be ambushed at that purple smoke.[50]

Calley's is not an isolated story. Lieutenant Colonel Anthony Herbert, a former enlisted man in the Korean War who worked his way through the ranks, noticed incredible disjunctions between officers' commands given in helicopters and real situations on the ground:

> The rule of thumb [for command] in the infantry had always been to be at the critical place at the critical time — to be where the action could best be influenced — and not up at 1,500 feet, giving directions to move men from Point A to Point B in fifteen minutes. There might be a dense wall of jungle, as well as other human beings who were determined not only to prevent your movement from Point A to Point B but to kick your ass off Point A if possible.[51]

Herbert was a battalion commander in the 173rd Airborne Brigade, one of the army's elite paratrooper units that had been converted to "airmobile" (helicopter-intensive) units. As a battalion commander, Herbert was responsible for four field companies, a headquarters company, and a heavy-weapons company. The brigade was composed of five "maneuver battalions" like Herbert's, plus numerous support battalions for logistics and combat services. In essence then, Herbert accuses his peers and superiors of gross incompetence, of practicing a managerial form of warfare where technological fetishism took the place of strategic and tactical thinking: "In any other war, the 'hover and observe' tactics of the commanders would have been fatal, but this was the Indian War, as General Allen liked to call it. We had the Sharps rifles and they had the bows and arrows."[52]

But the weapons, transport, and communications superiority of U.S. forces in comparison to the Vietcong and People's Army Vietnam forces could rarely be brought to bear. The massiveness of U.S. firepower, the routineness of its "assembly line" orientation, and management's distance and disregard of the ground troops in many instances rendered its firepower advantages irrelevant on the battlefield. The organization of Technowar allowed the enemy to know American soldiers' locations. Intelligence information from Vietnamese villagers was also crucially important, as was information from the more organized Vietcong spy network within ARVN and the GVN. Consequently, rather than being offensive strategy, search-and-destroy became a series of defensive operations — reactions to enemy ambushes. Official statistics gathered in 1966 show that around three-fourths of all contacts with VC and NVA forces were initiated by the enemy. Strategic offensive at the abstract level turned into tactical defense in reality. The Office of Systems Analysis in the Department of Defense created the following typology of combat engagements from low-level field reports and debriefings:

Table 5.2

TYPES OF ENGAGEMENTS IN COMBAT NARRATIVES

| *Type of Engagement* | *Percentage of Total* |
|---|---|
| 1. Hot landing zone. Enemy attacks U.S. troops as they deploy on battlefield. | 12.5 |
| 2. Organized enemy attack against U.S. static defense perimeter. | 30.4 |
| 3. VC/NVA ambush or encircle and surprise a moving U.S. unit, using what is evidently a preconceived battle plan. | 23.3 |
| 4. A moving U.S. unit engages the enemy in a dug-in or fortified position: | |
| a. The main engagement comes as a surprise to the American tactical commander because the enemy is well-concealed and has been alerted, either by observations of our unit or by our engaging apparent stragglers nearby. | 12.5 |
| b. The U.S. tactical commander has reasonably accurate knowledge of enemy positions and strength before committing his strength. | 5.4 |
| 5. U.S. unit ambushes a moving enemy unit. | 8.9 |
| 6. Chance engagement, both sides surprised. | 7.1 |
| TOTAL | 100.1 |

SOURCE: *The Pentagon Papers: The Senator Gravel Edition* (Boston: Beacon Press, 1971), vol. 4, p. 462.

The enemy's overwhelming dominance in combat initiative continued throughout the major American ground war. National Security Memorandum 1 on "The Situation in Vietnam" (December 1968) noted: "Three-fourths of the battles are at the enemy's choice of time, place, type, and duration. CIA notes that *less than one percent* of nearly two million Allied small unit operations conducted in the last two years resulted in contact with the enemy and, when ARVN is surveyed, the percentage drops to one tenth of one percent."[53]

This disjunction between search-and-destroy as offensive strategy in

Technowar theory and the lived reality of ground combat as a series of enemy ambushes was of great concern to combat soldiers. In the novels, memoirs, and oral history testimonies by American soldiers, story after story demands that the expendability of ground troops be understood as a major structural feature of Technowar. Marine medic Douglas Anderson begins with an analysis of search-and-destroy:

> The very idea of the search-and-destroy operation is one of enormous logical fallacy. You send a patrol out in order to get it ambushed, in order to mark a target with a smoke rocket from a helicopter so jets can come in and napalm the area. In other words, you have to get ambushed before you can find the enemy. Now, this immediately gives them a chance to inflict damage and then get out of the way. The VC were smart enough to know that it was going to take two or three minutes at fastest to get a Huey out there, so they could kill a couple of people and split before anybody got there. We proceeded to mark the target where we thought the fire had come from. Meanwhile, the VC were eating their hamburgers in Danang. It happened time after time. An incredible drain.[54]

Some soldiers saw the use of ground troops as "bait" as a necessary sacrifice or cost of production for producing a high enemy body count. Army Captain Michael O'Mera says:

> But there was no alternative. The battalion commanders had no alternative, the brigade commanders had no alternative. The division commander had no alternative because he was told to produce body count, and the only way he would do it was to make their ground units "bait."
>
> They made their ground units bait by sending them into the swamps, into the jungles, into the rice paddies where they would search for the enemy and at night set up in a night logger or a combat patrol position, and from this position they were most likely to be attacked. This is where the enemy would most likely hit them. They were bait. They were there strictly to make contact with the enemy and hopefully not take any casualties, but unfortunately in every one I can ever recall they did take casualties and great body counts did come from it.[55]

Other soldiers, particularly those in armored units, tend to blame the noise of their vehicles rather than command ineptness for their high casualties. As one squadron (armored battalion) commander of armored personnel carriers told a former infantry lieutenant who was joining the unit: ''Tracks [APCs] are different than what you're used to; they're noisy. You can hear 'em coming. I want at least one gook [Vietnamese] for every track we lose.''[56] Another armored soldier rhetorically asked, ''Can you imagine the noise of sixteen tracked vehicles? For sure, there aren't any surprise attacks on the enemy. Usually, they're waiting and well dug in.''[57] Westmoreland's imagined ''firepower and psychological impact'' did not communicate to the foreign Other. General Donn A. Starry reported in *Mounted Combat in Vietnam* that around 75 percent of armored vehicle losses came from mines rather than in pitched battles.[58]

A great many soldiers, though, saw war-managers as directly responsible for their deaths. Management did not care whether labor lived or died, only about producing a high enemy body count. United States lives were quite secondary to primary production of enemy deaths. Story after story from infantry soldiers concerns commanders who knew large enemy formations were in a given area, but did not tell their subordinates because they did not want them to be cautious. Stan Goff talks about night patrols in his army unit:

> Night movement, that was a suicidal patrol. That was one of the worst patrols you could ever go out on. The purpose of it was for you to walk up on Charlie and for him to hit you, and then for our hardware to wipe them out. We were used as scapegoats to find out where they were. That was all we were — bait. They couldn't find Charlie any other way. They knew there was a regiment out there. They weren't looking for just a handful of VC. Actually, they'd love for us to run into a regiment which would just wipe us out. Then they could plaster the regiment and they'd have a big body count. The general gets another damn medal. He gets promoted.[59]

Another soldier, Herb Mock, a squad leader in the 25th Infantry Division, had the same experience:

> Fullback 6 [radio code name], just an example of a colonel who wasn't worth a shit. He'd been watching too many General Patton movies. What he wanted to do was promote himself, and he didn't give a damn who it cost or what it cost. He did not want to win, he just wanted to look good. He wanted you to follow the regulations because that looks good. He wanted a body count because that looks good.
>
> He liked to send people in without them knowing the enemy would

be there because we wouldn't be as cautious and more likely to get in shit. And his actions were . . . in fact, I talked to him . . . it was because Ditch got killed — he died in my arms on that trail. The colonel knew they were there, but he didn't tell us about the NVA base camp. I was told afterward by an officer that he knew. And that's when I went to see him. I asked him if he knew they were in there. And he said yeah.[60]

Steve Hassna, a sergeant in the 101st Airborne Division in 1967, was not positive his platoon had been set up by higher command, but he wondered.

When the platoon walked up to that mound and found a full regiment sitting in the damn thing, they backed right out. The point man and the platoon leader both died, right off the top, wwwhhtt!!, they're gone. There's only maybe 23 or 24 guys in my platoon to begin with. The initial burst just about wiped us out. I think there were maybe 15, 16 men left in my platoon after the whole fucking thing was done and that's a squad and a half. . . .

In that accidental battle [ambush] we took a lot of casualties in my platoon. With proper intelligence some of those men would not have died. We often weren't told the proper intelligence, or the intelligence was misleading, or it was wrong, or it was right and we didn't listen — so we ended up wrong. Twenty-six people walked into a regimental C.P. There's 2,000 people in there. I've thought from time to time that possibly, very possibly — and I wouldn't nearly think that the military would ever sacrifice lives to find out if the enemy is in a particular place — possibly the platoon was sent in there to get it going. "Let's send our people in there and if they catch any shit, we'll just have our Phantoms go in." Because there was close artillery and jet cover instantly.[61]

Producing a high body count was crucial for promotion in the officer corps. Many high-level officers established "production quotas" for their units, and systems of "debit" and "credit" to calculate exactly how efficiently subordinate units and middle-management personnel performed. Different formulas were used, but the commitment to war as a rational production process was common to all. General Ewell, for example, set up standards to determine satisfactory "kill ratios" for different units:

Table 5.3
BODY COUNT RATIOS IN THE 9TH INFANTRY DIVISION

| Ratio Allied to Enemy Dead | Skill Level of Unit |
|---|---|
| 1 to 50 and above | Highly skilled U.S. unit |
| 1 to 25 | Very good in heavy jungle<br>Fairly good U.S. unit in open terrain<br>Very good for ARVN in open terrain |
| 1 to 15 | Low but acceptable for U.S. unit |
| 1 to 10 | Historical U.S. average |
| 1 to 6 | Historical ARVN average |

SOURCE: Lieutenant General Julian J. Ewell and Major General Ira A. Hunt, Jr., *Sharpening the Combat Edge* (Washington, D.C.: Department of the Army, 1974), p. 212.

Normal production rate for Ewell's units was thus killing ten enemy soldiers for every U.S. soldier killed! Rewards and punishments were distributed around that norm. The army's 25th Infantry Division routinely sponsored a "Best of the Pack" contest for all platoons in the division. Command specified the elements of success and failure quite clearly.

Note how the point system makes deaths and captured ratios and inspections all equivalent to each other. The only unusual feature of this unit's contest was the relatively high value given to American deaths — 500 points. In some other units U.S. casualties did not even count as a production cost or measure of unit efficiency. Robert Johnson, Jr., obtained the Military Performance Indicator chart for the 503rd Infantry Division. Credits included enemy body counts, prisoners of war, and U.S. reenlistments. Debits included accidents, courts-martial, sicknesses, and all kinds of disciplinary problems. Credits minus debits equals the index of efficiency. The five columns on the right in Table 5.5, page 115, are for each maneuver battalion.

Reports like this were created every month; the above is one from March 1969. Five battalions is roughly one brigade. The brigade commander could thus measure his battalion commanders each month. Battalion commanders could perform the same or a similar evaluation on their subordinate company commanders, and company commanders in turn could index their platoon leaders — the first and second lieutenants

Table 5.4
"Best of the Pack" Contest
in the 25th Infantry Division

---

Points Awarded for the Following:

5 – per man per day above 25 on an operation
10 – each possible body count
10 – each 100 lbs. of rice
15 – each 100 lbs. of salt
20 – each mortar round
50 – each enemy individual weapon captured
100 – each enemy crew served weapon captured
200 – each tactical radio captured
500 – perfect score on CMMI (inspection)
1,000 – each prisoner of war

Points Deducted for the Following:

50 – each U.S. WIA (wounded in action)
500 – each U.S. KIA (killed in action)

SOURCE: Gloria Emerson, *Winners and Losers* (New York: Random House, 1976), p. 65.

---

at the point of production. At the other end of the scale, division commanders weighed the performances of their three or four brigade commanders. Above them, senior war-managers, commanders in charge of two or more divisions (a corps) and the general staff at MACV in Saigon, determined productivity of generals commanding divisions. The officer corps became a vast numerological chart, where at each level of the hierarchy every officer was weighed according to his war production.

These evaluations largely determined promotions. The further a man advanced in the officer corps, the less his chances of promotion became. At the lower levels, institutional pressures for middle-level commanders with some experience demanded mass advancement in rank, but at higher levels, competition became intense. Army promotion figures for the Vietnam War are as follows:

This chart is deceptive in some ways. Only a very hot, "productive" company commander ever stood a chance of promotion to battalion commander. The vast logistical apparatuses of the military created thou-

Table 5.5

MILITARY PERFORMANCE INDICATOR CHART
FOR 503RD INFANTRY DIVISION

|  | *1/503* | *2/503* | *3/503* | *4/503* | *1/50* |
|---|---|---|---|---|---|
| Indicator BC + (5 × PoW) Contacts × 200 | 157 | 710 | 148 | 338 | 56 |
| Percentage first term reenlistments × 100 | <u>107</u> | <u>80</u> | <u>111</u> | <u>0</u> | <u>100</u> |
|  | 264 | 790 | 259 | 338 | 156 |
| AWOL (absence without official leave) × 3 | 66 | 9 | 30 | 42 | 6 |
| DR (delinquency report) × 2 | 56 | 32 | 28 | 112 | 6 |
| Accident × 3 | 27 | 9 | 3 | 9 | 12 |
| Malaria × 5 | 35 | 15 | 70 | 85 | 10 |
| Narcotics × 5 | 30 | 30 | 90 | 30 | 5 |
| Article 15 (discipline) × 1 | 50 | 3 | 41 | 35 | 21 |
| Summary Court-Martial × 2 | 4 | 0 | 2 | 0 | 2 |
| Specific Court-Martial × 3 | 30 | 12 | 9 | 15 | 0 |
| General Court-Martial × 15 | <u>0</u> | <u>0</u> | <u>0</u> | <u>0</u> | <u>0</u> |
|  | 298 | 110 | 273 | 328 | 62 |

RECAP  1) 2/503: 790 − 110 = +680
           2) 1/50:  156 − 62  = + 94
           3) 4/503: 338 − 328 = + 10
           4) 3/503: 259 − 273 = − 14
           5) 1/503: 264 − 298 = − 34

SOURCE: Robert Bowie Johnson, Jr., with Mike Betzold, from "Testimony from War's Trigger End," *Washington Monthly*, August 1971, p. 30.

sands upon thousands of staff positions; most occupants of these positions wanted combat commands because combat commands were absolutely essential for promotion. At the height of the war, the army had only over 100 battalions in Vietnam, while there were close to 2,500 lieutenant colonels in the pool competing for those 100 to 130 battalions. At the next level up, the ratio of applicants to positions became worse. By the early 1970s the army only had seventy-five or so brigade-

Table 5.6
PROMOTION IN THE ARMY OFFICER CORPS

| Rank | Highest Command Position | Percent Promoted |
|---|---|---|
| Second Lieutenant | Platoon Commander | Over 99 |
| First Lieutenant | Company Executive Officer | 95 |
| Captain | Company Commander | 93 |
| Major | Battalion or other Staff | 77 |
| Lt. Colonel | Battalion Commander | 50 |

SOURCE: Maureen Mylander, *The Generals: Making It, Military Style* (New York: Dial Press, 1974), pp. 75–76.

equivalent commands in Vietnam for colonels, while 2,000 of the 6,000 colonels in the army were serious competitors for these jobs. For those relative few who survived the cut-off between colonel and general, the structure did not open any farther. In the early 1970s around 200 major generals (two star) were in competition for thirteen division commander positions.

Given the large number of managers in competition for relatively few jobs, competition became intense, particularly at the key structural level, command of the infantry maneuver battalion. Battalion commanders had only a six-month tour of duty to begin with — as opposed to the normal tour of one year in Vietnam for enlisted men. If they didn't produce high body counts immediately, they were threatened with replacement. According to Professor Francis West of the Naval War College, a battalion commander "had a 30 to 50 percent chance of being relieved of command because [of failure]. If you were a division commander, however, you had less than a 5 percent chance of being relieved of command, given your resources."[62] A division commander could "play" with the numbers, rearrange them to signify productivity. But to signify his own success, a division commander demanded that his battalion and brigade officers follow the "rules" and produce a high body count. Threats to battalion commanders became very explicit. In *The Lionheads,* a fictional account of General Ewell's 9th Infantry Division, Josiah Bunting describes Ewell's treatment of the brigade commander with the lowest body count:

"IV Corps [Mekong Delta] below the River is lousy with VC. The MRB gets mortared two nights out of three. Your body-count is a standing joke. Tell you what, Robinson, you have *one week to pro-duce*. . . ."

Colonel Robinson knows — it is as simple as this — that he will be relieved unless he achieves a good body-count based on a major contact, and though he hates Lemming [Ewell] he knows the General can ruin him, can keep him from being a general, can keep him from riding through Persepolis, can make it difficult for him to keep paying his son's tuition at Cornell, can keep him from commanding a division himself some day, can vindicate his own wife's hatred for what he has been doing with his professional life, can make him a retired colonel selling fire insurance, with a Legion of Merit in his buttonhole. Can ruin him. The prospect is discomforting even to George Robinson.[63]

On the other hand, if ''Robinson'' and the other middle-management officers used their troops as the human ''bait'' called for in Technowar strategy, then many rewards were available. Simply flying in their command and control helicopters above effective anti-aircraft range became a way of earning prestigious medals. Cincinnatus notes that by February 1971 (close to the end of the major U.S. ground war) the army had given out 1,273,987 awards for bravery. Around 800,000 of these awards were Air Medals, emblems previously given out only to those who served in an extraordinary way as a member of an aircraft crew. But in Vietnam Air Medals were distributed simply for flying a set number of missions in a ''war zone.'' One chaplain described how officers manipulated criteria for receiving the award:

Think of Air Medals. A guy goes up for a five-minute flight in a perfectly peaceful area, and that counted toward an Air Medal. He does everything he can so he can get up in the air and get another Air Medal. It was easy and it was cheap. It was the kind of war-type mentality in Vietnam where some acted as if it was a play war — but elsewhere people were dying.[64]

Senior management fared better at such games. One colonel received a Silver Star — a very prestigious medal — for flying a helicopter full of frozen turkeys into a Special Forces camp for Thanksgiving. Other senior commanders were awarded medals for taking potshots at Vietnamese on the ground. In 1969 of fifty-seven army generals returning from Vietnam, fifty received the Distinguished Service Medal, commonly known as the ''general's good conduct ribbon.'' Twenty-six received either the Silver Star, the Distinguished Flying Cross, or the Bronze Star. Of the 345,000 enlisted men who returned to the United States that year, only about 30,000 received decorations. Only one of the citations the generals received was for ground combat, and apparently just being on the ground was what the citation was for: "It was from this vantage point that he felt he could best estimate and determine more fully the tactical situation. . . . Regardless of the continuous and heavy volume of rockets, automatic weapons and mortar fire, he was on the ground inspiring and giving confidence. . . ." The general got an award for being on the ground and getting shot at.

*New York Times* correspondent Gloria Emerson ironically reviews and summarizes the citations accompanying the medals:

> The generals are always flying their command and control helicopters in extremely hazardous flying conditions, with complete disregard for their own personal safety, to assist and direct rifle companies on the ground in contact with the enemy. The generals do it all. They arrange for artillery and air support, they sight enemy positions, they order the door gunners to open up, they give tactical guidance, they bring in more ammunition, they get out the wounded.[65]

Citations usually had the same ending. Actions by the officers were "in keeping with the highest traditions of military service and reflect great credit upon himself, his unit, and the United States Army." One general even received a Silver Star for a totally fictitious incident. The Awards and Decorations office of his division created the citation to give the general a medal as his tour in command was over!

Few ground troops were deceived by such fabrications and false awards. One soldier found his whole battalion trapped in a vertically walled canyon: "Everybody was pretty scared, except for the battalion commander, who was in his chopper."[66] Another trooper comments on the banality of medals: "Medals are a farce. Our Colonel got an Air Medal, which is a pretty impressive medal. He got an Air Medal for flying over a fire fight. Well, we were in it. He was up so high you could hardly see the helicopter."[67] Those soldiers who became wounded on search-and-destroy missions to fulfill their commanders' needs for high body counts give particularly bitter testimony. A man who lost his foot says:

> It's one thing to be in Nam huntin' Charlie and another to be there in some air-conditioned trailer. A lot of them guys don't have to sweat none. They fly around in them command choppers once in a while

and then they go back to Saigon or somewhere and live it up. Nobody give a shit what happened to us grunts. I mean they just didn't really care. Just so everything looked okay and none of the wheels chewed anybody's ass — that was all that mattered to 'em. I mean they kept givin' you all that fucking bullshit about helpin' the fucking gooks ain't gonna do nothin'. The main thing was that the wheels look good. Shit, I lost my foot going into a fuckin' village that the sergeant kept trying to tell the captain was just one big fuckin' booby trap. But the captain, he was new, and the battalion commander wanted the village checked and we had to go chargin' in there so the captain wouldn't look bad. Now I ain't got no foot, mister, and what for? I'll tell you why, because the Army don't give a shit about guys like me. . . . I wish I'd gone AWOL.[68]

Another soldier lost his arm: "His amputated arm had been shattered by a captured U.S. Bouncing Betty mine [a mine that reaches waist-high before exploding] while he was on a search and clear mission near the demilitarized zone. He had been leading a platoon searching vainly for Vietcong to kill and add to the unit body count."[69] Stories from soldier memoirs and interviews with journalists all point to the same pattern of men being wounded for their officers' advancement. A third amputee says:

Well, we was out on patrol looking for VC. We never saw none, just old women and kids. But our captain wanted to look real good so he had the platoon sweeping the paddies and going through the hoochies [GI slang for Vietnamese houses] to try and get a prisoner or body. . . . I come to this little old fence and I started to push open a busted-up gate so I could get behind the hootchie and there was this goddam noise and I got knocked down and then I passed out. They told me it was a frag grenade that some gook bastard had hooked to the gate — it really blew the shit out of me.[70]

A lieutenant in Ewell's 9th Infantry lost his eyes: "I was up behind the point walking along a little trail when the point man snagged a tripwire. All I remember was hearing a blast from the right and that was all she wrote. They told me later we walked into a U.S. made Claymore mine that was rigged alongside the trail. What still gets me, though, is why the hell we had to be out there like a bunch of clay pigeons trying to up the body count figures on some graph back at U SAR V [U.S. Army Vietnam Headquarters]." The lieutenant further indicates he went blind trying to meet his production quota: "I knew if I went in without a body count or at least a prisoner I'd be on the shitlist, so I kept the patrol out." [71] Army doctor Ronald J. Glasser heard many such stories from wounded soldiers he saw in Japan. The punishment for nonproduction was continual duty: "Some units were given a quota for a week, and if they didn't get it, they were just sent out again." [72]

Command pressure for determining productivity included ordering body counting missions either in the midst of combat operations or in the immediate aftermath when the battlefield was still a highly dangerous place. So many soldiers were either killed or wounded on body counting missions that the Department of the Army included an extensive account of incidents as a way of warning officers in its pamphlet *Vietnam Primer: Lessons Learned* (1967).

> *Item.* A U.S. rifle company in a good defensive position atop a ridge is taking a steady toll of an NVA force attacking up hill. The skipper sends a four-man patrol to police weapons and count bodies. Three men return bearing the fourth, who was wounded before the job was well started. Another patrol is sent. The same thing happens. The skipper says, "Oh, to hell with it!" *Item.* In Operation Nathan Hale three men working through a banana grove were hit by sniper fire. They were counting bodies. *Item.* In Operation Paul Revere IV a much-admired line sergeant was killed, and two other enlisted men were wounded, and a lieutenant barely escaped ambush, when the four together were "tidying up" the field. They ran into a stay-behind party planted in a thicket on the morning after the fight. [73]

The authors, retired General S. L. A. Marshall and Colonel David Hacksworth, said nothing about the production model of war and the war-managers' competition for promotion. Instead, their recommendations placed responsibility on lieutenants and captains — the "small unit commanders" — to defy their superiors: "If he believes that a present, but unmeasured danger forbids body counting or that a more urgent military object should come first, he need only have the courage of his own convictions in coming to that decision. No one may rightly press him to trade bodies for lives." [74] Yet the war-managers continued to do just that. Years later, one anonymous general confided in a survey of army generals who served in Vietnam: "I shudder to think how many of our soldiers were killed on a body-counting mission — what a waste." [75]

Technowar thus suffered from severe internal contradictions in its big-unit search-and-destroy operations. United States military officers conceived of themselves as business managers rather than combat leaders. Enlisted men were seen as a kind of migrant labor force of only marginal importance. They were marginal in that artillery, jet fighter-bombers, and helicopter gunships were officially responsible for producing enemy deaths, while infantry and armored cavalry became the "fixing force." Enlisted men were also marginal in that with the shift to the production model of war and the managerial officer corps, senior and middle-level officers became fixated on their individual career advancements with little attention given to troop welfare. Traditional military social bonds between troops and their commanders deteriorated. Soldiers instead became "costs of production" for Technowar as a whole while virtually "free" to any given war-manager. Casualties could be replaced by increasing Selective Service or draft quotas each month. Draftees as a percentage of those killed in Vietnam rose each year: 1965, 16 percent; 1966, 21 percent; 1967, 34 percent; 1969, 40 percent. These figures are for the U.S. military on the whole. Taking the army separately finds 62 percent of 1969 battle deaths and 70 percent of 1970 battle deaths from draftee ranks.[76] But regardless of whether an enlisted man was drafted, or joined because of draft pressures, or joined out of genuine desire, he was still conceptualized as a small production cost in a vast war machine run by management for management.

This abstract technological and production-oriented approach permeated all phases of war. For example, the concept of producing mass enemy deaths through high-technology, capital-intensive weapons assumed an empty, transparent kind of battlefield — as if comparing U.S. and NVA weapons systems on paper — and finding U.S. weapons could saturate an area more quickly. But in the real world, nature existed in its concrete, raw form. Rainy weather, for instance, grounded U.S. planes and helicopters. Thomas Bird describes what happened to the 1st Air Cavalry Division during the 1965–1966 Ia Drang Valley battle:

> The joke of Ia Drang Valley is, If you can't bring a chopper in to give air support, what good is it? If they can't fly because it's too humid or because the weight they are carrying won't let them get off the ground or they'll burn up too much ammo to go out and resupply and get back to base camp, what good is it? Then you're down on the enemy's level and they are masters there.[77]

Another soldier describes his unit's shock when they discovered the unit that ambushed them was dug into a mountain valley to keep U.S. jets away:

> Like valleys where you're pinned down. A lot of times we've had jets come in over the top of us, when it was hard to hit them any other way. They couldn't come across because of the mountains and stuff. They release the bombs right over our heads. And you can see the bombs. They'd be going towards us. And we're saying, "Ooh, fucking things just don't drop." But they like carried on the momentum of the speed they're going. They go in front of you. They blow up. That takes a lot of skill on an estimate. And a lot of fucking luck. The gooks choose this type of thing because they know that our jets can't come into a valley this way and make it. Because there's a mountain there and they can't get up. So they set up their defenses so they can shoot down the planes as they're coming in.[78]

Psychiatrist Charles J. Levy heard this story from a patient. Levy classified it as an example of "inverted warfare," the sense in which American common sense on how the world operates was reversed or inverted in Vietnam. The jet aircraft represents America's mastery of scientific principles concerning how nature works. To see the aircraft's efficacy vanquished by the *technologically* primitive technique of burrowing into a mountain inverts the normal Technowar order. Levy says: "The rationale for much of American technology had been the conquest of nature. But in Vietnam, the VC/NVA used nature for the conquest of technology."[79]

By far the most important Vietnamese use of nature was their use of the *earth*. Vietnamese villagers and Vietcong cadres and NVA troops all built thousands of miles of elaborate tunnels inside the south. The more sophisticated tunnel networks stretched from the northern supply routes along the Ho Chi Minh Trail in Cambodia to the very outskirts of Saigon. Hundreds, if not thousands, of more locally oriented tunnels hid Vietcong troops and supplies from U.S. search-and-destroy operations, artillery barrages, and air strikes. The Vietcong's tunnel system totally confounded American commanders.

General Fred Weyland, commander of the 25th Infantry Division, selected Cu Chi as headquarters for his division in 1966. As the general explains his choice, "I selected Cu Chi as an area that was well away from the populated center of Saigon, to act as a sort of lightning rod for the enemy. We picked the specific area because of the topography. It was the one place that was above the water table, where we could put trucks and tanks without having them sink out of sight during the monsoon season."[80]

Unfortunately for the general, the very topography sufficient to support Technowar was also sufficient for a vast tunnel system. One American adversary, Captain Nguyen Thanh Linh, describes how U.S. forces responded to their first encounter with attack from Vietcong hidden in the earth: "They were so bewildered, they did not hide or take defensive positions. They did not know where the bullets had come from. We kept on shooting. . . . Although their fellows kept falling down, they kept on advancing. They should have retreated. They called for artillery. When the first shells landed we simply went into the communications tunnels and went on to another place. The Americans continued advancing, but we'd gone." In recalling all his battles, Linh says of the tunnels, "They are something very Vietnamese and one must understand what the relationship is between the Vietnamese peasant and the earth, *his earth*. Without that, then everything here is without real meaning."[81]

Unable to see outside Technowar, war-managers often attempted to destroy "raw nature" with its mountains and forests and places to hide. They tried to create a physical terrain equivalent to the abstract, mathematical space of 1,000 meter by 1,000 meter grid squares necessary for jets and artillery to find orientation. Technowar attempted to defoliate Vietnam with herbicides as a way of reorganizing nature to meet its needs, rather than to see the contradiction of its project. Another of Ronald Glasser's patients told him what happened:

> Let me tell you about that defoliation program. It didn't work. No, I mean it. It ain't done a damn thing it was supposed to do. I'll give 'em there are a lot of dead people out there because of it, but not theirs — ours. The whole idea was to prevent ambushes, to clear the area. Some idiot somewhere sold somebody the idea that if the gooks couldn't hide, then they couldn't ambush you, and they bought the idea, I mean really bought it. The trouble with the whole thing is that the VC and NVA use guns in their ambushes instead of bows and arrows. Nobody mentioned that. They don't have to be sitting on top of you to pull off an ambush. An AK-47 round is effective up to 1,500 meters and accurate up to 600. So we'll hit an area, like along a busy road, billions of gallons of the stuff, and pretty soon there's nothing except for some dead bushes for fifty or even 300 meters on

both sides of where the road or track used to be. So the gooks will start shooting at you from 300 meters away instead of five, only now you're the one that ain't got no place to hide. Ever try running 100 meters or 200? It takes time, and they're firing at you the whole way. And I mean the whole way.[82]

Note how intended protection created a larger killing zone. In theory, defoliated territory was perfect for helicopter observation by war-managers and quick marshaling of planes and artillery. But at ground level soldiers had to run out of the barren zone to survive. Unable to produce the desired number of enemy deaths because the Technowar apparatus was so visible to a hostile population, the war-managers sought a solution by applying more force, more technology. Technowar must produce victory: debit can be transformed into credit by increasing war production. Contradictions became compounded. The foreign Other repeatedly took the "bait" while the traps backfired. Senior officers got medals and the troops got killed.

Thus far, analysis of search-and-destroy has concerned only how the production model of war, with its split between management and labor, suffered from structural contradictions that both mitigated American technological superiority against actual enemy combatants and rendered ground troops expendable. However, there are several other important dimensions of ground Technowar that must be explored to understand this complex system of power and knowledge. First, the production system with its precise reports of how many bodies were found on operations created the *appearance* of highly rational, scientific warfare. Body counts, weapons/kill ratios, charts of patrols conducted, helicopter and jet plane missions flown, and artillery rounds fired — all the indices of war production created at various command levels — presented Vietnam as a war managed by rational men basing their decisions on scientific knowledge. Statistics helped make war-managers appear legitimate to the American public.

The appearance of a science-governed war in turn helped make Vietnam seem like a lawful war. Rational men do not engage in systematic slaughter but fight real enemies — the foreign Other invading from without, trying to "take over" the sovereign state of South Vietnam. The representation of Technowar as a law-governed war was enhanced by command's proliferation of numerous and lengthy regulations determining conditions under which American forces could bomb, shell, and otherwise engage the enemy. Yet these rules had little truth in practice.

War-manager pressures for high body counts led to both systematic falsification of battle reports, routine violation of the rules of engagement and regulations covering treatment of prisoners, and systematic slaughter of Vietnamese noncombatants. The production model of war simultaneously destroyed both its own troops and the Vietnamese people, but it could not produce victory. Instead, as the war progressed, the increasing death and destruction, together with the accumulating "layers" of official lies throughout the chain of command, created conditions for Technowar's decay and collapse through internal contradictions.

The simplest aspect of false reporting concerns the many cases when troops and commanders invented enemy body counts out of thin air. Lieutenant William Calley says that one day his battalion commander threatened to relieve him from command of his platoon unless he became more productive. In response, Calley ordered his sergeant to have the platoon open fire on the surrounding jungle. Artillery fire was called in to repel the pseudo-attack. And when the "mock little firefight" was over, "I called in a body count: three and a combat loss of some compasses. It was near inventory time and I had lost those compasses somehow." [83]

One of Cincinnatus's informants has a similar story at company level. "I know one unit that lost 18 men killed in an ambush and reported 131 enemy body count. I was on the ground at the tail end of the battle and I saw five enemy bodies. I doubt if there were any more." [84] Moving up the chain of command, Captain Greg Howard describes the pressures his division commander put on his battalion commander in late 1968. Captain Howard is testifying before Congressman Ronald Dellums's unofficial hearings on war crimes in Vietnam:

> Our 3rd Battalion, 22nd Infantry, had not been getting the body count that the other battalions in the division had, and General Williamson told that battalion commander, Lieutenant Colonel Carmichael, that he had better start *producing* or we would get a battalion commander in that battalion that could produce. Colonel Carmichael got the message loud and clear.
>
> Approximately two weeks later his fire base was attacked. *He called in that night a body count of 312 and he had taken one wounded.* We flew out the next morning, I flew with General Williamson the next morning. We landed and counted the bodies around the perimeter of that base camp, and there were 30-plus North Vietnamese bodies and a few wounded prisoners.

General Williamson questioned him a bit further, and said I understood you have 312 body count and I see 30-plus here, where are the
other bodies? Colonel Carmichael then gave a vague statement of,
well I had an ambush patrol in a particular location on the map and
they saw 100 Viet Cong moving across an open field that night in
preparation for attack and we called in a lot of artillery fire out there,
and we counted those 100.

He gave instances like that which amounted to 312. It was obvious
to everybody that that was a lie. But General Williamson had put so
much pressure on the colonel to produce the body count, the man had
no choice. He is forty-five years old and he probably has two kids to
send to college, and General Williamson, recognizing that he had placed
this pressure on the battalion commander, accepted this lie.[85]

Both the colonel and the general meet their production quotas in terms
of reporting high body counts. Both become eligible for rewards. Indeed, in some stories, fabricating enemy body counts becomes an activity one party conducts to "reward" another party for doing something.
General Williamson's acceptance of the lie is a tacit reward for Colonel
Carmichael's submission to his will. In other cases body counts appear
as compensations, as imaginary credits to take the place of real-life
debits. As Lieutenant Calley says, "I knew damn well, *Weber's dead.
A boy in the second platoon has no legs anymore. A boy in the third
platoon* — I had to do it. I wrote in the after-action report [concerning
a U.S. artillery barrage that hit no one], 'VC body count six.' "[86]

At higher command levels the numbers just got larger. In one incident, an assistant division commander ordered a high enemy body count
for a company that had taken heavy casualties so "we can tell the survivors they did well."[87]

Beyond simple fabrications of body counts come inferential counting
rules, rules that a unit followed as "standard operating procedure" but
that were not part of official doctrine. An inferential counting rule is a
rule that a company uses to infer numbers of enemy dead according to
some found object or sign — an enemy weapon, a blood trail, a dis-
membered body part, or other mark of enemy presence. Inferential
counting rules tended to maximize enemy body count. Severed limbs
signified a whole body for counting purposes. One senior officer upset
with the body count heard a lower-level field officer tell "of an experience where he almost had to get in a fist fight with an ARVN adviser
over an arm, to see who would get credit for the body, because they

were sorting out pieces. . . . It just made him sick to the stomach that he was put in such a position that a body was so important to the next higher headquarters or to the division, that he had to go down and argue over pieces of a body to get credit for it.''[88]

In another case Martin Russ, author of *Happy Hunting Ground,* describes the problems one captain faced counting body parts and estimating deaths:

> Later he [the colonel] told Bizelle he wanted to see all the bodies he reported. Bizelle looked shamefaced and said he actually found only parts of bodies. ''But there's a long trail of blood,'' he added. ''And you can see where they stacked them before taking them up the mountain.''
>
> ''You've no idea how many?''
>
> ''I didn't measure the density of the gore, no sir, if that's what you mean.''
>
> Suggins said, ''There's hands and feet and hunks of meat all over, but the main housing groups [body trunks] are just gone.''[89]

The captain estimated fifty dead from the severed limbs his unit found. Missing bodies created a real problem. Enemy units dragged their fallen comrades from the field when possible, and friends and relatives likewise buried civilian casualties. Encountering Vietnamese graves while on operations was consequently a common occurrence for many U.S. units. Such encounters gave rise to another counting rule — counting graves as part of a unit's body count even if they were newly arrived in the area — counting them *twice.* One of Glasser's patients said, ''He'd heard about units of the 101st [Airborne — elite unit] burying their kills on the way in and digging them up again to be recounted on the way out.''[90] Captain Michael O'Mera, of the 25th Infantry Division, says units often doubled their bodies and graves as a rule of thumb: ''Another way, you come across the graves and you call in the number of graves you find. If you come across dead bodies, you count dead bodies. You resweep the area, recount the numbers, *double it,* and call it on in.''[91]

Robert Mall, an enlisted man in another unit, says a common inferential counting rule concerned finding enemy weapons: ''. . . in counting a weapon captured is counted as five bodies. In other words, if you shoot a guy who's got a gun and you get that gun, you've shot six people.''[92] Conversely, many U.S. units decided that if they shot a large number of munitions into an area, then these rounds fired signified that a certain number of enemy troops were killed. Captain O'Mera gives an example involving ground radars and the blips of light showing up on the screens:

> We would reference reports constantly and it was usually a Second Brigade policy that I know, they would detect 20 to 25 persons, perhaps it could have been trees moving — it could never be substantiated — 20 to 25 persons stationary, no less.
>
> Artillery was fired and the brigade would report 12 body count. *It was practice for them to take half the number on the radar screen and count it as a body count.* The next day when troops would sweep the area there would be nothing there. Yet this was accepted and it was good, because the pressure was on and this is what they had to do. This was the only way they could come up with it.[93]

Journalist Dale Minor found the same kind of extrapolation being done in units he visited: "When the battle is over and reporting time has come, a probable 'kill figure' is extrapolated from the estimated density of enemy troops hit by a known or approximate number of artillery and mortar rounds, bombs and rockets."[94] To make the body count even more imaginary, such extrapolations were often conducted by every military unit participating in a particular battle. A pacification official once complained that in his province, "Whenever several agencies combined in a single operation, it appears to be common practice for each to claim 100% of the results."[95]

These fabrications and inferential counting rules are not simply a deviation of Technowar, something that could be reformed leaving the system intact. Maximizing productivity — and therefore *reporting* high body counts — was essential both for individual commanders and for Technowar as a whole. To the war-managers, the deployment of this massive apparatus of planes, helicopters, artillery, and troops without a "product" became an *unthinkable* contradiction. The fetishism of advanced war technology where the mere appearance of Technowar will help persuade the NVA and the NLF "that they cannot win" in practice persuaded the war-managers that they could not lose: *the bodies must be out there, somewhere.* The visible presence of the superior war-production apparatus created a conceptual "wall" in which all contrary data from the real world became transformed into information that affirmed Technowar as successful even as it failed. Consequently, a "double-reality" became structurally produced by Technowar, a system of official reports full of scientific-looking production indices, and the reality of lived experience. The gap between these two realities in turn created the space for further falsification.

Nowhere is the discrepancy between Technowar practice and official representation more pronounced than in the rules of engagement. Taken at the broadest level, ROE (as they are called in the military) attempt to regulate relations between U.S. and enemy forces and the civilian population. More specific rules govern clearance procedures before opening fire. United States military personnel received two pocket-sized cards when they arrived in Vietnam providing rules for acceptable conduct with the civilian population and captured enemies. One card was called "Nine Rule" and the other was "The Enemy in Your Hands." The first card said:

> The Vietnamese have paid a heavy price in suffering for their long fight against the communists. We military men are in Vietnam now because their government has asked us to help its soldiers and people in winning their struggle. The Viet Cong will attempt to turn the Vietnamese people against you. You can defeat them at every turn by the strength, understanding, and generosity you display with the people. Here are nine simple rules:
>    1. Remember, we are guests here: We make no demands and seek no special treatment.
>    2. Join with the people! Understand their life, use phrases from their language and honor their customs and laws.
>    3. Treat women with politeness and respect.
>    4. Make personal friends among the soldiers and common people.
>    5. Always give the Vietnamese the right of way.
>    6. Be alert to security and ready to react with your military skill.
>    7. Don't attract attention by loud, rude or unusual behavior.
>    8. Avoid separating yourself from the people by a display of wealth or privilege.
>    9. Above all else you are members of the U.S. Military Forces on a difficult mission, responsible for all your official and personal actions. Reflect honor upon yourself and the United States of America.[96]

In summary these rules call for U.S. forces to respect Vietnamese and win their allegiance by their virtuous and friendly conduct. "The Enemy in Your Hands" also had a straightforward message succinctly articulated by President Lyndon Johnson: "The courage and skill of our men in battle will be matched by their magnanimity when the battle ends.'' One section of the card provides English-Vietnamese translations for phrases necessary to control prisoners. The rest of the card reads:

As a member of U.S. military forces, you will comply with the Geneva Prisoner of War Conventions of 1949 to which your country adheres. Under these Conventions:

*You can and will:*
Disarm your prisoner
Immediately search him thoroughly
Require him to be silent
Segregate him from other prisoners
Guard him carefully
Take him to the place designated by your commander

*You cannot and must not:*
Mistreat your prisoner
Humiliate or degrade him
Take any of his personal effects which do not have significant military value
Refuse him medical treatment if required and available

[Side Two]

THE ENEMY IN YOUR HANDS
1. *Handle him firmly, promptly, but humanely.*
   The captive in your hands must be *disarmed, searched,* secured and watched. But he must also be treated at all times as a human being. He must not be tortured, killed, mutilated, or degraded, even if he refuses to talk.
2. *Take the captive quickly to security.*
   As soon as possible evacuate the captive to a place of safety and interrogation designated by your commander. Military documents taken from the captive are also sent to the interrogators, but the captive will keep his personal equipment except weapons.
3. *Mistreatment of any captive is a criminal offense. Every soldier is personally responsible for the enemy in his hands.*
   It is both dishonorable and foolish to mistreat a captive. It is also a punishable offense. Not even a beaten enemy will surren-

der if he knows his captors will torture or kill him. He will resist and make his capture more costly. Fair treatment of captives encourages the enemy to surrender.

4. *Treat the sick and wounded captive as best you can.*

    The captive saved may be an intelligence source. In any case he is a human being and must be treated like one. The soldier who ignores the sick and wounded degrades his uniform.

5. *All persons in your hands, whether suspects, civilians, or combat captives, must be protected against violence, insults, curiosity, and reprisals or any kind.*

    Leave punishment to the courts and judges. The soldier shows his strength by his fairness, and humanity to the persons in his hands.[97]

Note the redundancy in these rules. This multitude of rules can essentially be reduced to one imperative: Treat any captured combatant as a person for whom the war is over — by surrendering they are more like civilians than combatants in terms of their category classification. "Nine Rules" and "The Enemy in Your Hands" specify American behavior toward Vietnamese that fall under two abstract categories, namely a civilian population and captured enemy troops. The rules imply that determining who is a civilian and who is a captured enemy soldier is completely clear — that individual Vietnamese can be readily distinguished by signs of their dress, conduct, and demeanor to allow ready classification into civilian, enemy, or captured enemy. But only in the far northern provinces, War Zone I, or I Corps, and along the border with Cambodia was it generally clear who was the enemy. Troops belonging to the People's Army of Vietnam, or NVA as the Americans called them, wore distinct uniforms and often operated in relatively unpopulated areas. In such cases battles between the United States and the foreign Other offered few problems in determining who was who.

However, these battles comprised only part of American military encounters with Vietnamese. In his memoir, *A Soldier Reports,* General Westmoreland spoke of how he had to withdraw troops from the border areas and assign them to populated areas of Vietnam: "In reality, despite my policy of using American units to oppose the enemy's main forces, more American troops were usually engaged on a day-to-day basis, helping weed out local opposition and supporting pacification process, than were engaged in the big fights."[98] MACV's two cards issued to every arriving American soldier, in conjunction with a massive series of memos issued to military war-managers, make it *appear* that U.S. military forces followed stringent rules of engagement.

In actual warfare, the practical rules of engagement were based on the physical appearance and activities of Vietnamese. According to American reasoning, certain signs signified that an individual was an enemy Vietcong. In social theory, the rules that link "signs," or signifiers, such as Vietnamese dress and activities, with categorical placements, such as "friend" or "foe" — "signifieds" in social theory — are called "codes." Codes designate rules that link many different signifiers with the same category or meaning. Rules of engagement are thus codes. At issue, then, is what were the practiced codes of war as opposed to the official rules of engagement found in cards and numerous memos issued from high command.

Vietnamese peasants throughout the country routinely wore as their everyday dress garments Americans described as "black pajamas." Yet for many units "black pajamas" signified that the individual was a Vietcong. Journalist Jonathan Schell overheard one soldier report to his captain: "We killed four VC this morning, sir. We turned around and saw that these guys were following us. They saw that we had spotted them, and we fired, and they took *evasive action*. We got all four of them though. They didn't have weapons, but they were wearing the short VC type black-pajama uniforms, and they were definitely of military age. No question about that, sir." [99]

Clothing was but one possible dimension among many used to determine Vietcong status. Some U.S. units payed particular attention to Vietnamese bodies for signs of their political affiliation. General Harry Kinnard, at the time commander of the 1st Air Cavalry, decided troops on patrol should look deeply into the eyes of the foreign Other: "It occurred to me that perhaps we would be able to identify the guerrillas — a farmer by day and a fighter by night — by the dark circles under his eyes." [100] Other commanders had their troops look at the hands of the peasants, a palmistry of sorts. Those who had many calluses were probably farmers; those with fewer calluses were considered Vietcong suspects and were taken prisoner. Other U.S. units looked at *feet* rather than palms: "In the villages you look at the ankles and feet of the young men. If they were covered with scratches watch out, they were usually Viet Cong." [101] Pity the unfortunate man who walked in the jungle while chasing a loose pig or chicken.

Shoulders comprised another important body part for some U.S. units.

Frederick Downs, author of *The Killing Zone,* explains his unit's practice of semiotics.

> Since all young Vietnamese males were supposed to be in the army, any strays in the area had to be Vietcong. Again, amid much yelling and protest from the accused, we tied his hands behind his back and brought him along also. I was pleased so far with the success of this patrol. One of the men ripped the man's shirt away from his shoulders to check for marks on his back from carrying a pack. This would be a sure sign that he was a Cong. We all knew the Cong transported rice and ammo on their backs. I was never sure this was a good idea. We also carried packs and we never had any marks from them — but we always checked anyway. You could never tell.[102]

Soon Downs discovered his mistake concerning the young man with indentations in his shoulders:

> The next day I was surprised to see the two men we had taken prisoner the day before standing in a group of men. As they told their story, the village men kept glancing in our direction. I called the captain to find out the status of those two men. He told me that the old man had been a records keeper in the area for the land boundaries, sort of a county clerk. The young man had been on leave from his ARVN unit.[103]

At least the man was still alive. Physical characteristics were passive signifiers and their presence was not often interpreted as life threatening. Physical movement — particularly running — often spelled deadly danger to U.S. forces. Story after story in the "ground-level" book collection of novels, memoirs, and lengthy interviews by journalists tells of U.S. troops firing on Vietnamese because the Vietnamese were running away from them. W. D. Ehrhart, a marine, describes his shot:

> We'd been out nearly three hours. Aside from a few water buffalo standing around asleep on their feet, we hadn't seen much of anything. Everyone but us obviously had sense enough not to be out in heat like this.
>
> And then I saw the figure in black pajamas running along a paddy dike about 300 meters ahead and to the left. "Got one!" I hollered.
>
> "Ten o'clock. He's mine."
>
> The muttered warning to halt — regulations: "Dung lai!" Drop to

one knee. Safety off. Sight in. Squeeze. Crack! The figure in black went flying like a piece of paper in a gust of wind.

"Get some!" Morgan shouted.

"Nice shot," said Newcome.

When we reached the body, it was sprawled in one of those impossible awkward postures only people who die violently while in motion are capable of assuming. I nudged the corpse face-up with my boot. It was a woman of indeterminate age, perhaps fifty-five to sixty.

"Stupid gook," said Wally. "What'd she run for?" [104]

Gary Battles adds his testimony to the dangers of running:

But a woman and child were running across, and the captain goes, you know, "There. They are running."

Well, free-fire zone, anyone running in Vietnam — well, if they are running they are wrong. They are enemy. And we shot. Like a whole squad opened up, and I don't think they really hit them. But then one guy drew up a careful bead and the woman went down. The next morning we went out and we could see the cap of the child that was bloodied and you could see where the mother had dragged the child away. [105]

Jonathan Schell, writing for the *New Yorker*, reported that the marines tried to warn Vietnamese villagers about the dangers of running from Americans by distributing thousands of leaflets with the message: "The Marines are here to help you. Do not run from them! If you run, they may mistake you for a Vietcong and shoot at you." [106] But apparently the leaflet had little effect. People ran because they were afraid.

Complementing these ground-level identification rules are ones used by Forward Air Control pilots (FACs). FAC pilots flew slow, propeller aircraft at low altitudes in search of Vietcong and NVA forces. When they found a target, they then marked it with a highly visible white phosphorus rocket to guide fast-moving jet bombers in for bomb runs. Jet fighter bombers flew so fast that they could not identify targets on the ground by themselves. Given the tremendous firepower of jet fighter-bombers and their massive use in Vietnam, FAC semiotics or identification rules are of great consequence. Schell spent several weeks flying with different FAC pilots. Some of the signs trained pilots looked for were:

FAC: If they run is one way. [107]

FAC: It's almost a fact that anything out in the open is friendly, so anything you see in the trees you suspect is unfriendly, because it might be VC.[108]

FAC: Now look down there. See how someone has built the trail around the [bomb] crater? This is the kind of sign you look for.[109]

FAC: I guess you can call it a kind of intuition. I think I can just about smell a VC from 5,000 feet by now. Like everything else, some people have got the knack and some people don't. Some people wouldn't be able to tell a VC no matter how long they tried.[110]

On many occasions American forces didn't have to bother trying. If an area was officially declared a "free-fire zone" then any ground or air unit could assume that anyone seen there was an enemy. In 1969 Westmoreland reported that no civilian deaths occurred as a result of American Technowar in areas declared free-fire zones — a simple tautology that begs the crucial issues of how free-fire zones were determined and who was really in them. Garry Battles attempted to answer the question of who made the free-fire zone maps for the Dellums committee hearings: "Yes, we have maps of our area where the free-fire zones were. . . . I can't say who does it. I would like to know."[111] More important, what identification rules did he use? Sometimes Vietnamese district and province chiefs charted zones for the Americans. ARVN leaders in Saigon made sure that no province or district chief was ever from the same area he ruled; their interests were not aligned with the local populace. Once Jonathan Schell overheard an ARVN general delight as a village was being evacuated and then burned by U.S. forces. He declared, "Good! Good! They are all VC. Kill them!"[112] Schell overheard another Vietnamese colonel responsible for controlling U.S. artillery fire and bombing missions: "I learned that his method of giving clearance in an American military operation was not to review the targets of individual air strikes or shellings but to give the American ground commander a blanket clearance before the operation was launched."[113]

Illusions of perfect spaces where everyone was the foreign Other allowed Technowar to apply its advanced war technology without qualms. Much of the firepower dumped in free-fire zones was officially classified as "harassment and interdiction" fire. No specific targets existed for harassment and interdiction fire; planes dumped their bombs on whatever looked promising and artillery commanders fired at will. General Harry Kinnard reports that when he took command of a large artillery unit, "A 1st lieutenant appeared with a coordinate square; inspecting a map, he selected, at random, points in the area where nighttime firing was authorized, and then measured off the coordinates for firing. This had been the method of choosing intelligence targets in that zone for the preceding several months." [114] Harassment and interdiction fire went unobserved — no U.S. observers were there to see who or what was hit. In theory, since the free-fire zones were filled with enemies, then it was good to harass them and interdict their movements with random fire. In 1966, nearly two-thirds of all artillery shells fired and bombs and rockets dropped by planes were classified as H&I missions. In the first six months of 1967 the figure was 45 percent. [115]

In this way war-managers could meet their production quotas. First Lieutenant Michael J. Uhl described the ammunition flow in and out of his camp:

> I don't know exactly how many rounds of ordnance had to be expended from the 11th Brigade base camp every day, but I know there was a convoy that came in, I believe, several times a week with new supplies of 175, eight-inch, 155, 105 Howitzers, four-deuce [4.2-inch-diameter shell] mortar, etcetera. So they constantly had to make room for the new stockpile of ordnance, and every night they were firing harassment and interdiction. [116]

Cincinnatus's informants repeated the same emphasis on the need to fire all their rounds. One artillery captain noted "We had a real trucking problem in hauling ammo to our firing batteries. But the ammo kept coming whether we had targets or not." [117] Another commander saw the real outcome of such massive firings into Vietnamese areas:

> We were supposed to shoot it just because we had it. Maybe artillery was the answer in World War II, when there were real targets to aim at — enemy artillery or fortresses or fortified positions or massed enemy troop formations or even bridges. In Vietnam there were none of those things, and for the most part, artillery fires were a waste. They did nothing but kill a lot of innocents and alienate us from those we were supposedly trying to help. [118]

Note the contradiction. War-managers receive promotions and medals for meeting or surpassing production quotas in rounds fired and bombs dropped, while Vietnamese civilians are killed and maimed — and driven toward allegiance with the enemy. There is still one further twist. Vietcong and NVA forces routinely made mines from American "duds," those munitions whose fuses failed to detonate upon impact. Artillery shells had a dud rate of 2 percent, while B-52 bombs had a dud rate of 5 percent. According to Marine Colonel William Corson, U.S. dud rates were fairly high as part of McNamara's economic rationalization of the military: "Additional comparisons between the fuses on our mortar and artillery rounds and those fired by the enemy are also revealing. Our fuses are cheaply made with cheap materials and consequently have a *'cost-effective'* reliability rate."[119] By 1967, Technowar's massive bombardments in conjunction with cost-effective fuses produced around 800 tons of dud munitions each month. At the same time — the first six months of 1967 — 17 percent of all U.S. casualties were from enemy mines, some 539 killed and 5,532 wounded.[120] Often these mines came from U.S. munitions. Lieutenant William Calley described an instance:

> The day we got orders to My-Lai, we had services for Sergeant Cox. A well-liked soldier in Charlie company — well, we never lost a soldier who wasn't liked. I haven't the vaguest idea why he had picked up a 105 artillery shell with a bamboo handle on it. A lieutenant said, "Put that goddamn thing down," but it went off: it blew him to hell. It had been booby-trapped.[121]

At times U.S. forces saw rules of engagement not as constraints upon their activities but as categories to be appropriated for deliberately killing people who they knew were noncombatants. Identification rules became a "cover" for perverse killing. Warrant Officer David Bressum, a helicopter gunship pilot, described how rules were used in his unit, 1st Squadron 9th Air Cavalry (regiment), 1st Air Cavalry Division. The 1/9 was "Colonel Kilgore's" unit in Francis Ford Coppola's film on the Vietnam War, *Apocalypse Now*. Bressum's testimony has several component stories:

> To begin with, I would like to go over my unit's interpretation of the rules that we operated under.
> One rule was if we were to spot a suspect we had to call back for clearance in order to fire upon him. If we saw a man running across a field with a rifle and pack, or if we just suspected an individual, it was necessary to call back for clearance. However, if we were to call

back for clearance, normally a man running across a field can dive into a ditch in a matter of seconds, so what we normally do, we always fly in teams of two aircraft and the higher aircraft would go ahead and call back for clearance, while the lower aircraft would go ahead and try to kill the individual.

And if we received clearance, then we would report it as a kill. If we did not receive clearance, we would just forget about it. This happened all of the time. We were just working under these rules.

We had another rule, the use of evasive action. Anyone taking evasive action could be fired upon. Evasive action was never explained to me. It normally entailed someone running or trying to evade a helicopter or any fire.

My unit, the gunships in my unit had installed MP sirens, police sirens on the helicopter and we used these for psychological effect, to intimidate people.

There is one incident I recall where we flew over a large rice paddy, and there were some people working in the rice paddy, maybe a dozen or fifteen individuals, and we passed over their heads and they didn't take any action, they were obviously nervous, but they didn't try to hide or anything. So we then hovered a few feet off the ground among them with the two helicopters, turned on the police sirens and when they heard the police sirens, they started to disperse and we opened up on them and just shot them all down.[122]

Another such story was uncovered by political scientist Guenter Lewy. A gunship made a low pass over a Vietnamese "junk," or boat, near the coast. Crew and passengers jumped overboard into the sea after this low, threatening pass. According to Lewy's sources, "The chopper apparently viewed this behavior as *prima facie* (at first sight) evidence of guilt and proceeded to attack."[123] United States forces thus consciously created conditions specified by rules of engagement to open fire and produce a body count.

Ground troops also engaged in creative interpretations. One rule said that legitimate Vietnamese civilians obeyed a curfew in their villages. One of Daniel Lang's informants, Sven Erikson, described how his unit interpreted the curfew:

Occasionally, official orders were used for justifying gratuitous acts of violence. Thus early in his tour of duty, Erikson recalled, GIs in his unit were empowered to shoot any Vietnamese violating a 7 p.m. curfew, but in practice it was largely a matter of individual discretion whether a soldier chose to fire at a stray Vietnamese hurrying home a few minutes late to his hootch.[124]

Soldier Thomas Cole of the Americal Division told the Dellums committee of a similar interpretation:

> Another instance back in April of 1967 I got a rear job, in a mortar platoon and in the brigade fire base, LZ Bronco. It was on a hill called Montezuma. At the time it was about the middle of April, sometime around the middle of April.
>
> We got a call for fire anyway. It was 6:30 in the evening, still daylight. Well, they said that there was VC out there and they called in to us so we fired out there and killed off seven of them.
>
> Well, the word came back to us that we killed seven rice farmers carrying their hoes, trying to make it back to the village.
>
> Well, we set up this six P.M. to six A.M. curfew time. It was set up for them. If they were out working their fields, even if it was in broad daylight, they were liable to get killed and we did kill these seven people.
>
> You know, these people didn't carry wrist watches, so they didn't have any idea what time it would be.[125]

Nor did the Vietnamese villagers have an absolutely positive sense of just how far fifty meters was. Some units guarding villages imposed a fifty-meter limit on how far a villager could move from the village after curfew. Vietnamese peasants did not have indoor plumbing. They normally defecated in their rice paddies to fertilize the soil. One of Dr. Charles Levy's patients told the story:

> But this was some fucking phony place between Chu Lai and Danang. And it was curfew out. At night gooks can't walk more than approximately fifty paces from their village. And they can't fuck around. They have to carry a torch at night if they move around. If they don't they can be shot. And if they move away from that village they can be shot.
>
> There was three guys in the bunker and it was the most forward position in our perimeter. B was there sleeping. And the other guys were awake. There were boots [new soldiers].

So they said, "Corporal B, some fucking body up there with a light." . . .

He says, "They can leave the village. They can walk fifty paces. He's probably just taking a shit." . . .

B said, "One more fucking step and then I'll give it to him. If he don't turn around or stop."

And the gook walked. And he let him have it. He shot a hundred round [machine gun] belt into that fucking slope. He just pumped rounds in. The whole belt he shot in there. . . .

The next morning they had a patrol go outside and find him. Right at dawn. And it was easy to find 'cause he was out in these dried up rice paddies.

And he was completely shot to shit. All hundred rounds must have hit him. He was completely perforated. He looked like a fucking piece of cheese. And he was about ninety-nine years old too. He hadn't a thing on him, like military. Like grenade or any type of booby trap anywhere near him. And he's a village elder. That kind of thing.

It didn't do a hell of a lot for our public relations.[126]

The fifty-meter rule is but one example of a territorial rule of engagement as an excuse to open fire. One soldier told of how a river boundary was violated with encouragement by command:

Our base was pretty quiet. Sometimes you'd be going up to guard mount and the commander would tell us, "Look, we haven't had many kills in a long time. So let's go down to the village and shoot somebody and drag them back across the river." You weren't supposed to shoot them unless they were on our side of the river. He didn't say it in those words exactly, he just said, "Hey, you know, you guys want a day off, we got to be getting more kills." He'd kind of hint.

Guys wanted more days off. I did too, but not enough to kill people. My squad never did it. We used to go down to the village and shack up when we were supposed to be working on ambush. But some of the guys would just go down to the village and mow down some people, including women and kids, and drag them back across the river. Look what we killed.[127]

Ground troops could kill Vietnamese only a few at a time. Helicopter gunships produced much more. But really big kills, according to regulations, necessitated heavy airpower. By the rules of engagement or official written code, Forward Air Control pilots were required to leaflet a village before an air strike was called in, unless the air strike was in support of ground troops under fire. FAC pilots interpreted this to mean "once warned, always warned." If a leaflet notifying a village of the possibility of air strikes had ever been dropped on a village, then thereafter it could be struck without warning for an indefinite time period. One pilot explained the difference in productivity between warned and unwarned strikes: "We give the people at least a good ten or fifteen minutes to get out before we put in a strike. But it's the immediate strike [without warning] that gives the best results. That's where you get your K.B.A.'s."[128] K.B.A. stands for "Killed by Air," a body count credited to airpower accounts. Military units thus fulfilled their production quotas while at the same time the written rules of engagement provided the appearance of law-governed combat. It didn't even matter if peasants could *read* the leaflets. According to Helen Emmerich, a *San Francisco Chronicle* reporter:

> At dusk the helicopters came, . . . dropping thousands of leaflets. . . . Colonel William Kitterman said they were warning leaflets, urging the villagers to move out before dark. . . . No one came out. . . . Kitterman put down the glasses [binoculars] and looked at me. "Well, they had their chance. Now, we just assume they're VC." . . . I finally asked a [marine] gunnery sergeant why the villagers hadn't come out after the leaflets were dropped. He took a hard drag on his coffee, looked around, then whispered to me, "Look, don't say I told you this — but don't you know — they couldn't read the leaflets."[129]

At times all pretenses vanished. Search-and-destroy meant just that, search and destroy whatever and whoever was found. Ultimately all of the arbitrary identification rules on official documents became replaced by one simple code, the "Mere Gook Rule": *"If it's dead and it's Vietnamese, it's VC."*

Some journalists captured the duality well. Michael Herr said of U.S. involvement: "Hearts and Minds, Peoples of the Republic, maintaining the equilibrium of the Dingdong by containing the ever encroaching Doodah; you could also hear the other, some young soldier speaking in all bloody innocence, saying, 'All that's just a load, man. We're here to kill gooks. Period.' "[130] Similarly, Martin Russ saw that the inevitable reduction of all Vietnamese to gooks made the rules of engagement and other efforts to regulate U.S. forces pointless:

I wonder where you draw the line. Do you say, go ahead and kill your gook but don't burn him up afterward? and don't shoot him between the eyes if he's still alive? These boys are here to kill gooks and let's face it, there are no gradations. You either do it or you don't, but whether you happen to enjoy it is beside the point, militarily speaking. And I think it's too much to expect an American just out of Hick City High to distinguish between guerrillas and civilians; they all look alike, they all dress alike, they're all gooks. [131]

Willingness to destroy all Vietnamese found expression in war culture. Jokes, popular sayings and songs all embodied the prime rule of Vietnamese as the enemy. An assortment is provided below:

*Hunting Culture by Helicopter Gunship Pilots and FAC Pilots*
Only we can prevent forests. [Defoliation Unit] [132]

Vietnam, man. Bomb 'em and feed 'em, bomb 'em and feed 'em. [133]

Squirrel hunting. Cong-zapping. Turkey-shoot. [134]

How can you shoot women and children? It's easy, you just don't lead 'em so much. [135]

Air sports. Nothing finer, you're up there at two thousand, you're God, just open up the flexies and watch it pee, nail the slime to the paddy wall, nothing finer, double back and get the caribou. [136]

I do like to see the arms and legs fly. [Colonel George Patton III] [137]

Bomb the schools and churches.
Bomb the rice fields, too.
Show the children in the courtyards
What napalm can do.

Strafe the town and kill the people.
Drop napalm in the square.
Get out early every Sunday
And catch them at their morning prayer.

Throw candy to the ARVN
Gather them all around
Take your twenty mike-mike [20mm automatic cannon]
And mow the bastards down.
— Forward Air Patrol pilot song [138]

*Dead Vietnamese*

Believers[139]

Crispy-Critters [napalmed Vietnamese][140]

No more boom-boom [sexual intercourse] for that mama-san.[141]

When we kill a pregnant woman, we count it as two VC, one soldier and one cadet. [FAC joke][142]

We had this one dude who would go out shooting people, then yell, "snake!" Like don't worry, I just killed a snake next to the trail.[143]

*Solutions to War*

What you do is, you load all the Friendlies onto ships and take them out to the South China Sea. Then you bomb the country flat. Then you sink the ships.[144]

I'd like to burn the whole country down and start again with Americans.[145]

"Burn the whole country down." The soldier was certainly in the right place. Some units even had "Zippo inspections" to make sure their lighters worked:

And I would say approximately two-thirds of the entire company had Zippo lighters. We held them up, lit them, demonstrated that they were filled and would burn, then put them away. . . . When we went out, I would say at least 50 percent of the villages we passed through would be burned to the ground. There was no difference between the ones we burned and the ones we didn't burn, it was just that where we had time, we burned them. . . . The entire village, for about a quarter of a mile, was on fire with illumination grenades or Zippo lighters. Everything was burned. Everything was torn down. All the animals were killed.[146]

The soldier in question was from the 5th Marine Regiment, nicknamed the "Burning Fifth Marines." But the Burning Fifth was not alone. Another soldier reported: "They [mortars] blew it all to pieces. We went through afterwards and you could find pieces of arms lying there, pieces of bodies, crater holes, the village itself was on fire — straw huts on fire. The ones that weren't being burned we burned ourselves."[147] And still another said, "We made it quite a habit of where we could . . . to put the Zippos to roofs."[148] Lieutenant Frederick Downs described his unit's missions:

It was a search and destroy mission, which meant we searched all the hootches and then burned them down. Whether a single farmer's hootch or a whole village — all were burnt. The few Vietnamese we found in the area were women, children, and old men who had been left behind. When we started to burn their particular hootch, they would start wailing, crying, and pulling at our clothes. We didn't harm the people, but the orders were to destroy all the dwellings, so we did.[149]

Search-and-destroy reduced villages to barren places. With the houses burned, the wells were often destroyed so that people and animals would have no water to drink. One of Michael Herr's informants described search-and-destroy:

Shit, last three patrols I was on we had fucking orders not to return fire going through villages, that's what a fucked-up war it's gettin' to be anymore. My last tour we'd go through and that was it, we'd rip out the hedges and burn the hootches and blow up all the wells and kill every chicken, pig and cow in the whole fucking village. I mean, if we can't shoot these people, what the fuck are we doing here?[150]

Apparently some units found well destruction to be one of their most difficult assignments. Lieutenant William Calley reports that the twenty-pound satchels of TNT given his unit for well destruction only made them deeper, rather than destroying them.[151]

Another battalion in Calley's unit, the American Division, succeeded in blowing up wells on their operations. The key seems to have been sealing the top of the well so that the blast charge would not all go out the top. Daniel Barnes described the technique:

[A suspected VC] went into a village and a woman and an old man were there and there was some animals around and so on. Well, they [American Division soldiers following VC suspect] started to interrogate her and she naturally was, the word was "no bik" which meant that she didn't want to say anything. So she kept saying "Nothing. Nothing." "No bik. No bik. No bik." So they decided that they would throw her down a well, so they did it. Two or three guys dumped her down a well and she was screaming and hollering and an old man came from somewhere, I don't know where. But he was screaming and yelling because they had thrown her down the well. So they threw him down too. Well, they were both down the well then. Then along with those two they started throwing in — well, there was a pig that went down the well, and a couple of ducks, and a few other things. They tried to get a calf, but it wouldn't get in there. So they had this calf halfway in there, stuck in the well. . . .

As I walked away, I walked around the corner, I heard an explosion and I came back and there was scattered debris and bricks from the well all over the place. So I figured that someone had thrown a grenade that caused the problem, most likely a grenade.[152]

Burning villages and blowing up wells appear to be the most common forms of destruction. However, on really thorough operations there was still more to come: "I started firing, and, then they came in, some other cats after we left, and they came in with bulldozers. Just destroyed the whole village. Half of it was destroyed, and it was like it was never there. I mean there was a big hole dug and all those bodies were thrown in it and then, pst, we moved on."[153] And finally, for the ultimate, salt followed the bulldozers: "What was left after the burning was dynamited, it was plowed into the ground, and the ground was salted."[154]

Burn; blow; bulldoze; salt: Some American units even had mottoes indicating that they understood that search-and-destroy operations created enemies among the Vietnamese survivors. James D. Henry, a soldier in the 35th Infantry Regiment of the 4th Infantry Division, said that: "A friend of mine in A company, which was our sister company, said one time that when A company goes into a friendly village, if it's not VC when they go into it, it's VC when they leave."[155] Another soldier said:

If the people don't treat you right when you walk through that village you can give them hell. They give you that snotty look. They won't say nothing to you, but they're a little cold. We expected for them to run out and welcome us like that World War II type of thing. "Hey GI. Yay, you the Americans." But they were a little standoffish.

As soon as we step outside the village, the captain radios in, "We're under heavy contact." Then right away, those Phantom jets come in and drop those 500-pound bombs. The village is leveled down and we go on to the next one. That's our Search and Destroy. If there wasn't an enemy out there, we made it be the enemy.[156]

If those Vietnamese who survived search-and-destroy operations became Vietcong, then why should Technowar allow any survivors? The "Nine Rules" pocket card specified adherence to the Geneva Convention and called for good contacts toward all Vietnamese who happened to be under U.S. military control. But "Nine Rules" was just a card, a representation of legal Technowar, not an enforced standard of conduct. To the contrary, story after story reports that many units' standard operating procedure was to *destroy everything and everyone*. Sergeant James Daley recalled:

> "When you come into an enemy village," we were told [by training instructors in the United States], "you come in opening fire. You kill everything that's living — women, children, and animals." And when we asked how to tell an enemy village from a friendly one, we were instructed that an enemy village was any village from which you were fired upon. Even if only one round was shot by only one person — that village was an enemy village as far as the army was concerned. And that meant you killed everyone. You destroyed everything.[157]

Shad Meshad, a psychologist who served in Vietnam and later worked for the Veterans Administration, described what he heard from soldiers in Vietnam and afterward back in the United States:

> Guys would come in, and tell me no more than, "I'm tired of fighting this war." I'd try to find out what the war was for them, and generally some of it would come out, including some of the guilt. They'd suffered several catastrophes, probably, and were already in the numbing stages. "I've done a lot of killing, and I'm not sure it's right."
>
> They'd been on sweeps of villages, with orders to leaving nothing living, not even chickens and [water] buffalos. Well, what the fuck did that mean, following orders like that? Wasn't it Lieutenant Calley who created the stir in the first place? They were doing a Calley every day.
>
> They'd be out on a mission and call in strikes. Napalm would be sprayed and the people would be burning. Sometimes they'd put them out of their misery. The guys who did that are still coming into the Vet centers with it 12 years later.[158]

Sergeant Joseph Grant of the 1st Infantry Division said he was ordered not to take any prisoners: "Yes. Often. On search and destroy missions. They told us to kill anything that moves. The order was if you do take a prisoner he is your baby. You must feed him from your own rations. So we killed everybody."[159] Terry Whitmore, a marine, described one execution:

> I just happened to be standing alongside the officer when the radio man said, "Look, sir, we got children rounded up. What do you want us to do with them." The guy says, "Goddam it. Marine, you know what to do with them. Kill the bastards. If you ain't got the goddam balls to kill them, Marine, I'll come down and kill the mother-fuckers myself." The Marine said, "Yes, sir," and hung up the phone. About two or three minutes later I heard a lot of automatic fire — and a lot of children screaming. I heard babies crying. I heard children screaming their fucking lungs out.[160]

Charles Locke, of the American Division, described an instance where command only wanted a body count because only body counts, not prisoners, counted in Technowar's reward structure:

> When we caught up with them we fired at them. One was killed — he wasn't really killed, he was shot through the shoulder and through the jaw. He was wounded.
> We stopped and called the colonel and told him we had one wounded dink, you know, and that we wanted him to send a chopper. The colonel says, "Is that what I heard you say? Wounded?"
> And the sergeant said, "No."
> And they blew his head off.
> Before we left on this mission the captain of the company had told us definitely do not take any prisoners. He didn't want to hear about any prisoners. He wanted a body count. He said he needed seven more bodies before he could get his promotion to major.[161]

One of Cincinnatus's informants said his unit's policy was "Kill them if they try to surrender — we need the body count."[162] Going by the rule "If it's dead and it's Vietnamese, it's VC," dead people become more valuable than live people.

Just as the captain got his promotion to major when he met quota, enlisted men got passes for dead Vietnamese. Jimmy Roberson of the army's 1st Division said, "It was in the First Division, if you killed a certain number of enemy you got a three-day pass, but you had to bring back the ears [to prove the kills]. . . . They would send you to a place where there wasn't too much fighting, like on the beach where you would get mortar attacks. It's a recreational center there."[163]

Journalist Michael Herr indicates that the marines similarly rewarded troops whose productivity exceeded the norm in terms of bodies counted. He describes the scene at China Beach, along the Bay of Danang:

> It was a place where they could go swimming or surfing, get drunk, get stoned, get laid, get straight, groove in the scivvie houses, rent sailboats, or just sleep on the beach. Sometimes it was just an in-country R&R, a vacation, and sometimes it was a reward for outstanding service, for exceptional bravery. Some Marines, the ones who were more than just good in a firefight, would get here as often as once a month because their company commanders did not like having them around between operations.[164]

Killing prisoners, particularly wounded prisoners, seems to have been standard practice in many ground units. Lieutenant Colonel Anthony Herbert took the exceptional step of changing the reward structure in his battalion of the 173rd Airborne Brigade in an attempt to generate more prisoners and fewer bodies:

> I also stressed that we were changing the body count policy. There would be no more in-country R and Rs for "dead dinks." From now on, I said, the R and Rs would be for live prisoners and only for live prisoners. We needed intelligence badly, and you only get intelligence from live people. The trooper would get five days for a legitimate POW, with one day subtracted for each cut, bruise, or contusion on the prisoner. *The better the condition of the merchandise, the more we were willing to pay for it.*[165]

More than the desire for a body count prompted mass killing. Vietnamese survivors not only had a good chance of becoming Vietcong, they also might talk about what happened to their village. Although the rules of engagement were basically intended for maintaining the appearance of a law- and morality-governed war for the news media and the American people, the possibility always remained that somehow Vietnamese would bring legal charges against Americans. (There were a few such cases during the war.) As one veteran described the relation between the official legal representations and the actual acceptable code of conduct for U.S. troops: "You can do anything you want as long as you don't get caught."[166] An artillery captain described to Cincinnatus the double-reality in his unit: "There used to be a regulation in Vietnam covering everything. At the battery [artillery company] level, I ignored most of them. No one cared at battery level. Now, if something had gone wrong, they would probably have hung me because of regulations I was violating. But as long as things went smoothly, no one cared what I did." [167] A squad leader interviewed by Mark Baker for his book *Nam* told of the legal dangers he faced and his commander's advice on how to avoid legal challenges:

> I got close to being court-martialed in Vietnam for shooting some kids. Of course, we thought they was VC. We were out on an ambush. Headquarters called and said they were getting sniper fire from this village and we were to go over there for a little Search and Destroy mission. They said, "Sweep through it." So we did.
>
> I was the squad leader. Burned all the rice and burned down a few hootches. We shot two or three kids that were running across the rice paddies, because it was dark and we thought they were carrying rifles. I beat up this old man. He was giving me a hard time. I beat him up and I was getting ready to shoot him, when somebody came over and told me that he was the fucking village chief.
>
> When we got back my whole squad had to write up like a statement. But the CO [commanding officer] told me, he said, "They had all better coincide. They better match up to what you said." So we all got together and we made up the same story and it was cool. We had brought a couple of prisoners back that time. The CO, he told me, "Next time, remember, dead men tell no tales. Don't bring back no prisoners." [168]

But in the grand order of things, those dead kids and beaten-up village chief were minor. The squad leader learned his lesson and the war went on:

> It wasn't too long after that, one of our platoons got in a firefight with the ARVN by mistake up on some hill. Platoon leaders killed the Vietnamese captain by mistake. Then some other company attacked a church full of people, killed them and burned down the church. The CO comes over to me and says, "Well, now you ain't the only one that's fucked up. They're going to forget about you now."
>
> That God damn Search and Destroy. They send you out to do it, then they want to fucking bust you for it. [169]

The writings of soldiers and freelance journalists contain two additional explanations of why troops sometimes became so willing to kill all Vietnamese. One is sexual pleasure in killing people — a subject explored in the next chapter. The other concerns revenge. In search-

and-destroy operations, normal combat involved U.S. forces walking into ambushes, booby traps, and mines. Men were killed by an unseen enemy. Troop frustration mounted as U.S. casualties increased. Recall Calley's story that Sergeant Cox's memorial service was held the day his company received orders for the My Lai operations. According to Calley, those orders from Captain Medina were "to go in rapidly and to neutralize everything. To kill everything." He recalled asking, "Captain Medina? Do you mean women and children, too?" According to Calley, Medina replied, "I mean everything."[170] Dr. John A. Parrish recounted the frustrations of a marine lieutenant in Vietnam and how his unit responded to the contradictions of Technowar; they didn't need orders:

> You walk through the fucking bush for three days and nights without sleep. Watch your men, your buddies, your goddam kids get bobby trapped. Blown apart. Get thrown six feet in the air by a trap laid by an old lady and come down with no legs. And the only thing he says to you is, "I'm sorry, lieutenant." And then he dies. Watch them die as you get more and more tired, and more and more scared, and more and more freaked out by no sleep. Watch the Bouncing Betty rip up three good men and watch your fucking corpsman bleed to death while he's trying to drag himself up to the other two.
>
> You finally take the fucking ville. The villagers welcome you and cheer you and then your men continue to die each night.
>
> All you want to do is sleep. And stay alive. And keep your men alive. All you want to do is sleep and not die. If you gotta kill every yellow thing that moves to do that you will. And you won't stop till you're out of ammo or your gun barrel burns your hands and every possible yellow shit is dead or gone. And then you think of your sarge and your corpsman and your buddy and you start in on the water buffalo and the huts and the dogs and chickens.[171]

Faced with obliteration by the American war machine, many peasants had no choice but to join the Vietcong — and thus maintain the traditional Vietnamese struggle to drive foreign rulers out. Oftentimes U.S. forces actually were facing village populations that were hostile. And oftentimes Vietnamese combatants did not look like soldiers. Steve Hassna described one aspect of the dilemma of to-shoot-or-not-to-shoot:

> Old men and women would sit by the side of the trail saying, "Oh hello GI, hello GI." And they'd count and count. They'd tell the local

VC cadre that 50 Americans just went that way. Before the GIs ever got to where they were going, the word had spread. Well, do you shoot an old man sitting by the side of the trail? Whether he's a trail watcher or not? Do you shoot him? My viewpoint is that I am an infantry soldier; I seek out, engage, close with, and destroy the enemy. The enemy is not an old man sitting by the side of the trail.[172]

Hassna thus chose to retain the conventional definition of the enemy even though he realized it might lead to his unit's being ambushed. At the same time he was disturbed by the deviations from what he was taught to expect. In another section of his oral history narrative he told of his shock on examining the Vietnamese bodies after a battle:

> We referred to the VC as "Victor Charlie" or just "Charlie." But then we called him Mr. Charles out of respect. And sometimes Mrs. Charles was with him. And there were a bunch of dead women on the top of that hill along with the men. And I thought, "Wow, they are hard!" That was real equality! Their determination weakened us. We were fighting against somebody we couldn't beat. They knew the country and we didn't. They were just kicking our asses all over the place. And even when we kicked theirs, they shocked us with their determination.[173]

So the old Vietnamese fought, and the women fought — and the children fought, too. Former marine W. D. Ehrhart said: "Two weeks ago, Saunders and I were driving through Hoi An, right through the middle of town, and a god-damned kid maybe eight or nine years old runs up and tries to flip a grenade into the jeep. A grenade! I had to blow 'im away. A little kid. It was really bad, you know. My kid brother's only twelve."[174]

Similar stories have been recorded. Technowar projects the foreign Other as like itself, another technologically equipped bureaucratic hierarchy, but with less production capacity. Since Vietnamese nationalism and social revolution were theoretically invisible to the war-managers, then troops had little or no orientation toward combat where they were the real aliens and entire populations were fighting against them. Sent into combat as expendable bait to activate a killing machine, the troops found themselves attacked by enemies they could not see. With no clear targets except villages that might or might not be enemies, many soldiers saw dead Vietnamese as the only way to guarantee survival. Yet this massive killing of civilians drove Vietnamese toward the Vietcong.

Technowar thus produced a spiral of death, a series of contortions killing both Americans and Vietnamese, but it did not produce a victory.

War-managers always represented Technowar as both productive and law-governed. No matter what the battle, or how openly deceptive the falsifications, U.S. forces always won. One military clerk described his experiences of writing and rewriting reports to sustain the illusion of victory:

> The first [report] was from the facts at hand, from information we had collected, as objective as could be. Then we sent it in, and always it came back, doctored. This was SOP — standard operating procedure — for the time I spent as BDE [brigade] historian. The result is that the battle news is edited and revised until it's acceptable to higher-ups. I've been ordered to write open lies on our civil aid programs, such as increasing fifteen English classes to three hundred to make it look good to the politicians and the people back home. I've been ordered to raise the figures for food distribution in refugee villages. I've also had to retype battle reports for the 503rd Engineering, 22 June, Hill 875, where the whole time sequence was destroyed in the wording of the report and vital facts omitted by the commanding general of the 173rd, thereby turning an NVA victory over superior American forces into a U.S. victory.[175]

Nearly everyone in the Technowar bureaucracy had a superior who demanded increased production. Given that "optimism" was official policy, then turning in an optimistic report affirmed the reality of official policy and was rewarded. Conversely, a "negative" report — one in which the U.S. lost a battle or did not meet quota in some sphere of war production — became an act of disloyalty, of dissent from official goals and disrespect for superiors. To those who had little or no experience of the real war because of their high managerial positions, then reality became only a matter of words and numbers representing commitment to their system. Men began to believe all of their own lies. As Major William I. Lowry wrote after the war: "Duplicity became so automatic that lower headquarters began to believe the things they were forwarding to higher headquarters. It was on paper, therefore, no matter what might have actually occurred, *the paper graphs and charts became the ultimate reality.*"[176]

And there were many graphs and charts produced by military managers. If the combat arms can be conceptualized as the manufacturing sector of Technowar, then the various intelligence agencies can be conceived of as the "bankers." Certainly Major General Joseph A. McChristian saw the joint army, navy, marine, air force intelligence unit at MACV headquarters as the central treasury of intelligence, the grand bank of knowledge for war production:

> Every scrap of information, every written report, is to the intelligence officer as nickels and dimes are to a banker. It takes a lot of them to make the business profitable. Every piece of information must be accounted for like money and confirmed or refuted as genuine or counterfeit. When an intelligence analyst receives an unconfirmed report, he cannot let it go. He must confirm it or refute it. From numerous reports the order of battle of the enemy is constructed and updated. The enemy order of battle includes his composition, disposition, strength, training status, morale tactics, logistics, combat effectiveness, and miscellaneous information such as unit histories, personality files, uniforms, and insignias.[177]

McChristian's book, *The Role of Military Intelligence 1965–1967,* is part of the Department of the Army's Vietnam Studies series. McChristian says that the central bank of Technowar truth increased production as the years went by. More real money was certified, more accounts audited, more truth produced for the manufacturing sector: "During 1966 it was a big day when 100 pounds of reports were printed. By early 1967 the daily volume averaged 1,400 pounds of reports, with every indication of greater volume in the future."[178] The order of battle includes estimating enemy strength and subtracting from that figure how many Vietnamese soldiers United States forces killed. McChristian never says how reports by other war-managers were treated. Consequently, a few questions need to be asked.

Were all the Vietnamese killed who were wearing black pajamas counted as dead VC? Did the dead have circles under their eyes or scratches on their ankles or indentations on their shoulders? What about those shot while running? Or those caught in the open after curfew or without an identification card or more than fifty meters from the village? What about those in the free-fire zones? Were the old man and woman at the bottom of the well classified as dead Vietcong? What about the dead ducks and chickens and water buffaloes? (Some units said they reported animal deaths as part of the body count.) How did central banking treat all the estimates made where U.S. forces could only find body parts or weapons or blood trails? Or those instances where numbers were just invented to make some survivors feel good or some midlevel war-manager look productive to his superior?

Apparently central banking, too, lived by the rule, "If it's dead and it's Vietnamese, it's VC." All the separate manufacturing accounts in central banking were marked credit. Technowar proved that it was productive. In the spring of 1967, General William Westmoreland announced that the "cross-over point" had been reached. Victory was only a matter of time.

CHAPTER 6

# The Tet Offensive and
# the Production of a Double Reality

Each year General Westmoreland submitted troop requests and budget estimates to his superiors — the Joint Chiefs of Staff, the secretary of defense, the senior White House staff, and the President. Fiscal years began in July; the debate on troop increases for 1968 began in March 1967. In 1966 Westmoreland had wanted 124 maneuver battalions and their logistical support units for 1967, a grand total of 555,741 authorized troop spaces. Senior officials reduced this figure to 470,366 troop spaces for 1967. He submitted basically the same request for fiscal year 1968, but with the important modification that these 555,741 spaces be structured to add two and one-third combat divisions. If he secured this significant increase in combat troops, then additional logistical units could be added later — it would be difficult to deny requests for supporting combat troops already in the field. Ideally, though, Westmoreland wanted a Technowar factory of even greater dimensions. According to memos in the *Pentagon Papers,* "The optimum force required to implement the concept of operations and to exploit success is considered 4⅔ divisions or the equivalent; 10 tactical fighter squadrons with one additional base; and the full mobile riverine force. The order of magnitude estimate is 201,250 spaces in addition to the 1967 ceiling of 470,366 for a total of *671,616.*" [1]

In April 1967, Westmoreland presented his case to President Johnson. First he noted that with 470,000 troops "we will not be in danger of being defeated but it will be nip and tuck to oppose the reinforcements the enemy is capable of providing. In the final analysis we are fighting a war of attrition in Southeast Asia." Production had to increase if the war was to be brought to a victorious conclusion: "Unless the will of the enemy is broken or unless there was an unraveling of the VC infrastructure the war could go on for five years."[2] Force increases of two and one-third divisions would reduce that time to three years, while the optimum war factory would require only two years to produce victory. Westmoreland thought the Vietcong and NVA might reinforce their troops if the Americans increased theirs, but he was confident U.S. forces could maintain a production rate beyond the "cross-over" point. Military intelligence had determined that "The VC and DRV strength in SVN now totals 285,000 men. It appears that last month we reached the cross-over point in areas excluding the two northern provinces. *Attrition will be greater than additions to this force.*"[3]

Note how this report presents Technowar as a production system that can be rationally managed and warfare as a kind of activity that can be scientifically determined by constructing computer models. Increase their resources and the war-managers claim to know what will happen. What constitutes their knowledge is an array of numbers — numbers of U.S. and allied forces, numbers of VC and NVA forces, body counts, kill ratios — numbers that appear scientific. Yet these numbers, the official representations of Technowar, had no referent in reality. During 1967 and 1968, the contradictions created by systematic falsifications of official reports exploded. In February 1968, at the very moment when war-managers saw American victory as inevitable, the Vietcong emerged in full power. The ensuing debacle momentarily exposed the vast gulf between warfare at ground level and Technowar's representations of it. Eventually war-managers regained control and sustained the lie of victory. This process of creating the appearance of Technowar victory in 1967–1968 will be examined step by step.

To begin, not all war-managers readily accepted Westmoreland's prediction. When McNamara became secretary of defense for the Kennedy administration, he established the Office of Systems Analysis to review military programs for cost-efficiency — the ultimate debit/credit accountant's office. OSA enforced troop allocations to make sure the armed services did not send more troops to Vietnam than had been allocated. Alain C. Enthoven describes their management technique:

> To motivate the Joint Chiefs of Staff to hunt for deadwood without being prodded, the Systems Analysis Office developed what was called the "Debit/Credit Account," which permitted the accumulation of personnel spaces from deleted units as a credit to be drawn on as new requirements developed. . . . Although the services normally kept a

Table 6.1
ESTIMATED WEEKLY ENEMY LOSSES FOR DIFFERENT FORCE LEVELS

|  | *Program IV Force [1967]* | *MACV "Minimum Essential" Force* | *MACV "Optimal" Force* |
|---|---|---|---|
| Peak losses* | 3,118 | 3,404 | 3,696 |
| Average losses** | 2,121 | 2,265 | 2,460 |

Defense Intelligence Agency and United States Intelligence Board estimate of enemy capability to sustain losses indefinitely = 3,265

*Based on January–March 1967 enemy losses to all causes
**Based on Calendar Year 1966
SOURCE: *The Pentagon Papers: The Senator Gravel Edition* (Boston: Beacon Press, 1971), vol. 4, p. 458.

credit balance [unfulfilled allocation] in the Debit/Credit Account, they were allowed to go in the hole from time to time. The only requirement was that at the end of each calendar quarter the *accounts be brought into balance.*[4]

The Office of Systems Analysis conducted some of the most rigorous accounting audits of Technowar. Their study questioned whether introducing more U.S. ground troops and airpower would result in killing Vietnamese faster than the Vietcong and NVA could replace casualties. Although OSA did not comprehend the social dynamics of the war, they could see that even by its own logic, the production model of war could not produce victory.

This complex chart warrants careful examination. The cross-over point can only be reached with MACV's optimal force and only then during extraordinary battle periods. The difference between the projected 3,696 bodies and losses the foreign Other could sustain "indefinitely" (3,265) is 431. As Enthoven says, "Even at a decrease in enemy forces of 431 per week, *over 10 years would be needed to eliminate the enemy.*"[5] In the same memo to the secretary of defense he enclosed "Types of Engagements in Combat Narratives," a table presented in the previous chapter. The study showed that the foreign Other determined the time and place of battle in over 80 percent of all encounters with U.S. infantry forces. Enthoven pointed out a horrible truth to senior war-managers: "These results imply that the size of the force we deploy has little effect on the rate of attrition of enemy forces."[6] There is no reason to presume that the North Vietnamese and Vietcong would choose to engage in battles and take casualties at a rate that would totally deplete their forces and grant victory to the Americans.

Note how problematic Westmoreland's vision of victory has become. However, Enthoven's statistical projections and his commentary still accept the basic logic of Technowar; the war seems rational to him. While clearly victory is not at hand, Enthoven's chart shows massive enemy casualties. Enemy losses are projected from body counts reported in 1966 and 1967. The *Pentagon Papers* contains a chart of losses from 1966.

Not only was the body count accepted as accurate, but it was further *multiplied by 1.5, meaning a 50 percent increase!* In this way an entire apparatus of lies was constructed. Numbers become the base for generating more numbers and differences between numbers become the debit or credit of defeat versus progress. Numbers as the definitive signs of truth outlive verbal commentary that expresses doubts as to their validity. The VC/NVA loss chart for 1966 was included in McNamara's 17 November Draft Memorandum for the President. The secretary of defense wondered about the figures: "Moreover, it is possible that our attrition estimates substantially overstates actual VC/NVA losses. For example, the VC/NVA apparently lose about one-sixth as many weapons as people, suggesting the possibility that many of the killed are unarmed porters or bystanders."[7]

But once stated, the implications are not expounded; instead, the

Table 6.2
1966 VC/NVA Losses
*(weekly averages)*

| Estimated Losses | 1st Quarter | 2nd Quarter | 3rd Quarter | October | Last 4 Quarters plus October |
|---|---|---|---|---|---|
| Killed* | 1,505 | 1,370 | 1,805 | 1,915 | 1,585 |
| Captured | 130 | 145 | 170 | 545 | 175 |
| Military defectors** | 580 | 430 | 355 | 470 | 470 |
| Total est. losses | 2,215 | 1,945 | 2,330 | 2,930 | 2,230 |

* 1.5 times recorded "body count"
** 2 times recorded military defectors
SOURCE: *The Pentagon Papers: The Senator Gravel Edition* (Boston: Beacon Press, 1971), vol. 4, p. 370.

question is dropped and discussion shifts to another subject. This same phenomenon of institutionalizing and compounding false numbers occurs with the enemy order of battle figures, reported by Westmoreland at 285,000 troops. In December 1966, CIA analyst Samuel Adams began examining information used to compile the OB. Much to his surprise, he found little documentation in support of the established numbers. Instead, information entered into official files years earlier was recirculated as the years went by. South Vietnamese sources gave 103,573 men and women as members of part-time guerrilla forces in 1964; the figure remained constant through 1966. A CIA study conducted in 1965 said that political cadre numbered 39,175. Service troops numbered 18,553 according to the Joint Chiefs of Staff, while main-force combat troops totaled around 110,000. Added together, the total came to just over 271,000.[8]

Adams did not like this figure. Not only was it based on old intelligence, but it was such a low figure that according to official body counts, the Vietcong should already be decimated. Obviously, someone was still alive to contest American forces severely. After examining more recent captured enemy documents, Adams concluded that the order of battle for Vietcong and NVA forces should be doubled to around 600,000 men and women. Adams's superior, George Carver, sent him to an order of battle conference in Honolulu convened by General Earle Wheeler, chairman of the Joint Chiefs of Staff. Military intelligence officers working for General Westmoreland had also come up with a new estimate. Colonel Gains B. Hawkins said, "You know, there's a lot more of these little bastards out there than we thought there were."[9] Hawkins served as chief of General Westmoreland's order of battle intelligence section. His new figure was 500,000. Adams at first thought the new figures would be recorded and that the dispute was over. However, nothing was released to the public afterward.

On March 9, 1967, General Wheeler cabled General Westmoreland to warn him of the dangers this new estimate posed to Technowar: "If these figures should reach the public domain they would, literally, blow the lid off Washington. Please do whatever is necessary to insure that these figures are not repeat not released to news media or otherwise exposed to public knowledge."[10] Westmoreland complied. In April he told President Johnson that the cross-over point had been reached. In May his intelligence chief, General McChristian, showed him new estimates for Vietcong guerrilla forces and political cadre that were significantly greater than the old figures. According to McChristian, "After reading the cable, General Westmoreland said to me that if he sent it to Washington it would be a 'political bombshell.' ''[11] The cable was not sent.

During May the central consortium of U.S. intelligence agencies met to write an official National Intelligence Estimate on ''The Capabilities of the Vietnamese Communists for Fighting in South Vietnam.'' Adams and Carver wanted a figure ''in the half-million range.'' The military's representative, George Fowler of the Defense Intelligence Agency, a joint service military intelligence agency, protested: ''Gentlemen, we cannot agree to this estimate as currently written. What we object to are the numbers. We feel we should continue with the official order of battle.''[12] Debate between military and CIA analysts went on for weeks. At one point, a military officer told Adams, ''You know, our basic problem is that we've been told to keep the numbers under 300,000.''[13]

In an attempt to reach a consensus, George Carver went to Saigon in September 1967 to confer with military and civilian officials. In particular, Carver approached Robert W. Komer, at the time President Johnson's personal representative in Vietnam, a man with ambassadorial status formally in charge of pacification programs. Komer thought the order of battle should eliminate as *categories* for consideration all Vietcong local guerrilla and militia forces. He described such forces as ''low-grade, part-time hamlet self-defense groups, mostly weaponless.''[14] His choice of abolishing Vietcong guerrilla forces and the subsequent endorsement of this theoretical abolition by other important commanders warrant explication. Recall that in the deep logic of mechanistic anticommunism and Technowar, the foreign Other's military forces are like those of the United States, except with less technology. The United States military did not have part-time guerrillas as an integral part of its forces. Theoretically abolishing them followed this constant pattern of projection. Second, by U.S. reasoning the local guerrillas were the logical category to abolish, since their low level of war technology made them less of a threat than main-force Vietcong and North Vietnamese units. Because the social world is abolished in Technowar, abolishing those military forces closest to the people — indeed, local militias were literally the local people — makes complete sense.

Carver soon received a cable from Richard Helms, director of the Central Intelligence Agency, ordering him to reach agreement with the military — to accept their figures. Later General Creighton Abrams (Westmoreland's deputy) cabled General Wheeler also to suggest that local guerrillas be eliminated as a category from the order of battle. The Board of National Estimates followed this policy and so approved a new official figure of 299,000 foreign Others. No dissent was allowed in the National Intelligence Estimate. When the conference had opened in May, Helms informed participants that no dissenting footnotes with different figures would be included. The war-managers thus went on record with the 299,000 figure and theoretically abolished all local guerrilla forces from consideration as part of "The Capabilities of the Vietnamese Communists for Fighting in South Vietnam."

Other leading officials similarly contributed to eliminating Vietcong by edict. When General McChristian's tour as chief of intelligence for MACV expired in September 1967, he was replaced by Brigadier General Phillip B. Davidson, Jr. Davidson told Westmoreland that the crossover point had been reached and told his intelligence analysts that henceforth all order of battle estimates would be cleared by him: "The figure of combat strength and particularly of guerrillas must take a steady and significant downward trend as I am convinced this reflects true enemy status. Due to the sensitivity of this project, weekly strength figures will hereafter be cleared personally by me." [15] After the military had won its struggle with the CIA, Davidson continued to exercise tight control of all estimates. He sent out a form for intelligence analysts under his supervision controlling all changes in the order of battle: "This addition of [blank] in enemy strength does not increase total enemy strength in excess of that agreed upon at the September 1967 CIA/DIA/MACV Enemy Strength Conference." [16] Thus Davidson declared by managerial command that there could be no more than 299,000 Vietcong troops. Even for additions that did not threaten the ceiling, Davidson required four officers to sign the report before forwarding it to him — that is, to risk their careers by offending him with additions.

By October, MACV was in the final stages of preparing a press release containing the new order of battle figures and reports of Technowar's impending victory. Ambassador Ellsworth Bunker thought the draft still contained a minor reference to guerrillas that might "mislead" people. He sent Walt Rostow a secret cable calling for eliminating any mention of these 120,000 guerrillas to "forestall many confusing and undesirable questions." [17] At the time Rostow was commanding a "psychological strategy committee" in the White House to present the Vietnam War to the public as favorably as possible. Rostow agreed to eliminating all references to local guerrillas. He even asked a researcher in the White House to create a report showing progress in pacification programs. The researcher refused, prompting Rostow to say, "I'm sorry you won't support your President." [18]

In November President Johnson asked General Westmoreland to return to the United States to speak on war progress. On the fifteenth, Westmoreland arrived at Andrews Air Force Base near Washington, D.C., and announced: "I am very, very encouraged. I have never been more encouraged in the four years that I have been in Vietnam. We are making real progress. Everyone is encouraged." [19] The next day he addressed a closed session of the House Armed Services Committee and offered victory within two years.

On the twenty-first, General Westmoreland addressed the National Press Club. He said that Phase II (American buildup and counterattack) was nearly completed, and that elimination of enemy main-force units was now in progress and success the inevitable conclusion: "With 1968, the new phase is now starting. We have reached an important point when the end comes into view." [20] Westmoreland implied that the time between the present production rate and when combat would become a matter of "mopping up" was not long. "Mopping up," cleansing Vietnam of the enemy, would take only two years for a small, residual force. Scholars and journalists agree that Westmoreland's campaign was effective. According to journalist Don Oberdorfer: "The success of November 1967 convinced many Americans that their fears and doubts had been erroneous and that the end was indeed in sight. For the moment, the revival of public confidence stemmed the erosion of support for the war." [21]

Thus by the fall of 1967, war-managers lived with multiple systematic falsifications, some created by subordinates at ground level, others by superior commanders at battalion, brigade, division, and corps levels, and still more systematic falsifications imposed by senior officials at MACV, the Pentagon, and the White House. False body counts made Technowar appear highly productive. The new order of battle both reinforced this illusion and presented a smaller enemy whose decimation was predictable.

One other factor contributed to U.S. delusions about war progress in the fall of 1967. That spring, North Vietnamese and Vietcong forces slowly began disengaging from combat with U.S. forces. As this trend continued throughout summer and fall, U.S. commanders saw enemy withdrawal as proof of their forthcoming victory. Since Technowar ran at full production, then the enemy must run at full production, too.

According to former military analyst Daniel Ellsberg, this reliance upon operational contacts as a key measure dates to American escalation in the 1950s.

> Since so great a part of U.S. and GVN knowledge of enemy activities comes from operational contacts, there seems to be an irresistible tendency for U.S. commanders to believe that data concerning contacts reveals enemy capabilities; i.e., that lessened VC combat operations indicate lessened capability. Another mechanism, then: U.S. optimism grows during VC "inactivity" — periods when VC activities are of a sort we do not observe — reaching a peak, ironically, when extreme VC quiescence reflects intense preparations for an explosion.
>
> Crisis periods, then, are typically preceded by high points in U.S. official expectations. Thus, peaks of U.S. optimism occurred in late 1953 (just before Dien Bien Phu), 1958 (when guerrilla warfare was about to commence), early 1963 (when the VC had been studying the vulnerabilities of the strategic hamlet program, and meanwhile infiltrating massively), and late 1967 (during last-minute recruiting and preparations for the Tet offensive, including feints at the borders).[22]

The disengagement of the Vietcong marked preparation for a massive, nationwide attack scheduled to begin January 31, 1968, the first day of Tet (the lunar new year), the principal Vietnamese holiday season. On that day, according to Vietnamese custom, the first person who came "calling" in your home was an omen for your forthcoming year. Historians differ in what Vietnamese Communists hoped to achieve with this attack. The "minimal gains" interpretation suggests that the Vietcong hoped that by attacking the cities — hitherto exempt from combat except for commando attacks and occasional rocket bombardments — ARVN forces would withdraw from the countryside to defend cities. Rural areas would then be open for Vietcong political and military operations. City dwellers would be shown U.S. and GVN impotence. A massive attack would force the United States to recognize its limits, and negotiations toward American withdrawal would begin. One major resolution passed by leading VC and NVA commanders supports this interpretation; it says in part: "At a certain time we can apply the strategy of fighting and negotiating at the same time, in order to support the armed struggle, and thus accelerate the disintegration of the puppet army and regime, and create more conditions favorable for our people to win a decisive victory."[23] A Tet offensive would thus shift the direction of the war toward long-term victory, but would not mean the end of the war.

Scholars closely associated with the U.S. military or civilian war-managers view these Tet ambitions differently. Former Army General Dave Richard Palmer contends that the North Vietnamese recognized that the United States had reached the cross-over point and thus "sensed that time was on the side of the enemy, that a continuation of the protracted war of attrition would inevitably lead to defeat."[24] To avoid this, Communist leaders theorized that a massive nationwide attack would trigger a general uprising by the people. Palmer says this Vietnamese concept of a general uprising was "the orgasm of revolution."[25] Vietcong troops would control large sections of cities and large towns. Some ARVN units would defect and others would disintegrate. The GVN would collapse and a coalition government would be formed. United States forces would have to retreat to coastal enclaves before leaving Vietnam for good. In this view, the foreign Other hoped to bring an immediate end to the war. A poem Ho Chi Minh sent to diplomats across the world and read on radio in late December and early January is said to indicate their true intent:

> This spring will be far better than any spring past,
>   As truth of triumph spreads with trumpet blast.
> North and South, rushing heroically together, shall smite
>   the American invaders.
> Go forward!
>   Certain victory is ours at last![26]

On January 31, 1968, Vietcong troops attacked five of the six major cities, thirty-six of forty-four provincial capitals, sixty-four of 242 district capitals, and numerous airfields, munitions dumps, and other military and economic facilities. A Vietcong commando team destroyed part of the American embassy in Saigon. Both ARVN and U.S. military forces retreated to the cities. Vietcong forces held parts of towns and cities for weeks. Much to their surprise, the United States immediately began shelling and bombing urban areas. One U.S. Army major surveyed the former city of Ben Tre after bombers had leveled it and said, "We had to destroy the town to save it."[27] In Saigon, 9,580 dwellings were destroyed, with thousands of civilian casualties. MACV's inspector general subsequently attributed most damage to U.S. forces. Much of Hue, the ancient capital of Vietnam, was also destroyed. Vietcong forces rounded up and executed several hundred GVN leaders during the weeks they held the city, while U.S. airpower killed several thousand civilians. Tet was a major battle from the beginning of February until early March, after which fighting slowly eased and cities returned to U.S.–GVN control. Few U.S. or ARVN soldiers returned to the countryside until late spring and summer.

Tet came as a surprise. American leaders really believed they had beaten the Vietcong by the autumn of 1967; they had become trapped in their own web of systematic falsifications. Captured documents indicating that a national attack was forthcoming were dismissed as *unbelievable*. As one U.S. Army intelligence officer said, "If we'd gotten the whole battle plan, it wouldn't have been credible to us." [28] A major booklet issued to Vietcong political and military cadre was entitled "For an Understanding of the New Situation and the New Tasks." It outlined a threefold mission of hitting important U.S. military facilities, trying to cause ARVN to collapse, and generating popular support for the general uprising. United States intelligence received this pamphlet on November 25, 1967. On January 5, MACV distributed a press release based on captured documents. The headline read: "Captured Document Indicates Final Phases of the Revolution at Hand." A partial translation said:

> Use very strong military attacks in coordination with the uprisings of the local population to take over towns and cities. Troops should flood the lowlands. They should move toward liberating the capital city, take power and try to rally enemy brigades and regiments to our side one by one. Propaganda should be broadly disseminated among the population in general, and leaflets should be used to reach enemy officers and enlisted personnel. [29]

The very same Vietcong forces that leading war-managers theoretically abolished in the order of battle debate took part in Tet. CIA analyst George Carver attended a meeting with McNamara on February 4, 1968. McNamara noticed that approximately half of the enemy units participating were not listed on the official order of battle. [30] Few People's Army of Vietnam (PAVN or NVA) took part in the attack. Missing units were nearly all Vietcong guerrillas who had been previously abolished!

Westmoreland and his associates proclaimed enemy defeat during the Tet Offensive. MACV estimated that from 67,000 to 84,000 enemy troops attacked and 45,000 had been killed. Even though many deaths were from units that MACV had previously eliminated from the enemy's credit account, all new bodies were *subtracted* from the official order of battle. By this reasoning, MACV issued a new OB on March 15 declaring only 204,000 enemy troops remained! Showing victory while American and ARVN forces retreated took much work. One high-ranking intelligence officer attached to MACV's order of battle section describes it in letters to his wife. Naval Commander James Meacham, chief of OB studies, thought their efforts were doomed:

> March 2, 1968: Tomorrow will be a sort of day of truth. We shall then see if I can make the computer sort out the losses since the Tet Offensive began in such a manner as to prove that we are winning the war. If I can't we shall of course jack the figures around until we do show progress. Every month we make progress here. . . . The MACV bunch is definitely on the defensive (mentally as well as militarily).
>
> March 13: You should have seen the antics my people and I had to go through . . . to make the February enemy strength calculations come out the way the general wanted them. We started with the answer and plugged in all sorts of figures until we found a combination the machine could digest, and then we wrote all sorts of estimates showing why the figures were right which we had to use. And we continue to win the war.
>
> March 21: We had a crash project to prepare a briefing for the press on enemy strength as of 29 February — complete with viewgraphs. . . . I have never in my life assembled such a pack of truly gargantuan falsehoods. The reporters will think we are putting on a horse and dog show when we try to sell them this crap.[31]

His foreboding was warranted. Important leaders saw problems with the numbers. Arthur Goldberg, the United States ambassador to the United Nations, was not impressed when he heard that the Vietcong had suffered 45,000 killed during February and early March. He asked his military briefers what the estimated ratio of enemy wounded-to-killed was. Officers replied that they normally counted 3.5 Vietnamese wounded for every digit in the body count; by this reasoning the enemy suffered 157,500 wounded. Goldberg noticed that this arithmetic signified the enemy's bankruptcy — only one-third of its forces remained if the official order of battle was accepted.[32] Yet in his communications with the Joint Chiefs of Staff, Westmoreland presented requests for troops that far exceeded his 1968 budget of 525,000 soldiers. Four objectives for 1968 were presented in this request:

— First, to counter the enemy offensive and to destroy or eject the NVA invasion force in the north;

— Second, to restore security in the cities and towns;

— Third, to restore security in the heavily populated areas of the countryside;

— Fourth, to regain the initiative through offensive operations.[33]

General Earle Wheeler went to Saigon on February 23. On the twenty-seventh he delivered a report to President Johnson stressing how demanding winning the war would be. United States forces needed to guard cities: "It is clear that this task will absorb a substantial portion of U.S. forces." United States forces also needed to help ARVN leave the cities and go fight the VC: "MACV estimates that U.S. forces will be required in a number of places to assist and encourage the Vietnamese Army to leave the cities and towns and reenter the country. This is especially true in the Delta [the most populous area]." Most important, there were not enough American troops to sustain production past the cross-over. According to Wheeler, ". . . MACV does not have adequate forces at this time to resume the offensive in the remainder of the country, nor does it have adequate reserves against the contingency of simultaneous large-scale enemy offensive action throughout the countryside."[34]

Pentagon war-managers recommended 206,756 additional troop "spaces" on top of the 1968 ceiling of 525,000. These extra forces would include three combat divisions, another 300 to 400 tactical fighter-bombers (fifteen squadrons), and increased navy ships. In response, President Johnson initiated an "A to Z" review, presided over by men who either previously or currently held powerful positions determining United States foreign policy. Robert McNamara had resigned late in 1967. His heir, Clark Clifford, directed the Senior Informal Advisory Group, or the "Wise Old Men." At lower levels of the military and State Department apparatus, a new series of studies examining past practice and recommendations for the future was commissioned.

According to an intelligence organization in the Department of Defense, the International Security Agency, prospects for increased production were limited:

> Even with the 200,000 additional troops requested by MACV, we will not be in a position to drive the enemy from SVN or destroy his forces. . . .

The more likely enemy response [to U.S. escalation], however, is that with which he has responded to previous increases in force levels, viz., a matching increase on his part. Hanoi has maintained a constant ratio of one maneuver battalion to 1.5 U.S. maneuver battalions from his reserve in NVN of from 45–70 maneuver battalions (comprising 40,000–60,000 men in 5–8 divisions).

Even if the enemy stands and fights as he did before Tet, the results can only be disappointing in terms of attriting his capability.

Over the past year the United States has been killing between 70 and 100 VC/NVA per month per U.S. combat battalion in theater. *The return per combat battalion deployed has been falling off,* but even assuming that additional deployments will double the number of combat battalions, and assuming that the kill-ratios will remain constant, we could expect enemy deaths, at best, on the order of 20,000 per month, but the infiltration system from North Vietnam alone could supply 13,000–16,000 per month, regardless of our bombing pattern, leaving the remainder — 4,000 — to be recruited in South Vietnam — a demonstrably manageable undertaking for the VC.[35]

If the enemy could afford such production, ISA staff doubted that the United States could: "We will have to mobilize reserves, increase our budget by billions, and see U.S. casualties climb to 1,300–1,400 per month. Our balance of payments will be worsened, considerably, and we will need a larger tax increase — justified as a war tax, or wage and price controls. . . ."[36] On March 25, the Senior Informal Advisory Group received an order of battle briefing by CIA analyst George Carver. He presented the case for doubling the OB to 600,000 and noted that since most U.S. and GVN forces had retreated to towns and cities, GVN rural pacification no longer existed. ISA had also made this point emphatically. President Johnson noticed an abrupt change in the group after this briefing. He tracked down Carver and had him repeat his performance on March 28. That same day Johnson rejected Westmoreland's request for an additional 206,000 troops, instead establishing a 1968 ceiling of 549,500 spaces, roughly 24,500 more than originally planned. Three days later he made his decision public and announced he would not seek a second presidential term.

Note, though, that Westmoreland was *only* limited to 550,000 troops. Establishing such a high level is not the same as ending the war and withdrawing U.S. forces. To the contrary, the war and the bureaucratic struggle over enemy order of battle and the cross-over point both continued. In April the CIA and MACV held another OB conference. The CIA wanted a 600,000 figure, including local guerrillas. Military war-managers insisted on low figures. Westmoreland said: "There is a much larger issue involved here than intelligence methodology. The acceptance of this inflated strength . . . is contrary to our national interest. The effect that its inevitable public announcement would have on the American public . . . is obvious." [37] Westmoreland won this struggle. Estimates of Vietcong forces remained low in military documents and press releases. Mechanistic anticommunism with its concept of the foreign Other invading the sovereign state of South Vietnam prevailed. Questions concerning how the Vietnamese class structure and history of resistance toward invaders could generate a strong guerrilla force and mass political organizations for farmers, women, youth, and other social groupings were dismissed. [38]

However, even within this conceptual universe, reports on productivity demonstrated systemic flaws. Thomas Thayer, of the Office of Systems Analysis, drew attention to several important studies conducted in the latter half of 1968. First, if North Vietnam increased the percentage of its population in the military to a figure equal to South Vietnam, it could double its forces. Even by accepting the incredibly high body count projected by MACV during the first six months of 1968 — the Tet Offensive and its spring second wave — then the DRV could fight for up to *thirty years* before its manpower account went bankrupt. Vietcong forces could only fight for another three and a half years, a figure reflecting the order of battle, but three and a half years of fighting at Tet levels meant tremendous American casualties. Even these projections failed to note that the enemy also controlled the pace of battle, and could thus control their casualty rate. Thayer reports:

> A statistical analysis after the 1968 offensives indicated that the VC/NVA had much more influence over fluctuations in both their combat deaths and U.S. combat deaths than did the allied forces. It concluded that the VC/NVA held the basic military initiative in South Vietnam because they could alter the combat death levels by changing the frequency and intensity of their attacks. Changing the tempo of allied operations had little effect.
>
> The correlation between VC/NVA attacks and their own combat deaths did not change much after the 1968 offensives. This suggests that there was little change in the VC/NVA's ability to alter their level of combat deaths by changing their levels of attacks. Before 1968,

they could presumably control about 85 percent of the fluctuations; after 1968, they seemed to have some control over about 75 percent of the changes, *enough to frustrate the allied attrition strategy.*[39]

Even by accepting the "Mere Gook Rule" way of counting enemy casualties, the military could not win. Although the cross-over point fails to indicate the complexities and contradictions of Technowar, the inability to make a "profit" signifies failure by its own most crucial definition. Technowar did not produce victory; it could not produce victory with more troops fighting for *decades.* By late 1968, senior officials had been receiving versions of this report for four years. Secretary of Defense Robert McNamara doubted the prospects of victory in his original troop allocations in 1965 and projections for future years. Office of Systems Analysis staff showed in 1966 that increased forces would not reach the cross-over point, as did 1967 calculations for Westmoreland's troop requests for 1968. Nor did calculations performed in 1968 show how victory could be produced.

In November 1968, Richard Nixon was elected President; a new team of senior civilian war-managers assumed command. What happened to all these studies when the uppermost levels of the bureaucracy changed? Journalist Seymour Hersh touched upon this question in his investigation of Henry Kissinger, *The Price of Power.* After Nixon appointed him as national security adviser, Kissinger asked the Rand Corporation to prepare a list of policy options for Vietnam. Daniel Ellsberg, who then worked at Rand and had written part of the *Pentagon Papers,* prepared a list of policy options which did not include any U.S. action leading to victory. Kissinger and his colleague Thomas C. Schelling noted this absence. Ellsberg replied to their inquiry, "I don't believe there is a win option in Vietnam."[40] Ellsberg did include a complete withdrawal option. Later on, Kissinger and his staff dropped the withdrawal option from copies presented to other government officials. Defeat remained unthinkable.

Nevertheless, Kissinger adopted one of Ellsberg's ideas. Ellsberg told him that when Robert McNamara became secretary of defense in 1962, he administered a 96-item questionnaire to high-level war-managers designed both to show them he knew defense issues and to ferret out views of different bureaucratic factions. Ellsberg believed that the questionnaire had helped McNamara take control. Kissinger similarly wanted to take control, so Ellsberg was commissioned to help design, administer, and analyze responses to a lengthy questionnaire. The document was known as "National Security Study Memorandum No. 1," and consisted of a 28-question survey and 548 pages of responses from government agencies. Both the survey and the responses received high-security classification. According to Seymour Hersh, "Nixon and Kissinger never relied on NSSM 1 and its replies except as a method of forcing the bureaucracy to do busywork and removing it from decision making."[41]

But the summary of responses demands explanation. The summary's unnamed author or authors indicate a general breakdown of responses into two groups. One group, which included MACV, CINCPAC (commander in chief, Pacific), the Joint Chiefs of Staff, and the staff of the American embassy in Saigon, saw victory as possible with increased resources. Group B, the CIA, the secretary of defense (including Systems Analysis), and the State Department, found bankruptcy. But apparently both groups concurred in analyzing "VC/NVA Manpower."

> It is generally agreed that the NVN/VC manpower pool is sufficiently large to meet the enemy's replenishment needs over an extended period of time within the framework of current rules of engagement. According to the JCS, "The North Vietnamese and Vietcong have access to sufficient manpower to meet their replenishment needs — even at the high 1968 loss rate of some 291,000 — for at least the next several years. . . . Present operations are not outrunning the enemy's ability to replenish by recruitment or infiltration." Enemy losses of 291,000 in 1968 were roughly balanced by infiltration and recruitment of 298,000. North Vietnamese manpower assets include 1.8 million physically fit males aged 14–34 of whom 45% are in the regular forces (475,000) and paramilitary (400,000) forces. 120,000 physically fit males reach draft age each year and 200,000 military and labor personnel have been freed by the bombing halt from defensive work. The potential manpower pool in SVN is estimated at half a million men and recruitment, while down, is running at approximately 3,500 per month. Enemy maintenance of the current commitment of 300,000 new men per year requires that the Allies inflict losses of 25,000 KIA per month, or 7,000 more than the current rate. MACV considers current Allied force levels adequate to inflict such casualties if the enemy chooses to engage.[42]

Using JCS estimates rather than Systems Analysis, the foreign Other can fight at 1968 levels for "at least the next several years." Again, these estimates assume the body count numbers have referential validity. Near equality between the enemy's debits and credits — 291,000 in debits versus 298,000 in credits — also seems dubious. The low estimate of potential Vietcong (a 500,000 "labor" pool) again indicates acceptance of MACV order of battle estimates and equally dubious figures for GVN pacification. After years of fighting women and old people, and occasionally children, the assumption remains that the only fighters are men from fourteen to thirty-four. But even using false figures designed to present productivity in the most positive light, MACV and JCS find that they run a deficit, only 18,000 Vietcong and NVA killed per month when the cross-over point necessary to break even is 25,000! The authors quote the JCS survey response: "It will be exceedingly difficult in 1968 for Allied forces to attrite the enemy at 1968 levels."[43]

Summary responses also suggest problems for GVN pacification programs. Although the Joint Chiefs of Staff and Westmoreland's command in Saigon thought the VC were completely destroyed and that GVN forces would control 90 percent of the population in 1969, the other auditors in OSD (Office of the Secretary of Defense), CIA, and the State Department saw things differently. NSSM 1 summary said that OSD concluded:

> (1) "The portions of the SVN rural population aligned with the VC and aligned with the GVN are apparently the same today as in 1962 [a discouraging year]: 5,000,000 GVN aligned and nearly 3,000,000 VC aligned."
> (2) "At the present, it appears that at least 50% of the total rural population is subject to significant VC presence and influence."
> CIA agrees, and State (INR) goes even further, saying: "Our best estimate is that the VC have a significant effect on *at least two-thirds of the rural population*."[44]

These estimates approximate reports submitted for Clifford's "A to Z" review. George Carver's briefing to the Senior Informal Advisory Group, and later the President, had included a CIA "Monthly Pacification Report" for February indicating that the program had collapsed in forty of the forty-four provinces! CIA officer William Colby halted dissemination of this report before he left Washington to take charge of pacification. ISA's manpower projection on enemy abilities was accompanied by an assessment of pacification. It saw "expulsion of GVN presence and influence from the rural areas, showing up on the pacification maps as a 'red tide' flowing up to the edges of the province and district towns, and over some of them."[45] Even in areas where the

GVN government was not completely driven away, ISA analysts thought that ARVN forces would be "even less likely than before" to aggressively search for local Vietcong companies and battalions. Consequently, "in that environment, informers will clam up, or be killed; the VC will get more information and cooperation, the GVN less; officials and police will be much less willing to act on information on VC suspects and activities."[46] It is difficult to imagine a more threatening assessment.

Many crucial studies demonstrating Technowar failure thus came to the attention of leading war-managers in the year following the 1968 Tet Offensive through March of 1969. President Johnson, Defense Secretaries Robert McNamara and his Democratic successor, Clark Clifford, and General Westmoreland all left their respective positions in this period. President Nixon, Defense Secretary Melvin Laird, and General Creighton Abrams (formerly Westmoreland's deputy) replaced them. National Security Study Memorandum No. 1 indicates that these men and their second echelon knew that a significant section of the government bureaucracy thought Technowar bankrupt and had considerable empirical evidence and traditional debit-credit production logic to demonstrate their case.

Yet *defeat was unthinkable:* debit could always be changed to credit by increasing war production. MACV's reports of massive productivity either beyond the cross-over point or close to it and projections of pacifying 90 percent of the Vietnamese within the year were "empirical" findings that resonated with a whole way of conceptualizing and acting upon the world.

Full ground operations continued — search-and-destroy as an assembly line — until U.S. forces began major reductions in late 1971. Note the distribution of U.S. casualties. From 1965 through 1967 the United States suffered 15,895 killed and 52,200 wounded. Nineteen sixty-eight brought 14,615 killed and 46,800 wounded. Remaining years of U.S. search-and-destroy (1969–1971) produced 14,998 killed and 52,900 wounded.[47] These figures are not restricted to ground operations alone, but instead include all U.S. combat casualties from different subassemblies of Technowar. Much of the national news media, particularly network television news, and many historians saw the Tet Offensive, the Senior Informal Advisory Group's denial of Westmoreland's request for a troop increase, and the subsequent beginning of peace talks as definitive evidence that ground war had ended. This erroneous assessment was aided by President Nixon's 1969 announcements calling for "Vietnamization'' of the war, providing more weapons to ARVN. More weapons went to ARVN to give them indisputable technological superiority, but ground war did not end in 1968. United States troops continued to fight and die.

In May 1974, the Fletcher School of Law and Diplomacy (a distinguished school for aspirants to the U.S. foreign service) held a conference called ''The Military Lessons of the Vietnam War.'' It was an ''in-house'' conference; only major war-managers and military researchers connected with the defense establishment attended. Two participants made note of the conventional belief that U.S. ground war had ended in the spring of 1968. Ambassador Robert Komer said: ''I was there when General Abrams took over, and remained as his deputy. There was no change in strategy whatsoever. In fact, he said he didn't intend to make any changes unless he saw that some were necessary. The myth of a change in strategy is a figment of media imagination; it didn't really change until we began withdrawing.''[48] Professor Francis West of the Fletcher School concurred with Komer's judgment. West had formerly served in the Office of the Secretary of Defense during the Nixon administration as a White House fellow and had previously served with the marines in Vietnam:

> If one asks what the difference is between what General Westmoreland did and what General Abrams did, I am not sure that anyone could really make the case of saying that a great difference existed. I think that another myth was perpetrated on the American public following the Tet offensive. Tet-68 occurred and we all drew a lesson — we had lost the war and we were going to get out. When did we get out of the war? Four years later. Four years later we had ended up spending more money after Tet-68 than before it, and having just as many casualties. This allowed General Abrams to do things that General Westmoreland could not do, because the public, at this point in the war, believed that the war was going to end. I think that there is great irony in terms of how the press reported that whole phenomenon.[49]

A second viewpoint of the effects of the Tet Offensive begins with the Tet-ended-U.S.-ground-war position and builds on it an extraordinary edifice. Conservative scholars and military men accept Westmoreland's contention that the United States unequivocally won Tet; they thus take MACV's order of battle for the Vietcong and the Vietcong body count as valid indices of real developments. United States and

GVN armed forces won Tet as a military offensive, but the American news media incorrectly portrayed it as a defeat. Peter Braestrup's *Big Story* serves as the textual reference for how the media portrayed Tet in Vietnam and Washington.[50] In this line of reasoning, since the United States won Tet militarily and the media incorrectly portrayed it as a defeat, thus promoting public sentiment for a negotiated peace settlement, then *in effect the war-managers were robbed of an imminent victory*.

Some conservatives go on to assert that not only was the U.S. military victory stolen by the media, but that the North Vietnamese allowed the United States to win in the first place! North Vietnam wanted all Vietcong killed so that when it invaded no local Vietcong would be alive to oppose it! Sir Robert Thompson expounded one variant of this position at ''The Military Lessons of the Vietnam War'' conference:

> Certainly one can sum up that offensive by saying militarily it was a dreadful defeat for them, but psychologically it was an extraordinary victory. Certainly it destroyed the Vietcong militarily — that is, the Vietcong regular forces and the Vietcong regional forces, which the North Vietnamese had the good sense to put into the front of the offensive, and it was the Vietcong who took most of the casualties. In other words, the Vietcong were no longer a possible regional rival to the NVA in South Vietnam.[51]

Whereas Thompson saw Vietcong decimation as a beneficial accident accruing to the North Vietnamese, General Frederick Weyland (a major U.S. force commander during Tet) saw the offensive as North Vietnamese treachery toward their southern comrades.

> Applying the test of *cui bono* (for whose benefit) it can be seen that the real losers of Tet-68 were the South Vietnamese Communists (the Vietcong or PRG) who surfaced, led the attacks, and were destroyed in the process. . . . Just as the Russians eliminated their Polish competitors [with] the Warsaw Uprising, the North Vietnamese eliminated their southern competitors with Tet-68. They thereby insured that the eventual outcome of the war would be a South Vietnam dominated and controlled, not by South Vietnamese Communists, but by the North Vietnamese.[52]

Just as Robert Komer and General William Westmoreland's staff advocated theoretical abolition of the Vietcong before Tet, Sir Robert Thompson, General Frederick Weyland, Colonel Harry Summers, and others declared the abolition of the Vietcong after Tet. In both cases, the theoretical abolition of the Vietcong leaves Technowar fighting its preferred foe, a devilish Other who devours its own children. Abolishing the Vietcong before the Tet Offensive was necessary to present Technowar as highly productive, with victory in sight; abolishing the Vietcong afterward was part of a more convoluted effort to explain American defeat as cunning Oriental deception, a psychological gimmick tricking the news media and through them the American public. Recall Kissinger's warning that Third World, pre-Newtonian societies had a subjective mentality that "offers great flexibility with respect to the contemporary revolutionary turmoil. It enables the societies which do not share our cultural mode to alter reality by influencing the perspective of the observer — a process which we are largely unprepared to handle or even perceive."[53] Unable to explain Technowar failure against an underequipped foe, the war-managers present Americans as the naive victims of clever magicians. Technowar won, but the foreign Other's magic made victory disappear.

Vietcong losses during the Tet Offensive decimated many main-force battalions; many units never reconstituted themselves to full strength from local recruits. After Tet, considerably more People's Army of Vietnam (NVA, in American terms) forces appeared on the battlefield, both as main-force units and as replacement troops inside Vietcong units. Ho Chi Minh undoubtedly would have preferred an overwhelming victory in 1968 leading to GVN collapse and rapid American withdrawal. Certainly, Vietcong political cadre and soldiers wanted complete victory and were severely damaged in many areas by their considerable losses. In these respects the conservative assessments of Tet have truth.

But Ho Chi Minh had been fighting over fifty years by 1968. Would such a man think that one battle would end the war when Vietnamese history showed protracted struggle over thousands of years as the only way to expel foreign invaders and unify the country? By 1968 Vietnamese Communist party leaders and their prominent generals had been fighting together for nearly *thirty years*, first against the Japanese, then the French, then against the United States. Their objective over these thirty years remained the same: national reunification and social revolution. Their strategy called for mobilizing peasants to support armed struggle. Would such a party deliberately destroy all those organizations and troops most closely connected with southern peasants, workers, and intellectuals when people were their major resource for survival and eventual victory?

Evidence suggests that the war-managers were both conscious and unconscious of creating a double-reality, a war at ground level and a much different paper edifice for Saigon and Washington headquarters. How could they be both conscious and unconscious simultaneously? The notion contradicts, the conventional concept of an individual who knows truth from falsity and chooses to lie.

George Orwell called this conscious/unconscious process "doublethink." In his novel *1984* the protagonist, Winston Smith, reads a book outlawed by the government, "The Theory and Practice of Oligarchial Collectivism." An excerpt of the book — an essay in the novel — is provided. Most of the essay concerns systematic falsification.

> *Doublethink* means the power of holding two contradictory beliefs in one's mind simultaneously, and accepting both of them. The Party intellectual knows in which direction his memories must be altered; he therefore knows that he is playing tricks with reality; but by the exercise of *doublethink* he also satisfies himself that reality is not violated. The process has to be conscious, or it would not be carried out with sufficient precision, but it also has to be unconscious, or it would bring with it a feeling of falsity and hence of guilt. Doublethink lies at the very heart of Ingsoc [acronym for English socialism, the government in 1984], since the essential act of the Party is to use conscious deception while retaining the firmness of purpose that goes with complete honesty. To tell deliberate lies while genuinely believing in them, to forget any fact that has become inconvenient, and then, when it becomes necessary again, to draw it back from oblivion for just as long as it is needed, to deny the existence of objective reality and all the while to take account of the reality which one denies — all this is indispensably necessary. Even in using the word *doublethink* it is necessary to exercise *doublethink*. For by using the word one admits that one is tampering with reality; by a fresh act of doublethink one erases this knowledge; and so on indefinitely, with the lie always one leap ahead of the truth.[54]

*George Orwell, 1984 (New York: New American Library, 1961), pp. 176-177*

Doublethink necessitates a network of people in bureaucratic positions. For example, a platoon commander reporting a false body count to his company commander knows he is lying; the report is a conscious deception by the lieutenant. But the lieutenant's lie is made "legitimate" or "truthful" by the captain's acceptance of the false body count even though the captain knows it is false. The company commander then recommends that the lieutenant be rewarded. Division headquarters gives the lieutenant a medal and promotes the captain to major because all of his platoon commanders are highly productive under his leadership. When the lieutenant and captain receive their rewards for false body counts, then the lies have become institutionalized truths; the rewards "erase" the first conscious lies. Doublethink constitutes a mode of systematic falsification. Second-order lies created through bureaucratic exchanges of reports and rewards provide the dynamic to keep lies moving "always one leap ahead of the truth." By having their own lies eventually return back to them as institutionalized truths and rewards (promotions, medals, high-level reports echoing low-level fabrications), individuals within the system could retain "the firmness of purpose that goes with complete honesty."

In Orwell's *1984* the real historical record vanished down the "memory hole," a sophisticated disposal and incinerator for all documents presenting facts different from those recently enthroned. MACV's distortion of the VC/NVA order of battle and all of the fabricated battle reports involved similar disregard of objective reality and the concomitant destruction of records not supporting Technowar progress. War-managers also made frequent use of the "memory hole." However, bureaucratic doublethink did not make the real war in Vietnam literally vanish, leaving only false records that did not really matter. To the contrary, the war's history demonstrates that official self-deceptions consistently led to disaster.

With the introduction of full-scale warfare from 1965 on, the war-managers' mechanistic conceptual universe and doublethink process created larger-scale, more convoluted contradictions between the official war and the real war. North Vietnamese and Vietcong leaders took advantage of these contradictions in their strategy of revolutionary war. Westmoreland's success in late 1968 and 1969 in reconstituting the appearance of victory was a tremendous achievement, but in taking doublethink to greater heights even greater contradictions were simultaneously created, as well as the grounds for more resounding failures.

Doublethink promoting the appearance of Technowar as both law governed and science governed helped war-managers overpower their political critics in the United States and maintain full war production. Numerous MACV directives concerning the rules of engagement gave most observers the impression that the war was being fought with considerable respect for civilian lives and property. Political scientist Guenter Lewy concludes from his examination of official files that "MACV directives sought to strike a balance between the force necessary to accomplish the mission of U.S. forces in Vietnam and the need to reduce to a minimum the casualties and damage inflicted on the civilian population.''[55] To support his conclusion, Lewy cites MACV memos beyond the "Nine Rules" card given to soldiers. One 1965 directive instructed U.S. military advisers to ARVN to "make every effort to convince Vietnamese counterparts of the necessity for preservation of the lives and property of noncombatants.''[56] Another 1965 program for newly arriving American troops told them that "respect for civilian life was not only a matter of basic decency and legality, but was also essential for winning the hearts and minds of the people.''[57]

Telford Taylor, former chief American prosecutor at the Nuremburg War Crime trials of Nazi war-managers, looked through MACV's rules of engagement and found them "virtually impeccable.''[58] Army Lieutenant General W. R. Peers also viewed the files in conjunction with his appointment to head an army commission of inquiry into the My Lai massacre and its cover-up by superior officers. He concluded, "In every instance I am aware of the intent was unquestionable: to minimize noncombatant casualties and prevent destruction of property.''[59]

With such an abundance of rules, reports of U.S. forces killing civilians appeared as *deviations* from the rules, either "accidents," or isolated incidents far from normal war conduct. Rather than examining the production model of war and the operating system of rewards and punishments within the military, attention thus became displaced toward how "deviations" occurred. The structure of Technowar remained invisible; inquiry shifted toward administrative efforts and troops' "understanding." Lewy says, "Even though the ROE were republished every six months to insure maximum visibility to all U.S. personnel during their tours of duty, the distribution of the rules to lower levels was often inadequate.''[60] General Peers had the same assessment: "The problem with these and other comparable regulations, however, was that it was difficult to define rules to cover every possible situation and have them understood by all the troops, and it was even more difficult to make sure they were implemented. The constantly changing situation and the rapid rotation of personnel magnified the problem in Vietnam.''[61]

In 1969 newspaper and television news coverage of massive killings of civilians at My Lai focused attention on the military's rules of engagement. Since the military's paper edifice had previously framed My Lai in terms of deviations from the rules, senior commanders emerged untainted — Lieutenant William Calley was convicted and publicized as the one man who ever committed murder on a search-and-destroy operation in Vietnam. Further institutional corrections involved issuing more rules and better training. Lewy quotes from a new army training manual written and issued after My Lai was exposed: "If you disobey the rules of engagement, you can be tried and punished for disobedience of orders. The disobedience may also be a war crime for which you can be tried and punished." [62] Note how responsibility shifts toward low-level troops (like Calley and his platoon) as opposed to generals and their strategy of warfare.

General Peers also thought that increasing mandatory annual training on the Geneva and Hague conventions to two hours a year plus three short films would help decrease deviations from official rules. Rewriting rules in simpler language for these lectures would also help: "The most important aspect of the new instruction is that it is brought down to the soldier's level. Previous instruction materials were so condensed, and written in such legalistic terms, that they were both boring and difficult to comprehend." [63] Peers concluded: "In sum, the Army responded swiftly to improve its policy directives and training with respect to the Law of War and the conventions. The problem in the future will be one of enforcement." [64]

But who will enforce the law when the law was never meant to be enforced? Calley was the only one convicted; charges against men in his platoon and against his superiors who covered up the massacre were dismissed.

While Calley was being tried and the army was writing new training manuals, Lieutenant General Julian Ewell was in command of the 9th Infantry Division in the Mekong Delta (1968–1969) and later served as corps commander for all U.S. forces in the Saigon region (II Corps). The army issued new training manuals while Ewell was rationalizing the production of death with statistical analyses and production quotas! Ewell even kept track of how many medals men received each month as an index of their efficiency. A new training manual threatening a court-martial for violating the rules of engagement is much less intimidating to a soldier than the realization that his unit will be left in the field unless its production quota is met. Falsely defining civilian deaths in terms of deviations from laws allowed the military to offer a false solution of more laws. A lie times a lie equals a doublethink truth.

Soldiers went through several months of basic training and more advanced instruction in their combat specialty (infantry, armor, artillery). Changing the manuals and showing some films did not change the *real lessons* taught by drill instructors and superior commanders. Several soldiers testifying before the Dellums committee hearings in April 1971 reflected upon how their training prepared them for unrestrained killing in Vietnam. Some were from Calley's division, the Americal Division. They wanted to show the army's institutional involvement in promoting massacres as opposed to the press and trial presentations focusing on Calley as an isolated deviant. Gary Battles said:

> I went from AIT [Advanced Infantry Training] and when I got out from there I went to Vietnam.
>
> Upon arrival in the Americal Division, we were sent to a briefing camp. We had seven or eight days to see what it was like in Vietnam, to learn how to stay alive, so to speak, at this training camp. It was a refresher, to get used to the climate, and so on.
>
> During this period they had classes and at each and every one of the classes there — there was a microphone in front of the speaker, just like in front of me — but we were told that "the only good gook is a dead gook, and the more gooks you kill, the more slant-eyes you can kill in Vietnam, that is the less you will have to worry about them killing you at night."[65]

Daniel Notley, also of the Americal Division, described his basic and AIT training:

> I had my basic training in the infantry at Fort Polk, Louisiana. I went through most of the training as the other guys went through. The complete dehumanization of a person in preparation for the Vietnam war.
>
> Now in this training they referred to the Vietnamese as dinks or gooks. The impression was that they were something less than human.
>
> I had a drill sergeant in AIT reply to a question, "What is it like over there?"; and he told us, he said, "It is like hunting rabbits and squirrels."[66]

Daniel Barnes said he was following his family tradition when he entered the army:

> So I went in with the idea of going into the Army that it was more of a privilege rather than more of a sacrifice, which is what it turned out to be.
>
> I went in with the respect for it and so on. After getting through basic training where the main word was, "Kill. Kill. Kill." all the time, they then pushed it into your head twenty-four hours a day.

Everything you said — even before you sat down to eat your meals, you had to stand up and scream, "Kill," before you could sit down and eat. Which I didn't think was very right.[67]

Charles David Locke said that during his AIT at Fort Jackson the "Kill" chant had a second line, "Kill, and kill without mercy."[68] Novels and memoirs by soldiers contain chants taught in basic and advanced training.

Ambushes are murder and murder is fun![69]

VC, VC kill, kill, kill. Gotta kill, gotta kill, gotta kill, 'cause it's fun, cause it's fun.[70]

Marines are killers.
We kill. We kill.[71]

I want go to Vietnam
Just to kill ol' Charlie Cong
Am I right or wrong?
Am I goin' strong?[72]

This is my rifle and this [penis] is my gun.
One is for killing, one is for fun.[73]

And then there is Lieutenant Calley's version of what he learned at Officer Candidate School:

It was drummed into us, "Be sharp! On guard! As soon as you think these people won't kill you, ZAP! In combat you haven't friends! You have enemies!" Over and over at OCS we heard this, and I told myself, I'll act as if I'm never secure. As if everyone in Vietnam would do me in. As if everyone's bad.[74]

Training taught fear of the enemy and sometimes promised pleasure as well. Once in Vietnam, soldiers found themselves immersed in racism with great pressure to produce, as epitomized in the "Mere Gook Rule": "If it's dead and it's Vietnamese, it's VC." A paper edifice could be readily "corrected" by the war-managers by adding more papers; that was the function military law served. The war continued while changed rules presented the appearance of policy change.

A similar doublethink process of keeping the lie "always one leap ahead of the truth" occurred in the military's handling of prisoner interrogations. As was the case with rules of engagement, MACV issued a pocket card, "The Enemy in Your Hands," for all troops and lengthier memos for divisional, brigade, and battalion headquarters. Most directives emphasized the illegality of harming prisoners. MACV Directive 20-4, dated 27 April 1967, called attention to Army Field Manual 27-10, The Law of Land Warfare, July 1956.

> A "grave breach" of the Geneva Conventions constitutes a war crime. Some examples of "grave breaches" are as follows (when committed against persons taking no active part in the hostilities, including members of armed forces who have laid down their arms and those placed *hors de combat* by sickness, wounds, detention, or any cause): Willful killing, torture or inhuman treatment, willfully causing great suffering or serious injury to body or health.[75]

At the same time military intelligence specialists were taught torture as a method of interrogation. But torturing techniques never appeared in military intelligence manuals. Instead the intelligence curriculum had a dual structure, a "legal" education in the formal educational materials, and an illegal education taught orally by instructors. Story after story confirms this split.

> I remember at Ford Holabird Intelligence School in Maryland, I never saw any regulation; I never read any directive; I never read any Army Manual that outlined for us torture methods.
>
> However, after the regular classes or after any particular classes, say, on interrogation, the men in the class would gather outside with the instructor and say, "Tell us, what is it really like?"
>
> Then they would tell you the incidents of men being thrown out of helicopters, electrical torture, beating, etcetera. But it was never official policy.[76]

Interrogators most often faced Vietnamese whose combat status and political allegiance was uncertain. The Americans rarely knew Vietnamese language, Vietnamese culture, or Vietnamese history, but they were responsible for ascertaining who was a Vietcong and who was a "civilian." Peter Martinsen, formerly a POW interrogator with the 11th Cavalry Regiment, describes how he learned to determine a civilian from a Vietcong:

> As mentioned earlier, you get a person into your presence for interrogation, and this person is classified as a detainee and it is up to the interrogator to determine just exactly what he has, whether you

have a legitimate POW, whether you have a rallier from the other side, called a "Chieu Hoi," whether you have a civil defendant, which is a breaker of the civil laws of Vietnam, or whether you have an innocent civilian.

And this is where the torture comes in Vietnam. There are many specific instances that I can recall, the first of which was a very brutal use of force in October '66, after we just lost a man in an ambush from our unit. The 11th Cav rounded up several detainees, one of which was of draftable age, and we were quite certain he was either a Vietcong or sympathizer, and he was taken into a tent and we proceeded with the interrogation. I proceeded to beat the man about the face, and got no effect from this.

The lieutenant came in and asked me if I had broken the prisoner — that is the term, to break a prisoner — asked me if I had broken the prisoner yet, and I replied that I hadn't, and he says, "Let's wire him up and see what happens."

This is something that is not taught in the intelligence school, as a matter of being on the curricula, but it is done more or less in an insidious way. After every class you have a smoke break and then you ask the instructor, an officer or senior enlisted man, "How do you interrogate a prisoner who will not talk?" And the answer is invariable, you take a field telephone, wire it up around the man's testicles, you ring him up and he always answers. It is known as the Bell Telephone Hour. You won't find it in the curriculum, though.[77]

During the Dellums committee hearings, Michael Uhl was asked if interrogators ever received manuals "that would tell you exactly what to do and what not to do in the interrogation of a prisoner?" Uhl replied that yes indeed they received such manuals, but that the one man who tried to follow the manual and MACV's regulations was relieved of his position.

Yes. In fact, the ultimate irony was that the man who was the interrogation officer, and as I stated before, already has testified publicly, was relieved of his position for attempting to follow the book. He attempted to apply the regulations as they were stated in the classifying [of] detainees.

By doing so, he came out with something like 99 percent of the people being classified as innocent civilians. Now every time he classified somebody as an innocent civilian he [commanding officer] would come back to him, "Interrogate him again."

It would happen two, three, or four times in a day. He was under constant harassment; he was always being called up first to the brigade S-2, later to the division commander of military intelligence.

Eventually, when in fact after several months he did not allow electrical torture in his unit any more, he was relieved.[78]

Military interrogators received rewards for producing enemy prisoners of war, much like battalion, brigade, and divisional commanders received rewards for producing a high enemy body count. Finding innocent civilians generated no rewards from the military stratification system. Uhl said, "There was tremendous pressure on the interrogation officer to classify everybody that was not captured with a weapon who would then be classified as a prisoner of war, as a civil defendant."[79] A civil defendant was a Vietnamese who had violated a Vietnamese law. The identification of civil defendants counted as productive interrogator work.

Torture helped produce confessions permitting classification as prisoner of war or civil defendant. Martinsen said the method of producing guilt through torture was known as the "Americal Rule": "And the 'Americal Rule' applied, although it wasn't called that then, and the standard joke is, if he wasn't a Vietcong then, he sure as hell is one now. And this is just what occurred."[80] Marine John Muir reported that the ARVN interrogators accompanying his unit realized that their torture was creating VC and found a solution: "We hesitated to use ARVN interpreters because their method of questioning people was to slap them upside the head with a revolver or shoot their foot off and say, 'You VC?' Sooner or later, after losing enough pieces, the guy would say yes and then he'd be shot because now he's guilty, you know."[81]

A common American version of this practice involved taking Vietnamese detainees up in helicopters for "Flying Lessons" or "Half a Helicopter Ride." Journalist Mark Baker interviewed one soldier who described what happened to three Vietnamese detainees in a chopper with an American intelligence officer:

> The first gook wouldn't talk. Intelligence gives you a signal, thumb toward the door, and you push the guy out. The other two gooks look to see this guy going out the helicopter door.
>
> If the second guy didn't look like he wants to say something or he's lying, the intelligence officer says, "This guy out the door." You'd kick him out, because you're supposed to do what these intelligence officers tell you to do. They're speaking for the Army. The last prisoner is crying and he's leaking like a typewriter. He's talking

Vietnamese like crazy. That's human nature. This guy is running his mouth. You can't keep him from talking. You'd have to gag him to make him shut up. . . .

Before we get back to the base camp, after this guy do all the talking and the intelligence officer document everything, they kick him out the door anyway. Even the good gook, they'd give the word on him and throw him out the door.[82]

One of Jonathan Schell's informants told a similar story: "Another time, I seen them get a bunch of VC's in a chopper. They push out one first, and then tell the others that if they don't talk they go out with him. And they talk."[83] Missing prisoners could easily be classified as suicides or attempted escapes. Prisoners killed during ground interrogations were often dumped in the countryside so a combat unit could include them as enemy killed in action for their body count.[84]

Changing the language or terminology of official reports provided war-managers another way of keeping the lie "always one leap ahead of the truth." In early 1966 the 1st Air Cavalry Division conducted a search-and-destroy mission in Binh Dinh province. The mission has the code name "Operation Masher," an appropriate name, considering the 141,712 artillery rounds fired during the operation. At the Honolulu Conference in February 1966, President Johnson demanded the name be changed because of adverse publicity: "I don't know who names your operations, but 'Masher.' I get kind of mashed myself."[85] Subordinate war-managers subsequently changed the name to "Operation White Wing," as if the troops were engaged in peace negotiations.

By late 1965 senior officials had decided that the term "free-fire zone" had to be eliminated because it accurately conveyed the sense of unrestrained firing and bombing. To replace "free-fire zone" came "specified strike zone," meaning that province chiefs had to give clearance. But province chiefs routinely cleared areas for free-fire zones: the rules of engagement were not changed for specified strike zones, although the term had connotations of controlled rather than unlimited firing. The terminology "harassment and interdiction" for artillery and bombing missions into free-fire zones was similarly abolished as a category early in 1968. In its place came "intelligence targets." General Douglas Kinnard's previous story of taking over an artillery unit where targets were picked at random referred to the selection of "intelligence targets." Only the words were different from harassment and interdiction, not the practice.

In 1968 this practice reached a new level when "search-and-destroy" was abolished. To Westmoreland, search-and-destroy was "nothing more than an operational term for a tactic." Although the general saw "nothing contradictory or brutal about the term, many people, to his surprise, came to associate it with aimless searches in the jungle and the random destroying of villages and other property."[86] Such an accurate fit between the term and actual practice had to be changed; one report says that Supreme Justice Abe Fortas first recommended that search-and-destroy as a term be dropped and that General Earle Wheeler agreed with him.[87] Westmoreland says that John Charles Daly, then head of the Voice of America, brought the matter to his attention.[88] In any case, the order went down the line. Josiah Bunting describes one lieutenant colonel's reaction to this general's semantic instructions in his novel, *The Lionheads*.

> "By the goddam way, Robertson, MACV has changed the fucking name: it is not search and destroy anymore. It is search and *clear*, or if your plans officer is a wise-ass, 'reconnaissance-in-force' is acceptable. Only stop sending my G-3 people OPLANS [operational plans] with 'search and destroy' written in as the mission. Clear?"
>
> Quite clear, General. Do not destroy the enemy or the hamlets they occupy at night; clear them. See that clown down there in his sampan, the one riding low in the water? *Clear* him. Then clear your weapons. We don't want people riding in choppers with their weapons not cleared. Clear? Clear. Robertson thinks of Danny Kaye; get in, get on with it, get it over with, and get out. Get it. Got it. Good.[89]

"Ambush" was also abolished by Westmoreland. It had too definite a meaning; to say U.S. forces were "ambushed" meant that they were attacked without warning, that the Vietcong or NVA had the tactical initiative. To say that the Vietnamese had the initiative implied that they might win, and that was unthinkable. Therefore, Westmoreland ordered the word eliminated from military reports and press releases. Instead, U.S. forces were said to have "engaged the enemy on all sides" or were "meeting engagements on all sides."[90] No sense of battlefield advantage was implied by this new phrase.

MACV tried to make sure that official language changes not only occurred in the military reporting machine, but in the news media. To insure uniformity between military and media, they routinely issued vocabulary tables listing correct and incorrect terms. War photographer Philip Jones Griffiths includes one in his photo collection, *Vietnam, Inc.*[91]

PROPER TERMINOLOGY DETERMINATION
LET'S SAY IT RIGHT!

| INCORRECT TERMS | CORRECT TERMS |
| --- | --- |
| South Vietnam | Republic of Vietnam (RVN) |
| Democratic Republic of Vietnam | North Vietnam |
| South Vietnamese Army | Army of the Republic of Vietnam (ARVN) |
| People's Army of North Vietnam | North Vietnamese Army (NVA) |
| People's Liberation Army | Vietcong (or if appropriate, North Vietnamese Army — NVA) |
| Ruff-puff | Regional Forces Popular Forces (RF/PF) |
| Mercenary | Civilian Irregular Defense Group (CIDG) soldier or volunteer |
| VC tax collectors | VC extortionists |
| Search and destroy | Search and clear |
| Body count | Enemy deaths or EN killed |
| U.S. troop withdrawal | Redeployment (or replacement) |
| Hamburger Hill | Hill 937 |
| Troops used to bait the enemy | Never to be used |
| Deserter or defector (VC) | Rallier or returnee |
| Free-fire zone | Pre-cleared firing area |
| Ambushed | Engaged the enemy on all sides |
| Booby trap | Automatic ambush |
| "Hearts and minds of the people" | "Develop community spirit" or equivalent descriptive phrases |
| Vietnamization | Favorable term for the process of turning over our efforts to the Vietnamese people |
| Five o'clock follies | MACV daily briefings (or daily press briefings) |

From MACV's perspective, control over war language helped their requests for additional resources. Deep criticism was impossible if one accepted the military's language. For example, how could the "Mere Gook Rule" exist if the word "gook" was proscribed? Philosopher Ludwig Wittgenstein's famous aphorism, "The limits of my language mean the limits of my world," shows its merits here.[92] Military language made ground war disappear from official reports and news media coverage reliant upon the military.

However, not all war-manager doublethink achieved its goal. For many soldiers, language manipulation fostered disenchantment. For Bunting's character, Colonel Robinson, bogus euphemisms created one more erosion of meaning in his world. The switch from one term to another — mere paperwork for war-managers — falsified the reality for those whom war was a real risk, and at times made their lives more dangerous.

Take the question of "combat strength," the ratio of combat to logistical personnel. Officially, military tables of organization call for 32,000 command and logistical workers to support one combat division of 16,000 men. Westmoreland's 1968 *Report of the War in Vietnam* claimed great advancement in decreasing this customary ratio of support to combat personnel:

> The level and responsiveness of logistical support in Vietnam is a tribute to the dedication, imagination, and initiative of our logisticians at all echelons. Even more remarkable is the fact that, as the quality and quantity of support increased, the proportionate strength of our support elements declined. By constantly analyzing requirements and capabilities, consolidating functions, and refining procedures, the support ratio was reduced from about 45 percent in 1966 to about 40 percent in 1967.[93]

In his autobiography the general repeats himself, adding that "When compared with the 43 percent ratio experienced in World War II and Korea, this decline represented a remarkable achievement."[94] The Vietnam numbers are highly dubious. Most observers say at most only *one of ten* men in Vietnam was a combat trooper. Instead, Westmoreland's figures were generated by playing with definitions concerning who was "serving in a combat role." Lieutenant Colonel Anthony Herbert studied "field strength" of the 173rd Airborne Brigade. The 173rd had additional logistical units attached to it. Herbert's study refers to the organic unit.

> The 173rd was the largest brigade in Vietnam, with over 10,000 men attached to it. It was, according to the manual, a combat brigade with absolutely no dead weight. But it was a humbug. There were five so-called battalions in the Brigade, and not one of them had more than 600 physically present for duty. Out of a total of 10,000 men,

then, there were no more than 3,000 at battalion level, which means that some 7,000 people were assigned to support roles: steakhouses, pizza huts, clubs, headquarters, the General's mess, artillery, engineers, etc. Even among the approximately 3,000 at combat level, not all were out looking with their rifles. Some were, of course, but the battalions had their "rear areas" just like the Brigade, with their own steakhouses, their own clubs. Each battalion was composed of five companies, one of them a makeshift outfit responsible for heavy weapons — which left four companies for walking. No company in any battalion in the Brigade had more than seventy-five men physically present ready to go. Thus, each battalion fielded about 300 combat troopers, except that each battalion assigned one company to guard its base of operations each day. That left a maximum of 225 men available for the field, or 1,125 on a Brigade basis. And that would have been on a good day with everybody out and everybody with a rifle — but everybody didn't carry a rifle. Some toted radios, some stayed back and typed, some worked in company supply, some were "fireflies," the daily helicopter resupply lifts, and some just plain screwed off. So an average day, the 173rd Airborne Brigade could field approximately 800 men — if all its battalions were out. In the year I was in the Brigade, all its battalions were never out.

Assuming four out of five battalions went out on an average day, then the unit fielded roughly 600 men out of 10,000. The 173rd ran at 6 percent combat troop, and 94 percent support troop, not far from the common 10 percent estimate, but far from Westmoreland's figures. Westmoreland's definition is more inclusive than Herbert's focus on combat infantry, but still the discrepancy is considerable. Herbert says that the 173rd Brigade commanders were under pressure from MACV to report a high proportion of its men assigned to combat roles, or "field strength." Internal brigade regulations called for no less than 98 percent of all men to be assigned to combat roles.

How was this tremendous discrepancy overcome? According to Herbert, brigade commanders created a new category of combat roles, called "reaction force." The reaction force on paper was an internal reserve, meaning that if any battalion of the 173rd needed immediate reinforcement either to pursue an advantageous contact with the enemy or to help overcome a highly threatening enemy attack, then the "reaction force" could be deployed. Brigade commanders placed all men whose official job descriptions were not declared "noncombat" in the reaction force.

However, no one was actually ready for immediate deployment. As Herbert said, "I've filled in those reports [for reaction force] myself and they truly look magnificent. All the guys at the steakhouse: In the Field; all the guys at the clubs: In the Field; the life guards at the Esther Williams pool: In the Field." Herbert said that even though he knew how doublethink falsification was being conducted, the semblance of rationality and the repetitiveness of official forms were difficult to shake off: "It was so *mesmerizing* that when I later took over a battalion myself, I had to add another column to my reporting procedure just to keep things straight." Lieutenant Colonel Herbert called his new column of debit and credit "Ass in the Grass," and it did not appear in official MACV reports.[95]

Twofold dangers fell upon ground troops from such command falsifications. Reserve combat troops are crucial units. Reserve troops can either make an offensive breakthrough in a battle going well for a commander or prevent disaster in a battle approaching an enemy breakthrough. To create an imaginary reserve force and convince oneself that such a force really exists is extremely dangerous. Herbert does not say whether the illusion actually caused deaths in the 173rd, but the principle of creating false reserves was probably widespread; it made complete sense from a war-manager perspective.

Second, treating understrength combat units as if they actually were functioning at full strength resulted in commanders overestimating their actual strength. Herbert indicated that of the 600 men in each battalion, at most 225 were ready for combat on an average day. Even using command figures for field strength, Department of Defense systems analyst Thomas Thayer calculated that the dispersion of U.S. forces into either logistical troops or combat troops guarding fixed facilities meant that U.S. combat forces were outnumbered by a ratio of 1.4 to 1.[96] This figure was created by accepting MACV's order of battle for VC/NVA forces. If the CIA's order of battle is accepted, and Herbert's estimation of actual combat strength is accepted as indicative of U.S. ground forces, then the conclusion is that the army and marines often fought battles in which they were highly outnumbered. This conclusion is reinforced both by military statistics showing that most engagements were initiated by the enemy and that Mao Tse-tung and Vo Nugyen Giap explicitly called for "concentration of forces" when attacking. Command doublethink thus fed directly into strategy practiced by the foreign Other.

And soldiers consequently suffered. Normal expectations were reversed. Walking into ambushes did not meet expectations of a technologically superior U.S. force obtaining the military offensive. Nor did the willingness of higher command to treat subordinates as low-cost or no-cost expendables conform to expectations of minimal respect. Double-reality or unreality permeated ground troops' experience in multiple ways.

United States forces repeatedly encountered Vietcong and People's Army of Vietnam soldiers equipped with U.S. munitions. Corruption in the government of South Vietnam will be examined thoroughly in the next two chapters. Here it is sufficient to point out that the U.S. practice of treating the GVN as a sovereign nation allowed corruption to flourish. Ground troops became enraged when they realized that their foe was also equipped by the United States. John Muir of the 1st Marine Division in 1966 described what happened in one instance when ARVN began fighting each other over South Vietnamese politics:

> Before the ARVNs abandoned the encampment at Henderson Trail, we had given them 36,000 Bouncing Betty mines. When they came back there were 36,000 60-millimeter Bouncing Betty mines missing. The VC just came right in and picked them up, and we had to go out and find them one at a time. Meaning, BOOM. . . .
>
> They were trip mines. All you had to do was bury them and pull the pin. You could rig them sixteen different ways. Step on them and they usually go off waist-high. It's a 60-millimeter mortar round, called a daisy cutter, with a super-fast fuse, designed to go off in a flat disc explosion. Bouncing Betty. . . . It's supposed to cut you in half, groin level. It's a psychological thing. Everybody would hit them. They were up in trees, they were all over. The VC had a picnic, just like decorating a Christmas tree. Yeah. Goody time.[97]

Other times war matériel was stolen by ARVN commanders and sold on the black market. Jonathan Polansky, a scout for the 101st Airborne, was amazed at what he found in a tunnel complex on the Laotian border:

> We went into one cavern. The tunnel alone was big enough for trucks to go through underground. Thousands of rooms full of American equipment — boots, fatigues, cots, ponchos, helmets. They seemed to have more of our supplies than we had back at Camp Eagle. We called B-52s on the whole complex. It was right on the Laotian border. It seemed to be a final waylay station of pulling a unit down to the South. Most of the equipment probably came from the black mar-

ket and pilfering from the bases. All new equipment. Better stuff than we had.[98]

If the Vietcong didn't have enough money to buy something they wanted, U.S. war-managers and corrupt ARVN officers provided them with a way to accumulate savings. Part of the "Chieu Hoi" surrender program for Vietcong defectors included paying cash for war equipment.[99] A grenade was worth thirty dollars. Grenades kept showing up at the local Chieu Hoi center, but there was no way Lieutenant Colonel Anthony Herbert could be certain from where they came, since he had given case after case to a local ARVN commander. Finally, Herbert and an assistant painted grenade fuses before giving them to ARVN. Marked and distributed on Monday, most returned by Friday: "So we gave the grenades to Nim, he gave them to his troops, they divvied them up among relatives and friends, and what didn't continue on to the VC their kids brought back to us for $30 apiece. John Q. Citizen had bought them twice."[100] Some U.S. troops paid more heavily. Many of the casualties of mines and booby traps were hit by American-made munitions.

Rarely, though, does one encounter stories of U.S. soldiers being shot by Vietcong using M-16 rifles. Part of the explanation can be attributed to the North Vietnamese effort to supply both Vietcong and PAVN soldiers with the 7.62mm by 39mm (cartridge case) AK-47 assault rifle. Having troops using the same weapon made resupply easier and in combat having all troops using a weapon different from the enemy meant easier distinction of "friend" from "foe." M-16 rifles were also not popular with the Vietcong because they routinely jammed, often causing death to the user. In Robert Roth's novel, *Sand in the Wind*, a soldier warns a new replacement about the M-16:

"How many [rifle] magazines do you have?"

"Eight, that's all they issued me."

"You'll need at least twenty. Most of the guys carry twenty-five. You can get some more when somebody gets medivacked or goes to the rear. They take twenty rounds; but if you don't want your rifle to jam, just put in eighteen. We're one of the first battalions to get M-16's and they jam a lot easier than 14's. Don't *ever* let me catch you with a dirty rifle. Clean it every chance you get. The last time Golf Company hit the shit, we had to recover the bodies. I saw three guys with bullets in their heads and their M-16's lying next to them, half taken apart. When them rice-propelled motherfuckers come at you and your rifle jams, you ain't gonna have time to take it apart and clean it. . . ."[101]

Lots of men never had the time. Shell casings overexpanded when fired and did not eject to clear the chamber for the next round. Marine Tim Holmes said:

> One of our dudes got hurt. His rifle fired a round and then it didn't eject it. The shell expanded and then it pushed another one right in there and it blew up. He was all bloody; that was our first casualty. You see, M-16's jam a lot. You're firing maybe two magazines real fast so it's hot as hell. Then you shove another one in and you fire some more. You stop, but you don't pull the bolt back so the M-16 doesn't eject the cartridge. That happened to me twice and I got a new rifle.[102]

W. D. Ehrhart and his fellow marines also had problems. Ehrhart recalled, "Wally said Row's sixteen jammed on him; he was tryin' to bang the casing out with a cleaning rod when he got it."[103] Later on Wally's M-16 jammed: " 'Look at this fuckin' piece of shit.' " According to Ehrhart, "He had his M-16 broken at the breach. A shell casing minus the rear end was stuck in the chamber, and another round had been driven on top of it."[104] Some soldiers wrote their congressmen and senators. One said, "We left with 250 men in our company and came back with 107. Practically every one of our dead was found with his rifle torn down next to him."[105] Another reported that out of fifty rounds he had fourteen malfunctions. One marine wrote to Senator Gaylord Nelson questioning who was responsible:

> The weapon has failed us at crucial moments when we needed fire power most. In each case, it left Marines naked against their enemy. Often, and this is no exaggeration, we take counts after each fight, as many as 50% of the rifles fail to work. I know of at least two Marines who died within 10 feet of the enemy with jammed rifles. No telling how many have been wounded on that account and it is difficult to count the NVA who should be dead but live because the M-16 failed. Of course, the political ramifications of this border on national scandal. I suppose that is why the Commandant and all the bigwigs are anxious to tell all that it is a wonderful weapon.[106]

It took a special congressional subcommittee of the Armed Services Committee to investigate what was wrong with the M-16 and why U.S.

ground forces had been issued weapons that did not work. Army and marine officials insisted that the M-16 was fine, but that troops did not clean it properly. High-ranking officers involved in testing, approving, and lobbying for the M-16 thereby retained umblemished records.

Committee investigators found several important army-mandated changes creating the M-16 from the original AR-15 test rifle. The number of grooves in the barrel was changed so that the rifle would fire a bullet following a stable trajectory in weather colder than 65 degrees below zero — a bizarre requirement. Army officials also required that the bolt mechanism be changed to permit manual chambering of a cartridge. While this addition sounds highly reasonable given the subsequent history of jamming, air force and marine ordnance specialists who had tested the AR-15 for three years thought that the additional mechanical complexity contributed to breakdowns.

But these changes were responsible for only some M-16 malfunctions. More important, the army changed gunpowders used in the 5.56mm ammunition. This change in gunpowder made the M-16 fire at a much faster rate in full-automatic usage than the weapon's design and preferred ammunition had intended. Increased stress from faster cyclic rate helped produce more jams than the original AR-15 design and ammunition. Second, army-mandated ammunition did not burn completely upon firing; it consequently left much powder residue in the firing chamber. By firing more rapidly than designed and leaving more powder residue than tolerated by design, the AR-15 transformation into the M-16 failed. Congressman Richard Ichord's committee discovered that the army knowingly let Colt Firearms (who held the license to manufacture the M-16) test weapons and pass army design criteria using ammunition specified by designer George Stoner rather than ammunition the army procured for use in Vietnam:

> Undoubtedly, many thousands of these were shipped or carried to Vietnam, *with the Army on notice that the rifles failed to meet design and performance specifications and might experience excessive malfunctions when firing ammunition loaded with ball propellant* [emphasis in original]. . . . The rifle project manager, the administrative contracting officer, the members of the Technical Coordinating Committee, and others as high in authority as the Assistant Secretary of Defense for Installations and Logistics knowingly accepted M-16 rifles that would not pass the approved acceptance test. . . . Colt was allowed to test using only IMR propellant at a time when the vast

majority of ammunition in the field, including Vietnam, was loaded with ball propellant. The failure on the part of officials with authority in the Army to cause action to be taken to correct the deficiencies of the 5.56mm ammunition borders on criminal negligence.[107]

"Borders on criminal negligence" comprises a harsh indictment by congressional committee standards, but it remained an empty accusation. The ball powder was slightly modified, but no switch to the designer-intended gunpowder occurred. Olin-Mathieson produced ball powder while Du Pont made the intended IMR powder. Journalist James Fallows pointed to corporate interests at stake in military contracts, but found no conclusive evidence of "fixing." Army officials also initiated an M-16 modification program (M-16A) that lined the firing chamber with chromium to reduce powder residue fouling. But no war-manager suffered, while several hundred to several thousand U.S. and later (from 1968 on) ARVN troops were killed or wounded because of jammed weapons. No soldier expected his country to arm him with highly defective weapons and cover up those who were responsible. Fighting a war with defective weapons when soldiers knew that the United States was the richest nation in the world was part of the "unreality" of Vietnam. Soldiers called the M-16s "Mattels," after plastic toy guns produced by the Mattel Corporation in the 1950s and 1960s. It was one way of making a joke out of a grim situation. "If it's Mattel, it's swell," went the old TV ads.

According to U.S. Army doctrine, ground troops were deployed as the "reconnaissance force" to contact the enemy. Once the battle began, then air strikes, artillery, and tanks could be called in to produce high enemy body counts. Oftentimes commanders so desperately wanted body counts that they were not concerned if their own troops were in the way. Psychologist Shad Meshad tells of a Long Range Reconnaissance Patrol soldier who no longer trusted his superiors: "With all these fears growing in him, for good reason, he had recently been put over the edge by the way his buddy had gotten wasted. He had been on a team that was setting up a B-52 strike. His buddy was on the Recon team that called in the strike. A pick-up to bring them out had never been arranged. The whole team was wiped out by this 'friendly fire' or friendly bomber." [108]

A marine medic found he was treating casualties caused by U.S. officers: "Our own officers sent tanks over our own wounded. I mean, the brass would kill our own people, as well as kill the others. Misdirected artillery, tanks moving in destroy a bunker and it would run over our own wounded without regard or not they were laying there, and it really got to the point of the ridiculous all the time. Things like this were always happening." [109]

Men became upset when these things happened, but superior officers did not think "friendly fire" warranted concern; it was to be expected and faced as part of a soldier's duty:

> I was working as a radio operator. We had this officer plot the map wrong. We were a landing zone. And you send your patrols out looking, like search and destroy missions. He moved them from checkpoint three, and he plotted the map wrong. And then an observer got on our freq and asked us where our men were. The lieutenant called in and told them where he had the map plotted. So he called back to Danang and got an air strike.
>
> They dropped napalm that killed the whole platoon. Eighteen guys. I felt like I was responsible. I felt bad because they were my friends.
>
> A quota came in for in-country R and R. I was supposed to stay two days and I stayed twenty-seven. I went AWOL. I had to. My head was really out of place. But they didn't think so. They gave me battalion office hours [administrative punishment]. Busted me [reduced rank].
>
> I should've never went AWOL, they said. They said, I "should've took it like a marine." The same exact words. I can remember, "Should've took it like a marine." [110]

"Should've took it like a marine" refers to a sexual identity fostered by the Marine Corps, namely, that a man should attend to his duty as defined by his superior officers; fidelity to hierarchy supposedly honors the dead far more than removing oneself from the war and questioning that hierarchy. But this phrase absolves the officer corps from responsibility.

Stories of bombs falling on U.S. troops because of incorrect coordinates occur frequently enough to point to a major flaw in teaching officers how to determine their location and read maps. Shad Meshad found fighter pilots in his area to be a distant and seemingly deranged group of people. Eventually barriers came down and an F-4 phantom fighter-bomber pilot explained their wild behavior: " 'We can't get good coordinates in this fucking mess,' he told me, 'so we keep cooking our own men. Every time I give support fire I just pray they're not gonna tell me I hit the forward observer.' ''[111]

Stories from soldiers just pour out; there are so many stories of Americans accidentally killing Americans. Oral history archivist Clark Smith found Steve Hassna, of the 101st Airborne, an insightful informant on this subject:

> I was blown up three different times by artillery and all three times it was American. One time we were at the bottom of a hill, getting ready to assault up the hill to take pressure off a company of the 2nd/five-o deuce. They were getting pretty badly mauled on top of this hill. A 105 battery started firing for effect. So the support artillery that was supposed to come in and help soften the area for us, hit us. These artillery people were 1,000 meters off their map sheet. There are four guns in an artillery battery. They have a fan-shaped area or gun sheath that they fire into. They can fire say, 90 degrees to 120 degrees. The gun sheaths are overlapping. The sheath is plotted on a map sheet. The artillery people were outside their gun sheath and totally off their map sheet. I was standing in the middle of a creek bed looking up in the air. The artillery round hit the water I was standing in. They dropped four rounds right on top of us. The rounds just walked right down the line of men in my company and wounded three people. We thought the Vietnamese were attacking, so we just opened a main frequency and started yelling, "Check fire, we have wounded. Who's firing on us? What's going on?" That's when we found out the rounds were our own support. So we had to pull back into a night position to extract the wounded. This meant that we did not assault the hill we were supposed to, and, consequently, the infantry on top of the hill sustained 33 dead and 65 wounded over and above what they had before we came to try and relieve them. So the whole battle was a fiasco. And I don't think the American people were ever informed about the fact that we were killing our own people. This kind of thing happened over and over. Often you didn't know who was shooting at you or for what reason. It was just totally insane.[112]

And finally there were the close-up killings, not a matter of distant jet fighter-bombers or artillery batteries, but infantrymen firing upon infantrymen. Lieutenant Colonel Herbert said that a lieutenant once took a patrol out for a night ambush. The lieutenant set up the ambush and then walked in front. While in radio contact his men reported that they heard noises and requested permission to open fire. He granted permission and was immediately killed — he had given the order to fire on himself! Herbert said: "If ever a legitimate study is made of that war, most Americans will be stunned to learn that we killed a hell of a lot of our own people, once again a failure directly traceable to poor leadership. All it took was the sound of a booby trap or the sighting of movement and we were prone to open up, to fire into the jungle and brush in every direction. We did it over and over again—to ourselves."[113]

Much war culture reflects upon the "unreality" of Vietnam, the sense in which nothing seemed to meet preconceived concepts of rationality. Soldiers always spoke of what they were going to do when their one-year tours of duty were up and they returned to "the world." Vietnam by implication was "unworld," another place. Two common names for Vietnam were "Brown Disneyland" and "Six Flags Over Nothing"; the country was like a playground or amusement park where social rules had been suspended, but the fun was gone. Journalist Donald Kirk found poems written on latrine walls questioning how far things would go:

> Kill one, they call you a murderer
> Kill thousands, and they'll call you a conqueror
> Kill them all, and they won't call you anything!

> We the UN known
> Do the UN Godly
> For the UN Grateful!

> I been going
> Downhill every [sic]
> Since I been in
> This Lost World
> But I haven't gotten
> To the bottom yet.[114]

Even when things went "right," at the same time they went "wrong." While body counts signified productivity on war-manager charts, fighting for abstract numbers left no sense of accomplishment. Steve Hassna bitterly recalled what it felt like to give up ground occupied after taking heavy casualties:

> We never held anything. We would lose thirty people to take a hill
> and then walk right off the damn thing and go to another hill and lose

another thirty people and walk off that hill. And we would go from one hilltop to the next all over that country — over and over again. There was only a couple of times that we could claim that we had an infantry victory over forces we were fighting — in the sense that we overran a base camp that they were in and kicked their ass.[115]

War practices and rules did not make "sense." One helicopter door gunner recalled that toward the end of the war, his chopper was delivering machine-gun and rocket fire to an infantry company that had been ambushed and surrounded. Nearly thirty helicopters and several navy jets flew in to give assistance. A one-star general commanded relief efforts. He wanted to orchestrate all air cover before six P.M., the time a cease-fire had been arranged by negotiators at the Paris Peace Conference. The door gunner listened to what messages were transmitted by the surrounded ground troops: "Everybody is talking, including some poor bastard on the ground, who is saying, 'Save our ass, please.' There's another radio operator down there who has managed to get his ass shot. He's laying next to an open mike, moaning and begging for help. Mostly it's that one word over and over again, 'Help, help.' "[116] But six o'clock came and all the helicopters and jets went home and the ground troops were left to die. The door gunner took his machine gun off its cable suspension, threw it on the floor, switched off his radio communications, and "just sat there in the silence." But later he became even more upset upon hearing the reaction of other crew members. Somebody asked, "Hey, what's wrong? Why are you acting this way?"

Their reaction made me start to realize things were not right. Later that night the crew chief, a good buddy of mine, came over and said, "What have you been doing?"

"What do you mean?"

"You're acting really weird. The pilots asked me to talk to you. You on any drugs?"

"What do you mean? You were just there. Didn't you hear? Are you deaf? Don't you realize what just took place? We left those guys to die. Because of a six o'clock truce which nobody gives a rat's ass about, except maybe in Paris where they're sitting around arguing about the size of the table. You're asking me if I'm stoned out on something? You think I'm weird? How weird are you?"

"Hey, okay, sorry we asked. Take it easy. Never mind. You're not on drugs. All right, we'll leave you alone."

They thought I was skulled out on something. That was the only logical explanation they could come up with. I saw that things weren't right. Maybe this wasn't Sgt. Rock [a comic book war hero] after all. I still liked flying and I liked being a door gunner, but from that point on, I felt something was really wrong here. I couldn't pick it out. It was just strange.[117]

This soldier's bewilderment was shared by many. Eventually a phrase evolved expressing distance from the war. "There it is," was the phrase, an indexical comment both pointing out some war event and questioning it. One lieutenant explained what the term meant to his troops: "You get an attitude. They can kill you, but they can't eat you. Don't sweat the small stuff. My men used to say, *'There it is.* There it fucking is, Lieutenant.' Like, what are you going to tell me, what are you going to show me? What is it in the scheme of things that is going to give me any more insight on this whole situation? You ain't showing me shit. Dead is dead. That's it. That transcends day to day living."[118]

At least one GI expression explicitly acknowledged how the structure of rules was at variance from their expectations. The phrase was "Good for you" and it was used in the doublethink way of acknowledging that an activity was wrong but that saying the phrase transformed into a positive deed. One commentator on the usage and meaning of "Good for you" begins by telling about his first search-and-destroy operation.

Now, I was behind the radio operator and as we moved into the vill nobody said anything but all of a sudden these guys started shooting. They were shooting women and kids. Now there weren't any men there. But these men were just shooting. They didn't say anything, and I was — I was in a state of shock almost. . . .

They killed these ten people, you know, about approximately ten people. Like I was — it was so traumatic, you know, I couldn't believe it. I was like in a state of shock and these guys did this so systematically like it was something done so many times before, it was easy. It didn't bother them, at least it didn't appear to bother any of them.

You know the crime has been done and it is condoned, or it is covered up, and you get the impression that if this was not right, that someone would make an attempt to stop it, and since no one makes an attempt to stop it, this is the way it is supposed to be. *"Good for you"*: that was the common expression. Here you can go ahead and shoot them for nothing. As a matter of fact, it's even smiled upon.

*Good for you.* Everything is backwards. That's part of the unreality of the thing.[119]

Technowar's creation of a double-reality presented soldiers with the opportunity of unrestricted behavior. In this world without rules some found pleasure: "The people in our unit would come with knives and cut off the ears of the dead enemy and put them in alcohol jars and keep them in their hootches, and the guy with the most ears was the guy that was looked up on the most. . . . Another thing, the fingers are pretty popular too, cutting off fingers and putting those in alcohol jars."[120]

Other units where collecting was practiced sometimes put their trophies on strings: "The guys would carry ears on strings. In the hootches they had them hanging from the ceiling. In the infantry units the hootches that were quarters for twelve might have ten strings. They were very proud of how many ears they could rack up."[121] And at least one soldier carried his body parts in a sack. "And he would say things like 'I got me another one. I got me another little slant-eye.' . . . He sat beside me on my bed. Next thing I know, he opens up the bag and three or four heads fall out on the bed — they were cut off at the neck."[122] The pleasure of killing also had extrinsic rewards: "It was in the First [Infantry] Division, and if you killed a certain number of enemy you got a three-day pass, but you had to bring back the ears. He would bring back the heads. . . . They kept giving him medals."[123]

Raping women provided another means for some soldiers to demonstrate their power over Vietnamese.

> Once in a while if we were out on a long patrol, and we hadn't seen a girl for a long time, maybe four or five of us would go into a village and take a girl and bring her out to the jungle. . . . Explain to her to lie on the ground and don't scream, otherwise she'll be killed immediately, and however many guys there are — well, they all do what they want. And if the guys are in a good mood they let her go. If not they kill her.[124]

Once raped, a woman could be destroyed many ways. Shooting was the quickest; other methods took longer and inflicted much more pain:

> The girls were unconscious at that point [after repeated rapes]. When they finished raping them three of the GIs took hand flares and shoved them in the girls' vaginas. . . . No one had to hold them down any longer. The girls were bleeding from their mouths, noses, faces, and vaginas. Then they struck the exterior portion of the flares and they

exploded inside the girls. Their stomachs started bloating up and then they exploded. The stomachs exploded and their intestines were just hanging out of their bodies.[125]

Other women were burned to death: "One day I was driving a back road and a guy comes over and says he needs some gas; didn't say why. . . . The girl is stripped and she's tied to two wooden stakes. I don't know what they had done to her before I got there. They pour gasoline all over the girl and light it. . . . And they just stand there and watch her burn up."[126]

Units that routinely engaged in murder, rape, and mutilation made sure that no soldier would press charges and make senior commanders investigate matters they would rather ignore. Fear of being killed by one's fellow soldiers was another part of the unreality. The soldier who spoke about ear collections said that those who chose not to participate "knew that if they protested about the ear collections that they might get shot in the back next time they went out on a patrol, so there were no complaints."[127] The soldier who explained the meaning of "Good for you" said that his unit wanted his commitment written in blood:

> My squad leader, well, he looked at me and he told me that there comes a time when people have to commit themselves or get involved and become one of them, and to become one of them he told me, "Well, this is a good time for you to try your canister rounds [giant shotgun shells for M-79 grenade launcher]."
>
> Well, I was scared for one thing and I was upset, I was in shock plus I was scared because the whole thing — well, he said, "This is a good time for you to try out your canister rounds."
>
> It was like — it seemed as though he was saying, "All right, the rest of us have committed ourselves. Now it's time for you to commit yourself and if you don't you are not one of us and if you are not one of us *you are one of them."*
>
> Well, I was actually scared for my life. Because this is not an unusual thing. I was really scared for my life. From my own people.[128]

Explicit and implicit threats against men often worked. However, threats did not keep men from thinking. Recognition that either other soldiers or themselves were being aroused by warfare often provided the shock necessary to break away from routine, unthinking participation. As the soldier who witnessed the gasoline burning of the woman said, "Then all my ideas about kill the enemy, patriotism, gung-ho, that all went down the drain."[129] A prisoner interrogator recalled the progress of arousal when questioning a captive: "It's so horrifying to recall an interrogation where you beat the fellow to get an effect, and then you beat him out of anger, and then you beat him out of pleasure."[130] One man began to recognize how dehumanization began while watching some soldiers torture rats:

> They set out cages, sometimes as many as seventy-five, and filled them with rodents. Then they'd mock the villagers with simulated Buddhist rituals and pour on gasoline and set the rodents afire. Everyone grinned while the rodents screamed. For the first time, I saw the connection. When harmless creatures have to be tortured in this way, it's easy to move over to takin' out on the human bein's.[131]

In other instances, soldiers became moved by encounters with Vietnamese that pointed out how far from humane conduct they had journeyed. Something happens that makes the foreign Other a real person, and seeing the Other as real changes one's self-perception. One of Dr. Charles Levy's informants recalled watching an old Vietnamese man die:

> It just fucks your head somehow like that same day when the mine went off an old man, he was about eighty years old, got hit in the head with a piece of shrapnel. A gook.
>
> When we came back after the mine sweep he was outside his hootch. And all his relatives and friends were sitting around and crying and shit.
>
> And we laughed.
>
> And human beings don't do things like that. But we stayed there and we fucking laughed until he died. So it turns you into some sort of fucking animal.[132]

Another soldier ran over a Vietnamese boy with his truck. He told his story to Eric Herter.

> He said they were encouraged to drive fast and scare people, to show them that the Marines were in charge. If they hit people, that was okay; it was all part of the game. *And he said that he didn't count the number of people he ran over with his truck.* But then he ran over a boy on a bicycle, maybe about 15 years old. Somehow the kid got tangled up in the wheels. Dennis got out of his truck and

walked around and looked at this kid who just stared back at him with an absolutely level stare. He didn't say anything, just stared at him, like, "Why did you do this to me?" and Dennis just walked away and wouldn't get back in his truck.[133]

For Dennis the war was over. He still had several months left, but his psychological involvement in projecting U.S. military power or personal power was gone. It was as if he had signed a separate peace treaty. Disengagement even hit men who truly liked what they were doing. Tim Holmes enjoyed his work as an interrogator with the 13th Interrogation Translation Team of the 1st Marine Division in 1969. He extended his tour to twenty months so that he could *"make money"* for the marines: "Getting reliable info is called *'making money.'* "[134] Holmes said his interrogations routinely involved hitting people: "Interrogation in the broadest sense of slapping happened 90% of the time. The said slappee ended up slap-happy. My job is to make them very aware that I am in the position of superiority, that I hold their fate in my hands, which I did."[135] Holmes said that "making money" involved being "really methodical by going over every little thing" during interrogations. With correct information, enemy positions could be determined and air strikes summoned. A solid hit meant that the interrogator had made money. The bigger the target, the bigger the war-production apparatus put into motion, the more money got made: "If it's a big unit, they'll use B-52's. *And getting a B-52 strike is making the most money.*"[136] Holmes said he was highly productive up until the day he interrogated one Vietnamese woman:

Towards the end of my time in Vietnam a girl was brought in who was about 16 or 17 years old. She lived in a village that was a free fire zone. Some of her people living out there wouldn't move. I started interrogating her. I was slapping her around the hootch and beating her and she shit in her pants. She was very embarrassed about shitting in her pants. She was trying to wipe it up and she's trying to use the bottom of her pants. And I stopped. I said, "Where's your father?" "He's dead." "How was he dead?" "Killed by artillery." You hear this a million times. Always someone's killed by artillery. And so the next question, "Whose artillery?" And they look at you: "American," of course. I heard it a million times. Well, it just so happened that this time it just hit me, dong, American! Why are we killing all these people? These people aren't soldiers. I'm beating on this girl and it all hit me. I'm beating up this girl, for what? What the fuck am I doing? I just felt like a shit. It was as if for the first time I was looking at myself. Here's this guy, slapping, beating on this girl, for what?[137]

He never found a satisfactory reason; Technowar's magic spell was gone and the Vietnamese were real people: "I wasn't a very good interrogator from that time on. I lost all motivation."[138] Instead, he became more interested in Vietnamese culture. He tried to make friends with men and women he interrogated, but found they were not interested. So instead he translated Vietnamese poetry from captured soldiers' diaries:

> And on the human side, the VC and NVA all wrote poetry. Of course all Vietnamese write poetry. Every soldier has a goddam poetry book; it's just a little notebook. And they're so goddam mushy, sentimental, really fine. They're all writing about how far away from home they are and wishing they could see their moon rather than this strange moon and they miss the flowers of their home. I remember one, "Oh Da Nang, I am in love with you." It was like Da Nang is a woman and they're gazing from the mountain at the lights of Da Nang and wishing they could be coupled together. It was really fine. I really dug it.[139]

Holmes spoke Vietnamese and had a noncombat job. His position was such that he had the ability to distance himself psychologically from the war and still stay alive. Ground troops did not have this option; for them the decision to make a separate, private peace treaty meant that their actions in the field had to change. "Search-and-avoid" was one common coping mechanism for troops no longer interested in fighting. As the name implies, it involved acting in such a way as to make contact with enemy forces unlikely. Journalist Donald Kirk went on one search-and-avoid mission: "Still, since someone must go on patrol down there, two or three GIs absentmindedly pick up M-79 grenade launchers and squeeze off a few rounds. 'If anyone's there, it'll scare 'em away,' one of them remarks."[140] Faking night patrols was another method of search-and-avoid. Men would go outside the camp perimeter a few hundred yards and spend the night rather than going on patrol.

> So we sat and talked, and Kam says, "Man, look, we ain't going out there. Them mother-fuckers will catch us out there, man. Listen, here's what we are going to do." So the four men they'd get the radio and take it inside this little hootch that we'd built. And the radio man he'd get inside the hootch and the four men with him. And we'd wait

in that hootch all night, smoke, talk, do anything we wanted. But about every hour or so the radio man would say, "Ssshh." [141]

Silence was necessary for fake radio reports back to company headquarters; no one would be talking on a real combat mission. Beyond search-and-avoid as a way of getting out came self-inflicted wounds. Robert Sanders talked about anger and frustration in the 173rd Airborne in 1968 and 1969:

> We talked about it everyday. All the guys felt the same way. We just weren't accomplishing anything. In fact, some guys were so depressed and disgusted that they was killing themselves. Some guys were taking hand grenades and blowing themselves away. They couldn't stand the strain anymore. It was really heavy. I don't think a lot of this stuff was reported. Guys would just kill themselves, and the army would probably send the stats home that the guy was killed or missing in action. [142]

Note his speculation that the doublethink system functioned to cover up self-inflicted wounds. There are certainly many stories and testimonies indicating that heavy casualties were produced by desperate men. One medic reported that eleven men in his platoon shot themselves. Robert Rawles, of the 1st Air Cavalry Division, said search-and-destroy turned inward after "we got fire fights after fire fights."

> Thinking back on the training, all they told us to do was kill. "KILL! KILL!" "What is the spirit of the bayonet?" "TO KILL!" It was just a bummed-out trip. And I just didn't go for it, you know. I can remember this one instance where this guy, he was so depressed, he was walking in the boonies and he said, "I'm going home today." I said, "How you going to do it?" "I'm going home today, man. I can't hardly think no more, all this killing and stuff." So he was walking. The next thing I knew, I heard a gunshot. Boom. Pow. He had shot himself through the ankle, through the foot. He said, "I finally made it home." And I thought about doing that to get back home. [143]

A lieutenant described how his platoon disintegrated through self-inflicted wounds.

> Other than that, outward reactions among my men were invisible. To outsiders, they were mostly phlegmatic, stupid-looking even; deep down, it was quite another thing. Finally, things got too much for

some of the guys; several tried deliberately to get wounded. I saw one man casually stand up in a fire fight and get it through the head. Another stood up, too, and only got it in the leg and arm. He was sent to a hospital in Japan and everybody thought he was the luckiest guy in the world because he was safe and free again.

Other men tried to get malaria. They would refuse to take their pills. One of my sergeants slept with his arm outside his poncho. He got the bug and was hospitalized for three months. He was then returned to our outfit but his malaria re-occurred, and finally he was sent to a safe job.[144]

The lieutenant said that he kept asking himself, "What am I doing here?" and felt guilty sending his men on mine-clearing and other extremely hazardous missions that were sure to result in their dying. Noticing that higher commanders were rarely present during operations, he said he mostly "just felt abandoned." Men wanted out from being "wasted" on search-and-destroy missions. Sometimes men who could not bring themselves to shoot or otherwise wound themselves had their friends perform the honors. In Robert Roth's novel, *Sand in the Wind*, Valdez, knowing that the next day he has to return to the Arizona, a free-fire zone, says to his friends: "I want you to tell my brother to stay home and take care of my parents, not to join the Crotch. . . . I'm not coming back from the Arizona. Ain't no way I can make it." Valdez only has two more weeks left before returning to the United States. But premonitions have great significance. As another character, Forsythe, said, "C'mon man, you know what the story is: If you think you're gonna get it, you will."[145] Believing this, Valdez's buddies persuade him to let them break his finger so he won't have to go into the Arizona. It is a difficult struggle involving several failed attempts but finally:

Valdez leaned forward on his hands to get up and leave. The sound of the hammer's dull thud was followed by an anguished but muffled scream. While Valdez writhed on his back in pain, he was somehow able to kick Childs in the crotch. Now there were two moaning figures on the ground, and three hysterical ones above them. Chalice came running out of the bunker, nervously asking what was going on. No one had the ability nor desire to tell him, and the only words spoken were those of Valdez. "Childs, you motherfucker, you crippled me. . . . I'll kill you. My hand is *destroyed*. . . . Oh, *God* it hurts. . . .

Thanks, Childs. Thanks. . . . I should kill you. *God* it hurts. . . . Thanks, man. Thanks." [146]

Valdez now has an injury serious enough to send a soldier home, but not to cripple him permanently. Short of such immobilizing wounds, soldiers had to be wounded *three times* before they were allowed to go home. A man wounded once or twice was rehabilitated and then sent back to battle. Childs had already been wounded twice when he decided the war was over for him. With three weeks left, he has a friend use a can-opener on his arm: "Hamilton ripped the C-ration opener from Childs's dog tag chain and gashed his arm, at the same time yelling, 'Corpsman, up! Corpsman, up!' " [147]

Soldiers would not report their own attempts to get out of the war. Instead, self-inflicted casualties show up in the official categories of wounded in action, accident, or other legitimate casualty classifications. Those listed as wounded in action would even get Purple Heart medals.

Not all disgruntled soldiers were willing to mutilate themselves. Nor were they willing simply to hope that they would survive their tours of duty. Instead, a significant portion of the U.S. Army and Marine Corps began to attack their own officers and senior sergeants. Officers and sergeants who either risked men's lives needlessly for their own career advancement or who abused the privileges of higher rank became targets. One marine in an artillery unit tells how his fellow soldiers became enraged when their new commander began a contest with another unit on who had the most beautiful camp. Troops spent much time arranging the appearance of their cannons. "That fucking fool made us build him a porch outside his tent. And he had an umbrella sent from the States. He would sit there and sip drinks and stuff and overlook his domain. While the fucking guys would be out there killing themselves." All of a sudden, this artillery unit began to suffer from "enemy" attacks at night:

That's when the shit started to hit the fan. We started having war calls which is like at midnight everybody in the outfit starts opening fire screaming "Gooks in the wire." In the barbed wire fences. And then you try to kill any of the lifers that you don't like.

So we tried to get the CO a couple of times with a machine gun. One time his rack took nine holes. His cot; nine bullet holes. He dove out of it and got away. Everybody would be shooting so he couldn't check weapons.

And they'd be throwing grenades at the wire and shit and yelling, "Gooks in the wire. Gooks." And they'd blow the siren and then run around. And then half the guys would be facing out where it's shooting. The other half of the guys would be waiting for a lifer to come out of the tent.[148]

Eventually someone rigged a booby trap to the captain's tent, but it blew the legs off the wrong man: "It was the executive officer, Captain J. Captain K was the one we wanted to get. He was a fucking asshole. But J, it was just as good to get J 'cause he sucked too. They both sucked."[149] Fragging stories often indicate that soldiers posted *reward money* for whoever killed or wounded the targeted officer or senior sergeant. James D. Nell said that he saw officers executed "five or six times" in 1968–1969. "Grunt will put a price on his head, one hundred, two hundred dollars on his head. The first one that kills him got that much money." Executions occurred "Next time he was out on a mission. Everybody would know it was going to happen. They would just wait until he was in the right position."[150] Getting an officer into position was often difficult. One soldier complained that after all his effort in trying to shoot his captain, his M-16 misfired:

Dear Congressman,
    I take pen in hand to complain about my piece. After months of assiduous care and maintenance of the weapon (M-16) it failed to function at a critical moment endangering my life and the lives of other men in this company. Last night, at 0300 hours [3 A.M.] I had a clear, unobstructed shot at the captain. To my chagrin, the weapon misfired. It may be weeks before I get another crack at the bastard and in the meantime I am subjected to the ridicule of my associates and can kiss good-bye the $2,000 in the company pool.
                                                One Mad G.I.[151]

Ten thousand dollars appears to be the highest reward offered. This reward was for the assassination of Major General Melvin Zais, commander of the 101st Airborne (Airmobile) Division, for ordering an attack on Hill 937 in May 1969. Hill 937 was known as Hamburger Hill by the troops, because the battle turned fifty-six of them into dead hamburger and 420 into wounded hamburger.[152] After reaching the top, troops destroyed enemy bunkers and were then ordered to leave. Enemy body count was reported as 505 back at command headquarters. Zais's tour of duty as division commander expired that same month; no one collected the reward.

Just how widespread assaults on American commanders were is of great interest. Beginning in 1969, the Pentagon began keeping statistics on confirmed fragging incidents.

War-managers reported that 80 percent of these attacks involved assaults on officers and noncommissioned officers; it was not a pattern of low-level enlisted men attacking one another. Over 500 confirmed assaults seems like a large figure, but in all probability the actual number of attacks upon commanders was much higher. Dr. Charles Levy found that Marine Criminal Investigating Department statistics showed over twenty fraggings within the 3rd Marine Division in the first eight months of 1969. Levy also found a "confidential message" from the commander of all marines in Vietnam that at least as many fraggings had occurred in the 1st Marine Division, the other marine unit in Technowar. Assuming that rate held for all U.S. units, then Levy estimates that over 500 attacks occurred in the first eight months of 1969, whereas the official figure is 96 for the entire year.[153] Levy's projection may not be completely valid, but widespread warfare between disgruntled soldiers and their commanders is noted in several sources. Lieutenant Colonel Anthony Herbert describes the casualties in his battalion of the 173rd Airborne before he took command in early 1969: "There had been two attempts on the previous commander's life. There had been quite a few fraggings in the battalion, of both officers and senior enlisted men. One man had both legs blown off; seven people had been wounded by a grenade, and a Claymore mine had been thrown right at the tactical-operations center — a mine to kill the staff, for Christ's sake."[154]

Table 6.3
FRAGGING INCIDENTS CONFIRMED BY PENTAGON

| Calendar Year | Number of Assaults | Deaths |
|---|---|---|
| 1969 | 96 | 39 |
| 1970 | 209 | 34 |
| 1971* | 215 | 12 |

*First 11 months
SOURCE: David Cortright, *Soldiers in Revolt: The American Military Today* (Garden City, N.Y.: Doubleday, 1975), p. 44.

Commanders had nothing to gain by reporting attacks against either themselves or other officers and noncommissioned officers in their units, since fraggings indicated failures in leadership. Many unit commanders probably wrote "wounded in action" or "killed in action" on reports of casualties they knew had been inflicted by their own troops. The Pentagon in turn tried to minimize those few reports they did receive by counting only grenade-caused casualties, literal "fraggings," rather than including attacks on superiors by all means, including the use of rifles and machine guns, and the sabotage of helicopters. Sociologist John Helmer found that 58 percent of the veterans he interviewed replied "yes" to the question "Did you ever personally know of a fragging incident *in your unit* directed against NCOs or officers?" [155] Veterans in his sample had previously served in combat infantry units.

Much evidence indicates that once fraggings began occurring with some frequency, the threat of violence often made commanders "back off" from previous practices of either troop harassment or highly dangerous combat tactics. David Cortright, author of *Soldiers in Revolt,* found that "the unexpected appearance of a grenade pin or the detonation of a harmless smoke grenade frequently convinced commanders to abandon expected military standards. Once a commander was threatened by or became the actual target of a fragging, his effectiveness and that of the unit involved were severely hampered." [156] Soldiers often spoke bluntly to their superiors. Steve Hassna witnessed his friend Gene Shroth confront a bully sergeant who wanted an enemy weapon Shroth had captured:

> Anyway the sergeant told him, "When I get back to the rear, I'm gonna have you on every dirty detail I can find." Gene looked at him and said, "You gotta get back to the rear first, Sarge." And when Gene got back to the rear, the sergeant wasn't in sight; he didn't hassle the man one bit. He realized, "Well, if I give shit to that man, in the middle of a firefight something might go wrong, and the next thing you know, it's body bag time for me." People left Gene alone. They knew he didn't have "Black Mariah" stenciled on his machine gun for nothing. [157]

An actual assassination also meant an implied threat against all "survivors." As James D. Nell said in response to the question "Did this [killing] tend to bring about a change in attitude on the part of surviving officers?": "Oh, yes. They started using their heads right quick. They would stop messing with the troops." [158] A new phrase described negotiations between enlisted men and their superior officers. "Working it out," signified that troops no longer automatically obeyed orders, but instead actively participated in deciding what the unit would do. And sometimes when things couldn't be worked out, whole units mutinied. On August 26, 1969, a company of the 196th Infantry refused to march down a mountain slope after several days of combat and high casualties. In December 1970, an infantry platoon of the 501st Infantry refused to move out of their night defensive positions when ordered by their battalion commander.[159] By Department of the Army statistics, courts-martial for "certain acts of insubordination, mutiny, and willful disobedience" increased from 252 in 1968 to 382 in 1970. Administrative punishments ordered by commanders (under Article 15 of the Uniform Code of Military Justice) increased from 137 for every thousand men in the military to 183 per thousand in 1972.[160] The number of infractions reported was undoubtedly much smaller than the actual acts of insubordination and sabotage.

Given that the senior officer corps saw themselves as "management" and the ground troops as "labor" in the production model of war, then one can legitimately speak of a "labor" revolt in reference to what David Cortright calls the "quasi-mutiny." Class conflict between management and labor became transposed into the military domain. In warfare the struggle did not concern wages or working hours or retirement benefits; here class conflict between "working-class" grunts and war-managers centered on the soldiers' unwillingness to die for war-managers. For some soldiers, Vietnam duty became a deeply radicalizing experience. Such men later founded Vietnam Veterans Against the War in Vietnam. Other "radicalized" men did not become politically active, but still had vastly different political perspectives than when they first entered the military. And still other GIs did not become politically conscious, but acted to save themselves and their fellow troopers. Class conflict does not necessarily imply full class consciousness among the working class. As the helicopter door gunner said, ". . . I felt something was really wrong here. I couldn't pick it out. It was just strange."

Class conflict between labor and management was also related to the social origins of soldiers sent to Vietnam. In reflecting upon World War II, military leaders had concluded that scientific progress had been threatened by having too many college-educated men serving in combat (and dying) in comparison to the total college-educated pool.[161] Therefore, when Selective Service was renewed in 1948, college attendance constituted a draft exemption. Selective Service established a whole array of exemptions to "channel" American men toward higher education and occupations that the military thought would contribute to the national defense. A 1965 Selective Service policy statement explained the theory:

> While the best known purpose of Selective Service is to procure manpower for the armed forces, a variety of related processes takes place outside delivery of manpower to the active armed forces. Many of these may be put under the heading of "channeling manpower." Many young men would not have pursued a higher education if there had not been a program of student deferments. Many young scientists, engineers, tool and die makers, and other possessors of scarce skills would not remain in their jobs in the defense effort if it were not for a program of occupational deferment. Even though the salary of a teacher has historically been meager, many young men remain in that job seeking the reward of deferment. The process of channeling manpower by deferment is entitled to much credit for the large amount of graduate students in technical fields and for the fact that there is not a greater shortage of teachers, engineers, and other scientists working in activities which are essential to the national defense.[162]

College deferments lasted until 1973, when the Selective Service System instituted a lottery method for determining who was going to be drafted. Graduate school deferments lasted until 1968. Thus college-educated men were able to minimize their exposure to the draft, as well as pursue legal means of securing an exemption through conscientious objector status, or physical or psychiatric exemption. Social science research has shown a strong relationship between a man's parental class position and the educational level he achieves. The higher the class position and the higher the income and education of his parents, then the greater the chances are of a young man's finishing high school and college. Sons of the upper-middle class did not enter the military and go to Vietnam in the same proportions as did the sons of the working class. Lawrence M. Baskir and William A. Strauss have conducted the most extensive study relating a man's family background and education to his chances of fighting in Technowar.

Note that an individual from a low-income family has over twice the likelihood of serving in a combat capacity than does a man from a high-income family. Another study found that of the hundreds of thousands of men drafted in 1965–1966, only 2 percent were college graduates![163] Once in the military, army records show, an enlisted man with a college

Table 6.4

LIKELIHOOD OF VIETNAM-ERA SERVICE

|  | Military Service | Vietnam Service | Combat Service |
|---|---|---|---|
| Low-Income | 40% | 19% | 15% |
| Middle-Income | 30% | 12% | 7% |
| High-Income | 24% | 9% | 7% |
| High School Dropout | 42% | 18% | 14% |
| High School Graduate | 45% | 21% | 17% |
| College Graduate | 23% | 12% | 9% |

SOURCE: Lawrence M. Baskir and William A. Strauss, *Chance and Circumstance* (New York: Alfred A. Knopf, 1978), p. 9.

degree had only a 42 percent chance of going to Vietnam, while high school graduates had a 64 percent chance and high school dropouts faced 70 percent odds.[164] At each level of the filtering process leading toward the point of war production — the ground forces — progressively fewer men with college educations serve. Those who were from the lower levels of the social stratification system served in the most dangerous jobs (ground troops). And they died in those jobs. Sociologist Maurice Zeitlin and his associates found that nearly 29 percent of all men from Wisconsin who died in Vietnam were from poor families, while only 15 percent of men in high school came from poor families. Therefore, they died in *twice* their proportion of men their age.[165]

Only 2.4 percent of the Wisconsin casualties were black men, but Wisconsin is an unusually "white" state, with only 1.8 percent of all males between five and eighteen being black. Taking the United States as a whole, black men died in greater numbers than their proportion of the population. Twenty-four percent of army deaths in Vietnam in 1965 were black men's deaths. The next year the figure declined to 16 percent, and by 1968 black casualties from all military services totaled 13 percent.[166] A Department of Defense campaign to reduce the disproportionate presence of blacks in combat units apparently had some effects. Originally the army had made a special effort to draft minorities. The Armed Forces Qualification Tests given to all prospective volunteers and draftees classified people in one of five mental categories according to test scores. People scoring in categories I–III were automatically taken, while those scoring in Category V were automatically rejected. During peacetime, military recruiters tried to limit the number of men inducted with Category IV scores, but once the ground war started in 1965 these standards were lessened. The military was encouraged to drop its standards by civilian officials in Lyndon Johnson's administration. Political scientist Daniel Patrick Moynihan chaired the Task Force on Manpower Conservation in 1964 and found that the military rejected around 600,000 men each year who were school dropouts. Moynihan published a study on black family structure the next year, 1965. He was disheartened by the "disorganized and matrifocal family life" in black communities. Suddenly he saw how the military could get the men it needed and how blacks could become real men for the first time:

> There is another special quality about military service for Negro men: It is an utterly masculine world. Given the strains of the disorganized and matrifocal family life in which so many Negro youth come of age, the Armed Forces are a dramatic and desperately needed change; a world away from women, a world run by strong men of unquestioned authority, where discipline, if harsh, is nonetheless orderly and predictable, and where rewards, if limited, are granted on the basis of performance. The theme of a current Army recruiting message states it as clearly as can be. "In the U.S. Army you get to know what it means to feel like a man." [167]

Moynihan wrote this extraordinarily paternalistic encomium when he was an assistant secretary of labor.

Military life also took these newly made black men off welfare and gave them job skills and the means for upward mobility:

> Military service is disruptive in some respects. For those comparatively few who are killed or wounded in combat, or otherwise, the personal sacrifice is inestimable. But, on balance, service in the Armed Forces over the past quarter century has worked greatly to the advantage of those involved. The training and experience of military duty is unique; the advantages that have generally followed in the form of GI Bill mortgage guarantees, federal life insurance, Civil Service preference, veterans' hospitals and veterans' pensions are singular, to say the least. [168]

To help more black men receive the fruits of military life, a special remedial education program was set up for Category IV recruits; 40 percent of all blacks scored in Category IV. Secretary of Defense Robert McNamara called it Project 100,000. The "subterranean poor . . . have not had the opportunity to earn their fair share of this nation's abundance, but they can be given an opportunity to return to civilian life with skills and aptitudes which for them and their families will reverse the downward spiral of decay.'' The war-managers would produce highly productive men, men with earning capacities *"two or three times what it would have been had there been no such program."* [169]

Recruitment standards changed; 240,000 Category IV test-scorers officially entered the military under the program's auspices from 1966 to 1968. Additional Category IV recruits entered the military but were not registered with the program. Some troops received remedial instruction in reading and some were placed in special training programs to get them through basic and advanced schools. But mostly these men, 40 percent of whom were black, took assignments in the combat arms (infantry, armor, artillery) and half of those in the army and marines went to Vietnam. [170] The great welfare program was a hoax; Technowar needed an ever-increasing labor supply at the point of production. Standards were changed so that those at the bottom of the racial and economic system of power could fight and die in Vietnam.

However deficient in test scores, many members of what Douglas Glasgow terms "the black underclass" understood completely where they were and why they were there. [171] David Cortright's investigations in *Soldiers in Revolt* found that "of all the troops in Vietnam, the most rebellious were the blacks. As was the case throughout the armed forces, black GIs in Vietnam were militant leaders of the GI resistance, posing great problems for American commanders." [172] War-managers attempted to contain black rebellion by sending them to military prisons. Prisons in Vietnam became locales for massive revolts. On August 16, 1968, marine inmates at the Danang brig (prison) rioted and seized control of the central compound for twenty hours. Full control over the prison was not obtained for several days. Two weeks later the massive army prison at Long Binh, holding 710 prisoners (in an area designed for 502), erupted. Fighting between military police and inmates protesting the living conditions went on for several hours. Later, a work strike was conducted by approximately 200 black inmates, and a smaller group maintained control of one prison section for nearly a month. Cortright describes how black nationalism manifested itself in these actions: "During the occupation, the militants reportedly simulated African dress and customs and transformed their tiny holding into a kind of liberated African state." [173]

The list of racial epithets applied to black soldiers by many white

troops was longer than the list for Vietnamese. Besides the old favor-
ites, "coon," "nigger," and "spade," there were "reindeer," "Mau
Mau," "jig," "spook," "brownie," and "warrior." Even without
slander, the message came through. David Parks, author of *G.I. Diary*,
said he heard the call: "The FO [forward observer]'s job is one of the
hairiest in the mortar platoon. He's on more patrols because an FO is
required to be with the patrolling squad at all times, and there are only
three FOs to cover sixteen squads. The odds are against him. Sgt. Paul-
son hand picks the men for this job. So far he's picked only Negroes
and Puerto Ricans. I think he is trying to tell us something."[174] Stanley
Goff heard the news from his friend Piper:

> At that particular time, most of the whites depended on the brothers
> to fight. That's how it got to be. And he [Piper] and every brother
> knew that, too. His thing was, "Don't let them use you all the way
> to the grave." And that was what they were really doing. He told us,
> "The government is sending us over here. When we get here, we're
> doing the most fighting." Piper was trying to make us see how they
> were using us. Here we were doing all the fighting out of proportion
> to our number. Anyway, that's what he was preaching. That was his
> lesson. He was enabling us to understand the system as he saw it and
> to realize that all the money that was being poured into the Nam could
> have been used to clean up the ghetto. He was politically oriented and
> just a hell of a guy.[175]

Drafted from the underclass and sent to die as grunts in combat units,
the black men's audacious revolt was punished by their white commanders. According to the National Association for the Advancement
of Colored People, black soldiers received 45 percent of all "less-than-
honorable" discharges issued in the Vietnam era.[176] A bad discharge
rating is a stigma that lasts for a lifetime — a way of keeping someone
at the socioeconomic bottom.

Other minorities, particularly Hispanics, also served and died in Vietnam in larger proportions than their ethnic and racial groups are represented in the United States. Ralph Guzman studied Hispanic deaths in
Vietnam as a percentage of total deaths suffered by men from the south-
western states of California, Arizona, New Mexico, Colorado, and Texas.
From 1961 through March 1969, casualties with Spanish surnames comprised around 19 percent of the total killed in Vietnam from southwest-
ern states. This figure is significantly higher than the U.S. Bureau of

the Census figures of 11.8 percent total Hispanic population of the Southwest and 13.8 percent of all males from seventeen to thirty-six.[177] Neither stories from ground troops nor academic studies indicate whether Chicano soldiers participated in the revolt against Technowar. But their high death rate again makes clear how Selective Service and the military division of labor reproduced the stratification system.

When confronted with the breakdown and revolt of U.S. forces in Vietnam, war-managers and scholars associated with the military sought to find explanations either in specific practices that could readily be reformed or in factors outside the military domain. According to one school of thought, the breakdown and revolt of U.S. forces in large part resulted from managerial policies rotating enlisted men in and out of Vietnam for one-year tours of duty and having officers command units for only six months. The constant changeover of men and commanders at all levels of a unit meant that few solid relationships developed among the men. Previous scholarship on American soldiers in World War II, principally Samuel Stouffer's famous work, *The American Soldier*, found that U.S. troops fought to preserve the lives of men in their primary group while ideological reasons for fighting were of much less importance.[178] By this reasoning, since men were always moving in and out of a unit, no primary group was formed and morale deteriorated. Richard A. Gabriel and Paul L. Savage contend in *Crisis in Command* that rotating units back and forth rather than individuals would have made more sociological sense: ". . . the rotation policies operative in Vietnam virtually foreclosed the possibility of establishing fighting units with a sense of identity, morale and strong cohesiveness. The assignment of individuals as opposed to *unit*, DEROS dates, plus the frequent rotation of officers, made it clear that the policy was virtually every man for himself."[179] DEROS is an acronym standing for Date Estimated Return Overseas Service. Every soldier knew his or her DEROS when arriving in Vietnam.

A related argument against individual rotation contends that the one-year tour of duty helped create American casualties because competent troops with experience were always being replaced with fresh troops from training camp. Thomas C. Thayer, of the Systems Analysis Office in the DOD, made this argument by inferring from casualty charts: "Twice as many troops died during the first six months of their tour as in the second half. After the first month, the number of deaths decline as the tour progresses, without exception."[180]

Some soldier narratives confirm both arguments against the rotation policy. Thomas Bird of the 1st Cavalry Division complained his August 1965–August 1966 tour was too short:

> Toward the end of my tour, when I started knowing what I was doing in the jungle and started knowing what to do under fire, it was just about time to go home. If that happened to me — if I was just getting good in the jungle and really knew what to do and I was going home — what good is it? I'm going to be replaced by a guy who is as green as I was when I got here, and by the time he gets good at it he's going to be replaced by a guy who is green. It's no wonder we never got a foothold in that place.[181]

Steve Hassna in turn talked about how he withdrew from close contact with his fellow soldiers after he was severely wounded (by American artillery) and returned from the hospital to find a completely new unit:

> When I got back to my company, I didn't know anybody. Everybody I knew was either dead or gone. And that's when I closed up. I sat by myself, I ate by myself, people didn't talk to me, I didn't talk to them. When new guys would come in, they'd be so scared they just wanted to make friends with everybody. They'd come up and start talking to me and I'd say, "I don't want to know your name, I don't want to know where you're from, I don't want to know about your girl friend — because if you die, and I know you, then I die too! So stay away from me!" Right there, that's a breakdown in morale; that's a breakdown in team effort. It means "I am going to survive." My attitude was: I will work with you for our joint survival, but when I see you get hit laying next to me, I'm pissed because you're dead, but at the same time I'm thinking "it's better you than me." And that's what started happening to American troops in Vietnam.[182]

Presumably, if Hassna's unit had been rotated out of the line and given time for the wounded to recuperate and for new troops to be trained and assimilated into the web of social relations, then Hassna or other soldiers would not withdraw from contact. With the primary group restored, U.S. units could have kept on fighting indefinitely — at least that is the implication.

Westmoreland personally established the one-year tour for the army. In so doing he explicitly gave as his reason his estimate that only a short tour would keep up soldier morale. He expected a prolonged war;

fresh troops were needed. His memoir, *A Soldier Reports*, says: "In keeping with my belief that it was going to be a long war, the one-year tour gave a man a goal. That was good for morale." [183]

The general's assessment of giving a man a "goal" also finds much confirmation in novels, memoirs, and journalist reports. The fallacies of Vietnam quickly became apparent to many soldiers. With victory against the mythological foreign Other vanished as a motive for fighting, personal survival became the goal. As one of Mark Baker's informants in *Nam* said: "One of the first things you realized when you got to Nam was that you weren't going to win this war. There was no way we could win doing what we were doing. After the first month, me and everybody else over there said, 'I'm going to put in my twelve months and then I'm getting the fuck out of here. It's not worth it.'" [184] Time in Vietnam became a countdown. Soldiers always knew exactly how much time they had left in the field, when they could go back to base areas for "processing" and when the "Freedom Birds" (planes) left to take them home. Michael Herr described one marine's focus on time in-country:

> Like every other American in Vietnam, he had his obsession with Time. (No one talked about When-this-lousy-war-is-over. Only "How much time you got?") The degree of Day Tripper's obsession, compared with most of the others, could be seen in the calendar on his helmet. No metaphysician ever studied Time the way he did, its components and implications, its per-second per seconds, its shadings and movement. The Space-Time continuum, Time-as-matter, Augustinian Time: all of that would have been a piece of cake to Day Tripper, whose brain cells were arranged like jewels in the finest chronometer. [185]

The knowledge that he would leave Vietnam after one year seems to have *restrained* many a soldier from taking action against his superiors. If Day Tripper could not think of the countdown as a way out, then what would he have done? There is no certain answer, but Westmoreland's analysis that the one-year tour helped morale in a long war has much merit. Discipline may well have broken down earlier without the one-year tour as a safety valve for extreme discontent. Second, while the argument that individual rotation vitiated social relationships in fighting units has much merit, the evidence suggests that men nevertheless fought and took risks for other soldiers to whom they had no "primary group" attachments. One of Dr. Ronald J. Glaser's characters in *365 Days,*

Sergeant Mayfield, describes this strange army that fought without en-
thusiasm.

> Strange war. Going for something they didn't believe in or for that
> matter didn't care about, just to make it 365 days and be done with
> it. They'd go, through; even freaked out, they'd go. They'd do what-
> ever he told them. Three mornings in a row after lying in the mud all
> night, they got up and pushed the gooks back so the choppers could
> get the wounded out. They charged, every time, just got up and went,
> right over the RPG's [rocket-propelled grenades] and AK's [assault
> rifles]. No flags, no noise, no abuse. They just got up and blew them-
> selves to shit because it had to be done. The same with ambushes.
> They'd do it, and if led right, they'd do it well. But they always let
> him know somehow that they would rather be left alone; it would be
> OK if they caught the gooks, but if they didn't that would be fine too.
> At first it had been disconcerting — troopers who didn't care but
> who'd fight anyway, sloppy soldiers smoking grass whenever they
> could, but would do whatever was asked. Skeptical kids who made
> no friends outside their own company and sometimes only in their
> own squads, who'd go out and tear themselves apart to help another
> unit and then leave when it was over without asking a name or taking
> a thanks, if any were offered.[186]

While not the vision of fraternity called for by reformists such as
Gabriel and Savage, neither is it a vision of complete anomie — a
normlessness where individuals are alone and unguided by any values.
For that matter, the soldiers' revolt was not an example of rotation-
induced anomie, either. Strong social integration among soldiers was
needed to place bounties on the heads of their commanders and take up
company-wide collections for the killer. Social integration among soldiers turned against the war-managers — a fact hidden by the reformist
argument about the effects of rotation.

A second argument that tends to minimize the internal conflicts in
Technowar concerns drug use. Marijuana usage remained quite high
throughout the war; heroin came into widespread use from 1968 on.
And much opium and amphetamines and barbiturates and psychedelic
drugs were also available. While no war-manager or analyst blamed the
breakdown solely on drug use, there was a sense that drugs bore a major
responsibility for poor U.S. military performance. And there are some
stories supporting this position. Lieutenant Colonel Anthony Herbert reports that an entire infantry company got stoned on marijuana and hash-

ish and was overrun by the Vietcong, with few survivors.[187] No doubt other such disasters occurred.

However, in the war literature more soldiers testify about drugs helping them cope with the war in one way or another than tell about drug-induced military dysfunctions. For example, one soldier testified how drugs made the destroy part of search-and-destroy easier:

> And like there was a big squabble, you know, and like the next thing I know they told me, some cat told me, that we best go out and smoke, because we might have to be doing something. . . . [The sergeant said] "We're going to get them, we've got to finish them all." . . . The next thing I know it was a few people, there was a platoon of us with them M-16s, and I don't know who started it off, somebody started firing. So I started firing. . . .[188]

And Michael Herr met a Long Range Reconnaissance Patrol scout who said drugs made the search part of search-and-destroy easier:

> I knew one 4th Division Lurp who took his pills by the fistful, downs from the left pocket of his tiger [camouflage] suit and ups from the right, one to cut the trail for him and the other to send him down it. He told me that they cooled things out just right for him, that he could see that old jungle at night like he was looking at it through a starlight scope. "They sure give you the range," he said.[189]

Drug usage implies that someone or some group is out of control while using the drug. From the perspective of high-level war-managers, the soldiers' insurrection meant that they were out of officers' control. Since the command stratification system is taken as both "natural" and legitimate by commanders, blaming revolt on "foreign" substances has resonance with their position. Much conflict between officers and enlisted men was caused by drugs. Military attempts to search men and barracks for drugs often resulted in fraggings. But to take conflicts surrounding drugs as indicative of purely drug-inspired, irrational revolt is completely wrong. Substance abuse both helped and hindered Technowar in different ways, but drugs were not the cause of military breakdown.

And finally war-managers and their allies have one more alien influence to explain why their own army turned against them — namely, the antiwar movement, the counterculture, the black nationalist movement, the news media, and other social forces that did not fully support them.

Political scientist Guenter Lewy points the finger in his treatise, *America in Vietnam:*

> Disenchantment with the Vietnam war on the part of the media, "peace" demonstrators and anti-war statements on the part of prominent public officials could not but create a climate of doubt and lack of sense of purpose which posed a severe challenge to dedication and discipline.
>
> Growing permissiveness in American society and an increase in social pathology, such as a rising crime rate and widespread attitudes of disrespect toward authority and law enforcement, undoubtedly played an important role.[190]

Professor Lewy is correct in some ways, but like the breakdown-as-drug-induced explanation, blaming domestic dissent sets up a "pure" military that was subverted from without — drug pushers, radicals, and liberal news people all became a new set of foreign Others. Such finger-pointing cannot explain Technowar's failed strategy, systematic lying, and disregard for its own troops. In the spring of 1968, Lyndon Johnson and his associates concluded that the war could not be won and began limited peace negotiations. President Nixon continued these negotiations and slowly began withdrawing troops even though his administration still sought military victory.

By 1968 it had become clear to many ground troops that Vietnamese reunification would not be stopped by their deaths. Acts of insubordination, resistance, and fragging occurred throughout the war, but beginning with 1968 they became more common. By 1969 and 1970 soldiers had established a two-front war, one against the Vietcong and NVA and another against their commanders. Conventional wisdom says that withdrawal preceded revolt — in Lewy's words, "During the years 1970–1972 the feeling of not wanting to be the last man killed in a war that was closing down appeared to have a detrimental effect on morale and discipline." [191] But understanding American withdrawal in terms of breakdown and revolt by ground troops also has much merit. War-managers could not fight a war with troops who killed their commanders; as the revolt spread, the United States had no choice but to withdraw its ground combat forces and find other means to fight.

# CHAPTER 7

# Forced Draft: Urbanization and the Consumer Society Come to Vietnam

B Y the end of the war there were an estimated 21 million bomb craters in South Vietnam. Air force planes sprayed 18 million gallons of herbicide containing dioxins on some 6 million acres — around one-seventh of South Vietnam's total land area, and a much higher proportion of its most fertile cropland and richest forests. An additional 1,200 square miles of territory were bulldozed flat, stripped of all life.[1] Nearly 10.5 million people either abandoned their homes because of fighting or had them destroyed. Given this devastation, a question must be asked: How could war-managers reconcile their professed goal of defending South Vietnamese "sovereignty" at the same time the American military was destroying the very country and people they were supposed to protect?

Two partial answers have been provided. First, victory was conceptualized as killing the North Vietnamese army at a faster rate than the Democratic Republic of Vietnam could infiltrate troops; by exhausting the foreign Other on the debit-credit scale, the enemy would go bankrupt and lose the war. Second, career advancement was the primary concern of much of the senior officer corps. Since the decimation of land and people did not count in the evaluation criteria used by superiors in determining promotions, the bleak contrast between the doctrine of protection and real destruction was not much questioned.

Instead, the destruction of both the country and its people was rewritten on another set of ledgers. This second set was known officially as "nation-building" or "pacification" and more informally as "winning hearts and minds" or "the other war" (in contrast to search-and-destroy). These phrases were in part just new names for the old practice of counterinsurgency, the attempt to establish physical control over the people and win their loyalty to the GVN regime. Pacification war sought to provide all refugees with at least minimal food, clothing, housing, and medical care; these goods would in theory "pacify" the displaced rural population gathered in ARVN-guarded camps and city slums. At another level of economic intervention, pacification war contributed to importing thousands upon thousands of cars, motorcycles, televisions, stereos, refrigerators, and other modern consumer goods for a more affluent class of Vietnamese.

This "other war" attempted to restructure the country from a rural agricultural society into a modern urban society with consumerism as a major source of psychological satisfaction. Just as the military had appropriated the logic of advanced capitalist production for reorganizing its internal structure and concept of war, so too did leading civilian and military officials come to conceive of pacification in terms of establishing and promoting American-style mass media, advertising, and consumerism.

Destruction was but the necessary first step in reconstruction. This shift in conceptual language from the production of destruction to the production of development and consumption allowed war-managers to rationalize what they were doing. The ravaging of Vietnam was formulated in what appeared to be scientifically informed, rational policy oriented toward economic development. Social science terms such as "resource allocation" and "forced-draft urbanization" made the doublethink process much easier; these words constituted a rhetoric of progress without reference to the devastated reality. In the midst of war, Vietnam vanished; in its place came the magical representation of a developing nation headed toward "takeoff."

Within the logic of the domino theory, all of South Vietnam's problems came from beyond, the place where the foreign Other lived. Westmoreland's references to the Vietcong in his memoir, *A Soldier Reports,* all seek to minimize the importance of internally generated military and political enemies. In one place, he refers to them as "termites": ". . . I occasionally likened the political subversives and guerrillas to termites persistently eating away at the structural members of a building, analogously, the structure of South Vietnamese government. . . ."[2] These termites were only a secondary enemy for the ordinary ARVN units to engage; the primary war against the NVA "bully boys" was fought by Americans in the border areas. In another instance, Westmoreland thinks the Vietcong were nothing more than bandits and thugs: "Fundamental to pacification was security, and as long as insurgents were raiding, robbing, molesting, and killing, in South Vietnam, the government forces would have to spend their time keeping the enemy out of hamlets and villages rather than improving the welfare of the people."[3]

From this perspective of the Vietcong as criminals comes the idea of pacification as a kind of "police action," whereby popular allegiance to the GVN is created by police-military action against criminals. When ARVN can physically control an area, then it will become pacified.

Jeffrey Race, a former U.S. Army adviser to the GVN in Long An province, calls this approach a *"reinforcement* strategy" in that the official response to Vietcong attacks is not to address the social conditions which help generate peasant support for the Vietcong, but to reinforce the local government bureaucracy with more military units to reestablish "tactical security" in an area.[4] The power of the government is based on its ability physically to control people from above, rather than to create what Race calls a "sympathetic environment," an alliance with the populace.[5]

In this logic of control, pacification became impossible once enemy resistance outpaced GVN ability to "reinforce" local government forces under attack. With Vietcong attacks taking place all over the country in 1964 and 1965, and Vietcong recruitment increasing significantly, then few areas could be reinforced. With the introduction of hundreds of thousands of American troops armed with incredible firepower in 1965 and 1966, another option presented itself to save pacification war from bankruptcy.

If there were not enough troops and police to guard every hamlet and every village, then perhaps the Vietnamese civilians could be persuaded to move to refugee camps and cities where they could be more readily guarded. As the term "people's war" indicates, Communist revolution requires close contact with the people for intelligence, logistical support, and recruits. Mao Tse-tung once poetically referred to the guerrillas' relationship to the populace as analogous to that of "fish" who swam in the "sea." If large areas of countryside were drained, guerrillas would in theory lose contact with the people. Guerrilla forces would then be isolated and defeated by conventional American and South Vietnamese soldiers.

By 1966 and 1967, war-managers began to articulate a policy of refugee production. Westmoreland wrote:

Until now the war has been characterized by a substantial majority of the population remaining neutral. In the past year we have seen an escalation to a higher level of intensity in the war. This will bring about a moment of decision for the peasant farmer. He will have to choose if he stays alive.

Until now the peasant farmer has had three alternatives. He could stay put and follow his natural instinct to stay close to the land, living beside the grave of his ancestors. He could move into an area under government control, or he could join the VC. Now, if he stays put, there are additional dangers.

The VC cannot patch up wounds. If the peasant becomes a refugee he does get shelter, food and security, job opportunities and is given a hope to possibly return to the land. The third alternative is life with the VC. The VC have not made good on their promises; they no longer secure areas. There are B-52 bombings, the VC tax demands are increasing, they want more recruits at the point of a gun, forced labor to move supplies. The battle is being carried more and more to the enemy. Our operations have been designed to make the first choice impossible, the second attractive, and to reduce the likelihood of anyone choosing the third to zero.[6]

In other words, the destruction of the countryside was a kind of "negative conditioning" for the peasants. Social scientist Charles Wolf explained the psychology of destruction as penalty: "Confiscation of chickens, razing of houses, or destruction of villages have a place in counter-insurgency efforts, but only if they are done for a strong reason: namely, to penalize those who have assisted the insurgents."[7] Another social scientist claimed that destruction of villages lowered morale and was thus effective negative reinforcement: "The point is that this rubs in the accuracy of modern artillery and has been found to be an effective way of lowering morale and the will to resist. The technique travels quickly by rumors since the uprooted have to find homes in other villages until they can re-build their own."[8]

Such behaviorism was often coupled with a "labor" economics approach. The production of refugees decreased the "manpower" supply for the enemy. Robert Komer, head of American pacification programs in 1967–1968, wanted to "step up refugee programs deliberately aimed at depriving the VC of a recruiting base."[9] Nicholas Katzenbach, undersecretary of state in 1966, also called for military operations to "stimulate a greater refugee flow through psychological inducements to further decrease the enemy's manpower base.''[10] In one formulation, there is even a sense that the United States should produce refugees in a cost-effective manner; a State Department memo suggested that "Measures to encourage refugee flow might be targeted where they will hurt the VC most and embitter people toward the US/GVN forces least."[11]

The actual generation of refugees involved three different destructive practices: intensive bombing and shelling; chemical destruction of crops and forests; and physical removal of villagers by ground troops. Of the three techniques, bombing and shelling seems to have been the most productive. One recurrent theme in the *Pentagon Papers* was Westmoreland's continual requests for additional B-52 sorties. These requests were often granted and the B-52 became a very important weapon. With a bomb load of around 28 tons per plane, a three-plane mission covered an area half a mile wide and several miles long. "Free-fire" or "specified-strike" zones, where the populace was suspected of supporting the National Liberation Front, were subject to massive B-52 attacks. Oftentimes after these raids additional American aircraft dropped psychological warfare leaflets. One common leaflet showed a picture of a B-52 on one side and had the following text (English version) on the reverse:

> As has been announced before, when the plane returns to sow death, you will have no more time to choose. Be sure to follow the example of 70,000 compatriots who have used the free-movement pass to return and re-establish a comfortable life in peace; or stay to die in suffering and horrible danger. All who stay will never be able to know when other bombs will fall. Be sure to be wise and don't be undecided any more. Be sure to use the free-movement pass of the Government printed on this leaflet and hurry to return to the righteous cause.[12]

Other leaflets did not presume the recipient was necessarily a Vietcong, but quite often the consequences of not heeding the message was the same. Captain Robert B. Johnson described one flyer: "On one side of the leaflet I remember there was a picture of a B-52 bomber, and the other side said in Vietnamese, 'Come to the New Life Hamlet, come to peace, freedom, and justice.' Of course, the message was clear to the people in the countryside; leave your homes or we will kill you."[13] Thousands upon thousands of Vietnamese were killed in these attacks. In 1966 *New York Times* reporter Neil Sheehan traveled with General Westmoreland for several months. As they traversed the country Sheehan became concerned about the number of Vietnamese civilian casualties and asked Westmoreland if he too was worried. The general replied, "Yes, but it does deprive the enemy of the population, doesn't it?" [14]

MACV attempted to calculate the number of Vietnamese killed and wounded on the basis of admissions to South Vietnamese provincial hospitals. By this criteria casualties from American bombing and shelling totaled 18,811 in 1967, 28,052 in 1968, 16,183 in 1969, and 8,607 in 1970. [15] The war-managers' counting method does not include casualties produced in areas controlled by the National Liberation Front, since by military definition these free-fire zones had no civilians, only enemy troops! Nor does the military definition of civilian casualty include anyone treated by any other medical facility or any estimate of those who are either killed outright, die before reaching medical care, or have wounds which are never treated. Military counting rules maximized the number of enemy soldiers killed and minimized civilian casualties; in this way it appeared to be both efficient and humane. Using different procedures for estimating civilian casualties, a U.S. Senate subcommittee estimated that actual civilian casualties ran from 100,000 a year in 1965 to 300,000 in 1968. [16]

While bombing and shelling produced refugees by threatening immediate, violent death, chemical destruction of Vietnamese crops produced refugees by threatening slow starvation. The program was known as Operation Ranch Hand. The U.S. Air Force used American aircraft, but Vietnamese *markings* were put on the planes and a Vietnamese was required to fly along in each aircraft. This slight subterfuge was undertaken to avoid problems with international law forbidding destruction of food intended for civilian consumption.

A 1967 air force study noted that the objective "was to separate the VC from the people by forcing refugee movements into GVN controlled areas. Intelligence reports document the success in achieving this objective." [17] Another military study made that same year also noted the high refugee flow produced by crop destruction, "and as a result, the VC suffered manpower shortages for support purposes." [18] Several years later, after additional millions of gallons of herbicide were sprayed, the war-managers again affirmed the program: "The crop destruction program made an effective contribution to the overall resource-denial program. The enemy's combat effectiveness was reduced as a result of the missions." [19]

But just who was this "enemy" whose "combat effectiveness" was reduced? According to one close observer of the resource-denial program, nutritionist Jean Mayer, children were the first to die when crops were destroyed. After them came old people. Babies were third in line — they died when the mother's milk dried up. Adult women had a chance for survival if they were strong enough to leave the area. Adult men in armed groups (the VC), were far more mobile than old people or women with children and babies. Guerrillas who could move when food was short were least affected by crop poisoning.[20]

The third method for producing refugees used troops to surround a village suddenly and announce to its people that their lives in the country were over. Colonel William Corson described how the process occurred in one village:

> Loudspeaker bullhorns were used to call the people from their homes and fields, where the rice harvest was due in three weeks. As the crowd of old men, women, and children assembled, amidst great confusion, the spectacle worsened. Those who failed to move with sufficient alacrity were prodded with clubs and bayonets. When "the word" was passed about what was to happen, a groan escaped from the people because they knew their crops would either be destroyed or rot in the fields. . . . When the destination of Cam Lo was announced another groan arose from the crowd.
>
> The first groan resulted from the peasants' fear that they were to be turned into paupers and stripped of their dignity as productive human beings. The second groan is a little harder for an American to understand fully because of our frontier heritage of migration. . . . Over 90 per cent of the residents of Trung Luong had never traveled farther than ten kilometers from their homes. They feared Cam Lo would not be "California" but rather a point of no return. Furthermore, the natives of Trung Luong were Buddhists who because of their religious beliefs were greatly concerned about dying in a strange place. They believe quite strongly in the necessity of being buried in their own family burial plots in order to achieve the Buddhist version of heaven. This fear, added to the loss of their fields and the length of the trip, was sufficient to demolish the people.[21]

One Rand Corporation study found that three-fourths of the peasants whose crops were poisoned explicitly hated the United States and the GVN.[22] Another study demonstrated that a great many refugees interpreted the government's production of refugees as a sign of government weakness — a correct interpretation — and consequently did not support the regime.[23]

David Ross, an army medic involved in the pacification program, conveyed the sense in which the Americans did not recognize the Vietnamese as people:

> When Americans are talking about Vietnamese or people in India or somewhere similar, it's not like we're looking at them like they're our next-door neighbors. If someone came to our neighborhood and burned all of our houses and most of our possessions and put us in flying saucers which we'd never seen before and zipped us across the universe, setting us down somewhere in a tent city in the middle of a sandbox with wire all around us, I guess we might not be too excited about it.[24]

Refugee camps were not exciting in the sense of a new and wonderful life. One American soldier described the camp where former residents of Ben Suc were sent after the town was destroyed by the pacification program:

> I saw that resettlement camp, and it looked to me very similar to a Nazi concentration camp. Double barbed wire fences, machine gun towers. You could not get in or get out. These people were existing only, they were given just enough rice to keep alive; they were given Army blankets that the American Army was getting ready to destroy because they were worn out; they were living in tents that were damaged, almost useless, and there were American Military Police guarding this concentration camp initially, and then the South Vietnamese Army took over. And they started shooting without warning anybody that was within a certain area of the fence.[25]

Virtually all unofficial testimonies by soldiers who witnessed life in these camps speak of extreme poverty in a prisonlike environment. Another soldier reported:

> You have a lot of wooden and tin huts, you know, just built together haphazardly. Usually the ground is bare: no vegetation or anything, no trees. So there is also a barbed-wire fence surrounding them, and only one entrance. . . . If they get any food, they certainly do not show it, because all the ones that I have seen they looked like they were starving, and they were dressed in rags. . . . I would say that the medical and sanitary conditions are very primitive. I mean by anyone's standards. I could not say that I ever saw anyone die of

starvation, but I saw people who looked like they were about to die of starvation.[26]

Jonathan Schell reported that in the northern part of the country in 1967, out of 68 camps established for refugees, "50 had no schools, 46 had no latrines, and 42 had no medical dispensary."[27] The northern sector, "I Corps," was precisely where Undersecretary of State Katzenbach ordered the military to produce more refugees. Refugees were created and then collected in concentration camps. But at the same time official military reports conceptualized refugees as people who *voluntarily* left their homes because they supported the South Vietnamese regime. Marine command history on pacification operations in I Corps during 1967 reads: "The presence of an estimated 539,000 refugees in CTZ [Corps Tactical Zone] at the close of October is a reflection of the growing confidence of the Vietnamese people in their government."[28] Similarly, the GVN officially reported all refugees as "compatriots who have fled from communism," regardless of the refugees' actual motives.[29]

Although doublethink satisfied war-managers, it did not satisfy hundreds of thousands of Vietnamese who spent years in the camps. Many became too physically weak and psychologically defeated to move elsewhere. For many others, however, the first preference was to return home. This choice had its difficulties. Since the vacated villages and countryside had either been declared free-fire zones before or after the refugees moved, then anyone returning home was a "legitimate" target. As one American soldier explained, "But there are insufficient facilities for the people in the refugee camps, so they come back, and they're automatically considered VC. Then we give it to them."[30]

Even if a man or woman was not killed directly by military action, he or she faced serious problems getting enough food. Many crops were bombed; others were destroyed by herbicides. Or a peasant might return home to find that his fields and fruit trees had been bulldozed away. Once an entire island, or at least 8,039 acres of it, was bulldozed. The after-action report stated, "Go Noi Island had been converted from a densely populated, heavily wooded area into a barren wasteland, a plowed field. In that, the operation was a success."[31] General Westmoreland had been an early advocate of bulldozers, particularly the largest ones known as "Rome plows." He claimed that bulldozing not only destroyed secret enemy bases, but also "cleared" the land for Vietnamese peasants to grow crops — a form of nation-building.[32] But there are no published records of bulldozed land being used for agricultural production, only accounts of destruction.

Returning home was thus not a viable option. Instead, the light at the end of the tunnel pointed toward the cities, where the modern Vietnam was being created. Millions took this path.

Technowar had its roots in the ascendancy of high-technology, capital-intensive production in the United States. In a similar, but not identical, way, urbanized development was taken as an appropriate model for development of South Vietnam. By far the most advanced, wide-ranging formulation of the new urban Vietnam was written by the noted political scientist Samuel P. Huntington. Examining the war after the massive Tet Offensive of February 1968, Huntington attempted to find a rationale for justifying destruction of the countryside. He first noted that rural pacification appeared to have failed: "The fragility of the whole pacification effort was reflected by the extent of its at least temporary collapse during the Tet offensive, despite the fact that the offensive was directed at the cities rather than the pacification cadres." After noting this failure, however, Huntington articulated a new theory of American warfare in which rural pacification becomes irrelevant. In contrast to the famous British counterinsurgency theorist, Sir Robert Thompson, who characterized the Chinese and Vietnamese practices of "People's Revolutionary War" as immune "to the direct application of mechanical and conventional power," Huntington thought that the American war machine was successful: "For if the 'direct application of mechanical and conventional power' takes place on such a massive scale as to produce a massive migration from countryside to city, the basic assumptions underlying the Maoist doctrine of revolutionary war no longer operate. The Maoist-inspired rural revolution is undercut by the American-sponsored urban revolution."[33]

Huntington estimated that by 1968 approximately 40 percent of the 17.2 million people in South Vietnam lived in cities of 20,000 or more, a figure several times higher than the early sixties when 85 percent of the South's populace lived in rural areas — a society of landlords and peasants, susceptible to "rural revolution." In the newly expanded cities, former peasants would find an exciting new economy:

> The rural poor, on the other hand, may well find life in the city more attractive and comfortable than their previous existence in the countryside. The urban slum, which seems so horrible to middle-class

Americans, often becomes for the poor peasant a getaway to a new and better way of life. For some poor migrants, the wartime urban boom has made possible incomes five times those which they had in the countryside. In one Saigon slum, Xom Chua, in early 1965 before the American build-up, the people lived at a depressed level, with 33 percent of the adult males unemployed. Eighteen months later, as a result of the military escalation, the total population of the slum had increased by 30 percent, but the unemployment rate had dropped to 5 percent and average incomes had doubled. In several cases urban refugees from the war refused to return to their villages once security was restored because of the higher level of economic well-being which they could attain in the city. The pull of urban prosperity has been a secondary but not insignificant factor in attracting people to the city.[34]

Through this formulation, the massive destruction of lives, crops, and homes is theoretically abolished: the war disappears. In its place, *rural poverty* is eliminated and urban prosperity created through a benevolent warfare-welfare apparatus. Life is equated to income and incomes are "five times those which they had in the countryside," and once in the city, "wartime urban boom" keeps them moving upward. Everyone but the enemy wins in this trip to modernity. People get richer and the United States "may well have stumbled on the answer to 'wars of national liberation.' "[35]

In their memos, reports, and books, war-managers repeatedly dismissed destruction and celebrated war as a constructive development enterprise. Technowar required a massive logistical infrastructure for its high-technology, capital-intensive warfare. Property controlled by Americans for their administrative headquarters, barracks, and supply depots totaled hundreds of thousands of acres. On this property the United States constructed billions of dollars' worth of buildings and roads. These base areas became a major part of the new Vietnam.

In many areas basic construction materials were not available. The massive port facility at Cam Ranh Bay was constructed on sand dunes. Before the base could be built, roads had to be built, and road-building required rocks — even rocks were not readily at hand: "As one commander explained, 'Rock was the word over here. I woke up in my sleep saying, Rock, rock, rock.' "[36] Eventually he found the necessary rock in a quarry opened and later abandoned by the French for their war. Nor was there any good source of fresh water — wells had to be dug. Nor was there any wood for making frames to shape the concrete.

There were forests across the bay, but "this territory had become a sanctuary of the Viet Cong, who used it as a rest area. It would have been expedient to set up a sawmill there, but such an operation, it was feared, would aggravate the enemy and invite serious attack, thus increasing the already demanding security requirements of the engineers."[37]

Eventually everything was brought in from abroad. Piers were prefabricated by the DeLong Corporation in Charleston, South Carolina, and towed across the oceans to Vietnam. Fuel tank farms were installed and pipelines for tankers were laid. Warehouses for war supplies and barracks for soldiers and hospitals for wounded and runways to move everyone in and out quickly were all constructed. Cam Ranh Bay became a *city*.

As a city, it required service personnel, people to do menial jobs associated with construction, laundry, and food preparation.

> Because of the absence of a local labor pool in the Cam Ranh Bay area, General Westmoreland in April 1965 recommended to the government of Vietnam that it resettle refugees and displaced persons there. The recommendation was well received and the government began planning for the relocation of approximately 5,000 Vietnamese in a model village to be built at Ba Ngoi across Cam Ranh Bay from the peninsula. Settlers began to arrive at the village as early as July 1965 and soon provided much needed support for various engineer activities in the area. By mid-1968, the population of the village had climbed to over 15,000.[38]

The logic of displacement exemplified in this passage characterizes most official writings. Rather than examining destruction of the counryside, U.S. officials instead saw employment opportunities for the Vietnamese. The Vietnamese had the privilege of employment in the construction and operation of base areas which would be used to drive more Vietnamese out of the countryside! By concentrating on employment as an abstract issue, war-managers could write the history of war in Vietnam as the transition between "traditional" and "modern" society.

American-style "nation-building" made road construction a primary index of national development. In the summer of 1966, General Westmoreland speeded construction when he told U.S. officers that they were too reliant on helicopters and afraid of using the roads — a mark of timidity, a failing of military virtue. Roads were built to U.S. standards of weight and traffic flow. By the spring of 1970, approximately 11,000 out of 26,000 U.S. Army engineers in Vietnam were building roads or "lines of communication." Roads were touted as proof of American benevolence. According to official histories, these roads were not primarily built for war:

> One purpose of the highway program was to facilitate the movement of military supplies and increase the flexibility of tactical maneuvers. In previous wars when adequate roads were lacking temporary military roads were constructed solely to meet military needs. In Vietnam, however, the nature of the war and the tactics employed were very different from those of previous American conflicts. The desire of the United States to improve the economic and social conditions of the people as well as to improve the military situation fostered the development of dependable roads of good quality.
>
> Even more important was the contribution the program made to the pacification effort. By making travel easier and safer, communication between the villages and the cities — socially, economically, and politically — was increased. New and better roads enabled the farmer to transport his products farther and faster. Goods from cities could reach more and more rural markets and thereby contribute to raising the standard of living in these areas. Engineer bridge builders were gratified to witness the surge of civilian traffic across their roads and bridges.[39]

The roads U.S. engineers built were used by civilians, but road traffic did not legitimate Technowar. That refugees walked away from poisoned fields and burned homes on roads capable of sustaining thousands of two-and-one-half-ton troop trucks did not make their losses any less severe, nor did hard-surfaced roads and new bridges cause Vietnamese refugees to love the men who destroyed their traditional lives. Nevertheless, war-managers and their hired researchers became mesmerized by the spectacle of American construction. Reports relayed the good news that when the war ended, the Vietnamese would inherit a vast treasure chest of developed goodies, a whole new country — rather than horizon-to-horizon bomb-craters.

> In some respects the task of building a military base is comparable to that of building a town. Perhaps the major difference is that bases are planned to serve specific ends, while towns are usually unplanned and grow on the basis of expediency rather than purpose. Typical

military bases contain cantonments, storage facilities, roads, electric
power plants, communications centers, water supply and sewage systems, and provisions for security. Bases may also include airfields,
ports, and fuel storage and distribution facilities. We can look back
now to some of the outstanding base facilities and related engineering
left to our Vietnamese allies.[40]

Eight major airfields suitable for large jets were built with materials
strong enough to last for decades and furnished with control towers, fuel
tanks, hangars, and other facilities. By November 1967, at least ninety
other runways had also been constructed, but from "expedient surfacing
materials" of less durable nature and thus less promising for future development purposes.

Deep-water ports dotted the South Vietnamese coast. Besides Cam
Ranh Bay, another new port facility was built across from Saigon Harbor, a dock known as Newport. Additional deep-water berths were built
for existing ports at Danang, Qui Nhon, Vung Tau, and Vung Ro. According to the Joint Development Group, "the ports, airfields, highways, and railroads built or repaired under military auspices will amply
satisfy the needs of an expanding national development."[41]

Not only would Vietnam have airfields and ports, it would also have
more wells and better water. As the author of *Base Development* says,
"A massive well-drilling program has accompanied the buildup of
American forces in Vietnam. . . . Between July 1966 and September
1967, contractors drilled 233 successful wells and 48 test holes at twenty-
five sites." Not only did the military meet its "production goal of fifty
gallons per man per day for intermediate and field cantonments and a
hundred gallons per man per day for temporary cantonments," the records it left pointed the way to water, water everywhere in the future:
"Besides wells now in production, the records of the well-drilling program will be valuable to geologists and engineers charged in peacetime
for developing Vietnam's water resources."[42]

Americans also developed Vietnam's waterborne sewage systems.
Military standards called for building waterborne sewage systems for
bases classified as "temporary" (meaning they were to last at least four
years, as opposed to the two more primitive levels of encampment, "field"
and "intermediate"). In these two lower levels, fecal matter was burned
with diesel fuel in cutaway 55-gallon drums. Troops did not like such
bonfires in their base towns: "Morale was adversely affected by this
dense, foul, black smoke generated during burning." In particular,

Americans were especially upset by those occasions when Vietnamese "local-hire personnel" were not available for disposing of Vietnamese fecal matter associated with their employment in American base areas: "Troops were particularly disgruntled when they had to burn out latrines restricted to Vietnamese workers."[43] Sewage development, then, aided relations between the allies, as well as laying the foundation for future urban progress.

And then there were the buildings the Americans were also going to leave behind; "Pentagon East," the headquarters of Military Assistance Command Vietnam, was the star piece:

> "Pentagon East," as the MACV command post has been called, was constructed near Tan Son Nhut Airport. Its network of two-story prefabricated buildings provides air-conditioned working space for 4,000 men. In addition to cantonments and utilities, it includes mortar shelters, security fences, and guard towers. The headquarters complex for USARV (United States Army, Vietnam) was constructed at Long Binh, sixteen miles from Saigon. It occupies twenty-five square miles and houses 50,000 soldiers at a cost of more than $100 million.[44]

The Americans also brought air-conditioning. Technowar *required* air-conditioning for its computers: the military's machines were no more rugged than their civilian counterparts. But air-conditioning went far beyond special rooms for computers or cooled hospitals for the wounded — the cool world of refrigerated air became a way of life. Although regulations attempted to control who was authorized to live or work in air-conditioned units, the citylike atmosphere of base camps did not lend itself to clear demarcations of "need." Those who did not officially qualify for air-conditioners were quite capable of buying their own machines from military PX (postal exchange) stores or from the Vietnamese.

Along with refrigerated air came refrigerated fresh and frozen food. Only those few soldiers actually in combat (approximately 10 percent) had to eat C-rations or other precooked food. All garrison troops in logistical bases ate A-rations, "including fresh fruits, vegetables and milk in accordance with the monthly Continental U.S., Master Menu."[45] To meet milk and ice cream requirements, the military called for Meadowgold and Foremost Dairies to build major processing plants. An additional forty or so small ice cream plants were also constructed to "provide ice cream as far forward as possible."[46]

Taken together, the air-conditioners for barracks and offices, the refrigerators and freezers, and the personal appliances owned by soldiers made for incredible electrical demands. By the late 1960s, eleven oceangoing petroleum tankers were converted into generating plants for American bases along the coast. Even with this addition, the military could not meet the demand for electricity, and the purchase of 145 different types of generators was necessitated.

For its major generating needs the military often contracted American corporations such as Vinnel Corporation or Pacific Architects and Engineers to provide generators and operating personnel. Even the army's divisional base camps often had electricity provided by civilian contractors; military dependency on urbanlike environments as both staging and rest areas was that great.

These massive demands for electrical generating capacity in turn heightened demands for petroleum products. Although statistics are not broken down into how much fuel was used for actual combat operations and how much was used for generating electricity for air conditioners and food storage facilities, Lieutenant General Joseph M. Heiser's volume, *Logistic Support,* documents an incredible expansion:[47]

These increases are signs of progress, just like other indices of urbanization and ''nation-building.'' Within this subdivision of military discourse, Technowar as a regime of power and knowledge organized to produce maximum destruction is *displaced* by official representations of Technowar as social and economic development: urbanization goes *up;* incomes go *up;* American-grade highways and roads go *up;* modern ports and runways go *up;* electrical generating capacity goes *up;* fuel

Table 7.1
COUNTRYWIDE PETROLEUM
CONSUMPTION
*(In thousands of barrels)*

| Date | Quantity |
|------|----------|
| 1964 | 2,700 |
| 1965 | 6,785 |
| 1966 | 21,850 |
| 1967 | 36,280 |
| 1968 | 43,650 |
| 1969 | 41,725 |
| 1970 | 36,450 |

storage capacity goes *up*. War is made to appear as a series of projects to transform Vietnam into the mirror image of the United States.

Not only is the destructive war in the countryside dropped from consideration, but the actual process of urbanization and the place of new urban areas in the social structure of the war becomes distorted to the point where the war is actually incomprehensible.

War-managers were concerned about inflation caused by the influx of American troops and dollars. According to Deputy Ambassador William Porter's August memo to Robert Komer, "Fiscal year 1966 was a year of inflation. Money supply rose by 72 percent and Saigon working class cost of living index by 92 percent."[48] Although a devaluation of the GVN's currency, the piaster, from 60 to 118 piasters per dollar as the official exchange rate reduced the money supply considerably, war-managers feared the effects of United States escalation in 1967. Budget figures of debit and credit between government policies that *increased* money supply and policies that *absorbed* money from circulation did not balance. Estimates projected that the U.S. and South Vietnamese forces would spend 175.9 billion piasters while absorbing only 131.8 billion. Deputy Ambassador Porter ended his bad-news message tersely: "We consider a gap of this magnitude to be unacceptable in light of current U.S. policies."[49]

Soon his immediate superior, Ambassador Henry Cabot Lodge, joined the inflation debate. Lodge called for a piaster expenditure "ceiling" of 58 billion, 42 billion for American military and 16 billion for American civilian agencies. This figure was 16 billion piasters greater than 1966 expenditures, but was still less than the 75 billion military and civilian officials wanted to spend to support escalated activities. Lodge strongly defended his lower figure by declaring that inflation could be comprehended only "in the light of the American soldier's life." Clearly his life could be imperiled several ways:

A) The most obvious is defeat in battle.

B) But in this country, a wildcat, soul destroying inflation which means that the Vietnamese military personnel cannot make both ends meet and thereby the Vietnamese armed forces lose fighting quality could also jeopardize our own troops.

C) Also, an inflation which results in thousands of adults demonstrating in the streets (where formerly we have had only rock-throwing teenagers), with the resulting political instability leading to the over-throw of the government, could be an even more pressing danger — more so even than defeat in battle. Indeed, RAND [Research and Development Corporation] reports indicate that Viet Cong prisoners no longer believe they can be victorious in battle, but are counting on overthrowing the government in Saigon. This is the political danger inflation can cause.[50]

In Lodge's formulation, the danger of losing Vietnam does not come from destruction, but from an inflationary war machine that would cause Vietnamese to shift sides to the enemy when they could not balance their accounts. Lodge fears insolvency; the war will be lost for sure if the country goes bankrupt.

He was not alone in this thinking. Secretary of Defense McNamara also feared inflation; in one memo he even justified turning down Joint Chiefs of Staff troop requests for 1967 in terms of the inflation additional forces would cause.

> The burden of inflation falls most heavily on just those Vietnamese — the ARVN and GVN civil servants — upon whose efficient performance our success most heavily depends. Unless we rigidly control inflation, the Vietnamese Army desertion rate will increase further and effectiveness will decline, thus at least partially cancelling the effects of increased U.S. deployments. Further, government employees will leave their jobs and civil strife will occur, seriously hindering both the military and the pacification efforts and possibly even collapsing the GVN.[51]

In McNamara's thinking, a major increase in troops would increase the production of destruction, but no "profits" would accrue from this escalation since there would be higher "costs of production" — inflation and the resulting debits of increased ARVN desertion and even the collapse of the South Vietnamese government. McNamara wanted a *cost-effective* Technowar, a war machine located at that ideal point on the marginal utility curve where increased production equaled increased costs. In his words to the Joint Chiefs of Staff, "The plan I am approving at this time for budgetary planning appears to me to be the maximum consistent with my reasonable hope of economic stability."[52]

One primary management tool developed to fight inflation was called the Commodities Import Program. Sponsored by the United States Agency for International Development, it provided loans to Vietnamese businessmen to import *consumer* goods. Presumably increased consumer goods — increased buying of motorcycles, stereos, refrigerators — would take money out of circulation. Decreased money supply would permit prices for staples such as rice and cloth to remain stable. AID paid off exporting firms immediately; South Vietnamese businessmen then paid off their AID loans after the commodities had been sold. The Commodities Import Program achieved great popularity among the Vietnamese. In the *Pentagon Papers,* discussions abound on Vietnamese pressure to increase funds allocated to CIP each year and American eagerness to comply and get the Vietnamese to increase imports. In the fall of 1966, Robert Komer cabled Ambassador Lodge concerning negotiations in Washington with Governor Hanh, head of the Republic of Vietnam's national bank, telling Lodge that the United States was pressuring the South "hard to spend rapidly growing foreign exchange reserves on imports." The negotiated agreement called for a payback in which U.S. tax dollars given to Vietnam would be spent on importing commodities from U.S. corporations:

(1) GVN will use all gold and foreign exchange available to it in excess of $250 million, not including commercial bank working balances, to finance invisibles [unlisted, off-budget items] and imports, including import categories now financed by the U.S.

(2) GVN will place at least $120 million of its reserves in U.S. dollar instruments of at least 2 year maturity.

(3) During U.S. FY [fiscal year] USG will make available at least $350 million of grant aid for imports [CIP], not including PL 480 Title 1 Commodities [free foodstuffs]. Any portion of the $350 million not required for such imports will be used during U.S. FY 67 as grant assistance for economic development projects.

(4) Within the balance of payments accounts, the amounts or categories to be financed by each of the governments will be determined through joint consultation on a quarterly basis.

In June, the two governments had negotiated rules governing CIP. The GVN asked for and received assurance that "The USG would liberalize the Commodity Imports Program to cover all importers' requests." [53]

The United States thus provided funds to finance imports, but had no say over what was imported or to whom import licenses were granted. In 1964 the CIP budget was $95 million; in 1966 it increased to $350 million; by 1970 the figure was up to $750 million.[54] Recall that the idea behind the program was to *take money out of Vietnam,* to decrease inflation by providing modern consumer goods. The provision of consumer goods also perfectly fit the idea of the United States as the sponsor of an "urban revolution" in Vietnam; by making Vietnam like America, Vietnam would be "pacified" and suffer no inflation.

At this point the simple dynamics of American "development" aid to Vietnam end and the "double-reality" comes into view. Increasing aid to the Commodities Import Program should have meant that more and more money was eventually taken out to pay for imports the program financed. To the contrary, the war-managers' representation of American aid as part of a progressive drive toward "modernity" hides an incredibly corrupt economy in which *crime* constituted the primary economic activity. What is at issue is another political economy, one in which there is no distinction between "public" and private interest, a political and military apparatus oriented toward using American support for private profit.

Money clarifies the relationship between the United States and the Republic of Vietnam. Taking 1966 as an exemplary year, the official rate of exchange between the United States and Vietnam for government and government-sanctioned corporate transactions was 84 piasters to the dollar, while individuals exchanged their dollars at 118 piasters to the dollar. In theory, the United States government and American corporations under contract with the U.S. government were subsidizing the Republic of Vietnam through this differential exchange rate.

At the same time, on the black market the exchange rate in 1966 averaged over two times the official rate, at minimum over 200 piasters per dollar. Throughout the war the black market piaster-dollar exchange rate remained at least twice as high as the official rate, and often went much higher. In 1970, for example, while the official exchange rate remained at 84 piasters per dollar for "organizations" and 118 piasters per dollar for individuals, the black market rate went over 500 piasters per dollar.

There was also a third "currency" involved, "Military Payment Certificates," the currency issued to all U.S. soldiers and American employees of U.S. corporations. By issuing troops and employees supposedly nonnegotiable "certificates" rather than dollars while they were stationed in South Vietnam, it was thought that money would not be spent but circulated back toward the United States. The MPC script became another currency on the black market, exchanged at the rate of at least two MPCs per dollar.

Analyzing the institutional mechanisms by which different currencies flowed from legal to illegal channels at various exchange rates leads to a more complete understanding of the social structure of the war. Obtaining a license to import goods financed by the Commodities Import Program customarily involved bribing the South Vietnamese government. With the license, a Vietnamese could exchange piasters at the official exchange rate of say, 118 piasters for the dollar. With those dollars he or she could "pay" the exporter — many times obtaining massive kickbacks in the process. Exporters had an interest in doing business with AID-financed Commodity Import Program business deals; they were paid immediately by AID. The importer could then both sell the consumer goods — motorcycles or television sets or antibiotic drugs or whatever — at the black market ratio of piasters per dollar, and exchange whatever kickback dollars were obtained at the black market rate. By having multiple currencies at different exchange rates, the United States was fostering institutionalized mechanisms that encouraged systematic corruption because the profit rates were so high.

American soldiers and civilian contractors could *legally* use some of the institutional mechanisms for multiplying currency. An American employee of a corporation in Vietnam could cash his or her paycheck on the illegal market for Military Payment Certificates, receiving the illegal exchange rate of, say, two MPCs per dollar. Cornelius Hawkridge, who worked for a U.S. trucking company as an investigator of fraud, told journalist James Hamilton-Patterson of the many ways to multiply checks:

> As Hawkridge had discovered in Qui Nhon much of the art lay in the conversion. There were several ways of getting hard value for MPCs. One could, for instance, buy travellers' cheques (provided one bought a cheap air ticket to carry round in order to comply with the regulations governing the issue of travellers' cheques). One could buy the air ticket itself with them. One could order cars in the United States with MPCs in Vietnam, then cancel the order and ask the American manufacturer to refund the dollars to one's U.S. account. There were thousands of luxury items to be bought in the PX, to say nothing of stocks and bonds and tax-free diamonds. One could even buy property through companies represented in the PX. Clothes could be ordered from Hong Kong tailors at a huge saving.

In short the whole system of Military Payment Certificates was carte blanche for the world's money-changers. It provided a convenient vehicle for manipulation and the loser was always the United States; more specifically, the American taxpayer. MPCs had been devised for use only by the military or U.S. government employees as a strictly non-negotiable currency; in Vietnam they ended up as an indeterminate currency halfway between the dollar and the piaster, although by no means at par with the dollar because a hundred MPCs could earn a hundred and fifty dollars.[55]

The gist of Hawkridge's message concerns the movement from legal currency to black market exchange to legal exchange as a way of making money: legal currency > "illegal" transaction > "legal" transaction. By using a variety of exchange mechanisms, *money can be multiplied without producing anything.* Individuals high in the South Vietnamese civil and military establishment, together with high-ranking American military officers and civilian officials, had the opportunity to maximize exchanges.

Tracking down and naming organizations and individuals involved in these massive currency manipulations is difficult; competent criminals do not leave massive paper trails. The logic of who was involved in such structural corruption, however, is not difficult to follow. In the passage quoted below, Hawkridge's soliloquy presumes knowledge that "Prysumeen" is the name stamped on the vast majority of all checks cashed on the black market in South Vietnam, and that Mr. Ameen is a renowned black-market banker — renowned in the sum of two billion dollars net worth over a twenty-year history of currency manipulations involving U.S. aid to Asian countries. Hawkridge is speaking to Senator Abraham Ribicoff:

> All right. Suppose the manager of U.S. corporation working in Vietnam cables his head office in the States saying that he will need a million dollars for next month's payroll. He tells the parent company to pay the million dollars into an account named Prysumeen at 44 Wall Street and to send the deposit slip out to Vietnam instead of the money. All right so far?
>
> Fine.
>
> So then the manager in Vietnam hurries round to one of the Indians like Mr. Ameen and gives him the slip for a million dollars. In return, Mr. Ameen will give him at least two million dollars' worth of piasters. So now, in exchange for a single piece of paper from New York,

the manager has enough money to pay this month's payroll and next month's if he wishes, although next month he can repeat the same procedure. The spare million he plays with. Net result: a fortune for him, the payroll paid, and a million dollars which never left the U.S. for the Prysumeen account. Nasty question number three: who pays income taxes on that million? I've estimated by my own figures that there is probably getting on for sixty million dollars in that one account alone, the majority of it from large U.S. corporations. So. Who pays?

This time there was a long silence.

Can it be, said Hawkridge tiredly, that some of our giant corporations, the backbone of the U.S. economy, are busily salting away private fortunes while our GIs are being shot up? That while the average man is crippled with taxes these people whose accounts are never audited join the ranks of Paul Getty and H. L. Hunt, rich enough to buy immunity? And on top of that, don't forget the connivance without which it couldn't be done. There must be someone in the know in the Head Office: nobody pays a million dollars of a corporation's money into an unknown bank account just at the request of a manager out in Vietnam. Also, someone in the Internal Revenue is being kind enough to overlook the Prysumeen account. How much is that attack of myopia worth, I wonder?[56]

In Hawkridge's experience, not only individuals but entire corporations took advantage of the dual exchange rate to multiply their financial holdings. Foreign governments operating in Vietnam used the same dual exchange rates as well. The United States paid for tens of thousands of Korean and Thai soldiers. According to MACV regulations, these troops were supposed to be paid in piasters at the official exchange rate. However, the American army colonel in charge of the Paymaster's Office in Saigon for paying foreign troops found that these regulations were readily circumvented. The conversation cited below takes place on an airplane flying from South Vietnam and Thailand; the plane is full of Thai officers, each officer possessing a large briefcase. The colonel is talking to Hawkridge:

"I'm in charge of paying the Thais fighting in Vietnam and the bastards won't take their pay in piasters. Their officers — these guys, as a matter of fact —" he jerked his head at the passengers, "took one look at the piasters and flatly refused to accept them. Well, regulations say pay 'em in piasters, but they still wouldn't take the stuff.

They marched off and a bit later MACV rang up and told me to pay them in any currency they wanted." He shrugged. "They wanted green, so I had to give 'em green."

Hawkridge nodded comprehendingly.

"The usual racket?"

"The usual racket," the Colonel agreed. "The officers would come in and collect their men's pay in U.S. greenbacks. They'd take the money straight round to the Indian dealers and buy enough piasters to pay off their troops. The rest of the dollars they pocket themselves and fly them back home to Thailand. That's what these guys here are doing. Bet you anything."[57]

When he walked down the plane's aisle, Hawkridge saw one officer's open briefcase; just as the colonel thought, it was filled with twenty-dollar bills. The paymaster did not say whether the same practice held true for the Koreans and Filipinos, but the financial incentive was the same. Moreover, the South Korean and Filipino governments negotiated favorable terms for sending their troops to Vietnam: for every man they sent, the United States agreed to pay his military salary as well as to hire a South Korean or Filipino civilian to work in Vietnam at American wages, $8,000 to $10,000 a year.[58] These civilian employees, too, used the black market. One even introduced investigator Hawkridge to the Indian money-changers: "I'm a Korean, Mr. Hawkridge, and I'm entitled to send home every month a certain proportion of my salary in dollars. So I go down to the money-changers, give them my salary cheque and get a fifty per cent mark-up in MPCs. That way I send off a thousand dollars and keep the other $600. In fact, Mr. Hawkridge, I get two salaries."[59]

Hawkridge put most of the pieces of the black market puzzle together. He noted that the exchange rate for the entire country was set every day at 8:30 A.M. He also noted that the leading Indian money-changers had virtually endless quantities of new piaster notes available within fifteen minutes' notice. There was also the hint dropped during a conversation with Mr. Ameen, one of the leading Indian black market bankers: "The Americans are immensely generous, but more immediately there are a number of very sympathetic people in the GVN."[60] Hawkridge tried to get a more definite explanation of "how is it that whenever we withdraw our MPCs and issue new ones you already have an unlimited supply within twenty-four hours? It has always puzzled me."[61]

Ameen did not reply, but the answer beckons: leading officials of the Republic of Vietnam participated in the black market currency exchange. To the Vietnamese, the American fiction of treating Vietnam as a sovereign state presented virtually endless opportunities for individual or group financial gain. Government and military positions were also *business* positions, ways of channeling monies and goods coming into Vietnam for the war effort into the black market for individual riches. When the United States government gave the GVN dollars for an artificially low exchange rate to pay for piasters the U.S. needed for its activities in Vietnam, GVN officials could then readily double their money by selling the dollars on the black market.

All the war-managers' talk of reducing inflation is completely bogus. Vietnam becomes *represented* as a developing nation whose problems of inflation are being solved through the rational planning of civilian consumption, but the new urbanized Vietnam was based on *systematic corruption*. The structure of dual exchange rates was only the financial half of this urban economy; the other half revolved around the theft of war supplies for sale on the black market and the provisions of "illegal" substances and services.

Theft was a principal business activity of many government personnel. According to William J. Lederer, a former navel officer turned journalist and novelist, the contents of all ships bound for Vietnam were put up for sale on the world market weeks before the ships actually arrived:

> The vice-director of the port of Saigon, Chung Duc Mai, and his boss know which American ships and what American cargoes will be coming to Saigon. They control the unloading. Perhaps two weeks before an American freighter arrives in Saigon, the contents of the American vessels have been broadcast among various possible customers. There are many. The Vietcong is one, the North Vietnamese are another, and sometimes Red China, or perhaps a middleman in Hong Kong, or any nation in the world who needs the cargo and is willing to pay a high enough price.[62]

The underground did not follow one uniform routine; once in harbor, different ships met different fates. Oftentimes ships did not dock immediately, but remained at anchor offshore for months. In these cases the cargoes were loaded onto small boats for the first leg of their black market journey. In other instances, the ships unloaded as scheduled and their cargoes were then taken from the dock area.

There are many stories of cargoes headed for Cambodia. Lederer and his Vietnamese guide, an old friend named Tran Trong Hoc, observed two modes of theft and shipment. The first began with an American freighter unloading its cargo onto barges. According to Tran, "Those barges belong to a Vietnamese company owned by a couple of Vietnamese generals. *You Americans pay for the use of those barges. You Americans pay for the privilege of sending ammunition and food and war supplies to this country* [Lederer's emphasis]."[63] The investigators watched the cargo loaded on trucks that "had been U.S. Army trucks, but now they were painted a slightly different shade of brown."[64] They observed that the truck drivers were getting "restless." Tran interprets: "Ordinarily time means very little to us. Therefore when Vietnamese drivers are nervous about a schedule, it means only one thing. They are about to go through VC territory. The VC are paid off to let a convoy come through at a specified time. If the convoy is early or late, the truck might be blown up."[65]

Soon a Vietnamese army jeep arrived to lead the convoy. A member of the government's intelligence service then gave each driver "an official document which says that the materials in the truck are being delivered to the South Vietnamese Intelligence Forces and are for the use of the Intelligence Forces."[66] This documentation got the truck past all road sentries, including the rare American checks. The trucks drove to Cambodia where they were met by a convoy of Cambodian cargoes. American electronic equipment from the ship was loaded on Cambodian trucks and, in turn, Vietnamese trucks were loaded with "tons of Red Chinese merchandise. There is no attempt to disguise anything. Everything is marked clearly in large cardboard cartons. The boxes contain toothbrushes, tooth powder, vitamins, imitation fountain pens, and thermos bottles, among other things."[67] These Vietnamese trucks were then driven to a warehouse in Cholon (outskirts of Saigon) owned by a Chinese businessman.

On another day, Lederer and Tran watched a huge riverboat being loaded with "sheet metal, U.S. rice, U.S. cement, U.S. ammunition, U.S. oil" and other American war supplies. It routinely left for Cambodia every sixth day and returned with contraband. The ship had official documents provided by one of the Vietnamese intelligence branches. Tran pointed out how difficult it was for the U.S. Navy to detect fraud: "All your goddam Navy can do is glance at the document with the

Intelligence Force's letterhead and Thanit's [a Vietnamese commander] signature. So, of course your Navy permits the ship to go on. How in hell does the U.S. Navy know the ship's carrying black-market material stolen from the U.S. Army?"[68] The steamship company running these smuggling missions to Cambodia was chartered by the Vietnamese navy.

Hawkridge even found some American military men doing business. A lieutenant made him a friendly offer: "We run this weekly convoy to the Cambodian border delivering munitions to the troops. There's a lot of stuff; I don't reckon the U.S. Army would miss the odd personnel carrier or M-60. If you give me the money, I'll get you what you want. You can buy anything at the border, anything at all."[69] From all accounts of corruption, the business in stolen supplies along the Cambodian border appears to have been tremendous.

Not everything was shipped out; Vietnam remained a massive market. Much war material was stolen as it was transported. American military and civilian agencies hired American corporations to provide trucking services. Equipment Incorporated, a subsidiary of Sea-Land Corporation, received a contract to haul supplies. There were so many supplies that the company hired 1,500 drivers to run 400 trucks twenty-four hours a day. By agreement with the Vietnamese and American governments, Equipment Incorporated had to hire Vietnamese drivers. Hawkridge reported that within the first month all 400 trucks had been stripped of their parts or stolen. Cargoes did not fare much better:

> The opportunities for hijacking and pilfering were unsurpassed. The drivers were usually in collusion with either the Vietnamese Security Police, the ARVN or the regular police. Mostly, the wanted cargoes were marked actually inside the Saigon port area by the Vietnamese security guards. These signs would be spotted by the drivers and hijackers so it was always known well in advance which load to misdeliver or waylay. Running four hundred trucks twenty-four hours a day, Equipment Incorporated quickly lost a staggering amount of goods; so much, in fact, that this single contract provided the basis for most of the black market supplies on sale in South Vietnam.[70]

Convoys leaving with fifty trucks often reached their destinations with only a dozen. Sometimes trucks were found abandoned, other times they just disappeared. Disguised by timbers and pieces of galvanized steel roofing that made them resemble huts, stolen vehicles escaped surveillance by American helicopters long enough to move their cargoes and be stripped for parts, the chassis cut into pieces to make identification impossible. In 1967, Equipment Incorporated tried running convoys in groups of twelve trucks with machine gun–equipped military jeeps in front and back. In response, some truck drivers deliberately cut their ignition wires, pulled off the road, and complained of mechanical failures. The armed military jeeps continued with the remaining trucks of the convoy, leaving the "disabled" truck and cargo for thieves.

United States Army administrators ruled that all thefts of American supplies by Vietnamese should be reported first to an American liaison officer, who in turn would notify Vietnamese police. Whether or not any given incident actually got reported was doubtful. Even when the "suspect" was reported, police involvement in organized theft often eliminated meaningful action. Under these circumstances, American military police were reluctant to get involved. Hawkridge once caught a driver taking a truckload of C-rations to enemy territory. When the American military released the suspect, Hawkridge asked why. In response, the Americans complained of "Aw, too much paper-work."[71] The suspect said that he didn't care whether the Americans attempted to have him prosecuted or not:

> However, this man knew enough English to point out that it made no difference whether or not they turned him in because his brother-in-law was the judge in Tu Duc and he would be released even before they had time to get home again. So they freed him too, a few hours after he had stolen a truckload of C-rations for the Viet Cong. The following day, he was back driving again for Equipment Incorporated.[72]

Since the Republic of Vietnam gave virtual license to steal war supplies, stopping theft was impossible so long as the United States treated its own creation — the GVN — as a sovereign state. Consequently, although the United States adhered to the "sovereign state paradigm" to avoid charges of colonizing Vietnam, one cost of this fictional sovereignty was massive theft. All the investigators seem to have been awed both by the quantity of illicit merchandise and by the fact that the American officials seemed totally unwilling to do anything about the problem.

When Cornelius Hawkridge got his job with Equipment Incorporated, he decided he needed a gun. An American colonel in Qui Non directed him to the local black market, a block-long shopping center:

> The entire market as well as the shops in the surrounding side streets was stacked with every conceivable kind of U.S. military equipment.

C-rations, K-rations, drink, clothing, guns, cannons, shells, cases of grenades, television sets, washing-machines . . . the mounds seemed limitless. Hawkridge walked all round it slowly. Shirts with the PX marking still on them, but now much cheaper. Cigarettes by the million. Wondering what limits there were he asked a Vietnamese stall-holder whether he could buy a tank.

"Tanks are a bit difficult right now," the man admitted, "but how about some armoured personnel carriers? Or helicopters, of course. We can't provide very many just off the cuff but we can get hold of some more if you would like to place an order. *Perhaps I can interest you in a heavy duty truck?*" [73]

Hawkridge had been hired to guard heavy-duty trucks, to stop the theft that allowed the vendor's casual offer. He ran back to the American colonel with a startling report: "Did you know, Colonel, that there's enough material in that market to put an entire U.S. division in the field for a month?" [74] The colonel said yes, he knew this, and he also knew that the United States was fighting a guerrilla war and that providing an open market of war supplies for the enemy was certainly bad form, "But there's an agreement between the U.S. and the Vietnamese governments that Americans are not allowed to police the country. This is a police matter. We have no jurisdiction." [75]

William Lederer arrived in Vietnam needing basic clothes and boots for the field, only to find that the American military store, the PX, didn't have any for sale. He was directed to the black market in Saigon:

The place looked like a U.S. Army ordnance ammunition depot. Everything seemed to be painted brown and smell either of oil or fresh paint. Ordnance equipment was arranged in orderly lines, and neatly printed price tags hung from everything. Automatic rifles were $250. A 105-mm. mortar, sample only (if a customer wanted one, he could pick it up at the Cholon godown), was priced at $400. *(I wondered if the mortar which blew off my friend Clint Moreau's legs was purchased here.)* [Lederer's emphasis] There were about a thousand American rifles of different kinds standing neatly in racks. M-16's cost $80. On one side of the lift were uniforms of all services, including the U.S. Air Force. There was even U.S. Navy diving equipment. [76]

Everything was available on the black market — everything that the United States supplied. By 1970 the U.S. Army estimated that over

500,000 tons of rice that the United States sent to Vietnam had been
stolen. Such a vast amount was the equivalent of 50,000 ten-ton trucks
disappearing, an imaginary convoy stretching 238 miles.[77] The Vietnamese officer corps stole the rice intended to pacify the populace that
was supposed to give them political support!

Much cement sent to Vietnam also was stolen. Cement was an essential war commodity, necessary for runways, mess halls, bunkers, houses,
hospitals, and virtually every other construction endeavor. Hawkridge
once found 40,000 stolen bags. Lederer tells about finding cement meant
for 10,000 refugees: "The Vietnamese lieutenant colonel who received
the cement sold it on the black market in Hue. U.S. officials knew about
this. But they were unable or unwilling to stop it or do anything about
it."[78]

Roofing intended for huts to be built by refugees was another stolen
commodity. According to marine Colonel William R. Corson, when the
initial request for 18,000 tons of "tin roof" was received by the Arthur
D. Little management consulting firm in 1967, they found that AID's
purchase of 18,000 tons of galvanized steel plate was "at least eight
times more than could be used to satisfy all of the valid demand in
Vietnam. Indicating clearly and in considerable detail every possible use
for steel plate, the report estimated that for civilian roofing requirements
1,000 or 'even 2,000 tons could be going into such uses. Even so the
*over-all supply and demand discrepancy would still be very large.*'"[79]
If the overall supply and demand was large at 2,000 tons, then 18,000
tons must be regarded as a figure derived by Vietnamese black market
manipulators.

Modern consumer goods imported either by the Commodity Import
Program or the PX system were also available on the black market.
General Westmoreland had conceived of building up the PX system so
that U.S. troops would spend their money there rather than contribute
to inflation by spending money in the local economy.[80] In reality, the
PX system permitted the importation of thousands of tons of consumer
goods. All U.S. military personnel, U.S. civilians, and foreign civilian
and military personnel directly hired by the U.S. government were entitled to purchase each year "one television set, two radios, two still
cameras, one movie camera, one movie projector, one slide projector,
one stereo tape recorder, one refrigerator, one washing machine, one
spin dryer, two watches. . . ."[81] Eventually, anyone with PX privileges could buy expensive items such as diamonds, bonds, real estate,
and automobiles. By this legal mechanism, consumer goods were sent

to Vietnam, where they were often stolen in massive quantities while in transport or storage.

Rarely did war-managers openly discuss corruption. In volume 2 of the *Pentagon Papers* there is a circumscribed discussion; the American embassy in Saigon reported the following agreement with the GVN in June 1966:

> The United States Military Agency appointed by COMUSMACV [General William Westmoreland, Commander, U.S. Military Assistance Command, Vietnam] . . . shall forthwith assume responsibility and all necessary authority for . . .
>
> A. The receipt and discharge of all AID-financed commodities consigned to CPA.
>
> B. The obtaining of customs clearances and all other clearances . . . for such commodities.
>
> C. The storage and warehousing of such commodities in transit as necessary.
>
> D. The transport of such commodities to such first destinations, including GVN holding areas and/or CPA ministerial depots as may be designated by USAID/CPA.[82]

At first glance it would seem that the United States was taking over the ports and was making a major effort to eradicate corruption. Although the *Pentagon Papers* indicates that these provisions were agreed upon by the GVN, at the same time entirely different negotiations are indicated for October 1966. The *Pentagon Papers* treats this second set of negotiations very briefly, but their implications are astounding. The June agreements are in effect nullified:

> Ky kept talking about infiltration whenever McNamara brought up the subject of the port. Finally, Ky said he had solved the port problem by telling the Minister of Finance "to write a decree to get rid of the mafia which was dominating the port."
>
> That did not solve the problem; the Embassy kept pressing. On November 2, Ky promised a tough decree on port management and a deliver-or-get-fired order to the General who had been put in charge of the port after the June agreement. (Accepting merely this order would permit further delay before any change in the system, of course.) Later on in November, Ky changed port charges and accepted some

increase in U.S. military personnel there; but both GVN and MACV strongly resisted any increase in MACV responsibility for the port.[83]

The *Pentagon Papers* quotes a State Department source advocating cutting off aid to the GVN. The rest of the interchange culminates in an extraordinary reconciliation with the GVN, confirming it as legitimate:

> There is already an interchange of information on the working level between Ky's investigative staff and our responsible people in USAID. We doubt GVN would respond positively to the idea of joint US/GVN inspectorate to work on AID diversions. This would touch very sensitive areas. While we want to expose and cut diversions to maximum extent possible, we doubt that this rather public way is best suited to achieve GVN cooperation.[84]

By December, U.S. officials had become so oriented toward satisfying the GVN that the *Pentagon Papers* summarized: "On December 3 [1966], Lodge and Ky had an 'amiable discussion' on corruption and Ky agreed to study and consider all these suggestions." American warmanagers knew that vast amounts of both war supplies and nation-building "pacification" materials were routinely stolen from ports and warehouses even though they were officially guarded by ARVN troops. For MACV to resist responsibility for guarding its own supplies suggests tacit acceptance of corruption. Ky's promise to have the GVN minister of finance "write a decree to get rid of the mafia which was dominating the port" was a joke, an insult to the Americans — no decree was going to stop theft organized by the South Vietnamese government, nor was an "amiable discussion" on corruption going to solve anything. Such notations represent corruption as a minor problem to be solved by small negotiating committees between the United States and the Republic of Vietnam and thus unworthy of further mention.

These evasions did not satisfy those who investigated corruption. Both of Lederer's closest informants thought that corruption was sanctioned by the United States. A Vietnamese economist called attention to Americans who profited by the war: "It is true that officials in the Vietnamese government are corrupt. But they could not be this way without considerable cooperation from American officials. If your Department of Internal Revenue would check up on the hidden earnings of several thousand Americans over here during the last fifteen years, you would be in for some surprises."[85] Tran Trong Hoc thought that "America is doing everything to lose the war. It makes a big show, spending billions, has thousands of its men killed, but *really down deep is trying to lose* [Lederer's emphasis]. . . . Whenever you allow these Vietnamese big-shot crooks to enrich themselves at the expense of the common good, at the expense of the common people, do you know what you are doing? You are helping the Vietcong to win the war!''[86] Both Vietnamese thought that since the United States was such a powerful country in comparison to Vietnam, the corruption must have been approved; they could not imagine a contradictory system in which the Americans took Vietnamese ''sovereignty'' seriously enough that they found themselves in a situation totally out of control.

Hawkridge also thought that the relationship between the two countries was determined by the United States, in particular exchange rates between them: ''Firstly, consideration must be given to the fact that the U.S. heavily overvalued the Vietnamese piaster since the start of the intervention, thereby giving the opportunity to every dubious character inside or outside the South Vietnamese government to make a fortune overnight. No-one will ever convince me that the weak South Vietnamese government forced the strong U.S. government to overvalue the piaster.''[87]

There is much merit to the assertion that the United States willingly participated in a systematically corrupt relationship with its creation, the Republic of Vietnam. Although the overvaluation of the Vietnamese currency was justified in terms of shoring up the GVN, in terms of economic rationality, the black market exchanges did not create a ''strong'' Vietnamese currency. To allow black market currencies to continue indicates official acceptance of money-making by manipulating Vietnamese and American regulations. MACV's refusal to guard Vietnamese ports and warehouses also indicates willing participation in corruption.

Sometimes congressional committees dared to probe the political economy of Vietnam, but they never saw just how massive corruption was, how many billions of dollars were involved. In 1966 the Senate Permanent Subcommittee on Investigations examined financial records of the great construction consortium for American projects in Vietnam, RMK/BRJ (Raymond, Morris-Knudsen, Brown, Root & Jones), reporting that the combine ''did not appear to use necessary foresight to obtain sufficient personnel to handle the influx of material, nor did they apparently take other proper steps to insure receipt, storage, theft protection, and accountability for shipments.''[88] By July 1966, $45 million worth of materials were missing. By May of 1967, the General Accounting Office's review of RMK/BRJ found that around $120 million was missing.[89] Yet nothing was ever done except to reward more contracts and periodically revise the figures for lost materials.

The same Senate subcommittee also looked into the Agency for International Development's Commodity Import Program. In 1966, Vietnam imported enough antibiotics for all Southeast Asia; investigators concluded that the Vietcong and other Communist forces received many shipments. There were also findings of "kickbacks," situations in which the Vietnamese imported merchandise bought from exporters under the stipulation that a good portion of the AID money paid to the exporters was "kicked back" to the importer. By 1968, American, West German, and British pharmaceutical companies paid back over one million dollars to AID for various discrepancies in their accounts[90] — considering the vastness of corruption involved, small change.

A senior sergeant-major in the U.S. Army, William O. Wooldridge, was caught in a plot involving the theft of several hundred thousand dollars from soldiers' entertainment clubs in Germany. Wooldridge and several other sergeants used this money to form a company that sold supplies at inflated prices to NCO (noncommissioned officer) clubs in Vietnam. Still little money was involved in comparison to major black market operations. The occasional revelation of corruption turned corruption into a seemingly solvable problem. Never was the basic legitimacy of the Republic of Vietnam called into question.

Why would the war-managers willingly acquiesce in the theft of so much American aid, especially when it sometimes ended in the grasp of the enemy? There are two versions of the "willful participation" thesis. The first posits that all the groups making money off systematic corruption lobbied to create and maintain a structure that they could manipulate. Lederer reports that quite a few people had an interest in the new urban economy feeding off American aid. According to his research, the rank order of group participation in the black market in terms of profits made and number of people involved was:

1. South Vietnamese generals and officials.
2. South Vietnamese businessmen who are friends of the Vietnamese in official power.
3. The National Liberation Front (Vietcong).
4. American black-market operators.
5. North Vietnamese agents.
6. Nationalist Chinese businessmen, both in Vietnam and in Taiwan.

7. Korean troops, businessmen, and officials.
8. Filipino troops, businessmen, and officials.[91]

Hawkridge's research shows the additional presence of Indian bankers and American corporations. The personal plunder theory explains the activities of GVN officials and other "businessmen," but it does not explain what American war-managers as a whole were receiving in return for setting up a corrupt system that seemed to destroy or at least hamper the continual production of Technowar.

Could it be that the leading GVN officials in effect demanded a corrupt system as their price for participating in the war? In other words, American war-managers *bought* the GVN officer corps as managers to organize a South Vietnamese army. The *price* American war-managers paid for their mercenary army was an unofficial aid system totaling hundreds of billions of dollars, which could be readily appropriated by the South Vietnamese officer corps and leading businessmen. These men got wealthy and in return permitted destruction of the countryside and the deaths of their lower-class peasant countrymen. "Buying" an army also fits the logic of Technowar and its emphases of debit and credit, war as an assembly line of death. By this reasoning, American officials could not "control" corruption because the South Vietnamese realized that the Americans *had to buy them to continue the war.* Therefore, the Vietnamese elite refused all efforts to "lower the price" by controlling corruption.

There is one more possible explanation for American participation in large-scale theft of American war supplies, namely the contradictions of what has previously been called the "sovereignty paradigm." If Vietnam was conceptualized by the war-managers as a sovereign nation being invaded from the "outside" by the foreign Other, then the United States had to respect the sovereignty of its creation — the GVN — and accede to its demands. In other words, the United States constantly had to avoid all situations in which it became apparent that the United States was the foreign Other in Vietnam. More concretely, the United States could not take any radical action that might lead to the collapse of the GVN regime, because if the government completely collapsed, then the South would be directly ruled by the United States, in contradiction to the justification of U.S. presence in Vietnam as assistance to a sovereign nation seeking to avoid Communist "takeover."

At the lower levels of the U.S. civil and military hierarchies, failures to intervene and stop Vietnamese theft and other forms of corruption were routinely explained by American officials in terms of the constraints official regulations imposed concerning Vietnamese sovereignty. Stories of U.S. restraint appear over and over again in texts by major investigators. William Lederer slowly came to understand the situation. He was first upset by Vietnamese boys wanting protection money to watch his jeep parked in front of the PX in Cholon. The PX officer replied to his angry complaint:

> The street is Vietnamese territory. We are guests in this country. We have no jurisdiction over anything that happens in the street. Those kids can sell stolen PX merchandise out there and we can't touch them. Only the Vietnamese police can do anything. . . .
>
> I assure you there's nothing we can do. We are the guests in this country . . . and that's the way General Westmoreland has ordered it.[92]

Paying a few piasters to Vietnamese boys was minor, but Lederer kept hearing the same explanation even as the stakes became progressively higher. He ran across an American adviser to the Saigon police who was trying to stop the police practice of extracting money from peasants who sold food in the Saigon marketplace. The police adviser was soon told by his superior from AID to stop complaining: "After all, this is their country, not ours."[93] Later on, another American official chastised the police adviser severely: "Remember, we are guests in this country. You are here to advise police on law enforcement techniques, not to interfere with their personal behaviors."[94] Stopping corruption was thus beyond the American domain. In particular, Americans were encouraged *not to report* corrupt actions; in this way corruption would eventually *disappear* from official forms as a "debit" and reappear as another problem solved. Even major corruption could be erased:

> The name of the chief of the Department of Supplies for Vietnam was Tran Do Cung. He turned down the request from the American government to unload the rice ship — even though the country was close to famine in some areas. Instead, he gave orders that ships carrying Honda motor scooters be given first priority for unloading.
>
> Tran Do Cung received a 5 per cent kickback on every Honda landed in Vietnam. The U.S. Embassy and the U.S. military knew about this. I asked an Army colonel why we didn't do anything. "How could we do anything? It's their country, isn't it?"[95]

Again and again in the war literature there are stories of taking abuse from Vietnamese allies the United States was supposed to be defending. The Vietnamese were adept practitioners of doublethink in their relations with Americans. Corruption involving rental of Vietnamese facilities to the U.S. government was common. Buildings were routinely reclassified to meet specifications for maximum rent increases according to official rules designed to hold down costs:

> The second rented house I looked at had four miniature bedrooms. It had one room which *might* be called a bath. It consisted of a toilet bowl and a shower. The shower had only cold water. There was no sink. Two of the bedrooms each had a basin with cold water. The house was designated by the Vietnamese as a "three-bathroom house." By Vietnamese zoning law, if a house has three "bathrooms" it can be designated as a hotel. If it is a hotel, the rent can be raised, and the minimum is $100 per month per room. This small, miserable shack was listed as a *three-bathroom hotel,* and the U.S. government was paying $400 per month for it. There was no wallpaper. The plaster was cracked. There was a garbage dump within fifteen feet of the front door. In America this shack could not possibly have gotten by even a bribed health inspector.[96]

Having rented thousands of these shacks and buildings, in many instances the United States went on to pay incredibly high electrical bills. Lederer encountered a U.S. Navy "chief," the equivalent to a senior sergeant in the army hierarchy, who explained how the cost of electricity was determined:

> You see that generator? It provides electricity for this building which has quarters and offices used by our armed forces. It's our building, on lease from the Vietnamese. We pay rent for it. Well, that U.S. Army generator makes the electricity for our building.
> We make the electricity because the power supplied by the Vietnamese is unreliable. We run our cables through the meter, and we have to pay South Vietnamese what the meter reads at the end of the month. We have to pay the South Vietnamese for the electricity which we generate. . . .
> The Vietnamese say they'll throw the United States out of the building if we don't comply. So we comply and pay them for the electricity we generate. What's more, if we pay without a squawk and everything goes smoothly all up and down the line, some colonel or general

gets a commendation for his "unselfish devotion to duty and cooperation" when his tour is up at the end of the year.[97]

Americans were not only the victims of crime. Americans were also
*buyers* on the black market; in particular they bought women and they
bought drugs. After Saigon fell in 1975, the Democratic Republic of
Vietnam claimed that an estimated 200,000 Vietnamese women had become prostitutes during the war.[98] That figure may be high, but Vietnamese refugees displaced from the countryside and working-class city
dwellers needed money to survive. Prostitution was the way many women
supported their families. Eric Herter, a former USAID official stationed
in the Mekong Delta, describes some of the social dynamics involved:

> I think the thing that touched me the most was the way that they
> would allow themselves to get very emotionally involved with guys.
> They'd done themselves in as far as Vietnamese society was con-
> cerned. Even their family would give them a certain amount of dis-
> tance for being a prostitute and they would be doing this for their
> family nine times out of ten. The family would be poor and the girl
> would be good-looking. How virtuous is it to remain virtuous when
> by so doing she was depriving her family of more money than her
> father could make. The greater virtue lies in giving up her "virtue"
> and, in a sense, sacrificing herself, sacrificing her life. Vietnamese
> women are raised with the idea of being a mother, being a wife, with
> a very idealistic sense of it. There's practically no divorce in Vietnam
> and when people get married, they get married with the greatest kind
> of sentimental attachment. They really believe in the institution of
> romantic love. So these girls had thrown that away and, in a sense,
> were on their own.[99]

Vietnam novels and memoirs are full of similar accounts of Vietnamese women supporting their families through prostitution. Lieutenant
William Calley says of one woman he knew: "I could pay her $10,000
and she would send it, every cent, to her mother, that's how the Vietnamese are."[100] Yvonne's mother had been a prostitute for French troops.
Another soldier expressed his anger more bluntly: "Vietnam may be
one big whorehouse, but the only thing degrading is that women have
to fuck in order for whole families to survive."[101]

American money and mobility created a multitiered sexual marketplace. The most expensive "call girls" catering to the higher echelons
of civil and military officials often had operations to make their eyes

appear more Caucasian. Relatively few women had such elite courtesan positions. For women of peasant and urban working-class origins, the most stable position was that of "hootch girl" or "house-mouse." Sometimes these terms were used by American soldiers to refer to the Vietnamese women who cleaned their barracks in rear-area bases. At other times the terms indicate the widespread practice whereby women cleaned, cooked, had sexual relations — virtually lived — with Americans in these base areas for as long as the soldiers stayed. Women "came with" living quarters; new soldiers inherited women from departing soldiers. When Colonel Anthony Herbert arrived at An Khe, the base commander congratulated him: "And by the way," he chortled, "wait until you see the one you're getting. She is a doll, a real doll. She'll be in tomorrow."[102]

Sometimes soldiers also supplied their friends with names of prostitutes with whom they spent their weeklong rest and relaxation "leaves." Although most soldiers traveled to Hong Kong or Taiwan or Thailand for their leaves, "in-country" leave business remained strong. One soldier told the story of his relationship: "But I did go to a hotel with her for a week, and she explained to me I should find her another man so she could send money back to her family. And the last I heard of her she had been through dozens of guys, still earning money, still supporting the whole family back home."[103]

There were also "bar girls," women who worked in bars selling "Saigon tea" to American soldiers and civilians. The woman's objective was to prolong conversation with the customer, encouraging consumption of weak, green tea at expensive prices before negotiating a price for herself. Bar girls were required to split their fees with bar owners. According to Mike McGrady, a *Newsday* reporter, these women earned at least $700 a month in the mid-1960s, an amount far higher than officially paid to the country's premier ($350).[104]

But most prostitutes worked in brothels, virtual sex factories where the turnover of customers was rapid, the pay low, and the life brutal. Known as "massage parlors" by their public signs and advertisements, they were places men went for "steam and cream," or "short-time" or "boom-boom." Sometimes brothers and sisters or even children of these women served as their pimps. Just getting paid could be a problem for these women — encounters with soldiers often turned hostile. Lieutenant Calley reports that a man in his platoon hit a prostitute in an effort to get twenty dollars back because she would not have sex with everyone in the platoon *twice* for the money.[105]

Sometimes soldiers cooperated with the prostitutes' demands for more money; even false affection was better than hostility:

"Hey Chris, you souvenir me two dollar?"

"What?" he spat the word through his teeth as he grabbed for his shirt.

"Five dollar for Mama-san. You souvenir Hue now."

Oh, the bite. He should have known. He knew perfectly well, because Chief had told him, that the girls kept fifty percent and Mama-san got fifty percent, and this was just a trick to get him to pay more. "No." He flung down the word, stepped over, and started out of the little enclosure.

"Cheap Charlie!" The words bit into him. They were mean and hard, a total switch from what the girl had been.

Then he thought of the room full of people and that wise-ass Ragland. What if she got out there and said something. They'd surely all laugh. Maybe the other Vietnamese would make a fuss. What should he do? More angry than ever, he ripped out his wallet and took out two dollars, threw them down on the bed and turned to go. Just as instantly as her mood had swung hard, now it swung back.

"Chris, you numba one," she cooed. "Come see Hue boo-coo times. No butterfly." He felt like throwing a grenade, but he set his face in a blank mask and walked back to the room.[106]

On other occasions sexual encounters became violent. Some Vietnamese women were shot and killed; others were beaten. Pat Faherty portrays one marine's violence against a woman when the thin illusion of romance vanished and her alienation became evident:

Turning to her customer, she gave the basic gook name and threw out her entire English vocabulary. "You pay."

"You'd never suspect she loves Americans," Crash joked to the leeching kid who waited to handle the financial end of the deal. . . .

When Crash crawled in, she was out of her robe, sitting up with her legs spread open, her arms at her side and an impatient stare on her face.

She made him uneasy as he fumbled to undress, positioned himself and kept an eye on his belongings at the same time.

He took her left hand and kissed it. She laughed at him. He stroked her nipples and gently edged to the center of the bed. Her expression turned to a blank-eyed smirk. Her body remained still and stiff.

"You're beautiful," Crash whispered rising to his knees.

He swung!

His right fist caught her solidly where her arm joined her shoulder. Her head hit the wall. Her face contorted. She rolled over on her side clutching the rapidly disintegrating point of impact.

He grabbed her neck jerking her towards him. The look on her face turned from terror to hate. He took longer than usual to finish. Finally getting back up to his knees, he threw the spent rubber at her, turned and pissed on the wall.[107]

Pervasive prostitution by Vietnamese women as a means of survival did not help the Americans win allegiance from Vietnamese. As one American soldier said, "The Vietnamese hate us also because the whole thing is turning into a big brothel . . . Saigon is a large whorehouse. It is. I was there. I saw it. Bien Hoa is, too. Xuan Loc is too."[108] McGrady once read a Vietnamese newspaper editorial on the disastrous consequences of raising school tuition: "As the school fees go to new highs, the parents will send only the boys to school and the girls will stay home. And what will these illiterate girls do? Be snack-bar girls, prostitutes, or employees for Yankee firms?"[109] So many women either became prostitutes or had emotionally bonded sexual relations with American men that Vietnamese men started a rumor that Americans brought "shrinking bird [penis] disease" to Vietnam. This "disease" caused severe sexual dysfunctioning among Vietnamese men.[110] Impotence does not pacify anyone.

Nevertheless, much *money* was made off prostitution; it was an integral component of the new urban society. In some areas, the Vietcong routinely taxed brothels: "Going downtown on the weekend was an adventure. . . . We were being protected by the NLF in town because 20,000 people, each spending $20 a weekend was a huge source of income through their taxation system."[111] In other areas, brothels were taxed by Vietnamese police and ARVN units. Hawkridge discovered that General Nguyen Ngoc Loan, head of the Military Security Service and the National Police, was involved in "taxation" of Saigon brothels: "By the way, his police were being trained by the U.S. and trained well; every hour on the hour the police jeeps make their rounds of the Saigon whorehouses to collect their dues."[112] In other cities and towns different military units took their cuts. Prostitution was part of the organized criminal social structure.

Drugs were another major commodity. While the central foci of

Technowar were the ground war in South Vietnam and the bombing campaign in the north, another war took place in Laos. The Central Intelligence Agency ran that war using mountain-dwelling Meo tribesmen — whose main crop was opium poppies — as their primary ground fighting force. The CIA provided the Meo arms, ammunition, and air transport. It paid them only low wages but sanctioned its subsidiary, Air America, to transport poppies to Vientiane, the Laotian capital, and other major cities, where they were refined into a crude opium base. Planes from both the Royal Laotian Air Force and the South Vietnamese air force then flew the pulp to Bangkok, Saigon, and other Asian centers for further refinement and packaging. According to Alfred W. McCoy in his superb work, *The Politics of Heroin in Southeast Asia*, the South Vietnamese civil and military leadership was heavily involved in the narcotics business. General and subsequent president of the Republic of Vietnam, Nguyen Van Thieu ran one major operation, while Nguyen Cao Ky — at times air marshall, premier, and vice-president — ran another. General Loan of the police and intelligence networks was also active in the heroin trade as a member of Ky's group.[113]

Hundreds of thousands of Americans and Vietnamese became addicted to heroin. The drug was so common that competition between brand names developed, principally between two "#4" grade products (extremely pure), Double U-O Globe Brand and Tiger and Globe Brand heroin. A plastic vial cost between two and five dollars and was readily available in the urban shantytowns outside of major American bases.

No systematic research on the marijuana and other drug trades in Vietnam has emerged. Because marijuana was grown locally, there might have been a more open market in the sense of many "firms" being involved. On the other hand, the same political and military forces involved in the heroin trade no doubt regulated production, wholesaling, and retail distribution of marijuana. Unlike the United States, where marijuana is sold in leaf form in plastic bags, in Vietnam the drug came in cigarette packages:

> Childs reached in his pocket. "I thought you'd like it, Hamilton."
> He pulled out a cellophane pack containing ten cigarettes. They were a little shorter than Pall Malls. He lit one and took a big drag. Chalice began to grin: There was no mistaking the aroma. . . .
> Hamilton cut in, "Saving roaches is great back in the world, but it's a waste of time out here. We get the grass we want for ten cents a joint."[114]

Ten cents per marijuana cigarette may not seem like much, but the American market was huge. In the 1971 Department of Defense drug survey conducted by the Human Resources Research Organization, it was found that 50.9 percent of army troops stationed in Vietnam had used marijuana in the previous year; 13.8 percent reported that they smoked pot every day.[115] In combat units usage was higher than overall rates. One sample of front-line troops in the 173rd Airborne Brigade found that 35 percent smoked more than once a week and 19 percent smoked every day.[116] For some of these troops, smoking every day meant smoking during every waking hour. Robert Roth described such a man preparing for a major operation:

> We got the word one day that the whole battalion was going into the Arizona [a Vietcong area near Da Nang] and we'd be there in a couple of months. The Arizona's the only place you can't get grass, and if he ran out, Tony knew he'd go nuts, so he bought five hundred joints to take with him. Half his pack was filled with grass. A week after we went in, we got a new guy in our squad, also named Tony. It was kinda confusing so we started calling Tony 5, Tony 5. He was stoned the day we went into the Arizona, the day we came out, and all the days in between.[117]

Retail selling of many drugs was often conducted by women and children; drugs were just things they sold, along with PX goods and beer and soda pop and pornographic pictures and the inside story on how to find the best prostitutes. For people near the bottom of the retail chain, constant small-scale buying and selling was not the path to upward mobility. Huntington's glowing reports on rapidly increasing incomes concealed the horrible reality that for most people in the American-sponsored "urban revolution," life was just a matter of surviving. For example, getting shoes or boots shined might be a small matter to the soldier, but to thousands of Vietnamese children, every shoe shine was of major importance. Larry Hughes described how business was transacted at his base.

> G.I. would walk to the gate carrying a pair of boots and the kids would stampede. Such screaming and yelling in broken English you wouldn't believe! These kids were not shining shoes to earn spending money. Like, this was it. Give your boots to one kid and the others hit you with some pretty ripe language. All these kids were filthy, but

each had at least one article of clothing recognizable as having once been worn by an American G.I.

The kid with the boots would run back across the street to squat down and spit-shine toe and heel. When the kid returned your boots a bargaining session started. Here's where the influence of the Vietnamese store owner was felt. The kid would ask an insane price of one or two hundred piasters. You had to harden your stomach before talking a Vietnamese kid out of a fantastically high price. You had to forget about feeling sorry for kids who had it rough. Then you looked them in the eyes and said, "Bullshit! Too much! Number-ten shine!" After that the bargaining was easy.

The kid demands 100 piasters and refuses to accept anything less. You take a 50-piaster note out of your pocket and that's all there's going to be. The kid says no. You try sticking the money in his pocket but he'll have none of it. The kid spits, curses, and kicks at the dirt. There is no reasoning.

You throw the money in the dirt and grab the boots. The boy is crying. At the last second and just before one of the bigger shoeshine boys makes a grab for it, the kid takes the money he would not take. He walks back across the street to face the store owner. The tears flood his eyes.[118]

The last means of survival in the new Vietnam consisted of going through garbage dumps. According to Michael Kukler, a former chief information noncommissioned officer for MACV in Saigon, poor men and women volunteered to collect the approximately 75,000 tons of garbage that were collected from the Saigon streets every day. "They wanted to be in the bottom of the garbage truck. Here they could sort out and save the edibles in a clean white cloth and let it drip until they got off duty. Eating out of a garbage can is the only way for the poor to survive."[119]

Kukler's story concerns Saigon, but from other accounts it seems certain that Vietnamese in all urban areas, especially those living near massive American bases, routinely searched through garbage dumps for food and shelter: "Some people built shacks of cardboard boxes, on which the same markings would be repeated again and again. (The walls of several houses read 'COMBAT MEAL COMBAT MEAL COMBAT MEAL' from top to bottom.)"[120]

Officially, most people at the bottom of the new urban Vietnam eventually ceased to exist. In 1966, when the first criticisms involving the production of refugees were articulated publicly, the official refugee count fell from 1,400,000 to 268,000 by the end of the year. Such an incredible shift was accomplished simply by changing categories. Several hundred thousand people were *reclassified* as "resettled in place," even though their place might be a camp or a shantytown hut made from C-ration boxes.[121] By late 1967, the numbers were back up, so another tactic for erasure was attempted. This time General Westmoreland's "Combined Campaign Plan for 1968" called for commanders to be sure that "military operations did not needlessly generate more refugees."[122] But refugees still continued to be generated — in Guenter Lewy's words, "this problem continued to haunt the American Command."[123] American pacification officials then abolished the word "refugee," creating a new term, "war victims." In 1970, a leading United States Agency for International Development official named John Hannah addressed a major meeting of the International Rescue Committee on the success of his agency; there were only "205,000 refugees left in all of South Vietnam."[124]

By erasing the official presence of those at the bottom, the war-managers' constant talk of "urbanization" and "nation-building" was made to appear legitimate. All production indices of development — ports, runways, electrical generating plants, sewage systems, cars, refrigerators — took their place on the ledger of Technowar as contributing to a progressive development upward from zero. Technowar's urbanization of Vietnam looked good; the country appeared to be becoming a modern society complete with "pacifying" affluence.

Yet the doublethink process had its limits. Although the American and Vietnamese war-managers nearly eliminated the destruction of the countryside from their official representations, *much of the countryside really was destroyed and millions of people actually became refugees.* Similarly, despite the efforts of officials to eliminate the poor by manipulating categories, the poverty of life in urban Vietnam was real. While facile talk of the "American-sponsored urban revolution" might be well received among government officials and segments of the international press and public opinion, it did nothing for Vietnamese living in urban poverty. They still continued to make a living by selling drugs or stolen merchandise or by selling themselves or by going through garbage dumps. Technowar urbanization did not create a "pacified" populace; it just created misery for the majority of the people and great wealth for those ARVN officers and civilian officials who organized the black market.

# CHAPTER 8

# Pacification War in the Countryside

SEVERAL different programs were also developed for attempting to control and pacify the rural populace without actually removing them from their villages and lands. In the Hop Tac operation, pacification was to spread outward from Saigon like a "giant oil spot" or concentric "rings of steel" — the terms used by American embassy officials. In this way the capital city would be made safe; the enemy could not reach the "center" from outside if the distance to be traversed was too great. Ambassador Lodge proposed the Hop Tac program in June 1964; by September Vietnamese troops began implementing it. After a year of search-and-destroy missions, patrols, speeches, and material aid, little progress was reported.

Reasons for failure were reported by an American embassy official who analyzed social and political problems outside the dominant paradigm. He pointed out that although the idea of "concentric circles" looked good in terms of a *representation on a map,* "The concentric phase lines around Saigon do not adequately take into account existing areas of GVN strength and existing Viet Cong base areas; rather they commit the GVN to a continual expansionary effort on all sides of Saigon simultaneously, an effort which is beyond its capabilities." [1]

The official also indicated that Americans failed to see the *political problems* of their formulating a plan for Vietnamese pacification: "The staff planning for the plan was done almost entirely by the United States, and then translated into Vietnamese. It is, in the eyes of many Vietnamese, 'the plan of the Americans.' " [2] No Vietnamese could thus claim credit for the program if it succeeded. Since credit was not possible, few Vietnamese leaders wanted to devote resources to Hop Tac. The embassy analyst reviewing the program thought that the only leader who might even be interested was General Nguyen Khanh — a man whom the Americans had previously forced out of office and a political foe of the American ally, Prime Minister Ky! The Americans who conceived Hop Tac did not understand the political deployment of ARVN troops and GVN province officials: "Since it surrounds Saigon (but does not include it), every political tremor in the capital is felt in the neighboring area . . . the [ARVN] High Command has created chains of command in the area which are clearly designed primarily to prevent coups, and only secondarily to pacify the countryside. Another example: in the last 11 months, 24 out of 31 district chiefs and five out of seven province chiefs have been changed."[3]

Even as early as the fall of 1964, then, pacification programs met failure by conceiving ARVN as a mechanistic fighting organization like the American military, rather than understanding ARVN to be a network of political factions, each with its own agenda. Second, as the metaphors of "oil spot" and concentric "ring of steel" signify, American pacification officials saw their task as keeping a foreign enemy away from the people rather than coping with the people's insurgency against the GVN and the class structure.

By late 1965 and early 1966, the United States had framed the problems of pacification in terms of inadequate coordination among U.S. and GVN war-managers and as the lack of material resources. Pacification had to become more efficient and production had to be rapidly expanded. These concerns were first mentioned at a conference near Warrington, Virginia, attended by many American military and civilian officials responsible for formulating and implementing war policy. The conference concluded with a call for "a single focus of operational control and management over the full range of the pertinent U.S. efforts in order to gear all such U.S. activities and resources effectively into implementation of the rural construction concept."[4]

Senator William Fulbright, chairman of the Senate Foreign Relations Committee, began hearings on Vietnam in early February 1966; one session on February 4 involved severe interrogation of David Bell, an AID official. Later in the day the White House announced that a special U.S.–GVN conference on pacification was soon to be held in Honolulu. Johnson even announced that he was bringing Secretary of Health, Education and Welfare John W. Gardner and Secretary of Agriculture Orville Freeman to Honolulu for their advice on welfare and agricultural projects.

Participants at Honolulu stressed achieving production quotas. Ambassador Lodge wanted pacification statistics to increase from the official number of "about 52% to about 66% by the end of the year."[5]

South Vietnamese General Nguyen Duc Thang had a whole list of quotas to achieve in 1966: "All provinces have promised to the government that 75 percent of the following facts maybe can be accomplished by the 1st of January 1967: Pacification of 963 new hamlets [*new* hamlets? — refugee camps]; pacification of 1,083 existing hamlets; building of 2,251 classrooms; 913 kilometers of road; 128 bridges; 57 dams; and 119 kilometers of canals."[6] President Lyndon Johnson made it clear to all his American subordinates and Vietnamese allies that he wanted a massive increase in pacification production in 1966:

> You men who are responsible for these departments, you ministers, and the staffs associated with them in both governments, bear in mind we are going to give you an examination and the finals will be on just what you have done.
>
> In paragraph 5; how have you built democracy in the rural areas? How much of it have you built, when and where? Give us dates, times, numbers.
>
> In paragraph 2; larger outputs, more efficient production to improve credit, handicraft, light industry, rural electrification — are those just phrases, high-sounding words, or have you coonskins on the wall. . . .[7]

In Johnson's reasoning, democracy was "built," much like "credit, handicraft, light industry, [and] rural electrification," and war-managers would be evaluated on how much they built in 1966. Indeed, the group decided to use the term "social construction" instead of "pacification" to indicate the spirit of the projects.

Lodge appointed his deputy ambassador, William Porter, in charge of all American programs falling under the "pacification" or "social construction" rubric. Porter saw his job as coordinating existing American pacification efforts; he did not try to establish direct command over different bureaucracies. By some accounts his approach was successful. Henry Kissinger, for example, concluded his report after a July 1966 visit that "the organization of the Embassy has been vastly improved since my last visit [in 1965]. The plethora of competing agencies, each operating their own program on the basis of partly conflicting and largely uncoordinated criteria, has been replaced by an increasingly effective structure under the extremely able leadership of Bill Porter. Porter is on top of his job."[8]

Back in Washington, President Johnson appointed Robert W. Komer as his special assistant for pacification in March 1966. Komer's job was like Porter's except that he was responsible for handling bureaucracies in Washington. Komer's bureaucratic position was superior to Porter's in that while Porter was subordinate to Ambassador Lodge, Komer reported to the President. He presented his major analysis in August 1966. It was entitled "Giving a New Thrust to Pacification." The new thrust conceptualized pacification in terms of productivity. Its introductory paragraph reads:

> There is a growing consensus that the U.S./GVN pacification effort needs to be stepped up, that *management of our pacification assets is not yet producing an acceptable rate of return for our heavy investments,* and pacification operations should be more abreast of our developing military effort against the NVA and VC main force. The President has expressed this view, and so has Ambassador Lodge among others.[9]

Komer made the case for pacification in his memo: "Chasing the large units around the boondocks still leaves intact the VC infrastructure, with its local guerrilla capability plus the weapons of terror and intimidation. . . ." Unless these people were defeated, then American progress in "containing inflation," and building democracy would not succeed. It was as if pacification war was a giant, inefficient conglomerate ready for takeover from an outside firm with a new, tough management. The takeover might be risky, but the risk had to be taken since the potential for profit was there:

> Yet another reason for stressing pacification is that the U.S. is supporting a lot of assets in being which are at the moment poorly employed. Even the bulk of ARVN, which increasingly sits back and watches the U.S. take over the more difficult parts of the war against main enemy units and bases, might be more effectively used for this purpose. . . . Thus, even if one contends that pacification as I have defined it is not vital to a win strategy, *stepping up this effort would add little costs and might produce substantial pay offs.*[10]

Well before this transition occurred, though, other important war-manager factions presented their views on the need to reform ARVN and make it the essential component of pacification war. The U.S. Army report commissioned in 1965 by the chief of staff was submitted in March 1966. Entitled "PROVN — The Program for the Pacification and Long-Term Development of South Vietnam" — the report called for focusing at more local levels: " 'Victory' can only be achieved through bringing the individual Vietnamese, typically a rural peasant, to support willingly the GVN. The critical actions are those that take place at the village, district, and provincial levels.''[11] To help achieve this goal, the PROVN study group called for abolishing the divisional military structure of ARVN, breaking it into smaller military units under the province chiefs. Similarly, American ground combat units were to come under the command of the "Senior U.S. Representative at the provincial level."[12] PROVN also wanted a single command structure for all U.S. civilian and military forces, with the American ambassador filling the top.

By August 1966, Westmoreland and his staff agreed that ARVN should be directed toward pacification or "Revolutionary Development" (RD). Westmoreland's memo to the Joint Chiefs of Staff for his fall of 1966 and spring of 1967 battle plan called for a division of labor between American and ARVN forces: "The growing strength of US/FW [Free World] Forces will provide the shield and will permit ARVN to shift its weight of effort to an extent not heretofore feasible to direct support of RD. . . . The priority effort of ARVN forces will be in direct support of the RD program; in many instances the province chief will exercise operational control over these units. . . . This fact notwithstanding, the ARVN divisional structure must be maintained. . . ."[13] Note the continuity in reasoning. Even at the very moment ARVN was being shifted away from combat with the foreign Other in terms of big-unit engagements, Westmoreland insisted that it retain an organizational structure mirroring that of the Americans. At the same time, the retention of the ARVN divisional structure allowed the power bases of ARVN leaders to remain intact as well, making it impervious to subsequent American requests for reform.

The idea of shifting ARVN's mission to pacification while simultaneously reforming it finds its most emphatic exposition by Robert McNamara. The secretary of defense thought that big-unit warfare had severe limits in terms of influencing the Vietnamese; pacification was instead the true "center" of the conflict.

> The large-unit operations war, which we know best how to fight and where we have had our successes, is largely irrelevant to pacification as long as we do not lose it. By and large, the people in rural areas believe that the GVN when it comes will not stay but that the VC will; that cooperation with the GVN will be punished by the VC; that the GVN is really indifferent to the people's welfare; that the low-

level GVN are tools of the local rich; and that the GVN is ridden with corruption.[14]

This was an extraordinary statement for an American war-manager, especially for the leading advocate of a "management science" approach to rationalized, high-technology, capital-intensive warfare. If the deep logic of Technowar can be visualized as a "grammar" of some kind, then McNamara's statement here can be viewed as "ungrammatical," or maybe even a "foreign language." All the problems between the GVN and the Vietnamese people were problems of *social relationships*, questions of class structure, culture, and political power; none of these problems were solvable by either the production of death or the production and distribution of commodities. McNamara went on to outline both the limits of U.S. involvement in pacification and the need for major structural reforms in both the GVN and ARVN:

> The U.S. cannot do this pacification security job for the Vietnamese. All we can do is "massage the heart." For one reason, it is known that we do not intend to stay; if our efforts worked at all, it would merely postpone the eventual confrontation of the VC and GVN infrastructures. The GVN must do the job, and I am convinced that drastic reform is needed if the GVN is going to be able to do it.
>
> The first essential reform is in the attitude of GVN officials. They are generally apathetic, and there is corruption high and low. Often appointments, promotions, and draft deferments must be bought; and kickbacks on salaries are common. Cadre at the bottom can be no better than the system above them.
>
> The second needed reform is in the attitude and conduct of the ARVN. The image of the government cannot improve unless and until the ARVN improves markedly. They do not understand the importance (or respectability) of pacification nor the importance to pacification of proper, disciplined conduct. Promotions, assignments and awards are often not made on merit, but rather on the basis of having a diploma, friends, or relatives, or because of bribery. The ARVN is weak in dedication, direction and discipline.
>
> Not enough ARVN are devoted to area and population security, and when the ARVN does attempt to support pacification, their actions do not last long enough; their tactics are bad despite U.S. prodding (no aggressive small-unit saturation patrolling, hamlet searches, quick-reaction contact, or offensive night ambushes); they do not make good use of intelligence; and their leadership and discipline are bad.[15]

McNamara both points to the social structure leading to American failure in Vietnam and runs away from the logical conclusions of his indictments. The secretary of defense explicitly says that the United States cannot conduct pacification war; he sees the logical conclusion of major American involvement in that sphere: "if our efforts worked at all, it would merely postpone the eventual confrontation of the VC and GVN infrastructures." Yet while McNamara realizes that the United States cannot pacify the Vietnamese people, he points to a GVN and ARVN structure that cannot pacify the populace either. Note how deep his indictments of the South Vietnamese civilian administration and military establishment go. The GVN officials "are generally apathetic, and there is corruption high and low." ARVN doesn't understand the importance of pacification, has a corrupt structure of promotion rather than a merit system, fails to "make good use of intelligence," and is generally "weak in dedication, direction and discipline." From these paragraphs the war seems lost; the war-managers appear to have come to their senses and to be ready to initiate American withdrawal.

But at the very moment McNamara pointed to the failure of the GVN and ARVN and the inability of the United States to substitute for an internal political structure having the allegiance of the peasant majority — at that moment he also began moving away from these realizations. The next paragraph reads:

> Furthermore, it is my conviction that a part of the problem undoubtedly lies in bad management on the American as well as the GVN side. Here split responsibility — or "no responsibility" — has resulted in too little hard pressure on the GVN to do its job and no really solid or realistic planning with respect to the whole effort. *We must deal with this management problem now and deal with it effectively.*[16]

McNamara thus turned pacification into a management problem to be solved just when he was about to break out of the paradigm. His "ungrammatical" statements on the social structure of the GVN were thus "corrected." The "problems" were serious, but they were problems capable of being solved, depending upon the effort; the greater the input, the greater the output. In McNamara's terms, "The odds are less than even for this task, if only because we have failed so consistently since 1961 to make a dent in the problem. But, because the 1967 trend of pacification will, I believe, be the main talisman of ultimate U.S. success or failure in Vietnam, extraordinary imagination and effort should go into changing the stripes of that problem.''[17] By the end of his memo, McNamara had fully reestablished a homology between his "empirical" reports and the deep logic of Technowar. The reformulation of the social breakdown of the GVN and ARVN into a management problem was but the first step. From despair over social contradiction, McNamara ended by endorsing the Vietnamese leadership. Thieu and Ky had fortunately "expressed agreement with us that the key to success is pacification and that so far pacification has failed." All of a sudden, major progress appeared upon a two-year horizon:

> Ky will, between January and July 1967, shift all ARVN infantry divisions to that role. And he is giving Thang, a good Revolutionary Development director, added powers. Thieu and Ky see this as part of a two-year (1967–1969) schedule, in which offensive operations against enemy main force units are continued, carried on primarily by the U.S. and other Free World forces. At the end of the two-year period, they believe the enemy may be willing to negotiate or to retreat from his current course of action.[18]

Although McNamara corrected the deviant twist of his memo from crisis toward inevitable progress, the dangerous implications of his comments warranted rebuttal by other war-managers. George Carver, special assistant for Vietnamese affairs to CIA director Richard Helms, pointed out the full implications of the secretary of defense's attack upon ARVN and the GVN:

> We agree with Secretary McNamara's prognosis that there is little hope for a satisfactory conclusion of the war within the next two years. We do not agree that "the odds are less than even" for enlivening the pacification program. If this were true, the U.S. would be foolish to continue the struggle in Vietnam and should seek to disengage as fast as possible. We think that if we establish adequate management and control on the U.S. side and ensure that the Vietnamese follow through on redirecting their military resources as promised, there are at least fair prospects for substantial progress in pacification over the next two years.[19]

Again note the power of Technowar as logic. If McNamara's criticisms were correct, then the United States would inevitably lose the war. However, since defeat was unthinkable within the discourse of the war-managers, then victory had to be possible. If victory had to be possible, then the path to progress or victory resided in the system of

production — "adequate management and control" together with the
Vietnamese redirection of resources, as if the ARVN were a machine
that just needed to be pointed in another direction. In reality, the social
structures of ARVN and the GVN did not disappear, but were hidden
from consideration.

For the highest levels of the officer corps the war offered many ways
of getting rich. No wonder the secretary of defense was concerned about
ARVN "promotions, assignments and awards" being made on the basis
of "friends, or relatives, or because of bribery." If the military hierarchy was a series of business opportunities, then it follows that positions were bought and sold.

The officer corps of ARVN had a specific class and cultural background. Senior commanders often had long histories of association with
the French. They were from land-owning families or part of the urban
merchant class. They had college degrees and practiced Catholicism.
Many leading officers were from the north, having come south after the
Geneva agreements. In contrast, most rank-and-file enlisted men were
from poor peasant families, had little formal education, and practiced
Buddhism. Officers often saw their troops as another opportunity to make
money, rather than as men whose respect they wanted to win. For example, ARVN troops normally had to pay their officers for food they
received; oftentimes they had to pay more than official prices. Officers
also often accepted bribes from their troops. A "flower soldier" was a
trooper who paid his commander a bribe while he worked at another
job. A "phantom soldier" was a soldier who had deserted, but whose
commander did not report him missing so that he could collect the missing man's pay.[20]

The peasant soldier in ARVN's pacification war was thus near the
bottom of the Vietnamese class structure. The sons of the rich either
became officers or bribed their way out of military service altogether.
There was no one-year tour for the ARVN soldier. He remained a trooper
for the duration of the war or until he reached forty-two years of age,
meaning that in all probability he either faced being killed or wounded
or else he deserted. In 1966 nearly 20 percent of ARVN deserted. The
next year nearly 78,000 out of an army of 350,000 left. Throughout the
war desertion remained a constant structural feature; percentages varied
greatly according to unit. ARVN combat units had desertion rates around
two and a half times higher than those for the armed forces as a whole;
in some years one-third of the army left.[21]

One American military commander called ARVN's military tactics "search and avoid." It was not that officers and enlisted men were incapable of finding the NLF and NVA troops, but rather that senior officers chose not to fight. Marine Colonel William Corson points to the ARVN 25th Division in 1966. At the end of the year the division commander reported that his 13,000 men inflicted seventeen casualties upon the enemy, while suffering seventy casualties themselves. Fifty casualties came from jeep and truck accidents rather than combat. In contrast, the U.S. Army 25th Division, operating in the same area, suffered over 1,000 men wounded and over 200 killed in combat operations.[22] Contact with the enemy was not in the peasant soldier's interest, because he had a lifetime of war in which he risked death. Nor was it in the interest of higher commanders, because in the political economy of ARVN, military victory was not readily exchangeable for rewards, and a clear-cut military defeat often meant that the commander would be replaced and thus lose economic opportunities inherent in high rank and established position.

From ARVN's perspective, the shift to pacification operations removed the burden of combat and increased their market. *New York Times* correspondent Malcolm Browne outlined the opportunities for making money:

> You [ARVN officer] may have been able to collect a rice haul of taxes from some hamlet one month, but there's no automatic need to turn this tax money in to your bosses, if you're discreet. You can keep it, and claim that you couldn't get your tax-collection team into the hamlet because the Viet Cong was too strong there.
>
> To make sure the hamlet makes no trouble about all this, you can always feed headquarters an "intelligence report" that a Viet Cong regiment has camped in the hamlet, along with the recommendation the whole thing ought to be blown off the map immediately. Generally, this will be done, and the Skyraiders [fighter-bombers] will be over in a day or two to bomb the town to rubble.[23]

Presumably this is the kind of activity signified by McNamara's indication that "the attitude and conduct of the ARVN" needed to be reformed. But from the standpoint of the Vietnamese officer corps, there was no incentive for change; the class structure gave them power. Year after year, study after study pointed to ARVN's contempt for the peasant population. A 1967 U.S. State Department study noted that ARVN had poor morale, poor leadership, and had "poor relationships with the population who, on the one hand, have had little reason for confidence in the ability of the military to afford any of them any lasting protection and, on the other hand, have all too frequently been victimized by them."[24] A 1969 study by the National Security Council found that the GVN's military had committed crimes ranging from chicken-stealing to murder and rape in nearly half the hamlets in the country.[25] In 1971 a Rand Corporation study concluded that ARVN attitude toward the populace depended on how well equipped the military unit in question was: "When soldiers have helicopters they seem to worry less about the disposition of the population along the roads they would otherwise have to travel. When they have armor, the attitudes of the villagers seem less important."[26] Another report conducted in 1971 concluded by saying that ARVN thefts, shakedowns, and other crimes were "widespread and detrimental to the pacification program."[27] ARVN did not win the "hearts and minds" of the peasantry; it pacified no one. The senior officer corps had no class interest in pacification. Unfortunately, enlisted men, often from peasant backgrounds themselves, did not overcome their own victimized condition, but instead sought out others to victimize.

These studies, however, like McNamara's original indictments of the Vietnamese leadership, were pushed aside and discarded. They did not become part of the official knowledge for war-manager action, since in Technowar, the possibility of increased production always held the possibility of great victory.

A report by Robert Komer exemplifies such a production orientation. Komer celebrated the sheer massiveness of Technowar. His August 1966 memo ended by cheering:

> Wastefully, expensively, but nonetheless indisputably, we are winning the war in the South. Few of our programs — civil or military — are very efficient, but *we are grinding the enemy down by sheer weight and mass.* And the cumulative impact of all we have set in motion is beginning to tell. Pacification still lags the most, yet even it is moving forward.
>
> Indeed, my broad feeling, with due allowance for over-simplification, is that our side now has in presently programmed levels all the men, money and other resources needed to achieve success. . . .[28]

By the end of 1966, Komer overcame his "over-simplification" in a detailed report entitled "Vietnam Prognosis for 1967–1968." He called for the United States and the GVN to "mount a maximum effort in 1967–1968 and make it so. The key is better orchestration and management of our Vietnam effort — both in Washington and Saigon."[29] In particular Komer thought that the Vietnamese military needed to be managed better, just as he had said in his August memo: "Our most important under-utilized asset is the RVNAF. Getting greater efficiency out of 700,000 men we're already supporting and financing is the cheapest and soundest way to get results in pacification."[30] Komer thought that the Vietnamese would be mesmerized by the presence of so much American-sponsored action and so many American things in Vietnam: "By themselves, none of our Vietnam programs offer high confidence of a successful outcome (forcing the enemy to fade away or to negotiate). *Cumulatively,* however, *they can produce enough of a bandwagon psychology among the southerners* to lead to such results by end-1967 or sometime in 1968."[31] Like a good accountant, Komer saw the psychological "credit" of the bandwagon related to a corresponding "debit" on the enemy side: "These efforts will reinforce each other in *convincing the Southern VC and Hanoi that they are losing.*" Pacification had to be productive; there was no other choice; "At any rate, do we have a better option?"[32]

In April of 1967, President Johnson announced that pacification war was going to be reorganized into one vast holding company, the Civil Operations and Rural Development Support, or CORDS as it was commonly called. Johnson also exercised option number 2 in Komer's August 1966 outline of possible management options — CORDS was placed under General Westmoreland's command in MACV, with a civilian deputy to serve as chief administrator for all pacification activities. Komer received the initial appointment as chief of CORDS. On the day he left to assume command, he wrote a memo calling for the reform of ARVN: "We have trained and equipped over 650,000 (and for so little cost that it is a good investment in any case). But can't we greatly increase the return?" All that was required to make ARVN profitable was to "Insist on jacking up RVNAF leadership at all levels. . . . A massive attack on it could *pay real short-run dividends.*"[33]

Komer moved quickly to establish CORDS as the management organization for all pacification war activities. On May 13, four days after President Johnson signed National Security Action Memorandum 362 establishing CORDS, Komer addressed American military commanders at Cam Ranh Bay. According to the U.S. Army's official history, *Reorganization for Pacification Support,* Komer did not outline a specific program for winning the allegiance of the Vietnamese people, but instead "talked of the use of mass and of no single solution but many programs unified in a 'comprehensive package.' "[34] Within months many disparate pacification programs organized by the Joint U.S. Public Affairs Office (JUSPAO), the Agency for International Development, the Central Intelligence Agency, and the U.S. Army's various advisory programs to the South Vietnamese military were all collected within a single joint civilian and military management structure.

The resulting collection of programs can be roughly divided into four groupings. First, a whole series of endeavors concerned the production and dissemination of propaganda; incredible efforts were made to construct entirely new media systems for the Vietnamese. A second set of enterprises focused on distributing food and other supplies to the rural populace, a pacification-through-consumption approach. The third area involved an array of paramilitary programs designed to control the rural populace through violence; these programs ranged from providing arms, ammunition, and pay to local militias to the formation of spy networks and assassination teams. The fourth grouping consisted of ways to measure and monitor the net effects of all the other programs, the construction of statistical indices to measure the percentile of the Vietnamese population who were "pacified."

Land reform was not included among these projects. Komer did not succeed in getting the Agency for International Development to transfer the program to CORDS. There is no reason to think CORDS pacification managers would have been more successful than AID staff in persuading the South Vietnamese to conduct major land reform — land reform went against class interests of leading members of the GVN. However, it is important to notice that land reform was absent from the horizon of thought and action for the CORDS staff when they were officially responsible for managing virtually all American programs concerning rural pacification. In contrast, the National Liberation Front or Vietcong regarded land reform as central to securing peasant support for their cause.

From 1965 through 1972 over *fifty billion* leaflets were distributed in South and North Vietnam and along the Ho Chi Minh Trail in Laos and Cambodia; this vast sum was the equivalent of more than 1,500 leaflets per person in both the north and the south.[35] In 1969 the military and civilian propaganda apparatuses produced over 10.5 billion leaflets, 4 million pamphlets, 60,000 newspaper articles, over 24.5 million posters, and nearly 12 million magazines.[36]

Recall Ambassador Henry Cabot Lodge's solution to pacification in the countryside: "Saturate the minds of the people with some socially conscious and attractive ideology, which is susceptible of being carried out."[37] But there was no consideration of just what the Vietnamese might feel was a "socially conscious and attractive ideology." Instead we talked to ourselves. One famous program conducted in 1968 consisted of distributing brown paper grocery bags to merchants. Each bag had a political message, much like the advertisements often seen on American grocery bags and milk cartons. For example, one sack attempted to persuade the Vietcong to return to the GVN side by showing a sad mother, wife and daughter eating together. The caption read:

> We miss you at the evening meal!
> We miss you at every evening meal; your Mother,
> Your child and I are waiting for you.[38]

But Vietnamese did not use grocery bags. People traditionally carried their purchases in plastic netting or cloth squares; merchants wrapped purchases for consumers in whatever kind of paper was available. With the provision of brown paper grocery bags, brown paper became a common wrapping material. Messages were often shredded before being read; grocery bags had a place in American consumer culture, not Vietnamese.

Along with grocery bags came the sex-and-politics approach to pacification. Various military units attached to MACV designed several leaflets aimed at persuading the Vietcong to stop fighting on the grounds of sexual deprivation. One leaflet showed a Vietnamese woman in a bikini with her bra straps slipping off her shoulders. The title of the leaflet was "Don't Deny Yourself the Right to Be a Man." The text read: "Right now your only satisfaction is that you hope you are able to stay alive through the terrifying Army of the Republic of Vietnam attacks. Don't deny yourself the right to be a man. Return to a life of happiness and personal freedom. Rally to the open arms of the Government of Vietnam. Why do you deny yourself the satisfactions of life?"[39]

Vietnamese considered these leaflets in poor taste and not sexually alluring. Bare breasts did not have the same sexual connotations in Vietnam as they did in the United States; the leaflet was an autoerotic exercise. Since the Vietnamese as people were invisible, then their own configurations of sexual desire and sexual ethics were likewise invisible to American psychological war-managers.

Another set of leaflets addressed to enemy soldiers dealt with death themes; they included pictures and sketches of heads torn from bodies, mass graves, skulls roasting in flames, corpses in various stages of decomposition and mutilation, with flies and maggots evident. In 1967, it was learned that many defectors from the Vietcong "felt that these grisly pictures reflected unfavorably on the Republic because the government seemed to be gloating over the deaths of fellow Vietnamese."[40] Nevertheless, even after it was shown that death-message leaflets had serious unintended consequences, the American military continued to produce them in vast quantities. According to the principal historian of American propaganda efforts in Vietnam, Lieutenant Colonel Robert W. Chandler, these leaflets "may well have unwittingly reinforced Communist allegations testifying to the callousness of the Saigon government."[41]

One year American psychological war-managers even tried to play Santa Claus to children living in the Democratic Republic of Vietnam (North Vietnam). A child's packet was designed containing needles, cloth, paper tablet, T-shirt, and towel — all inscribed with some political message. During November and December of 1965, approximately 15,000 of these kits were parachuted over the North.[42] Children's T-shirts complete with inscriptions, another development of American consumer culture, so became a form of subversion!

In 1972, a campaign to demoralize North Vietnamese was waged on the grounds that war caused inflation. The United States military created leaflets that looked like the DRV's banknote, the "dong." Millions of these dong-leaflets were distributed over the north. The English translation of the leaflet read:

> Dear Comrade,
>
> You may lose all your property earned by your hard work, sweat, and tears. The Party is wasting the money-property of the people in the desperate war. While the war is going on, you don't feel like buying anything, but when the war is over, the country devastated, the money which the people are saving will be worthless.
>
> Be alert for a currency exchange — It may happen again.[43]

This last sentence, "It may happen again," referred to 1959, when the Communist government devalued the currency at the rate of 1,000 old dong notes for one new note. The inflation rate in the early 1970s was nowhere approaching that of the economic collapse of the 1950s. By 1972 the United States Air Force and Navy had dropped several million tons of bombs on North Vietnam. People lived off subsistence agriculture, imports, and small-scale, decentralized manufacturing facilities. What little normal industrial production the DRV had was destroyed by bombing by 1972; the massive destruction of the economy and the physical infrastructure of the society (buildings, bridges, and so forth) was readily evident to the people. Sending fake money with an anti-inflationary message ignored these years of bombing. It was as if Vietnam were another consumer society like America, that just happened to be fighting in a land far from its own domain, and that this fighting was causing a strain on the economy.

Few American psychological warriors spoke Vietnamese. In 1970, after five years of major ground combat, one survey found that only six out of 132 civilians at the JUSPAO headquarters in Saigon could speak Vietnamese at a minimally functional level.[44] No comparable figures are available for fluency among the American military assigned to propaganda operations with JUSPAO, but Chandler reports that it was not until 1970 that the U.S. Army included a rudimentary Vietnamese language course in its twelve-week program for training psychological warfare operatives. CORDS received graduates from the State Department's yearlong course in Vietnamese, but their numbers were few and they arrived late in the war.

Consequently, the Americans were nearly totally dependent on Vietnamese for translations of their propaganda programs. One study found that the Americans simply picked up Vietnamese translations and gave them to the printer. Until late 1966 no one "pretested" leaflets with Vietnamese not directly employed by either the U.S. or GVN. After 1966, one participant reported the problem was solved: "After 1966 very few *'bad'* products were put out or in existence very long without being picked up by quality control at some level."[45] Other studies, though, pointed to structural flaws in the production process. Janice Hopper found that her Vietnamese informants complained of leaflets written in literary Vietnamese, rather than peasant sociolects. Politically speaking, the "literary language has a potential for the negative communication to the peasant audience of a reinforcement of traditional beliefs that the Saigon Government has no real concern with rural man and the hinterlands."[46] Similarly, other Vietnamese found that the translators employed by the Americans translated literally, on a word-for-word basis, rather than conveying the sense of the American message in a Vietnamese way. Literal translation meant that the messages all had what the JUSPAO staff called either "foreign imprint" or "American smell."[47]

The GVN equivalent to the Joint U.S. Public Affairs Office was known as the Vietnamese Information Service. The VIS was supposed to bear major responsibility for creating propaganda; in theory most problems created by American mirrorlike projections of their culture upon Vietnam were to be solved by having Vietnamese take major responsibility for creating original texts. However, the idea of a fully functional VIS was also part of the same American mirrorlike projection. In reality, the Vietnamese Information Service was corrupt. According to Harry D. Latimer, of the twelve men who directed the ministry between 1964 and 1971, "Some . . . were hacks, others among the most corrupt of Vietnamese officials."[48] When the ministers changed, other high-level positions also changed. At the top, then, the VIS was but a series of political payoff appointments for various factions. At lower bureaucratic levels, appointments went to sons and daughters of the dominant social class. This finding comes from Barry Zorthian, the director of JUSPAO: "Among VIS psywar trainees . . . are numerous sons and daughters of persons of local affluence, most of whom fill administrative-clerical positions at VIS province headquarters. VIS personnel sent for training often enough are sent merely to fill a district quota, and no use is made of specialized training they receive."[49] Oriented toward finding a soft job — a draft-exempt job until 1968 — these lower-level appointments were either unwilling to or incapable of doing good work.

In 1967, only twenty-five people were responsible for gathering information used to form conceptions of the Vietcong, NVA, and rural Vietnamese. The Department of Defense also found that "most intelligence specialists in 1967 were not knowledgeable about JUSPAO's requirements."[50] Among the thousands of American intelligence operatives in Vietnam, few were gathering information for propaganda purposes. Fifty billion leaflets were *produced,* but there was no staff for intelligence gathering, no knowledge of the language, and no knowledge of the culture.

Conventional materials such as leaflets and magazines did not satisfy the desire for high-technology communications. Print belonged to the eighteenth and nineteenth centuries. Television was the predominant means of mass communications in the United States. Several different officials take credit for establishing television in Vietnam. Presidential adviser Walt Rostow seems to be the first sponsor. David Halberstam reports that in the early 1960s "Rostow in particular was fascinated by the possibility of television sets in the thatch hutches of the world, believing that somehow this could be a break-through."[51] Recall Rostow's major work, *The Stages of Economic Growth,* with its prescription of high levels of consumption as the antidote to the "disease" of communism. Previously Rostow had created several important political advertising slogans for presidential campaigns — ''Open Skies for Ike'' for Eisenhower's 1956 campaign and ''The New Frontier'' and ''Let's Get This Country Moving Again'' for Kennedy in 1960.[52]

At the Manila conference in October 1966, Nguyen Cao Ky requested President Johnson's help in bringing television to Vietnam: ''Johnson immediately turned to the group of aides following us and called out 'Where's the USIS [United States Information Service] man?' He told the official what I had said and added, 'Premier Ky is right. Do something right now, please.' Within a month the Americans had television in Vietnam.''[53] The presidential order was so emphatic that propaganda war-managers did not even wait until ground stations were constructed before beginning their broadcasts. Instead, television transmitters were placed in cargo planes trailing antennas in the sky! President Johnson was deeply concerned about his personal television image and how network television news presented his administration. He had a special television console in the White House that had three screens. According to testimonies from his aides, he often watched all three screens simultaneously, shifting audio from network to network by remote control.

General William Westmoreland says nothing about the influences and contributions of Walt Rostow or Nguyen Cao Ky or Lyndon Johnson in bringing television to Vietnam. Instead, *A Soldier Reports* offers his leadership on the issue. He proposed a television network primarily to permit the Vietnamese government to broadcast to the people and secondly to provide entertainment programs to U.S. forces in base camps. Some channels were for the Vietnamese, and other channels for the Americans. Apparently, though, Vietnamese refugees became deeply involved in American programs: ''When some of the refugees from the village of Ben Suc slipped away from their refugee camps to return to Ben Suc, TV prompted them to come back. They said they missed seeing 'Gunsmoke' [a popular Western for nearly twenty years].''[54]

Ben Suc's destruction by American forces and the removal of its inhabitants have been described previously. It was one of those places that was bombed, shelled, dynamited, burned, bulldozed, and the raw earth salted so nothing would ever grow there again. Its inhabitants were removed to one of those refugee camps where the huts were constructed of empty cardboard C-ration boxes, thus providing the graphic design COMBAT MEAL COMBAT MEAL COMBAT MEAL from bottom to top. Refugees leaving those camps found themselves classified as Vietcong by the American military since their village was now a free-fire zone and, by definition, only enemy troops lived in free-fire zones. Returning home they found defoliated crops. Notice how in Westmoreland's comments television serves as a "credit" to outweigh previous "debits" of destroyed lives.

Much effort was made to ensure that Vietnam received television. AID monies went to importers seeking to bring TV receivers into the country. Hawkridge astutely noted that the mid and late 1960s was the time when the American public was switching from black and white to color television sets. Manufacturers had hundreds of thousands of old sets they wanted to sell — by 1971, about half a million of these sets went to Vietnam. For poor villages, CORDS distributed around 3,500 community-viewing sets. And for remote areas, the war-managers came up with solutions: "Other techniques used included mobile television with music, news, and propaganda; motorized sampans were used to reach villages not serviced by roads. Each sampan contained a TV set or a movie projecter and a Honda generator. The sampan would move into an area by day where the crew would talk to the villagers, giving them a TV show in the evening."[55]

References to programming content on Vietnamese television are usually vague. Peter Watson, the researcher who reported on mobile television, did not say any more on content than "music, news, and propaganda." Robert Chandler, author of *War of Ideas: The U.S. Propaganda Campaign in Vietnam,* reported that about half of the programming was "produced solely for enjoyment, including news, interviews, musicals, dramas, speeches, children's shows, soap operas, and special events coverage." How such a wide variety of programs could be summarily categorized as apolitical is apparent from the researcher's source — the JUSPAO bureaucracy who produced the programs. Their conception of political programming was the story of a North Vietnamese soldier who found life in Saigon so pleasant that he defected.

Television worked no better than printed material in pacifying the rural population. Propaganda replaced or overcame reality only on the balance sheets of the war-managers. Chandler notes his agreement with the thesis that "more deaths and misery probably were brought about by Allied firepower than Communist terrorism."[56] He then goes on to state briefly the consequences of this death production: "The Republic's image suffered as a result, for the National Liberation Front was quick to take advantage of the people's resentment over the death and destruction wrought by Allied military operations."[57] Nor could the leaflets accompanying the defoliation missions successfully persuade the people to "Set your mind at ease, because these chemicals do not harm your health or lives."[58] Chandler reported on the unfortunate failure of propaganda here:

Unfortunately, such explanations probably fell on deaf ears, since the population's doubt was based more on emotion than on reason. Some illnesses were reported as a result of the herbicides, but Americans diagnosed these symptoms as associated with hysteria and suggestive in origin. Regardless of the actual cause of the maladies, the important psychological point was that the sick believed themselves to be ill from the defoliant chemicals.[59]

Agent Orange contained dioxin, a powerful carcinogenic chemical. People were harmed by defoliation missions; Vietnamese children are still being born with deformities, as are children of many American soldiers. Published in 1981, Chandler's work still adhered to the United States government position of no ill effects. He believed the leaflet; the Vietnamese watched their relatives, neighbors, and farm animals get sick.

Despite its efforts, the United States could not create a popular government. The reforms promised in leaflets and radio and television shows never occurred. The leaflet showing President Thieu upholding the constitution of the GVN did not keep people from knowing that he ordered the abolition of hamlet elections after winning the presidency in an unopposed race. Doublethink served to sustain the bureaucracy, not to win the allegiance of the people. The disjunction or chasm between the various American and GVN bureaucracies and the rural populace was never overcome. Just who was the Other who was to respond to the leaflet "This is Your Home, Keep it Clean. Please Put Trash in Trash Cans"?[60] Recall Lady Bird Johnson's campaign to beautify the United States in the 1960s and the accompanying antilittering drives. The Great Society wanted a clean war.

Accompanying the distribution of propaganda messages came the distribution of commodities. (CORDS took over many programs formerly run by the United States Agency for International Development.) Stealing AID commodities was not just an urban phenomenon; theft also occurred at province and district levels. Hawkridge once asked a Catholic priest running a refugee camp what had happened to aid the camp was supposed to receive.

"Stolen," said the priest simply. "It's taken by the Vietnamese government. Time and again we have applied to AID for various items and we know they have been issued and dispatched, but they very seldom reach us." He indicated some sacks which had been stitched together and now served as a curtain in the doorway for a nearby hut. They were printed with the AID emblem. "Even the rice is stolen and we have to buy it back from the Vietnamese officials to keep the refugees alive. The AID people know, of course, but nothing gets done. We were allotted some corrugated metal roofing but the officials stole that as well."[61]

In an attempt to reach beyond Vietnamese province and district chiefs toward establishing a government presence in hamlets and villages, CORDS increased the Revolutionary Development Cadres program. Revolutionary development teams were composed of fifty-nine people, divided into three security squads of eleven persons each and twenty-five civic-action cadres. According to the GVN minister of Revolutionary Development, the RD program was "determined to realize a social revolution in the rural area [sic], aiming at destroying the present gloomy, *old life* and replacing it with a *brighter and nicer new life.*"[62] Note the concept of social life tacit in the minister's formulation of the Revolutionary Development program. A "new life," the result of the Revolutionary Development, does not mean transforming social relationships, but is instead analogous to a new consumer durable, a "brighter and nicer" commodity replacing a "gloomy, old" one. In practice, the provision of new objects was about all Revolutionary Development teams could give peasants, even though they were officially supposed to stay in a hamlet for six months to fulfill the "Eleven Criteria and Ninety-eight Works for Pacification."

1. Annihilation of the Community Underground Cadres
2. Annihilation of the Wicked Village Dignitaries
3. Abolishing Hatred and Building Up a New Spirit
4. The Administration and People's Democratic Organizations
5. To Organize and Struggle Against VC
6. Illiteracy Campaign
7. Health
8. Land Reform
9. Development of Agriculture and Handicraft
10. Development of a Communications System
11. A Meritorious Treatment of the Combatants[63]

The list sounds like a program for the construction of a liberal welfare state. The GVN was not that kind of government; it was a highly militarized market regime, at once dependent upon the United States for economic and military aid and contemptuous of the United States. The ruling class of the GVN established policies for its benefit, not to please thousands of American advisers and leading American war-managers in Saigon and Washington. Taking the criteria one by one, a translation of what was possible for the Revolutionary Development cadres to achieve becomes more visible. Some criteria, especially number 1 ("Annihilation of the Communist Underground Cadres,") and number 5 ("To Organize and Struggle Against VC"), refer to paramilitary activities, the third area of CORDS technological intervention, and will be discussed later.

Criterion number 2 involves eradication of corruption. Since the entire regime was systematically corrupt, reports emanating from the hamlet and village level were only rarely acted upon by those entrenched at higher levels. As one Revolutionary Development team leader explained: "This is the most difficult task of all. They are all tied in with one another from the generals right down to the hamlet. We report them, but nothing ever happens."[64] Criterion number 3, the creation of a "New Spirit" refers to the propaganda activities recently discussed. In number 4, a reference to building "People's Democratic Organizations," severe problems were encountered by teams because many peasants had been burned in their previous participation in government programs, such as agricultural development, and were less willing to contribute. Land reform, number 8 on the list, rarely occurred, and when it did it often meant the return of the landlords to collect back rents.[65] "Meritorious Treatment of the Combatants," number 11, meant distributing medals and naming streets for local ARVN combatants. The practical horizon for doing something worthwhile consisted of working on health, illiteracy, handicraft, and communications (numbers 6, 7, 9, and 10).

Often these projects became translated as constructing buildings and distributing various objects. For example, the illiteracy campaign translated into building schools and the health campaign translated into building clinics or dispensaries. On paper, this approach toward providing important public services appears to be highly progressive, but in reality the schools and dispensaries were seldom *staffed*. William Lederer once asked a team leader what his group had accomplished; in reply he pointed to a new school building and a health clinic. Lederer's version of the exchange follows:

"These were the first things we did. We made a school and a dispensary." We inspected the two small buildings, which were empty.

"When do the doctor or nurse come?" I asked.

"There is no doctor or nurse. The province chief said they are not available. Not now anyway. Maybe next year."

"How many children are in school?"

"None yet. We have no teacher."

I asked him what good the buildings did the village.

"It's good for the spirit of the village to have a school and a dispensary even if there are no doctors or teachers."

I said, "When the government reports say that so many schools and dispensaries have been established, are they like these?"

"Yes," he said, "mostly. But you must remember we are a nation at war and you can't do everything at once. And the buildings are useful. They can be used as storehouses until the teachers come." [66]

No doubt the buildings could be used as storehouses, but whether the teachers and doctors ever came is questionable. It is only certain that these empty buildings were reported as schools and clinics. On American and Vietnamese pacification reports the number of schools and medical clinics thus constantly increased.

Lederer was not alone in his findings. Marine Colonel William Corson had a similar conversation with an American CORDS official in another province:

A CORDS/USAID official boasted to me about the number of classrooms they had built in Tam Ky, which is the provincial capital of Quang Tin province. He brushed aside the graft which had occurred as a result of the construction and the lack of teachers and students for the classrooms as being "political considerations" beyond his concern. It did no good to ask the purpose of his effort — though I tried — because from his warped perspective the classrooms were an end in themselves, never a means. [67]

From the CORDS/AID perspective, the ability to *report* that a classroom had been constructed was the objective; reported numerical progress on paper ensured upward mobility for the bureaucratic official. Material goods distributed or constructed were ultimately no more than empty signifiers, like the propaganda messages; they had no referent in social reality. The CORDS bureaucracy once again confused the self-promoting paper universe with the lived reality of rural Vietnamese.

Conversely, the GVN regularly withdrew from use important material goods it had previously distributed on the grounds that the political labels or signs attached to supplies no longer had the correct signifying message. Don Luce, an American teacher serving with a private aid organization, International Voluntary Services, explained one early erasure. To begin, "The American aid office passed out yellow strategic hamlet pins, strategic hamlet stamps, strategic hamlet matchbooks, and strategic hamlet school notebooks. All bore the strategic hamlet symbol, a flaming torch of freedom." [68] Recall that the Diem regime had sponsored the Strategic Hamlet program in the early 1960s. After the November 1963 coup against Diem, the new regime retracted all materials with the Strategic Hamlet symbol and references to Diem and either destroyed them or put them away in warehouses. Don Luce wanted the notebooks for English-language classes he taught Vietnamese children. The new minister of education, however, refused his request. Anything associated with Diem or the Strategic Hamlet program went into the "memory hole," to use George Orwell's term for the destruction of historical records.

It was as if the American war-managers and their GVN allies thought that a change in names in pacification programs would ensure a new success after each previous failure. Name changes in the pacification war occurred at least every two years starting from the French effort: Reconstruction, Civic Action, Land Development Centers, Agglomeration Camps, Agrovilles, Strategic Hamlets, New Life Hamlets, Hoc Tap (Cooperation), Chien Thang (Victory), Rural Construction, Revolutionary Reconstruction, Revolutionary Development. [69] With each name change, all bureaucratic forms and material goods with the old name had to be replaced. In this way the lie attempted to stay "at least one step ahead of the truth." Each system of signifying messages was always a series of progressive victories for the Vietnamese and American war-managers; when they were defeated, the name was just changed.

Many different paramilitary units were formed during the Vietnam War. Only three projects will be discussed here in the context of CORDS organized pacification war: local militias known as the Regional and Popular Forces; the assassination program known by its code name, "Phoenix"; and the program to get members of the National Liberation Front to defect to the GVN.

To begin, it is crucial to understand that the entire Revolutionary Development cadre program was basically under the control of the Central Intelligence Agency. According to Thomas W. Scoville, the author of *Reorganization for Pacification Support,* "Just how jealously the CIA guarded its prerogatives was apparent from a memorandum of understanding which gave the CIA station chief and the Revolutionary Development Cadre Division, a CIA official, wide authority and veto power over planning, programming, funding, and operating the Revolutionary Development Cadre program."[70] In many ways CORDS was simply a front organization for the CIA. William Colby, a career CIA officer, was appointed Robert Komer's deputy from the beginning, and Colby later succeeded Komer as director of CORDS in late fall of 1968. In his autobiography Colby says that when President Johnson gave him ambassador status for his directorship of CORDS, he was "on leave without pay" from the CIA. A mere eight pages later, though, Colby says in an aside that "An incidental effect of having CORDS run this program [Phoenix], as well as the other paramilitary operations of the CIA station, was that the station could concentrate on the penetration of the Communist apparatus both unilaterally and with the Special Branch [GVN counterintelligence service]."[71] Both American soldiers attached to MACV and the CIA's Revolutionary Development cadres shared responsibility for training the Regional and Popular Forces, while the CIA alone ran Phoenix.

Regional and Popular Forces were formed in 1966 as one response to ARVN's high desertion rate. Since most deserting soldiers returned to their native provinces and villages, it was thought that local militias might be one way to retain some military presence. Regional Forces were organized in company strength units with official rosters of 140 men; they were supposedly available for patrolling their home provinces (there were forty-four provinces). Popular Forces were basically village militias, small units of at most forty or fifty men. In 1966 170,000 belonged to Regional Forces while another 150,000 belonged to Popular Forces.[72]

RF/PFs or "Ruff-Puffs" as they were sometimes called by Americans, suffered high casualties. Thomas C. Thayer, a former analyst with the secretary of defense's Office of Systems Analysis, reports that although territorial forces represented at most half of the Republic of Vietnam Armed Forces, they suffered from 55 to 66 percent of South Vietnamese military deaths. In return, they inflicted about 30 percent of the total casualties suffered by Vietcong and North Vietnamese forces. Even by treating estimated enemy casualties as "true" (a false assumption), the results still show that the territorial forces did not fare well.

RF/PFs have been conceptualized in retrospect as the most *cost-efficient force* for the US-GVN side. Thayer makes his case by saying:

Adding cost data to the assessment of effectiveness suggests that the RF/PF, *dollar for dollar*, were the most effective large force in killing VC/NVA troops in South Vietnam. The figures indicate that the RF/PF accounted for 30 percent of the VC/NVA combat deaths inflicted by RVNAF forces, but for less than 20 percent of the RVNAF program budget costs. More startling, the territorial forces accounted for 12–30 percent of all VC/NVA combat deaths, depending on the year, but for only 2–4 percent of the total program budget costs of the war.[73]

Thayer's next paragraph begins by saying "These are macabre calculations, because they purport to equate dollars and deaths, which is nonsense. . . ." Yet the production ratios of dollars and deaths spent for enemy deaths is exactly what interests Thayer. Note the phrase "dollar for dollar"; its customary usage is a metaphor for return to investment, profit earned per dollar of investment. He has just expressed the basic logic of Technowar, mapping the capitalist production system onto military conduct. "Deaths per dollar" is really what Thayer is referring to, both produced enemy deaths, and dollar cost of Ruff-Puff deaths. Ruff-Puffs died cheaply. Even alive, Regional and Popular Forces received only about one-half the salary paid to regular ARVN soldiers, which is to say one-half of very little — when they were paid, since GVN officials often stole RF/PF salaries. When local militia soldiers died, the costs of supporting their survivors were extremely low. Marine Colonel William Corson explains:

The RF and PF suffer three to four times the casualties of the ARVN, receive half the pay of the ARVN soldier, and are victimized by GVN officials in getting disablement and death benefits. For example, widows of RF and PF soldiers killed in action are supposed to receive a year's pay to be paid in monthly installments beginning four months after their husband's death. In Phong Bac [province] we found out that the payments were delayed as much as eight to ten months, and few widows ever received more than two or three payments. Furthermore, until we "persuaded" the district chief to pay the benefits in accordance with the law, he had been deducting a significant percentage to defray his costs of office. Petty despotism exists to some extent in any bureaucracy, but in Vietnam it runs rampant.[74]

Thayer's thrill over the relative inexpensiveness of the Regional and Popular Forces resulted from the Vietnamese stratification system. Peasants were not important to upper-class ARVN officers; no economic rewards were given for cooperating with RF/PF. Thus there was no incentive to risk casualties and spend military resources by helping the local militias when they were attacked.[75]

Such structural factors were invisible to senior war-managers and their advisers. The second half of the sentence offering Thayer's modest objection to the equation of deaths and dollars reads "but they do serve to point up the incredibly unbalanced allocation of resources within the allied war effort." In other words, the war-managers failed! Technowar capital was not distributed properly for maximum cost-efficient production! Thayer gasps at what proper management might have accomplished:

> The attrition objective alone would seem to have called for more resources and emphasis for the territorial forces. If 30 percent of VC/NVA casualties can be had for only 4 percent of the resources, what might have happened if the allies had allocated 10 percent of the resources to RF/PF? The potential effects might have been staggering. And the RF/PF role in establishing territorial security has not even been put into the calculation yet.[76]

In a war based upon supposedly scientific decision-making oriented toward maximum production of death, then the small allocation of resources for RF/PF does indeed appear to be the result of poor business decisions by war-managers. But just as Technowar cannot conceive of the power of the Vietnamese peasant insurgents fighting with the Vietcong, so too did it remain blinded to the possibility of significantly arming rural people to fight on its side. The idea of low-tech peasants either defeating or offering major support to the most advanced technological power on earth was unthinkable to Americans. Additionally, the GVN's upper-class social base could not conceive of seriously arming and supporting its class antagonists, the peasantry, in units that might readily slip out of its control. Thus allocating much more resources to the RF/PF would never have been a major option for either U.S. or GVN war-managers.

Journalist Harvey Meyerson reports that during his year in Vinh Long province few Ruff-Puffs went on operations. Of the approximately 10,000 troops in the province, around 7,000 were stationed in former French bunkers or in newer facilities. Another 1,000 troops spent their time either as maintenance and supply troops for soldiers occupying fixed positions or as the province chief's personal bodyguard. This left 2,000 RF/PF for offensive operations — a seemingly large number at once reduced by its dispersion over province territory.[77]

Colonel Corson, one early organizer of Regional and Popular Forces, confirms Meyerson's observations on RF/PF tactical deployment. Corson notes that the casualties so valued by American public relations officers and statistical analysts like Thayer as indices of combat aptitude were often the result of poor deployment by South Vietnamese commanders, not signs of commitment and high-production by troops.

> The Joint U.S. Public Affairs Office (JUSPAO) in Saigon loves to propagandize the "efforts" of the RF's by pointing to the relatively large numbers of casualties they suffer in comparison with regular ARVN units. However, what is omitted in this rhapsody of phony-baloney is the fact that the great bulk of the RF casualties are incurred because of their temerity and unwillingness to seek out the enemy. It may be bad form to shoot "sitting duck" in England, but the VC are not under such a compunction when they attack the RF.[78]

Another example of Ruff-Puff failure comes from journalist Martin Russ, a marine veteran of the Korean War. The Marine Corps ran a small program in which marine squads (twelve soldiers and a medic) were assigned to live in Vietnamese villages and form Popular Force platoons. Many soldiers, journalists, and scholars regard the Marine Combined Action Platoon program as the closest the United States ever came to a viable pacification strategy, in that it attempted to forge alliances with peasants. However, often marine and army war-managers resisted implementing "civic-action," meaning helpful relations with the peasants. Russ interviewed one marine commander who regarded his CAP units as simply more conventional troops:

> He said two things that impressed me. First, he wanted to make sure I understood his three CAC's [Combined Action Companies] were military units. "I use them as outposts," he said. He scoffed at the whole civic-action concept. To him the CAC's are tactical units tactically deployed. The other thing that impressed me was his opinion on how to win the war: invade the North and take over. "Without the support of Hanoi," he said, "the Viet Cong would wither away." He's forty-three and doesn't know nothing.[79]

The stories that Corson, Meyerson, and Russ narrate all point to the structural consistency of Technowar. Even when war-managers made their greatest efforts to secure rural support, the military continued to conceive of security as an ever-expanding network of forts and conventional units designed to keep the foreign Other out. The enemy is always a machinelike entity coming from the outside. All forces are arrayed in a series of inside-outside dichotomies: Popular Forces keep the foreign Other out of the village; Regional Forces keep the foreign Other out of provinces; ARVN and U.S. troops defend national borders; and American fighter-bombers strike the foreign Other in the outside itself. Defending boundaries within boundaries within boundaries, Technowar always needed more troops, more forts, more planes, to keep the foreign Other out.

Yet back within their villages, RF/PF peasant soldiers remained at the bottom. The financial compensation offered for their services was not adequate. They well understood that they were regarded as inexpensive labor. Ignored and abused, they never became a stable force, but instead deserted regularly, particularly during massive enemy attacks.

In 1967 the Central Intelligence Agency proposed that all American military and civilian intelligence agencies, together with all South Vietnamese intelligence agencies, create a new common pool of information on the organization and membership of the National Liberation Front. At first the project was known as ICEX — Intelligence Coordination and Exploitation Program. When Robert Komer became head of CORDS in 1967, he arranged for ICEX to fall under CORDS auspices. He also picked a new name for the program, calling it Phoenix, or Phung Hoang in Vietnamese, meaning "all-seeing bird." [80]

CORDS in general and the Revolutionary Development cadres in particular served as the organizational cover for intelligence penetration to the village level. One official task of the RD cadres was to take a "census" or count of the local populace. Before they left the village, cadres were supposed to recruit someone to fill a new GVN position called "Census Grievance." Publicly, the Census Grievance office was supposed to perform census tasks for the GVN and listen to peasant reports on corrupt GVN officials. In reality, the Census Grievance man reported on anyone he thought supported the National Liberation Front. Anyone who complained about the GVN, the ARVN, or landlords subsequently was reported as a Vietcong supporter.

Such individuals became "VCI suspects," meaning members of the Vietcong "infrastructure." "Infrastructure" was a concept developed primarily by an employee of the United States Information Agency, Douglas Pike. Pike did not see the National Liberation Front as a social movement generated by the inequities of the social structure and the country's traditional resistance against foreign control. Instead, he followed the logic of mechanistic anticommunism, but with a slight variation — he considered the peasants important. The National Liberation Front was but a mechanical instrument of the foreign Other, and it must be stopped because the "techniques" of the NLF were instrumentally effective. Note the title of his first major book: *Vietcong: The Organization and Techniques of the National Liberation Front of South Vietnam.*[81] The VC were an *efficient machine;* American victory necessitated taking apart the machine, piece by piece or rather individual by individual.

To smash the enemy machine required another mechanized system. The massive intelligence-gathering apparatus involving GVN agencies, together with Census Grievance operatives, constituted the reporting component of the system. Actually to "neutralize" VCI, the CIA constructed another paramilitary unit. Originally they were called "Counter-Terror Teams"; members were recruited from Vietnamese prisons! Later the name was changed to Provincial Reconnaissance Units, since the original name too accurately conveyed their purpose — to serve as assassination teams operating from lists compiled by intelligence agencies. To ensure productivity, Komer instituted what former CIA analyst Douglas S. Blaufarb calls the "preferred management technique" of the Vietnam War, the quota.[82] Vietnamese units were paid according to how many names they generated and how many VCI were "neutralized."

Assessments concerning their effectiveness differ considerably. Political scientist Guenter Lewy quotes one American province adviser who contended that Phoenix was basically an elaborate reporting machine. American officials provided "buildings, desks, typewriters, file cabinets, index cards, dossiers, etc. It was inevitable that the program would develop a strong clerical slant. Now, the intelligence is often accumulated, cross-indexed, properly analyzed and filed. That is the end of the process."[83] Blaufarb wrote that Phoenix managers assumed "that the various competing and jealous Vietnamese intelligence services could be forced to cooperate, share information, and contribute qualified personnel to a combined effort."[84] Robert Komer, after he left CORDS and went to work as an analyst for the Rand Corporation, found that Phoenix was a "poorly managed and largely ineffective effort."[85] From the perspective of these former officials, Phoenix was thus another wasteful, unproductive apparatus, but not a particularly harmful enterprise.

Other reports, however, make it apparent that many Vietnamese were either killed, tortured, or extorted by Phoenix operatives. Mike Beamon participated in the Phoenix program as a U.S. Navy SEAL. SEAL refers to Sea, Air, Land; they were the navy's elite commando unit, formed in the early 1960s as the navy's response to U.S. Army Special Forces. Beamon described several different operations in Al Santoli's oral history collection, *Everything We Had*. Sometimes SEALs operated with Provisional Reconnaissance units, striking villages deep in Vietcong territory:

> Sometimes we'd go out with a whole pack of mercenaries. They were very good going in, but once we got there and made our target [killing the man or woman], they would completely pillage the area, which created a lot of ruckus. They would rob everything. It was a complete carnival going back, so we would try to get way ahead of them so they could have their little carnival and if they got ambushed they'd have to deal with it.[86]

On other operations SEAL units conducted assassinations with only Vietnamese scouts:

> The other kinds of missions we went on were more with our team. Our team was fifteen SEALs, but we would usually break into groups of seven. Assigned to us were LD&Ns, basically SEAL-trained Vietnamese. I would usually scout with a Vietnamese person. Those kinds of targets consisted sometimes of ambushes. I can remember ambushing a lot of tax collectors. After they made all the collections, you'd hit them in the morning and rob them of all the money and, of course, kill them. And then report that all the money was destroyed in the fire fight. They'd carry a thousand dollars at a time. So we'd have quite a party.[87]

Sometimes the target wasn't killed immediately, but was instead kidnaped. SEALs entered homes at night and took them away.

> With that motion I would take the gag, grab it from behind their head, the knife under the throat, and literally pick them up just by the head. They were small people, usually sleeping in their black pajamas, and I'd just pick them up and carry them out. Now, if anybody moved in the hootch, the other scout with me, who's Vietnamese,

would start talking to them very quietly. He'd have them all lay down on the ground, face down. By then I'd have the person outside. I'd have his elbows secured behind his back. I would pass him to the prisoner-handler. . . . I would usually sit by the hootch for about five minutes and listen and, while I was doing that, hook a grenade on the door, flatten the pin and run a fishing line across the door so if anybody opened it up, they would drop the grenade and of course they would be killed.[88]

According to Beamon, many SEAL assassinations and kidnapings were conducted to make it appear that the Vietcong did the killing. SEALs normally carried no identification and learned to look like the Vietcong. "I had no identification on me except for a morphine syringe around my neck. If I was hit, I'd shoot morphine. My number was 50, it was on all my clothes. My face was completely painted out black. Often I would wear a black pajama top. I learned to walk like a Viet Cong, move like a Viet Cong, think like a Viet Cong."[89] By making violence appear to be work of the Vietcong, the Americans hoped to destroy political relations between VC cadre and peasants. Beamon reported that the Rand Corporation studied effects from these special operations: "We had Rand Corporation people with us. Rand would get this information and do extrapolations on it. It was called perturbation research, perturbation meaning if you go into one village and assassinate the village chief and make it look like the Viet Cong did it, then that'll have ramifications throughout the system."[90]

American officials have denied that assassinations or kidnapings took place in the Phoenix program. In William Colby's autobiography, *Honorable Men,* he said that in 1969, when he was head of CORDS, he "issued a directive on the subject of assassination and other equally repugnant activities." The memo stated that Phoenix operatives "are specifically not authorized to engage in assassinations or other violations of the rules of land warfare. . . ."[91] Since the directive explicitly forbade such activities, then any investigation would find the official records legally impeccable. Colby went on to say that in 1971 he reported to a congressional committee on what Phoenix had accomplished. From mid-1968 through mid-1971 some 28,000 VCI were captured and another 20,000 were listed as killed. He clarifies the numbers: "But the word was 'killed,' not 'assassinated,' and I went on to clarify that the vast percentage of these — over 85 percent — were killed in combat actions with Vietnamese and American military and only about 12 percent by police or other security forces."[92] Are the SEALs and their hits included in the reference to "other security forces"? Note how effectively the official version marginalizes the program.

The GVN issued much higher statistics for Phoenix casualties, 40,994 "suspected enemy civilians."[93] Given the quota system for reporting VCI suspects and casualties, the GVN figure seems highly questionable. However, even the Democratic Republic of Vietnam says that Phoenix created problems for local Communist cadres. Journalist Seymour Hersh interviewed North Vietnamese foreign minister Nguyen Co Thach on why they refused an American negotiation offer in 1969.

> A third reason for not taking the new offer seriously, Thach said, was the weakness of the Vietcong troops in the South. The Central Intelligence Agency's assassination program in South Vietnam, known as Operation Phoenix, had slaughtered far more than the 21,000 officially listed by the United States. "We had many weaknesses in the South," Thach said, "because of Phoenix." In some provinces, 95 percent of the Communist cadre had been assassinated or compromised by the Phoenix operation.[94]

War-managers wanted to keep Phoenix activities secret. Nor would any official want attention drawn to the Provincial Interrogation Centers, run by Vietnamese Special Police and "advised" by the Central Intelligence Agency. CORDS later provided cover for the CIA through its Pacification Security Division. As Blaufarb said in regard to Phoenix, "Furthermore, while the concept was American, the execution was largely Vietnamese."[95] In August 1971, the CIA had twenty-six men "providing advice on professional techniques of interrogation."[96]

But CIA management and staffing of Phoenix did not mean that the apparatus truly distinguished between uninvolved civilians and Vietcong political cadres. Quotas encouraged systematic falsification. The Vietnamese intelligence forces, including their network of informants, were also quite willing to extort money from other Vietnamese. One means of extortion involved threatening to turn someone in unless they paid a monthly fee. Army First Lieutenant Michael J. Uhl told of his experience as a counterintelligence officer. His testimony comes from the Dellums committee hearings.

> I would like to just say several words about the reliability of intelligence information. Again, we did not speak the language; we knew nothing of the culture. We used to pay informants whose motives we could in no way know — for all we know, they could have been

opportunists. We found on many occasions that the information we were getting was as result of a grudge.

A man would tell us that another man was an infrastructure member, member of the cadre, and the reason he would tell us that is because we would find out that our agent had been bribing this man and saying that if you don't pay me a certain number of piasters every month, I am going to turn you over to military intelligence as an infrastructure member. The information that we got was unverified, always, always unverified, always classified as unverified. It was unverifiable. There was no way we could verify it.

Nevertheless, it was continuously used as input into air strikes and artillery strikes. At the end of the day, any information we could not react to on an immediate basis we would send to the S-2 [battalion intelligence officer], or to the artillery liaison officer. That night the coordinates that we provided through our agent reports would be used, would be fired on and often these coordinates overlapped civilian populated areas.[97]

Phoenix did not regularly involve itself with bombing or artillery strikes, but the principle of unverifiability regarding intelligence information applies generally. Even former CIA analyst Blaufarb reported that Vietnamese intelligence agencies sought to "preserve the system and its benefits for the individuals and groups that controlled it, the benefits being understood to include in many cases the opportunity to squeeze the population and to appropriate the resources made available by the Americans."[98] Bribing or extorting people by threatening to report them as VCI was but one aspect of corruption. Listing people killed in other military actions as VCI for fulfilling the quota was another.

Arresting peasants who only paid taxes required by the Vietcong or who joined their mass organizations provided an additional opportunity for extortion. Blaufarb regretfully reported that "Bribery and official indifference together with the shortage of facilities led to many Vietnamese being released soon after their apprehension. One estimate made by Phoenix advisors stated that in 1969 only 30 percent of the suspects brought in through the Phoenix mechanism were eventually sentenced and served jail terms."[99]

Former SEAL Mike Beamon offered one final twist to the question of efficiency. He questioned just where his target list came from: "It is my feeling that later on we were hitting people that the Viet Cong wanted us to hit, because they could feed information through us and other

intelligence sources to the CIA and set up a target that maybe wasn't a
Viet Cong but some person they wanted to wipe out, might have been
a South Vietnamese leader. I didn't understand Vietnamese. The guy
could've said he was President for all I knew. He wasn't talking with
me. I had a knife on him. So it was absolutely chaos out there. Here
we are, their top unit. It was absolutely insane.''[100] Reflect for a moment upon the CIA's estimate that around 30,000 Vietcong successfully
infiltrated the Saigon regime.[101] How the CIA estimated successful in-
filtrations is unclear, since by definition a successful infiltration would
be unrecorded; nevertheless the figure is large enough to indicate that
the GVN had significant problems in maintaining secrecy. No doubt
intelligence services were primary VC targets; that is the way intelligence operations have traditionally operated. Beamon's speculations are
plausible.

The problem of determining what actually happened also characterizes a CORDS program called the "third-party inducement plan." Beginning in November 1969, pacification commanders offered peasants
financial rewards for persuading members of the National Liberation
Front to surrender. The higher the rank of the defector, the more lucrative the payment to the third party who induced the defection. Defectors
or prisoners got a good deal from GVN wardens and their American
advisers. Former "enemies" spent a month and a half in relatively nice
camps, with food, clothing, shelter, and medical care provided. They
also received political indoctrination by leaflets and television shows
created by propaganda warriors. After the six-week indoctrination, they
were given two sets of clothes, some money, and were then released.
Camps all across the country soon became filled.

Harvey Meyerson investigated the program in Vinh Long province.
Only 5 percent of the defectors had served with the NLF for more than
one year. Of that 5 percent, only half were from that province: "The
so-called 'Open Arms' program had scarcely touched the Viet Cong
hard core. The Viet Cong who were collapsing were fresh recruits."[102]
Meyerson explains that the VC changed their recruitment policy following their victory in the Tet Offensive of 1968. In more open control
than ever before, the NLF inducted many men and women who were
not politically motivated. The NLF also began confiscating government
identity cards that summer, meaning that a person without a card became a ready target for ARVN or American troops. Meyerson inquired
what percentage of defectors were coming in under the third-party

inducement plan. The American adviser to whom he addressed the question replied: "Sir, I have the statistics for this week. We received sixty-two returnees. And I am happy to say, sir, that every one of them came in through [the] third party inducement plan."[103]

Afterward he talked to one American overseeing interrogation: " 'It's amazing how little most of them know,' the interrogator said. 'I talked to a squad leader yesterday who couldn't remember anything he had done for the Viet Cong.' "[104] The squad leader was fourteen years old. He reported that he had served with the enemy over a year. A relative turned him in to the program. In December 1968, Meyerson went back to find out one more statistic: the percentage of defectors who returned to their home hamlets after being released. Of 145 "defectors," all but three went home.[105] For a true VC defector, the return home would have been fatal — his former comrades would have killed him.

For pacification managers, the most important question became how to measure the net effect of their activities: how many peasants were under GVN "control"; how many moved from the debit to credit side of the anti-Communist ledger. According to William Colby, in 1966 Robert McNamara asked the Central Intelligence Agency to create a "technique by which to measure trends in pacification, and it developed the Hamlet Evaluation [Survey] to do so."[106] Robert Komer later defined HES as "a system for detailed monthly evaluation of pacification on a hamlet by hamlet basis, identifying problem areas for management attention and monitoring a hamlet/population base of 12,600 hamlets."[107]

Field representatives for HES were United States senior military advisers at the district level. At the time there were 242 districts in South Vietnam and military advisers were assigned to 222. Advisers were given worksheets on which they were to evaluate the "progress" of pacification on eighteen indicators:

### Hamlet Evaluation Survey Categories

#### SECURITY

*Vietcong Military Activity*
1. Village guerrilla unit
2. External forces
3. Military incidents affecting hamlets

*Vietcong Political and Subversive Activities*
4. Hamlet infrastructure
5. Village infrastructure
6. Activities affecting hamlet

*Security (Friendly Capabilities)*
7. Hamlet defense plan and organization
8. Friendly external force assistance
9. Internal security activities

DEVELOPMENT

*Administrative and Political Activities*
1. GVN government management
2. Census grievance information
3. Information/psyop [psychological warfare operations] activities

*Health, Education and Welfare*
4. Medical services and sanitation
5. Education
6. Welfare

*Economic Development*
7. Self-help activity
8. Public works
9. Economic improvement programs[108]

Adviser reports went to Saigon, where they were processed by a computer into composite scores. These scores were then ranked according to a system in which numbers signified degrees of security. Michael Klare obtained the grading code from MACV documents.

"A" Hamlet: A superhamlet. Just about everything going right in both security and development.

"B" Hamlet: High-grade hamlet. Effective twenty-four hour security. Adequate development. No VC presence or activity.

"C" Hamlet: VC military control broken. Relatively secure day and night. Most of VC infrastructure identified. No overt VC incidents — VC taxation may continue. Economic improvement programs underway.

"D" Hamlet: VC frequently enter or harass at night. VC infrastructure largely intact. GVN program just beginning. Strictly contested.

"E" Hamlet: Definitely under VC control. Local GVN officials and our advisors don't enter except on military operation. Most of population willingly or unwillingly supports VC.[109]

HES appears rational: taken at face value, it seems impossible that the reality of pacification war could escape CORDS officials given such an exhaustive, month-by-month evaluation process. Note the similarity between the evaluation security categories and the grades on a student's report card. Substitute an "F" for the "E" and consider the VC as delinquents or dropouts and you have a kind of school grading system. The question then becomes who did the grading and under what conditions. To begin, senior district advisers, like most U.S. military and civilian government employees, had one-year assignments. Advising was not considered an important task that would help one advance up the ranks in the officer corps. Sometimes senior advisers helped their subordinates by getting them transferred into more prestigious positions. Harvey Meyerson asked one commander about this system:

> I asked the senior advisor why. With disarming frankness he explained that he did it because he liked the major and wanted to help his career. The post as liaison officer [with the Vietnamese] carried no credit for "combat" or "command." As a subsector team leader in an enemy zone he would get both. Of course this meant transferring him just when he was beginning to be useful, it meant restarting the painfully slow confidence-winning process with a new liaison officer, but that couldn't be helped. No matter how outstanding his performance as liaison officer the major's career would have suffered had he stayed on.[110]

Vietnamese corruption often created additional problems for American military men staying in advisory and liaison positions. Westmoreland's directive to American advisers to stop reporting corruption, "lest they get a reputation as spies and lose their leverage with their counterparts," had strong implications for the HES system and the pacification efforts it supposedly measured.[111] William Lederer asked staff officers in one province he visited why the senior adviser, a colonel, did nothing about rampant Vietnamese corruption. In reply a major said:

> Hell, the colonel is just about the most experienced U.S. advisor in Vietnam. Of course he knows what's happening. But what can he do? If he interferes with the Vietnamese, man, he's had it. He, like all the other advisors for the past twelve years, has been ordered to "get

along with the Vietnamese.'' If the poor son of a bitch does what is his duty to do, the ARVN command will complain to MACV and he'll never make general. He'll be punished by the U.S. Army for doing his duty.[112]

How was the colonel honestly going to evaluate pacification in his district when he had been ordered to not report corruption and faced career trouble if he did report problems? Leading war-managers made it impossible for the reporting mechanism to function as intended; the system created illusions that it represented as — and believed to be — scientific ''fact.''

Hamlet evaluation took place in district headquarters with rural hamlets literally out of sight. A senior adviser normally visited only one-fourth the hamlets in his district a month. Visits to individual hamlets customarily lasted a few hours. Once in a hamlet, most American advisers were totally dependent on their interpreters. The Vietnamese saying ''If you fail at everything else, you can become an interpreter for the Americans'' in practice meant that many interpreters spoke marginal English. One informal study by Lederer found few Vietnamese interpreters who knew over 500 English words.[113] Understanding questions Americans wanted to ask villagers was often difficult for men with this level of English fluency. Second, many interpreters were former refugees from the north who came south after the 1954 division of Vietnam at the seventeenth parallel. They often spoke with a northern accent or spoke a different Vietnamese dialect. Vietnamese is a tonal tongue; inflections mean everything. Consequently, southern peasants often mistrusted the interpreters and did not fully understand what they were saying. Similarly, interpreters often could not understand what peasants said in response. Even assuming that interpreters had adequate linguistic skills, there was no guarantee that translations from Vietnamese to English were accurate. Most interpreters were formally employed by GVN and ARVN officials, not directly by Americans. They had primary allegiance to their Vietnamese bosses, not to American advisers.

In other words, advisers based their analyses on surface appearances — on those elements that could be categorized on Hamlet Evaluation Survey worksheets. Many soldiers, civilian pacification officials, and journalists have spoken of how survey forms led to misrepresentations.

In point of fact there had been *no* overt military incidents for several months against Cam An, but the hamlet's residents were being taxed regularly by the Vietcong. Each of the peasants who travelled the four miles to the capital to market his fish and rice carried with him a Vietcong tax receipt to insure his safe conduct through the "enemy" lines.[114]

The figures on population so precisely noted by Komer's HES take no account of the number of able-bodied men in a hamlet, nor of their loss. Several "C" hamlets located in Quang Ngai province were moved up to a "B" grade in August 1967 because there had been no "VC-initiated incidents" (shootings) during the preceding month. However, during the preceding month the Vietcong had entered the hamlets and marched off every able-bodied man living there. When I [Colonel Corson] mentioned this fact to the Sub-Sector Advisor he defended the grading with the statement that "according to the instructions there had been no Vietcong military activity."[115]

[There was a hamlet that] contains a cluster of people rated as "B" on the HES *and* the 312 Main Force VC Battalion. The VC and the local Government forces have reached a tacit accommodation; they avoid each other without openly recognizing these arrangements. When the VC do come into the populated area to collect taxes, propagandize or otherwise terrorize the people, the people do not report to the authorities: they are frightened. The paddies farmed by the people are next to the VC area. The people paint the Government flag on their doorposts, participate in PSDF (in an accommodating manner) and their children learn the National Anthem. The VC, however, still hold a veto power over the life and death issues in this hamlet. With no reported incidents and overt pro-Government responses by the people, the HES marks this a "B" hamlet.[116]

Nowhere in the HES is it asked if RF/PF are carrying out their missions. . . . [These units] receive good intelligence and utilize it effectively; when they know the enemy is coming to a hamlet they simply avoid them by withdrawing or defending in the wrong direction.[117]

Like the schools with no teachers, the categories of the Hamlet Evaluation Survey were empty. To give a hamlet a high grade one month, then a lower one the next, then a higher grade the month thereafter provides a false knowledge of actual social relationships.

The most perverse exercise of turning people's lives and deaths into ledger entries involved American payment (known as "solacium" payments) for deaths and damages inflicted on Vietnamese. USAID and CORDS officials spent much time correcting accounts. Eric Herter, an army private assigned to USAID, described the payment plan:

> The refugee advisor went out all over the province largely to areas where there'd been battles. He would assess the value of the people's destroyed houses and dead livestock and pay people off. For example, an adult civilian over 15 years old who was killed was worth $35 to their family; a child under 15 was worth $14.40. The United States government paid people off for their dead children, or their dead husbands and wives, or whatever, at the rate of $35 or $15, depending on their age.[118]

With accounts settled, survivors were presumably ready to be influenced by whatever else pacification war had to distribute — as if the sorrow of having one's loved ones killed could be compensated by a few dollars, as if money paid for grief and, with grief gone, the peasantry was ready to move to the credit side of the ledger if further inducements were offered. The very discontinuity of the various debit and credit ledgers blinded the accountants. Jonathan Schell commented eloquently:

> Many optimistic Americans, including reporters as well as military men and civilian officials, tended to set off the destruction caused by the military effort against the construction resulting from civil-affairs effort, seeing the two results as *separate but balanced* "sides" of the war; and, looking at our commitment of men and materials, they were often favorably impressed with the *size* of the constructive effort, almost as though it were being carried out in one country while the military effort was being carried out in another. But, of course, the two programs were being carried out in the same provinces and the same villages, and the people who received the allotments of rice were the same people whose villages had been destroyed by bombs. The Vietnamese civilians felt the effects of the two programs not as two abstract "sides" of the war but as a *continuing experience in the single reality of their daily lives,* and, from their point of view, the aid given them by the Americans and the South Vietnamese government amounted to only a tiny measure of compensation (although extravagant promises were made in the leaflets and in other propaganda) for enormous losses and suffering. Many Amer-

icans, both civilian and military, tended not to see beyond the particular program they were involved in.[119]

The production model of war had no concept of legitimacy, of loyalty, of allegiance, in any deep sense; instead it attempted to produce control by force, distribution of commodities, and public relations slogans. HES counted refugees in camps and cities as securely pacified. By the fall of 1967, this amounted to four million people. Around the same time, the official estimate said that 75 percent of the South Vietnamese population, 12 million people, were pacified. This figure was created by adding 4 million refugees to one million Vietnamese who · worked for Americans, plus one million serving in the South Vietnamese military or police, plus 2.4 million living around Saigon, and finally some 4 million people living in "A," "B," or "C" hamlets.[120] Pacification war was represented as victorious toward the end of 1967.

The National Liberation Front emerged from the space provided by the contradictions of Technowar during the Tet Offensive in 1968. A cease-fire had been agreed upon, but the NLF instead attacked in mass strength across the country. The NLF offensive operations demonstrated to the Vietnamese that the Saigon regime could not provide security even in the country's most densely populated areas. They surely made their point in the countryside — ARVN battalions, Revolutionary Development cadres, and most American forces withdrew to defend cities. This was the moment when the real village world knocked on the district adviser's door. NLF forces passed through hundreds of "A" and "B" hamlets without their presence being betrayed by the populace when they were in transit to the cities; NLF forces now even had daytime control over rural Vietnam.

During the Tet Offensive Komer said, "The pacification program is intact, the Vietcong bypassed the hamlets to attack the cities,"[121] as if tens of thousands of Vietcong could approach the cities without passing through hamlets. In February 1968, the master chart showed that the GVN controlled only 35 percent of the population. March showed another low number. The American advisers were still living in the cities; they guessed that their former prizes belonged to the foreign Other. In the spring, ARVN troops moved back into the countryside. April showed 41 percent of the country controlled, May flowered with 44 percent; June triumphed with 52 percent.[122] Each month the figures went higher. The return of ARVN, the RDs, and American advisers to the countryside meant the return to the realm of the visible, and the visible looked good only because the NLF was recovering from its losses; there were fewer "incidents."

Major institutions that use systems of numerical representations about their "product" are able to make important claims about those numbers. Since the institution is normally considered legitimate, it is assumed that the numbers are produced in "good faith," according to rules adhered to by institutional workers. This means that the numerical distribution, the percentage of cases in various categories, is on the *whole* accepted as accurate. Consequently, when anyone challenges the distribution, say by telling stories of NLF presence in hamlets that have high pacification ratings, these stories can be *dismissed* as isolated deviations, individual lapses in a legitimate rule-governed process. A sophisticated institution can claim that they have even statistically accounted for such deviations through the statistical measure called "the standard deviation."

Note the immense power of the institution in such situations. A critique of numerical representation can proceed only through the analyses of concrete cases, because *only through concrete cases can the systematic failure of the institution to grasp concrete reality be explained.* Yet at the same time the institution can use its legitimacy to claim the validity of the abstract representations as a whole. Komer did this in responding to a network television news reporter in December 1968:

> I think you've got to look at the trends. I've never denied that there are plenty of things going wrong in this country. But I believe if you look further enough back you can see that the situation back in 1964 was a lot worse than it was by 1967, and when I draw the *balance sheet*, it seems that the *pluses* outweigh the *minuses*. That's why I can say that on the *average* things are going better and you can give the instances in which they are going worse. I don't think that we really have a disagreement.[123]

At the time Komer spoke, the newly released "relatively secure" figure ("A," "B," and "C" hamlets) was 73.3 percent, an all-time pacification high. What Komer did not say, however, was how that figure was produced. In November 1968, the Accelerated Pacification Program began. One month earlier MACV had found itself deeply worried about the prospect of the NLF demanding a cease-fire at the Paris Peace Conference and then claiming to represent large sections of the country, particularly the Mekong Delta, which ARVN had not yet "regained." To counter this nightmare, MACV declared that pacification cadres would attempt to establish a minimal presence in as many hamlets as possible. The RD cadres originally scheduled to stay in a village for six months now were to stay only six weeks. What was to be accomplished in those six weeks? There were four official criteria, but as one American adviser said, "The name of the game is planting the government flag"[124] — and thereby producing high numbers. In December, all these newly "pacified" hamlets were added to the total count to produce the most successful year in the history of pacification war.

Komer was replaced by William Colby in December 1968. Colby accomplished two objectives in his tenure at CORDS. First, he increased Phoenix production. Second, he helped introduce and test a new version of the famous Hamlet Evaluation Survey; war-managers and scientists had decided that the previous survey left too much room for the subjectivity of advisers making reports. To correct "subjective and multi-dimensional" HES problems, the army awarded contract DAAH-70-C0009 to Control Data Corporation. Control Data developed "HES 70," "a highly integrated *man-machine* interface," which would solve the previous problems of subjectivity by being "objective and uni-dimensional."[125] Some objective and unidimensional questions on the new survey are given below:

> Do any households in this hamlet own a TV set?
> Are there any organized activities for the youth of this village (4T, boy scouts, sports, etc.)?
> Do any households in this hamlet own *motorized* vehicles (such as motor-cycles, motorized sampans, cars, etc.)?
> Can Western medicines, particularly the more common antibiotics, be purchased locally by village residents?
> Is there a surplus of goods or food-stuffs produced in the village for sale outside of the village?[126]

As the minister of Revolutionary Development said, pacification aimed to destroy "the present, gloomy, *old life* and replacing it with a *brighter and nicer new life*." The consumption of commodities would win the war. The commodities mentioned in the new survey were available to some people: city prostitutes who sent money home; drug pushers; workers who could steal from the PX system or import warehouses; peasants who turned in grenades or their relatives for money. Those participating in the mode of war production could buy Hondas and TV sets and antibiotics. Every Honda signified a pacified consumer. Years later, Colby reflected favorably on how HES motivated Vietnamese officials:

The variety of their alibis soon paid tribute to their imagination, the subtlety of their efforts to influence their American advisors spoke well of their potential as diplomats, but they soon discovered that the easiest and best way to affect the ratings of their hamlets was actually to do some of the things that the system measured — send a platoon to establish a permanent post in the vicinity or train and arm a small self-defense group.[127]

Of course Vietnamese officials made their numbers comply to American requests. By the time of HES 70 they had years of experience. Even during the Kennedy administration they had understood what was necessary. Former Assistant Secretary of State Roger Hillsman reported:

> " *'Ah, les statistiques!'* one of the Vietnamese generals exclaimed to an American friend. 'Your Secretary of Defense loves statistics. We Vietnamese can give him all he wants. If you want them to go up, they will go up. If you want them to go down, they will go down.' "[128]

Although top war-managers remained hermetically sealed in their headquarters buildings where social reality and numerical representations achieved union, some field-workers distinguished between official and lived realities. Lieutenant William Calley was one such man. After My Lai, Calley retired from his line infantry company and applied to become his battalion's S-5, the civic action officer. He said to his battalion commander, "I'm tired of killing them, sir. I want that job."[129] At first he was enthusiastic:

> They haven't running water, gas, or electricity, and God knows if you showed them a TV set. It's almost unreal there, and I had been there for months without seeing it. I knew, I can win if I can make these people aware of their prospects. Of the comforts that a democracy offered them. God, if our society was as great as I thought, the Vietnamese just would gobble it up. And would say, "Let's get it! Let's kick out the communists now! Let's go!"[130]

Calley got going. He showed John Wayne's film *The Green Berets*. He built wells. He vaccinated people. He introduced soap. He started a sewing class and got five prostitutes out of jail to work in the new company. Everything went well with one exception. Pigs had been given to a farmer named Ky. Ky raised these pigs and sold them to his neighbors. The problem was that there was not enough food for the pigs.

Calley solved this problem by getting the battalion cook to save his "wet-waste" — potato peels, onion shells, outer lettuce leaves, and so forth. The lieutenant bribed the cook into taking ten garbage cans full of waste to town each day by giving him authorization to use a "laundry shop" (whose relationship to brothels has been explored previously).

He soon received reports that the pigs were still starving. Surprised, he went to town to investigate. It seems that Ky had appropriated the garbage and was selling it at five cents for a number ten can. When Calley arrived, Ky attacked him: "You cheat me! No get enough on Sunday! No get enough any day!" Calley tried to explain that the food was free, for everyone, that Ky could not sell it. Ky replied "I can! I'm the pig man here." In response, Calley reflected on his actions as S-5:

> It just isn't right, I thought. I had been showing the Vietnamese how capitalism could — I almost said "imperialism" could. But that's really it: I had been making the rich people richer, that's all. I had gotten those pigs, and Ky was being a gangster about them. I had built wells, and rich people now were fencing them off. I had helped some of the village chiefs make $100 a day from prostitutes, liquor, and pot. I had helped the Vietnamese people, sure: the greedy ones.[131]

So Calley learned. Others, however, never did. The production model of war was so deeply ingrained in their minds that even its ultimate failure was conceptualized in the logic of capital accumulation. A few years after he returned to the United States, Robert Komer got a grant from the Defense Advanced Project Agency to study the organization and management of counterinsurgency war. Komer worked with the Rand Corporation, probably the most important social science think tank doing government contract research. Rand published his report. It is aptly entitled *Bureaucracy Does Its Thing: Institutional Constraints on U.S.–GVN Performance in Vietnam*. In the concluding chapter, "What Institutional Lessons Can Be Learned?" he writes: "As this study suggests, the U.S. did not get comparable *value* for its massive aid to the GVN."[132] Pacification war was a bad investment to be written off.

# PART III

# Death from Above

CHAPTER 9

# Air War over North Vietnam: Bombing as Communication

D URING World War II the United States dropped over two million
tons of bombs and other munitions from aircraft. From 1965 through
1973, the United States dropped *at minimum* over eight million tons of
munitions from aircraft onto Southeast Asia.[1] The air war over Southeast Asia was thus the largest air war in world history. The United
States did not use atomic weapons, but eight million tons is the equivalent in explosive force to 640 atomic bombs of the size used at Hiroshima.[2] Paradoxically, the air war over North Vietnam is conventionally
regarded as the most "limited" phase of a limited war.

Two aspects of the air war warrant immediate attention. First, its
command structure differed considerably from ground and pacification
subsystems. Westmoreland and Komer, the respective commanders for
ground and pacification wars, were dependent upon President Johnson,
Secretary of Defense McNamara, and their advisers for approval or rejection of basic plans. Below them, command structure followed formal
bureaucratic lines, with operational decisions being made within military bureaucracies.

In air war, however, President Johnson extended his powers as Commander in Chief to include considerable control over which targets could
be struck, when they could be struck, and how hard. Bombing was
conceptualized as a *way of communicating* to the North Vietnamese;
control was exercised by top civilian officials. To help decide how
bombing could best communicate American intent, the executive branch
commissioned multitudes of studies from intelligence agencies, outside
consultants, and the military. Year after year, study after study addressed questions of what to bomb, how much to bomb, and what previous bombing had or had not accomplished.

Second, if in mechanistic anticommunism the foreign Other is always invading or subverting a country from outside and if, according to Technowar, the enemy exists only as a technobureaucratic apparatus, then North Vietnam's small industrial base, transportation system, and military depots were logically *the prime targets* for American war efforts. The United States had the most technologically advanced fighters, bombers, communications systems, and munitions in the world — and it had more of them than any other nation — while the North Vietnamese had a small air force of old planes and no sophisticated anti-aircraft forces (in the beginning). The disparity between forces could not have been greater: the foreign Other was logically defeated before the first bombing mission.

Plans were made for the heavy bombing of North Vietnam in the spring of 1964. Known as CINCPAC OPLANS 37-64, the program envisioned three distinct phases. Phase I principally concerned South Vietnam. There, the United States would begin more sustained ground and air operations, at times crossing over into Laos and Cambodia. Phase II concerned North Vietnam. The United States would bomb and conduct commando operations under the rubric of "retaliation," publicly linking each attack in the north to some Vietcong action in the south. Once the world was accustomed to such attacks, the retaliation cover would be dropped and the bombing would gradually escalate until the DRV surrendered during negotiations. This was Phase III.[3]

Elements of Phase I went into practice during the year. The CIA's patrol-boat raids on the North Vietnamese coast were designed to make them turn on their coastal radars so that the electronic warfare destroyers *Maddox* and *C. Turner Joy* could learn where these radar sites were. A map of radar sites was necessary before sustained bombing could begin. These raids of course led to the Gulf of Tonkin "incident" and the subsequent congressional resolution endorsing escalation in the name of self-defense. In preparation for Phase II, thirty B-57 bombers were sent to South Vietnam, yet the timing for beginning regular bombing of North Vietnam remained in question. On November 1, 1964, when the Vietcong attacked the Bien Hoa airfield and destroyed twenty-seven of the thirty B-57s, killing five Americans and wounding seventy-six, the Joint Chiefs of Staff favored utilizing the occasion to inaugurate the second phase. President Johnson, however, had run for office pledging that he would not escalate the war.

The question of timing was also linked to the decision that OPLANS 37-64 was to be a joint project of the United States and the Republic of

Vietnam (GVN). The plan assumed at least a moderately stable regime, and U.S. officials hoped that increased war efforts would help overcome the regime's divisive internal politics. But the fall of 1964 and the early winter of 1965 were not stable times. Military losses from defeat and desertion had been extensive from summer on through the year. Other troops, particularly elite ground forces and air force units, were removed by their commanders for "coup duty," either preparing to conduct a coup or preparing to resist one.

And finally, there was the timing of the Russians. On February 16, 1965, Soviet Premier Alexi Kosygin arrived in Hanoi. The next day, Vietcong destroyed more B-57s at Pleiku. Although no one in the administration saw Kosygin as directly responsible, his presence provided an opportune moment for the United States to display airpower that would communicate the disparity between forces. Consequently, on February 7 and 8, American and South Vietnamese planes bombed targets listed as barracks on the official Joint Chiefs of Staff targets list.[4]

A White House statement made after the bombing declared that "The key to the situation remains the cessation of infiltration from North Vietnam and the clear indication that it is prepared to cease aggression against its neighbors." "Appropriate reprisal action" was stressed in the announcement.[5] Thus the United States was at the very edge of Phase II.

The space between Phase II and Phase III was crossed quickly. On February 10, Vietcong attacked American barracks in Qui Nhon. United States casualties there were the highest in the war. Within a day American and Vietnamese planes again attacked the north. This time, all talk of "retaliation" and "reprisal" vanished; the terms "response" and "air operations" appeared for the first time.[6] Such semantic changes appear slight; however, they are the surface manifestation of a move toward full warfare.

Between the first and second air attacks that February, presidential assistant McGeorge Bundy and his study group (Assistant Secretary of State John McNaughton, White House aide Chester Cooper, and Leonard Unger, chairman of the Vietnam Coordinating Group) issued their recommendations. The report was entitled "A Policy of Sustained Reprisal." Shortly thereafter, Ambassador Maxwell Taylor issued his own assessment of "Graduated Reprisals." Admiral Ulysses S. Grant Sharp, commander of all U.S. forces in the Pacific (CINCPAC was his acronym), in turn followed with a "Graduated Pressures" statement. The Joint Chiefs of Staff called for an "Eight-Week Program."

For the Bundy group, sustained bombing of the north allowed the United States to speak effectively in the south:

> There is one grave weakness in our posture in Vietnam which is within our power to fix — and that is the widespread belief that we do not have the will and force and patience and determination to take the necessary action and stay the course.
>
> This is the overriding reason for our present recommendation of a policy of sustained reprisal. Once such a policy is put in force, we shall be able *to speak* in Vietnam on many topics and in many ways, with growing force and effectiveness.[7]

Bombing the north would affect "the will of Hanoi to direct and support the VC," but "the immediate and critical targets are in the South — in the minds of the South Vietnamese and in the minds of the Viet Cong cadres."[8] Air war, then, was seen as a form of psychological warfare: the vast technocapital of air power had power far beyond physical destruction; its mere appearance was a form of power.

What were the expected effects of this powerful appearance? To begin, defeat in the south and its accompanying mood of "pessimism" would be psychologically changed into optimism. "It seems very clear that if the United States and the Government of Vietnam join in a policy of reprisal, there will be a sharp immediate increase in optimism in the South, among nearly all articulate groups."[9] Having provided cause for optimism, the United States would then press for actions to make *real* victory possible:

> This favorable reaction should offer opportunity for increased American influence in pressing for a more effective government — at least in the short run. Joint reprisals would imply military planning in which the American role would necessarily be controlling, and this new relation should add to our bargaining power in other military efforts — and conceivably on a wider plane if a more stable government is formed. We have the *whip hand* in reprisals as we do not in other fields. . . .
>
> The Vietnamese increase *in hope* could well increase the readiness of Vietnamese factions to join together in forming a more effective government.[10]

In essence, then, bombing would solve the contradictions of the sovereignty paradigm. It would simultaneously overcome the privatized nature of the regime and lead to a genuine public government and allow the United States to control this same government! Moreover, just as the South Vietnamese would go "up" by these new policies, the Vietcong would go "down," thus forming a new balance in the ledger: "We think it plausible that effective and sustained reprisals, even in a low key, would have a substantial depressing effect upon the morale of Viet Cong cadres in South Vietnam." [11]

Bundy and his associates believed that the odds of success for the bombing program were "somewhere between 25% and 75%," but "measured against the *costs* of defeat in Vietnam, this program seems *cheap*. And even if it fails to turn the tide — as it may — the *value* of the effort seems to us to exceed its *cost*." [12] And what was this surplus value from the investment in air war? To begin, air war would communicate to the American people and the rest of the world American resolve: "At a minimum, it will damp down the charge that we did not do all that we could have done, and this charge will be important in many countries, including our own." [13]

Second, "surplus" value would accrue on a global scale in that even if air war failed, it would demonstrate "U.S. willingness to employ this new norm in counter-insurgency." [14] Bombing "will set a *higher price* for the future upon all adventures of guerrilla warfare, and it should therefore somewhat increase our ability to deter such adventures." [15] Bombing will thus produce a global "credit," even if Vietnam is a failure, a "debit."

"A Policy of Sustained Reprisal" is a remarkable document. By simply signaling the disparity between opposing forces through a relatively low-level bombing campaign, the United States would at once significantly help South Vietnamese morale, help form a genuine national government in the south, control this new government, depress the enemy, protect itself against charges of inaction from domestic critics, and deter all future wars of national liberation. Air war would succeed where all previous policies had failed.

While Bundy and his associates emphasized the communicative powers of air war in the south, Maxwell Taylor emphasized the communicative powers of bombing to North Vietnamese leaders. In air war the very same bombs can be dropped for different reasons. In Taylor's assessment, the primary target was the "will of Hanoi leaders." The United States should conduct a "gradual, orchestrated acceleration of tempo measured in terms of frequency, size, number and/or geographical location of the reprisal strikes and related activities. . . . The exact rate of acceleration is a matter of judgment but we consider, roughly speaking, that each successive week should include some new act on our part to increase pressure on Hanoi. . . ."[16] The United States would present to leaders of the Democratic Republic of Vietnam a "vision of inevitable, ultimate destruction if they do not change their ways."[17] Casualties and physical destruction would not have a "decisive bearing upon the ability of DRV to support VC," but instead would operate as psychological warfare, "as a measure of their discomfort."[18]

Once sufficiently impressed with this vision of "inevitable, ultimate destruction," the foreign Other would then negotiate on terms highly favorable to the United States. The United States would demand that the "DRV return to strict observance of 1954 accords with respect to SVN and the 1962 agreement with respect to Laos — that is, stop infiltration, and bring about a cessation of VC armed insurgency."[19] Although Taylor thought that bombing would help morale in the south — "fortunately the requirements for building morale in the South are roughly the same as those for impressing Hanoi leaders with the rising cost of their support of the VC" — note that in his theory the war can be won *without* GVN participation.[20] Between Bundy and Taylor there is thus a consensus to bomb and a consensus that bombing communicates; but at the same time, there is a vast difference concerning audiences.

The military's contribution at this point was not as theoretically developed. Admiral Sharp simply expressed concern that the public justification for bombing, the "reprisal" cover, not interfere with the real policy of sustained attack, or "graduated pressures." The more "correct" term had the "connotation of steady, relentless movement toward our objective of convincing Hanoi and Peiping of the prohibitive cost to them of their program of subversion, insurgency and aggression in SE Asia."[21] He further warned against the dangers of premature negotiations, declaring that the American political program would be successful "in proportion to the effectiveness of the military pressures program itself."[22]

The Joint Chiefs of Staff took responsibility for planning the actual program. Four fixed targets in the north would be hit each week for an eight-week period. These targets would be attacked "in the order of ascending risk to the attacking forces and are attacked at a frequency that assures that continuous and regular pressure is maintained against the DRV."[23] During the first eight weeks, all targets would be below the nineteenth parallel, thereby excluding the capital city of Hanoi and the port of Haiphong. The JCS commented on possible Chinese and/or Soviet intervention in the form of volunteers, planes, and anti-aircraft missiles, but on the whole they thought these contingencies to be manageable. Indeed, the concluding paragraph of the JCS report exudes confidence: "It is the opinion of the Joint Chiefs of Staff that the program herein proposed will demonstrate to the DRV that continuation of its direction and support of the insurgencies will lead progressively to more serious punishment. If the insurgency continues with active DRV support, strikes against the DRV will be extended with intensified efforts north of the 19th parallel." [24]

Note the peculiar form of this confidence. Just as the JCS has finished saying that the eight-week program will satisfactorily demonstrate to the Vietnamese that it is logical to negotiate on American terms, the staff then goes on to propose *more* bombing if such negotiation offers are not forthcoming. The Taylor–military version of communicative bombing, with its premise that the Vietnamese will see the "vision of the inevitable, ultimate destruction" present in the first few attacks, ultimately has *no internal limits other than ultimate destruction*. The potential for a vast air war is inscribed in the opening discourse on *limited* bombing.

Despite this flurry in early February, the bombing campaign did not move to full operations. President Johnson had called for all air operations against the north to be joint U.S.–GVN strikes. Joint operations had been part of the Bundy group's recommendations to build the GVN through air war. Ironically, the inital Rolling Thunder strikes had to be canceled because of a coup against Khanh, the factional leader in Saigon during the winter of 1964. The South Vietnamese air force could not regularly fly during coup periods because of political commitments to one or another faction.

Ambassador Taylor subsequently became quite perturbed about the irregular timings of the bombing campaign against the north. For bombing to communicate to the Vietnamese enemies, it had to follow a pattern or code they could decipher. Irregular attacks did not form a bombing message code: "What seems to be lacking is an agreed program covering several weeks which will combine the factors, frequency, weight and location of attack into a *rational pattern* which will convince the leaders in Hanoi that we are on a dynamic schedule which will not remain static in a narrow zone far removed from them and the sources of their power but which is a moving growing threat which cannot be ignored." [25]

To better form a bombing code, the provision of Rolling Thunder requiring all attacks to be composed of both American and South Vietnamese aircraft was eliminated. Air war could thus be more regularly

conducted by American aircraft alone, since Vietnamese political instability and withdrawal of their planes for coup duty would no longer stop
American attacks against the north. One principal reason for joint bombing had been its projected effects on morale and political unity in the
south. In eliminating this requirement, a gap emerged in the explanation
of why bombing the north would achieve quick victory.

This gap was immediately filled by *another* set of reasons. Both the
Taylor and Bundy elements had concentrated on what bombing signified, on what it communicated to various foreign Others. Little attention
was paid to what one actually bombed, the physical target. Even Taylor,
whose primary target was the will of the Hanoi regime, gave little thought
to what destruction was necessary. At first, he actually thought it did
not matter, that any target pattern was adequate: "If we support the
thesis (as I do) that the really important target is the will of the leaders
in Hanoi, virtually any target north of the 19th parallel will convey the
necessary message at this juncture as well as target 40."[26] Given the
communicative theory of bombing, virtually anything would be adequate since the concern was not literal destruction, but the signifying
message of potential destruction.

Still, some literal target system had to be selected. In March 1965 the
"LOC interdiction concept" was developed. "LOC" stands for "lines
of communication," meaning railways, highways, barges, bridges, trucks,
and the like. These targets had military significance. What is so interesting, though, is the American estimation of what these destroyed targets would connote, of what their signifying message would do to the
will of the regime, the primary target. Ambassador Taylor and General
Westmoreland explain:

> The Viet Cong's intensive efforts against lines of communications
> would make strikes against DRV LOC's highly appropriate at this
> time. In view of heavy traffic recently reported moving south, such
> strikes would also be militarily desirable. Moreover, these attacks by
> interrupting the flow of consumer goods to southern DRV would carry
> to the NVN man in the street, with minimum loss of civilian life, the
> message of U.S. determination.[27]

The Joint Chiefs of Staff concurred. In their late March recommendations for a twelve-week bombing campaign against North Vietnamese
lines of communications they stated: "This initial program should bring
home to the population the effects of air strikes since *consumer good(s)*

[sic] will be competing with military supplies for the limited transport.[28] The consumption model of pacification war has been seen before. It should come as no surprise to see the projection of American consumption values onto the North Vietnamese. With consumer goods in short supply or completely gone, the populace would be disgruntled, and this alienation would in turn affect the "will of the regime."

It is also important to see how war-managers always find reasons to bomb. In the beginning, the Bundy group had theorized air war as a means of improving morale in the south, overcoming the contradictions of the sovereignty paradigm, depressing the VC, and so forth. When the provision requiring that all air strikes be joint U.S.–GVN ventures was canceled because the South Vietnamese air force was too busy with coup and anticoup duty, then half of the communicative theory of bombing was rendered invalid before bombing really began. Yet rather than reflecting upon their failed theory, American war-managers instead developed another rationale. Demoralization from scarcity of consumer goods in the north "balances" failure of GVN performance in the south. Such balancing is rarely made explicit; it is, rather, a property of the "deep structure" of mechanical logic. United States airpower was so great that it *must* lead to victory. *Possession* of this technocapital could thus indirectly generate numerous rationales for its productive and eventually victorious employment. It is *inconceivable* to the war-managers that the apparatus could not win. This inconceivability indirectly generates multiple theories in which victory through airpower *is conceivable*. A failed rationale always finds ready alternative replacements.

Senior officials questioned how much bombing would be necessary to convey the signifying messages and what bombing could be *exchanged for* in negotiations. The North Vietnamese would either recognize the threat of "inevitable, ultimate destruction" as connoted by the "program of progressive military pressure" and consequently negotiate, or else bombing would escalate to ultimate destruction. Communicative bombing is a *logic of domination or torture:* the foreign Other can only recognize its *subordination* to superior American Technowar. Within the theory, no other response is imaginable. By late March and early April, numerous quantitative proposals on bombing abounded within the administration. Walt Rostow favored bombing major electrical power stations. North Vietnamese leaders would be presented "with an immediate desperate economic, social, and political problem which could not be evaded."[29] Rostow considered this proposal moderate, since its objective was not to destroy the industry of the Democratic Republic of Vietnam but only to "paralyze" it. Lights would go out; in the darkness the foreign Other would see the power of Technowar.

A full array of quantitative options was presented by Assistant Secretary of Defense John McNaughton. The first program called for one or two "mission days" each week, each mission having a hundred planes, the targets each week moving closer to Hanoi and becoming more important. In addition to these raids, each week three "armed reconnaissance" missions against trucks, boats, and anything else moving in the "lines of communication" were to be conducted.[30]

Alternative bombing plans offered more. One option called for a twelve-week program attacking all targets except "population" centers. A second alternative included bombing the population as well, avoiding only the central airport in Hanoi. McNaughton also listed options of blockading ports with mines or ships and significantly increasing bombing in Laos.[31]

President Johnson's decision came on April 6, in National Security Memorandum No. 328, section nine:

> Subject to continuing review, the President approved the following general framework of continuing action against North Vietnam and Laos:
>
> We should continue roughly the present slowly ascending tempo of ROLLING THUNDER operations, being prepared to add strikes in response to a higher rate of VC operations, or conceivably to slow the pace in the unlikely event VC slacked off sharply for what appeared to be more than a temporary operational lull.
>
> The target systems should continue to avoid the effective GCI [ground control interception] range of MIGs. We should continue to vary the types of targets, stepping up attacks on lines of communication in the near future, and possibly moving in a few weeks to attacks on the rail lines north and northeast of Hanoi.
>
> Leaflet operations should be expanded to obtain maximum practicable psychological effect on the North Vietnamese population.
>
> Blockade or aerial mining of North Vietnamese ports needs further study and should be considered for future operations. It would have major political complications, especially in relation to the Soviets and other third countries, but also offers many advantages.
>
> Air operations in Laos, particularly route blocking operations in the

Panhandle area, should be stepped up to the maximum remunerative rate.[32]

Substantively, the decision followed McNaughton's first plan, the "program of progressive military pressure" with its call for major strikes against fixed targets each week together with armed reconnaissance missions. This was the mildest option presented. However, the "continuing review" pointed toward further bombing.

War-managers soon made the logic of domination and subordination more explicit. President Johnson explained that "limited" bombing resembled sexual relations with women. Columnists Evans and Novak reported the special briefing:

> Employing a vivid sexual analogy, the President explained to friends and critics that the slow escalation of the air war in the North and the increasing pressure on Ho Chi Minh was seduction, not rape. If China should suddenly react to slow escalation, as a woman might react to attempted seduction, by threatening to retaliate (a slap in the face, to continue the metaphor), the United States would have plenty of time to ease off the bombing. On the other hand, if the United States were to unleash an all-out, total assault on the North — rape rather than seduction — there could be no turning back, and Chinese reaction might be instant and total.[33]

The foreign Other is thus a woman. Johnson makes a distinction between seduction and rape, but rape sometimes follows rejected seduction. She "deserves" it. Rejection equals humiliation, a loss of "reputation," and as John McNaughton wrote as a preamble to his bombing options, the American aim in Vietnam was "70% — To avoid a humiliating US defeat (to our reputation as guarantor)."[34] Within a sexual culture based on male domination, seduction is seen as legitimate and rape as sometimes legitimate, sometimes not legitimate, but both are acts of male power and possession on the same continuum. McNaughton concluded, "If the DRV will not 'play' the above game, we must be prepared to risk passing some flash points in the Strike North program. . . ."[35]

In late April, McNamara, Bundy, McNaughton, Taylor, Wheeler, Sharp, and Westmoreland met in Honolulu. Although there were disagreements in many areas, McNamara reported that a consensus was reached on bombing: "Ambassador Taylor stated what appeared to be a shared view, that it is important not to 'kill the hostage' by destroying the North Vietnamese assets inside the 'Hanoi do-nut.' ''[36]

The personalizing transformation of a target into a "hostage" was inherent in communicative bombing; the United States bombs North Vietnam to communicate with its leadership. But a "hostage" is not simply any Other, but an Other *possessed* by the dominant party. Possession comprises part of the structural relationship in sadomasochistic sexuality. Although violence in such relationships for the most part occurs as theatrical display and fantasy, the limit to real violence is death, because, as literary theorist George Bataille says, at that point the "slave" can no longer "recognize the conqueror so as to satisfy him. The slave is unable to give the master the satisfaction without which the master can no longer rest."[37] Thus it is important not to "kill the hostage," because a dead hostage could not recognize its subordination to superior American Technowar. As McNamara says in his report, "The strategy for 'victory' proposed by Ambassador Taylor, General Wheeler, Admiral Sharp and General Westmoreland is to *break the will* of the DRV/VC by denying them victory. Ambassador Taylor put it in terms of a demonstration of Communist *impotence,* which will lead eventually to a political solution."[38]

From April 1965 Rolling Thunder bombarded the north. The unit of measurement for such missions is known as the "sortie," which is equal to a single flight by one plane. Month after month, the sortie rate for combat missions in the north gradually increased: 3,600 in April; 4,000 in May; 4,800 in June. By year's end, 55,000 sorties had been flown against North Vietnam, and this figure represents only about one-third of air war in Indochina. Bombing in Laos had increased from around 500 sorties a month in June to over 3,000 a month by December.[39] In the south, bombing by B-52s was introduced. Each plane carried around thirty tons of bombs. Code-named Arc Light, they illuminated the path toward the end of the tunnel.

Geographical limits to bombing were constantly extended. The old Provisional Military Demarcation Line, the boundary between north and south, had been set at the seventeenth parallel. At first air strikes were confined to the nineteenth parallel, then extended to the twentieth, then extended further to 20 degrees, 33 minutes north. Beyond this limit lay the "Hanoi-Haiphong donut" where the hostage lived and the "China buffer zone," the Chinese–North Vietnam border.

In August 1965, McNamara ordered the Central Intelligence Agency and the Defense Intelligence Agency to list targets damaged or destroyed during Rolling Thunder and to estimate damage in monetary terms. In December they released 1965 CIA "Appraisal of the Bombing of North Vietnam." Target categories are given first:

*Power plants.* 6 small plants struck, only 2 of them in the main power grid. Loss resulted in local power shortages and reduction in power available for irrigation but did not reduce the power supply for the Hanoi/Haiphong area.

*POL storage* [petroleum-oil-lubricants]. 4 installations destroyed, about 17 percent of NVN's total bulk storage capacity. Economic effect not significant, since neither industry nor agriculture is large user and makeshift storage and distribution procedures will do.

*Manufacturing.* 2 facilities hit, 1 explosive plant and 1 textile plant, the latter by mistake. Loss of explosive plant of little consequence since China furnished virtually all the explosives required. Damage to textile plant not extensive.

*Bridges.* 30 highway and 6 railroad bridges on JCS [Joint Chiefs of Staff] list destroyed or damaged, plus several hundred lesser bridges hit on armed reconnaissance missions. NVN has generally not made a major reconstruction effort, usually putting fords, ferries, and pontoon bridges into service instead. Damage has neither stopped nor curtailed movement of military supplies.

*Railroad yards.* 3 hit, containing about 10 percent of NVN's total railroad cargo-handling capacity. Has not significantly hampered the operations of the major portions of the rail network.

*Ports.* 2 small maritime ports hit, at Vinh and Thanh Hoa in the south, with only 5 percent of the country's maritime cargo-handling capacity. Impact on economy minor.

*Locks.* Of 91 known locks and dams in NVN, only 8 targeted as significant to inland waterways, flood control, or irrigation. Only 1 hit, heavily damaged.

*Transport equipment.* Destroyed or damaged 12 locomotives, 819 freight cars, 805 trucks, 109 ferries, 750 barges, and 354 other water craft. No evidence of serious problems due to shortages of equipment.[40]

The two intelligence agencies estimated damage to total $63 million, divided between $36 million in damage to "economic" targets and $27 million to "military" targets. This is significant considering that North Vietnam's total gross national product was $1.6 billion in 1965. Commentary accompanying these indices of capital loss or "debit" spoke eloquently of "problems" created:

> In addition to this measurable damage, the bombing was reported to have "disrupted" the production and distribution of goods; created "severe" problems and "reduced capacity" in all forms of transportation; created more "severe problems" in managing the economy; reduced production; caused "shortages" and "hardships"; forced the diversion of "skilled manpower and scarce resources" from productive uses to the restoration of damaged facilities and/or their dispersal and relocation and so on.[41]

According to analysts, bombing had created management problems for the enemy war-managers. However, the DRV refused to recognize its subordination! By December 1965, the United States still remained close to defeat even though it introduced ground combat troops and expanded its total forces to around 200,000 men. North Vietnam responded by stationing an estimated 17,000 troops in the northern provinces along the "demilitarized zone" while the indigenous National Liberation Front increased its forces from 140,000 in 1963 to well over 500,000 in 1965.[42] Internal growth in the south was more important than the contribution of the foreign Other. The bombing campaign had not succeeded.

The CIA-DIA analysts explained failure in terms of *limits* to bombing: "[Losses] still remain small compared to the total economic activity and the major industrial facilities have not been attacked."[43] Another CIA report quantified what the limits had excluded: ". . . almost 80 percent of North Vietnam's limited modern industrial economy, 75 percent of the nation's population, and the most *lucrative* military supply and LOC targets have been effectively insulated from air attack."[44] To make "money" required increased bombing.

Military leaders had been lobbying for greater bombing ever since the first bombs were dropped. When the Democratic Republic of Vietnam was first "targeted" by the Joint Chiefs of Staff in 1964, only 94 targets were listed. Only eight targets were industrial installations; nothing more was thought worth hitting. By the end of 1965, though, the JCS had expanded its definition of significance to include 24 industrial targets,

18 of them small power plants used for irrigation and street lighting. The target list expanded to 240, over twice the original list. Even this figure was restricted by an administration decree that no more than two targets could be added each week. Of these 240 targets, 134 were bombed at least once by the end of December.[45] Most "targets" not bombed were either in the Hanoi-Haiphong "donut" or else along the Chinese border.

One hundred thirty-four is a larger number than 94, by 40. However, 134 is a *smaller* number than 240, by 106. By this play of numerical representation the Joint Chiefs of Staff created another abstract quantitative space, *a space of bombs not dropped*. This debit explains the failure of air war to be productive. The *lucrative, remunerative* targets are all in the *space of bombs not dropped*. In this space *the foreign Other lives*.

This numerical play can be repeated indefinitely. The closure offered by exactly 106 targets not bombed can be opened up to limitless bombing by increasing the number of targets. Target list increases occurred throughout the war. What appears as the scientific assessment of bombs not dropped is only a numbers game played by the military to increase the production of air war.

Before war-managers could increase bombing, they thought that another kind of appearance was necessary, the appearance of an honest American effort toward peace. McNamara wrote President Johnson in late November of 1965:

> It is my belief that there should be a three- or four-week pause in the program of bombing the North before we either greatly increase our troop deployments to Vietnam or intensify our strikes against the North. The reasons for this belief are, first, that we must lay a foundation in the mind of the American public and in world opinion for such an enlarged phase of the war and, second, we should give North Vietnam a face-saving chance to stop the aggression.[46]

The sense in which the pause was for political appearances only can be discerned in most memoranda. John McNaughton had an honest title in his contribution "Hard-Line Pause Packaged to Minimize Political Cost of Resuming Bombing." McNaughton demanded extraordinary actions from the DRV and the NLF to avoid more bombing.

    a. The DRV stops infiltration and direction of the war.

    b. The DRV moves convincingly toward withdrawal of infiltrators.

    c. The VC stops attacks, terror and sabotage.

d. The VC stops significant interference with the GVN's exercise of government functions over substantially all of South Vietnam.[47]

This program demanded capitulation: "The truth of the matter, however, is that the hard-line objective is, in fact, capitulation by a Communist force which is far from beaten, has unlimited (if unattractive) reserves available in China, and is confident that it is fighting for a just principle."[48] There was little likelihood that the Communist forces would negotiate and ruin plans for increased bombing. The major problem McNaughton foresaw was ridicule of the United States by nations who saw through the bogus negotiating position. For this possibility the author suggested "that the hard-line objectives should be blurred somewhat in order to maximize favorable public reaction, even though such blurring would reduce the chances of DRV acceptance of the terms."[49] The bombing pause tried to win public opinion, not generate negotiations.

Only two problems were left in stage-managing the bombing pause. The first necessitated making sure commanders in Vietnam did not take the pause seriously. This was taken care of in a State Department memo to the embassy in Saigon: "The prospect of large-scale reinforcement in men and defense budget increases of some twenty billions for the next eighteen month period requires solid preparation of the American public. A crucial element will be clear demonstration that we have explored fully every alternative but that the aggressor has left us no choice.[50]

The second problem concerned how to resume bombing without discrediting the fake peace efforts. McNaughton proposed to begin with the lines of communication, which could be "identified as militarily required interdiction" — the constant attempt to stop enemy movement southward. After a few weeks, "Later strikes could then be escalated to other kinds of targets and to present or higher levels." In this way the United States could "maintain a 'military' cover," and "avoid the allegation that we are practicing 'pure blackmail.' "[51]

A thirty-seven-day bombing pause took place in late December 1965 and January 1966. Behind the public spectacle of peace-seeking, war-managers debated escalation. The target that was chosen should come as no surprise. Technowar conceives war to be a struggle between two machinelike, technobureaucratic apparatuses. And what do industrial machines require for functioning? In American terms, they require POL — petroleum, oil, and lubricants. Bombs would make the Vietnamese run out of gas. The "Great POL Debate" began.

# CHAPTER 10

# Structural Dynamics of Escalation in Theory and Practice, 1966–1967

B Y July Rolling Thunder had been under way for three months. Pressure from the Joint Chiefs of Staff for immediate bombing of virtually all targets on their master target list had been constant since the first bombs were dropped. What was new in July 1965 was a Select National Intelligence Estimate calling for increased bombing. SNIE is the name given to papers written by the coordinating body of most U.S. intelligence agencies, the United States Intelligence Board. The board did not think strikes in the Hanoi-Haiphong donut and along the Chinese border by themselves would do much. However, there was one target system they thought might have a "critical impact."

> If, in addition, POL targets in the Hanoi-Haiphong area were destroyed by air attacks, the DRV's capability to provide transportation for the general economy would be severely reduced. It would also complicate their military logistics. If additional PAVN [People's Army of DRV] forces were employed in South Vietnam on a scale sufficient to counter increased US troop strength [which the SNIE said was "almost certain" to happen] this would substantially increase the amount of supplies needed in the South. The Viet Cong also depend on supplies from the North to maintain their present level of large-scale operations. The accumulated strains of a prolonged curtailment of supplies received from North Vietnam would obviously have an impact on the Communist effort in the South.[1]

At the time McNamara considered such attacks to be potentially counterproductive; there was "a real possibility than an attack on the Haiphong petroleum supply would substantially increase the risk of Chinese participation." McNamara speculated that the Vietnamese enemy might retaliate in kind, launching "an attack on the petroleum dumps outside of Saigon that contain eighty percent of the petroleum storage for SVN."[2] Such an attack would cripple the American war effort and disrupt the growing "service" economy. The secretary of defense consequently opted for "incremental escalation," which would "emphasize the threat."[3] This was in July.

By late fall, when it was clear that Rolling Thunder had not been successful, the Joint Chiefs of Staff took to the offensive:

> We shall continue to achieve only limited success in air operations in DRV/Laos if required to operate within the constraints presently imposed. The establishment and observance of de facto sanctuaries within the DRV, coupled with a denial of operations against the most important military and war supporting targets, precludes attainment of the objectives of the air campaign. . . . Thus far, the DRV has been able and willing to absorb damage and destruction at the slow rate. Now required is an immediate and sharply accelerated program which will leave no doubt that the US intends to win and achieve a level of destruction which they will not be able to overcome.[4]

The space of bombs not dropped would vanish in their plan: all major ports, five key electrical power plants, all major airfields, all major supply depots, most public ministries, rails, roads, waterways — all would be destroyed by bombing. So would the POL system. According to the Joint Chiefs, "Attack on this system would be more damaging to the DRV capability to move war-supporting resources within country and along the infiltration routes to SVN than an attack against any other target system."[5] What made such strikes even more attractive was that the JCS estimated that 97 percent of North Vietnamese POL supplies were concentrated in a mere thirteen sites, four of which had already been hit. Destroying the rest would definitely mean bad news: "Recuperability of the DRV POL system from the effects of an attack is very poor. Loss of the receiving and distribution point at Haiphong would present many problems. It would probably require several months for the DRV, with foreign assistance, to establish an alternate method for importing bulk POL, in the quantities required."[6]

However, at the very moment when some aspects of intelligence estimates indicated great profit from increased production of air war, doubts about the ability of the United States to end the war through bombing began to be articulated by those very same intelligence agencies! In the deep logic of mechanistic anticommunism and Technowar, the foreign

Other is another bureaucratic machine with war technology, but is much less technologically advanced than the United States. By this reasoning, destroying North Vietnam's meager POL facilities would cripple its puny war machine and economy. But the same intelligence analysts who thought in these conventional terms were beginning to break out from this paradigm, to see that the DRV was different from what customary American projections determined it to be. Intelligence memos became contradictory; the very next paragraph in the JCS estimate after the comments on poor DRV recuperability of its POL system says: "An alternative to bulk importation would be the packaging of POL at some point for shipment into NVN and subsequent handling and distribution by cumbersome and costly methods over interdicted LOCs. Loss of bulk storage facilities would necessitate the use of small drums and dispersed storage areas and further compound the POL distribution problem."[7]

A "costly" alternative for the North Vietnamese, not profitable according to the accounting standards of corporate capitalism, was coming into view. If the Vietnamese saw gasoline and oil as essential goods in themselves, rather than commodities on a market, then steps could be taken to hide POL despite the increased financial costs:

> Current evidence shows that the DRV has in progress an extensive program of installing groups of small POL tanks in somewhat isolated locations and throughout the Hanoi area. Photographs reveal groups of tanks ranging in number of 16 to 120 tanks per group. The facilities are generally set into shallow excavations and are then earth-covered leaving only the vents and filling apparatus exposed. This construction was observed at several places in the Hanoi area in August and appeared to be an around-the-clock activity. . . . In addition, considerable drum storage has been identified.[8]

This latter report on the alternative POL complex was not in the main body of the Joint Chiefs of Staff memorandum, but rather in the appendix. However, the JCS attempt to curtail debate over the probable success or failure of air strikes against North Vietnam's POL facilities failed. Many intelligence analysts were beginning to recognize that North Vietnam really was not an industrialized nation and was not fighting according to Technowar logic.

The Central Intelligence Agency's principal analytical group, the Board of National Estimates, did not see capitulation by the North Vietnamese resulting from either POL strikes or the total bombing plan proposed by the Chiefs. At best, POL strikes might embarrass the north: "We believe that the DRV is prepared to accept for some time at least the stress and difficulties which loss of the major POL facilities would mean for its military and economic activity. It is unlikely that this loss would cripple the Communist military operations in the South, though it would certainly embarrass them."[9] Nor did the board believe the total attack wanted by the JCS would achieve its desired end. Closed ports simply meant supplies would have to be off-loaded into small boats. Even in the face of complete destruction of central POL depots, the board contended, the north might expand the war rather than quit:

> Prudence would seem to dictate that Hanoi . . . should choose
> . . . to reduce the effort in the South, perhaps negotiate, and salvage
> their resources for another day. We think that the chances are a little
> better than even that this is what they would do. But their ideological
> and emotional commitment, and the high political stakes involved,
> persuade us that there is an almost equal chance that they would do
> the opposite, that is, enlarge the war and bring in large numbers of
> Chinese forces.[10]

Unhappy with a political analysis showing the Vietnamese will to resist, McNamara called for yet another study, one which would confine itself to *technical* problems presented to the DRV by attacks on Haiphong Harbor and other POL storage facilities. The resulting study restates (in "technical" language) the split between those who thought in Technowar terms and those who thought North Vietnam was not an industrial country fighting a mechnanized war. Handling oil in small tank trucks, boats, and drums would not be cost efficient for the north: "The economy would suffer appreciably from the constant disruption of transportation. This . . . would somewhat curtail the output of the DRV's modest industrial establishment and complicate the problems of internal distribution."[11] Despite these internal problems, the study concluded that POL strikes would not stop the north's assistance to the south. Note the reason why:

> The loss of stored POL and the dislocation of the distribution system would add appreciably to the DRV's difficulties in supplying the Communist forces in the South. However, we have estimated that the Communist effort in South Vietnam, at present levels of combat, *does not depend on imports of POL and requires only relatively small tonnages of other supplies (say 12 tons per day, on an annual basis)*. Accordingly, we believe that adequate quantities of supplies would

continue to move by one means or another to the Communist forces in South Vietnam, though the general supplies would not move as fast and it would hence require more to keep the pipeline filled.[12]

Someone had made an important discovery. With no tanks, no helicopters, no jets, no heavy artillery, indeed almost none of the artifacts of capital-intensive Technowar, the Vietcong in the south did not use POL and required relatively few external supplies. In American terms, twelve tons a day could be transported in *one* tractor-trailer rig, *five* two-and-a-half-ton military trucks, or fifteen three-quarter-ton capacity pickups. Even if this daily tonnage figure was way too small, the order of magnitude was so low that multiplying the estimate by ten only gives 120 tons a day, a figure that could have been transported by fewer than ten tractor rigs, forty-eight two-and-a-half-ton military trucks, or 160 pickup trucks. Daily estimates, either the CIA's twelve-ton figure or a higher number, must be multiplied to grasp what weekly or monthly requirements were, but still the required supplies and transport were tiny compared to U.S. supplies. Stopping such few goods by crippling large POL storage tanks became a dubious enterprise to some intelligence analysts. The real foreign Other was beginning to emerge beyond the conceptual bounds imposed by Technowar.

Additional studies conducted during the POL debate confirm the difference. One Joint Staff–Defense Intelligence estimate calculated that although the North Vietnamese had a bulk POL capacity of 179,000 metric tons, its annual need for POL products totaled only 32,000 metric tons, indicating that it would be extremely difficult to cripple the system through bombing.[13] This study also indicated that a dispersed POL system could suffice for the nation's needs. Another Select National Intelligence Estimate examined what would be the likely results of hitting both POL facilities and major electrical power plants. It also concluded that although such strikes would probably "paralyze" North Vietnamese industry, this still would not seriously affect war in the south "because so little of what is sent south is produced in the DRV, an industrial shutdown would not very seriously reduce the regime's capability to support the insurgency." And once again, the study contended that the destruction of POL storage facilities could be readily overcome: "Importation of POL would be a key problem, but would be surmountable in a comparatively short time, probably a few weeks, since quantities involved would not be large, even if increased somewhat over previous levels."[14]

How then was this true difference of the foreign Other overcome and subsumed back into Technowar? In part the answer resides in the familiar play of numerical representation. The CIA study cited in the section on the fake bombing halt of 1965–1966, the one which lamented that "almost 80 percent of North Vietnam's limited modern, industrial economy, 75 percent of the nation's population and the most lucrative military supply and LOC targets have been effectively insulated from air attack," proved to be quite influential to McNamara.[15] He, too, believed that the DRV's power resided in its ability to deliver consumer goods to its citizens:

> In the longer term, the recommended bombing program . . . can be expected to create a substantial added burden on North Vietnam's manpower supply for defense and logistics tasks and to engender popular alienation from the regions should shortages become widespread. While we do not predict that the regime's control would be appreciably weakened, there might be an aggravation of any differences which may exist within the regime as [to] the policies to be followed.[16]

McNamara had left the presidency of Ford Motor Company to become secretary of defense. It should also be recalled that his first claim to fame resulted from his role as a statistician for the army corp's strategic bombing campaign of Western Europe during World War II.[17] McNamara was not the only war-manager to have experience with strategic bombing in World War II. Walt Rostow had also picked bomb targets during that war. He firmly believed in POL strikes:

> From the moment that serious and systematic oil attacks started, front line single engine fighter strength and tank mobility were affected. The reason was this: it proved much more difficult, in the face of general oil shortage, to allocate from less important to more important uses than the simple arithmetic of the problem would suggest. Oil moves in various logistical channels from central sources. When the central sources began to dry up the effects proved fairly prompt and widespread. What look like reserves statistically are rather inflexible commitments to logistical pipelines.
> With an understanding that simple analogies are dangerous, I nevertheless feel it is quite possible the military effects of a systematic and sustained bombing of POL in North Vietnam may be more prompt and direct than conventional intelligence analysis would suggest.
> I would underline, however, the adjectives "systematic and sus-

tained.'' If we take this step we must cut clean through the POL system — and hold the cut — if we are looking for decisive results.[18]

Conventional intelligence analysis was on the verge of recognizing that the enemy did not use POL in the south and that little POL was used in transporting supplies southward since relatively few supplies were sent southward. In time, conventional intelligence analysis might even have recognized that it was the United States and the forces it equipped that required 73,881,000 barrels of POL in 1965, another 112,995,000 barrels in 1966, and still more barrels, 146,697,000 in 1967.[19] Mechanized, air-intensive war required such vast quantities.

Rostow was not alone in his memory of World War II. General William W. Momyer, former air force chief of staff, former commander of the U.S. Air Force in Southeast Asia, and a former bomber group commander during the Second World War, stressed the lessons of that war in his memoir, *Air Power in Three Wars*. The question of POL strikes comes first:

In World War II the destruction of the synthetic oil plants and related war goods had such a deleterious effect on the fighting ability of the German armed forces that Reichminister Albert Speer said the oil attacks of 1944 brought about the decision of the war. It had become only a matter of time until the German Army would have ground to a halt for lack of supplies for its armoured and mechanized divisions. The Allies, thus, had placed the German Army in serious logistical problems before the invasion.[20]

Momyer then outlines the full concept of air interdiction as it developed:

From these lessons of World War II, the concept of interdiction developed: (a) Strike the source of the war material; (b) concentrate the attacks against the weak elements of the logistical system; (c) continuously attack, night and day, the major lines of communication supporting the army in the field; (d) inflict heavy losses on enemy logistics and forces before they approach the battlefield where the difficulty of successful interdiction is greatest; (e) keep continuous ground pressure on the enemy to force him to consume large quantities of logistics.[21]

Rostow, Momyer, Westmoreland, and the Joint Chiefs of Staff all applied this concept to Vietnam. Search-and-destroy attempted to make

the Vietcong and NVA fight large-scale battles that would use up supplies. By hitting the Vietnamese POL dumps and lines of communication to the south, Technowar would create a logistical crisis for the
enemy, which in turn would lead to their surrender. As early as 1965,
when Westmoreland and the Joint Chiefs of Staff announced search-
and-destroy, they considered a sizable air war to be "an indispensable
component of this overall program."[22] Ground war and air war are thus
interdependent subsystems; each "calls" for the other. Both follow the
same logic.

This return to the U.S. experience in World War II marks another
development in military doublethink. Doublethink can be extended to
events in the past, as Orwell explains in his description of the "Party's"
vision of history in *1984:*

> Past events, it is argued, have no objective existence, but survive
> only in written records and in human memories. The past is whatever
> the records and the memories agree upon. And since the Party is in
> full control of all records, and in equally full control of the minds of
> its members, it follows that the past is whatever the Party chooses to
> make it. It also follows that though the past is alterable, it never has
> been altered in any specific instance. For when it has been recreated
> in whatever shape is needed at the moment, then this new version *is*
> the past, and no different past can ever have existed.[23]

*George Orwell, 1984 (New York: New American Library, 1961) p. 176*

Orwell elucidates the incredible mental gymnastics necessary for
doublethink: "To tell deliberate lies while genuinely believing in them,
*to forget any fact that has become inconvenient,* and then, when it becomes necessary again, to draw it back from oblivion for just so long
as it is needed, to deny the existence of objective reality and all the
while to take account of the reality which one denies — all this is in-
dispensably necessary."[24] Forgetting *any fact which has become inconvenient* is important to our understanding of the war-managers' dreams
of WWII.

When World War II ended in Europe, one of the highest-priority intelligence missions concerned gathering information about the effects of
strategic bombing against military and economic targets. Eventually 316
volumes of the *United States Strategic Bombing Survey* were published.
Strategic bombing over Germany failed. Bombing raids killed 155,846
British and American airmen, but German war production was not significantly affected by the bombing, nor was German morale broken.[25]

Albert Speer, minister of production for the Third Reich, confirmed the failure: "After two and a half years, in spite of the beginning of heavy bombing, we had raised our entire armaments production from an average index of 98 for the year 1941 to a summit of 322 in July 1944."[26] Speer even conceded that bombing might have caused a drop in war production by 9 percent as the survey claimed, but he pointed to a possibly different effect of bombing: "On the contrary, from my visits to armaments plants and my contacts with the man in the street I carried away the impression of growing toughness. It may well be that the estimated loss of 9 percent of our production capacity was amply balanced out by our increased effort."[27]

Speer recalled only one occasion when strategic bombing presented insurmountable difficulties to the Germans:

> On May 8, 1944, I returned to Berlin to resume my work. I shall never forget the date May 12, four days later. On that day the technological war was decided. Until then we had managed to produce approximately as many weapons as the armed forces needed, in spite of their considerable losses. But with the attack of nine hundred and thirty-five daylight bombers of the American Eighth Air Force upon several fuel plants in central and eastern Germany, a new era in the air war began. It meant the end of German armaments production.[28]

By late July of 1944, Speer reported, bombing had destroyed 98 percent of Germany's aviation gasoline plants. By November the Germans restored production to 28 percent of prebombing production levels, some 1,632 metric tons daily. Germany also had considerable reserves.[29] Flights by German fighters were curtailed. Without POL, the Luftwaffe could not adequately defend German industry against further bombing raids, and German armored divisions could not pursue their Blitzkreig strategy of assault.

But what of the Vietnamese? North Vietnam had no refineries, only storage dumps. The north had no massive air force to protect a nonexistent armaments industry. The north had no tanks, planes, or helicopters in the south. The Democratic Republic of Vietnam was not Germany in the Second World War, yet this is what the foreign Other was cast to be, and even then the lessons of the *Strategic Bombing Survey* were largely forgotten.

Despite McNamara's and Rostow's recommendations, POL facilities were not struck immediately. The spring of 1966 saw major social upheaval in South Vietnam. Three years earlier Buddhist protests against Diem had considerable influence in prompting a military coup. This time the uprising was not as large, but it still threatened the government. Buddhists in Hue and Danang, together with the commanding Vietnamese general for the northern sector of the country, all revolted against the central government; they sought a neutralist policy for South Vietnam. Premier Ky and military forces loyal to him destroyed some of this opposition; other elements were placated by a government promise to move more quickly toward constitutional democracy. Leading American officials did not think it was wise to escalate during these political convolutions.

The spring of 1966 was also a time when many different nations attempted to find a peaceful settlement for Southeast Asia. A Canadian diplomat named Chester Ronning made two trips to Hanoi as a go-between for the United States. France, Rumania, Egypt, India, and the Netherlands — among others — made efforts to get negotiations going. Secretary General U Thant of the United Nations also tried.[30] No one succeeded. The North Vietnamese were not willing to negotiate while being bombed, and the United States was not willing to stop bombing before negotiations.

On April 16, William Bundy, the assistant secretary of state, submitted a paper on the political consequences of U.S. failure in Vietnam. It did not matter if the United States failed because the regime was internally divided and lacked popular support from its people:

> Faced with this reaction, we must still conclude that Thailand simply could not be held in these circumstances, and that the rest of Southeast Asia would probably follow in due course. In other words, the strategic stakes in Southeast Asia are fundamentally unchanged by the possible political nature of the causes for failure in Vietnam. The same is almost certainly true of the shockwaves that would arise against other free nations — Korea, Taiwan, Japan, and the Philippines — in the wider area of East Asia. Perhaps these shockwaves can be countered, but they would not be mitigated by the fact that the failure arose from internal political [sic] causes rather than any US major error or omission.[31]

Bundy was restating the domino theory, replacing fallen dominoes, popping corks, and chain reactions with "shockwaves." The *Pentagon Papers* noted two additional studies. George Carver, of the Central Intelligence Agency, formulated an American policy that was not solely anti-Communist, but instead required "some measure of responsible political behavior on the part of the South Vietnamese themselves including, but not limited to, their establishment of a reasonably effective government with which we can work."[32] In this approach, American withdrawal was justified on grounds that the Vietnamese government was inadequate — a radical difference. The final paper was presumably written by John McNaughton. Entitled "Politics in Vietnam: A 'Worst' Outcome," the work accepted the assumption that South Vietnam and Thailand would "fall" to communism, but that different lines of containment would protect Asia.[33]

But neither Carver nor McNaughton held sway among the elite. On April 21, President Johnson announced that although "Vietnam must seem to many a thousand contradictions," the United States was committed to helping it emerge "free from the interference of any other power, no matter how mighty or strong." Questions concerning Vietnamese political and social structure were postponed indefinitely. In his words, the "normal processes of political action" would "someday, some way create in South Vietnam a society that is responsive to the people and consistent with their traditions. . . ."[34]

Given this structural logic, escalation against North Vietnam would follow. On April 27, Maxwell Taylor submitted his recommendations to the President, a paper entitled "Assessment and Uses of Negotiation Blue Chips." Taylor was concerned about the exchange value of bombing in negotiating. He thought that the United States and the foreign Other had a pile of *poker chips*. Bombing was the big American chip, worth all military activity by the National Liberation Front and the People's Army of Vietnam: "Hence, I would be inclined to accept as an absolute minimum a cessation of Viet Cong incidents and military operations (their a and b), which are readily verifiable in exchange for the stopping of our bombing and of offensive military operations against Viet Cong units (our a and b).[35] To stop bombing before negotiations would consequently waste purchasing power:

> Such a tabulation of negotiating blue chips and their *purchasing power* emphasized the folly of giving up any one in advance as a precondition for negotiations. Thus, if we give up bombing in order to start discussions, we would not have the *coins necessary to pay* for all the concessions required for a satisfactory terminal settlement. My estimate of assets and values may be challenged, but I feel that it is important for us to go through some such exercise and make up our collective minds as to the *value of our holdings* and how to play them.[36]

Defining the war in economic logic precludes the possibility that the enemy might well see Vietnamese national unity in terms beyond debit and credit. Mr. Taylor was not alone in his reasoning. William Bundy at the State Department even thought Taylor to be a bad shopper, unaware of the full power of Technowar dollar: ". . . I have myself been inclined to an *asking price,* at least, that would include both a declared cessation of infiltration and a sharp reduction in VC/NVA military operations in the South."[37]

On June 29, 1966, Rolling Thunder went after POL facilities. Haiphong Harbor lost 80 percent, while the large tank farm in Hanoi was reduced to nothing. Air war increased to 8,100 sorties per month for North Vietnam and 10,100 per month for Laos. Every known POL site was hit; it was a "strangulation program."[38] Initial statistics indicated successful bombing. By the end of July, the Defense Intelligence Agency placed 70 percent of NVN's known bulk storage capacity as destroyed, together with 7 percent of dispersed sites. By December 1966, things looked even better. Admiral Sharp reported that in 1966 air war had destroyed 3,903 POL areas while damaging 4,481 others. Air war had also destroyed or damaged some 9,500 water vehicles, 2,314 railroad vehicles, 4,084 motor vehicles, 122 ports, 8,304 buildings, and thousands of other targets.[39]

However good these numbers looked, there were other numbers indicating failure. The Democratic Republic of Vietnam still had "about 26,000 metric tons storage capacity in the large sites, about 30–40,000 tons capacity in medium-sized dispersed sites, and about 28,000 tons capacity in smaller tank and drum sites."[40] Recall that North Vietnam only needed an estimated 32,000 metric tons to meet its minimum annual needs. CIA analysts saw the accounting problem. Although over 50 percent of bulk storage capacity had been destroyed, "it is estimated that substantial stocks still survive and that the DRV can continue to import sufficient fuel to keep at least essential military and economic traffic moving."[41]

Conventional intelligence analyses conducted before POL strikes had indicated likely failure, but these reports had been pushed aside by belief in advanced war technology. With the failure of the strikes, Technowar entered a protracted crisis: the *unthinkable* had actually occurred. At first Secretary of Defense McNamara thought the problem resided in the intelligence agencies and their reports, rather than the bombing. In the summer of 1966 he called for a special convocation of war scientists, men who had created many high-technology, capital-intensive weapons. Sponsored by the Institute for Defense Analysis, the Jason group, as it was called, held a high-level summer camp to consider bombing over North Vietnam. The results challenged Technowar:

> In view of the nature of the North Vietnamese POL systems, the relatively small quantities of POL it requires, and the options available for overcoming the effects of U.S. air strikes thus far, it seems doubtful that any critical denial of essential POL has resulted, apart from temporary and local shortages. It also seems doubtful that any such denial need result if China and/or the USSR are willing to pay greater costs in delivering it. . . .
>
> Since less than 5 percent of North Vietnamese POL requirements are utilized in supporting truck operations in Laos, it seems unlikely that infiltration south will have to be curtailed because of POL shortages; and since North Vietnamese and VC forces in South Vietnam do not require POL supplies from the North, their POL-powered activities need not suffer, either.[42]

The Jasonites' reports were not confined to the POL question alone. In their summary these scholars indicated that war-managers must understand that North Vietnam was not an industrial economy like the United States.

> As of July, 1966 the U.S. bombing of North Vietnam (NVN) had had no measurable direct effect on Hanoi's ability to mount and support military operations in the South at the current level.
>
> Although the political constraints seem clearly to have reduced the effectiveness of the bombing program, its limited effect on Hanoi's ability to provide such support cannot be explained solely on that basis. The counter-measures introduced by Hanoi effectively reduced the impact of U.S. bombing. More fundamentally, however, North Vietnam has basically a subsistence agricultural economy that presents a difficult and unrewarding system for air attack.
>
> The economy supports operations in the South mainly by functioning as a logistical funnel and by providing a source of manpower. The industrial sector produces little of military value. Most of the essential military supplies that the VC/NVN forces in the South require from external sources are provided by the USSR and Communist China. Furthermore, the volume of such supplies is so low that only a small fraction of the capacity of North Vietnam's rather flexible transportation network is required to maintain the flow. The economy's rela-

tively underemployed labor force also appears to provide an ample manpower reserve for internal military and economic needs including repair and reconstruction and for continued support of military operations in the South.[43]

The next major finding concerned empirical evidence against the theory of communicative bombing, with its emphasis on influencing the will of the regime:

> . . . initial plans and assessments for the ROLLING THUNDER program clearly tended to overestimate the persuasive and disruptive effects of the U.S. air strikes and, correspondingly, to underestimate the tenacity and recuperative capabilities of the North Vietnamese. This tendency, in turn, appears to reflect a general failure to appreciate the fact, well-documented in the historical and social scientific literature, that a direct, frontal attack on a society tends to strengthen the social fabric of the nation, to increase popular support of the existing government, to improve the determination of both the leadership and the populace to fight back, to induce a variety of protective measures that reduce the society's vulnerability to future attack, and to develop an increased capacity for quick repair and restoration of essential functions.[44]

Pearl Harbor and the Battle of Britain were both well known to senior officials and military commanders. The Jasonites were simply pointing out war-manager doublethink — the foreign Other is both like us when convenient and not like us when convenient.

They had one additional criticism. Namely, the *methodology* used by war-managers was not adequate. No one could know what quantity of bombs would be adequate to force submission:

> The fragmented nature of current analyses and the lack of an adequate methodology for assessing the net effects of a given set of military operations leaves a major gap between the quantifiable data on bomb damage effects, on the one hand, and policy judgments about the feasibility of achieving a given set of objectives, on the other. Bridging this gap still requires the exercise of broad political-military judgments that cannot be supported or rejected on the basis of systematic intelligence indicators. It must be concluded, therefore, that there is currently no adequate basis for predicting the levels of U.S. military effort that would be required to achieve the stated objectives — in-

deed, there is no firm basis for determining if there is *any* feasible level of effort that would achieve these objectives.[45]

This study caused McNamara's "disenchantment" with bombing. However, the Jasonites did not leave the secretary of defense totally unequipped. Instead, they recommended that a gigantic, electronic minefield be constructed along the demilitarized zone to keep the foreign Other out. The field would be composed of advanced electronic sensors, some for detecting heat, others for detecting noise, which would radio reports to a command center, which would in turn dispatch aircraft. Portions of the barrier were later constructed in Laos.

The end of 1966 found air war in crisis. Approximately 148,000 sorties had been flown. Out of 242 targets on the Joint Chiefs of Staff target list, 185 had been hit.[46] A major effort had been made against POL facilities, and it had failed. McNamara consequently opposed any further escalation, recommending only that the program be stabilized. The vast productive apparatus of Technowar had failed in its most capital- and technology-intensive phase of warfare.

However, the internal dynamics of air war discourse were far from exhausted. In 1967 the Joint Chiefs of Staff and their military subordinates made their greatest efforts yet to close the space of bombs not dropped, to hit every possible target in the Democratic Republic of Vietnam, to reduce the master target list to *zero*. All "self-imposed restraints" were to be abandoned, leaving "only those minimum constraints necessary to avoid indiscriminate killing of the population."[47] By removing these constraints, "lucrative," "remunerative" targets could be destroyed, thereby restoring profit. By late February, war-managers had created three bombing packages for presidential review. Listed as options A, B, and C, the three packages outline levels of destruction:

Examine the list with particular emphasis on option C, the military's maximum program. Here is a vision of total attack. The last remnants of North Vietnam's industrial sector would be destroyed. Agriculture would be severely damaged as well — North Vietnam relied upon dikes and levees for rice cultivation, its food staple. Several highly populated river valleys and coastal areas would be flooded. And most of all, ports would be destroyed. No longer could the foreign Other rely on help from a still more "outside," more foreign, Other. As Admiral Sharp said, "A drastic reduction of external support to the enemy would be a major influence in achieving our objective. . . ."[48]

Against this table of projected destruction another table was con-

Table 10.1

JOINT CHIEFS OF STAFF BOMBING OPTIONS FOR 1967

| A B C | *I. Military Actions Against North Vietnam and in Laos* |
|---|---|
| | A. Present programs |
| | B. Options for increased military programs |
| | 1. Destroy modern industry |
| X X X | — Thermal power (7-plant grid) |
| X X X | — Steel and cement |
| X X | — Machine tool plant |
| | — Other |
| X | 2. Destroy dikes and levees |
| | 3. Mine ports and coastal waters |
| X X | — Mine estuaries south of 20° |
| X X | — Mine major ports and approaches, and estuaries north of 20° |
| | 4. Unrestricted LOC [Lines of Communication] attacks |
| X X X | — Eliminate 10-mile Hanoi prohibited area |
| X X | — Reduce Haiphong restricted area to 4 miles |
| X | — Eliminate prohibited restricted areas except Chicom [Chinese Communist] zone |
| X X | — Elements of 3 ports (Haiphong, Cam Pha and Hon Gai) |
| X | — 4 ports (Haiphong, Cam Pha, Hon Gai and Hanoi Port) |
| X X | — Selected rail facilities |
| X X | — Mine inland waterways south of 20° |
| X | — Mine inland waterways north of 20° |
| X X | — 7 locks |
| | 5. Expand naval surface operations |
| X X X | — Fire at targets ashore and afloat south of 19° |
| X X | — Expand to 20° |
| X | — Expand north of 20° to Chicom buffer zone |
| | 6. Destroy MIG airfields |
| X X X | — All unoccupied airfields |
| X X | — 4 not used for international civil transportation |
| X | — 2 remaining airfields (Phuc Yen and Gia Lam) |

SOURCE: *The Pentagon Papers: The Senator Gravel Edition* (Boston: Beacon Press, 1972), vol. 4, pp. 145–146.

structed by one official stung by the POL debate. John McNaughton took figures produced by conventional intelligence analysis and did some simple addition and subtraction. He worked under the assumption of total attack given in option C.

Table 10.2
NORTH VIETNAM'S POTENTIAL FOR OBTAINING IMPORTS
BEFORE AND AFTER U.S. ATTACK
*(Tons per Day)*

|  | Potential Now | Potential after Attack |
|---|---|---|
| By sea | 6,500 | 650 |
| By Red River from China | 1,500 | 150 |
| By road from China | 3,200 | 2,400 |
| By rail from China | 6,000 | 4,000 |
| TOTAL | 17,200 | 7,200 |

Without major hardship, the need for imports is as follows:

| | |
|---|---|
| Normal imports | 4,200 |
| If imports replace destroyed industrial production | 1,400 |
| If imports replace rice destroyed by levee breaks | 600–2,500 |
| TOTAL | 6,200–8,100 |

SOURCE: *The Pentagon Papers: The Senator Gravel Edition* (Boston: Beacon Press, 1972), vol. 4, p. 155.

McNaughton's tabulations are extraordinarily revealing. Even during a maximum bombing campaign, the DRV could secure enough supplies. Such an intensive bombing campaign would cripple a complex industrial society such as the United States, but North Vietnam was not a complex industrial society! Given the relatively small amount of supplies needed and the redundancy of the transportation system, North Vietnam could function even after severe attacks and continual follow-ups.

Struggles between war-managers looking at different "bottom lines" continued through the rest of 1967. Intelligence agencies wrote several reports on bombing failure and the proposed alternatives. Some reports addressed the idea that enough bombs would cause the foreign Other to recognize its subordination. Below are some CIA examples:

Twenty-seven months of US bombing of North Vietnam have had remarkable little effect on Hanoi's overall strategy in persecuting the war, on its confident view of long-term Communist prospects, and on its political tactics regarding negotiations. The growing pressure of US air operations has not shaken the North Vietnamese leaders' conviction that they can withstand the bombing and outlast the US and South Vietnam in a protracted war of attrition. Nor has it caused them to waver in their belief that the outcome of this test of will and endurance will be determined primarily by the course of the conflict on the ground in the South, not by the air war in the North.

Morale in the DRV among the rank and file populace, defined in terms of discipline, confidence, and willingness to endure hardship, appears to have undergone only a small decline since the bombing of North Vietnam began.[49]

Short of a *major invasion* or *nuclear attack,* there is probably *no* level of air or naval actions against North Vietnam which Hanoi has determined in advance would be so intolerable that the war had to be stopped.[50]

Other CIA reports concentrated on bomb damage and ways in which damage was usually either repaired or circumvented:

The destroyed petroleum storage system has been replaced by an effective system of dispersed storage and distribution. The damaged military targets systems — particularly barracks and storage depots — have simply been abandoned, and supplies and troops dispersed throughout the country. The inventories of transport and military equipment have been replaced by large infusions of military and economic aid from the USSR and Communist China. Damage to bridges and lines of communications is frequently repaired within a matter of days, if not hours, or the effects are countered by an elaborate system of multiple bypasses or pre-positioned spans.[51]

For example, in southern North Vietnam the road system in 1965–1966 had a potential for shipping 450 tons a day. Despite heavy bombing, the system had been expanded by 1967 to handle up to 740 tons a day. Actual usage, though, was much *less.* In 1965 and 1966, the system averaged less than thirty trucks or an estimated 85 tons a day, only 20 percent of its total capacity. With the new expanded road systems, 85 tons represented only around *9 percent* of the total capacity.[52] Therefore, even if a very intense campaign could reduce road capacity by 50 percent, the system could still handle roughly five times more than was needed!

In June of 1967, the Central Intelligence Agency withdrew from debates concerning the Joint Chiefs of Staff target option programs. The agency had concluded that *no conceivable conventional bombing campaign* could significantly deter shipment of supplies southward to the extent that revolutionary war in the south would be seriously affected. Having reached this conclusion, the agency stopped making recommendations on bombing.

On the whole, though, the military's program of bombing until no targets were left unstruck held precedence in policy circles. By the end of May, fourteen out of twenty electrical power plants on the JCS target list had been repeatedly bombed with the President's approval; these raids destroyed 87 percent of North Vietnam's total electrical generating capacity.[53] Many other industrial and logistical targets were also struck.

Having achieved significant success, the military pressed harder for the full program (option C). General Wheeler, chairman of the Joint Chiefs of Staff said, "The bombing campaign is reaching the point where we will have struck all worthwhile fixed targets except the ports. At this time we will have to address the requirement to deny the DRV the use of the ports."[54] According to Townsend Hoopes, undersecretary of the air force, reconnaissance flights consistently showed that *no military supplies* came through ports. Weapons and munitions instead entered North Vietnam overland through China.[55] Nevertheless, the ports were "open," and the internal dynamics of the air war discourse tended toward closure from all "outside" connections and an empty target list.

By August, dominant military managers were so frustrated that they took the extraordinary step of going public. Their allies in Congress, particularly Senator John Stennis, chairman of the Senate Armed Services Committee, opened hearings on air war. All leading military warmanagers involved in the bombing campaigns were invited. Theirs was a familiar story. Bombing stopped the North Vietnamese from *doubling* troops in the south. Bombing required 500,000 North Vietnamese to work continually on repairs. Bombing significantly slowed down infiltration of men and materials.[56]

The military attacked "gradualism" — what has been called the communicative theory of bombing. They attacked "self-imposed restraints" and most of all they attacked the space of bombs not dropped. By this time the JCS master target list had grown to 427 targets, a massive increase from 98 in 1965 and 242 in 1966. Of these 427 targets, 359 recommended for destruction immediately, 302 had already been hit once or more.[57] This left 57 "lucrative" targets that would restore profitability to Technowar.

Testimonies before the Stennis Committee became another contest between differing "bottom lines." McNamara noted that the Vietnamese had an agrarian economy. Recent strikes had destroyed most major electrical plants, but then total capacity for the entire nation had been *less* than the single power plant in Alexandria, Virginia. Some 2,000 small diesel-powered generators had proved sufficient to provide the enemy's electrical needs.[58] The secretary of defense described the limited supplies needed in the south and how much redundancy was built into the transportation system. He even spelled out the real bottom line, the ability to import sufficient goods despite destruction of ports and continual attacks against lines of communication.

But the committee preferred the military bottom line:

> In our hearings we found a sharp difference of opinion between the civilian authority and the top-level military witnesses who appeared before the subcommittee over how and when our airpower should be employed against North Vietnam. In that difference we believe we also found the roots of the persistent deterioration of public confidence in our airpower, because the plain facts as they unfolded in the testimony demonstrated clearly that civilian authority consistently overruled the unanimous recommendations of military commanders and the Joint Chiefs of Staff for a systematic, timely, and hard-hitting integrated air campaign against the vital North Vietnamese targets. Instead, and for policy reasons, we have employed military aviation in a carefully controlled, restricted, and graduated build-up of bombing pressure which discounted the professional judgment of our best military experts and substituted civilian judgment in the details of target selection and the timing of strikes. We shackled the true potential of airpower and permitted the build-up of what has become the world's most formidable antiaircraft defenses. . . .[59]

Military war-managers were "professionals" and "experts," versus civilian war-managers with their implied amateurism. The spectacle of a "shackled" productive apparatus complete with a numerical space of bombs not dropped was thus sufficient to confirm the escalatory dynamics of air war.

President Johnson succumbed. By the end of October strikes had been conducted against all but five targets in the fifty-seven spaces of bombs not dropped. The target list, however, continued to grow. Another seventy targets were added. The production apparatus could always find another "lucrative" target not hit. Only ports still remained off-limits.

Just as the Stennis hearings were confirming the recommendations of the military, the Jasonites presented another summer camp report. This report was *not* made public:

> As of October, 1967, the U.S. bombing of North Vietnam has had no measurable effect on Hanoi's ability to mount and support military operations in the South.
>
> The bombing campaign has not discernibly weakened the determination of the North Vietnamese leaders to continue to direct and support the insurgency in the South.
>
> We are unable to devise a bombing campaign in the North to reduce the flow of infiltrating personnel into SVN.[60]

Zero, zero, zero — air war had failed to achieve its objectives despite several hundred thousand sorties flown and millions of bombs expended. If the Light at the End of the Tunnel could not be generated by bomb blasts, then perhaps there was no possibility of light at all, only an abyss. Out of the abyss came the Tet Offensive of February and March 1968. During the offensive and its aftermath numerous study groups reviewed the war; the *Pentagon Papers* called it an "A to Z" review. Although the military wanted an additional 200,000 soldiers for Vietnam and heavily increased bombing of the enemy, their call for escalation was temporarily restrained.

On March 30, 1968, President Lyndon Johnson announced that he was curtailing bombing to south of the twentieth parallel. He also said that he would not run again for president and that he would try to generate peace negotiations. One State Department official later commented on the move toward peace: "Something had to be done to extend the lease on public support of the war."[61] In its cable message to American ambassadors, the administration's actual assessment was made clear: "You [American ambassadors] should make clear [to American allies] that Hanoi is most likely to denounce the project and thus free our hand after a short period. Nonetheless, we might wish to continue the limitation even after a formal denunciation, in order to reinforce its sincerity and put the monkey firmly on Hanoi's back for whatever follows." They were confident that the monkey would travel north: "Insofar as our announcement foreshadows any possibility of a complete bombing stoppage, in the event Hanoi really exercised reciprocal restraints, we regard this as unlikely."[62] In the war-managers' assessment, there was little risk of negotiations. Even the temporary halt cost little; the weather was going to be bad over North Vietnam and planes could be readily rerouted to Laos:

> In view of weather limitations, bombing north of the 20th parallel will in any event be limited at least for the next four weeks or so — which we tentatively envisage as a maximum testing period in any event. Hence, we are not giving up anything really serious in this time frame. Moreover, air power now used north of 20th can probably be used in Laos (where no policy change planned) and in SVN.[63]

General Momyer, commander of the 7th Air Force, later wrote: "I supported the proposal for a bombing halt because I realized that the weather alone would probably cause us to cancel all but a few hundred sorties. . . ."[64] The bombing halt was intended to pacify American and world opinion at little cost to future air war.

However, the Vietnamese responded to the negotiations offer, thereby spoiling the trap. Late in October, Johnson announced the complete halt of bombing over the north. Although the gesture was a political ploy to help Democratic party candidate Hubert Humphrey in the November elections, the gesture failed in that Richard Nixon was elected president and another group of civilian war-managers took control. Two points should be noted at this juncture. First, despite the public proclamations, there was no real bombing halt in the sense that fewer planes dropped fewer bombs over Southeast Asia. As the administration memo to its ambassadors indicated, production was redistributed to targets in Laos and South Vietnam.[65]

Second, the internal dynamics of air war with its inherent tendency toward escalation and false closure toward an ever-increasing target list was not *publicly* discredited. The air war discourse remained intact, complete with a space of bombs not dropped, ready to be appropriated again.

# CHAPTER 11

# The Structure of Air Operations

At each moment of escalation, the highest war-managers decided upon both the general target categories to be hit and the *rate* of production, the number of sorties that would be flown in a given time period. In 1965 Assistant Secretary of Defense John McNaughton wrote about increasing sorties from the average of 3,000 per month to 4,000 a month in 1966. His numbers were too low. By October of 1966, Robert McNamara reported that "Attack sorties in North Vietnam have risen from about 4,000 per month at the end of last year to 6,000 per month in the first quarter of this year and 12,000 at present." He considered this rate too high; there were a "marginal 1,000 or even 5,000 sorties" per month that were unproductive.[1] To cut back on production would thus increase efficiency.

From the perspective of senior officials, the sortie rate is a managerial device for controlling air war. However, from the perspective of subordinate commands, a sortie rate is a *production quota*. Similarly, in air war, promotion among the officer corps was dependent upon meeting one's sortie rate quota or rather to report the best production statistics. Pressure to report a high sortie rate affected virtually every phase of air operations.

Classical military doctrine calls for unity of command over all air forces operating in a given area. In this way planes can be moved quickly as target priorities change, allowing the highest commander either to concentrate his planes for a mass attack on a single target or to disperse them to many targets.[2] Given the geographical size of the Democratic Republic of Vietnam and the range of most U.S. aircraft, air war over the north logically called for one commander. American forces never achieved this unity.

The 7th Air Force stationed in Thailand and the 7th Fleet stationed in the South China Sea were the two major air services used to bomb

North Vietnam. From time to time, air force and marine planes from Danang (in northern South Vietnam) were also used.

Competition between the air force and the navy for targets and sorties was so great that the commander of all U.S. military forces in the Pacific (including Southeast Asia) divided the sortie figure allotted for each two-week unit of Rolling Thunder operations between the two services. North Vietnam was divided into six separate target zones, called Route Packages. The air force got Route Packages I, V, and VIA, while the navy got II, III, IV, and VIB.[3] Note that the division of Route Package VI on the map opposite allows each service its own especially "lucrative" target area, Hanoi for the air force and Haiphong for the navy. The entire Route Package system was designed to allow each service to reach its quota.

Management techniques utilized by the army had their counterparts in the navy and air force. General Curtis LeMay, commander of the Strategic Air Command (nuclear bombers and missiles) in the 1950s, was one of the leaders in the "scientific" management movement in the military. When he subsequently became air force chief of staff in 1961, the emphasis on quantitative measurement and the centralization of control over operating forces was extended throughout the air force, including the Tactical Air Command that later managed fighter-bomber missions over North Vietnam.[4]

Just as the production model of war governing ground operations created a double-reality, so did a double-reality emerge in air war. Air war resembled ground war in that the emphasis on maximizing sorties led to indiscriminate killing of both the target population and the pilots who flew missions.

Fighter-bombers need good weather to find and hit a target. The standard criteria call for clouds no lower than 10,000 feet and horizontal visibility of at least five miles. Given these conditions, a group of fighter-bombers can begin their dive toward the target at 10,000 feet, release their bombs between 7,500 and 6,000 feet, and then pull out of the dive between 6,000 and 4,000 feet. With this attack approach, a fighter-bomber will put *half* its bombs in a circle 400 to 450 feet in diameter while the other bombs will be dispersed in a circle of much greater diameter.[5] This dispersed pattern defines "precision bombing" or a "surgical strike" under optimal conditions.

From December through mid-May, weather over North Vietnam was far from optimal. Winter and spring were monsoon season, when clouds were present at 6,000 feet or less (often at 1,500–1,800 feet) and hori-

# Air Force and Navy
# Bombing Route Packages

CHINA

NORTH VIETNAM

VI A

VI B

V

Haiphong

HANOI

IV

III

II

I

GULF OF TONKIN

HAINAN

LAOS

THAILAND

SOUTH VIETNAM

CAMBODIA

GULF OF SIAM

SOUTH CHINA SEA

N

miles  0   50   100   150   200
km    0   50  100  150  200

20°

16°

12°

G.W.WARD

102°        106°        110°

zontal visibility was most often less than five miles. Flying under these conditions was hazardous. It was made worse by command pressure to produce. Colonel Jack Broughton, an air force F-105 fighter-bomber pilot stationed in Thailand, explains:

> We sure telegraphed our punches. There were not all that many targets in that area, and it did not take too many smarts to figure out about where the force was headed, especially when we headed them there *day after day,* making them fly up to the target before making the go or no-go decision on weather *we knew was not acceptable,* turned over the target and then came back the next day to try again.[6]

Command pressure to fly in bad weather to maintain a high sortie rate extended to all kinds of units, even to the A-1 prop-driven planes assigned to fly low over the Ho Chi Minh Trail in Laos. Air Force Captain Richard S. Drury reports that one night before his squadron was supposed to take off he asked the Forward Air Control pilot what the weather was like over the trail. The man replied, "There's nothing there. The weather's so bad I never saw any ground at all. Flew around for three hours in the storms for nothing. There's no reason to go there now. It's rained so much that the trail is closed anyway, no trucks, nothing. I'm sure you'll be canceled. Just taking off and landing is bad enough."[7] So informed, Drury spoke to the lieutenant colonel commanding his unit about the futility of the night's assignment. The colonel replied: "Obviously you don't understand the big picture, Captain. If you knew what was really going on you'd see why you're going out there. It's simply a matter of dropping ordnance and flying sorties. The more we drop the better we do and also the Defense Department looks at what we used during this time period and projects our future finances and allotments on that figure. If we cancel flights then we drop less ordnance, use less fuel and oil, and get less next time."[8]

Competition between services and within each service for targets and sortie quotas made bad weather *invisible,* but even if command had not been obstinate, the previous division of North Vietnam into separate target zones for each service made rerouting difficult. The air force could not routinely fly into a navy Route Package if its own zones were under bad weather, nor could the navy fly into an air force Route Package if its zones had bad weather.

Air Force General Momyer later admitted to a Senate committee hearing that this often led to air force planes being sent on missions to Laos that were not necessary. Air force units often fulfilled their sortie quotas on bad weather dry runs and low-priority targets only to find that when the weather broke their sortie quota was used up and they could not fly any more missions until a new allotment was given.[9]

In late 1965 and 1966, the competition between air force and navy commanders was so intense that planes were sent on missions with virtually no bombs. Sorties continued, and each commander reported air activity to his superiors. But operational consequences were disastrous. As Colonel Broughton says, the United States was "sending kids out to attack a cement and steel bridge with nothing but 20-millimeter cannon, which is like trying to knock down the Golden Gate Bridge with a slingshot. Stupid missions like that cost us aircraft and people."[10]

Frank Harvey, a freelance reporter working for *Flying* magazine, reported identical findings:

> Later, I talked with a couple of nearly apoplectic F-4 pilots at Danang who told me they had recently gone out on a four-plane mission carrying a very small bomb load. "We risked eight guys," one pilot said to me, gritting his teeth in anger, "when we could have hung the whole load on one plane — risking only two people — and done the job better."
>
> "Then why send out four planes?" I asked.
>
> "Damned if I know, unless it's just to keep our sortie rate high," the pilot said disgustedly. "But I'll tell you this: It's a goddam crime."
>
> I had heard about this sortie business out on *Constellation* [aircraft carrier]. Navy pilots had told me they could do a better job with a few A-6s, operating in the safety of darkness, than with all those Skyhawks skimming around with light loads in daylight.
>
> So while it didn't seem possible, it appeared that the Navy was trying to out-sortie the Air Force, and the Air Force was trying to out-sortie the Navy. The guys who were flying the sorties took a dim view of it.[11]

The people doing the fighting were expendable to senior commanders who needed a high count. Virtually every phase of air operations was oriented toward expansion. Failure of no-bomb and bad-weather missions could be used just as well as self-designated successful missions to justify requests for *more sorties*. General William Momyer discusses Rolling Thunder raids on railroads:

> The Kep–Thai Nguyen line remained blocked during both the 1965–1968 and 1972 campaigns from repeated attacks against marshalling

yards at various points. These yards were the largest the Vietnamese had except for the Yen Vien and Hanoi classification yards. Immediately after each attack, the North Vietnamese always made a major effort, particularly at Kep, to get a through-line open. This work was little different from the German and Chinese attempts to restore traffic on main arteries in Europe and Korea. The fact that the line was blocked one day didn't mean we could write it off for even a week.

Because of the frequency of repair, reconnaissance missions and reattacks were all-important considerations. Reconnaissance was essential to establish the condition of the target, for it wasn't prudent to run a strike into a high threat area, even when cleared by the JCS, until we knew the strike would have a worthwhile target.

Another rail line segment, the Haiphong-Hanoi line, was frequently attacked along its forty miles. Task Force 77 [aircraft carriers] was responsible to keep this line interdicted, especially at Hai Duong, the key choke point on this line. Since most of the bulk products such as food, clothing, fuel, and essential civilian commodities entered through Haiphong, interdiction of this line put stress on the distribution system centered in Hanoi.

The longest segment of the overall rail system ran from Hanoi to Vinh; from Vinh to the DMZ the line was unusable. From Hanoi to Vinh the line was 165 miles long, parallel to the coast, and in open terrain most of the way. It was, therefore, vulnerable to attack by air and from naval gunfire. Generally, we kept the line interdicted so extensively below Thanh Hoa that the enemy resorted to a shuttle operation between the cuts. Trucks bridged the gaps of destroyed track, and, as elsewhere except during the bombing halt, movement took place during darkness. Because the mountains were about 25 miles from the rail line, moving supplies into the excellent cover along the karst was a relatively safe operation.[12]

Note the definition of success the general is using. A target is never destroyed once and for all. Instead, each target must be hit constantly: "The fact that the line was blocked one day didn't mean we could write it off for even a week." Each new target taken on means that the sortie rate increases not by a simple $x$ number of additional sorties, but by a $5x$ or $10x$ or $50x$ number of sorties per year, depending on how often the target must be restruck! And even then, railroad lines were either repaired or replaced and the traffic still flowed toward its destinations.

In 1966, the year of the great assault against the petroleum-oil-lubricants facilities, the air force and navy reported 3,903 POL areas destroyed and another 1,065 damaged, for a grand total of 4,481.[13] What the report does not say is just what some of those POL dumps actually were. Frank Harvey reports air war's operational success in this area: "The North Vietnamese have made every effort to counter our bombing by dispersal of their oil in 55-gallon drums spaced out at intervals along back roads, and have also stored them in bomb craters. We have bombed and strafed these dispersed stores of oil with considerable success — particularly the drums stored in craters, which have been ignited by dive bombing and strafing with 20mm cannon."[14]

Thus a dispersed POL system is hidden in bomb craters which are then bombed, which creates more craters for oil to be hidden in, which in turn means air war will need to produce more sorties to drop more bombs over larger areas of bomb craters which means that more new bomb craters will be created in which the foreign Other can further disperse his POL which means air war needs more sorties. Each new target not only requires a 5x or 10x or 50x increase in sorties just to hit it year round, but also calls for even more sorties since each new target hit results in the enemy's dispersion of that target into a plurality of targets spread over a wider area.

Faced with target systems that gradually fragmented into a thousand parts, the American high command became obsessed with anything that looked like a concentrated target. By far the most famous was Thanh Hoa Bridge. Thanh Hoa Bridge was seventy miles south of Hanoi, part of the 165-mile rail line running from Hanoi south to Vinh. Two officers describe it in the official air force monograph *The Tale of Two Bridges:*

> The new bridge at Thanh Hoa was called the Ham Rung (or Dragon's Jaw) by the Vietnamese. It was 540 feet long, 56 feet wide, and about 50 feet above the river. The Dragon's Jaw had two steel truss spans which rested in the center on a massive reinforced concrete pier, 16 feet in diameter, and on concrete abutments at the other ends. Hills on both sides of the river provided solid bracing for the structure. Between 1965 and 1972, eight concrete piers were added near the approaches to give additional resistance to bomb damage. A one-meter gauge single railway track ran down the 12-foot wide center and 22-foot wide concrete highways were cantilevered on each side.[15]

Thanh Hoa Bridge was considered a "bottleneck," meaning that if something happened to it a large transportation and distribution system beyond the bridge would be affected. The bridge was deemed to be a "lucrative" target and much effort was placed on knocking it down.

Unfortunately, the bridge did not have a cost-effective design. It had been built by Chinese and Vietnamese in the 1950s and their construction and engineering methods were such that the bridge was stronger than it had to be to support the weight that would cross it. French-designed bridges fell when hit properly with bombs, but Thanh Hoa Bridge did not. Hundreds upon hundreds of sorties were flown against the bridge from 1965 until the bombing halt in 1968. Traffic over the bridge could be stopped temporarily, but never was a span dropped. Since the bridge was a favorite target, more and more anti-aircraft weapons were moved into the area. The Vietnamese claim that over one hundred American planes were shot down on bombing attacks over the bridge.[16] American military command never released any figures. The official monograph only quotes one pilot: "The general area looks like a valley on the moon."[17]

During the 1965–1968 Rolling Thunder campaign, a legend circulated among air force and navy pilots: "The world was composed of two spring-loaded hemispheres, hinged somewhere under the Atlantic and held together by the Thanh Hoa bridge; if the bridge was severed, the world would fly apart."[18]

Finally, in 1972, when massive bombing was resumed and munitions included laser-guided and television-camera-guided bombs with lock-on targeting devices, Thanh Hoa Bridge was destroyed. A pilot told Stuart H. Loory what happened next:

> And then, what many pilots believed to be true was confirmed. The North Vietnamese made no effort to repair the bridge. It was not an important link in the transportation network at all. It had little military significance.
>
> "There's a ford a few miles upstream," one pilot told me in the fall of 1971, before the bridge was destroyed. "It's not a legitimate target. They don't need it to move their supplies."[19]

Thanh Hoa Bridge was ten miles from the coast; the river was neither uniformly wide nor deep. Besides the ford, there was at least one pontoon bridge. The last paragraphs of *The Tale of Two Bridges* read:

> With the help of technology and training, airmen with determination, courage and professional skill finally were able to bring the "Tale of Two Bridges" to a convincing close. Their story is but one of

many in the long Vietnam experience where airpower was applied and the report came back. . . .

"Mission accomplished!" [20]

In the spirit and practice of doublethink, the authors had previously reported that the North Vietnamese "also built pontoon bridges in the vicinity to provide a by-pass while the bridge was unusable." [21] The pontoon bridge was composed of segments that could be taken apart and hidden during the day and then reassembled for night usage.

Thanh Hoa Bridge was but the most dramatic example of a false target that gave the Vietnamese the opportunity to shoot down American aircraft. There are many more mundane examples. Captain John Trotti, a Marine Corps F-4 phantom fighter-bomber pilot, found the railyards at Vinh barren except for anti-aircraft guns:

> Our job was to neutralize the air defenses at the marshalling yards northeast of Vinh for a flight of four Air Force 105s coming in from their base in Thailand. This was my third trip to Vinh that month, and each time it had been to pin down the guns while an Air Force or Navy flight took out the real target. At first, the role of spear carrier rankled, but I had mellowed in the realization that while I'd seen plenty of guns, I had yet to spot vehicles or material at the staging site. [22]

This was in April 1966. Yet the same pattern persisted over two years later when Trotti returned for a second tour of duty. Flights along the Ho Chi Minh Trail fought enemy "tree farms" or forests: "There we bombed Ho Chi Minh tree farms in the open, catering to someone's seemingly insatiable demand for toothpicks. Most often there was a gun site hidden in the lumber, and then we got to come back and report guns in the Ho Chi Minh tree farm in the open. Heck of a deal." [23]

Yet such missions were reported by staff officers as productive attacks on "hidden storage areas" and "suspected truckparks." [24] Trotti says that on many occasions when pilots weren't sure what they'd hit, those responsible for bomb-damage assessments would base their reports on what ordnance was dropped: "The attitude they seemed to have was that if you expended 'X' amount of ordnance over 'Y' territory you would receive 'Z' results. QED. Granted there was information in these reports, but a dearth of understanding, so it was as if there was a wall between the decision makers and the operating forces they controlled." [25]

Command wanted to report not only that a given target had been destroyed in the sense that it could no longer perform its function, but that it had been *100 percent destroyed*. This push toward a pseudo-objective numerical closure led to repeated attack. Colonel Broughton explained the results:

> Unfortunately, hit or miss, we often find ourselves repeatedly fragged [ordered] against targets that have already been bombed into insignificance except for the defenses that are left, and reinforced, to capitalize on our pattern of beating regular paths to each target released from the "Restricted" list.
>
> They figured if the Americans want to keep coming back here again and again, they might as well move in all the guns they can and get as many of us as possible.[26]

Mission control had become so centralized that pilots had little to say about how aircraft could best approach targets. Command not only repeatedly sent planes out to the same target, but ordered the very same flight plan, including time and flight approach, despite the loss of surprise and flexibility the colonel speaks of. The processing of reconnaissance photographs of bomb damage was also criticized by Colonel Broughton:

> If the bomb damage assessment by one of the many reconnaissance vehicles available does not satisfy all concerned as to what you saw or claimed, back you go. Perhaps the greatest source of irritation along this line is the interpretation of the photos the reconnaissance aircraft bring back. You can have as many assessments of damage as you have viewers of the pictures. Unfortunately, the groups known as photo interpreters are not always of the highest level of skill or experience, and their evaluation quite often does not agree with that of the men doing the work. I have bombed, and seen my troops bomb, on specific targets where I have watched the bombs pour in and seen the target blow up, with walls or structures flying across the area, only to be fragged right back into the same place because the film didn't look like that to the lieutenant who read it way back up the line. I have gone back on these targets and lost good people and machines while doing so, and found them just as I expected, smashed. But who listens to a stupid fighter pilot?[27]

On the other hand, a former air force intelligence officer told of reading a report by four pilots who said that they had bombed a railroad line and seen several "secondary explosions." The intelligence officer then looked at the films taken during the strike: "Later, when the aerial photos are available, the interpreters see a different picture. Nothing in or around the tracks has been destroyed. The secondary explosions turn out to have been large piles of loose dirt blown into the air by the bombs and scattered along the tracks, making the line look as if it had been destroyed. In reality, the railroad can be put back into operation with a few shovels." [28]

Similarly, pilots attacking truck convoys often overestimated the effectiveness of their strikes. Take the hypothetical case of a four-plane mission. The first pilot claims three trucks destroyed and two damaged; the second, four trucks destroyed and three damaged; the third, four destroyed and four damaged; the fourth pilot claims he destroyed five trucks and damaged four. This makes sixteen trucks destroyed and thirteen damaged, or over seven trucks hit per sortie. However, as the intelligence officer warned: "Experience showed — whenever the pilots' reports could be checked against photo intelligence — that the total usually fell far short of the pilots' claims because two or more pilots would list the same truck." [29]

Both Colonel Broughton and Captain Blachman, the intelligence officer cited above, are probably right in their respective cases. Intelligence analysts often corrected the pilots' tendencies toward reporting maximum productivity, yet at the same time military intelligence analysis suffered from its own structural problems. As pointed out previously, analysis was the *least prestigious* and least powerful job with the fewest promotional opportunities. What counted in the intelligence field was the *collection or production* of data. Collection departments received most agency budgets and collection departments represented their progress in terms of how many "bits" of information they collected, or how many hours of radio messages were recorded. Since their work was so tangible and measurable, collection departments got the most. [30] As one senior staff member of the National Security Council said, "95 percent of the U.S. intelligence effort has been on collection, and only 5 percent on analysis and production [interpretation]." [31] Because of the lack of resources and low prestige associated with analysis, interpretations were uneven in quality beyond the real uncertainties inherent to the intelligence project.

There was a larger discrepancy between what pilots and intelligence analysts publicly said about targets struck and what the Vietnamese said. War-managers publicly maintained that no civilian targets were inten-

tionally struck — other than war related industry — and that many pre-
cautions were taken to avoid hitting civilian areas. General Momyer said
that the North Vietnamese shot indiscriminately while the United States
practiced restraint:

> The pressure to hold down damage to civilian targets prevented
> missions that would have been run in World War II and Korea. These
> restrictions made it essential to limit the probability that bombs would
> impact outside the prime target area. Although North Vietnamese pro-
> paganda hammered the theme that U.S. bombing was directed at ci-
> vilian targets, never in the course of the war was a target selected for
> any reason other than its military significance. Inevitably, in combat
> some bombs are dropped out of the target area. These cases, however,
> result from improper release, jettisoning because of enemy fighters,
> malfunctioning bomb racks, or, in some cases, from releasing ord-
> nance when the aircraft is in an improper altitude, thereby causing
> gross errors. Many of the North Vietnamese claims of civilian damage
> came about because their own anti-aircraft rounds and SAMs [surface
> to air missiles] missed their mark and impacted the ground. As far as
> we know, the North Vietnamese had no restriction on where SAMs
> or AAA [anti-aircraft artillery] could fire. They were sited for the best
> defense of a target, irrespective of the effect such weapons would
> have on their own civilians, despite the fact that a SAM that didn't
> detonate in the air was potentially a live bomb when it hit the ground.
> Unfortunately, we were unable to measure the self-inflicted damage
> from such firings.[32]

This is one view. Secretary of Defense McNamara once indicated that
the United States might be deeply involved in hitting civilian areas. He
was worried about "costs" of noncombatant casualties. The relevant
subsection is entitled "Bombing Purposes and Payoffs."

> The primary costs of course are U.S. lives: The air campaign against
> heavily defended areas costs us one pilot in every 40 sorties. In ad-
> dition, an important but hard-to-measure cost is domestic and world
> opinion: There may be a limit beyond which many Americans and
> much of the world will not permit the United States to go. The picture
> of the world's greatest superpower killing or seriously injuring 1,000
> non-combatants a week, while trying to pound a tiny backward nation
> into submission on an issue whose merits are hotly debated, is not a
> pretty one. It could conceivably produce a costly distortion in the

American national consciousness and in the world image of the United States — especially if the damage to North Vietnam is complete enough to be "successful." [33]

The Joint Chiefs of Staff took a different perspective on killing and seriously injuring 1,000 noncombatants a week. The Chiefs believed in the communicative theory of bombing and the idea that such bombing would break "the will of the regime." In their response to McNamara, they wrote that reduced bombing "would relieve the Hanoi leadership from experiencing at first hand the pressures of recent air operations which foreign observers have reported." [34]

Numerous foreign observers visited the Democratic Republic of Vietnam during the 1965–1968 bombing campaign. English and European doctors, scientists, intellectuals, and journalists made special inquiries on the targets and casualties of air war. Many of their reports were first collected for a "war crimes" tribunal held in Stockholm in 1967; subsequent reports were added for the 1971 collection, *Prevent the Crime of Silence*. Sections of their findings are presented below:

> Phat Diem has been described by some U.S. reports as a "naval base." It is clear on the ground that it is nothing of the sort, and it must unquestionably be clear as well, that it is not from the air. The town is in the heart of a Roman Catholic area, as is clear from the large number of spires which decorate the landscape. It seemed to me that Phat Diem has been subjected to a pretty systematic attempt to flatten all modern-looking stone and brick buildings. . . . No main road runs through Phat Diem, and the road which does go through the town runs east-west not north-south. There is no railway and no industry in the region. It is a fairly prosperous agricultural town, which used to be well-known for its handicrafts, especially basket-work. . . . We were informed that total fatal casualties in more than fifty raids on Phat Diem had been in the region of 100. But seventy-two of these had been suffered during the course of one sneak raid on the fourth church we visited; this raid, on 24 April 1966, had caught a congregation on the point of leaving a service, and it had been the first raid of the long series. [35]

We interviewed Dr. Oai, who witnessed the repeated bombing of the Quynh Lap leprosarium. The first raid occurred at 8 p.m. on 12 June 1965, the planes flying over and then returning to drop twenty-four bombs and fire missiles. A night nurse was wounded. The fol-

lowing morning, all patients had been evacuated, but at 1:45 p.m. on
13 June 1965 when some of the patients had returned, large numbers
of U.S. planes came over and bombed and strafed the hospital in turn.
The centre was demolished completely. In the following few days,
the Americans returned again and again until the sanitarium had been
completely destroyed. The raids of 12–21 June 1965 were reported to
have killed 140 patients in all. Dr. Oai was moved to another hospital,
while the remaining patients were dispersed to a variety of institutions. We also interviewed three other eye-witnesses — one man,
Hoag-Sinh, who had been wounded in one of the raids, Duong Thi
Lien and Vu Thanh Mui, two women. These corroborated the testimony of Dr. Oai in respect of the most important details — i.e., the
height of the planes, the fact that the bombs were followed up by
strafing of the patients and staff as they sought shelter. Dr. Oai, in
response to questions, asserted that there had been "at least seven"
low flying reconnaissance flights before the first bombings.[36]

We went on to visit Tu Ky hamlet in the village of Hoang Liet, in
the suburbs of Hanoi. We interviewed Nguyen Thi San, an elderly
woman of fifty-seven; she described the 2 December 1966 raid, ex-
plaining how the U.S. planes "dive-bombed and strafed." The school
here is a ruin, the ground pitted with many bomb craters. All round
this agricultural hamlet the ground is ploughed up with water-filled
craters, like a miniature Ypres or Paschendale. There is no military
target in sight. The Tu Ky pagoda [was] also badly damaged.[37]

On 18 January [1967], at 7 a.m., eighteen F-105s had attacked
[Viet Tri] with high explosive bombs, pressure bombs, time bombs
and CBU's [a canister containing several hundred grenade-type bombs,
which disperse over a wide area]. They struck the Roman Catholic
commune of Tien Cat and also the commune of Minh Dong, including
the hamlets of Gia Vuong and Minh Tan. Twenty people were killed
(seven male and thirteen female), including eight children. Fifty-one
were wounded (twenty-eight male and twenty-three female) including
fifteen children. One hundred and twenty-nine houses were demolished and eight were burned down. The school, the hospital and the
kindergarten were bombed. Dikes and sluices had also been attacked.[38]

Next morning, 29 January [1969], we received a report on the attacks on Phu Tho province. The province has a population of 640,000 and the city of Phu Tho has a population of 14,000 reduced by evacuation to 6,700. Repeated attacks on the city had been made since October 1965. On 22 November, starting at 2:15 a.m., thirty-one sorties were flown over the city. Ninety-five explosive bombs, some weighing 1,000 lbs., were dropped. These made craters as big as thirteen meters deep and thirty-seven meters in diameter. Rockets, missiles and CBUs were also used. Thirty-three people were killed (fourteen male and nineteen female) including one old person and six children. 282 houses were burned down or demolished. A school, a Buddhist temple, a hospital and a medical school had all been bombed.[39]

But the most traumatic experience was in the province of Thanh Hoa. It was 29 January 1967. . . . At four p.m. we visited the hospital, the first place on our itinerary. This was the hospital where we should have been at 2:30. At 3:00 p.m. it had been bombed and some of the patients killed. While they were being removed from the hospital and taken to the first-aid station, there was another attack and the first-aid station had been completely destroyed. Incendiary bombs had been used and some houses were still burning. There were embers and flames everywhere. We saw a large crater caused by an American rocket. Anti-personnel weapons had been used.

Two hundred homes had been damaged or destroyed, and 125 families were homeless.

A hospital with Red Cross markings and a first-aid station had been singled out and destroyed. If the shelters provided by the authorities had not been so effective, the casualties would no doubt have been higher. Half of Thanh Hoa had been evacuated in advance as well, and this too was fortunate. I have looked around for anything which could conceivably have been a military target in the town itself. There was no sign of any military object.[40]

In Dan Ly Village, Trieu Son district, about fifteen kilometers west of Thanh Hoa city, two hamlets, "Number Five" and "Number Nine" were bombed with pineapple-shaped CBU bombs on 13 March 1967. . . . We went to Dan Ly village on 19 March, a Sunday. We heard sobs and moans and in the twilight saw an old man sitting barefoot in the carbonized ruins of his garden. He had been living alone. He had lost everything, including his buffaloes, in the raid.

In hamlet "Number Five" there were 127 houses of which twelve were completely destroyed by fire caused by high explosive bombs. The raid took place at a time when the children had returned from school and the adults were returning to their work in the fields. Six persons were killed, among them two old women, and seven were wounded. Three of the wounded, all children, later died in the hospital.

The hamlet is in a flat delta landscape and surrounded by immense rice fields. The only military targets to be seen were the rifles which the peasants carry with them to the fields. Only pineapple-shaped CBU bombs had been dropped on this hamlet. The craters had not been counted when we came there. As one plane usually carries four canisters and four planes had taken part in the attack, the total number of small bombs was probably 6,000 to 8,000 against this single hamlet. Each small bomb contains 240 to 250 steel pellets. The total number of pellets against the population of hamlet "Number Five" was between 1.5 and 2 million. The casings break up into sharp, crystal-form fragments of different sizes. One can safely conclude that the number of fragments from these bombs is probably as great as the number of pellets.[41]

These bombings were highly productive: 250,000 to one million fragments and pellets per sortie for a four-plane "flight," the standard operational unit in air war. Some Vietnamese saw their children burn to death: "Madame Le Thi Tanh . . . , in the course of the bombings, saw her two children burnt in their house and was not able to go to their aid because three other air raids prevented all assistance by machine-gunning of the town. The Vietnamese wardens urged the poor woman to remain in the shelter with her two small children. She is plagued with the memory of the cries of her two children burning in their own house."[42] "[Mr. Le Qang Toai] described how his wife and two children (one of them five months old) had died. They were crushed as the sides of their shelter squeezed together due to the blast of a pressure bomb."[43] "A few houses from there we met Mr. Nguyen Van Hua, also with three small children. His wife had been running for their shelter when she was hit by a global-shaped CBU bomb which exploded on her head, killing her instantly. A few metres from the spot there was one half of a CBU canister."[44]

Two patterns of air war attacks emerge from these victim reports. The first concerns deployment of various munitions in an ordered sequence:

It was explained to us that the normal pattern of attack was to drop steel pellet bombs while people were trying to help the victims of the first attack. [45]

They are usually employed in a three stage raid: first comes observation, then bombardment with high explosives and/or napalm and then by CBUs (container [cluster] bomb units) containing the guava steel pellet bombs. [46]

From our shelters we watched the bombing which lasted about ten minutes, then we watched a second wave of planes return five to ten minutes later and bomb for about the same length of time. We were able to reach the spot only a few hours later — this time lapse being due to security measures — and were therefore able to ascertain the real nature of the target. This bombing was aimed solely against a district of Thanh Hoa located about five miles from the Ham Rong bridge, the only possible strategic target in this area. We saw the entire area in flames and completely destroyed; we also saw the little district hospital demolished by incendiary bombs. On the very spot we saw the craters made by missiles and rockets. By questioning the witnesses we learned the function of the second wave of planes: this second wave machine-gunned the rescue teams and the wounded who were being evacuated from the burning hospital. [47]

Bombing civilians with antipersonnel weapons was deliberate, not an accident of proximity to military targets and anti-aircraft weapons. Second, many schools, churches, and hospitals were subject to bombing attacks. Several such raids have been mentioned; other accounts confirm the pattern:

The main street and market were smashed flat, and among destroyed buildings I made out a church, a school and a pagoda. The water-control dam had obviously been bombed, and craters, as yet unfilled, were obvious nearby. [48]

Ninety-one houses were burned or damaged; forty-six were completely destroyed. One hundred and thirty meters of dikes were destroyed; the Roman Catholic church was severely damaged. [49]

On March 26 [1967] we visited a monastery for Jesuit nuns close to Thanh Hoa City. This had recently been bombed with demolitional (HE) [high explosive] bombs which had partly destroyed the monastery and damaged the vegetable gardens, where there are very large craters.[50]

The numerous churches which we have visited had been built in the western style, perfectly visible, with the bell towers very high, standing out clearly from the neighboring houses which are low and built of bamboo. The frequent attacks on these buildings also seem to indicate the objective was the place of worship, itself.[51]

Foreign observers who witnessed raids gave much thought to why these institutions were bombed. Recall the first story where the reporter speculated that there was a ''pretty systematic attempt to flatten all modern-looking stone and brick buildings.''[52] Wilfred Burchett commented:

All school buildings in Thanh Hoa province and the other coastal province I visited, together with all hospitals and sanatoria, had either been bombed to smithereens or had been evacuated in expectation of bombing. *Any large building of brick or stone in the countryside was an automatic target for American pilots,* doubtless reported back as ''barracks, military warehouses,'' and so forth. . . .

One of the most senseless examples of bombing I was to come across in Thanh Hoa province was on the road to Sam Son, a seaside resort where lots of rest homes for workers have been built up in recent years. A few miles from Sam Son itself, there was a fine Old Peoples Home, half a dozen or so *red-tiled, brick buildings.* It had also been bombed to rubble in a series of raids in July, 1965, and doubtless the destruction of another ''naval barracks'' was registered in Pentagon records.[53]

Abraham Behar also wondered about stone and brick buildings.

In a number of cases the school was only a part of a more widespread destruction. But there are more cases which make me think that there have been specific attacks against schools. It is important to realize that in villages made of bamboo or straw the school is one of the few modern buildings, and therefore perfectly visible from the air.[54]

The Vietnamese reported that by February 1967, 391 schools had been destroyed.[55] They also reported over eighty churches and thirty pagodas destroyed. Like schools, churches and other religious institutions were among the few large, modern structures in the Democratic Republic of Vietnam.

A convent of nuns at the town of Thanh Hoa was attacked at the beginning of this year and the main building was destroyed by heavy bombing. Another example is the seminary of Bo Lang. This seminary, situated in the district of Tinh Gia on the edge of the Gulf of Tonkin, is a *very large building several stories high,* completely isolated on the coast with numerous crosses which enable it to be easily identified. Since 1964 the seminary has been attacked from the air nineteen times. In the area we found numerous craters caused by heavy bombs of more than a ton. These craters measure up to thirty meters in diameter. The buildings are almost completely destroyed. There is only one wall left standing which continues to be hit periodically by batteries of the 7th Fleet which constantly patrols the adjoining waters. This seminary is completely isolated and very far from even a village. There is no objective which could be remotely considered military.[56]

Hospitals were in the third category of modern buildings. By February 1967, the DRV reported ninety-five health institutions had been destroyed. Several hundred doctors, patients, and staff were killed and wounded. Quynh Lap leprosarium alone had undergone thirty-six attacks in 1965 and 1966.[57]

Under which target category were such attacks reported? Burchett speculates that these buildings would be considered barracks of some sort. The closest category to that in General Westmoreland's and Admiral Sharp's *Report on the War in Vietnam* covering 1965 through mid-1968 is that of "military areas." In 1966 the report lists 118 military areas destroyed and 434 damaged.[58] Could the schools, hospitals, and churches be listed there? There is another category on the "Target Element Summary" sheet titled "buildings."

The only other categories that have higher numbers are "Motor Vehicle" and "Water Vehicle." Since only the government had motor vehicles in the DRV, then many motor vehicles were military targets. Fishermen had junks and sampans. Below is a report on a fishing village named Hai Thanh:

This fishing village has endured 1,620 bombs, 650 rockets, twelve missiles, and forty-one machine-gun attacks. There have been 162 homes burnt and 644 bombed out, eighteen junks completely de-

Table 11.1
BUILDINGS BOMBED IN NORTH VIETNAM, 1966–1968

| Year | Destroyed | Damaged | Total |
|------|-----------|---------|-------|
| 1966 | 4,903 | 3,363 | 8,304 |
| 1967 | 2,354 | 1,193 | 3,547 |
| 1968 | 532 | 232 | 764 |

NOTE: "Some fixed targets were restruck numerous times and damage to them may be reported above more than once."
SOURCE: Admiral U. S. G. Sharp, "Report on Air and Naval Campaigns against North Vietnam and Pacific Command-Wide Support of the War," in General William Westmoreland, *Report on the War in Vietnam* (Washington, D.C.: U.S. Government Printing Office, 1969), p. 29.

stroyed, and seventy-six damaged. There have been ninety inhabitants killed, of whom seven were burnt, and fourteen villagers have disappeared at sea. There have been eleven children younger than ten years old killed and five new-born babies killed.

Now, this little hamlet with a Catholic majority is situated on the coast of the Gulf of Tonkin, completely cut off the main road, far from any objective which could be considered military. The Second Commission of Inquiry visiting this village saw the beach where the fishing boats are tied up. It could not in any case be considered a proper port, but only a simple beach where several junks were pulled up on the sand. It would be difficult to believe that this little fishing village could be confused with a proper port which could have any military activity. All along the coast of the Gulf of Tonkin we saw many small fishing villages that had suffered the same kind of attacks.[59]

Thus far civilians have only been considered *victims,* but there was another twist to the tale. Wilfred Burchett reported: "It has become a nationwide duty to study plane silhouettes, to memorize characteristics of speed and altitude; to recognize planes by their sounds; to know how many lengths ahead of a certain type one must aim if it is in level flight and at which point of the nose to fire if it is dive bombing."[60] The DRV armed the entire population. Colonel Broughton commented on the inability to fly low to the ground because of anti-aircraft fire from peasants:

If he went down, he would have been faced with the intense small-arms and automatic-weapons fire that even extended down to hand-guns; and don't ever think that a handgun can't knock down a big bird if it hits the right spot. When the bugle blows and thousands of people lie on their backs and fire small-caliber personal weapons straight up in the air, woe be unto him who is unfortunate enough to stray through that fire.[61]

If a pilot can avoid being picked up on radar, "vanish" below the radar horizon from time to time, at altitudes of ground level to 3,000–4,000 feet, then radar-controlled anti-aircraft artillery and surface-to-air missiles cannot be used effectively against his airplane. In North Vietnam, many of the 37mm anti-aircraft artillery pieces and most of the 57mm, 85mm, and 100mm cannons were radar controlled. By denying American aircraft relatively safe air space, the civilian populace forced planes to face more sophisticated, radar-guided weaponry and prevented them from successfully carrying out real military missions.

The low-level air space was also needed by U.S. fighter-bombers and fighter escorts to outrun the enemy's MIG fighter planes. American aircraft tended to be electronically complex and consequently relatively heavy, requiring larger engines, which used more fuel than smaller aircraft. F-105 pilots operating out of Thailand needed to refuel in midair once on the way to the target and once again on the way back. Even after dropping their bomb loads, they were still not maneuverable.

The F-105, or The Thud, "was notorious for its ability to go downhill fast."[62] Part of the room for eluding a MIG fighter attack from behind was lost by the North Vietnamese control of low air space. Most F-105 flights had fighter escorts from F-4s. These planes were primarily designed for speed and a large weapons payload. They were also heavy and sometimes awkward even when equipped with air-to-air missiles rather than bombs. Moreover, pure speed is not important in contemporary air combat. One air force colonel actually resigned from the service because the air force would not publish a paper he had written on the subject. Below are the findings of that study:

Despite more than 100,000 sorties flown by Mach 2 capable aircraft over the skies of Vietnam —

Not one second of flight combat time at Mach 2.2 speed (or above) was recorded.

Not one second of flight combat time at Mach 2.0 speed (or above) was recorded.

Not one second of flight combat time at Mach 1.8 speed (or above) was recorded.

Almost no time at Mach 1.6 (or above) was recorded. (Seconds)

Extremely little flight time at 1.4 Mach (or above) was recorded. (Minutes)

Remarkably little flight time at 1.2 Mach (or above) was flown. (Hours)

The vast majority of military operations and all heavy combat maneuvering was done in the domain of speeds below 1.2 Mach. . . .[63]

Mach 1 is the speed of sound, at sea level 738 mph. Fuel consumption rises sharply as an airplane approaches Mach 1. The few pilots who reported combat time at Mach 1.6 all ran out of gas. As for Mach 2, according to the pilots' folklore, "An airplane will reach Mach 2 just in time to run out of fuel."[64]

Technowar produces aircraft to achieve an abstract, big-number speed, rather than to achieve the actual speed and quick maneuver flexibility needed in air combat. Such aircraft, with their electronics and complex engines, are difficult to maintain. To keep an F-4 fighter-bomber wing (70 to 75 aircraft) in operation required 70,000 different kinds of parts and a computer to run the supply system. The planes were so heavy that they required thick concrete runways. Not even steel planking on the ground was sufficient. The engines were so sensitive that men walked around with special trash bags called "FOD bags," meaning "foreign object damage bags." The base area had to be kept absolutely clean because anything an engine might suck in on takeoff could cripple it.

One colonel kept wondering why the Vietnamese did not send one plane a week to bomb his base at Danang, because one planeload was all it would take: "We're lucky the North Vietnamese ran such a poor war. Any Air Force with one tenth the power of ours, if they used it wisely, could cripple us."[65] The American air war was so complex in its logistic requirements that it could not withstand combat in its base areas. Fortunately for the Americans, although there were frequent mortar and rocket attacks on bases, air attacks never occurred. It may well be that the DRV and the U.S. had a tacit reciprocal understanding. Senior officials had placed severe restrictions on American attacks against

Vietnamese airfields. In George Ball's assessment, World War III might be triggered:

> The bombing of the airfields would very likely lead the DRV to request the use of Chinese air bases north of the border for the basing of North Vietnamese planes, or even to request the intervention of Chinese air. This would pose the most agonizing dilemma for us. Consistent with our decision to bomb the North, we could hardly permit the creation of a sanctuary from which our own planes could be harassed. Yet there is a general agreement that for us to bomb China would very likely lead to a direct war with Peiping and would — in principle at least — trigger the Sino-Soviet Defense Pact, which has been in force for fifteen years.[66]

Although some restrictions on bombing airfields were lifted in 1967, targets were still controlled by the White House. Fear of World War III receded somewhat, but fears of more limited air attacks against American bases remained.[67] The major part of the campaign against the north was conducted from bases in *Thailand*.

If an enemy aircraft had appeared over an American base, the chances were fairly good that no American plane would have been ready to intercept. The sortie rate was so high, the effort to meet the production quota of bombing attacks so great, that oftentimes air-to-air combat systems on fighter-bomber aircraft were not maintained. Although in theory an F-4 Phantom could be readily switched back and forth between bombing and air cover or "Mig Cap" roles, in practice radars and other electronic equipment necessary to activate air-to-air missiles were not routinely maintained if a squadron had been previously detailed to bombing runs.[68]

War-managers received regular reports from intelligence agencies and study groups concerning estimated dollar damage done to the Democratic Republic of Vietnam as compared to the estimated dollars spent by the United States in the bombing. In 1965 the Central Intelligence Agency and the Defense Intelligence Agency issued a summary, "Appraisal of the Bombing of North Vietnam": "According to this [report], the first year of ROLLING THUNDER inflicted $63 million worth of measurable damage, $36 million to 'economic' targets like bridges and transport equipment, and $27 million to 'military' targets like barracks and ammunition depots."[69] The *Pentagon Papers* does not include their estimate of American costs, but John McNaughton's calculations for the first year are present. The assistant secretary of defense thought that the 178 airplanes lost over the north cost about $250 million alone.[70] He did not give a dollar figure for operating costs or how much it would cost to replace the lost air crews. Another 1965 CIA study said that "direct operational cost of the program (i.e., production costs of aircraft lost, plus direct sortie overhead costs — not including air base or CVA [naval carrier groups] maintenance or logistical support — plus ordnance costs)" came to $460 million in 1965. All in all, the CIA calculated that it cost the United States $6.60 to inflict $1 worth of damage upon the DRV.[71]

During 1966 air war became even more expensive. A draft Memorandum for the President estimated that North Vietnam had suffered $140 million damage between the beginning of Rolling Thunder in February 1965 through October 10, 1966. At the same time, the memo estimated that American costs ran "at least $250 million a month at current levels."[72] From February 1965 through October 1966 is twenty-one months; the cost estimate is somewhere around $5 billion. The CIA's figures for American costs were lower, an estimated $1.247 billion, using the same accounting procedures used for 1965. Total damage to North Vietnam in their calculations came to $130 million, for a 1966 cost ratio of 9.6 to 1.[73]

In a 1967 summary, figures were presented for the entire three years. The Systems Analysis Office in the Defense Department reported that aircraft losses alone totaled over $6 billion, excluding operational costs, logistical base support, and the $500,000 it cost to train a new pilot to replace a casualty.[74] By November 1967, the air force alone had lost over 730 aircraft. North Vietnamese losses for three years of bombing were put at $164 million in capital assets destroyed and $294 million in lost gross national product.[75] But North Vietnam's debits were more than matched by credits from its allies:

> NVN has transmitted many of the material costs imposed by the bombing restrictions back to its allies. Since the bombing began, NVN's allies have provided almost $600 million in economic aid and another $1 billion in military aid — more than four times what NVN had lost in bombing damage. If *economic criteria* were the only consideration, NVN would show *a substantial net gain from bombing,* primarily in military equipment.[76]

Much of the equipment was anti-aircraft defense weapons: "Based on the CIA estimate of 5,300 metric tons per day import rate, it is notable that the enemy is willing to use up to *15% of his total imports* (by weight) in air defense." [77] Air war was beginning to look bankrupt.

There was one additional cost to North Vietnam that had not yet been computed: the estimated costs for employing several hundred thousand Vietnamese in air defense and repair capacities. United States military leaders made repeated references to these costs in their discussions with civilian war-managers. Admiral Sharp, commander of all Pacific air forces, saw manpower allocation as a principal benefit of bombing: "A primary effect of our efforts to impede movement of the enemy has been to force Hanoi to engage from 500,000 to 600,000 civilians in full-time and part-time war-related activities, in particular for air defense and repair of LOCs [lines of communication]." [78] Air Force General Momyer also thought highly of the labor dislocation inflicted by bombing: "Interdiction had an added benefit: it reduced the available enemy manpower. The labor force devoted to the maintenance of both rail and road systems included an estimated 500,000 troops and civilian militia plus another 175,000 committed to the country's air defense system. These were troops who could have been in combat units if not diverted to this task." [79] At the Stennis Committee hearing in August of 1967, military leaders said that bombing diverted the North Vietnamese. If bombing was stopped, then the DRV might double its force in the south and so require "as many as 800,000 additional U.S. troops at a cost of $75 billion just to hold our own." [80]

At the time the military itself estimated that the DRV only had about 50,000 troops in the south, the same figure as 1966. [81] Once again the war-managers were caught within their own reality of maximum production, projecting a foreign Other who was, like themselves, running at full capacity. But North Vietnam was not an industrial economy running at maximum production with full employment. Bombing had released many people for repair; an estimated 33,000 workers had lost their jobs when Vietnamese industry was destroyed while an estimated 48,000 women evacuated from cities were also available for work. The Chinese were thought to have sent around 40,000 to help out. But most of all, North Vietnam was a poor agricultural country, not an industrial one, and it had a young population. Of the estimated 750,000 people needed for bombing and air defense–related activities, over 90 percent could be accounted for just through population growth. [82] The rest could readily be absorbed from the agricultural sector: "Finally, additional workers could be obtained in North Vietnam from low productivity employment. In less developed countries, agriculture typically *employs more people than are really needed to work the land,* even with relatively primitive production methods. Also, further mobilization may be possible through *greater use of women* in the labor force.''[83]

The authors concluded that the need for 750,000 war-related workers ''appears to have been offset with no particular strain on the population.''[84] Wilfred Burchett had confirmed the Office of Systems Analysis findings a year or so earlier. He noticed that most people in the countryside were women. He asked a DRV Planning Commission official about this social transformation. The official replied, ''It is true, the women have largely taken over in the countryside. There is a labor shortage on the land. But don't forget that until recently surplus manpower was the main problem in the countryside.''[85] Burchett asked if economic decentralization really worked. The official replied, ''Yes, it can work and it does work. But it is not something you can find the answer to with cost accounting.''[86]

# CHAPTER 12

# The Redistribution of Air War: Laos, 1968–1973

R ICHARD NIXON became President in January 1969. As vice-president under Eisenhower, Nixon had favored American bombing and ground invasion at Dien Bien Phu. In 1962 he had urged Kennedy to escalate counterinsurgency war, to "step up the build-up." By 1964 he favored intervention into Laos and North Vietnam, and by 1966, his position called for sending half a million men to Vietnam.[1] In February 1968, while campaigning in the New Hampshire primary, Nixon called Vietnam *"the cork in the bottle of Chinese expansion in Asia."*[2]

Nixon presented himself as a "peace" candidate, promising that "the long dark night for America was almost over." His campaign successfully disseminated the idea that he had "a secret plan to end the war," and he was never really pressured by the press to reveal just what this secret plan was in even the most general terms.[3]

The "secret plan" was nothing more than an extreme version of the communicative theory of bombing. Nixon called it the "Madman Theory." He explained the theory to his assistant, H. Robert Haldeman.

> The *threat* was the key. . . . Nixon coined a phrase which I'm sure will bring smiles of delight to Nixon haters everywhere. . . . He said, "I call it the Madman Theory, Bob. I want the North Vietnamese to believe I've reached the point where I might do *anything* to stop the war. We'll just slip the word to them that "for God's sake, you know Nixon is obsessed about Communism. We can't restrain him when he's angry — and he has his hand on the nuclear button" — and Ho Chi Minh himself will be in Paris in two days begging for peace."[4]

During Nixon's first months in office, severe violations of the bombing halt over North Vietnam could not be entertained without endangering the Paris peace talks and the public appearance of an administration seeking peace. Under the new category of "protective reaction strikes," United States planes flew 37,000 sorties against North Vietnam in 1969.[5] Protective reaction implied self-defense; if reconnaissance planes were fired upon, then other American warplanes would attack. In practice, it meant that the United States could get away with limited bombing attacks and still not appear to be violating the bombing halt over the north. In the words of one Pentagon spokesman, "Look, these so-called reinforced protective reaction strikes amount to a limited, selected resumption of the bombing. They are limited in time and in geographic area."[6]

A mere 37,000 sorties were insufficient to maintain the threat; the full productive capacity of air war needed to be utilized. This political need in turn meshed with the desires of the air force and navy to maximize sorties. One war-manager explained the shift to targets in Laos and Cambodia offhandedly as "We couldn't just let the planes rust."[7] A more serious study compared airpower to a fire hose "running under full pressure most of the time and pointed with the same intensity at whichever area is allowed, regardless of its relative importance in the scheme of things."[8]

The war in Laos had its origins in the struggle against French colonialism. The 1954 Geneva Accords had found Laos in a condition roughly analogous to that of Vietnam. The Pathet Lao — equivalent to the Vietminh or Vietcong — controlled the two northern provinces of the country, while the Royal Laotian Government controlled the capital city, Vientiane, and portions of the southern panhandle. Supporters of the Royal Laotian Government largely came from wealthy families, interlocked with an officer corps who had fought with the French against the Pathet Lao.

Large-scale American efforts to support this government began soon after the French defeat. The American embassy staff grew from a dozen or so at the end of 1954 to forty-five by the fall of 1955 to over one hundred by the end of 1957.[9] These men were responsible for implementing a huge aid program of several hundred million dollars. The aid program did not succeed in creating popular allegiance for the Laotian government. Much was stolen or redirected by the Laotian elite for their own purposes; very little aid reached peasants.

The Geneva Accords had called for a coalition government in Laos uniting all factions. In 1956 the right-wing government resigned after its failure to negotiate with the Pathet Lao made the country more politically unstable. Prince Souvanna Phouma then became prime minister, pledging that "No effort shall be spared so that the negotiations with the adverse party [Pathet Lao] be crowned by the loyal reconciliation longed for by all."[10] By early August he succeeded in negotiating an agreement with the leader of the Pathet Lao, his half brother Prince Soupanuvong; the agreement called for a cease-fire, full political rights for Pathet Lao, and a neutralist foreign policy.

The United States cut all foreign aid — the debit and credit political ledger could not tolerate a coalition government. But the cessation of aid did not cause conservative change in Laotian politics, so after a month it was resumed. In early 1957 U.S. officials forced Souvanna Phouma out, but resulting convolutions soon brought him back to power. Toward the end of 1957, the coalition agreements went into effect. Prince Soupanuvong became minister of reconstruction and planning and another Pathet Lao leader joined the cabinet as minister of religion and fine arts.

This time the United States came up with a new aid program designed to increase American presence in the countryside. Called Operation Booster Shot, the plan called for wells, flood-control dams, repair of roads and public buildings, and so forth. Apparently, much money was also given to pro-Western candidates for use in the spring elections.[11] Once again, foreign aid did not work: American largess could not overcome political fragmentation. In May 1958, with 32 percent of the vote, Pathet Lao won thirteen of twenty-one seats in the National Assembly.

Again the United States terminated all aid. At the same time the Central Intelligence Agency launched a massive campaign to build a new right-wing coalition. The National Assembly was successfully bribed to vote against Souvanna Phouma, and in mid-August a new government was formed by Phoui Sananikone. The new prime minister immediately declared, "We are anti-communists."[12] Prince Soupanuvong and other Pathet Lao leaders were arrested. Pathet Lao troops scheduled for integration into the national army escaped at the last moment.

In April a new election was held under rules that allowed only 20,000 people to vote. The Pathet Lao were eliminated as a political force by gerrymandered districts and by increasing the fee a candidate needed to pay in order to file, and raising educational requirements for candidacy. Shortly before the election, military operations began in areas with Pathet Lao voting records.

The actual government was now headed by Kou Abhay. Earlier the Central Intelligence Agency's favorite military officer, General Phoumi

Nosavan, had launched a coup against Phouni Sananikone. State Department officials did not want Phoumi to become prime minister, for fear he would project a too "militaristic" image. The king was persuaded to name Kou Abhay to office, while real power would remain with General Phoumi. Within months, the new right-wing coalition was destroyed. By 1960 the Pathet Lao had spread throughout the countryside. Hundreds of villages had open PL administrations, while many more had underground political systems. American intervention and the rigged election alienated thousands more who had formerly been strict neutralists.

One alienated neutralist was Captain Kong Le, commander of a paratroop battalion. On August 8, 1960, Kong Le led his troops into Vientiane and deposed the government. His sentiments were neutralist: "I have fought for many years and have killed many men, but I have never seen a foreigner die." [13] To form a new government, Kong Le accepted the king's nomination of Souvanna Phouma as prime minister. Phouma came close to succeeding, but the Central Intelligence Agency instead reinforced General Phoumi with munitions, money, and advisers. The general formed a new political organization called the Revolutionary Committee and marched on Vientiane. After several days of fighting, Kong Le's paratroopers, joined by other Laotian troops, withdrew from the city. They were expected to go northward to Luang Probang, but at a crucial road junction about 100 miles north of Vientiane, Kong Le's forces turned east toward the Plain of Jars. In conjunction with Pathet Lao guerrillas they drove the CIA's right-wing forces off the plain.

The CIA had been actively sponsoring paramilitary forces in Laos since 1959, when the Eisenhower administration authorized Operation "White Star." White Star was a covert operation run by the Central Intelligence Agency to form a secret Meo tribesman army in northeastern Laos. It was hoped that this army would be more effective in fighting the Pathet Lao than government troops. CIA field agents or case officers and United States Army Special Forces on detached duty to the CIA provided basic leadership, training, and strategy. [14] Supplies were flown in by the CIA's proprietary airline, Air America. [15] Vang Pao, a Meo leader with an old record of fighting with the French against the Vietminh and Pathet Lao, was recruited to lead this secret army.

Operating from small Air America planes and helicopters, Vang Pao and American agents flew from one mountain village to another, making local tribespeople an offer that was difficult to refuse. In exchange for sending a few recruits into the new secret army, each village would receive guns, money, rice, and other food. Conversely, if they would not join, then the village would be considered hostile. As one Meo leader recalled, "Vang Pao sent us guns. If we did not accept his guns he would call us Pathet Lao. We had no choice. Vang Pao's officers came to the village and warned that if we did not join him he would regard us as Pathet Lao and his soldiers would attack our village." [16]

By participating in the secret army one particular trade advantage accrued to the Meo. Once airstrips were open, small planes operated by the Corsican mafia in Laos flew in regularly to buy up each village's opium crop.[17] Opium poppies had long been the leading cash crop for the mountain people. With the airstrips, crops could be marketed easily.

By 1962, the CIA and Vang Pao directed a "secret" army of 10,000 to 12,000 men. In response, the Soviet Union flew supplies to neutralist and Pathet Lao forces. President Kennedy seriously considered sending in American troops. In March 1961, three aircraft carriers were sent to Southeast Asia with 1,400 marines. Transport aircraft were sent to the Philippines to pick up troops there for possible airlift; troops in Japan also went on alert. The Joint Chiefs of Staff recommended utilizing a total force of 140,000 soldiers in Laos armed with tactical nuclear weapons. General Lyman Lemnitzer advised: "If we are given the right to use nuclear weapons, we can guarantee victory." [18]

Kennedy instead favored negotiated settlement at Geneva. On July 23, 1962, representatives from fourteen nations, including the United States, Great Britain, the Soviet Union, and the People's Republic of China, signed the "Declaration on the neutrality of Laos." Provisions called for withdrawal of all foreign troops. Supervision was assigned to the International Control Commission, a body composed of Western, Communist, and neutralist countries. On June 11, a new "national unity" government came into existence. Souvanna Phouma (the neutralist) became prime minister and minister of defense. Prince Soupanuvong (aligned with the Pathet Lao) got back his old job as minister of planning and reconstruction. General Phoumi (head of the right-wing faction) gained control of the Finance Ministry in addition to his military powers. Both Soupanuvong and Phoumi had the additional title of deputy premier, giving each of them veto power over cabinet decisions. Remaining cabinet positions were split, with four each to Pathet Lao and General Phoumi's supporters and four seats to men who were right-wing politicians, but neutralists in the sense they disliked General Phoumi.

The United States greatly increased overt and covert operations. The Agency for International Development constructed a "parallel bureaucracy'' of sorts, with a top USAID officer in each of the parallel ministries and each top officer controlling many subordinates. In effect, the USAID controlled public services. Laotians referred to the director of the Agency for International Development as the "second prime minister of Laos." [19]

The AID bureaucracy also served as cover for CIA activity. A USAID building was headquarters for the secret army, or Armee Clandestine, and other CIA paramilitary endeavors. AID contracted to the CIA airline, Air America, to deliver rice and supplies. AID also contracted with International Volunteer Service, Inc. IVS was a fundamentalist Protestant organization dedicated to relief work for refugees. IVS was also anti-Communist, providing crucial intelligence and logistical support to CIA operations in many instances and actual "cover" for CIA officers in other cases; [20] no clear boundary between CIA and IVS existed in Laos.

With so many layers of bureaucratic cover — USAID, Air America, IVS — the CIA was provided with just the *double-reality* it needed to maintain its secret army operations after the 1962 Geneva Accords. Some CIA operatives moved to Thailand and commuted to Laos every day. Others moved into AID, Air America, or IVS. The American embassy ruled that Air America flights to Meo villages for USAID supply runs constituted "humanitarian" aid and were exempt from the Geneva Agreements. Air America pilots had two names for rice they dropped on these humanitarian missions. "Soft rice" was actual rice; "hard rice" was guns and ammunition. A joke evolved about relations between the two rices: "No boom-boom, no rice." [21]

The new coalition government never really coalesced. General Phoumi attacked, aided by the secret army. In April 1963, Kong Le turned against the Pathet Lao, complaining that their political work was undermining his control over his troops. A year later the right launched another coup against Souvanna Phouma. This time the United States insisted that Souvanna Phouma remain *formally* in power. Otherwise the Geneva Agreements would collapse and the United States would be faced with an international confrontation at a time when the Soviet Union had lost interest in Laos. Laotian generals — members of a different faction from that of General Phoumi — announced that "in consideration of external policy" they would ask Souvanna Phouma to form yet another government. [22] Souvanna agreed, but the generals demanded that he merge the neutralist and right-wing armies, placing their favored junior officers into relatively powerful positions. At this point the remaining Pathet

Lao members in the government quit. In May 1964, the Pathet Lao attacked Kong Le's forces on the Plain of Jars and drove them out.

Pathet Lao soldiers had support from about half the populace, living in two-thirds of the country.[23] American military aid quickly escalated. The Laotian air force was augmented with an additional six T-28 aircraft, and American jets began reconnaissance flights over Pathet Lao territory. The Pathet Lao began shooting down these American jets, which in turn meant more planes were sent out on bombing runs. By the end of 1964, seventy-five American aircraft were stationed in Thailand for Laotian air war.[24] As the years went by, this number dramatically increased.

Laotian combat evolved into four distinct, but related, wars. The first, code-named Barrel Roll, concerned the bombing of northeastern Laos, including the Plain of Jars.[25] The second war concerned the secret army. Its major area of operations was also northeastern Laos. The third war was conducted by the Royal Laotian Army around major cities and towns. During the wet season, from May through October, the Royal Army advanced into the countryside under air support. During the dry season, from November through April, the Pathet Lao advanced on the new outposts of the Royal Army. (With no air transport available, the guerrillas had difficulty with their supply lines during the wet season.) The fourth war concerned American interdiction efforts along the western frontier of the country.

With Kong Le's defeat and routing from the Plain of Jars in the summer of 1964, the area was declared a free-fire zone. A few dozen planes appeared each day — mainly old propeller aircraft — and bombed targets in the forests. Few towns and villages were struck. For two years bombing gradually increased, but the target pattern remained the same. Planes sought Pathet Lao guerrillas and North Vietnamese troops (the maximum estimate was under 2,000) in the forests. In 1967, more jets appeared over the Plain of Jars and targets included *villages*. People began to live in caves deep in the forests.

Tremendous destruction began the next year. During the Tet Offensive of 1968, Pathel Lao and North Vietnamese forces launched concerted attacks throughout the northeast. On March 11, 1968, they captured a secret CIA radar installation built on a mountain near Phou Pha Thi, about 160 miles west of Hanoi. This installation had been responsible for guiding planes over Hanoi and the Red River Delta.[26] Three weeks later Lyndon Johnson announced the partial bombing halt over North Vietnam. The possibility of a direct connection between capture of "AN-

MSQ-77 Radar Controlled Directing Central'' and the bombing halt cannot be discounted.

Facing military defeat, Vang Pao and his CIA advisers decided to evacuate the Meo population rather than have them live in Pathet Lao areas. By relocating the Meo, Vang Pao would have a captive and totally dependent group from which he could "recruit." Such "recruiting" was desperately needed by 1968. Edgar Buell, the principal IVS official in contact with Vang Pao, described the secret army's condition in the early winter of 1968:

> Vang Pao has lost at least a thousand men since January 1, killed alone, and I don't know how many more wounded. He's lost all but one of his commanders. . . . A short time ago we rounded up three hundred fresh recruits. Thirty percent were fourteen years old or less, and ten of them were only ten years old. Another 30 percent were fifteen or sixteen. The remaining 40 percent were thirty-five or over. Where were the ones between? I'll tell you — they're all dead . . . and in a few weeks 90 percent of (the new recruits) will be dead.[27]

With the partial bombing halt in April 1968 and a total bombing halt in October (except for "protective reaction" missions), air war had now a surplus capacity for generating sorties. Many sorties continued to be directed toward the Plain of Jars. Estimates say around 230,000 tons of bombs were dropped over northern Laos in 1968 and 1969 alone, with 75,000 to 150,000 tons falling on the plain from 1964–1969.[28]

Forward Air Control planes flew at approximately 2,000 feet. Above them at 5,000 feet came propeller bombers, gunships, and flareships. Still higher, at approximately 10,000 feet, flew jet bombers, photo-reconnaissance planes, and various electronic-warfare aircraft. Tanker planes to refuel the fleet traversed the area at 20,000 feet. Way up at 35,000 feet came command and control aircraft directing the air war factory.[29]

Command and control planes were converted cargo planes filled with communications systems and staffed with large crews. Their mission consisted of determining whether or not a target identified by a Forward Air Control pilot met the rules of engagement. If the target was legitimate, then an attack was ordered. After the Plain of Jars was destroyed, a Senate Foreign Relations Committee researcher commented on the discrepancy between the rules and civilian destruction: "Given the apparent stringency of these rules of engagement, it is difficult to see how roads with civilian traffic, villages and groups of civilians could have been bombed, rocketed, or napalmed. It seems clear, however, that . . .

the system itself is so complicated that it cannot possibly be fool-proof.''[30]

He was going under the conventional assumption that rules of engagement in bombing had normative status. General Momyer, however, suggests that the rules of air war concerning Laos were approached as *problems to be solved*. Below he discusses the problem posed by the secret radar site in Laos used for directing bombing missions over the DRV:

> The MSQ [radar] at Site 85 which directed those attacks was unique because of certain political problems. Ambassador William H. Sullivan was reluctant to permit the site in Laos to provide control of aircraft over North Vietnam. His position was that to direct air strikes over North Vietnam from Laos would appear an escalation of the war, in that Laos could be viewed as a base of operations for attacks against North Vietnam. A unique technique was devised to satisfy this political objection; a C-135 relay aircraft, positioned in the Gulf of Tonkin near the 19th parallel, would relay instructions from the MSQ site in Laos to the strike aircraft. The short time delay in the relay operation was accommodated in timing the instructions to release the bombs.[31]

By creating many rules and a hierarchical series of checks and counterchecks, the appearance of air war as a rational, *law-governed* operation was maintained. Rules of engagement, like the numerical representation of the sortie rate with its connotations of a science-governed, managerially measured rational war, are a way of representing a war as a legitimate practice. Even when war-managers admitted deviations from rules, the deviations were presented as limited, contained actions necessary because of special circumstances. Major General Robert L. Petit testified before a Senate committee investigating the Laotian war: ''When the situation got close to desperate in June in Laos, certain restrictions were removed and we were allowed to use airpower in a little freer manner. We also had available what might be termed a sufficient quantity of airpower.''[32]

The Senate committee deemed his response appropriate. One senator suggested that if the United States continued to use airpower ''properly,'' then Laos could be held cheaply. From 1954 through 1959, Laos had received over $647 million in economic aid.[33] By 1969 it was estimated that air war over Laos cost two billion dollars.[34] Military aid to Laotian ground forces would substantially increase this figure. One estimate says that the CIA's secret army cost at least $150 million a year and that total military aid to Laotian ground forces was around $300 million a year.[35]

In November 1968, President Johnson terminated all bombing missions over North Vietnam. Surplus production capacity was rerouted to Laos; by 1969 nearly 300 sorties per day were directed to northern Laos (the region including the Plain of Jars).[36] This sortie rate is equal to the rate produced for the Rolling Thunder bombing campaign over the DRV at its height.

For the 50,000 to 60,000 peasants living in the Plain of Jars and the other 100,000 peasants living in the province, these relaxed rules of engagement meant disaster. One United Nations adviser, Georges Chapelier, reported what he witnessed:

> Prior to 1967, bombing was light and far from populated centers. By 1968 the intensity of the bombings was such that no organized life was possible in the villages. The villagers moved to the outskirts and then deeper and deeper into the forest as the bombing climax reached its peak in 1969 when jet planes came daily and destroyed all stationary structures. Nothing was left standing. The villagers lived in trenches and holes or in caves. They only farmed at night. All of the interlocuters, without any exception, had his village completely destroyed. In the last phase, bombings were aimed at the systematic destruction of the material basis of the civilian society. Harvests burned down and rice became scarce, portage became more and more frequent.[37]

In April 1969, when after months of heavy bombing, the Pathet Lao withdrew from the city of Xieng Khouang, southeast of the Plain of Jars, Vang Pao's forces flew into the city, raped, looted, and burned for a few weeks, and then evacuated when Pathet Lao counterattacked. When Vang Pao retreated, 10,000 to 15,000 people were forcibly evacuated. In August, after the heaviest bombing yet, the Pathet Lao withdrew completely from the plain. The evacuation operation by Air America aircraft was repeated, this time taking 15,000 to 20,000 survivors. One Air America pilot described the operation: "Whenever we got a foothold in the Plain of Jars, we hauled most of those people out of there in a C-130. You'd go in and they would be herded together like cattle until they were so squashed together we couldn't close the doors."[38]

From 1964 to 1969 the USAID carried approximately 130,000 people on its monthly dole list. By November 1969, some 230,000 were listed and in early 1970 the figure reached well over a quarter of a million. Each refugee was allotted thirty to forty dollars' worth of relief supplies for a year. One Senate study found that costs for 600 sorties (a small part of the total sortie figure) equaled the entire annual budget for USAID relief.[39]

Some refugee groups were placed on mountaintops beyond Pathet Lao reach. Others were stationed near the headquarters of the secret army at Long Cheng. Still others were removed to the western and northwestern parts of the country. The rest went to camps in the flat country around Vientiane. There they died from poor nutrition and poor medical care. Fred Branfman got the reports from survivors in these camps with the aid of Laotian interpreters. Below are their testimonies:

> I am a child of my village. I once saw a horse of great size and goodness. A man had ridden to his ricefield and was hit by the airplanes. Only the horse ran back to the village. We knew that this must mean the airplanes had shot him. I went with the grownups to look for him. But he was already dead in the field. When I saw this, I felt much pity for him. I saw his children and wife and cried together with them. Everyone missed this man.
>
> — fourteen-year-old child [40]

> My village stood on the edge of the road from Xieng Khouang to the Plain of Jars. There were ricefields next to the road. At first, the airplanes bombed the road, but not my village.
>
> At that time my life was filled with great happiness, for the mountains and forests were beautiful: land, water, and climate were suitable for us. And there were many homes in our little village.
>
> But that did not last long, because the airplanes came bombing my ricefield until the bomb craters made farming impossible. And the village was hit and burned. And some relatives working in the fields came running out to the road to return to the village but the airplanes saw and shot them — killing these farmers in a most heart-rending manner. We heard their screams, but could not go to help them. When the airplanes left, we went out to help them, but they were already dead.
>
> — thirteen-year-old child [41]

> Such is the life of the monks in the region of Xieng Khouang, a region of war. This truly did I see with my very own eyes: There was an old monk wounded and much blood flowed out, coloring his body red. For, one day we were in the pagoda, not having yet gone into the holes. And an airplane came and he was hit, along with a villager,

who thought of and worried about this old monk, whose death sad-
dened the hearts of the villagers.

— twenty-two-year-old woman[42]

This village woman was a person of good character. She spoke
softly and sweetly and never gave sorrow to any person for any reason. Why did she have to die so pitifully. She died in misfortune with
unsurpassed sadness. The outlaws in the airplanes did this, bringing
fear to our country such as we had never before seen. The airplanes
truly killed people at a time when we knew nothing about what was
going on. They came to do this, why? When you see this, how do
you feel about your own brothers and sisters and relatives? Would
you not be angry and concerned? Compare our hearts to yours. And
what are we to do?

— no age available[43]

In the area of Xieng Khouang, the place of my birth, there was
health, good earth, and fine weather. But then the airplanes came,
bombing the ricefields and the forests, making us leave our land and
ricefields with great sadness. One day a plane came bombing my rice-
field as well as the village. I had gone very early to harrow the field.
I thought, ''I am only a village rice farmer, the airplane will not shoot
me.'' But that day it did shoot me and wounded me together with my
buffalo, which was the source of a hundred thousand loves and a
hundred thousand worries for me.

— thirty-three-year-old man[44]

All we saw was the fire of the firebombs everywhere. One day I
saw the planes come and I ran out with my child. But my child's skin
was hit. I took him and ran for the forest. There were some other
people who tried to take their belongings and run out of the houses
with their children also. But the houses were old and big. They were
hit by the airplanes and burned and we were not courageous enough
to go back and get any more of our things. After that day I always
stayed in the holes in the forest, for I didn't have any house at all. I
made a very small shelter in which to stay.

— thirty-two-year-old man[45]

Air war on the Plain of Jars eliminated the space of bombs not dropped.
But did Technowar produce victory? Survivors of the bombing campaign reported that in 1965, when Pathet Lao cadres came to their vil-

lages seeking recruits, only about 25 percent of the young men and women volunteered. When bombing escalated, so too did successful recruitment. Survivors estimated that by 1968, 95 percent of the combat-age men and women joined the Pathet Lao. Toward the end, the Pathet Lao adopted a policy of leaving behind the last surviving son of a family to help his parents and younger brothers and sisters. Two thousand of these men were later impressed into Vang Pao's forces for use as cannon fodder.[46]

In 1970 the Pathet Lao retook the Plain of Jars despite attacks by B-52 bombers. The following year Pathet Lao and North Vietnamese overran Long Tieng, headquarters of the secret army and CIA operations in northern Laos. Close to 150,000 Meo had to be moved. By the end of 1971 Vang Pao's army was decimated: around 3,300 had been killed and another 5,400 wounded. This represents between a fourth to a third of his forces, which listed between 30,000 to 40,000 men.[47]

No longer could Vang Pao recruit so easily. Even the prospects of higher prices for opium — he had pushed out the Corsicans and had begun doing business himself in 1964 — no longer served as sufficient attraction. One village chief explained his refusal: "Vang Pao keeps sending the Meo to be killed. Too many have been killed already, and he keeps sending more. Soon all will be killed, but Vang Pao doesn't care."[48] The village chief further remarked that the rice drops had been stopped, but his people would no longer fight for Vang Pao, nor would they agree to become refugees.

Vang Pao saw the end coming: "We must stay here. We must die here. There is no place to go. For many years my people had a saying. They had it long before they left China. There is always another mountain, they said. My Father, there are no more mountains."[49] By the end of 1971 the secret army was finished. The Pathet Lao controlled the entire country except for major cities and their surrounding areas.

For some Laotian military men, however, 1971 was not a bad year. General Ouane Rattikone had been a member of the coalition of right-wing generals that overthrew General Phoumi's front government in 1964. Since then Ouane had increased his control over the heroin trade. In 1965 he ousted the Corsicans and in 1967 he won the famous Opium War in the region. By 1971 he had the largest, most efficient heroin refinery in the region, one capable of processing 100 kilos of raw opium per day. Ouane's trademark "#4" grade heroin, Double U-O Globe, was the favorite of American GIs in Vietnam.[50]

"We wired the Ho Chi Minh trail like a drugstore pinball machine, and we plug it in every night."[51]

— technician, Project Igloo White

While the Plain of Jars was destroyed, another bombing campaign was under way in southern Laos. The target was not a Pathet Lao region, but a complex network of roads and trails used by North Vietnamese to move men and supplies into South Vietnam. Known to the American military as the Ho Chi Minh Trail, it became the test area for the "electronic" or "instrumented battlefield."

This development dates back to the first Jason study in 1966. Jasonites found bombing to be ineffective. Nevertheless, as scientists and engineers with long working histories with the Department of Defense, they were deeply committed to high-technology warfare. To replace the bombing campaign over the north, the Jasonites recommended that an "electronic barrier" be constructed to literally keep the foreign Other out. In October 1966, McNamara recommended that one *billion* dollars be allocated for its construction.[52]

Part of the barrier concept called for American ground troops to monitor listening posts and other sensory devices directly south of the demilitarized zone. This idea was abandoned once troops were shelled by North Vietnamese artillery and it was realized that thousands of troops would be necessary to man the "McNamara Line."

However, the idea of seeding the Ho Chi Minh Trail in southern Laos with electronic sensory devices soon became a reality. Camouflaged as plants, thousands of monitors were dropped into Laos to listen for the noises of trucks, or the "pop" of small "gravel" mines. These small mines were not designed to kill or maim, but rather to make a distinctive noise when triggered. Other detection devices included seismic monitors, sensitive to any vibrations in the ground coming from movements. Infrared sensors measured changes in heat. "Urine sniffers" measured changes in the number of ammonia molecules present. These devices automatically radioed data to planes circling overhead, which in turn relayed the signals to computers at Nakhon Phanom, Thailand. This operation went on twenty-four hours a day, every day. Sensory devices had to be replaced often because their batteries did not last over a few weeks. Simply maintaining the field cost some $800 million per year.[53]

The computer bank at Nakhon Phanom was the center of the system. Once sensor readings passed programmed "threshold" points, a "target" would appear on war technicians' television screens:

A TV-type screen provides the Assessment Officer a map of the section of Laos under his control. Each of the roads used by the North Vietnamese in his area is etched on his screen. As the seismic and acoustic sensors pick up the truck movements their locations *appear as an illuminated line of light, called "the worm,"* that crawls across his screen, following a road that sometimes is several hundreds of miles away.

From there the battle becomes academic. The Assessment Officer and the computer confer on probable times the convoy or convoys will reach a pre-selected point on the map. This point is a *"box"* selected by the Igloo White team of experts at the ISC [Infiltration Surveillance Center]. Airborne at the moment are gunships and fighters. A decision is made as to the type of ordnance best suited for the area.[54]

The "box" was a set of map coordinates that could be radioed to aircraft. All of southern Laos was mapped into such boxes. Loran radio beacons then locked onto the planes' computers and navigation systems and automatically guided them to the target area. Planes either dropped their bombs automatically on command from the ground computer or pilots took manual control and used their aircraft-mounted surveillance devices to locate the trucks. Virtually all combat over the Ho Chi Minh Trail was at night. Daytime bombing had forced the enemy into darkness.

Note that a target appeared only as "an illuminated line of light" to ground controllers. Likewise to pilots using electronic warfare devices, targets appeared as marks on electronic screens. At the point when Technowar reaches its technological apex, it turns completely into a representation. Indeed, the very name for a "target" was *"target signature."* And when the "target" was destroyed, the lights on the screen went out. The representation disappeared:

His task now finished, the general had nothing more to do than wait for the results of the operation, which within twenty minutes of the launching of the raid were signalled simultaneously over the loudspeaker and on the big screen. The heavy breathing of the engines was abruptly smothered by the exploding of the first bombs. The roar lasted only a second, then gave way to absolute silence. At the same time the *red dots* and the *blue ribbon* of the convoy *disappeared from the screen.* The operation was over. The F-4's had played their role, on the whole, a modest one. The jungle ears were *out of commission;*

others would be dropped the next night. The convoy *must* have been severely hit, if not utterly destroyed.[55]

If a "target" is only the programmed threshold point and if a "destroyed" target also involves the destruction of the transmitting sensors, then how can one be sure that there really were trucks and men in the first place? Couldn't it be a herd of elephants or deer? Or couldn't Vietnamese use decoys to deceive sensors? Or, even if the Vietnamese really were detected, how could war-managers and technicians be sure they were destroyed when bombing raids destroyed the sensors that helped create the "target signatures"?

General Momyer thought interdiction in southern Laos was outstanding. Even before Igloo White became fully operational, the general reported that in 1966–1967 his planes sighted some 49,371 trucks and destroyed 7,194 and damaged 3,278.[56] This highly productive rate of destruction increased as Technowar became more sophisticated. From October 1970 through May 1971, the air force claimed to have destroyed 25,000 trucks and damaged many, many more.[57] The official rate of destruction for the most advanced gunship, the AC-130, with 20mm and 40mm cannon firing 6,000 rounds per minute and equipped with radar, low-light television, and infrared sensors, was 9.72 trucks destroyed per sortie.[58]

There is one problem with these statistics. If Technowar over the Ho Chi Minh Trail was that efficient, then southern Laos should have been completely littered with burnt-out trucks. Reconnaissance flights made the day after night strikes never found these burnt-out vehicles, at least not the thousands reported. General Momyer explains the discrepancy between pilot reports and reconnaissance flights: "Trucks destroyed/damaged — the statistics are subject to differences of interpretation. The difficulty in confirming a truck destroyed plagued the commanders of 7th Air Force throughout the war. The North Vietnamese were able to move trucks struck during the night into heavy jungle. Reconnaissance was not able, therefore, to provide the *desired evidence* on many missions as to the number of trucks destroyed/damaged."[59]

Granted that the enemy moved some trucks into jungle, how many people would be alive and functioning in a truck convoy hit by cannon, machine guns, cluster-bomb units, and napalm? Junior officers in the 7th Air Force came up with an appropriate answer. In the jungles of southern Laos lived the *Great Laotian Truck Eater*. This monster loved to eat dead and crippled trucks. Daylight reconnaissance flights could never find truck skeletons because the *Great Laotian Truck Eater* had devoured them before dawn.[60]

How many trucks were destroyed by Commando Hunt operations over southern Laos remains a Vietnamese secret. Evidence suggests North Vietnamese used decoys effectively. Many tribespeople in the Laotian panhandle were Vietnamese allies dating back to the war against the French. They located many ground sensors. Tape recordings of crickets and other jungle noises were placed next to sensors to conceal truck convoys. At the same time, tape recordings with truck noises were placed along different routes to promote attacks on fake convoys, sensors, and tape recorders. Should an air attack hit a convoy, North Vietnamese soldiers were trained to throw grenades and other explosives to falsely signify truck destruction.[61] Technowar bombed many real trucks located by its sensors and special army reconnaissance patrols, but it also fooled itself.

The United States Army knew at least some of the differences between real and imaginary successes in the air force's interdiction program. Given the relative failure of bombing, it wanted to invade southern Laos. By 1971 it was too late for direct American involvement. Consequently, the U.S. Army helped ARVN invade Laos in January, 1971. This operation was known as Lam Son 719.

"How can they *dream* of pushing through a couple of hundred miles of jungle and mountains in southern Laos, holding and occupying it. That might look very attractive *on the maps* they print in their newspapers. Perhaps it is of comfort to the U.S. public. But in fact they cannot do it."[62]

— General Nguyen Van Vinh
from an interview held in 1966

Invading and occupying southern Laos had been a favorite war-manager plan since the fifties. When intervention was contemplated in the early 1960s, a move across southern Laos to Thailand was considered. General Westmoreland and the Joint Chiefs of Staff recommended it to the Johnson administration several times. In the most grand versions, occupying Laos would be accompanied by the invasion of North Vietnam just north of the seventeenth parallel.[63] A solid line of Americans would keep the foreign Other out.

In May 1970, President Nixon ordered Cambodia invaded. That fall he approved plans for a winter 1971 invasion of Laos. Political reaction in the United States against the invasion of Cambodia, however, led to a law prohibiting the use of American ground troops in Cambodia or Laos. But the law did allow American airpower to be used. Nixon had previously called for "Vietnamization." South Vietnamese troops would replace American "labor" on the ground, while the United States would provide airpower for capital-intensive Technowar. In this manner American casualties would go down to a level acceptable to the American public while fighting continued.

Invading Laos was thus a South Vietnamese operation with American air support. But instead of air force and navy planes providing cover for operation Lam Son 719, the *army* took charge. At issue was a battle between the air force and the army over helicopter assaults. The air force insisted that helicopter success in South Vietnam was due only to limited anti-aircraft weapons. They contended that if helicopters met serious gun emplacements the aircraft would be shot down. Air force fighter-bombers should therefore strike any area before a helicopter assault, and air force officers should have control over helicopters.[64] Army officers argued that helicopter gunships provided necessary air support and that air force fighters weren't needed in large numbers.

Lam Son 719 so became another *"test"* in the laboratory. Lieutenant General James W. Sutherland commanded American army helicopter transports and gunships while Lieutenant General Hoaug Xuan Lam commanded Vietnamese ground troops. Sutherland had approximately 600 helicopters for use during the operation.

The attack plan was simple. About twenty miles northwest of Khe Sanh was Tchepone. Tchepone was supposedly the "center" of the enemy's logistic network. An old road called Route 9 ran between Khe Sanh and Tchepone. The plan called for one infantry division to move by helicopter north of the road and another infantry division to be airlifted into positions south of the road. These two divisions would conduct ground operations and establish artillery fire bases to protect the road. A third infantry division along with armor would then drive to Tchepone. If everything went well, ARVN would stay in Laos from early February through May.

North Vietnamese knew operational details long before the attack. All possible landing zones were covered. Artillery, tanks, and anti-aircraft guns were astutely positioned. Although no SAMs were in the area, southern Laos was full of PAVN heavy machine guns and anti-aircraft cannon, weapons that were serious threats to slow-moving aircraft. Air force commanders had quit sending propeller gunships there and had been using jets only for months! Moreover, the rainy season had come.

Weather was so bad that army helicopters could use only a few mountain valleys as air space on those days when they could fly at all. These valleys were ringed with enemy anti-aircraft.

By early March, five People's Army of Vietnam divisions had moved into battle. ARVN ground bases came under severe attack; some were completely overrun. South Vietnamese command structure began to break down; units received contradictory orders from different headquarters, and American helicopters had difficulty coordinating their flights with Vietnamese infantry. Worst of all, since the U.S. Army intended to use this operation to validate a new combat doctrine of using helicopter gunships as the principal source of fire support for infantry, little attention had been given to how Vietnamese units could call upon American fighter-bombers. Although the air force flew over 8,000 sorties in support of Lam Son 719, production was not adequate for the tasks at hand. By mid-March, orders were given to abandon fire bases north and south of Route 9. Soldiers often flew out of Laos holding on to the skids of American choppers.

Intelligence reports had stated that Route 9 was adequate and that its terrain was open for tanks and armored personnel carriers. In reality, the road was almost unusable. General Don Starry tells the story in his army publication, *Mounted Combat in Vietnam:*

> Intelligence reports had indicated that the terrain along Route 9 was favorable for armored vehicles. In reality, Route 9 was a neglected forty-year-old, single-lane road, with high shoulders on both sides and no maneuver room. Moreover, as the units moved forward they discovered the entire area was filled with huge bomb craters, undetected earlier because of dense grass and bamboo. Armored vehicles were therefore restricted to the road.[65]

The air force had ruined the army's campaign with its bomb craters. Confined to a narrow road where they could not maneuver, troops and tanks were easy targets. On March 19, armored units were ordered to withdraw. When one unit was ambushed in a stream, troops abandoned their vehicles, blocking the path. Already demoralized from previous high losses, units lost cohesion. ARVN entered Laos with 71 tanks and 127 armored personnel carriers; they got out with 22 tanks and 54 carriers.[66]

South Vietnamese losses came to over 2,500 killed and several thousand wounded. The U.S. Army says it lost 107 helicopters. This represents a loss rate per sortie of one-quarter of one percent, a rate the army says "compared favorably with the loss rate of high performance air-craft in Southeast Asia for the same period."[67] Army commanders counted a helicopter "lost" *only when the downed helicopter could not be recovered.* The air force estimated the number of helicopters shot down during Lam Son 719 "at 200 of more than 600 helicopters used."[68]

The air force looked upon the entire affair with satisfaction. In one history book, the air force perspective reads, "Past critics of air interdiction had often suggested that ground forces could achieve more effective results, but now they were less optimistic."[69] The air force could now return to bombing its sensors and watching the lights on the screens go out. There were even more trails and roads to bomb. While combat took place from Tchepone east to the Vietnamese border, the North Vietnamese expanded their road network west of Tchepone; infiltration was never stopped.

# CHAPTER 13

# Closing Out the War:
# Cambodia and North Vietnam, 1969–1973

A IR war over Cambodia begins with a military acronym— "COSVN."
COSVN was supposedly the Lao Dong, or Communist party headquarters for South Vietnam. United States commanders envisioned it as
a highly centralized command organization, just like MACV. In General
Westmoreland's words, "Both political and military operations were under
COSVN's *control.*" [1] If COSVN controlled all of the enemy's activities,
then COSVN must be a *big place.* The American Military Assistance
Command headquarters consisted of several acres filled with large buildings. Clearly, then, COSVN headquarters could be found and destroyed. And if headquarters were destroyed, then the enemy would be
left without a directing "brain," and its operations would be severely
curtailed. General Momyer describes some of the American efforts:

> . . . B-52's would bomb COSVN's probable location (which was
> to remain *elusive* throughout the war). Many times Westmoreland re-
> quested fighter strikes against a suspected location of COSVN, and
> on a few occasions he personally scheduled the B-52's against these
> suspected sites. Before scheduling such strikes, because of difficulty
> in locating the suspected area of the headquarters, RF-4's were dis-
> patched to reconnoiter the position. Most of the time the intelligence
> information was very scanty, and reconnaissance, both visual and
> photographic, failed to reveal the location of COSVN. Nevertheless,
> such information could not be dismissed since even an outside chance
> of knocking out COSVN was worth the effort. [2]

If intelligence consistently failed "to reveal the location of COSVN,"
there is some question as to whether COSVN really existed as an analog
to American headquarters. But it had to exist for the highest officials of

the U.S. war effort; it was impossible to a imagine a truly different foreign Other. Consequently, bombs were dropped regardless of evidence. Westmoreland requested that B-52 sorties be increased from 400 per month in 1965 to 1,200 per month by 1968. Each B-52 dropped from twenty to thirty tons of bombs. Westmoreland asked for B-52s because their bomb pattern over a large area was more regularly distributed and their bomb craters deeper than comparable bombs dropped by fighter planes. COSVN must be *completely destroyed,* not just hit.[3]

American war-managers never knew where COSVN was in any real, physical sense, but COSVN always had a *constant* location in military discourse. General Westmoreland describes Operation Junction City, a search-and-destroy mission to obliterate COSVN: "In only two instances did the enemy stand and fight, and the staff of COSVN *apparently* escaped across the border into a Cambodian *sanctuary.*"[4] In American military discourse, COSVN lived in the land beyond, *in the space of bombs not dropped,* the place where all "lucrative" and "remunerative" targets really were; the internal dynamics for escalating B-52 strikes are obvious.

Cambodia really was a sanctuary until 1969 and the North Vietnamese really did use territory along the Cambodian and Vietnamese border for infiltration. But did COSVN live there? Until 1969, war-managers thought COSVN lived in South Vietnam or Laos. On February 9, 1969, General Creighton Abrams — Westmoreland's replacement since the summer of 1968 — sent the Joint Chiefs of Staff a message. COSVN was now in Cambodia: "The area is covered by thick canopy jungle. Source reports there are no concrete structures in this area. Usually reliable sources report that COSVN and COSVN-associated elements consistently remain in the same general area along the border. All our information, generally confirmed by imagery interpretation, provides us with a firm basis for targeting COSVN HQs."[5]

President Nixon approved the strike but required secrecy. A "normal" B-52 strike inside South Vietnam would be made, but at the last minute, twenty-eight of the sixty aircraft would continue flying westward to Cambodia to bomb "Base Area 353." Code-named "Operation Breakfast," the strike against COSVN occurred on March 18, 1969.

A reconnaissance team was sent to survey results. Special Forces Lieutenant Randolph Harrison describes the briefing he received beforehand: "We had been told, as had everybody . . . that those carpet bombing attacks by B-52's [were] totally devastating, that nothing could survive, and if they had a troop concentration there it would be annihilated." Harrison and his men, however, were hit hard; only five out of eleven soldiers made it back and most were wounded. In Harrison's words, the bombing had the "same effect as taking a beehive the size of a basketball and poking it with a stick. They were mad."[6] Another recon team was ordered in, but the troops refused to go.

COSVN apparently got away — the space of bombs not dropped was quite large in Cambodia. Base Area 353 was only one of fifteen sanctuaries on the official chart. Hunting for COSVN continued. From March 1969 through May 1970, B-52s flew 3,630 sorties over Cambodia.[7] None of these sorties officially existed. No public mention was made by American war-managers; even official secret records showed that the raids took place over cover targets in South Vietnam rather than Cambodia.

Three political factors were involved in deciding on a secret bombing campaign. First, the Nixon administration had come to power with a campaign platform that called for ending the Vietnam War. A public campaign against Cambodia enacted two months after inauguration would be politically difficult. A campaign against Cambodia would also raise legal questions. The Gulf of Tonkin Resolution concerned Vietnam, not Cambodia — or Laos, for that matter. Antiwar-movement activity was also strong during this period.

In March 1969, the United States had an ambiguous relationship with the ruler of Cambodia, Prince Norodom Sihanouk. Sihanouk called his foreign policy "extreme neutralism." This term glossed a set of remarkable unofficial agreements. North Vietnam denied they utilized the Vietnamese-Cambodian border area and Sihanouk said little publicly. Their actual relationships were more intricate. The DRV imported supplies through the Cambodian port of Sihanoukville and utilized the Vietnamese-Cambodian border as a staging area. Cambodian elites, including the right wing, made vast profits off imports, and North Vietnamese kept Cambodia's left wing under tight control and far away from populated areas.[8] Sihanouk's coalition governments had both right- and left-wing elements. In 1967 a peasant revolt had broken out in one province and the prince ordered the revolt crushed. He subsequently moved his government to the right, and most left-wing ministers resigned to join the underground opposition, the Khmer Rouge. The prince practiced contradictory domestic politics, at once genuinely concerned over the peasantry and actively involved in maintaining political and economic advantages for family and friends.

Sihanouk did not publicly denounce the bombings. He made efforts to deal with both North Vietnamese and Americans, but was not successful. In March 1970, the army and the Cambodian upper and middle classes conducted a successful coup against Sihanouk while he was visiting France. His successor was Lon Nol, formerly minister of defense, serving at the time as prime minister. The Central Intelligence Agency was involved in the coup, although its exact role is disputed.[9] Lon Nol was pro-American and anti-Communist, despite considerable profits he made off arms trade at Sihanoukville.

The coup was not well received in the countryside, where Prince Sihanouk's populist efforts were deeply appreciated and where his status as monarch was revered. Lon Nol's brother, Lon Nil, was killed, his liver cooked and distributed to a crowd. In other cities Cambodian soldiers fired into crowds, killing and wounding hundreds.

But in Washington the coup was well received. B-52 bombing attacks against COSVN had failed. The "elusive" COSVN had escaped again and again. A new plan was put forth. Cambodia would be invaded by ground troops; search-and-destroy would have a new terrain. By April, General Abrams and other war-managers had convinced themselves that COSVN was really in Base Areas 352 and 353. Base Area 353 had been the site of the original B-52 attack. Together they had been subject to approximately 29,000 tons of bombs. However, the bombing attacks had been ineffective because COSVN was *really* twenty-nine feet underground in reinforced concrete bunkers. The *5,000* officials and technicians of COSVN were thus immune from B-52 attacks.[10] Initial intelligence reports on Base Area 353 had said "there were no concrete structures in this area."

By this time the reality of COSVN — or the unreality of COSVN — did not matter. Instead, the vast COSVN bunker fitted Technowar reasoning and a ground attack upon Cambodia allowed the military to remain *productive*. One of General Abrams's staff officers later explained: "South Vietnam was relatively tranquil then. We were looking for *something to do*."[11] In General Abrams's words, ARVN could handle most battles, but it would be good to use American troops "in most *productive* base areas, if U.S. policy permits."[12] Productive American attacks upon lucrative targets would bring a high return on Technowar investment.

For Nixon's administration, bombing Cambodia served *communicative* purposes. Early in April, Nixon received a briefing by Admiral John S. McCain, Jr., the CINCPAC who replaced Admiral Sharp. He was known as the "Big Red Arrow Man," because his maps invariably showed red arrows moving from China across Asia. The arrows were known as "McCain's claws."[13] The map Nixon saw showed red arrows or claws moving from eastern Cambodia, which was already colored *red,* onward past the capital city of Phnom Penh reaching toward Thailand.

In this manner Cambodia was erased, just as Vietnam had been erased years before. Cambodia became another abstract site, a space to be used for communicating American will to the world. Nixon said as much in his television address on April 30, 1970. There were introductory remarks about "cleaning out major North Vietnamese and Vietcong-occupied territories" and destroying "the headquarters for the entire Communist military operations in South Vietnam," but the speech revealed different concerns:

My fellow Americans, we live in an age of anarchy both abroad and at home. We see mindless attacks on all the great institutions which have created the free civilizations in the last five hundred years. Even here in the United States, great universities are being systematically destroyed. Small nations all over the world find themselves under attack from within and from without. . . .

If, when the chips are down, the world's most powerful nation, the United States of America, acts like a pitiful, helpless giant, the forces of totalitarianism and anarchy will threaten free nations and free institutions throughout the world. . . .

We will not react to this threat to American lives merely by plaintive diplomatic protests. If we did, the credibility of the United States would be destroyed. . . .

We will not be humiliated. We will not be defeated. It is not our power but our will and character that is being tested tonight. . . .

If we fail to meet this challenge, all other nations will be on notice that despite its overwhelming power the United States, when a *real* crisis comes, will be found wanting.[14]

As Jonathan Schell has noted, Nixon in effect said that Cambodia was not a *real* crisis, but instead a "test" crisis.[15] The real invasion was important only as a vehicle for the global significations mentioned in his speech. In this movement to global significance, Cambodia becomes an unimportant word in a long speech. Note also that the speech is very *tough,* very masculine. Nixon and administration officials talked about toughness during the invasion. Alexander Haig, chief of staff for

Henry Kissinger at the National Security Council, concluded a staff meeting by saying, "The basic substance of all this is that we have to be tough."[16] Kissinger said, "We're trying to shock the Soviets into calling a Conference and we can't do this by appearing weak."[17] "Let's go blow the hell out of them" were Nixon's words to the Joint Chiefs of Staff.[18] To members of Congress who were worried about mass protests following the invasion of Cambodia, the President said, "Don't worry about divisiveness. Having drawn the sword, don't take it out — stick it in hard. . . . Hit'm in the gut. No defensiveness."[19]

Administration officials worked hard to maintain the appearance of virility. Meanwhile, antiwar protesters opposed to invasion closed hundreds of colleges and universities. Massive demonstrations and riots occurred throughout the country. By mid-May, congressional opposition threatened continued war in Cambodia. Senators Frank Church and Sherman Cooper secured an amendment to the Foreign Military Sales Act requiring all American troops be withdrawn from Cambodia by June 30, 1970. No American planes could fly tactical air support missions for Cambodian forces, nor could American advisers be attached to Cambodian units.

In response war-managers played familiar doublethink games with categories. Tactical air strikes, like B-52 attacks, *did not officially exist anymore*, although 156 sorties were flown in May: such missions were categorized as "interdiction" sorties, that were allowable. Fighter-bombers were used instead of B-52s because, as General Abrams reported, "At this time it is not believed that the targets described are of sufficient persistence to qualify as *lucrative* Menu [B-52] targets."[20] He did not want to waste production capacity. American body counts in South Vietnam could also be changed. On May 28, 1970, Admiral William Lemos proposed that casualties decrease in July: "If necessary we must do it by edict."[21]

In President Nixon's June 30 speech, enemy body count numbered around 11,000 and vast quantities of supplies had been captured. "Vietnamization" was working; the South Vietnamese army had performed well, as had American forces. The President did not say anything about finding COSVN. Others had come to different conclusions. Kissinger's staff found that the withdrawal of American and South Vietnamese troops from their locations in Vietnam had left those areas vulnerable to guerrilla attack. Systems Analysis in the Department of Defense did not think Cambodian operations had crippled the NVA and Vietcong.

Although U.S. and ARVN cross-border operations have disrupted NVA operations in Cambodia to some extent, these operations have not substantially reduced NVA capabilities in Cambodia. Approximately 25% of the Vietnamese Communists' reserve stocks have been lost. Captured supplies can be reconstituted in about 75 days with the opening of additional supply routes through Laos and continued high level supply operations into the rainy season.[22]

Lon Nol was particularly disturbed about the effects of invasion. He fully realized that the Communists would be pushed *westward* toward populated regions. When Alexander Haig told him Americans would withdraw in June, he cried. By August, Cambodia was a free-fire zone for American and Vietnamese aircraft. Curtailment of sorties over North Vietnam meant that there was surplus production capacity for Cambodia. "Armed Reconnaissance" was a favorite category for such strikes. Pilots could bomb virtually anything they wanted. Air support for the Cambodian army was another favorite. Although the Cooper-Church Amendment had forbidden such strikes, they were simply reclassified as "interdiction" missions.[23]

In 1970 Secretary of Defense Melvin Laird attempted to control sorties over Cambodia by instituting a "banking" system like the one used over North Vietnam. Each service got a fixed number of sorties for a given period in the hopes that this quota would promote rational "resource allocation" against military targets.[24] Laird's proposal was not successful. He tried quotas only after failing to control sorties more directly. He wanted a sortie rate that was responsive to the actual military situation: "Anyone that addresses the problem starting with a set number of sorties doesn't understand the problem and isn't qualified to discuss it."[25] That he later came to endorse such a proposal marks the difficulty in controlling a system whose internal dynamics lead to ever-increasing demands for more production. For example, the Joint Chiefs of Staff ordered General Abrams to "conduct the most aggressive U.S. and R.V.N.A.F. [South Vietnamese air force] air campaign in Cambodia which is feasible. . . ."[26]

South Vietnamese air force pilots were willing to participate: Vietnamese hatred for Cambodians was intense. Previously it had been difficult to get South Vietnamese pilots to fly on Sundays. Now pilots paid bribes to superior officers who controlled flight assignments to fly missions seven days a week. ARVN was equally enthusiastic. It acted like a conquering army rather than an ally; bicycles, radios, motorcycles, and everything else which could be transported became bonus pay for troops.

Residents of eastern Cambodia fled. One hundred thousand Vietnamese who had been living in Cambodia went back to South Vietnam and its refugee camps; Cambodians went westward. Within months the populace of Phnom Penh doubled to 1.2 million. By December 1971, the Cambodian Ministry of Health calculated that over two million out of the entire population of seven million had become refugees; agriculture ceased in large areas. Inflation increased several hundred percent. Over 20 percent of the country's property was destroyed by the end of 1971. This was the product of 61,000 sorties flown by American and South Vietnamese pilots in 1971 and 23,800 sorties flown in 1970.[27]

At the time, the Khmer Rouge were estimated to have only a few hundred troops in their main-force units and several thousand part-time guerrillas. They were confined to the Vietnamese border. They had no firm social base with the peasantry, but instead were dependent upon the North Vietnamese for logistical support.

Soon after the invasion, three American journalists were captured by the guerrillas. One journalist, Richard Dudman, later wrote: "The bombing and shooting was radicalizing the people of rural Cambodia and was turning the countryside into a massive, dedicated and effective rural base. American shells and bombs are proving to the Cambodians beyond doubt that the United States is waging unprovoked colonialist war against the Cambodian people."[28] One report by the Defense Intelligence Agency estimated that the Khmer Rouge controlled a third of the people and two-thirds of the land. Main-force units numbered some 10,000 troops, supplemented by 35,000 to 50,000 guerrillas. Further growth was predicted: "Unless the Government is able to reassert its influence and maintain some semblance of control over the rural sector, the communist infrastructure will probably continue to grow."[29]

Sortie production should have grown upward from 61,000 in 1971. But in 1972, production over Cambodia unexpectedly fell to 25,000 sorties. North Vietnam made an unexpected move and air war was redistributed once again.

By December 1971, all PAVN units had been withdrawn from the south. Three People's Liberation Armed Forces divisions moved back to North Vietnam, two withdrew to Laos, and six were in Cambodia. Statistical indices of pacification progress consequently all rose. On the briefing charts in Saigon and Washington victory appeared once again. In the spring of 1972, the graphs fell. Most American ground troops had been withdrawn. Officials called for "Vietnamization." Toward the end of March, all divisions originally withdrawn went into battle. They were joined by new units. Attacks came directly across the DMZ; other fronts opened in the Central Highlands and northwest of Saigon.

ARVN went into immediate shock. The division below the demilitarized zone completely broke down; one regiment defected. By the end of April, Saigon was forced to commit its strategic reserve: 34,000 Rangers, 13,000 marines, and 10,000 airborne soldiers. Once these troops were committed, Saigon had no mobile forces to respond against renewed guerrilla warfare. Local troops — the Regional and Popular Forces — could not stand on their own. An estimated 70,000 militia soldiers were destroyed from April through June. Regular ARVN forces also lost 70,000 men through the same processes, making 140,000 casualties. For the first time in the war, American intelligence estimated the enemy won the body count; NVA and VC losses were put at 70,000.[30]

America sent hundreds of additional air force and navy aircraft to Southeast Asia. In March, sortie production for all South Vietnamese and American aircraft was 4,237. In April this figure *quadrupled* to 17,171, and in May it increased to 18,444. June saw a slight decline, with only 15,951 sorties. These sortie rates were for South Vietnam *alone*.[31] What was new about the American response concerned North Vietnam. From May through December, the space of bombs not dropped was closed. Technowar introduced its most spectacular weapon, the B-52 strategic bomber, to combat over the north. On April 6, B-52 attacks began. By the fifteenth, bombers hit Haiphong. On May 8, Nixon ordered the mining of North Vietnamese ports; mining would keep weapons "out of the hands of the international *outlaws* of North Vietnam."[32]

Former Undersecretary of the Air Force Townsend Hoopes had previously discovered that most weapons entering North Vietnam came across the Chinese border. Air Force General George Keegan found that mining and bombing did not achieve its intended results of isolating the North Vietnamese. According to him, the Russians "broke the blockade and found the means, despite the closure of the ports, to push through the largest tonnage of supplies through Mainland China in history. Instead of moving it down the rail lines, which were all disrupted, they moved it down roads and into the canals."[33] However, despite bombing's strategic failure, it had definite political impact. When Nixon ordered attacks, both the Soviet Union and the People's Republic of China were predisposed to grant him great latitude. It was the beginning of détente, and although the DRV's allies increased their material aid, they did not pressure the United States into concessions during negotiations.

At the beginning of the spring offensive, the DRV thought three different outcomes were acceptable. Each was a "compromise" but the DRV wanted to end the war "even if there was a compromise, but a compromise which permits us to make a step forward."[34] The most favorable compromise agreement would replace Saigon with a transitional coalition government until elections were held. Second choice consisted of a return to the "checkerboard" pattern of different zones ruled by the Provisional Revolutionary Government and the Republic of South Vietnam. Recall that this "checkerboard" plan was in effect before the Geneva Conference of 1954 reached a compromise consolidating forces into northern and southern zones. The last acceptable outcome only withdrew American forces, letting war continue among the Vietnamese.

From May through September, the North Vietnamese attempted to negotiate a settlement based on a coalition government without Thieu. Secretary of State Henry Kissinger would not negotiate on that basis. Although the B-52s no longer struck, there was much fear that the United States might launch an attack on dikes and flood the country. This fear eased in September, but summer had also seen an ARVN counteroffensive that limited further military advances.

On October 8, 1972, Le Duc Tho presented Kissinger with a detailed draft proposal of nine chapters and twenty-two articles. Article 1 stated that the United States was obligated to respect the "independence, sovereignty and territorial integrity of Vietnam as recognized by the 1954 Geneva Agreements."[35] Another crucial provision called for elections in South Vietnam within six months. Civilians would be able to move freely from the temporary zones controlled by the PRG and GVN. An "administrative structure," called the National Council of Reconciliation and Concord, would arrange elections and negotiate other political and military problems.

By October 12, negotiations were completed on most chapters. Kissinger first proposed that the text be initialed October 19, 1968, and signed a week later; he later wanted final signing on October 30. Only two issues remained. First, the DRV wanted the treaty to state when Vietnamese political prisoners would be released from Thieu's jails. In turn, the United States wanted to resupply the south with large quantities of weapons and munitions. *Publicly,* though, Kissinger announced that "Peace is at hand" on October 26. American presidential elections were scheduled for November 5.

No treaty was signed on October 30. In mid-October the Nixon administration sought first to delay signing until after the election and then, once the election was over, to reverse the terms. Many "delays" were *publicly* expressed in getting President Thieu of South Vietnam to go along. Kissinger stated that the United States would not allow Saigon veto power. Nevertheless, Thieu's objections clarified the treaty. The United States and its client had *lost the war;* the treaty demonstrated their defeat.

First, Thieu pointed out the full implications of allowing 300,000 North Vietnamese troops to remain in the south: "Because it's like recognizing their right to call themselves liberators, their right to say that Vietnam is one country, from Hanoi to Saigon. . . ." This made his own government illegitimate. The agreement put "the legal government of South Vietnam in the position of a puppet government installed by the Americans!" Furthermore, if the government was a puppet regime, then "It means considering the South Vietnamese army as a mercenary of the Americans." [36]

Article 1's demand that the United States respect the "independence, sovereignty, unity and territorial integrity of Vietnam as recognized by the 1954 Geneva Agreements" tacitly indicated that the United States had violated those principles. It also meant that the demilitarized zone was no longer a national boundary and so undercut Thieu's government's claim to sovereignty. Virtually *everything* in the agreements meant South Vietnam was no longer a sovereign nation. The National Council of Reconciliation and Concord was, in Thieu's terms, a "supragovernmental" body, and would therefore "nullify the whole parliament, as well as the Supreme Court, because it would be completely independent." [37] The council promised creation of a new constitution and government: "This council, having three equal segments with the same number of personnel, will supervise the two existing governments and organize a general election. This means a new constitutional assembly will be elected and there will be a new constitutional and a new system predetermined by the new constitution." [38]

Thieu was correct in his interpretations. His regime was not recognized as a sovereign entity by the treaty. As the DRV had said back in September, the treaty was based on a political-military reality that there were "two administrations, two armies and other political forces" in South Vietnam. The proposed elections offered Thieu and the Saigon elite a chance, but it was only a chance. Candidates from the Provisional Revolutionary Government — successor to the National Liberation Front — and candidates from Vietnamese political groups previously imprisoned by the regime would all be running for the new national assembly. Thieu did not want these elections. He had financed his last election through the heroin trade and won through fake ballots, use of the army, and jailing opponents to his party.[39]

Nor did American war-managers want an election in South Vietnam. Now that the American election was over, negotiations could be pursued differently. On November 20, Kissinger presented "revisions." The demilitarized zone would be restored as a boundary between nations, making the NVA's presence in South Vietnam illegal. Some North Vietnamese troops would have to be withdrawn. The National Council would become much less important. Elections would only be for a new president within the GVN's constitutional framework. All references to the Provisional Revolutionary Government were dropped. References to the "sovereignty of South Vietnam" were inserted in many places. It was as if the war had never occurred, much less been lost.

The foreign Other was cast in purely technobureaucratic terms, just like the United States and the Saigon regime. The zones of control for the Vietcong and the Saigon regime were to be determined by a *purely military count*. Only the ground where military forces stood counted as a zone and the NVA was to induct all Vietcong guerrillas into regular military units and provide a *list* of who and where they were![40] Hamlets and villages that had effective administration by Vietcong political cadre and only occasional guerrilla action thus would not count as PRG territory under the new proposals; the United States and Saigon claimed nearly 1,400 villages previously ceded to the PRG.[41]

To persuade the foreign Other to accept this defeat, the United States moved back to its original conception of history as a series of static points, each point a measure of the balance of forces at that moment. History could thus be easily changed by the introduction of more forces. Throughout November and December Kissinger promised "savage" bombing attacks if the DRV would not submit. Two versions of the ultimatum story exist. According to the United States, President Nixon sent an ultimatum to North Vietnam on December 15 and demanded a response within seventy-two hours.[42] The Vietnamese say that the ultimatum came on December 18, only a few hours before the first wave of B-52s appeared on their radar at 7 P.M. Le Duc Tho had returned from Paris only three hours previously.[43]

This bombing attack had an appropriately virile code name, Line-backer II. At the time the U.S. Air Force had approximately 400 B-52 bombers in the Strategic Air Command. Half were used in five nights of B-52 attacks over Hanoi and Haiphong. *Three-fourths of all B-52 crews* in the air force flew these missions.[44]

There are three major models of B-52 bombers. The G and H models are fairly similar. Pilots and other crew members had no great difficulty switching from one aircraft to another. However, there was a vast difference between the G and H models and their predecessor, the D model. The D model did not have powered controls. As Air Force General McCarthy described the flight experience, "Flying the B-52D has been compared to driving an 18-wheel truck without power steering, air brakes, or automatic transmission in downtown Washington during the rush hour."[45] Many B-52s in Southeast Asia were D models. These older planes had additional pylons put on their wings to increase their conventional bomb load.

For Linebacker II, air crews who normally flew G and H models were brought in with only a two-week course in flying B-52Ds. Conversely, many pilots in Thailand and Guam flying D models had to switch over to newer G and H models. Air force command adopted the principle of exchangeability to get maximum aircraft off the ground. An air crew had to take whatever model was available. For example, if a plane had problems during final checks before takeoff, the crew was transferred to whatever standby aircraft were available.[46] The principle of *maximum productivity* thus overruled any question of whether a crew was competent to fly the aircraft.

Each crew carried vast technical data *inside* the aircraft. Theoretically, they could read manuals on the long flight to Hanoi. One air force historian described the gear aboard:

> For the heavy bomber missions, in addition to survival vest, side-arms, and large boxes of rations, a crew would have several oversize briefcases crammed full of classified mission materials, several full sets of aircraft technical manuals, bombing computation tables, celestial navigation data, other professional gear, and a full complement of cold weather flying clothes. It seemed somewhat ludicrous to see a crew haul cold weather gear out to an aircraft in the middle of the tropics.[47]

During 1972 North Vietnam had improved its anti-aircraft capabilities. Its radar system could follow most aircraft. Surface-to-air missiles had been improved by more powerful warheads and made more mobile by devising suitable truck mounting. Their numbers had also increased. By late December, American intelligence estimated that Hanoi was defended by 850 SAM missile launchers. DRV officials had heard Kissinger's threats: evacuation of children began on December 4; large elements of the military and governmental bureaucracies were also removed.

On the first night several B-52s were shot down. Much technical data crew members were carrying in their briefcases was captured intact. Years later, the mayor of Hanoi, Tran Duy Hung, told the story:

> They had been assured it was what they called a "milk-run" operation. They thought they knew the limitations of the SAM-2 missiles. What they did not take into account was a Vietnamese secret of improving their efficiency. The pockets of the chief pilot shot down were *stuffed with technical data on the model he was flying.* He would never have been carrying it had there seemed the slightest risk of being shot down. It was very precious documentation for us because there were the latest B-52 D's and B-52 G's with no less than 17 electronic jamming devices to fool our radar warning system and especially conventional missile guidance systems. By the time the sun was up our electronic experts were working on how to counter those of the jamming systems which could affect the efficiency of our missile batteries.[48]

By sundown the next day a new strategy had been devised by the North Vietnamese. Missiles would be launched in salvos along flight paths. MIGs would attempt to locate the altitude, speed, and course direction of each three-plane "cell" on a bombing run. Salvos would be fired accordingly, thus either neutralizing electronic warfare measures by sidestepping them or severely reducing their effectiveness.

How many B-52s were shot down has been disputed. The air force claims that only fifteen bombers were lost and twenty-five more damaged.[49] North Vietnam gave a tally of thirty-four bombers lost over North Vietnam with many others either crashing at sea or elsewhere in Southeast Asia or returning to base as severely damaged aircraft incapable of further missions.[50] Some evidence supports this view. After high losses were experienced during the first few night attacks, a prolonged debate broke out. An official air force historian reports that at SAC headquarters in Omaha, Nebraska, "Such expressions as 'stop the carnage — we can't lose any more B-52's — it has become a blood bath' were commonplace."[51] The head of the Strategic Air Command,

General Meyer, favored further demonstration of virility: *"Press On!"* was his response.[52] More missions were flown, but other war-managers put pressure on Nixon to end B-52 attacks.

China and the Soviet Union made public statements indicating détente would end unless the raids ceased. Much of Western Europe denounced the assaults; even the Pope issued a condemnation. Elements of Congress promised to end the war by law. On December 30, Nixon ended the bombing and announced new negotiations. During those negotiations the United States surrendered virtually every reversal it had demanded during the November sessions. The completed draft was like the first one agreed to in October, the one Thieu interpreted as the end to legitimacy for his regime. Technowar failed, even after dropping 40,000 tons of bombs on Hanoi and 15,000 tons on Haiphong. Over 1,600 people had been killed and many more wounded, but their loss did not produce American victory. Still the bombing campaign was not over; just before the treaty was signed, Kissinger announced that the United States would continue bombing Cambodia.

With vast surplus capacity for sortie production, the air force soon flooded Cambodia with a bombing monsoon. In 1972, B-52s dropped slightly less than 37,000 tons, while fighter-bombers dropped 16,513 tons. During the next year these figures increased tremendously. In March, B-52s dropped over 24,000 tons, the next month 35,000 tons. In May they got up to almost 35,600 tons. Fighter-bombers showed more remarkable increases. They dropped almost 15,000 tons in April alone and increased to over 19,000 tons a month by summer. As the director of the Central Intelligence Committee later explained, "Cambodia then was the only game in town."[53]

Back in Phnom Penh, the game was played with *maps*. Lon Nol loved his maps. William Shawcross reports: "Lon Nol seemed to invest it [bombing] with supernatural powers, and air attachés at the United States embassy spoke with awe of his habit of simply *erasing from the map* any enemy unit he had ordered bombed."[54] Others played more dangerous games. Official maps were 1:50,000 in scale. One embassy official cut out a "box" to scale and put it on his map. A "box" was the area of impact for a three-plane B-52 raid. He found that in central Cambodia there was virtually no place one could put a box without hitting a village: "One night a mass of peasants from a village near Saang went out on a funeral procession. They walked straight into a 'box.' Hundreds were slaughtered."[55] The official does not say whether they were counted as "killed by air," but then one rarely knew in Cambodia; most strikes went *unobserved*. Cambodians were supposed to check each strike, but there were so many bombing runs that there was not enough time to check coordinates. One American involved said, "They never plotted anything. We could have given them the coordinates of the palace and they would have said 'yes.' "[56]

An air force pilot asked that he and his fellow pilots be given better maps. The 1:50,000 scale ones "lacked sufficient detail and currency to pinpoint suspected enemy locations with some degree of confidence."[57] He wanted 1:5,000 scale maps. They were never issued, but the lack of maps did not stop bombs from being dropped. Air war over Cambodia became so intense that the chief of the Targets Division, based in Thailand, declared that a threshold of military history had been reached: "In defiance of the 'conventional wisdom that air cannot take ground or hold it,' we have done it. . . . The Cambodian army is as hapless and helpless as could be imagined. The application of sound principles in the use of U.S. air by a determined Commander, skillful staff, and well trained and disciplined air crews took and held ground by making it *untenable* for the enemy."[58]

Khmer Rouge troops were stopped from taking the capital during the summer of 1973, but the country was bombed flat in the process. Phnom Penh had over a million refugees by midsummer; other cities were also refugee camps. Agriculture had been completely destroyed. Starvation and disease were everywhere, but little refugee aid was provided by the United States. Technowar had won and that was all that mattered. Cambodia had not become one of the dominoes; its ground had been decimated, but its name could be placed on the "credit" side of the ledger.

The war's dynamics were such that there was no logical end to bombing. However, an *external* limitation was imposed. The House of Representatives passed an amendment to the Supplemental Appropriations Bill on May 10, 1973, barring funds for bombing Cambodia after June 30; the Senate soon passed a similar version. Nixon vetoed the bill and Congress failed to override the veto; instead the majority pledged to attach the amendment to stop bombing to all legislation. Nixon then publicly promised to end bombing on August 15, 1973, and that's when it ended. By that date the U.S. Air Force had officially dropped 257,465 tons of bombs on Cambodia.[59]

PART IV
# The Perfect War

# CHAPTER 14

# Finding the Light at the End of the Tunnel

THE Paris Peace Treaty of 1973 did not bring peace to Vietnam. It marked yet another point in the homogeneous time of Technowar, a temporary balance of forces that could be redistributed. The treaty stated that there were two legitimate governments in the south, the Republic of Vietnam and the People's Revolutionary Government. President Nixon announced that the United States would "continue to recognize the government of the Republic of Viet-nam as the sole legitimate government of South Viet-nam." [1]

Shortly before the treaty was signed, the United States turned over its bases, munitions, and equipment to its allies. Several hundred aircraft were flown into the south and were turned over to the Vietnamese air force, making it the world's fourth largest. Billions of dollars in small arms, tanks, trucks, artillery, and other war items were shipped to ARVN during "Project Enhance." American military men suddenly "retired," only to be immediately rehired by American corporations with Department of Defense contracts for work in South Vietnam — $150 million in contracts to twenty-three corporations. [2]

By changing from military uniforms to civilian slacks and shirts, the United States considered itself to be in "accord" with Article 4 of the agreement: "The United States will not continue its military involvement or intervene in the internal affairs of South Vietnam." [3] By transferring legal papers having to do with its bases and equipment, the United States was in "accord" with Article 6, the provision calling for "dismantlement of all military bases in South Vietnam of the United States" and its non-Vietnamese foreign allies such as the Koreans and Australians. [4] One American official noted the Vietnamese shock when they learned that the United States had no bases to destroy or equipment to ship out: "General Tra seemed to be genuinely surprised." [5] As the

U.S. State Department report said, "We did not explain to the DRV negotiators our interpretation of the phrase 'of the United States.' "[6]

The treaty brought only public appearance of American withdrawal. To war-managers the treaty was another effort to change the representation, to shift signifying words and phrases and legal categories to create a text without reference to real American actions. While war's end was announced publicly, President Nixon *secretly* promised Thieu that the United States would "react very strongly and rapidly" and "with full force" if the South Vietnamese regime was threatened on the battlefield.[7] Although no specific American actions were listed, South Vietnamese rulers presumed this meant renewed bombing attacks.

On January 26, 1973, two days before the cease-fire deadline, Vietcong forces launched attacks. It was an attempt to consolidate "zones" of the Provisional Revolutionary Government, literally to "plant the flag" in hamlets that were politically sympathetic to the PRG, but where there were tacit agreements between National Liberation Front forces and ARVN forces. These were villages where ARVN forces could stay without being attacked, but with the understanding that they would not interfere with Vietcong administrations and popular organizations. By attacking these outposts, the PRG hoped to secure recognition from International Control Commission teams responsible for drawing boundaries between the PRG and ARVN.

Recognition was not forthcoming. Instead, most PRG flags became targets for a massive ARVN counteroffensive. By the spring of 1973, ARVN artillery units were firing an estimated 10,000 rounds a day into PRG zones; most shellings were classified as "harassment and interdiction."[8] Air strikes continued for the next year. By early March 1974, ARVN units had captured roughly 15 percent of the PRG zone and brought another 5 percent of the South Vietnamese population under Saigon control.[9]

This gain was misleading in several respects. Massive shelling and bombing produced additional refugees. Life in the new refugee camps was no better than in the old; as one new refugee said, "They have imprisoned us here. It's like they have put us in a cattle pen and left us to starve."[10] Agriculture had already been reduced by years of herbicidal spraying, bombing, and shelling. Recent assaults meant both that less land was cultivated and that new refugees must be fed.

Few refugees could be absorbed into the South Vietnamese urban economy. It had been a service economy geared toward American troops; when the troops left, jobs as interpreters, laborers, black market merchants and money-changers, hotel and restaurant workers, prostitutes and bar-girls vanished. Former CIA official Frank Snepp estimates that 17,000 Vietnamese jobs were dependent upon the American presence in 1973 versus 160,000 in 1966.[11] Although these figures seem low in that illegal jobs don't officially exist, the scale of reduction points to the unemployment problem. Extreme inflation accompanied economic collapse: in 1973, 65 percent, in 1974, even higher.[12]

Economic crisis gave rise to increased corruption. Nguyen Ngoc Huy, formerly a high GVN official at the Paris Peace Talks, published an essay outlining the military consequences of increased corruption:

> Except for a few special cases, in which officers look after their troops and help them surmount financial difficulties, the soldiers are unable to feed their families and no longer have the will to fight. They are demoralized because of the shameless exploitation by their superiors. . . . Generally speaking, the army has become a vast enterprise for corruption; even artillery support must be paid for. . . .
>
> As long as security was good and living standards decent the people tolerated corruption and inefficiency in government. These defects are becoming less and less tolerable as security and living standards decline and numerous large-scale scandals bring into the open the rotten character of the leaders of the regime. If Thieu continues to govern with the support of corrupt and incompetent men while rejecting any true dialogue with other non-Communists, it will be difficult for South Vietnam to win the struggle against the Communists, whether it is fought militarily or politically.[13]

Nguyen Ngoc Huy's fears concerning corruption find support elsewhere. The Defense Attaché Office — the American military body responsible for coordinating military aid programs — conducted a survey in mid-1974 of South Vietnamese troops; 92 percent reported that they could no longer provide food, clothing, and shelter for their families. DAO researchers saw that the economic crisis was related to severe "deterioration of performance" and questioned whether ARVN could be considered "a viable military force."[14] ARVN salaries had only gone up 25 percent in 1973–1974. Many troops deserted, an estimated 170,000 in 1974. The GVN rounded up 123,000 deserters in the same year, but a former deserter's motivation to fight is highly questionable.[15] Thus, although the GVN was pushing back the Provisional Revolutionary Government, its social base was threatened.

Embassy officials responded by denying that problems existed and then calling for increased American aid. CIA station chief Thomas Polgar tried to refute Nguyen Ngoc Huy. At first he asked one of his own analysts, Ms. Pat Johnson, to study ARVN morale. When Johnson's report confirmed Huy and the DAO, Polgar wrote his own assessment: "There is no strong evidence that the morale factor has at this stage significantly affected ARVN's combat performance. . . . There has been no interruption of basic public services. There have been no strikes. The mail gets delivered routinely, which cannot be said in some more advanced countries. . . . The three percent per annum population increase suggests both physical prowess and a hopeful view of the future." [16] The production of babies thus signified impending victory. This report replaced Johnson's; hers was never forwarded to Washington. CIA headquarters deemed Polgar's baby thesis extreme, but Ambassador Martin was impressed. He sent the report to the American embassy in Moscow where officials could forward it to the Russians to convince them how hopeless their cause was. [17]

Reports like this and the suppression of "negative" assessments caused bewilderment in the Saigon CIA station. One agent inquired just what agency policy was. In part, Polgar replied, "If the Ambassador, be it Martin or anyone else, asks me to provide, I will try to comply with his request, provided that such request is not illegal and would not interfere with my basic responsibilities." [18] Confirming official reality held precedence over dissenting views. The distance between deluding others and self-delusion was not far. In his office Polgar had a cartoon poster entitled "The last Viet Cong Offensive"; it showed an elephant with one enemy soldier loading a spear into its trunk while another soldier with a huge hammer prepared to hit its testicles. Underneath the cartoon the caption read "Heavy Artillery." [19]

In 1973 Congress had voted $1.29 billion for economic and military assistance for the 1974 fiscal year. Ambassador Graham Martin wanted $1.45 billion for 1975. He preferred a three-year massive infusion of American aid that presumably would allow the GVN to become self-sufficient. Here doublethink simultaneously became more convoluted and began to unravel as internal contradictions previously concealed became manifest. Martin's call for increased aid did not cohere with previous reports on ARVN and the Thieu regime. Why should aid be increased if all was well? Congress was highly skeptical of South Vietnam's proposed independence after twenty years of dependence. During a crucial congressional visit, Polgar departed from his usual policy of supporting

Martin and indicated how fanciful such prospects for independence really were.[20]

By the spring of 1974, Congress had already put a one-billion-dollar ceiling on aid for fiscal year 1975. In August, they cut this figure to $700 million. This decrease had both real and symbolic consequences. Pentagon officials had counted on massive appropriations to Vietnam as a way of financing other activities. The budget for the Defense Attaché Office, rather than coming out of the Department of Defense, was largely included in aid to the GVN military. DAO overhead expenses were some $250 million a year — the swimming pools, commissaries, and other luxury services were now taking away revenues that should have gone to essential war items.[21]

Major General John E. Murray, head of the Defense Attaché Office in 1974, saw the Light at the End of the Tunnel while viewing these budget figures. Murray fully subscribed to the production model of war. "You can roughly equate cuts in support to a loss in real estate. As the cutting edge of the FVNAF [Republic of Vietnam Armed Forces] is blunted and the enemy continues to improve its combat position and logistical base, what will occur is a retreat to the Saigon-delta areas as a redoubt."[22] A redoubt is a fort used to defend important territory; in effect, General Murray said that the northern two-thirds of the country would be lost. If American aid dropped below $700 million, then one could "write off the Republic of Vietnam as a *bad investment* and a broken promise."[23]

Nowhere in General Murray's thinking are questions of popular allegiance to the regime addressed or structural problems of corruption confronted. However, previous Americans had also failed to ask these questions. Advisers had instructed Vietnamese to fight a capital-intensive, high-technology war. To insist now after twenty years that they should fight a "low-budget" war was hypocrisy. General Murray discovered that his name was not on the promotion list for two-star to three-star advancement. With nothing to lose, he spoke his mind: "We set one standard for ourselves and another for the Vietnamese. If an American officer began to take casualties, he would stop and call in the air and artillery and generally blast the hell out of the enemy positions. Today the South Vietnamese are forced to hoard their air power and artillery, and so they get more people killed and wounded. It's not only sadistic, it's racist."[24]

Murray left Vietnam in 1974. Before his departure he lectured South

Vietnamese generals on the consequences of reduced American aid. According to Frank Snepp, he had influence: "The American military
commander had said they could not survive if U.S. aid slipped far below the $700 million level. With the worst now a reality, they became
ever more convinced their future was out of their hands and that all
depended on direct American support and intervention. Their morale
took on the very fragility of the American commitment itself."[25] Murray was equally pessimistic in his report to Admiral Noel Gaylor, com-
mander-in-chief of Pacific forces (Sharp's replacement at CINCPAC).
To Gaylor, Murray reported that the South Vietnamese regime would
be defeated — "maybe not next week or next month, but after the year
they are going to be through."[26]

With declining American aid, the constant ARVN practice of appro-
priating war supplies for sale on the black market had fatal results. The
Government Accounting Office found that over $200 million worth of
war materials sent in 1973–1974 were missing — missing in the sense
of "no record." Missing inventory included 143 "small warships," $2
million worth of ammunition, and $10 million worth of small arms.
Using a high figure of $250 for an M-16 rifle, $10 million worth of
rifles is 40,000 weapons — enough to equip three divisions. The GAO
also found that the Pentagon had written off an additional $44 million
in war supplies. Although $200 million was a good estimate of total
losses, there was no definite figure since there were no comprehensive
lists of what was in Vietnam![27] Unable to remove corrupt generals among
themselves, ARVN commanders instead reduced allocations to their
troops. They went to war with drastically reduced munitions and supporting air and artillery strikes and died as a result. General Van Tien
Dung, the chief of staff for the Vietnam People's Army, wrote in 1974
that Thieu was now forced to fight a "poor man's war."[28]

At the time the treaty was signed, the DRV was reluctant to start a
major military offensive. Their theory and practice of war called for
political supremacy over the military. The treaty was to shift conflict to
the political level. Organizations among Vietnamese peasantry, workers, and intellectuals were far more politically astute and had wider social bases for generating support than did Thieu's political party with its
base among large-scale landowners and Catholics from the north resettled in the south. Communists were also prepared to enter a coalition
with non-Communist opponents to Thieu. In their assessment, virtually
any regime was better than Thieu's.

Fear of renewed American bombing also made the political path more palatable. Although the DRV authorized the 1973 offensive to "plant the flag" in Provisional Revolutionary Government zones, this offensive only involved local guerrillas, not main-force units. Indeed, these units were restrained from combat until the spring of 1974.[29] Just as in 1967 and 1970–1971, when American and GVN forces seemed victorious, the 1973–1974 victories of ARVN should be seen in large part as a result of the Communist forces' deliberate withdrawal from battle. The North Vietnamese hoped that international pressure would force adherence to the treaty and push revolutionary struggle into the political realm. (A ready analogy can be found in the military silence from 1954 to 1959, a time when the Communists hoped to instigate internationally supervised elections.)

Yet as time passed, the DRV leaned toward "revolutionary violence." No progress was being made in diplomatic efforts, while the United States was slowly moving away from direct military intervention. Congress had officially halted all American bombing over Southeast Asia on August 15, 1973. In November it passed the War Powers Act, which prohibited presidential authorization of military involvement beyond sixty days without explicit congressional authorization. In December 1973, Henry Kissinger secretly met DRV representatives in Paris to discuss the peace treaty. According to Frank Snepp, Kissinger remarked that the DRV and the Provisional Revolutionary Government could not expect much in negotiation concessions since they had not demonstrated their power on the battlefield.[30]

In May 1974, negotiations between the DRV-PRG and the Republic of Vietnam broke down. Gareth Porter indicates that the breakdown resulted from a deliberate effort by the Thieu regime to increase its penetration of PRG zones and end the peace talks because they imparted legitimacy to the enemy. The PRG responded by releasing its main-force units to regain territory; by early fall, most lost ground was regained.[31] In August 1974, President Nixon resigned from office because of Watergate.

Nixon's madman theory of bombing was taken seriously by the DRV since he had ordered the December 1972 bombing raids over Hanoi and Haiphong; they always feared renewed attacks. With Nixon gone, conditions for military offenses seemed more favorable. In October 1974, the Political Bureau and Central Military Committee of the Vietnamese Communist party met to hear a presentation by the General Staff of the People's Liberation Armed Forces (PAVN). The first secretary of the Communist party, Le Duan, summarized the favorable circumstances for renewed revolutionary warfare and the unlikelihood of American intervention by saying, "Now that the United States has pulled out of the South, it will be hard for them to jump back in. And no matter how hard they may intervene, they cannot rescue the Saigon administration from its disastrous collapse."[32] This encouragement did not translate into a grand plan. Instead, objectives for 1975 were conceptualized as a series of possibilities, including the "liberation" of northern South Vietnam and securing two-thirds of the rice harvest from the Mekong Delta for Communist forces. The Communists also wanted an end to Thieu's regime and the formation of a more moderate government with whom negotiations could be held. On October 8, 1973, the Provisional Revolutionary Government radio station announced a PRG policy calling for "an end to the U.S. military involvement and interference in South Vietnam, the overthrow of Nguyen Van Thieu and his clique, and the establishment in Saigon of an administration willing to implement the Paris Agreements seriously."[33]

From December 18, 1974, through January 8, 1975, the Political Bureau met again. A Communist intelligence agent close to Thieu had received word that Thieu and his leading generals thought that the Communists would increase attacks, but would not approach the intensity of either the 1968 or 1972 offensives. It was expected that enemy forces would concentrate on small towns directly south of the DMZ and in the Mekong Delta. Frank Snepp notes that the CIA suspected that four members of Thieu's inner circle were possible Communist agents; however, two of these four suspects had received extensive CIA assistance in establishing their careers and intimacy to Thieu. The possibility of acute embarrassment thwarted efforts to move on those double agents; career advancement and agency reputation came before concern over enemy penetration.[34]

To the DRV, the intelligence agent's revelations had great significance. If Thieu expected an attack in either the far north or far south, then they should attack the middle. The Political Bureau decided on a mass offensive against Ban Me Thout, about 160 miles northwest of Saigon. Le Duan thought that the attacks in 1975 would lay groundwork for a total offensive in 1976. There was another option in the December two-year plan, though. In his book, General Van Tien Dung has the relevant passage in italics: *"if the opportune moment presents itself at the beginning or the end of 1975, we will immediately liberate the South in 1975."*[35] The concept of "opportune moment," or *Thoi Co* in Vietnamese, was a crucial enemy concept implying an offensive seizure of a situation beyond previously established military objectives.

On March 10, 1975, the NVA attacked Ban Me Thout. By late the next night, the city had fallen. President Thieu told his top generals of a new strategic plan entitled "Light at the Top, Heavy at the Bottom." The plan called for ARVN troop withdrawal from the northern part of the country, as well as withdrawals from the Central Highlands. Some troops would be brought south to Saigon, while others would hold onto major coastal cities such as Hue and Danang.

The commander in the Central Highlands of Military Region 2, Major General Pham Van Phu, told that the highlands could not be held without massive air support and replacement troops for casualties. These men and resources were not available — thus the decision to withdraw. In planning retreat, Phu and his staff found that all major roads were interdicted by the enemy. But there was an old, abandoned loggers' road called Route 7B, that as far as anyone knew had no Communist troops. No one knew if the road was usable or whether bridges crossing rivers, streams, and ravines were still intact. On March 15, ARVN divisions began their retreat along this abandoned road. Neither province chiefs nor Regional and Popular Forces were informed — as Montagnards rather than ethnic Vietnamese, they were considered expendable. When the populace became aware of the military pullout, widespread panic ensued. The next day the North Vietnamese army and local Vietcong troops intercepted retreating ARVN forces and their families. Officers abandoned their troops and the army disintegrated under attack.

Hue fell on March 25, and Danang went under five days later. In less than a month 150,000 South Vietnamese troops were taken out of the war. With morale and social cohesion gone, each individual acted for personal survival. What had begun as a campaign with limited political and military objectives became an all-out effort. On March 25, the Political Bureau met and sent new orders: "Our general strategic offensive began with the Tay Nguyen campaign. A new strategic opportunity has come, and conditions allow an early completion of our resolution to liberate the South. We resolve to rapidly concentrate our forces, technological weapons, and materials to liberate Saigon before the rainy season."[36] The rainy season began in late May or early June.

President Gerald Ford's administration had attempted to increase appropriations for Vietnam and Cambodia in January. At the time, though, requests of $300 million for Vietnam and $200 million for Cambodia were largely symbolic, as if public announcement of increased aid would consolidate client regimes. It is questionable whether such funds were even needed. Only $158.4 million of the $700 million appropriation for Vietnam had been spent. Moreover, a Department of Defense logistics team had found some missing war supplies: there were enough artillery shells to fire 18,000 rounds a month for a year. Ambassador Martin attempted to prove that Vietnam needed more aid because Communists were receiving more. Unfortunately, this debit-and-credit accounting exercise showed the opposite: $700 million in military aid for Saigon versus an estimated $300 million in military aid for the foreign Other.[37]

With the March disasters the administration tried again to change the accounts. At first Secretary of State Henry Kissinger supported a proposal to send $722 million in emergency military aid. At a press conference principally concerned with American relationships to Israel and Middle East negotiations he said, "We understand that peace is indivisible. The United States cannot pursue a policy of selective reliability. We cannot abandon friends in one part of the world without jeopardizing the security of friends elsewhere."[38] General Frederick Weyland, head of a special investigating team organized to determine South Vietnam's military needs, also phrased his request in terms of global symbolism:

> The governments of the world know the past, but they will surely see any present failure to support the Vietnamese in their current crisis as a failure of U.S. will and resolve. . . . Continued U.S. credibility, world wide, hinges on whether we make an effort, rather than on an actual successor failure. If we make no effort our credibility as an ally is destroyed, perhaps for generations.[39]

Thus the congressional approval of $722 million would in theory buy a global "credit," regardless of whether or not the Republic of Vietnam ended up on the credit or debit side of the ledger. It is not clear whether Weyland thought that this aid would achieve its "real" aims of reequipping four ARVN divisions composed of men whose units no longer existed and supplying all ARVN forces with enough to fight sixty days.

As days passed and disasters mounted, Henry Kissinger's public comments demonstrated a new concern: "Our objective is to bring about a military stabilization, but if that should fail and the worst should come to pass, then this request will also be the most effective way to bring about the evacuation of Americans and those Vietnamese to whom we have a moral responsibility." As Frank Snepp points out, Kissinger believed "that if a ransom was to be paid for American lives in Saigon, only a kingly sum would do."[40] Money could buy global respect; money could buy the reformation of ARVN; money could buy American lives.

Even in mid-April there was talk in Washington and Saigon about forming a new South Vietnamese government. Polgar didn't believe increased enemy radio messages around Saigon meant attack was imminent. As Frank Snepp reports, "There was a good possibility, he remarked to me on Thursday, that the Communists were merely 'spoofing' — that is, churning out bogus messages to mislead and frighten us."[41] Ambassador Graham Martin had rejected the idea of formulating careful plans for American evacuation. Even in his worst-case scenario, most Americans and their Vietnamese employees would ride buses across town to the Defense Attaché Office to be evacuated by helicopter. Riding buses across town presumed that while the government was falling, civil order in the streets would remain.

But then it all came down. The NVA and Vietcong advanced on Saigon. On April 30, 1975, orders came from Ambassador Martin to *burn all money* while helicopters from the 7th Fleet came in to evacuate. There are several bizarre stories concerning money on that last day. Concerning the embassy, the first goes like this:

> The Marines dumped the cash into metal drums at the far end of the compound, sprinkled on some gasoline, and struck a match.
> But just as the flames swirled through the first container, Bordreau [administrative counselor at the embassy] came running through the crowds. "Stop! Stop!" he shouted. The ambassador had changed his mind. He wanted to keep the money around a bit longer, in case he could work out a last-minute settlement.[42]

Martin thought that a few million dollars would be useful in buying a settlement with the foreign Other when they were winning total victory after thirty years of warfare. Everyone has his price. Over at the Defense Attaché Office there were also problems with burning money:

> Inside the DAO compound itself, a few hundred yards away, Nelson Kief, the DAO staffer from Pleiku, was even then calmly destroying his last classified files. He had just dipped into his last drawerful when he spotted two Army officers outside his window, pouring gasoline into two tin drums. That's a break, he thought to himself, and began bundling up the refuse. By the time he had lugged it outside, the officers had disappeared and the two drums stood unattended. Kief

sidled over to one of them and opened the lid — and nearly fainted at what he saw. Stuffed in the bottom, in neat little bundles, were millions in cash. The gasoline had soaked a few of the bills, but the rest seemed good as new.

Kief stared at the treasure a moment, not quite able to believe his eyes. He knew that earlier in the day General Smith had ordered the last of DAO's cash stocks destroyed. Evidently, what lay in the bottom of the drums was the bonanza itself, over three and a half million dollars in small bills. Only one thing was missing: the single match that would set them all ablaze.[43]

Nelson Kief didn't take any money. "So many other things, more basic, seemed far more important at that moment. The life I'd known for the past three years was disintegrating around me. Many of my Vietnamese friends had been lost. What the hell did I need money for, anyway?"[44] Back at the embassy, people discussed what things cost and what should be taken and what should be left for the Communists. A CIA man walked into one room with two Zenith transoceanic radios and said, "Want one? It's a shame to leave them for the Commies." Polgar replied by kicking a $700 General Electric two-way radio across the room and saying "Yes, take anything you can. The agency has already lost over five million dollars' worth of equipment in this place over the past two months."[45] Ambassador Martin gave up the idea that he could use embassy money for making a deal. For a second time, the money was ordered destroyed. One man saw it happen. Ed Bradley, a correspondent for CBS television news, barely got inside the embassy compound. He looked down a long corridor and saw a conference room illuminated by fluorescent light. Inside, men were burning four and three-quarters million dollars. Bradley remarked that he had finally found "the light at the end of the tunnel."[46]

# CHAPTER 15

# Surveying the Wreckage: The Limits of Conventional Criticism and the Reproduction of Technowar

S OCIETIES go to war, not disembodied foreign policies. After one has found the Light at the End of the Tunnel, the question becomes, "What does one see?" In American society the idea that Vietnam was a mistake of some kind or another was the prevalent conception at least through the early 1970s. This view prevailed not only among serious scholars, but also in public opinion polls. In August 1965, 61 percent favored the war and only 24 percent thought the effort to be an error. By April 1968, 40 percent favored the war while 48 percent saw it as a mistake. By May 1971, only 28 percent thought the war to be worthwhile.[1]

When the United States evacuated Saigon in the spring of 1975, the *Christian Science Monitor* declared that "Many voices, including this newspaper, regard the communist victory as a tragedy, believing the United States involvement in Vietnam to have been honorable, although the conduct of the war in both its political and military phases was fought with *mistakes and misjudgments.*"[2] The *Washington Post* editorialized similarly: "For the fundamental 'lesson' of Vietnam surely is not that we as a people are intrinsically bad, but rather that we are *capable of error* — and on a gigantic scale. That is the spirit in which the post-mortems on Vietnam ought now to go forward."[3] Anthony Lewis, a liberal columnist in the *New York Times,* cast his verdict in the same conceptual framework: "The early American decisions can be regarded as blundering efforts to do good. But by 1969 it was clear to most of the world — and most Americans — that the intervention had become a *disastrous mistake.*"[4]

David Halberstam went to Vietnam as a correspondent for the *New York Times*. His first book on Vietnam was entitled *The Making of a Quagmire* and was published in 1965.[5] Note the metaphor — "quagmire." A quagmire is a kind of swamp, a place where ground gives way once you step on it. Vietnam, then, is a place where things went wrong. Later Halberstam studied elite decision-makers in the Kennedy and Johnson administrations. He called his work *The Best and the Brightest* (1972) and it is about how "intelligent, rational men" ended up in that quagmire.

This formulation of "mistakes" leading to a "swamp" can be found in many other books. Chester L. Cooper, a former State Department official, wrote *The Last Crusade: America in Vietnam* (1970). Chapter 13 is entitled "Tragedy of Errors." He writes in reference to the Kennedy administration, "Once immersed in a swamp, however, it makes little difference whether one slid into it stylishly or not."[6] Townsend Hoopes, formerly undersecretary of the air force from 1967 to early 1969, writes about "The Slippery Slope" and how in 1965 "There was the President and there was the country — waist-deep in the Big Muddy."[7] His book is called *The Limits of Intervention* (1969), and he too argues "that our intervention in 1965 *was misconceived.*"

The most famous formulation of the mistake and quagmire thesis comes from Arthur M. Schlesinger, Jr. in his book *The Bitter Heritage: Vietnam and American Diplomacy 1941–1968* (1969). The relevant passage is worth quoting in full:

> And so the policy of "one more step" lured the United States deeper and deeper into the morass. In retrospect, Vietnam is a triumph of the politics of inadvertence. We have achieved our present entanglement, not after due and deliberate consideration, but through a series of small decisions. It is not only idle but unfair to seek out guilty men. President Eisenhower, after rejecting American military intervention in 1954, set in motion the policy of support for Saigon which resulted, two Presidents later, in American military intervention in 1965. Each step in the deepening of the American commitment was reasonably regarded at the time as the last that would be necessary. Yet, in retrospect, each step led only to the next, until we find ourselves entrapped today in that nightmare of American strategists, a land war in Asia — a war which no President, including President Johnson, desired or intended. The Vietnam story is a tragedy without villains.[8]

Note the key phrase — "We find ourselves entrapped today in that *nightmare.*" As a dream, a nightmare is not *real*. Also, as a dream, it is not something consciously willed or controlled. Instead, "we find ourselves *entrapped* today in that *nightmare.*" The nightmare entrapped the United States. Men only made small decisions. The nightmare is synonymous with the "morass" or "swamp" or "quagmire." Note Schlesinger's beginning sentence. The United States was *"lured . . . deeper and deeper into the morass."*

What is going on here? The war becomes conceptualized as some place *beyond* rational conceptualization — the "swamp," the "quagmire," the "nightmare." "Tragedy" is also a favorite, as if thirty years of American intervention in Vietnam were a Greek play in which the hero is struck down by the gods. In the face of the incomprehensible, absolution: fate decreed defeat.

Schlesinger absolves Lyndon Johnson. The footnoted sentence reads: "President Johnson has made his ultimate objective very clear: he does not seek, he has said, total military victory or the unconditional surrender of North Vietnam, but a negotiated settlement." The footnote reads: "One must *discount* flourishes like the presidential exhortation to the combat commanders in the officers' club at Cam Ranh Bay: 'Come home with that coonskin on the wall.' " [9]

To sustain the central assumption that the war was simply a series of mistakes or miscalculations by rational men, one must discount a lot. The coonskin has racial and sexual overtones. At the time of the Gulf of Tonkin Resolution in 1964, Johnson has been quoted as saying, "I didn't just screw Ho Chi Minh, I cut his pecker off." [10]

At times the intellectual convolutions taken to preserve the sense of rational men acting in a rational system reach unbelievable proportions. In 1979, former Department of Defense analyst Leslie Gelb wrote a book entitled *The Irony of Vietnam: The System Worked*. According to Gelb, the war contained a great paradox: "The paradox is that the foreign policy failed, but the domestic decision making system worked." [11] His explanation has two parts. The first concerns the familiar errors in judgment:

> For liberals, conservatives, and most Americans, however, the argument that a good system produced a disastrous policy is understandably galling. But the painful reality is that if the system failed, it did so in ways almost unavoidable in a democratic regime and represen-

tative institutional pattern of policy-making, or because no system can compensate for *errors in judgment* (or felt needs to gamble on unlikely possibilities) if those errors are pervasive among authorities. Failure of policy cannot automatically be the same as failure of the system; otherwise substance and process are indistinguishable.[12]

In proving how the system works, Gelb concentrates on Washington bureaucracies. He deals with Vietnam briefly. Concerning American and Saigon forces Gelb writes, "These anti-Communist forces could never translate their advantages in total air superiority, dominance in mobility and firepower, and a sizeable edge in manpower into victory. In fact they spent most of the time on the defensive until mid-1968. Something was wrong somewhere. Something always was wrong."[13] As for the other side, Gelb explains their victory: "And certainly Hanoi received massive doses of aid from the Soviet Union and China, although only a fraction of the aid the United States gave to France and Saigon. But something always went right for them somewhere."[14] The entire war has become unreal in these sentences and, since the war isn't real, it doesn't have to be explained.

Nevertheless, Gelb illuminates the entire error in judgment discourse. He summarizes the system that worked: "The system facilitated decision-making of means to reach the end of containment; that end remained virtually unchallenged within the executive branch. The system facilitated decision-making on ways to keep the *costs* as low as possible: the problem was the progressive *inflation* of the lowest possible *costs* of preventing Communist victory."[15]

This passage has a familiar ring to it. The foreign Other from outside, fallen nature, is to be contained. The "debits" and "credits" of mechanistic anticommunism are here, too. "Inflation" of blood and money, the fundamental problem of productivity in war, was a problem that just could not be solved by rational officials. Gelb is not alone in his accountant's reading of Vietnam as a mistake. Edwin S. Reischauer, a former American ambassador to Japan and distinguished Asian scholar, wrote an essay called "Back to Normalcy" after the fall of Saigon. Reischauer also views the big mistake in terms of poor economic forecasting: ". . . the real lesson of the Vietnam War is the tremendous cost of attempting to control the destiny of a Southeast Asian country against the cross-currents of nationalism. Southeast Asia is not open to external control *at a cost that would make this a feasible proposition* for any outside power."[16]

Sociologist Charles Kadushin discovered that this "pragmatic" opposition to the Vietnam War was the most prevalent position among the American intellectual elite. In his words, "The war in Vietnam was opposed by the overwhelming majority of the leading American intellectuals in our sample simply and solely because it did not 'work.' "[17] He quotes one respondent to exemplify this "pragmatic assessment": "You see, my position has always been non-ideological — simply practical. . . . If you want another metaphor, I'm in the position of a *businessman:* "don't open that store. You will go broke." It doesn't mean that this guy is anti-capitalist or something. He simply looks at the situation and arrives at the conclusion that *this enterprise cannot* succeed."[18]

Most scholarly work and media commentary focus on the mistakes of high-level civilian policymakers. But military conduct is also seen as a series of mistakes. Richard A. Gabriel and Paul L. Savage wrote *Crisis in Command: Mismanagement in the Army* (1978). As the subtitle suggests, their work is formulated in terms of mistakes: "The American Army is deeply rooted in our social structure, indeed perhaps too deeply rooted, and for this very reason was no more capable of anticipating and forestalling the *mistakes* it made than is any other social institution."[19]

The authors analyze careerism in the officer corps and the social/physical distance between officers in command and control choppers and grunts on the ground. There is much concurrence between their position and the current analysis. However, as in all error-in-judgment analyses, a point is reached where institutional order is affirmed and a portion of the war vanishes. For Gabriel and Savage, that point concerns Lieutenant Calley; they view Calley as an aberration, a result of an army policy mistake:

> Under the doctrine of "equity," a requirement that all officers must serve at least one tour in Vietnam, the quality of individuals allowed to hold commissioned rank steadily declined from year to year. Eventually, given a contrived "demand," the officer corps could correctly be described as both bloated in number and poorer in quality. One result was My Lai. Even the staunchest defenders of the Army agree that in normal times a man of Lieutenant Calley's low intelligence and predispositions would never have been allowed to hold a commission.[20]

Lieutenant William Calley's experiences, observations, and reflections have been quoted in previous chapters. In his autobiography he said that he did not consider himself to be a successful army officer. Gabriel and Savage's argument on how the production model of war and the army's own career-management orientation reduced the quality of the officer corps has great merit. However, casting Calley and the massacre at My Lai as isolated policy mistakes goes against both their own structural argument and the reports of many scholars, journalists, and soldiers. My Lai seems to have been a particularly well-organized massacre, but both explicit and implicit policies of killing civilians were evident in the everyday conduct of the war. The "Mere Gook Rule" and the harassment and interdiction artillery fires and the "killed by air" productivity charts all resulted in mass killings. To cast Lieutenant Calley as an isolated deviant renders ground war invisible. Even with the "best" management procedures, "errors" such as Lieutenant Calley's commission and assignment to combat platoon command are possible. The critique of Calley as a management error does not lead to the truth about the military system.

Other military studies informed by the military error-in-judgment model share similar limitations. In 1977, Douglas Kinnard, a retired army general who served in Vietnam, published *The War Managers*. It surveys army officers who were generals in Vietnam. The study was conducted in 1974; the questionnaire was confidential. Some of the questions and responses are given below.[21]

|  | *Percentage* |
|---|---|
| Were U.S. objectives in Vietnam prior to Vietnamization (1969) | |
| (1) Clear and understandable | 29 |
| (2) Not as clear as they might have been | 33 |
| (3) Rather fuzzy — needed rethinking as the war progressed | 35 |
| (4) Other | 3 |
| Was the search and destroy concept | |
| (1) Sound | 38 |
| (2) Sound when first implemented — not later | 26 |
| (3) Not sound | 32 |
| (4) Other or no answer | 4 |

Execution of search and destroy tactics was

| | |
|---|---|
| (1) Superior | 7 |
| (2) Adequate | 35 |
| (3) Left something to be desired | 51 |
| (4) Other or no answer | 7 |

Before My Lai became public knowledge [fall of 1969], the rules of engagement were

| | |
|---|---|
| (1) Carefully adhered to throughout the chain of command | 19 |
| (2) Fairly adhered to throughout the chain of command | 61 |
| (3) Not particularly considered in the day-to-day conduct of the war | 15 |
| (4) Other or no answer | 5 |

The kill ratio was based upon the body count. Was body count

| | |
|---|---|
| (1) Within reason accurate | 26 |
| (2) Underestimated | 3 |
| (3) Often inflated | 61 |
| (4) Other or no answer | 10 |

Careerism (i.e., ticket punching, rapid promotion in jobs, etc.) was

| | |
|---|---|
| (1) No problem | 9 |
| (2) Somewhat of a problem | 50 |
| (3) A serious problem | 37 |
| (4) No answer | 4 |

Note how critically these army generals have assessed the war. War objectives were not clear. Search-and-destroy was considered dubious by over half the generals, and execution "left something to be desired." Over 60 percent thought the body count to be inflated, and 87 percent thought careerism was a more or less serious problem. The anonymous questionnaires portray a far different war than do the twenty or so volumes in the army's Vietnam Studies series. Each volume concerns a specific military field, such as armor or airmobile operations, and each is written by a general. Yet the public war portrayed in these works consists of reports on the constant increase of war production over time, of how more artillery rounds were fired and more "bits" of intelligence filed into computer banks. The first sentence of each volume's foreword affirms the army's success: "The United States Army has met an unusually complex challenge in Southeast Asia." This challenge included "superimposing the immensely sophisticated tasks of a modern army in an underdeveloped environment," fulfilling "the basic needs of an agrarian population," and fighting against guerrillas and "well-trained and determined regular units."

No general ever spoke out about the serious problems indicated in the survey. No general ever resigned his commission. To the contrary, almost all got medals (at minimum the "general's packet," in grunt terms) and many received promotions. As the title of Kinnard's book indicates, these men were the army's "war-managers." They ordered reports rewritten, thereby turning real defeats and standoffs into paper victories. These men flew in command and control helicopters above anti-aircraft range. These men instituted the point system for kills, and systems of reward and punishment for over- and underproduction. They flourished in the military's doublethink system.

Lieutenant General W. R. Peers's official army inquiry into the My Lai massacre illustrates the classic split in the military between private assessment and official thought and action. In late November 1969, General Westmoreland, the army chief of staff, directed Lieutenant General Peers to head "The Department of the Army Review of the Preliminary Investigations of the My Lai Incident." The review was thus directed primarily not at what had happened at My Lai, but at the military reporting machine, at how higher levels handled original reports of a massacre.

Peers and his staff had difficulty reconstructing the reporting machine. Witnesses suffered from repeated memory failures. Reports that should have been filed were often missing. Discrepancies in reports were ignored by responsible authorities. The original official account of My Lai listed 128 Vietcong killed and only 3 weapons captured with only one American killed. These are kill ratios and weapons captured–kill ratios far out of line even by inflated standards. Peers found that official complaints registered by one American helicopter pilot and one Vietnamese lieutenant were never investigated. Instead, Peers found that Westmoreland's headquarters — Military Assistance Command Vietnam — had sent a letter of commendation to Calley's battalion for a job well done (high productivity).

The investigating staff was appalled. "Finally we came up with a list of thirty persons who, we felt, had known of the killing of noncombatants and other serious offenses committed during the My Lai operation but had not made official reports, had suppressed relevant information, had failed to order investigations, or had not followed up on investigations that were made." [22] This list included the commander of the Americal Division and several staff officers, the commander of the artillery unit that gave fire support, the commander and several subordinates of the 11th Infantry Battalion (Calley's battalion), the commander of Task Force Barker — the My Lai mission commander and his staff — and several other officers. Peers thought he had sufficient evidence to press charges against fifteen of these men.

Lieutenant Calley was found guilty of ordering and leading the massacre. He was first sentenced to life imprisonment. A military judicial review subsequently reduced his sentence to twenty years; the secretary of the army reduced it to ten. He was soon paroled to "house arrest." Finally President Nixon granted him a pardon. Captain Ernest Medina, Calley's company commander, was found not guilty, as was Captain Kotouc, commander of an adjacent company. Sergeant David Mitchell was also found not guilty of murder. Everyone else implicated in the My Lai affair, from the highest officers to the lowest enlisted men, had court-martial charges against them dismissed. The resolution of My Lai indicates that the army preserved institutional practices.

General Peers recognized that My Lai had ethical implications. When he turned in the results of his investigation, it was accompanied by a letter expressing serious concern about officer morality. Westmoreland immediately classified the letter "secret" and called for a staff study of military professionalism. This task was turned over to the Army War College. Westmoreland informed the War College of its new responsibility on April 19, 1970. The study had to be completed by July 1.

But the Army War College successfully mobilized to meet Westmoreland's deadline. A survey questionnaire was issued to 415 officers. Questions were aimed at discovering if there was significant difference between "ideal" army values such as honesty, integrity, bravery, justice, and responsibility, and "real" values practiced in the military. Responses from officers confirmed that "There are widespread and often significant differences between the ideal ethical/moral/professional standards of the Army and the prevailing standards. . . ." [23] "Prevailing standards" refers to ethics and practices necessary for career advancement. Former West Point graduate and CIA analyst Lewis Sorley dryly noted, "Content analysis of the narrative responses to the study found distortion of reports to be the most prevalent deviation from professional standards observed within the ranks of the officer corps.''[24] The doublethink system was apparently obvious to the officer corps.

Ironically, Westmoreland originally withheld the report so it could be read only by generals — and not by lower-ranking officers whose responses had been surveyed! To compound the irony, authors of the Army War College study noted that the army's atmosphere was such that problems exposed by the study were not ''self-correcting'' and that ''disloyalty to subordinates'' was endemic.

> The present climate does not appear to be self-correcting. The human drives for success and recognition by seniors, sustained if not inflamed by the systems of rewards and management which cater to immediate personal success at the expense of a long term consolidation of moral and ethical strength would appear to perpetuate if not exacerbate the current environment. Time alone will not cure the disease. The fact alone that the leaders of the future are those who survived and excelled within the rules of the present system militates in part against any self-starting incremental return toward the practical application of ideal values.[25]

Eventually restrictions on access to the study were lifted, but the *1970 Study on Military Professionalism* and its sequel, the *1971 Comprehensive Report: Leadership for the 1970s, USAWC Study of Leadership for the Professional Soldier,* remain texts without institutional practice. Technowar won the war; it was a *perfect war.* As General Westmoreland said, ''Good management is good leadership.'' Despite this failure, the War College and other military reform-oriented scholars and officers continued their researches. In 1976 the War College published *U.S. Army Unit Readiness Reporting.* ''Readiness Reporting'' concerns an important annual army report that calls for units to evaluate their ability. Evaluations cover how much equipment and how many people a given unit has in comparison to the ''full'' complement presented in organizational charts. How well trained each unit is is also an indicator of its ''combat-readiness.''

In the ''equipment'' category, a C-1 grade means that a unit has at least 90 percent of equipment in operational condition; C-2 means from 70 to 89 percent. C-3 (60 to 69 percent) is considered ''combat-ready,'' but with ''major deficiencies.'' In practice, this means that a tank platoon that is supposed to have five functioning tanks is considered ready with only three. Personnel-grading criteria are along similar lines, while the training question attempts to measure how many weeks of training it would take to become combat ready.

In a survey of junior officers conducted by the War College staff, 70 percent thought that "a unit's readiness report does not reflect the true readiness condition." Fifty-eight percent thought that their personal integrity was challenged by the evaluation system. Forty percent said that their judgments were influenced by "unjustified pressure" from superior officers. Some divisions were even found to have offered *classes* to their officers on how to fill out forms so that the highest possible grades could be given yet defended if questioned.[26] Not only was the moral atmosphere of the army degraded, but also the ability to fight had been so misrepresented that the system could not fulfill its instrumental goals.

David R. Segal, a civilian scholar, noted that the military does not distinguish "leadership" from "management." The army does not even include the word "leadership" in basic publications for officers, while in other publications it is used interchangeably with "command" and "management." The army's solution to this lexiconal deficiency is not really a solution: "Military leadership is the process of influencing human behavior so as to accomplish the mission of the organization."[27] This definition makes no distinction between the instrumental manipulation of organizational resources to achieve goals and the subjective relationships between officers and troops necessary to motivate a force.

Segal commented on "military community": "The military installation is increasingly less of a community and more of a *workplace* as large numbers of personnel move to off-post housing, do their shopping, and spend their leisure with their civilian peers." Hypothetically, "One could easily compute the cost of building the housing necessary to keep personnel on post," but from the military management-production stance "It is less easy to measure the benefits of maintaining a sense of community within a unit." Segal explained this decline in terms of the difficulty of measuring community in the management model: "The kind of management that is replacing leadership in the modern force has not included such elements in its calculus, however. In an era of cost-benefit analysis and systems analysis, factors that everyone knows are important, but that are difficult to measure, tend to be excluded."[28]

At least one army officer, Stephen D. Wesbrook, cited the disintegration of the American military forces in Vietnam as a starting point for his criticisms, the unwillingness of war-managers "to recognize that political factors have anything to do with soldiers' behavior in combat."[29] His own research in the late 1970s found that "a large percentage of Americans have traditionally regarded wars of colonialism or economic expansion as unjust. To the extent that an American soldier perceives a war to be motivated by these factors, he will also perceive hierarchical demands to be illegitimate.''[30]

In another study Wesbrook showed that the army recruited people in the 1970s and 1980s who were likely to see colonial and economic aspects of intervention in the Third World, namely working-class people and minorities. When the American economy began to collapse in this period, radical critics called the volunteer military a "poverty draft." Racial and ethnic minorities began to comprise upward of 40 percent in many military units. In Wesbrook's assessment, these were the "alienated" members of society, those whose lack of commitment to American society made it "impossible for the Army's leadership to exert the only kind of power that is likely to be effective in modern battle.''[31] Troops outnumber and outgun officers. Wesbrook's reference to the "only kind of power" refers to moral persuasion, the belief in legitimacy; he despaired at the inability of the military hierarchy to recognize such factors:

> The military establishment is also so overly concerned with the instrumental factors of war that it frequently neglects the moral factors; it emphasizes the capacity to fight rather than the will to fight. This is no more evident than in the indicators of combat readiness which the U.S. Army monitors. While keeping scores of statistics on equipment readiness and the state of training, it has not systematically asked whether soldiers trust and like each other, whether they have pride in their units and believe their units would support them in battle, whether they respect and trust their officers and political leaders, whether they know or believe in what they are preparing to fight for, or whether they have an underlying commitment to the worth of their larger political system.[32]

Major Wesbrook compared "unit readiness" in the United States Army to the readiness of the People's Army of Vietnam. He found that in heavy equipment the American military totally dominated the NVA. The NVA's victory, then, was the result of categories not conceptualized by the American military — questions of motivation and organizational cohesion: "the underarmed army, living in great physical deprivation, persevered to eventual victory. The enemy credited this perseverance to a strength produced by political purpose that was itself guided by political training. Perhaps it is time to believe him.''[33]

Wesbrook has great difficulty understanding why good relationships between troops and officers cannot be established by American military leaders. Army studies show that its career-management orientation leads to tremendous individual mobility within the military; in the late 1970s, army units suffered a 130 percent turnover of personnel each year — over 30 percent change in each unit every three months. Wesbrook calls for a "regimental system," whereby troops stay with one unit and units, as opposed to individuals, are rotated overseas. But for all his analytical astuteness, he fails to see why such a change is so difficult: "Such deference to cost factors and administrative efficiency in light of the critical role of primary groups and unit cohesion is inexplicable."[34]

So Wesbrook ends with the inexplicable; Segal ends with an era of cost-effectiveness and systems analysis; the War College ends with a system that is not self-correcting. Of these analyses, the War College comes closest to understanding that the basic production logic of both advanced capitalism and the military views a viable community (soldiers with strong social bonds to one another) as unimportant in contrast to sophisticated technological production and individual material gains.

German social theorist Jürgen Habermas makes analytical distinctions between "system" and "life-world."[35] "System" refers to *instrumental action*, which is governed by technical rules and scientific knowledge. Instrumental action or rationality is what Kissinger saw as the West's great achievement. To produce technically sophisticated war materials requires much scientific knowledge and technical expertise.

However, instrumental action does not preempt social reality. To the contrary, there is the vast "life-world," the world of values, norms, traditions — indeed, the whole world of socially shared meanings and processes among people by which a meaningful tradition and way of life are created. A government may well have the production capacity to destroy a peasant economy with its bombing attacks and provide refugees with modern consumer goods, but this does not imply that the government can force these refugees to believe in the moral worth of such a government. By the same logic, the United States military can provide troops with sophisticated weapons, but the production model of war does not concern itself with the "life-world" questions of history, meaning, and motivation that integrate soldiers into the military and make them willing to fight.

The failure of the military reform movement occurred within the same historical and institutional framework that has given renewed credence to the "self-imposed restraint" explanation of American military defeat in Vietnam. Military command saw both the foreign Other and its own troops as external objects to be manipulated. By blaming defeat on civilian war-managers, top military officials maintained the validity of their past practices toward both. Conversely, admitting the necessity of reform is on the same logical plane as admitting military defeat by the revolutionary armies because the Vietnamese fought better. The theory of self-imposed restraint thus solves two major problems for the officer corps. Insofar as defeat in Vietnam is accepted as self-inflicted, then Technowar and mechanistic anticommunism have not only reproduced themselves, but more importantly have made the intellectual case for increasing the military budget and allowing freer rein to military judgment in future American wars.

Drew Middleton, military correspondent of the *New York Times*, covered the Vietnam War and the military's reaction to its defeat in the 1970s. In January 1982, he published "Vietnam and the Military Mind" in the *New York Times Magazine*. He found that assessments by the officer corps — men who were captains and majors during the war and who now are colonels and generals — tended to center on the same basic vision. Most thought that the battles they had been involved with had ended in American victories. Defeat in Vietnam was thus not their defeat; consequently, blame must be placed elsewhere. Some blame was cast upon the mass media and the antiwar movement, but most was directed toward civilian war-managers — the Presidents and their chosen officials. In the military view, these men formulated policies of "self-imposed restraint" that caused defeat. President Johnson and his staff are criticized the most, since 1966 is taken to be the key year where victory was denied:

> What was needed, most officers believe to this day, was a more *realistic view* of the American involvement — the view that the United States was in Southeast Asia not simply to protect the people and Government of South Vietnam but to win a decisive victory against the *expansionist Communist regime in Hanoi*. This victory, it is felt, could have been won in 1966. The prevalent opinion — as it was among Army and Marine Corps officers I talked to at the time — is that, given sufficient logistical support and freedom of action, the American ground forces could have *invaded North Vietnam, seized the port of Haiphong and taken Hanoi.*[36]

Middleton explicitly asked officers about the consequences of such an invasion: "The argument that even that would not have ended the war

— that our troops would have been condemned to years of occupation duty and combat against guerrilla forces holed up in the jungles — finds no more support among officers today than it did then."[37]

The invasion of the north would have meant a fight to the death for every inch of territory. In 1966 only about 50,000 NVA troops were in the south. This means that the People's Army of Vietnam was in the north, along with hamlet, district, and province militias. In Giap's words, "We would welcome them. They will find themselves caught in people's war; they will find every village a hornet's nest. . . . Every citizen is an enemy killing combatant. Every house is a combat cell; every village or factory a fortress."[38] Historical Vietnamese resistance against the Chinese and French supports Giap's prediction.

The military fantasy of invasion as a way to win the war also ignores the reality of massive internal unrest and social revolution in the south. The Vietcong tremendously expanded their forces in the south in the 1963–1968 period. Yet, as Middleton paraphrases one military officer, "Too much effort, he was sure, was being expended on sideshows, such as programs designed to 'win the hearts and minds' of the South Vietnamese."[39]

Air Force Major General George Keegan expressed an even more extreme view of how "self-imposed restraint" caused American defeat. He thought that bombing alone could have produced victory in 1965:

> The tragedy of Vietnam is that the target system evolved in Washington was the most inept of any war in which modern air power has been committed. Contrary to the judgments held by 99 percent of our defense analysts and political leaders, I for one came out of that war convinced that a bombing campaign like Linebacker II — an eleven day campaign with B-52's, fighter-bombers, F-111's operating at night at two hundred feet, and jamming — could have brought the war to a close as early as 1965. North Vietnam could have been isolated from the battlefield in a matter of weeks and North Vietnam's wherewithal to fight in the South would have been reduced to such proportions that the ground defenders could have managed far more easily than they did.[40]

By the American military's own statistics, the Democratic Republic of Vietnam was isolated from the battlefield in 1965; only a few thousand NVA troops were stationed in the south, as opposed to over 200,000 local Vietcong guerrillas. In their review of 1965, the *Pentagon Papers* spoke of the necessity for a force of several hundred thousand U.S.

troops not in terms of countering an invasion from the north, but in stopping the formation of a provisional revolutionary government and preventing GVN internal collapse!

Fragmentary comments on how "self-imposed restraint" caused American defeat abound, but only two more cases will be examined. The first is from Senator Barry Goldwater, noting how the rules of engagement crippled American forces:

> It is unbelievable that any Secretary of Defense would ever place such restrictions on our forces. It is unbelievable that any President would have allowed this to happen. . . . I am ashamed of my country for . . . such restrictions to have been placed upon men who were trained to fight, men who were trained to make decisions to win war, and men who were risking their lives. I dare say that the restrictions had as much to do with our casualties as the enemy themselves.[41]

Goldwater's comments are quoted by important "revisionists" such as Guenter Lewy in *America in Vietnam* (1978), and Lewy in turn is repeatedly quoted by Norman Podhoretz in his work *Why We Were in Vietnam* (1982). In November 1982, Secretary of Defense Caspar Weinberger represented the Reagan administration at the dedication of the Vietnam veterans memorial in Washington, D.C. There, Mr. Weinberger proclaimed that the United States would never again ask its men to "serve in a war that *we did not intend to win.*"[42]

There is a more comprehensive version of the self-imposed restraint position in Colonel Harry G. Summers, Jr.'s book, *On Strategy: A Critical Analysis of the Vietnam War* (1982). The 1982 date refers to its commercial publication; apparently it had already been in classroom use at the Army War College. Colonel Summers begins by indicating the "paradox" of American victory in all battles, yet defeat in war:

> One of the most frustrating aspects of the Vietnam War from the Army's point of view is that as far as logistics and tactics were concerned *we succeeded in everything we set out to do*. At the height of the war the Army was able to move almost a million soldiers in and out of Vietnam, feed them, clothe them, house them, supply them with arms and ammunition, and generally sustain them better than any Army had ever been sustained in the field. To project an Army of that size halfway around the world was a logistics and management task of enormous magnitude, and we have been more than equal to the task. On the battlefield itself, the Army was unbeatable. In engage-

ment after engagement the forces of the Viet Cong and of the North Vietnamese Army were thrown back with terrible losses. Yet in the end, it was North Vietnam, not the United States, that emerged victorious. How could we have succeeded so well, yet failed so miserably? That disturbing question was the reason for this book.[43]

From literally page one Colonel Summers has assumed the managerial perspective and confirmed the military reporting machine; he takes these "victories" as established facts, exempt from critical scrutiny. From the beginning, the cause of defeat must be found *elsewhere*. This is a brilliant move by any rhetorical standard. From this beginning, the central thesis flows with compelling logic.

Summers's thesis is that there was no "real" guerrilla war in the south, nor were "pacification" and the creation of the GVN important tasks. Instead, nationalism and guerrilla war were but "screens" behind which the foreign Other could progress. Summers articulates this theme over and over again in his 200-page analysis. He quotes a foreign service officer who thought the Vietcong were just decoys: "In South Vietnam we responded mainly to Hanoi's *simulated* insurgency rather than to its real but controlled aggression, as a bull charges the toreador's cape, not the toreador."[44] Summers moans: "But instead of orienting on North Vietnam — the source of war — we turned our attention to the symptom — the guerrilla war in the south."[45] Having been tricked, Summers thought we deployed our forces incorrectly: "It caused the United States to deploy against a secondary force [guerrillas] and exhaust itself in the effort. It also employed the Army of South Vietnam to deploy in such a manner that it could not be massed to meet a North Vietnamese cross-border conventional attack."[46]

Summers ignores the historical record. As Westmoreland indicated in his memoirs, most American ground troops were deployed in the border regions; they were not engaged in pursuit of guerrillas. Giap indicated that this was his strategy — to draw American troops into relatively unpopulated areas so that guerrillas and political cadres could pursue their tasks.[47] There was no mass cross-border conventional attack until the spring of 1972, a full seven years after American ground combat troops had been committed.

But facts do not matter in Summers's argument; his rhetoric is compelling. He even accuses the North Vietnamese of lying in their own Communist party publications to deceive the United States: "Not only are their doctrinal manuals not available, the material that is available primarily reflects North Vietnamese declaratory strategy which was designed to continue the smokescreen of revolutionary war to mask their own aggression.''[48] The foreign Other publishes lies, a most attractive thought. Frank Snepp of the CIA indicates that the embassy failure to receive its normal Communist party publications in late winter and early spring of 1975 was a major reason for American analysts' failure to see the Light at the End of the Tunnel: the mails had been messed up.[49] Communist parties are strong on publishing, much like academicians. Summers is the *only* analyst who has accused the North Vietnamese of using their party publications as a way of deceiving Americans. Even if it were true, being taken in by a Communist party document is not much of a defense. Presumably, this is why governments have many intelligence agencies collecting and analyzing the same data.

Having demonstrated gross errors in fighting deceptive guerrillas, Colonel Summers indicates what should have been done. If "the strategic error was in calling for the reinstitution of pacification programs in Phase Two," then strategic correctness resided in "containing communist expansion." Summers quotes his mentor, General Dave Richard Palmer:

> In a seminar at the U.S. Army War College, he said that, together with an expanded Naval blockade, the Army should have taken the tactical offensive along the DMZ across Laos to the Thai border in order to isolate the battlefields and then deliberately assume the strategic and tactical defensive. While this strategy might have entailed some of the long-term costs of our Korean strategy [attrition warfare], it would (like that strategy) have furthered our political objectives in containing communist expansion.[50]

Summers's book offers nothing new, just the same old Technowar. There are no references to the *Pentagon Papers*, no references to the works of Mao and Giap, and no references to the hundreds of novels and memoirs published by soldiers or reports by feature journalists. As a "critique" that uses basically official information, the army's most advanced statement on Vietnam recapitulates dogma.

If failure in Vietnam is understood as the result of "not enough," then only continued military growth offers the possibility of foreign policy success. In fiscal year 1950, $13 billion went to defense. This figure increased to $47 billion by 1961, the increase marking a decade that included the Korean War, American assistance first to the French and later to Diem in Vietnam, and the buildup of strategic nuclear forces.

In 1968, $107.8 billion was allocated to the Department of Defense. Official costs for 1969 and 1970 were also high, $103.7 and $94.5 billion respectively, but by 1973, when the Paris Peace Accords were signed, outlays had dropped to $73.5 billion. Although "common sense" indicates that the military budget would fall further now that the war was over, 1974 and 1975 saw increases to $87 and $100 billion.[51] In 1976 James Earl Carter, Democratic candidate for president, promised a 5 percent reduction. Once elected, real military purchasing power exceeded inflation. By March 1980, this increase was presented as a significant accomplishment: "[whereas] defense spending dropped by one third in those eight years before I became President, outlays for defense spending [have] been increased every year."[52]

These increases did not buy American control over other countries. To the contrary, 1976–1980 contained several upheavals which lessened American hegemony. In Nicaragua the Sandinista National Liberation Front overthrew the Somoza family regime (the Somozas had been installed by U.S. Marines in 1933). In Iran, Mohammed Reza Pahlavi had come to power in a 1954 coup organized by the CIA. After his son's overthrow in 1979, American embassy officials were held hostage for over a year. Guerrilla war also broke out in El Salvador.

Ronald Reagan replaced Mr. Carter as President in 1980. During his campaign he promised to increase military expenditures and he has been faithful to his promise. By 1984, military planning called for spending around $200 billion. More important, the Reagan administration has called for spending $1.8 trillion between 1984 and 1988.[53] Historically, major weapons systems have cost over three times their original estimates. Recent systems have gone way beyond a threefold multiple.[54] Weapons procurement constitutes $670.8 billion of this $1.8 trillion. From 1980 through 1983, the rate of weapons procurement vastly exceeded the weapons and materials bought during the Vietnam buildup from 1965 to 1968.[55] In economic expenditures, the United States fought a more intense war in the early and mid-1980s than it did in the 1960s and plans to fight an even greater one in the late 1980s.

Industrial engineer and economist Seymour Melman analyzed relationships between defense expenditures and the U.S. economy. His findings help provide a grasp of what these large military budgets signify.

> By capital I mean production resources. The money expression we'll
> call finance capital. In the United States from 1951 to the present year

[1983], the finance capital allocated to the military functions in this society has exceeded, every year, the net profits of all corporations. That means that the state has become the principal controller of finance capital.[56]

Melman provides United Nations statistics comparing ratios of military expenditures to fixed capital (buildings, machinery) in several different countries. For example, in 1979 the United States spent $33 on the military for every $100 industry spent in securing the means of production; this ratio compares to $20 to $100 spent by West Germany and a mere $3.70 to $100 spent by Japan. Melman says that the Soviet Union does not publish detailed statistics, but he estimates a $66 to $100 ratio. From 1946 through 1981, the United States has spent $2,001 billion on defense and that from 1981 through 1988 it will spend another $2,089 billion. This means that from 1946 to 1985 United States military budgets will have surpassed "more than 100 percent of the material reproducible national wealth, which means *the money value of everything man-made on the surface of the United States*, excluding the money value assigned to the land." The Reagan administration's projections for increased expenditures will achieve parity yearly. By 1988 the United States will be spending $87 for the military for every $100 of fixed capital formation in the civilian economy.[57]

The rise of the military has had deleterious effects on the American economy. By 1965 many American corporations were emulating the defense contractor practice of "passing cost increases along to price rather than striving to offset them by their internal methods [to increase productivity]." American engineering has also adopted the military practice of designing objects that achieve "maximum" performance (on paper) regardless of cost. Consequently, American goods have become less competitive on both domestic and world markets. Industrial decline and high unemployment in traditional manufacturing areas have become important social problems. Defense expenditures together with interest payments on the national debt (a debt created through past wars and military expenditures) take up more than 60 percent of the federal budget. Remaining funds are no longer adequate to maintain basic public infrastructures — roads, railways, water and sewage systems, educational and health care systems, and so forth. Melman fears the projected military increases:

> My judgment is that in the course of attaining that level of use of capital for the military, the industrial system of the United States and

the infrastructure of American society will be driven to *conditions of deterioration so severe as to render it problematic* whether it's possible to plan, let alone execute, a return of ordinary workaday production competence.[58]

Thus, although Technowar has its social base in advanced capitalism, the historical record points to a contradiction between military growth to achieve world dominance and subsequent social deterioration. "Defense" no longer "defends." Structural conflict between Technowar and civilian society has emerged. Only radically different foreign and military policies can lead to a breakthrough in restructuring and revitalizing the public sector and the civilian economy, but mechanistic anticommunism and the production model of war still constitute the parameters of serious political discourse. Read carefully Major General William W. Hoover's 1982 testimony before the House Subcommittee on Procurement and Military Nuclear Systems describing U.S. strategic nuclear forces as an industrial enterprise:

The nuclear development and production programs are unique in government in that they constitute an integrated government-owned industry. . . . We are, ladies and gentlemen, talking about, in terms of assets and products, what would be a major U.S. industrial corporation — one that would rank in the upper quarter of the Fortune 500.

I would like you, therefore, to consider yourselves the board of directors of that corporation and my remarks to you the prospectus of our company's future. The record of this testimony will serve as our report to the stockholders — the American taxpayers.

*Assets:*
From the air, our production plant looks like a cross section of American industry. Once on the inside, one begins to see the extent and diversity of their capabilities.

*Product Line:*
Strategic weapons.
Long-range theater nuclear systems.
Battlefield nuclear systems.
Fleet air defense.

These systems constitute the near-term product line of our weapons industry. It is an impressive array, but as a product-oriented industry, we must ask: Can we keep up with the demand, and what about preparations for new products in the future?

*Investment Strategy:*

If I may ask you again to think of the weapons complex as a business, I believe you will agree that in responding to these challenges it is important that we consider not just the program's immediate needs, but rather our objectives, goals, and resource requirements in the context of a long-term investment strategy. Our aim is to:

1. Provide sufficient capacity to meet the current and planned production workload;
2. Increase personnel levels in the weapons laboratories;
3. Increase nuclear testing;
4. Restore the complex to modern industrial standards.

Mr. Chairman, in closing I want to say that this government-owned industry we are managing is basically sound. There is a strong demand for our products for the foreseeable future and, if we are prudent in our care of existing facilities and equipment and future acquisitions, it will be a strong competitor in the world for the long term.[59]

If nuclear production is oriented for the "long term," then increased production of conventional forces constitutes a short-term strategy.

Calls for new intervention in the Third World came before the Vietnam War ended. In 1974 retired General Maxwell Taylor published an essay in *Foreign Affairs* which said that international stratification between the wealthy Western countries and the poor Third World countries was increasing. Given this gap between rich and poor, the United States "may expect to fight for our national valuables against envious 'have-nots.'" Taylor presented a familiar solution: "In this troubled world which I have postulated . . . we shall need mobile, ready forces to deter, or in some cases, suppress, such conflicts before they expand into something greater."[60] Taylor's ideas are old ones, first articulated in chapter 8, "Flexible Response — A New National Program," of his book *The Uncertain Trumpet* (1960).

In 1979 Army Chief of Staff General Bernard W. Rogers announced plans for a "Unilateral Force" of 100,000 men prepared to fight in "the Persian Gulf, Middle East, Northeast Asia," and other non-European battlefields. Later the name was changed to "Rapid Deployment Force." In 1980, General P. X. Kelley publicly articulated deployment strategy for the RDF: "A pre-emptive strategy to me means that we get forces into an area rapidly, irrespective of the size, because once you get a force into an area that is not occupied by the other guy, then you have changed the whole calculus of the crisis, and he must react to you, and you not to him."[61] From 1980 to 1983, the Rapid Deployment Force grew from 100,000 to between 200,000 and 300,000 men.

Defense planning also called for more air transports, the C5-A and even newer planes, as well as more air tankers to refuel them. "Near-Term Prepositioning Ships" are to be loaded with equipment and stationed near potential sites of military interventions. Three hundred thousand marines are supposed to use these vessels. In summary, American military forces are being prepared for fast movement. The "self-imposed restraint" school concerning Vietnam has succeeded in doctrinally and technologically overcoming the "fault" posed by its own assessment that the United States did not intervene quickly enough with overwhelming firepower.

A "target zone" has been articulated by the Reagan administration — Central America. Revolution in Nicaragua and guerrilla war in El Salvador have been conceptualized by Reagan administration officials as conflicts in which the domino theory applies. In March 1983, President Reagan addressed the elite "Commonwealth" group in San Francisco:

> If they get a foothold, and with Nicaragua already there, and El Salvador should fall as a result of this armed violence on the part of guerrillas, I think Costa Rica, Honduras, Panama, all of these would follow.
>
> We believe that the government of El Salvador is on the front line in a battle that is really aimed at the very heart of the Western Hemisphere — and eventually at us.[62]

Public acceptance of Asian dominoes suffered from the fact that the Pacific Ocean separated Asia from the United States. The idea of these hordes of Asian Communists crossing the Pacific sometimes strained the limits of belief. Situating the premier domino within the American landmass solves this problem; the foreign Other will march northward from the south.

Low-intensity or "sublimited" warfare by the United States is already under way in Central America. Hundreds of millions of dollars' worth of military equipment was supplied to El Salvador from 1980 through 1986. Officially, there are fifty-five American military trainers in El Salvador, but this figure does not include CIA personnel, military men serving in El Salvador under "temporary duty" (as opposed to "permanent change of duty" classification), and "civilians" hired by American paramilitary corporations, but serving in an official capacity.

Comments on the Salvadoran military have a similar, negative ring. One analyst said: "At least 60 percent of the troops we have there are not there voluntarily. Even many of the ones who volunteer join because of socio-economic reasons. There is nothing better for them to do now, at least in the army they are going to have a bunk and food."[63] Once recruited, most soldiers receive only "on-the-job" training in search-and-destroy tactics.

To compensate for military failures on the ground, the United States reached for an old remedy. In 1984–1985, planes and bombs sufficient to escalate radically the air war in El Salvador were provided — nine A-37 jet fighter-bombers, two AC-47 gunships, at least ten 0-2 spotter planes, six Hughes 500 helicopters, and forty-three Bell UH-1 helicopters. By July 1985, this air armada was dropping at least forty tons of bombs a month together with several hundred air-to-ground rockets and many thousands of rounds of machine-gun fire.

To control the newly concentrated rural populace, a complementary CORDS-type program has also been implemented. As one U.S. military source said, "CORDS is probably the best analogy I can think of, although this plan has their [Salvadoran] own conceptions in it."[64] Consumption of beans and rice and possibly tin roofing will thus accompany rural destruction.

Neighboring Guatemala also has a counterinsurgency war under way. In 1954 the Central Intelligence Agency sponsored a coup against the elected president of Guatemala, Jacobo Arbenz Guzmán.[65] The United States provided extensive financial and military assistance until 1977, when President Carter cut off aid because of human rights violations. President Reagan renewed assistance in 1981. By 1982 the expanded program included some familiar terminology.

> "This entire area is Vietnamized," said Lieutenant Camilo Salvatierras. He was pointing on the map to an area north of Chajul in the highlands of Quiche Province in Guatemala. Lieutenant Salvatierras explained that "Vietnamized" means that "guerrillas have politicized the population."
>
> In the town of Nebaj, a Captain Hernandez told me, "The guerrilla is the peasant himself. We can't tell who they are." Hanging on the wall behind him was a map of Guatemala. Although it was partially covered with a red cloth, I could see the words "Hanoi," "Saigon"

and "Angola" printed in large letters. When I asked Hernandez about the names, he replied, "Oh, you are not supposed to see that. That's why it's covered. It refers to military areas."[66]

Officers believe that the tactics used in Vietnam were correct, but that the United States should have shown "more resolve." " 'We are a poor army, but we are strong like steel,' Captain Hernandez boasted." The man who replaced President Arbenz, General Carlos Castillo Armas, graduated from the U.S. Army Command and General Staff College at Leavenworth, Kansas.[67] Hundreds of other Guatemalan officers have also graduated from American military training programs.

Some Americans have even taught Guatemalans the names of pacification programs in Vietnam along with the strategy of confining population to controlled camps. Beatrice Manz, writing in the *Nation*, found that the New Life strategic hamlet program was alive and well:

> I asked a young woman at New Life how she had gotten there.
> "The army brought us."
> "What if you had refused to come?"
> "We would have died of hunger."
> "Why?"
> "Because we could no longer make fires to cook our food. They would have been detected by the army. We were afraid of the army. They would kill you. Even if they found you walking along the road, they would kill you."
> "Did the army burn your crops?"
> "No, they burned the houses. The *milpas* [cornfields] they cut down with machetes."[68]

The United States war against Nicaragua has been somewhat better reported than the insurgencies in El Salvador and Guatemala. In 1981 the CIA began recruiting former members of Somoza's National Guard. John D. Negroponte, American ambassador to Honduras, and General Gustavo Adolfo Alverez, head of the Honduran military, directed this operation. Originally, America planned to use Argentinian intelligence and paramilitary operatives to train Nicaraguan exiles, but Argentina withdrew in 1982 after the United States supported Great Britain in its war with Argentina over the Falkland, or Malvinas, Islands. At least fifty American soldiers replaced Argentinians as advisers and commanders of the new counterrevolutionary army.[69]

By the spring of 1983 an exile force of 5,000 to 7,000 men had been trained, equipped, and led into battle against the Sandinistas. At the same time the United States began conducting joint military exercises with Honduran soldiers near the Nicaraguan border. American military men left much equipment behind after the maneuvers for the Hondurans and the CIA-directed exile force; the war games were both practice for the Rapid Deployment Force and a "cover" for moving supplies to the "contras." The United States also dispatched electronic surveillance warships to the Gulf of Fonseca, a small body of water on the west coast of Central America bordering Nicaragua, Honduras, and El Salvador. Fifty air force personnel were assigned to operate a massive radar installation in Tegucigalpa, Honduras, capable of detecting and tracking aircraft for 200 nautical miles — a range sufficient to cover El Salvador, almost all of Nicaragua, and at least 60 percent of Guatemala.[70] Military construction engineers began work on at least six major airfields and scores of minor ones in 1983. Plans were made for building a $150 million port and base area on the Honduran Atlantic coast.[71] Runways, ports, and prepared bases mean that the Rapid Deployment Force can fly in, pick up its heavy weapons and tactical air support, and go to war — all from a safe rear area.

From 1983 through 1986, the United States consistently escalated its military activities against Nicaragua. Additional Big Pine maneuvers rotated thousands of U.S. troops in and out of Honduras and brought supplies to the contras. More runways were prepared and bases improved. The CIA's exile army has been increased to 15,000 to 20,000 men; their attacks inside Nicaragua have killed thousands, but have not won many adherents among the general populace. Faced with political defeat and military stalemate, the United States may well engage in further military escalation to change debit to credit. The history of Technowar certainly points in that direction.

Ten years after defeat in Vietnam, then, the United States once again prepares for war. If the war does not occur in Central America, then there is possible U.S. intervention against the growing insurgency in the Philippines, and if not there, then perhaps South Africa. In many ways, the particular country does not matter. As long as popular insurgencies that challenge vast economic inequality, racial and ethnic oppression, and fight for national independence continue to be conceptualized as bogus causes masking encroachment by a unified Communist machine, then the United States will find almost endless opportunities for another Vietnam.

A new war will not redeem U.S. defeat in Vietnam. There is no such thing as "new, improved" Technowar that will produce more value for the investment.[72] There is no way to move peasants 100 miles and place them in concentration camps without disrupting their lives. There is no way to torture people humanely. Nor can rules of engagement be devised that distinguish between guerrillas and civilians, since they live and work together and often are the same people.

Instead, another major war against a popular insurgency only offers the prospect of more death and destruction. The insurgents will suffer the most, but American soldiers will die, too. Since the same mechanistic theory of revolutionary war informs the war-managers today as it did over thirty years ago, and since the same organizational dynamics characterize today's military, the redeployment of Technowar can only result in another massive defeat. To finally understand the American defeat in Vietnam is to understand how the United States both created and became entrapped by a mythology and a war-production system. And with such understanding, changing the war system and mythology, and creating a more complex, humane, vision of the world, become compelling obligations.

APPENDIX

# The Warrior's Knowledge: Social Stratification and the Book Corpus of Vietnam

T HE warrior's knowledge as expressed in memoirs, novels, poems and plays by the soldiers, together with reports by oral historians and essay journalists, posits a literature about the war that contradicts the war-managers at virtually every level. Yet these narratives have failed to influence the conventional assessments by both the "error in judgment" and the "self-imposed restraint" schools. How can a major war like Vietnam be absorbed into the historical record without listening to those who fought the war, especially when over 200 books have been written by soldiers and their close observers?[1] What are the tacit rules governing "legitimate" knowledge about the war, and how have they marginalized and discredited the warrior's knowledge?

To investigate the warrior's knowledge within the corpus of Vietnam books requires examining the warrior's place within the system of social stratification. The rules that structure social acceptance or rejection of claims to serious knowledge cannot be simplistically reduced to the class and status position of an author, but neither can knowledge be understood totally free of its social context. Social position is particularly important in the study of war. As one soldier wrote in his book's introduction:

> I was also inhibited by the fact that I was a low-level actor in the over-all sweep of events that unfolded around me in Vietnam. Captains don't write the histories of wars — generals inherit that task. The whole world awaited General Westmoreland's memoirs, but who would be interested in the thoughts of one of the thousands of junior officers who served in Vietnam? Each time I was tempted to write, I reminded myself of this.[2]

A basic conceptualization of the relationships between knowledge and social stratification has been present throughout this analysis. War-managers are at the top of the stratification system. They think in instrumental categories taken from technology and production systems, and the business accounting rationales of the debit and credit ledger.

Those at the top of the stratification system had a virtual monopoly on socially accepted "scientific" knowledge. Conflict among different war-managers was quite common, yet these conflicts all occurred within the paradigm of Technowar and its technical knowledge about the war. Never was the "otherness" of the foreign Other really questioned, nor was the social world of the Vietnamese peasantry examined, nor were the terrible contradictions and double-reality facing U.S. soldiers in the field ever confronted. Debates at the top were only debates and struggles concerning the direction of Technowar, not a questioning of its basic assumptions.

Conversely, those closer to the bottom of the stratification system — the soldiers, the Vietnamese peasantry, and, in a way, the Vietcong and NVA — saw the world more in terms of social relationships where questions of "meaning" were more important. It was not as if these different groups shared the same homogeneous body of knowledge, but rather that their horizons for conceptualization concerned social relationships, not mechanistic formulations. For the Communist party, those relationships involved the dynamics of revolution — mobilizing and uniting the people to counter the technological superiority of the Americans. For the peasantry, those social relationships included their relationships with landlords and GVN officials, with the Vietcong, and with the Americans. For the American soldiers, both their relationships with the Vietnamese and with their own commanders formed the bases for their warrior's knowledge.

Soldiers' novels, memoirs, poems, and interviews repeatedly contradict the system formulations of Technowar. The warrior's knowledge falls under Michel Foucault's conception of *"subjugated knowledges."* Such knowledge is below the threshold of "scienticity," not in the sense that its propositions are poorly formed or that its claims to knowledge are always invalid, but rather that such stories or accounts do not follow the social and intellectual rules governing who can be a serious thinker and the correct form for serious ideas and important facts:

> On the other hand, I believe that by subjugated knowledges one should understand something else, something which in a sense is al-

together different, namely a whole set of knowledges that have been disqualified as inadequate to their task or insufficiently elaborated: naive knowledges, located low down on the hierarchy, beneath the required level of cognition or scienticity. I also believe that it is through the re-emergence of these low-ranking knowledges, these unqualified, even directly disqualified knowledges (such as that of the psychiatric patient, of the ill person, of the nurse, of the doctor — parallel and marginal as they are in the knowledge of medicine — that of the delinquent, etc.), and which involve what I would call a popular knowledge *(le savoir des gens)* though it is far from being a general, commonsense knowledge, but is on the contrary a particular, local, regional knowledge, a differential knowledge incapable of unanimity and which owes its forces only to the harshness with which it is opposed by everything surrounding it — that it is through the re-appearance of this knowledge, of these local popular knowledges, these disqualified knowledges, that criticism performs its work.[3]

"Genealogy" is Foucault's term for the systemic study of subjugated knowledge. Genealogies transform a particular corpus of subjugated knowledge according to the intervention of "erudite" or theoretical knowledge: "Let us give the term genealogy to the union of erudite knowledge and local memories which allows us to establish a historical knowledge of struggles and to make use of this knowledge tactically today."[4] Genealogies challenge the normal, established relationships between power and knowledge:

What it [genealogies of knowledge] really does is to entertain the claims to attention of local, discontinuous, disqualified, illegitimate knowledges against the claims of a unitary body of theory which would filter, hierarchise and order them in the name of some true knowledge and some arbitrary idea of what constitutes a science and its objects. Genealogies therefore are not positivistic returns to a more careful or exact form of science. They are precisely anti-sciences. Not that they vindicate a lyrical right to ignorance or non-knowledge: it is not that they are concerned to deny knowledge or that they esteem the virtues of direct cognition and base their practice upon an immediate experience that escapes encapsulation in knowledge. It is not that with which we are concerned. We are concerned, rather, with the insurrection of knowledges that are opposed primarily not to the contents, methods or concepts of a science, but to the effects of the centralizing powers which are linked to the institution and functioning of an organized scientific discourse within a society such as ours.[5]

An example of "the effects of centralizing powers" concerns funding of social science research on Vietnam. Colonel Corson reports that $650 million was spent between 1963 and 1968. Corson concluded from his extensive review of the research that "while it may be good politics to berate the Administration, it is poor business for a nonprofit think tank to come up with an analysis contrary to the interest of their paymaster."[6]

But the marginalization of the warrior's knowledge versus the hegemonic monopoly of Technowar within the terrain of intellectual discourse is only partially a result of the relationships between research institutes and government funding agencies. Relationships between the "centralizing powers" and the "functioning of an organized scientific discourse within a society such as ours" include other aspects of how a society organizes different kinds of knowledge. Three different divisions "separate" the official knowledge of Technowar from the warrior's knowledge.

The first level involves the preferred bureaucratic "sites" of knowledge. Technowar as a regime of mechanical power and knowledge posits the high-level command positions of the political and military bureaucracies as the *legitimate* sites of knowledge. Top-level knowledge is not considered to be one level among many in a complex system, but rather holds the structurally key position for knowledge: those at the top know "more"; they have access to all the reports funneled upward by the reporting machine with its prestigious technologies of communication — the photo reconnaissance and electronic intelligence information, the systems analysis studies of kill ratios and pacification reports, and all the other secret reports. From all this information, those at the top see "the big picture," the way in which all of the parts come together to constitute the whole. Those at the top make decisions and consequently "know" how and why decisions were made. Those at the top are "inside"; everyone else is "outside."

To the intellectual world, the memoirs and retrospective analyses of administration officials and high-ranking military men represent the means of incorporating Vietnam into the academic structure of disciplines — Vietnam as a case study for the intellectual progress of economics, political science, sociology, international relations, and history. To current and potential high-level decision-makers, knowledge by previous war-managers potentially bears upon future policies for war.

When academicians study the war they most often assume the *tacit* position of a high-level war-manager and make great note of their penetration to the bureaucratic "inside." The first page of the preface to Guenter Lewy's *America in Vietnam* is completely devoted to establishing his high-level access to "undisclosed," bureaucratic knowledge previously available only to commanding war-managers. The key paragraph reads:

> This book is the first work dealing with the Vietnam war which, in addition to *standard* sources, makes use of the *classified records* of the U.S. Army, Air Force, and Marine Corps — after-action reports of military operations, field reports and staff studies of the pacification effort and the Phoenix program, intelligence reports, investigations of war crimes, and the like. As one would expect, the picture that emerges is both novel and occasionally startling in both fact and significance.[7]

The standard sources in question are indeed the standard sources — other memoirs, retrospective analyses, and high-level reports previously released. Classified reports provide more production data. Social stratification designates command positions as the only legitimate sites of knowledge. The warrior's knowledge, emanating from lower-level officers and enlisted men is local and limited by definition, a mere inventory of "events" in comparison to the more generalized reports from the top. High-powered "truth" and high political-bureaucratic position go together.

Ultimately, the restriction of serious discourse to those who formerly held top-level positions or analysts who tacitly conceived and wrote their works from a high-level position tends to restrict the kind of theories offered as explanations. Where the "inside" is the only acceptable source of information, then analysis becomes the complete prisoner of the reporting machine because there is no "outside" from which to gain perspectives on how the system actually operated. Bureaucratic logic — the production model — becomes the invisible ground from which the error-in-judgment position formulates its criticisms of too much production or bankrupt production and the invisible ground from which the "self-imposed restraint" school sees the war in terms of too little production. In this way the limits of intellectual debates are confined to the basic parameters of Technowar. Lewy's special sources are official reports and his research attempts to demonstrate that the war was governed by science, management, law, and rational decision-making. This relation between research sources and rational war is not coincidental by any means, but instead represents how the regime of power and knowledge functions; power attempts to monopolize "truth" to legitimate itself.

In contrast, the warriors are spread throughout the hierarchy, from some colonels and majors, to more numerous captains and lieutenants and finally to the enlisted men. No single "logical structure of propositions" informs their memoirs and novels and poems. The grunt turned novelist may well make claims to knowledge concerning how the war was dishonestly conducted, yet simultaneously support the domino theory. The warrior's knowledge is not homogeneous; its insights and concepts and "supporting data" are not laid out in readily understood sequence, but are instead embedded in thousands of *stories*.

Regardless of propositional content, the story form marks the warrior's knowledge as marginal within the terrain of serious discourse. This third analytical level in studying the corpus of Vietnam concerns the form of discourse, or "genre" and "style." The socially accepted legitimate knowledge of Technowar follows the normal academic form of discourse. Such books are inevitably "nonfiction" and are divided into chapters with subtheses in each chapter and have footnotes, indexes, and bibliographies that situate the book in a referential field of other accepted works.

By contrast, the books comprising the warrior's knowledge all appear as completely separate entities, individual creations of their authors having no ostensible relationships among each other. The novel, the journalist's collection of insights and interviews with men in battle, the poem, and the low-level memoir are "genres" or forms of discourse that rarely cite other works. They are taken to be artistic endeavors, each work an expression of the imagination and writing ability of its author, rather than as claims to knowledge sharing similar insights and propositions to other "low-level" works.

Prose style in the top-level, generalized works of Technowar follows the normal academic practice as well. It is a prose style with a very unpoetic poetic, no puns, metaphors, or alliteration. Within university English departments, this type of writing is known as the "official style," and is the same educated prose style used throughout the major institutions of the society. Its relative homogeneity contrasts to the many different ways language is used by the soldiers.

One way to understand the difference is to note that the warrior's knowledge is most often written in *colloquial* language as opposed to educated prose; it is often *obscene* language as well. Some obscenities are the normal expletives, but words like "gook" and "crispy critters" tell the reader about a world different from the one described in official accounts of a war against communism, battles against Vietcong and NVA troops, and the categories of casualty reports. If all intellectual discourse must be written in "civil" terms, then the warrior's knowledge is automatically moved to the margins. And if all intellectual discourse communicates through the official style of writing, then the stylistic efforts of novelists, poets, and journalists *discredit* the claims to knowledge contained within their works. In other words, the regime of power and knowledge reads aesthetics as a definitive sign of no truth.

Technowar thus monopolizes "organized scientific discourse" through multiple, but centralizing relationships among high-level bureaucratic position, technobureaucratic or production logic in the structure of its propositions, and the conventional educated prose style. The debate on Vietnam occurs within this unity. As Foucault says, "Every educational system is a political means of maintaining or modifying the appropriation of discourse, with the knowledge and the powers it carries with it."[8]

Having established these fundamental contrasts between the official terrain of serious discourse and the warrior's knowledge, it is necessary to understand the structure of the "low-level" corpus in terms of how books differ according to their origin in the military hierarchy. Low-level officers, the lieutenants and captains, shared basically the same horizons of experience as did enlisted men — in combat, that is. The middle-level commanders, however, had some access to more senior war-managers as well as access to the experiences of their subordinates; battalion commanders in the ground war and squadron commanders in the air war had very wide-ranging experiences.

Marine Colonel William Corson, Army Lieutenant Colonel Anthony Herbert, and Air Force Colonel Jack Broughton exemplify officers at this level. They were all professional military men with experience in previous wars. In their books, all recollect experiences of falsification and pressures for increased production from high-level war-managers. They all saw how the production of war and systematic falsifications of the reporting machine were conducted at higher bureaucratic levels, yet at the same time these men demonstrated considerable knowledge of the war below them. They were professionals; they had advanced through the ranks yet had not forgotten or disdained the lived reality of actual warfare on their way up to more distant sites of command. Michael Herr provides a ready example of such a middle-level commander who became burnt out by the lies:

> The Intel report lay closed on the green field table, and someone had scrawled "What does it all mean?" across the cover sheet. There wasn't much doubt who had done that; the S-2 (intelligence captains and majors who had the wit to cut back their despair, a wedge to set against the bitterness). What got to them sooner or later was an inability to reconcile their love of service with their contempt for the war, and a lot of them had to resign their commissions, leave their profession.
>
> We were sitting in the tent waiting for the rain to stop, the major, five grunts and myself. The rains were constant now, ending what had been a dry monsoon season, and you could look through his tent flap and think about the Marines up there patrolling the hills. Someone came in to report that one of the patrols had discovered a small arms cache.
>
> "An arms cache!" the major said. "What happened was, one of the grunts was out there running around, and he tripped and fell down. That's about the only way we ever find any of this shit."
>
> He was twenty-nine, young in rank, and this was his second tour. The time before, he had been a captain commanding a regular Marine company. He knew all about grunts and patrols, arms caches and the value of most Intelligence.[9]

Since they would not conform to the system, these men could only resign or retire after their tours in Vietnam were over. Relatively few middle-level commanders have written about the war, but the ability of such renegades to grasp the operations of many different levels makes their contributions extremely important. The other group of professional military men who were below the top ranks, the senior sergeants, are virtually absent as authors or interview subjects.[10] The "lifers" did not break with the military.

Another social division demonstrated within the corpus is that between combatants and noncombatants. The warrior's knowledge is overwhelmingly a compendium of testimonies about combat. Combatants are far more present in the novels, memoirs, and interviews than are the vast majority of troops who served in maintenance depots, supply dumps, and clerical administration. Less than a handful of accounts by soldiers are available dealing with "In the rear with the beer" life in Vietnam.[11] Most combat books concern the army and marines; few books explore life in the air force, navy, and Coast Guard, other than prison narratives by pilots who were shot down and captured by North Vietnamese.

Race and ethnicity also constitute important social divisions in the warrior's knowledge. Blacks, Latinos, American Indians, Asian Americans, and other minorities are not present in the published accounts anywhere near the degree to which they were present in combat units. As of 1985, only one novel, one memoir, and two oral histories of black soldiers have been published. No book-length works by Latino, Indian, or Asian American soldiers have been published. Blacks as characters in novels and as interview subjects are fairly common, but Latino soldiers and other minorities are just barely present in stories by white authors.[12] The present book corpus does not provide adequate accounts of race relations among combat troops and commanders.

Thousands of American women served as nurses during the war, but as of 1985, only three pulp novels and one serious novel, together with one memoir, have appeared.[13] So few books do not sufficiently convey women's experiences and insights.

Thus far the discussion of how rank and other dimensions of social stratification structure the warrior's knowledge has been confined to narratives by military personnel. Equally important is the question of where journalists "fit in." To begin, there was a vast difference between journalists who worked for major news media institutions such as newspapers, newsmagazines, and the television networks, in contrast to those journalists who wrote feature articles for magazines.

The professional rules of what constitutes news virtually dictated that the news media would report on what the war-managers said about the war. News as a form of knowledge is professionally defined by journalists as what the highest levels of bureaucracies say about the world, not what people in subordinate levels have to say.[14] News media coverage of the war cannot be completely reduced to this formulation, but from the standpoint of how journalism contributed to the warrior's knowledge, feature writers are far more important than "news" personnel.

Journalists who registered with the public affairs office of Military Assistance Command Vietnam (MACV) received unofficial officer status, meaning they could eat and drink in facilities for officers. Most of the officer corps had college educations and officer rank has middle-class status. Most journalists also had college educations and journalism is a middle-class profession. Although the military often thought that journalists were hostile to them, they regarded journalists as people whose job was to converse with officers.

Some feature journalists deliberately associated more with the middle-level commanders, junior officers, and enlisted men rather than high-level war-managers. Although as journalists they often had access to the elite, they made a commitment to report the war "from below." Michael Herr indicates the difficulty he had in interviewing General Westmoreland and how estranged he felt from the more hierarchically oriented news media:

> My own interview with General Westmoreland had been hopelessly awkward. He'd noticed that I was accredited to *Esquire* and asked me if I planned to be doing "humoristical" pieces. Beyond that, very little was really said. I came away feeling as though I'd just had a conversation with a man who touches a chair and says, "This is a chair," points to a desk and says, "This is a desk." I couldn't think of anything to ask him, and the interview didn't happen. I honestly wanted to know what the form was for those interviews, but some of the reporters I'd ask would get very officious, saying something about "Command postures," and look at me as though I was insane. It was probably the kind of look that I gave one of them when he asked me once what I found to talk about with the grunts all the time, expecting me to confide (I think) that I found them as boring as he did.[15]

But the feature writers did not find the grunts boring; instead, they learned how to listen to their war stories and how to ask questions. They learned how to read the poems and prayers written on the latrine wall, helmets, and flak jackets. They learned how to speak the language of war as it was spoken from below. In their works, soldiers appear as real people, not as statistics in a casualty report released by headquarters.

The last divisions in the warrior's knowledge concerns differences between "forms of discourse," differences between memoirs, novels, interviews, and poems in their claims to knowledge. In terms of the modern terrain of what is considered to be serious knowledge, the customary "nonfiction" versus "fiction" dichotomy is the most important topic. Soldiers' memoirs and reports by magazine feature writers are marginal in terms of the usual social stratification of knowledge since they deal with lower levels of the hierarchy, but at least they are considered as potentially factual, as having some claims to knowledge. Novels and poems, as "fictional works," are customarily discredited as sources for cognitive claims.

The conventional "fiction" versus "nonfiction" classification of texts does not distinguish the horizons of experience provided for men and women at specific places in the world and the different ways of writing about those experiences. "Nonfictional" texts are thought to monopolize the representations of all real experiences. "Nonfictional" texts are thought to represent "what really happened," as opposed to "fictional" texts, which deal in matters that "never really happened"; experiences that are not real experiences, but only imaginary ones.

However, the structural horizons of experience created by the division of labor in Technowar are the same for both "fictional" and "nonfictional" accounts. It is not as if the men who wrote novels and the men who wrote memoirs were in different wars. "Gooks," "slants," "slopes," and "dinks" are found in all the different kinds of texts. Stories about soldiers who died because their M-16 rifles jammed in combat and stories about commanders flying well above the killing zone and collecting medals for their flights are found in both.

The differences between novels and memoirs occur mainly at the level of plot, or narrative sequence. Memoirs often follow the same pattern: entry into the military and progression through training; deployment to Vietnam; experiences in the war; and leaving after the author's one-year tour of duty is over. Plot development for novels shows more variation. Some follow the memoir pattern; others take the reader immediately to a combat unit in Vietnam, establish their characters, and then move through a series of battles in which some characters survive and other characters are killed. Some novels end like memoirs when the surviving characters go home; others end with their characters still in Vietnam, facing more battles. Voice is also different in memoirs and novels. Memoirs are invariably written in the first person, while novels are written in either first-person or third-person narrative.

But at the level of scenic description, there are rarely any differences between novels, memoirs, and journalist accounts. Whether from novels or memoirs, paragraphs, pages, and entire sequences of pages concerning how Technowar functioned are oftentimes virtually indistinguishable. Claims to knowledge occur at the level of specific events. Events are represented in scenic descriptions. This does not mean that every event described in a novel should be taken as literal truth, but rather that insofar as novels describe events as the consequences of structural patterns, then the "fictional" claims to knowledge deserve as much consideration as do the "nonfictional" assertions.

Captain Trippitt, Sergeant Martin, Chalice, Childs, and Tony 5 are all fictional characters in Robert Roth's novel, *Sand in the Wind*. Chalice says, "We lose twice as many men on ambushes than we get." Childs says, "What does he care? He only counts the Gooks he kills, not the Marines." Tony 5 responds. *"That's what they [higher command] put on his record."* In response, Childs says, "I wish somebody put KIA [killed in action] on his *record.*" [16] Robert Roth's character has just told the reader something important. Higher command will most likely officially report that Sergeant Martin, the man fragged in the novel, *died of combat injuries,* rather than indicating he was killed by his own troops. Who is going to say that Martin was killed by the troops? Certainly not Trippitt, since he desperately wants further promotions and a company mutiny will not look good on his *record.* The troops are not going to report that they killed him; premeditated murder of an American is a serious crime with a long statute of limitations. Will higher command investigate? How good will the battalion commander, brigade commander, and division commander look to their respective superiors in reporting that a marine company put a collective price on their captain's and sergeant's head?

Official fragging statistics exist; they have already been quoted in chapter 6: 126 in 1969; 271 in 1970; 321 in 1971 — for the army alone. Roth is making a claim to knowledge that the official statistics on the revolt of the ground troops are way too low. The official figures represent only those cases in which someone was caught or cases occurring in base areas far away from the enemy where it was clear that an American threw the grenade or pulled the trigger. In combat units, though, who is going to talk? If they talked, how would they stay alive?

Most Vietnam novels are written in a "realist" style. Narrative realism serves in part as a bridge between "fiction" and "nonfiction," but realism is not totally privileged in that other styles of writing are thereby discounted. Tim O'Brien's novel, *Going After Cacciato,* has a surreal plot and style. A soldier, Cacciato, decides to leave the war while on a mission near the Cambodian border; he travels across Asia, the Middle East, and Europe to attend the Paris Peace Talks. A lieutenant and a squad of men are ordered to go after him. In "reality," Cacciato had not deserted to walk across the world to Paris, but he is missing-in-action and the trek across Asia and Europe occurs as a fantasy in one soldier's mind. O'Brien highlights the soldier's hallucination by indicating just how tenuous were the boundaries between real and unreal, good and evil, in Vietnam. His claims to knowledge take the form of a litany:

They did not know even the simple things: a sense of victory, or satisfaction, or necessary sacrifice. They did not know the feeling of taking a place and keeping it, securing a village and then raising the flag and calling it a victory. No sense of order or momentum. No front, no rear, no trenches laid out in neat parallels. No Patton rushing for the Rhine, no beachheads to storm and win and hold for the duration. They did not have targets. They did not have a cause. They did not know if it was a war of ideology or economics or hegemony or spite. On a given day, they did not know where they were in Quang Ngai, or how being there might influence larger outcomes. They did not know the names of most villages. They did not know which villages were critical. They did not know strategies. They did not know the terms of the war, its architecture, the rules of fair play. When they took prisoners, which was rare, they did not know the questions to ask, whether to release a suspect or beat on him. They did not know how to feel. Whether, when seeing a dead Vietnamese, to be happy or sad or relieved; whether, in times of quiet, to be apprehensive or content; whether to engage the enemy or elude him. They did not know how to feel when they saw villages burning. Revenge? Loss? Peace of mind or anguish? They did not know. They knew the old myths about Quang Ngai — tales passed down from old-timer to newcomer — but they did not know which stories to believe. Magic, mystery, ghosts and incense, whispers in the dark, strange tongues and strange smells, uncertainties never articulated in war stories, emotion squandered on ignorance. They did not know good from evil.[17]

Should the aesthetic presence of alliteration be read as the definitive sign of no truth? Similarly, does the irony of a poem mean that it can make no claim to knowledge of what happened? Poetry in particular demonstrates the ways in which the war became divided and distanced within soldiers' minds. Below are two examples:

*The Fifty Gunner*
[.50-caliber heavy machine gun]

It came to his palms
And to his thumbs

Pressed hard
Against the trigger.

It came through
His hands,
And up his arms,
And across his shoulders.

Then, the telegraphed recoils
Set bouncing
The peace medallion
Dangling on his chest.

From his muzzle,
The huge bullets
Ripped flesh
From the running targets.[18]
— Frank A. Cross, Jr.

*Hunting*

Sighting down the long barrel,
I wait till front and rear sights
form a perfect line on his body,
then slowly squeeze the trigger.

The thought occurs
that I have never hunted anything
    in my whole life
except other men.

But I have learned by now
where such thoughts lead,
and soon pass on
to chow and sleep
and how much longer till I
    change my socks.[19]
— W. D. Ehrhart

What the warriors and their close observers have told us about the
war is far more important than the question of whether they wrote "fiction" or "nonfiction." All forms of discourse can serve as ways to

make serious claims concerning important facts or concepts, claims worthy of scholarly consideration. Feature-writing journalists make their contributions; "fictional" novels and poems make their contributions as well, regardless of the style in which they were written.

Finally, there are important aspects of the warrior's knowledge that do not lend themselves to theoretical appropriation for a genealogy of power and knowledge. It is difficult to convey the full presence of death in the memoirs, novels, poems, and interviews. As gruesome and horrible as the death accounts quoted have been, the quotations have all been abbreviated; nothing more was quoted after the analytical point at hand had been made. In a way this was necessary, but in a way it was wrong. My analysis has avoided the fundamental relationship between death and knowledge. Michael Herr tells a story about how long it took him to catch on. He is interviewing a member of a Long Range Reconnaissance Patrol, or "Lurp." Lurps were hardcore:

> "Didn't you ever meet a reporter before?" I asked him.
> "Tits on a bull," he said. "Nothing personal."
> But what a story he told me, as one-pointed and resonant as any war story I ever heard, it took me a year to understand it.
> "Patrol went up the mountain. One man came back. He died before he could tell us what happened."
> I waited for the rest, but it seemed not to be that kind of story; when I asked him what happened he just looked like he felt sorry for me, fucked if he'd waste time telling stories to anyone as dumb as I was.[20]

"He died before he could tell us what happened." Death determines much of what can be known and what will never be known. The dead cannot speak; their reports on Technowar will not be heard. Herr reports that he eventually got past the conventional limits on the relationship between death and knowledge. He doesn't seem to regard the breakthrough as an accomplishment, nor did he use his tape recorder to prove the events for scientific verification. Something just began to happen out there, somewhere:

> After a year I felt so plugged in to all the stories and the images and the fear that even the dead started telling me stories, you'd hear them out of a remote but accessible space where there were no ideas, no emotions, no facts, *no proper language,* only clean information. However many times it happened, whether I'd known them or not,

no matter what I'd felt about them or the way they died, their story was always there and it was always the same: it went, *"put yourself in my place."*[21]

"Put yourself in my place." How do the living put themselves in the place of the dead? It is a good question and no answer will be offered here. *

The present analysis of the war is just that, an analysis. For all of the violations against the terrain of serious discourse, the taboo against discussing real death has been followed. The analytical appropriation of the warrior's knowledge has its limits. In this corpus men and women live and die; the stories of their lives and their deaths have their truths beyond incorporation in any theoretical arguments.

\* How then can an observer or a stateside audience ever communicate as an equal to a combat participant?

# Notes

## 1. TRAILING THE BEAST

1. John Leonard's comments appear on the Avon paperback edition (1980) of Michael Herr's *Dispatches* (New York: Alfred A. Knopf, 1967).
2. See the Dell Publishing Company paperback edition (1979) of Tim O'Brien's *Going After Cacciato* (New York: Delacorte Press / Seymour Lawrence, 1978).
3. Arthur M. Schlesinger, Jr., *The Bitter Heritage* Greenwich, Conn.: Fawcett, 1968), pp. 58–59.
4. For a review of the Vietnam Syndrome and its replacement by new doctrines calling for U.S. military intervention in the Third World see Michael T. Klare, *Beyond the "Vietnam Syndrome": U.S. Intervention in the 1980s* (Washington, D.C.: Institute for Policy Studies, 1981).
5. The conference papers have been edited by Harrison E. Salisbury in *Vietnam Reconsidered: Lessons from a War* (New York: Harper and Row, 1984).
6. The review of some new American scholarship on Vietnam and how the war is being taught in American universities is by Fox Butterfield, "The New Vietnam Scholarship," *New York Times Magazine,* February 13, 1983. The review of novels concerning the Vietnam War is by Michiko Kakutani, "Novelists and Vietnam: The War Goes On," *New York Times Book Review,* April 15, 1984.
7. CBS News, "The Uncounted Enemy: A Vietnam Deception," January 23, 1982. General Westmoreland subsequently sued CBS for libel. The opening salvo is by Don Kowet, *A Matter of Honor: General William C. Westmoreland versus CBS* (New York: Macmillan, 1984).
8. See my review of the PBS series "Apocalypse Then," in *In These Times,* October 5–11, 1983.
9. Stanley Karnow, *Vietnam: A History* (New York: Viking Press, 1983), p. 11.
10. Myra MacPherson, *Long Time Passing: Vietnam and the Haunted Generation* (Garden City, N.Y.: Doubleday, 1984), p. 4.
11. Kakutani, "Novelists and Vietnam: The War Goes On," p. 39.
12. *New York Times,* May 29, 1984.
13. Guenter Lewy, *America in Vietnam* (New York: Oxford University Press, 1978), p. 451.
14. Ibid., p. 50.
15. Alain C. Enthoven and Wayne K. Smith, *How Much Is Enough?: Shaping the Defense Program, 1961–1969* (New York: Harper and Row, 1971), p. 297.
16. For an introduction to Foucault's work see *Power/Knowledge: Selected Interviews and Other Writings,* edited by Colin Gordon (New York: Pantheon Books, 1980).
17. John Morton Blum, *V Was for Victory: Politics and American Culture during World War II* (New York: Harcourt Brace Jovanovich, 1976), p. 123.
18. Ibid., pp. 144–145
19. For an analysis of "scientific management" and the rationalization of production in the United States see Harry Braverman, *Labor and Monopoly Capital* (New York: Monthly Review Press, 1976).
20. Henry A. Kissinger, *American Foreign Policy,* expanded edition (New York: W. W. Norton, 1974), p. 57.
21. Ibid., p. 54.
22. Max Weber, *The Protestant Ethic and the Spirit of Capitalism,* translated by Talcott Parsons (New York: Charles Scribner, 1958).

23. Kissinger, *American Foreign Policy*, pp. 48–49.
24. Karl Marx, *Capital: A Critique of Political Economy*, vol. 1: *The Process of Capitalist Production*, edited by Frederick Engels (New York: International Publishers, 1967), p. 72.
25. Karl Marx, *Grundrisse: Foundations of the Critique of Political Economy*, translated by Martin Nicholaus (Middlesex, England: Penguin Books in association with *New Left Review*, 1973), p. 706.
26. C. Wright Mills, *The Power Elite* (New York: Oxford University Press, 1956).
27. Seymour Melman, *The Permanent War Economy: American Capitalism in Decline* (New York: Simon and Schuster, 1974).
28. Henry A. Kissinger, *Nuclear Weapons and Foreign Policy*, published for the Council on Foreign Relations (New York: Harper and Brothers, 1957), p. 155.
29. Ibid., p. 155.
30. Ibid., p. 226.
31. Ibid., pp. 156–157.
32. Ibid., pp. 154–155.
33. Morris Janowitz, *The Professional Soldier: A Social and Political Portrait* (Glencoe, Ill.: Free Press, 1960).
34. Richard A. Gabriel and Paul L. Savage, *Crisis in Command* (New York: Hill and Wang, 1978), p. 20.
35. Quoted by F. M. Kail, *What Washington Said: Administration Rhetoric and the Vietnam War, 1949–1969* (New York: Harper and Row, 1973), p. 66.
36. Ibid., p. 85.
37. Gabriel Kolko, "The American Goals in Vietnam," in *The Pentagon Papers: Critical Essays*, edited by Noam Chomsky and Howard Zinn, vol. 5 of *The Pentagon Papers: The Senator Gravel Edition* (Boston: Beacon Press, 1972), p. 1.

## 2. LEGACIES OF RESISTANCE: VIETNAMESE NATIONALISM AGAINST THE CHINESE AND FRENCH

1. Frances FitzGerald, *Fire in the Lake: The Vietnamese and the Americans in Vietnam* (Boston: Atlantic–Little, Brown, 1972), p. 59.
2. Ibid., p. 14.
3. Ibid., p. 15.
4. David G. Marr, *Vietnamese Anticolonialism, 1885–1925* (Berkeley: University of California Press, 1971), p. 7.
5. Ibid., p. 12.
6. Ibid., p. 13.
7. Ibid., p. 14.
8. Bernard B. Fall, *The Two Viet-Nams*, 2nd rev. ed. (New York: Frederick A. Praeger, 1967), p. 18.
9. Marr, *Vietnamese Anticolonialism*, p. 24.
10. Ibid., p. 80.
11. Alfred W. McCoy with Cathleen B. Read and Leonard P. Adams II, *The Politics of Heroin in Southeast Asia* (New York: Harper and Row, 1972), pp. 74–76.
12. Marr, *Vietnamese Anticolonialism*, p. 46.
13. Ibid., p. 63.
14. Ibid., p. 67.
15. Ibid., p. 71.
16. Ibid., p. 44.
17. Ibid., pp. 118–119.
18. Ibid., p. 149.
19. Ibid., p. 167.
20. Ibid., p. 245.
21. Jean Lacouture, *Ho Chi Minh*, translated by Peter Wiles and Jane Clark Seiti, edited by Jane Clark Seiti (New York: Random House, 1968), p. 14.
22. Ibid., p. 20.
23. *Ho Chi Minh on Revolution: Selected Writings, 1920–1966*, edited by Bernard B. Fall (New York: Frederick A. Praeger, 1969), pp. 3–4.

24. Ibid., pp. 5–6.
25. Lacouture, *Ho Chi Minh*, p. 45.
26. Ibid.
27. Ibid., p. 46.
28. *Ho Chi Minh on Revolution*, p. 129.
29. Marr, *Vietnamese Anticolonialism*, pp. 264–265.
30. Lacouture, *Ho Chi Minh*, p. 73.
31. Ibid., p. 75.
32. Ibid.
33. Ibid., pp. 75–76.
34. *Ho Chi Minh on Revolution*, pp. 132–134.
35. Ibid., p. 82.

### 3. THE PERMANENT WAR BEGINS: 1940–1954

1. William J. Lederer, *Our Own Worst Enemy* (New York: W. W. Norton, 1968), p. 57.
2. Bernard B. Fall, *The Two Viet-Nams*, 2nd rev. ed. (New York: Frederick A. Praeger, 1967), p. 45.
3. Archimedes L. A. Patti, *Why Viet Nam?: Prelude to America's Albatross* (Berkeley: University of California Press, 1980), p. 17.
4. Fall, *The Two Viet-Nams*, pp. 26–27.
5. Patti, *Why Viet Nam?*, p. 18.
6. Ibid., p. 53.
7. Ibid., p. 55.
8. Ibid., p. 57.
9. Jean Lacouture, *Ho Chi Minh*, translated by Peter Wiles and Jane Clark Seiti, edited by Jane Clark Seiti (New York: Random House, 1968), p. 92.
10. Patti, *Why Viet Nam?*, p. 65.
11. Ibid., p. 70.
12. Ibid., p. 86.
13. Ibid.
14. Ibid., p. 88.
15. Ibid., p. 127.
16. Ibid., p. 129.
17. Ibid.
18. Ibid., p. 135.
19. Ibid., p. 129.
20. Ibid., pp. 144–145.
21. Ibid., p. 145.
22. Ibid., p. 187.
23. Ibid., p. 223.
24. Robert Shaplen, *The Lost Revolution* (New York: Harper and Row, 1965), p. 29.
25. Lederer, *Our Own Worst Enemy*, p. 42.
26. Ibid., p. 43.
27. Patti, *Why Viet Nam?*, p. 250.
28. Ibid., p. 251.
29. Ibid., p. 252.
30. Leslie Gelb with Richard K. Betts, *The Irony of Vietnam: The System Worked* (Washington, D.C.: Brookings Institution, 1979), pp. 34–35.
31. Patti, *Why Viet Nam?*, p. 120.
32. Ibid., p. 320.
33. Ibid., p. 350.
34. Ibid., p. 373.
35. Ibid., p. 374.
36. Lacouture, *Ho Chi Minh*, p. 119.
37. Patti, *Why Viet Nam?*, pp. 380–381.
38. Ibid., p. 381.
39. Ibid., p. 382.

40. Ibid.
41. Ibid., p. 393.
42. Gelb and Betts, *The Irony of Vietnam*, p. 42.
43. Bernard B. Fall, *Street without Joy* (Harrisburg, Penn.: Stackpole, 1964), pp. 174–175.
44. Patti, *Why Viet Nam?*, pp. 400–401.
45. Fall, *Street without Joy*, pp. 174–175.
46. General Vo Nguyen Giap, *Dien Bien Phu*, 3rd ed., revised and enlarged (Hanoi: Foreign Languages Press, 1964), p. 31.
47. Ibid., p. 31.
48. Patti, *Why Viet Nam?*, pp. 406, 418–421.
49. Philippe Devillers and Jean Lacouture, *End of a War: Indochina, 1954* (New York: Frederick A. Praeger, 1969), p. 20.
50. Fall, *Street without Joy*, p. 112.
51. Ibid., p. 354.
52. For an account of the battle see Bernard B. Fall, *Hell in a Very Small Place: The Siege of Dien Bien Phu* (Philadelphia, Penn.: Lippincott, 1967).
53. Giap, *Dien Bien Phu*, p. 86.
54. Devillers and Lacouture, *End of a War*, pp. 206–207.
55. The Geneva Agreements on the Cessation of Hostilities in Vietnam, July 20, 1954.
56. Devillers and Lacouture, *End of a War*, pp. 308–309.
57. Patti, *Why Viet Nam?*, p. 419.
58. Devillers and Lacouture, *End of a War*, p. 123.

## 4. AMERICA COMES TO VIETNAM: INSTALLING THE MECHANISMS, 1954–1964

1. Bernard B. Fall, *The Two Viet-Nams*, 2nd rev. ed. (New York: Frederick A. Praeger, 1967), p. 239.
2. Ibid., p. 243.
3. Philippe Devillers and Jean Lacouture, *End of a War: Indochina, 1954* (New York: Frederick A. Praeger, 1969), pp. 336–337.
4. Robert L. Samson, *The Economics of Insurgency in the Mekong Delta of Vietnam* (Cambridge: Massachusetts Institute of Technology Press, 1970), p. 29.
5. Wilfred G. Burchett, *Vietnam: Inside Story of a Guerrilla War* (New York: International Publishers, 1965), p. 178.
6. Samson, *Economics of Insurgency*, pp. 54–55.
7. Ibid., pp. 57–58.
8. Fall, *The Two Viet-Nams*, p. 257.
9. Ibid., p. 236–237.
10. William J. Lederer, *Our Own Worst Enemy* (New York: W. W. Norton, 1968), p. 57.
11. Burchett, *Vietnam: Inside Story of a Guerilla War*, p. 125.
12. Jeffrey Race, *War Comes to Long An: Revolutionary Conflict in a Vietnamese Province* (Berkeley: University of California Press, 1972), pp. 36–37.
13. Fall, *The Two Viet-Nams*, p. 318.
14. Brigadier General James Lawton Collins, Jr., *The Development and Training of the South Vietnamese Army, 1950–1972*, Department of the Army Vietnam Studies Series (Washington, D.C.: U.S. Government Printing Office, 1975), p. 2.
15. Race, *War Comes to Long An*, p. 78.
16. Burchett, *Vietnam: Inside Story of a Guerrilla War*, pp. 121–164.
17. Samson, *Economics of Insurgency*, p. 59.
18. Ibid., p. 67.
19. Race, *War Comes to Long An*, p. 129.
20. Samson, *Economics of Insurgency*, p. 74.
21. André Malraux, *Anti-Memoirs*, translated by Terence Kilmartin (New York: Holt, Rinehart and Winston, 1968), pp. 360–361.
22. Douglas S. Blaufarb, *The Counterinsurgency Era: U.S. Doctrine and Performance* (New York: Free Press, 1977), pp. 54–55.
23. Maxwell Taylor, *The Uncertain Trumpet* (New York: Harper and Row, 1960), p. 152.

24. Donald Duncan, *The New Legions* (New York: Pocket Books, 1967), pp. 146–148.
25. Michael T. Klare, *War without End: American Planning for the Next Vietnam* (New York: Alfred A. Knopf, 1972), pp. 48–49.
26. Walt W. Rostow, *The Stages of Economic Growth: A Non-Communist Manifesto* (Cambridge; Massachusetts Institute of Technology Press, 1960), p. 109.
27. Rostow is quoted in Blaufarb, *Counterinsurgency Era*, pp. 57–58.
28. Rostow, *Stages of Economic Growth*, p. 91.
29. Gregory Palmer, *The McNamara Strategy and the Vietnam War: Program Budgeting and the Vietnam War* (Westport, Conn.: Greenwood Press, 1978), p. 58.
30. Alain C. Enthoven, "Economic Analysis in the Department of Defense," *American Economic Review* 53 (May 1967), 418–419.
31. Ibid., p. 420.
32. Klare, *War without End*, p. 55.
33. Robert W. Komer, *Bureaucracy Does Its Thing: Institutional Constraints on U.S.–GVN Performance in Vietnam* (Santa Monica, Calif.: Rand Corporation, R-967-ARPA, 1972), p. 3.
34. Guenter Lewy, *America in Vietnam* (New York: Oxford University Press, 1978), p. 90.
35. Race, *War Comes to Long An*, p. 70.
36. Blaufarb, *Counterinsurgency Era*, p. 65.
37. General William Westmoreland, *Report on the War in Vietnam* (Washington, D.C.: U.S. Government Printing Office, 1969), p. 104.
38. Fall, *The Two Viet-Nams*, pp. 375–376.
39. Burchett, *Vietnam: Inside Story of a Guerrilla War*, p. 191. For other accounts of strategic hamlet collapse see his work, *The Furtive War: The United States in Vietnam and Laos* (New York: International Publishers, 1983) pp. 18–21, 96.
40. David Halberstam, *The Making of a Quagmire* (New York: Random House, 1965), pp. 301–302.
41. Ibid., p. 186.
42. Fall, *The Two Viet-Nams*, p. 334.
43. Ibid., p. 374.
44. Burchett, *Vietnam: Inside Story of a Guerrilla War*, p. 72.
45. Ibid., p. 61.
46. Colonel Francis J. Kelley, *U.S. Army Special Forces, 1961–1971*, Department of the Army Vietnam Studies Series (Washington, D.C.: U.S. Government Printing Office, 1973), p. 26.
47. Ibid., p. 20.
48. Leslie Gelb with Richard K. Betts, *The Irony of Vietnam: The System Worked* (Washington, D.C.: Brookings Institution, 1979), p. 90.
49. Burchett, *Vietnam: Inside Story of a Guerrilla War*, pp. 216–217.
50. For the official version of the Gulf of Tonkin incidents see *The Pentagon Papers: The Senator Gravel Edition* (Boston: Beacon Press, 1972), vol. 3, pp. 183–185.
51. Eugene V. Windchy, *Tonkin Gulf* (Garden City, N.Y.: Doubleday, 1971), p. 211.
52. *Pentagon Papers*, vol. 3, p. 722.

### 5. TECHNOWAR AT GROUND LEVEL: SEARCH AND DESTROY AS ASSEMBLY LINE

1. *The Pentagon Papers: The Senator Gravel Edition* (Boston: Beacon Press, 1972), vol. 2, p. 90.
2. Ibid., p. 92.
3. Ibid., vol. 3, pp. 308–315.
4. Leslie Gelb with Richard K. Betts, *The Irony of Vietnam: The System Worked* (Washington, D.C.: Brookings Institution, 1979), p. 105.
5. *Pentagon Papers*, vol. 3, pp. 730–731.
6. Ibid., vol. 4, pp. 296–297.
7. Ibid., pp. 632–633.
8. Cincinnatus, *Self-Destruction: The Disintegration and Decay of the United States Army during the Vietnam Era* (New York: W. W. Norton, 1981), p. 40.
9. *Pentagon Papers*, vol. 4, pp. 296–297.
10. Ibid., p. 306.

11. Ibid., p. 622.
12. Ibid., pp. 622–623.
13. David Halberstam, *The Best and the Brightest* (New York: Random House, 1972), p. 596.
14. John McNaughton, "Memorandum for General Goodpaster," *Pentagon Papers*, vol. 4, p. 292.
15. Ibid., vol. 3, p. 467.
16. Gelb and Betts, *The Irony of Vietnam*, pp. 135–136.
17. *Pentagon Papers*, vol. 4, p. 65.
18. Ibid., p. 173.
19. Ibid., p. 318.
20. Ibid., p. 314.
21. Gelb and Betts, *The Irony of Vietnam*, p. 139.
22. *Pentagon Papers*, vol. 4, p. 328.
23. William C. Westmoreland, *A Soldier Reports* (Garden City, N.Y.: Doubleday, 1980), pp. 277–278.
24. Jean Larteguy, *The Centurians*, translated by Xan Fielding (New York: E. P. Dutton, 1961).
25. *Quotations from Chairman Mao Tse-tung [Zedong]* (New York: Bantam Books, 1967), pp. 5–6.
26. Ibid., p. 43.
27. Ibid., p. 49.
28. Ibid., p. 85.
29. General William C. Westmoreland, "American Goals in Vietnam," in *The Lessons of Vietnam*, edited by W. Scott Thompson and Donaldson D. Frizzell (New York: Crane, Russak, 1977), p. 8.
30. Westmoreland, *A Soldier Reports*, p. 268.
31. Ibid., p. 233.
32. Ibid., p. 188.
33. Ibid., p. 186.
34. Ibid., p. 190.
35. Lieutenant General Julian J. Ewell and Major General Ira A. Hunt, Jr., *Sharpening the Combat Edge: The Use of Analysis to Reinforce Military Judgment*, Department of the Army Vietnam Studies Series (Washington, D.C.: U.S. Government Printing Office, 1974), pp. 236, 228.
36. Graff Henry, *The Tuesday Cabinet* (Englewood Cliffs, N.J.: Prentice-Hall, 1970), p. 82.
37. Dave Richard Palmer, *Summons of the Trumpet: U.S.–Vietnam in Perspective* (San Rafael, Calif.: Presidio Press, 1978), p. 144.
38. Ralph Littauer and Norman Uphoff, eds., *The Air War in Indochina* (Boston: Beacon Press, 1972), p. 52.
39. Palmer, *Summons of the Trumpet*, p. 141.
40. Cincinnatus, *Self-Destruction*, p. 67.
41. Ibid., p. 68.
42. Malcolm W. Browne, *The New Face of War* (New York: Bobbs-Merrill, 1965), p. 56.
43. S. L. A. Marshall, "Thoughts on Vietnam," in Thompson and Frizzel, eds., *The Lessons of Vietnam*, pp. 48–49.
44. Sir Robert Thompson, *No Exit from Vietnam* (New York: David McKay, 1969), p. 136.
45. Lewis Walt, *Strange War, Strange Strategy* (New York: Funk and Wagnalls, 1972), p. 33.
46. Cincinnatus, *Self-Destruction*, p. 70.
47. S. L. A. Marshall and Lieutenant Colonel David Hacksworth, *Vietnam Primer: Lessons Learned* (Washington, D.C.: Department of the Army, 1967; Sims, Arkansas: Lancer Militaria, 1984), p. 17.
48. Cincinnatus, *Self-Destruction*, p. 70.
49. Thompson and Frizzel, *The Lessons of Vietnam*, p. 143.
50. John Sack, *Lieutenant Calley: His Own Story* (New York: Viking Press, 1974), pp. 46–47.
51. Anthony B. Herbert with James T. Wooten, *Soldier* (New York: Holt, Rinehart and Winston, 1972), p. 268.
52. Ibid., p. 140.
53. *Congressional Record*, vol. 118, no. 76 (May 10, 1972), E4978.

54. Quoted by Al Santoli, *Everything We Had: An Oral History of the Vietnam War by Thirty-three American Soldiers Who Fought It* (New York: Random House, 1981), pp. 72–73.
55. Citizens Commission of Inquiry, ed., *The Dellums Committee Hearings on War Crimes in Vietnam: An Inquiry into Command Responsibility in Southeast Asia* (New York: Vintage Books, 1972), p. 71.
56. Ronald Glasser, *365 Days* (New York: George Braziller, 1971), p. 129.
57. Quoted by Charles J. Levy, *Spoils of War* (Boston: Houghton Mifflin, 1974), p. ix.
58. General Donn A. Starry, *Mounted Combat in Vietnam*, Department of the Army Vietnam Studies Series (Washington, D.C.: U.S. Government Printing Office, 1978), p. 79.
59. Stanley Goff and Robert Sanders with Clark Smith, *Brothers: Black Soldiers in the Nam* (Novato, Calif.: Presidio Press, 1982), pp. 32–33.
60. Santoli, *Everything We Had*, p. 179.
61. Clark Smith, ed., *The Short-Timers Journal: Soldiering in the Nam*, no. 1 (September–October 1980), 62.
62. Thompson and Frizzel, *The Lessons of Vietnam*, pp. 81–82.
63. Josiah Bunting, *The Lionheads* (New York: George Braziller, 1972), p. 49.
64. Cincinnatus, *Self-Destruction*, p. 162.
65. Gloria Emerson, *Winners and Losers: Battles, Retreats, Gains, Losses and Ruins from a Long War* (New York: Random House, 1978), p. 254.
66. Fred Halstead, *GIs Speak Out against the War: The Case of the Fort Jackson Eight* (New York: Pathfinders Press, 1970), p. 67.
67. Mark Lane, *Conversations with Americans* (New York: Simon and Schuster, 1970), p. 181.
68. Edward L. King, *The Death of the Army: A Pre-Mortem* (New York: Saturday Review Press, 1972), pp. 28–29.
69. Ibid., p. 29.
70. Ibid., p. 28.
71. Ibid., p. 30.
72. Glasser, *365 Days*, p. 37.
73. Marshall and Hackworth, *Vietnam Primer*, p. 48.
74. Ibid., p. 49.
75. Douglas Kinnard, *The War Managers* (Hanover, Mass.: University Press of New England, 1977), p. 75.
76. Emerson, *Winners and Losers*, pp. 254–255.
77. Santoli, *Everything We Had*, p. 43.
78. Levy, *Spoils of War*, pp. 69–70.
79. Ibid., 70.
80. Tom Mangold and John Penycate, *The Tunnels of Cu Chi: The Untold Story of Vietnam* (New York: Random House, 1985), p. 137.
81. Ibid., pp. 50, 66–67.
82. Glasser, *365 Days*, p. 227.
83. Sack, *Lieutenant Calley*, p. 47.
84. Cincinnatus, *Self-Destruction*, p. 81.
85. Citizens Commission of Inquiry, *Dellums Committee Hearings*, pp. 62–63.
86. Sack, *Lieutenant Calley*, p. 56.
87. Cincinnatus, *Self-Destruction*, p. 81.
88. Ibid., pp. 79–80.
89. Martin Russ, *Happy Hunting Ground* (New York: Atheneum, 1968), p. 83.
90. Glasser, *365 Days*, p. 34.
91. Citizens Commission of Inquiry, *Dellums Committee Hearings*, p. 72.
92. Halstead, *GIs Speak Out*, p. 63.
93. Citizens Commission of Inquiry, *Dellums Committee Hearings*, p. 72.
94. Dale Minor, *The Information War* (New York: Hawthorn Books, 1970), p. 47.
95. Guenter Lewy, *America in Vietnam* (New York: Oxford University Press, 1978), p. 80.
96. W. R. Peers, *The My Lai Inquiry* (New York: W. W. Norton, 1979), pp. 264–266.
97. Ibid.
98. Westmoreland, *A Soldier Reports*, p. 189.
99. Jonathan Schell, *The Military Half* (New York: Alfred A. Knopf, 1968), p. 165.

100. Philip Jones Griffiths, *Vietnam, Inc.* (New York: Collier Books, 1971), p. 50.
101. Clark Smith, ed., *The Short-Timers Journal: Aspects of Counter-Insurgency,* no. 2 (April–May 1981), 63.
102. Frederick Downs, *The Killing Zone: My Life in the Vietnam War* (New York: W. W. Norton, 1978), pp. 63–64.
103. Ibid., p. 65.
104. W. D. Ehrhart, *Vietnam-Perkasie: A Combat Marine Memoir* (Jefferson, Va.: McFarland, 1983), p. 87.
105. Citizens Commission of Inquiry, *Dellums Committee Hearings,* p. 168.
106. Schell, *The Military Half,* p. 20.
107. Ibid., p. 114.
108. Ibid., p. 97.
109. Ibid., pp. 120–121.
110. Ibid., p. 114.
111. Citizens Commission of Inquiry, *Dellums Committee Hearings,* p. 177.
112. Schell, *The Military Half,* p. 27.
113. Ibid., p. 84.
114. Kinnard, *War Managers,* p. 47.
115. Lewy, *America in Vietnam,* p. 99.
116. Citizens Commission of Inquiry, *Dellums Committee Hearings,* pp. 96–97.
117. Cincinnatus, *Self-Destruction,* p. 73.
118. Ibid., p. 77.
119. William R. Corson, *The Betrayal* (New York: W. W. Norton, 1968), p. 289.
120. Lewy, *America in Vietnam,* p. 101.
121. Sack, *Lieutenant Calley,* p. 85.
122. Citizens Commission of Inquiry, *Dellums Committee Hearings,* pp. 282–283.
123. Lewy, *America in Vietnam,* p. 121.
124. Daniel Lang, *Casualties of War* (New York: McGraw-Hill, 1969), p. 18.
125. Citizens Commission of Inquiry, *Dellums Committee Hearings,* p. 238.
126. Levy, *Spoils of War,* pp. 56–57.
127. Mark Baker, *Nam: The Vietnam War in the Words of the Men and Women Who Fought There* (New York: William Morrow, 1981), p. 191.
128. Schell, *The Military Half,* p. 84.
129. Helen Emmerich, *San Francisco Chronicle,* December 2, 1969.
130. Michael Herr, *Dispatches* (New York: Alfred A. Knopf, 1977), p. 20.
131. Russ, *Happy Hunting Ground,* p. 122.
132. Herr, *Dispatches,* p. 154.
133. Ibid., p. 10.
134. Schell, *The Military Half,* p. 45.
135. Ibid., p. 35.
136. Ibid., p. 62.
137. Lane, *Conversations with Americans,* p. 48.
138. Schell, *The Military Half,* pp. 52, 140.
139. Ibid., p. 45.
140. "Glossary of Terms Used by Vietnam Era Veterans," distributed by New Haven (Conn.) Vietnam Veterans Outreach Center, 1979.
141. Herr, *Dispatches,* p. 199.
142. Schell, *The Military Half,* p. 141.
143. Baker, *Nam,* pp. 195–196.
144. Herr, *Dispatches,* p. 59.
145. John Sack, *M* (New York: New American Library, 1967), p. 189.
146. John Kerry and Vietnam Veterans Against the War, *The New Soldiers,* edited by David Thorne and George Butler (New York: Collier Books, 1971), p. 50.
147. Lane, *Conversations with Americans,* p. 105.
148. Ibid., p. 113.
149. Downs, *The Killing Zone,* p. 31.
150. Herr, *Dispatches,* p. 29.
151. Sack, *Lieutenant Calley,* pp. 40–41.

152. Citizens Commission of Inquiry, *Dellums Committee Hearings*, pp. 219–220.
153. Lane, *Conversations with Americans*, p. 59.
154. Ibid., p. 86.
155. Ibid., p. 178.
156. Baker, *Nam*, p. 212.
157. Cincinnatus, *Self-Destruction*, p. 83.
158. Shad Meshad, *Captain for Dark Mornings* (Los Angeles: Creative Image Associates, 1982), p. 45.
159. Lane, *Conversations with Americans*, p. 193.
160. Ibid., p. 158.
161. Citizens Commission of Inquiry, *Dellums Committee Hearings*, p. 228.
162. Cincinnatus, *Self-Destruction*, p. 85.
163. Lane, *Conversations with Americans*, p. 60.
164. Herr, *Dispatches*, p. 164.
165. Herbert and Wooten, *Soldier*, pp. 246–247.
166. Vietnam Veterans Against the War, *The Winter Soldier Investigation: An Investigation into American War Crimes* (Boston: Beacon Press, 1972), p. 39.
167. Cincinnatus, *Self-Destruction*, p. 89.
168. Baker, *Nam*, p. 198.
169. Ibid., p. 198.
170. Sack, *Lieutenant Calley*, p. 89.
171. Ibid.
172. Smith, *The Short-Timers Journal*, no. 1, p. 80.
173. Ibid., p. 41.
174. Ehrhart, *Vietnam-Perkasie*, p. 56.
175. Murray Polner, *No Victory Parades: The Return of the Vietnam Veteran* (New York: Holt, Rinehart and Winston, 1971), pp. 55–56.
176. Cincinnatus, *Self-Destruction*, p. 57.
177. Major General Joseph A. McChristian, *The Role of Military Intelligence, 1965–1967*, Department of the Army Vietnam Studies Series (Washington, D.C.: U.S. Government Printing Office, 1974), pp. 9–10.
178. Ibid., pp. 37–38.

## 6.   THE TET OFFENSIVE AND THE PRODUCTION OF A DOUBLE REALITY

1. *The Pentagon Papers: The Senator Gravel Edition* (Boston: Beacon Press, 1972), vol. 4, p. 427.
2. Ibid., p. 442.
3. Ibid.
4. Alain C. Enthoven and Wayne K. Smith, *How Much Is Enough?: Shaping the Defense Program, 1961–1969* (New York: Harper and Row, 1971), pp. 275–276.
5. *Pentagon Papers*, vol. 4, p. 458.
6. Ibid., p. 462.
7. Ibid., p. 371.
8. Thomas Powers, *The Man Who Kept the Secrets: Richard Helms and the CIA* (New York: Alfred A. Knopf, 1979), p. 238.
9. Ibid.
10. Walter Schneir and Miriam Schneir, "The Uncounted Enemy: How the Enemy Cooked the Books," *Nation*, May 12, 1984, p. 571.
11. Ibid., p. 572.
12. Powers, *Man Who Kept Secrets*, p. 238.
13. Ibid., p. 239.
14. Schneir and Schneir, "The Uncounted Enemy," p. 572.
15. Ibid., pp. 572–573.
16. Ibid., p. 573.
17. Ibid., p. 574.
18. Ibid.
19. Don Oberdorfer, *Tet!* (Garden City, N.Y.: Doubleday, 1971), p. 105.

20. Ibid., p. 104.
21. Ibid., pp. 105–106.
22. Daniel Ellsberg, *Papers on the War* (New York: Simon and Schuster, 1972), p. 120.
23. Oberdorfer, *Tet!*, p. 52.
24. Dave Richard Palmer, *Summons of the Trumpet: U.S.–Vietnam in Perspective* (San Rafael, Calif.: Presidio Press, 1978), p. 165.
25. Ibid., p. 173.
26. Ibid., p. 181.
27. Peter Braestrup, *Big Story: How the American Press and Television Reported and Interpreted the Crisis of Tet 1968 in Vietnam and Washington* (Garden City, N.Y.: Anchor Press / Doubleday, 1978), p. 177.
28. Palmer, *Summons of the Trumpet*, p. 179.
29. Powers, *Man Who Kept the Secrets*, p. 242.
30. Ibid., p. 181.
31. Schneir and Schneir, "The Uncounted Enemy," p. 575.
32. David Halberstam, *The Best and the Brightest* (New York: Random House, 1972), p. 653.
33. *Pentagon Papers*, vol.4, p. 548.
34. Ibid.
35. Ibid., p. 561.
36. Ibid., p. 564.
37. Schneir and Schneir, "The Uncounted Enemy," p. 575.
38. Ralph W. McGehee, *Deadly Deceits: My Twenty-five Years in the CIA* (New York: Sheridan Square Publications, 1983), pp. 127–129.
39. W. Scott Thompson and Donaldson D. Frizzell, eds., *The Lessons of Vietnam,* (New York: Crane, Russak, 1977), pp. 88–89.
40. Seymour M. Hersh, *The Price of Power: Kissinger in the Nixon White House* (New York: Summit Books, 1983), p. 49.
41. Ibid., p. 50.
42. "National Security Study Memorandum No. 1, January 21, 1969" was entered into the *Congressional Record,* May 10, 1972, E4977–4981. It can also be found in Gareth Porter, ed., *Vietnam: A History in Documents* (New York: New American Library, 1979), p. 377.
43. Porter, ed., *Vietnam,* p. 378.
44. Ibid., p. 379.
45. *Pentagon Papers*, vol. 4, p. 561.
46. Ibid., p. 562.
47. These figures exclude more than 10,000 men who died in accidents or from disease and exclude all wounded who did not require hospitalization. See United States Bureau of the Census, *Statistical Abstract of the United States: 1984* (Washington, D.C.: U.S. Government Printing Office, 1984), p. 354.
48. Thompson and Frizzell, *Lessons of Vietnam,* p. 79.
49. Ibid., p. 83.
50. Braestrup, *Big Story,* pp. 508–530.
51. Thompson and Frizzell, *Lessons of Vietnam,* pp. 100–101.
52. Henry G. Summers, Jr., *On Strategy: A Critical Analysis of the Vietnam War* (Novato, Calif.: Presidio Press, 1982), p. 96.
53. Henry A. Kissinger, *American Foreign Policy,* expanded edition (New York: W. W. Norton, 1974), p. 57.
54. George Orwell, *1984* (New York: New American Library, 1961), pp. 176–177.
55. Guenter Lewy, *American in Vietnam* (New York: Oxford University Press, 1978), p. 233.
56. Ibid.
57. Ibid.
58. Telford Taylor, "Vietnam and the Nuremberg Principles: Colloquy on War Crimes," in *The Vietnam War and International Law* (Princeton, N.J.: Princeton University Press, 1976), vol. 4, p. 29.
59. W. R. Peers, *The My Lai Inquiry* (New York: W. W. Norton, 1979), p. 29.
60. Lewy, *America in Vietnam,* p. 234.
61. Peers, *The My Lai Inquiry,* p. 29.

62. Lewy, *America in Vietnam*, p. 241.
63. Peers, *The My Lai Inquiry*, p. 239.
64. Ibid., p. 239.
65. Citizens Commission of Inquiry, ed., *The Dellums Committee Hearings on War Crimes in Vietnam: An Inquiry into Command Responsibility in Southeast Asia* (New York: Vintage Books, 1972), p. 239.
66. Ibid., p. 181.
67. Ibid., p. 215.
68. Ibid., p. 228.
69. Philip Caputo *A Rumor of War* (New York: Ballantine Books, 1978), p. 34.
70. Mark Lane, *Conversations with Americans* (New York: Simon and Schuster, 1970), p. 38.
71. Ibid., p. 32.
72. Tim O'Brien, *If I Die in a Combat Zone* (New York: Dell, 1979), p. 56.
73. Gustav Hasford, *The Short-Timers* (New York: Bantam Books, 1980), p. 12.
74. John Sack *Lieutenant Calley: His Own Story* (New York: Viking Press, 1974), p. 28.
75. Peers, *The My Lai Inquiry*, pp. 261–262.
76. Citizens Commission of Inquiry, *Dellums Committee Hearings*, pp. 99–100.
77. Ibid., p. 144.
78. Ibid., pp. 101–102.
79. Ibid., p. 95.
80. Ibid., p. 50.
81. Al Santoli, *Everything We Had: An Oral History of the Vietnam War by Thirty-three American Soldiers Who Fought It* (New York: Random House, 1981), p. 25.
82. Mark Baker, *Nam: The Vietnam War in the Words of the Men and Women Who Fought There* (New York: William Morrow, 1981), pp. 205–206.
83. Jonathan Schell, *The Military Half* (New York: Alfred A. Knopf, 1968), pp. 43–44.
84. Citizens Commission of Inquiry, *Dellums Committee Hearings*, p. 86.
85. *Pentagon Papers*, vol. 2, p. 552.
86. William C. Westmoreland, *A Soldier Reports* (Garden City, N.Y.: Doubleday, 1980), p. 83.
87. Oberdorfer, *Tet!*, p. 314.
88. Westmoreland, *A Soldier Reports*, p. 83.
89. Josiah Bunting, *The Lionheads* (New York: George Braziller, 1972), pp. 66–67.
90. Robert Pisor, *The End of the Line: The Siege of Khe Sanh* (New York: W. W. Norton, 1982), p. 68.
91. Philip Jones Griffiths, *Vietnam, Inc.* (New York: Collier Books, 1971), p. 2.
92. Ludwig Wittgenstein, *Tractatus Logico-Philosophicus*, translated by D. F. Pears and B. F. McGuinness (London: Routledge and Kegan Paul, 1961), p. 115.
93. General William Westmoreland, *Report on the War in Vietnam* (Washington, D.C.: U.S. Government Printing Office, 1969), p. 147.
94. Westmoreland, *A Soldier Reports*, p. 244.
95. Anthony B. Herbert with James T. Wooten, *Soldier* (New York: Holt, Rinehart and Winston, 1972), pp. 140–141.
96. Thompson and Frizzell, *The Lessons of Vietnam*, pp. 90–91.
97. Santoli, *Everything We Had*, p. 27.
98. Ibid., pp. 190–191.
99. William J. Lederer, *Our Own Worst Enemy* (New York: W. W. Norton, 1968), p. 84. For background see Charles Wolf, *United States Foreign Policy and The Third World* (Boston: Little, Brown, 1967), p. 63.
100. Herbert, *Soldier*, pp. 284–285.
101. Robert Roth, *Sand in the Wind* (New York: Pinnacle Books, 1974), pp. 31–32.
102. Clark C. Smith, ed., *The Short-Timer's Journal: Aspects of Counter-Insurgency*, no. 2 (April–May 1981), 60.
103. W. D. Ehrhart, *Vietnam-Parkasie: A Combat Marine Memoir* (Jefferson, Va.: McFarland, 1983), p. 91.
104. Ibid., p. 179.
105. Pisor, *End of the Line*, p. 20.
106. James Fallows, *National Defense* (New York: Random House, 1981), p. 93.

107. Ibid., p. 91.
108. Shad Meshad, *Captain for Dark Mornings* (Los Angeles: Creative Image Associates, 1982), pp. 44–45.
109. Lane, *Conversations with Americans,* p. 211.
110. Charles J. Levy, *Spoils of War* (Boston: Houghton Mifflin, 1974), p. 40.
111. Meshad, *Captain for Dark Mornings,* p. 103.
112. Clark C. Smith, ed., *The Short-Timer's Journal: Soldiering in Vietnam,* No. 1 (September–October 1980), pp. 63–64.
113. Herbert, *Soldier,* p. 140.
114. Donald Kirk, *Tell It to the Dead: Memories of a War* (Chicago: Nelson-Hall, 1975), p. 4.
115. Smith, *Short-Timer's Journal,* no. 1, p. 41.
116. Baker, *Nam,* p. 253.
117. Ibid., p. 254.
118. Ibid., p. 118.
119. Citizens Commission of Inquiry, *Dellums Committee Hearings,* pp. 188–189. This is a composite quote. "Good for you" and rest of paragraph comes from a patient of Dr. Robert Jay Lifton's in *Home from the War* (New York: Simon & Schuster, 1973), p. 36.
120. Lane, *Conversations with Americans,* p. 67.
121. Ibid., pp. 120–121.
122. Ibid., p. 60.
123. Ibid.
124. Ibid., p. 95.
125. Ibid., p. 183.
126. Ibid., p. 123.
127. Ibid., p. 121.
128. Citizens Commission of Inquiry, *Dellums Committee Hearings,* p. 189.
129. Lane, *Conversations with Americans,* p. 123.
130. Peter Martinsen, "Testimony and Questions," in *Prevent the Crime of Silence: Reports from the International War Crimes Tribunal founded by Bertrand Russell,* edited by Ken Coates, Peter Limqueco, and Peter Weiss (London: Allen Lane / Penguin Press, 1971), p. 259.
131. Murray Polner, *No Victory Parades: The Return of the Vietnam Veteran* (New York: Holt, Rinehart and Winston, 1971), p. 84.
132. Levy, *Spoils of War,* p. 4.
133. Smith, *Short-Timer's Journal,* No. 2, p. 19.
134. Ibid., pp. 64–65.
135. Ibid., p. 63.
136. Ibid., p. 65.
137. Ibid., pp. 66–67.
138. Ibid., p. 67.
139. Ibid., p. 68.
140. Kirk, *Tell It to the Dead,* p. 63.
141. Lane, *Conversations with Americans,* p. 71.
142. Stanley Goff and Robert Sanders with Clark Smith, *Brothers: Black Soldiers in the Nam* (Novato, Calif.: Presidio Press, 1982), p. 134.
143. Santoli, *Everything We Had,* p. 155.
144. Polner, *No Victory Parades,* p. 69.
145. Roth, *Sand in the Wind,* p. 334.
146. Ibid., pp. 340–341.
147. Ibid., p. 562.
148. Levy, *Spoils of War,* pp. 33–34.
149. Ibid., p. 36.
150. Lane, *Conversations with Americans,* p. 242.
151. Larry G. Waterhouse and Mariam G. Wizard, *Turning the Guns Around* (New York: Praeger Publishers, 1971), p. 102.
152. Richard Boyle, *The Flower of the Dragon: The Breakdown of the U.S. Army in Vietnam* (San Francisco: Ramparts Press, 1972), p. 75.
153. Levy, *Spoils of War,* pp. 44–45.

154. David Cortright, *Soldiers in Revolt: The American Military Today* (Garden City, N.Y.: Anchor Press / Doubleday, 1975), p. 46.

155. John Helmer, *Bringing the War Home: The American Soldier in Vietnam and After* (New York: Free Press, 1974), p. 199.

156. Cortright, *Soldiers in Revolt*, p. 46.

157. Smith, *The Short-Timer's Journal*, no. 1, p. 60.

158. Lane, *Conversations with Americans*, p. 242.

159. Cortright, *Soldiers in Revolt*, pp. 35–39.

160. Ibid., p. 23.

161. General Dwight D. Eisenhower, "Memorandum for Directors and Chiefs of War Department General and Special Staff Divisions and Bureaus and the Commanding Generals of the Major Commands on Scientific and Technological Resources as Military Assets," in Seymour Melman, *Pentagon Capitalism: The Political Economy of War* (New York: McGraw-Hill, 1970), p. 232.

162. "Channeling" was one of ten documents in an orientation kit for local draft boards published by Selective Service in July 1965. See Waterhouse and Wizzard, *Turning the Guns Around*, p. 204.

163. Lawrence M. Baskir and William A. Strauss, *Chance and Circumstance: The Draft, The War and the Vietnam Generation* (New York: Alfred A. Knopf, 1978), p. 9.

164. Ibid., p. 10.

165. Maurice Zeitlin, Kenneth Lutterman, and James Russell, "Death in Vietnam: Class, Poverty, and the Risks of War," in *The Politics and Society Reader*, edited by Ira Katznelson et al. (New York: David McKay, 1971), pp. 55–57.

166. Baskir and Strauss, *Chance and Circumstance*, p. 8.

167. Daniel Patrick Moynihan, "The Negro Family: The Case for National Action," *The Moynihan Report and the Politics of Controversy* (Cambridge, Mass.: Massachusetts Institute of Technology Press, 1967), p. 42.

168. Ibid., p. 47.

169. Baskir and Strauss, *Chance and Circumstance*, p. 126.

170. Douglas G. Glasgow, *The Black Underclass: Poverty, Unemployment, and Entrapment of Ghetto Youth* (New York: Vintage Books, 1980).

171. For accounts of what happened to category IV soldiers see Paul Starr, *The Discarded Army: Veterans after Vietnam* (New York: Charter House, 1973), pp. 192–193; Cortright, *Soldiers in Revolt*, pp. 194–195; Baskir and Strauss, *Chance and Circumstance*, pp. 128–129.

172. Cortright, *Soldiers in Revolt*, p. 39.

173. Ibid., p. 40–41.

174. David Parks, *G.I. Diary* (New York: Harper and Row, 1968), p. 86.

175. Goff, Sanders, and Smith, *Brothers*, p. 30.

176. Baskir and Strauss, *Chance and Circumstance*, p. 139.

177. Ralph Guzman, "Mexican Casualties in Vietnam," *La Raza* 1 (1971), 12.

178. Samuel Stouffer et al., *The American Soldier: Combat and Its Aftermath*, vol. 2 of *Studies in Social Psychology in World War II* (Princeton, N.J.: Princeton University Press, 1949), pp. 105–191.

179. Richard A. Gabriel and Paul L. Savage, *Crisis in Command* (New York: Hill and Wang, 1978), p. 13.

180. Thompson and Frizzell, *The Lessons of Vietnam*, p. 210.

181. Santoli, *Everything We Had*, p. 43.

182. Smith, *Short-Timer's Journal*, no. 1, pp. 40–41.

183. Westmoreland, *A Soldier Reports*, p. 387.

184. Baker, *Nam*, p. 112.

185. Michael Herr, *Dispatches* (New York: Alfred A. Knopf, 1977), p. 112.

186. Ronald Glasser, *365 Days* (New York: George Braziller, 1971), pp. 32–33.

187. Herbert, *Soldier*, pp. 171–174.

188. Lane, *Conversations with Americans*, p. 58.

189. Herr, *Dispatches*, pp. 4–5.

190. Lewy, *America in Vietnam*, p. 159.

191. Ibid.

## 7. FORCED DRAFT: URBANIZATION AND THE CONSUMER SOCIETY COME TO VIETNAM

1. "Cost of the Vietnam War," *Indochina Newsletter* 18 (November–December, 1982), pp. 12, 9.
2. William C. Westmoreland, *A Soldier Reports* (Garden City, N.Y.: Doubleday, 1980), p. 187.
3. Ibid., p. 85.
4. Jeffrey Race, *War Comes to Long An: Revolutionary Conflict in a Vietnamese Province* (Berkeley: University of California Press, 1972), pp. 153–159.
5. Ibid., pp. 146, 188.
6. Reported by Nguyen Cao Ky, *Twenty Years and Twenty Days* (New York: Stein and Day, 1976), pp. 140–141.
7. Charles Wolf, *United States Foreign Policy and the Third World* (Boston: Little, Brown, 1967), p. 66.
8. Cited by Peter Watson, *War on the Mind: The Military Uses and Abuses of Psychology* (New York: Basic Books, 1978), p. 412.
9. *The Pentagon Papers: The Senator Gravel Edition* (Boston: Beacon Press, 1972), vol. 4, p. 441.
10. Guenter Lewy, *America in Vietnam* (New York: Oxford University Press, 1978), p. 113.
11. Ibid., p. 111.
12. Ralph Littauer and Norman Uphoff, eds., *The Air War in Indochina* (Boston: Beacon Press, 1972), p. 47.
13. Citizens Commission of Inquiry, ed., *The Dellums Committee Hearings On War Crimes in Vietnam: An Inquiry into Command Responsibility in Southeast Asia* (New York: Vintage Books, 1972), p. 42.
14. David Halberstam, *The Best and the Brightest* (New York: Random House, 1972), p. 550.
15. Lewy, *America in Vietnam*, p. 447.
16. Ibid., p. 445.
17. Ibid., p. 259.
18. Ibid., p. 260.
19. Ibid., p. 262.
20. J. B. Neilands et al., *Harvest of Death: Chemical Warfare in Vietnam and Cambodia* (New York: Free Press, 1972), p. 165.
21. William R. Corson, *The Betrayal* (New York: W. W. Norton, 1968), pp. 70–71.
22. Russell Betts and Frank Denton, *An Evaluation of Chemical Crop Destruction in Vietnam* (Santa Monica, Calif.: Rand Corporation, 1967), pp. 21–22.
23. Lewy, *America in Vietnam*, p. 112.
24. Al Santoli, *Everything We Had: An Oral History of the Vietnam War by Thirty-three American Soldiers Who Fought It* (New York: Random House, 1981), pp. 47–48.
25. Mark Lane, *Conversations with Americans* (New York: Simon and Schuster, 1970), p. 263.
26. David Kenneth Tuck, "Testimony and Questioning," in *Prevent the Crime of Silence: Report from the International War Crimes Tribunal found by Bertrand Russell,* edited by Ken Coates, Peter Limqueco, and Peter Weiss (London: Allen Lane / Penguin Press, 1971), p. 245.
27. Jonathan Schell, *The Military Half* (New York: Alfred A. Knopf, 1968), p. 61.
28. Lewy, *America in Vietnam*, p. 53.
29. Ibid., p. 108.
30. Schell, *The Military Half,* p. 42.
31. Lewy, *America in Vietnam*, p. 148.
32. Westmoreland, *A Soldier Reports*, p. 368.
33. Samuel P. Huntington, "The Bases of Accommodation," *Foreign Affairs* 46 (July 1968), p. 645.
34. Ibid., p. 649.
35. Ibid., p. 652.
36. Major General Robert R. Ploger, *U.S. Army Engineers, 1965–1967*, Department of the Army Vietnam Studies Series (Washington, D.C.: U.S. Government Printing Office, 1974), p. 44.
37. Ibid.
38. Ibid., p. 37.
39. Ibid., pp. 122–123.

40. Lieutenant General Carroll H. Dunn, *Base Development in South Vietnam, 1965–1970,* Department of the Army Vietnam Studies Series (Washington, D.C.: U.S. Government Printing Office, 1972), p. 143.
41. Ibid., p. 147.
42. Ibid., pp. 144–145.
43. Ibid., p. 84.
44. Ibid., p. 144.
45. Lieutenant General Joseph M. Heiser, Jr., *Logistic Support,* Department of the Army Vietnam Studies Series (Washington, D.C.: U.S. Government Printing Office, 1974), p. 190.
46. Ibid., p. 199.
47. Ibid., p. 73.
48. *Pentagon Papers,* vol. 4, p. 338.
49. Ibid., p. 339.
50. Ibid., pp. 340–341.
51. Ibid., p. 364.
52. Ibid., p. 365.
53. Ibid., vol. 2, p. 389.
54. Ibid., p. 318 for 1964–1965 and p. 389 for 1966–1967. For 1970 see James Hamilton-Paterson, *A Very Personal War: The Story of Cornelius Hawkridge* (London: Hodder and Stoughton, 1971), p. 211.
55. Hamilton-Paterson, *A Very Personal War,* p. 129.
56. Ibid., pp. 163–164.
57. Ibid., p. 183.
58. Ibid., p. 72.
59. Ibid., p. 77.
60. Ibid., p. 215.
61. Ibid., pp. 215–216.
62. William J. Lederer, *Our Own Worst Enemy* (New York: W. W. Norton, 1968), p. 97.
63. Ibid., p. 93.
64. Ibid.
65. Ibid., p. 94.
66. Ibid., p. 97.
67. Ibid., p. 96.
68. Ibid., p. 100.
69. Hamilton-Paterson, *A Very Personal War,* pp. 105–106.
70. Ibid., pp. 84–85.
71. Ibid., p. 92.
72. Ibid.
73. Ibid., p. 69.
74. Ibid.
75. Ibid.
76. Lederer, *Our Own Worst Enemy,* p. 84.
77. Hamilton-Paterson, *A Very Personal War,* p. 249.
78. Lederer, *Our Own Worst Enemy,* p. 116.
79. Corson, *The Betrayal,* pp. 221–222.
80. Westmoreland, *A Soldier Reports,* p. 326.
81. Hamilton-Paterson, *A Very Personal War,* p. 116.
82. *Pentagon Papers,* vol, 2, pp. 383–384.
83. Ibid., pp. 390–391.
84. Ibid., p. 391.
85. Lederer, *Our Own Worst Enemy,* p. 115.
86. Ibid., p. 101.
87. Hamilton-Paterson, *A Very Personal War,* pp. 193–194.
88. Ibid., p. 261.
89. Ibid.
90. Ibid., p. 269.
91. Lederer, *Our Own Worst Enemy,* p. 98.
92. Ibid., p. 82.

93. Ibid., p. 103.
94. Ibid.
95. Ibid., p. 114.
96. Ibid., pp. 111–112.
97. Ibid., p. 125.
98. "Cost of the Vietnam War," *Indochina Newsletter*, p. 12.
99. Clark C. Smith, ed., *The Short Timer's Journal: Aspects of Counter-Insurgency*, no. 2 (April–May 1981), p. 112.
100. John Sack, *Lieutenant Calley: His Own Story* (New York: Viking Press, 1974), p. 117.
101. Murray Polner, *No Victory Parades: The Return of the Vietnam Veteran* (New York: Holt, Rinehart and Winston, 1971), p. 117.
102. Anthony B. Herbert with James T. Wooten, *Soldier* (New York: Holt, Rinehart and Winston, 1972), p. 120.
103. Polner, *No Victory Parades*, p. 117.
104. Mike McGrady, *A Dove in Vietnam* (New York: Funk and Wangalls, 1968), p. 26.
105. Sack, *Lieutenant Calley*, p. 38.
106. William Turner Hugget, *Body Count* (New York: Dell Publishing, 1974), p. 179.
107. Pat Faherty, *The Fastest Truck in Vietnam by 1391116* (San Francisco: Pull Press, 1983), pp. 122–123.
108. Peter Martinsen, "Testimony and Questioning," in Coates, Limqueco, and Weiss, *Prevent the Crime of Silence*, p. 263.
109. McGrady, *A Dove in Vietnam*, p. 28.
110. Philip Jones Griffiths, *Vietnam, Inc.* (New York: Collier Books, 1971), p. 191.
111. Smith, *Short-Timer's Journal*, no. 2, p. 18.
112. Hamilton-Paterson, *A Very Personal War*, p. 197.
113. Alfred W. McCoy with Cathleen B. Read and Leonard P. Adams II, *Politics of Heroin in Southeast Asia* (New York: Harper and Row, 1972), pp. 149–222.
114. Robert Roth, *Sand in the Wind* (New York, Pinnacle, 1974), p. 59.
115. David Cortright, *Soldiers in Revolt: The American Military Today* (Garden City, N.Y.; Anchor Press / Doubleday, 1975), p. 29.
116. Ibid., p. 32.
117. Roth, *Sand in the Wind*, p. 60.
118. Larry Hughes, *You Can See a Lot Standing under a Flare in the Republic of Vietnam* (New York: William Morrow, 1969), p. 74.
119. Michael A. Kukler, *Operation Baroom* (Gastonia, N.C.; TCP Publishers, 1980), p. 27.
120. Schell, *The Military Half*, p. 62.
121. Hamilton-Paterson, *A Very Personal War*, p. 67.
122. Lewy, *America in Vietnam*, p. 113.
123. Ibid.
124. Hamilton-Paterson, *A Very Personal War*, p. 67.

8. PACIFICATION WAR IN THE COUNTRYSIDE

1. *The Pentagon Papers: The Senator Gravel Edition* (Boston: Beacon Press, 1972), vol 2, p. 525.
2. Ibid.
3. Ibid.
4. Ibid., p. 540.
5. Ibid., p. 549.
6. Ibid., p. 550.
7. Ibid., p. 552.
8. Ibid., p. 564.
9. Ibid., p. 565.
10. Ibid., p. 571.
11. Ibid., p. 576.
12. Ibid.
13. Ibid., p. 588.
14. Ibid., p. 595.

15. Ibid., p. 596.
16. Ibid.
17. Ibid., p. 597.
18. Ibid., pp. 597–598.
19. Ibid., p. 598.
20. Guenter Lewy, *America in Vietnam* (New York: Oxford University Press, 1978), p. 209.
21. Ibid., pp. 172–174.
22. William R. Corson, *The Betrayal* (New York: W. W. Norton, 1968), pp. 88–89.
23. Malcolm W. Browne, *The New Face of War* (New York: Bobbs-Merrill, 1965), p. 210.
24. *Pentagon Papers*, vol. 4, p. 399.
25. Lewy, *America in Vietnam*, p. 399.
26. Brian M. Jenkins, *A People's Army for South Vietnam: A Vietnamese Solution* (Santa Monica, Calif.: Rand Corporation, 1971), p. 9.
27. Lewy, *America in Vietnam*, p. 179.
28. *Pentagon Papers*, vol. 2, p. 575.
29. Ibid., vol. 4, p. 391.
30. Ibid.
31. Ibid.
32. Ibid.
33. Ibid., pp. 439–440.
34. Thomas W. Scoville, *Reorganization for Pacification Support*, U.S. Army Center of Military History (Washington D.C.: U.S. Government Printing Office, 1982), p. 63.
35. Robert W. Chandler, *War of Ideas: The U.S. Propaganda Campaign in Vietnam* (Boulder, Colo.: Westview Press, 1981), p. 3.
36. Ibid., p. 27.
37. *Pentagon Papers*, vol. 2, p. 530.
38. Chandler, *War of Ideas*, p. 19.
39. Ibid., p. 22.
40. Ibid., p. 48.
41. Ibid.
42. Ibid., p. 112.
43. Ibid., p. 122.
44. Ibid., p. 240.
45. Ibid., p. 243.
46. Ibid.
47. Ibid., p. 244.
48. Ibid., p. 32.
49. Ibid.
50. Ibid., p. 244.
51. David Halberstam, *The Best and the Brightest* (New York: Random House, 1972), p. 123.
52. Ibid., p. 157.
53. Nguyen Cao Ky, *Twenty Years and Twenty Days* (New York: Stein and Day, 1976), p. 81.
54. William C. Westmoreland, *A Soldier Reports* (Garden City, N.Y.: Doubleday, 1980), p. 245.
55. Peter Watson, *War on the Mind: The Military Uses and Abuses of Psychology* (New York: Basic Books, 1978), pp. 411–412.
56. Chandler, *War of Ideas*, p. 179.
57. Ibid.
58. Ibid., p. 182.
59. Ibid.
60. Ibid., p. 164.
61. James Hamilton-Paterson, *A Very Personal War: The Story of Cornelius Hawkridge* (London: Hodder and Stoughton, 1971), pp. 64–65.
62. Douglas S. Blaufarb, *The Counterinsurgency Era: U.S. Doctrine and Performance* (New York: Free Press, 1977), p. 227.
63. Corson, *The Betrayal*, pp. 296–309.
64. Jeffrey Race, *War Comes to Long An: Revolutionary Conflict in a Vietnamese Province* (Berkeley: University of California Press, 1972), p. 260.
65. Blaufarb, *The Counterinsurgency Era*, p. 230; Corson, *The Betrayal*, p. 162.

66. William J. Lederer, *Our Own Worst Enemy* (New York: W. W. Norton, 1968), pp. 145–146.
67. Corson, *The Betrayal*, p. 221.
68. Don Luce, and John Sommer, *Viet Nam: The Unheard Voices* (Cornell University Press, 1969), p. 147.
69. Lewy, *America in Vietnam*, p. 89.
70. Scoville, *Reorganization for Pacification Support*, pp. 45–46.
71. William Colby and Peter Forbath, *Honorable Men: My Life in the CIA* (New York: Simon and Schuster, 1978), p. 269.
72. Corson, *The Betrayal*, pp. 84–85.
73. Thomas C. Thayer, "Territorial Forces," in W. Scott Thompson and Donaldson D. Frizzell, eds., *The Lessons of Vietnam* (New York: Crane, Russak, 1977), p. 260.
74. Corson, *The Betrayal*, p. 87.
75. Thayer, "Territorial Forces," in Thompson and Frizzell, *Lessons of Vietnam*, p. 259.
76. Ibid., p. 260.
77. Harvey Meyerson, *Vinh Long* (Boston: Houghton Mifflin, 1970), p. 115.
78. Corson, *The Betrayal*, p. 85.
79. Martin Russ, *Happy Hunting Ground* (New York: Atheneum, 1968), p. 116.
80. Blaufarb, *The Counterinsurgency Era*, pp. 145–146.
81. Douglas Pike, *Vietcong: The Organization and Techniques of the National Liberation Front of South Vietnam* (Cambridge, Mass.: Massachusetts Institute of Technology Press, 1966).
82. Blaufarb, *The Counterinsurgency Era*, p. 246.
83. Lewy, *America in Vietnam*, p. 284.
84. Blaufarb, *The Counterinsurgency Era*, p. 246.
85. Robert W. Komer, "Impact of Pacification on Insurgency in South Vietnam," *Journal of International Affairs* 25 (1971), 53.
86. Al Santoli, *Everything We Had: An Oral History of the Vietnam War by Thirty-three American Soldiers Who Fought It* (New York: Random House, 1981), p. 204.
87. Ibid.
88. Ibid., p. 208.
89. Ibid., p. 205.
90. Ibid., p. 217.
91. Colby and Forbath, *Honorable Men*, pp. 270–271.
92. Ibid., pp. 81–82.
93. Seymour M. Hersch, *The Price of Power: Kissinger in the Nixon White House* (New York: Summit Books, 1983), p. 81.
94. Ibid., p. 81–82.
95. Blaufarb, *The Counterinsurgency Era*, p. 248.
96. Lewy, *America in Vietnam*, p. 287.
97. Citizens Commission of Inquiry, ed., *The Dellums Committee Hearings on War Crimes in Vietnam: An Inquiry into Command Responsibility in Southeast Asia* (New York: Vintage Books, 1972), p. 96.
98. Blaufarb, *The Counterinsurgency Era*, p. 247.
99. Ibid.
100. Santoli, *Everything We Had*, pp. 217–218.
101. Ralph W. McGehee, *Deadly Deceits: My Twenty-five Years in the CIA* (New York: Sheridan Square Publications, 1983), p. 156.
102. Meyerson, *Vinh Long*, p. 196.
103. Ibid., p. 197.
104. Ibid., p. 198.
105. Ibid.
106. Colby and Forbath, *Honorable Men*, p. 259.
107. Corson, *The Betrayal*, p. 232.
108. Ibid., pp. 232–233.
109. Michael T. Klare, *War without End: American Planning for the Next Vietnam* (New York: Alfred A. Knopf, 1972), p. 221.
110. Meyerson, *Vinh Long*, p. 153.
111. Westmoreland, *A Soldier Reports*, p. 83.
112. Lederer, *Our Own Worst Enemy*, p. 181.

113. Ibid., pp. 22–24.
114. Corson, *The Betrayal*, p. 236.
115. Ibid., p. 238.
116. Lewy, *America in Vietnam*, p. 194.
117. Ibid.
118. Clark C. Smith, ed., *The Short-Timer's Journal: Aspects of Counter-Insurgency*, no. 2 (April–May 1981), p. 25.
119. Jonathan Schell, *The Military Half* (New York: Alfred A. Knopf, 1968), p. 197.
120. Corson, *The Betrayal*, pp. 232–239; Lewy, *America in Vietnam*, p. 125; Thomas C. Thayer, "On Pacification," in W. Scott Thompson and Donaldson D. Frizzell, eds., *The Lessons of Vietnam* (New York: Crane, Russak, 1977), p. 233.
121. Corson, *The Betrayal*, p. 239.
122. Blaufarb, *The Counterinsurgency Era*, p. 262.
123. "CBS Evening News" December 16, 1968.
124. Meyerson, *Vinh Long*, p. 126.
125. Philip Jones Griffiths, *Vietnam, Inc.* (New York: Collier Books, 1971), p. 160.
126. Ibid., p. 161.
127. Colby and Forbath, *Honorable Men*, p. 260.
128. Roger Hillsman, *To Move a Nation* (New York: Dell Publishing, 1969), p. 523.
129. John Sack, *Lieutenant Calley: His Own Story* (New York: Viking Press, 1974), p. 135.
130. Ibid., p. 137.
131. Ibid., p. 142.
132. Robert W. Komer, *Bureaucracy Does Its Thing: Institutional Constraints on U.S.–GVN Performance in Vietnam* (Santa Monica, Calif.: Rand Corporation, 1972), p. 154.

9. AIR WAR OVER NORTH VIETNAM: BOMBING AS COMMUNICATION

1. Estimates on how many bombs were dropped over Southeast Asia differ considerably. Ralph Littauer and Norman Uphoff of the Cornell University Air War Study Group estimated that by the end of 1971 the United States had dropped 6.3 million tons of aerial munitions on Southeast Asia. See their work, *The Air War in Indochina* (Boston: Beacon Press, 1972), p. 11. The *Indochina Newsletter* offers a figure of 7.8 million tons of aerial munitions and 200,000 tons of naval shelling for the war as a whole. By adding aerial and naval bombardments the 8-million-ton figure used here as a minimum estimate was created. See "Costs of the Vietnam War," *Indochina Newsletter* 18 (Nov.–Dec. 1982): 12, 9. Yet the North Vietnamese indicate that these figures are way too low. In 1976 Dr. Hoang Dinh Cau, the DRV's vice-minister of health, told a meeting of the World Health Organization that the United States dropped 7.6 million tons of bombs on North Vietnam alone. By this reckoning, total tonnage for all of Southeast Asia would tally at least 15 million tons. See Gloria Emerson, *Winners and Losers: Battles, Retreats, Gains, Losses and Ruins from a Long War* (New York: Random House, 1978), p. 358.
2. This estimate excludes the thermal blasts and radiation given off by nuclear bombs.
3. *The Pentagon Papers: The Senator Gravel Edition* (Boston: Beacon Press, 1972), vol. 3, pp. 287–289.
4. Ibid., pp. 297–303.
5. Ibid., pp. 304–306.
6. Ibid., pp. 306–307.
7. Ibid., p. 311.
8. Ibid., p. 313.
9. Ibid.
10. Ibid., p. 314.
11. Ibid.
12. Ibid.
13. Ibid.
14. Ibid.
15. Ibid.
16. Ibid., p. 316.
17. Ibid.

18. Ibid.
19. Ibid., p. 317.
20. Ibid., p. 316.
21. Ibid., p. 318.
22. Ibid.
23. Ibid., p. 319.
24. Ibid., p. 320.
25. Ibid., p. 335.
26. Ibid., p. 336.
27. Ibid., p. 341.
28. Ibid., p. 343.
29. Ibid., p. 382.
30. Ibid., p. 349.
31. Ibid., pp. 349–350.
32. Ibid., p. 351.
33. Ibid., p. 354.
34. Ibid., p. 695.
35. Ibid.
36. Ibid., p. 358.
37. Jessica Benjamin, "The Bonds of Love: Rational Violence and Erotic Domination," *Feminist Studies* 6 (Spring 1980), 155.
38. *Pentagon Papers*, vol. 3, pp. 358–359.
39. Ibid., p. 384.
40. Ibid., vol. 4, pp. 55–56.
41. Ibid., p. 55.
42. MACV's Order of Battle called for 300,000. See the debate in chapter six.
43. *Pentagon Papers*, vol. 4, p. 57.
44. Ibid., p. 30.
45. Ibid., p. 59.
46. Ibid., p. 33.
47. Ibid., p. 37.
48. Ibid.
49. Ibid.
50. Ibid., p. 40.
51. Ibid., p. 45.

10. STRUCTURAL DYNAMICS OF ESCALATION IN THEORY AND PRACTICE, 1966–1967

1. *The Pentagon Papers: The Senator Gravel Edition* (Boston: Beacon Press, 1972), vol. 4, p. 25.
2. Ibid., p. 31.
3. Ibid., pp. 28–29.
4. Ibid., p. 60.
5. Ibid.
6. Ibid., p. 61.
7. Ibid., pp. 61–62.
8. Ibid., p. 62.
9. Ibid., pp. 62–63.
10. Ibid., p. 64.
11. Ibid., p. 65.
12. Ibid.
13. Ibid., p. 67.
14. Ibid., p. 69.
15. Ibid., p. 78.
16. Ibid.
17. Henry L. Trewhitt, *McNamara* (New York: Harper and Row, 1971), pp. 36–39.

18. *Pentagon Papers,* vol. 4, pp. 100–101.
19. Admiral U. S. G. Sharp, "Report on Air and Naval Campaigns against North Vietnam and Pacific Command-Wide Support of the War," in General William Westmoreland, *Report on the War in Vietnam* (Washington, D.C.: U.S. Government Printing Office, 1969), p. 57.
20. General William W. Momyer, *Air Power in Three Wars* (Washington, D.C.: U.S. Government Printing Office, 1978), pp. 163–164.
21. Ibid., p. 167.
22. *Pentagon Papers,* vol. 3, p. 481.
23. George Orwell, *1984* (New York: New American Library, 1961), p. 176.
24. Ibid., p. 177.
25. For an excellent summary of the *United States Strategic Bombing Survey* see Harold L. Wilensky, *Organizational Intelligence: Knowledge and Policy in Government and Industry* (New York: Basic Books, 1967), pp. 24–35.
26. Albert Speer, *Inside the Third Reich,* translated by Richard and Clara Winston (New York: Macmillan, 1970), p. 210.
27. Ibid., p. 278.
28. Ibid., p. 346.
29. Ibid., p. 350.
30. *Pentagon Papers,* vol. 4, pp. 81–88, 94–95.
31. Ibid., p. 89.
32. Ibid., pp. 89–90.
33. Ibid., pp. 90–91.
34. Ibid., p. 91.
35. Ibid., p. 96.
36. Ibid.
37. Ibid., p. 97.
38. Ibid., p. 109.
39. Sharp, "Report on Air and Naval Campaigns," in Westmoreland, *Report on the War in Vietnam,* p. 29.
40. *Pentagon Papers,* vol. 4, p. 110.
41. Ibid., p. 111.
42. Ibid.
43. Ibid., p. 116.
44. Ibid., p. 119.
45. Ibid.
46. Ibid., p. 136.
47. Ibid., p. 128.
48. Ibid., p. 144.
49. Ibid., p. 168.
50. Ibid., p. 180.
51. Ibid., p. 169.
52. Ibid., p. 184.
53. Ibid., p. 153.
54. Ibid., p. 170.
55. Townsend Hoopes, *The Limits of Intervention* (New York: David McKay, 1969), p. 257.
56. *Pentagon Papers,* vol. 4, p. 199.
57. Ibid., p. 201.
58. Ibid., pp. 201–202.
59. Ibid., pp. 204–205.
60. Ibid., pp. 224–225.
61. Gareth Porter, *A Peace Denied: The United States, Vietnam, and the Paris Agreement* (Bloomington: Indian University Press, 1975), p. 71.
62. *Pentagon Papers,* vol. 4, p. 270.
63. Ibid.
64. Momyer, *Air Power in Three Wars,* p. 27.
65. Ralph Littauer and Norman Uphoff, eds., *The Air War in Indochina* (Boston: Beacon Press, 1972), p. 168.

## 11. THE STRUCTURE OF AIR OPERATIONS

1. *The Pentagon Papers: The Senator Gravel Edition* (Boston: Beacon Press, 1972), vol. 4, pp. 125–126.
2. General William W. Momyer, *Air Power in Three Wars* (Washington, D.C.: U.S. Government Printing Office, 1978), p. 108.
3. Ibid., p. 94.
4. Frank Harvey, *Air War — Vietnam* (New York: Bantam Books, 1969), p. 149.
5. Townsend Hoopes, *The Limits of Intervention* (New York: David McKay, 1969), pp. 121, 149.
6. Colonel Jack Broughton, *Thud Ridge* (Philadelphia: J. B. Lippincott, 1969), pp. 63–64.
7. Richard S. Drury, *My Secret War* (Fallbrook, Calif.: Aero Publications, 1979), p. 150.
8. Ibid., p. 151.
9. Colonel James A. Donovan, *Militarism, U.S.A.* (New York: Charles Scribner's Sons, 1970), pp. 180–181.
10. Broughton, *Thud Ridge*, p. 25.
11. Harvey, *Air War — Vietnam*, p. 112.
12. Momyer, *Air Power in Three Wars*, pp. 186–187.
13. Admiral U. S. G. Sharp, "Report on Air and Naval Campaigns against North Vietnam and Pacific Command-Wide Support of the War," in General William Westmoreland, *Report on the War in Vietnam* (Washington, D.C.: U.S. Government Printing Office, 1969), p. 29.
14. Harvey, *Air War — Vietnam*, p. 177.
15. Colonel Belbert Corum et al., *The Tale of Two Bridges*, Monograph 1 of volume 1 of United States Air Force Southeast Asia Monograph Series (Washington, D.C.: U.S. Government Printing Office, 1976), p. 9.
16. Stuart H. Loory, *Defeated: Inside America's Military Machine* (New York: Random House, 1973), p. 338.
17. Corum et al., *Tale of Two Bridges*, p. 46.
18. Bernard C. Nalty, "The Air War against North Vietnam," in *The Vietnam War*, edited by Ray Bonds (New York: Crown Publishers, 1979), p. 93.
19. Loory, *Defeated*, pp. 338–339.
20. Corum et al., *Tale of Two Bridges*, p. 92.
21. Ibid., p. 46.
22. John Trotti, *Phantom over Vietnam* (New York: Berkeley Books, 1985), p. 21.
23. Ibid., p. 195.
24. Drury, *My Secret War*, p. 154.
25. Trotti, *Phantom over Vietnam*, p. 195.
26. Broughton, *Thud Ridge*, pp. 96–97.
27. Ibid., pp. 97–98.
28. Morris J. Blachman, "The Stupidity of Intelligence," in *Inside the System: A Washington Monthly Reader*, edited by Charles Peters and Timothy J. Adams (New York: Frederick A. Praeger, 1979), pp. 273–274.
29. Ibid., p. 273.
30. Major General Joseph A. McChristian, *The Role of Military Intelligence 1965–1967*, Department of the Army Vietnam Studies Series (Washington, D.C.: U.S. Government Printing Office, 1974), pp. 32–40.
31. Benjamin F. Schemmer, *The Raid* (New York: Harper and Row, 1976), p. 31.
32. Momyer, *Air Power in Three Wars*, pp. 179–180.
33. *Pentagon Papers*, vol. 4, pp. 171–172.
34. Ibid., p. 179.
35. Malcolm Caldwell, "Report from North Vietnam," in *Prevent the Crime of Silence: Reports from the International War Crimes Tribunal Founded by Bertrand Russell*, edited by Ken Coates, Peter Limqueco, and Peter Weiss (London: Allen Lane / Penguin Press, 1971), pp. 122–123.
36. Ibid., pp. 123–124.
37. Ibid., p. 127.
38. Lawrence Daly, "American Bombing in North Vietnam," in Coates, Limqueco, and Weiss, *Prevent the Crime of Silence*, p. 129.

39. Ibid., pp. 131–132.
40. Ibid., p. 135.
41. John Takman and Alex Hojer, "Bombardment of Civilians in North Vietnam," in Coates, Limqueco, and Weiss, *Prevent the Crime of Silence,* pp. 153–154.
42. Abraham Behar, "Summary Report of the Bombing of the Civil Population of the North," in Coates, Limqueco, and Weiss, *Prevent the Crime of Silence,* p. 167.
43. Daly, "American Bombing in North Vietnam," in Coates, Limqueco, and Weiss, *Prevent the Crime of Silence,* p. 131.
44. Takman and Hojer, "Bombardment of Civilians in North Vietnam," in Coates, Limqueco, and Weiss, *Prevent the Crime of Silence,* p. 152.
45. Daly, "American Bombing in North Vietnam," in Coates, Limqueco, and Weiss, *Prevent the Crime of Silence,* p. 130.
46. Jean-Pierre Vigier, "Technical Aspects of Fragmentation Bombs," in Coates, Limqueco, and Weiss, *Prevent the Crime of Silence,* p. 120.
47. Behar, "Summary Report of the Bombing of the Civil Population of the North," in Coates, Limqueco, and Weiss, *Prevent the Crime of Silence,* p. 158.
48. Caldwell, "Report from North Vietnam," in Coates, Limqueco, and Weiss, *Prevent the Crime of Silence,* p. 121.
49. Ibid., p. 132.
50. Martin Birnstingol, "Report from North Vietnam," in Coates, Limqueco, and Weiss, *Prevent the Crime of Silence,* p. 137.
51. Behar, "Summary Report of the Bombing of the Civil Population of the North," in Coates, Limqueco, and Weiss, *Prevent the Crime of Silence,* p. 165.
52. Caldwell, "Report from North Vietnam," in Coates, Limqueco, and Weiss, *Prevent the Crime of Silence,* pp. 122–123.
53. Wilfred G. Burchett, *Vietnam North* (New York: International Publishers, 1966), p. 19.
54. Behar, "Summary Report of the Bombing of the Civil Population of the North," in Coates, Limqueco, and Weiss, *Prevent the Crime of Silence,* p. 163.
55. Ibid., pp. 161–164.
56. Ibid., p. 165.
57. Ibid., pp. 159–160.
58. Sharp, "Report on Air and Naval Campaigns," in Westmoreland, *Report on the War in Vietnam,* p. 29.
59. Behar, "Summary Report of the Bombing of the Civil Population of the North," in Coates, Limqueco, and Weiss, *Prevent the Crime of Silence,* p. 168.
60. Burchett, *Vietnam North,* p. 113.
61. Broughton, *Thud Ridge,* p. 113.
62. Corum et al., *Tale of Two Bridges,* p. 36.
63. James Fallows, *National Defense* (New York: Random House, 1981), p. 45.
64. Ibid.
65. Loory, *Defeated,* pp. 342–343.
66. *Pentagon Papers,* vol. 4, p. 52.
67. See *Pentagon Papers,* vol. 4, pp. 245–257; Momyer, *Air Power in Three Wars,* p. 21–26.
68. Loory, *Defeated,* p. 341; Fallows, *National Defense,* p. 41; Trotti, *Phantom over Vietnam,* p. 36.
69. *Pentagon Papers,* vol. 4, p. 53.
70. Ibid., p. 53.
71. Ibid., p. 136.
72. Ibid., pp. 134–135.
73. Ibid., p. 136.
74. Alain C. Enthoven and Wayne K. Smith, *How Much Is Enough?: Shaping the Defense Program, 1961–1969* (New York: Harper and Row, 1971), p. 306.
75. *Pentagon Papers,* vol. 4, pp. 225–226.
76. Ibid., p. 226.
77. Ibid., p. 194.
78. Ibid., p. 230.
79. Momyer, *Air Power in Three Mars,* p. 190.
80. *Pentagon Papers,* vol. 4, p. 199.

81. Cincinnatus, *Self-Destruction: The Disintegration and Decay of the United States Army during the Vietnam Era* (New York: W. W. Norton, 1981), p. 55.
82. *Pentagon Papers*, vol. 4, p. 227.
83. Ibid., p. 228.
84. Ibid.
85. Burchett, *Vietnam North*, p. 58.
86. Ibid., p. 55.

## 12. THE REDISTRIBUTION OF AIR WAR: LAOS, 1968–1973

1. For Nixon's early positions on Southeast Asia see F. M. Kail, *What Washington Said: Administration Rhetoric and the Vietnam War, 1949–1969* (New York: Harper and Row, 1973), pp. 84–86. For his positions in the 1960s and 1970s see Jonathan Schell, *The Time of Illusion* (New York: Alfred A. Knopf, 1975).
2. William Shawcross, *Sideshow: Kissinger, Nixon, and the Destruction of Cambodia* (New York: Simon and Schuster, 1979), p. 86.
3. Schell, *Time of Illusion*, pp. 5–25.
4. H. R. Haldeman with Joseph Pimona, *The Ends of Power* (New York: New York Times Books, 1978), p. 86.
5. Shawcross, *Sideshow*, p. 93.
6. Ralph Littauer and Norman Uphoff, eds., *The Air War in Indochina* (Boston: Beacon Press, 1972), p. 180.
7. Ibid., p. 78.
8. Shawcross, *Sideshow*, p. 92.
9. Charles A. Stevenson, *The End of Nowhere: American Policy toward Laos since 1954* (Boston: Beacon Press, 1973), p. 29.
10. Ibid., p. 40.
11. Ibid., pp. 47–49. Also see Bernard B. Fall, *Anatomy of a Crisis* (Garden City, N.Y.: Doubleday, 1969), pp. 71–76.
12. Len E. Ackland, "No Place for Neutralism: The Eisenhower Administration and Laos," in *Laos: War and Revolution*, edited by Nina S. Adams and Alfred W. McCoy (New York: Harper and Row, 1970), p. 140.
13. Stevenson, *The End of Nowhere*, p. 93.
14. To my knowledge there is no full account of White Star. For fragmentary references see Stevenson, *The End of Nowhere*, pp. 125, 174, 184; and Benjamin F. Schemmer, *The Raid* (New York: Harper and Row, 1976), pp. 31–43.
15. Christopher Robbins, *Air America: The Story of the CIA's Secret Airline* (New York: G. P. Putnam's Sons, 1979).
16. Alfred W. McCoy with Cathleen B. Read and Leonard P. Adams II, *The Politics of Heroin in Southeast Asia* (New York: Harper and Row, 1972), p. 274.
17. Ibid., p. 277.
18. Stevenson, *The End of Nowhere*, p. 151.
19. Fred Branfman, "Presidential War in Laos, 1964–1970," in Adams and McCoy, *Laos: War and Revolution*, p. 261.
20. McCoy, Read, and Adams, *Politics of Heroin*, pp. 265–277; John Lewallen, "The Reluctant Counterinsurgents: International Voluntary Services in Laos," in Adams and McCoy, *Laos: War and Revolution*, pp. 357–376.
21. Robbins, *Air America*, p. 122.
22. Stevenson, *The End of Nowhere*, p. 197.
23. Ibid.
24. Ibid., p. 204.
25. Ibid., p. 210.
26. For a discussion of the importance of the radar site see General William W. Momyer, *Air Power in Three Wars* (Washington, D.C.: U.S. Government Printing Office, 1978), pp. 178–179. For an account of the Pathet Lao capture of the base see McCoy, Read, and Adams, *Politics of Heroin*, pp. 278–279.
27. Robert Shaplen, *Time out of Hand* (New York: Harper and Row, 1969), p. 348.

28. Estimates for bombing in northern Laos are in Littauer and Uphoff, *Air War in Indochina*, pp. 66–86. Fred Branfman estimates that 75,000 to 150,000 tons of bombs were dropped on the Plain of Jars. See his book, *Voices from the Plain of Jars* (New York: Harper and Row, 1972), p. 4.
29. Branfman, *Voices from the Plain of Jars*, p. 18.
30. Littauer and Uphoff, *Air War in Indochina*, p. 83.
31. Momyer, *Air Power in Three Wars*, p. 179.
32. Littauer and Uphoff, *Air War in Indochina*, p. 81.
33. Branfman, "Presidential War in Laos, 1964–1970," in Adams and McCoy, *Laos: War and Revolution*, p. 261.
34. Ibid., p. 255.
35. Ibid., p. 248.
36. Littauer and Uphoff, *Air War in Indochina*, p. 70.
37. Branfman, *Voices from the Plain of Jars*, p. 19.
38. Robbins, *Air America*, p. 143.
39. Stevenson, *The End of Nowhere*, p. 226.
40. Branfman, *Voices from the Plain of Jars*, p. 40.
41. Ibid.
42. Ibid., p. 73.
43. Ibid., p. 85.
44. Ibid., p. 97.
45. Ibid., p. 117.
46. Ibid., p. 21.
47. McCoy, Read, and Adams, *Politics of Heroin*, p. 281.
48. Ibid., p. 290.
49. Don A. Schanche, *Mister Pop* (New York: David McKay, 1970), p. 304.
50. McCoy, Read, and Adams, *Politics of Heroin*, pp. 242–354.
51. George L. Weiss, "Battle for Control of the Ho Chi Minh Trail," *Armed Forces Journal*, February 15, 1971, p. 19.
52. The Jason study on the electronic barrier and McNamara's recommendations are discussed in *The Pentagon Papers: The Senator Gravel Edition* (Boston: Beacon Press, 1972), vol. 4, pp. 120–126.
53. Ibid., p. 122.
54. Weiss, "Battle for Control of the Ho Chi Minh Trail," p. 22.
55. This is a fictional account. See Pierre Boulle, *Ears of the Jungle*, translated by Michael Dorby and Lynda Cole (New York: Vanguard Press, 1972), pp. 82–83. Bernard C. Nalty gives a nonfictional account in his essay, "The Air War on the Laotian Supply Routes," in *The Vietnam War*, edited by Ray Bonds (New York: Crown Publishers, 1979), p. 168.
56. Momyer, *Air Power in Three Wars*, p. 213.
57. Nalty, "The Air War on the Laotian Supply Routes," in Bonds, *The Vietnam War*, p. 170.
58. Momyer, *Air Power in Three Wars*, p. 212.
59. Ibid., p. 213.
60. Nalty, "The Air War on the Laotian Supply Routes," in Bonds, *The Vietnam War*, p. 170.
61. Boulle's plot in *Ears of the Jungle* concerns how the North Vietnamese were able to generate false signals and confuse the sensors.
62. Wilfred G. Burchett, *Vietnam North* (New York: International Publishers, 1966), pp. 134–135.
63. William C. Westmoreland, *A Soldier Reports* (Garden City, N.Y.: Doubleday, 1980), pp. 355–358.
64. Momyer, *Air Power in Three Wars*, pp. 321–324.
65. General Donn A. Starry, *Mounted Combat in Vietnam*, Department of the Army Vietnam Studies Series (Washington, D.C.: U.S. Government Printing Office, 1978), p. 191.
66. Momyer, *Air Power in Three Wars*, p. 324.
67. Lieutenant John J. Tolson, *Airmobility, 1961–1971*, Department of the Army Vietnam Studies Series (Washington, D.C.: U.S. Government Printing Office, 1973), p. 251.
68. Momyer, *Air Power in Three Wars*, p. 324.
69. Shawcross, *Sideshow*, p. 217.

13.  CLOSING OUT THE WAR: CAMBODIA AND NORTH VIETNAM, 1969–1973

1.  William C. Westmoreland, *A Soldier Reports* (Garden City, N.Y.: Doubleday, 1980), p. 68.
2.  General William W. Momyer, *Air Power in Three Wars* (Washington, D.C.: U.S. Government Printing Office, 1978), pp. 296–297.
3.  Westmoreland's memo calling for B-52 raids in South Vietnam is in *The Pentagon Papers: The Senator Gravel Edition* (Boston: Beacon Press, 1972), vol. 3, pp. 296–297.
4.  Westmoreland, *A Soldier Reports*, p. 269.
5.  William Shawcross, *Sideshow: Kissinger, Nixon, and the Destruction of Cambodia* (New York: Simon and Schuster, 1979), p. 19.
6.  Ibid., p. 25.
7.  Ibid., p. 28.
8.  Ibid., p. 64.
9.  Ibid., pp. 112–123.
10.  Ibid., p. 140.
11.  Ibid., p. 138.
12.  Ibid.
13.  Ibid., p. 136.
14.  Jonathan Schell, *The Time of Illusion* (New York: Alfred A. Knopf, 1975), pp. 90–91.
15.  Ibid., p. 91.
16.  Shawcross, *Sideshow*, p. 145.
17.  Ibid.
18.  Ibid., p. 152.
19.  Ibid., p. 153.
20.  Ibid., p. 135.
21.  Ibid., p. 172.
22.  Ibid., p. 173.
23.  Ibid., p. 214.
24.  Ibid., p. 213.
25.  Ibid.
26.  Ibid., p. 214.
27.  Sortie rates for 1970 are from Ralph Littauer and Norman Uphoff, eds., *Air War in Indochina* (Boston: Beacon Press, 1972), pp. 275–276. Sortie rates for 1971 are from Shawcross, *Sideshow*, p. 218.
28.  Shawcross, *Sideshow*, p. 175.
29.  Ibid., p. 249.
30.  Gareth Porter, *A Peace Denied: The United States, Vietnam, and the Paris Agreements* (Bloomington: Indiana University Press, 1975), p. 107.
31.  Colonel Donaldson D. Frizzell and Colonel Ray L. Bowers, eds., *Airpower and the 1972 Spring Invasion*, Monograph 3, volume 2, United States Air Force Southeast Asia Monograph Series (Washington, D.C.: U.S. Government Printing Office, 1978), p. 106.
32.  Schell, *Time of Illusion*, p. 241.
33.  W. Scott Thompson and Donaldson D. Frizzell, eds., *Lessons of Vietnam* (New York: Crane, Russak, 1977), p. 202.
34.  Porter, *A Peace Denied*, p. 115.
35.  Ibid., p. 122.
36.  Oriana Fallaci, "Thieu: An Interview," *New Republic*, January 20, 1977.
37.  Porter, *A Peace Denied*, p. 140.
38.  Ibid., p. 140.
39.  For a detailed account of Thieu's participation in the heroin trade see Alfred W. McCoy with Cathleen B. Read and Leonard P. Adams II, *The Politics of Heroin in Southeast Asia* (New York: Harper and Row, 1972), pp. 174–222. For accounts of Vietnamese elections see Wilfred G. Burchett, *Grasshoppers and Elephants: Why Vietnam Fell* (New York: Urizen Books, 1977), pp. 148–149. Also see Shawcross, *Sideshow*, p. 234.
40.  Porter, *A Peace Denied*, p. 151.
41.  Ibid., p. 108.
42.  Ibid., p. 156.
43.  Ibid., p. 156.

44. Ibid., p. 158.
45. Brigadier General James R. McCarthy and Lieutenant Colonel George B. Allison, *Linebacker II: A View from the Rock*, Monograph 8, volume 6, United States Air Force Southeast Asia Monograph Series (Washington, D.C.: U.S. Government Printing Office, 1979), p. 158.
46. Ibid.
47. Ibid., p. 22.
48. Burchett, *Grasshoppers and Elephants*, p. 162.
49. McCarthy and Allison, *Linebacker II*, p. 164.
50. Burchett, *Grasshoppers and Elephants*, p. 164.
51. McCarthy and Allison, *Linebacker II*, p. 85.
52. Ibid.
53. Shawcross, *Sideshow*, p. 265.
54. Ibid., p. 271.
55. Ibid., p. 272.
56. Ibid., p. 271.
57. Ibid., pp. 271–272.
58. Ibid., p. 297.
59. Ibid.

14.   FINDING THE LIGHT AT THE END OF THE TUNNEL

1. Gareth Porter, *A Peace Denied: The United States, Vietnam, and the Paris Agreements* (Bloomington: Indiana University Press, 1975), p. 186.
2. Ibid., p. 187.
3. Ibid.
4. Ibid., p. 320.
5. Ibid., p. 233.
6. Ibid., p. 171.
7. Ibid., p. 187.
8. Ibid., p. 255.
9. Ibid., pp. 264–265.
10. Ibid., p. 258.
11. Frank Snepp, *Decent Interval: An Insider's Account of Saigon's Indecent End Told by the CIA's Chief Strategy Analyst in Vietnam* (New York: Random House, 1977), p. 94.
12. Ibid., pp. 94, 116.
13. Ibid., pp. 118–119.
14. Porter, *A Peace Denied*, pp. 272–273.
15. General Van Tien Dung (Chief of Staff, Vietnam People's Army), *Our Great Spring Victory: An Account of the Liberation of South Vietnam*, translated by John Spragens, Jr. (New York: Monthly Review Press, 1972), pp. 8–9.
16. Snepp, *Decent Interval*, p. 120.
17. Ibid.
18. Ibid., p. 88.
19. Ibid., p. 85.
20. Ibid., pp. 147–148.
21. Ibid., p. 113.
22. Ibid., p. 108.
23. Ibid.
24. Ibid., p. 114.
25. Ibid., p. 115.
26. Ibid., p. 114.
27. Ibid., p. 103.
28. Van Tien Dung, *Our Great Spring Victory*, p. 17.
29. Porter, *A Peace Denied*, p. 266.
30. Snepp, *Decent Interval*, pp. 98, 121, 123.
31. Porter, *A Peace Denied*, pp. 262–268.
32. Van Tien Dung, *Our Great Spring Victory*, p. 20.
33. Porter, *A Peace Denied*, p. 269.

34. Snepp, *Decent Interval*, pp. 133–135.
35. Van Tien Dung, *Our Great Spring Victory*, p. 25.
36. Ibid., p. 97.
37. Snepp, *Decent Interval*, p. 161.
38. Ibid., pp. 237–238.
39. Ibid., pp. 306–307.
40. Ibid., p. 308.
41. Ibid., p. 420.
42. Ibid., p. 491.
43. Ibid., p. 536.
44. Ibid., p. 537.
45. Ibid., p. 546.
46. "CBS Evening News," April 30, 1975.

### 15. SURVEYING THE WRECKAGE: THE LIMITS OF CONVENTIONAL CRITICISM AND THE REPRODUCTION OF TECHNOWAR

1. John E. Mueller, *War, Presidents, and Public Opinion* (New York: John Wiley and Sons, 1973), p. 55. For additional polls see Hazel Erskine, "The Polls: Is War a Mistake?," *Public Opinion Quarterly*, vol. 34, no. 1 (Spring 1970), pp. 134–150.
2. *Christian Science Monitor*, April 22, 1975.
3. *Washington Post*, April 30, 1975.
4. *New York Times*, April 21, 1975.
5. David Halberstam, *The Making of a Quagmire* (New York: Random House, 1965).
6. Chester L. Cooper, *The Lost Crusade: America in Vietnam* (New York: Dodd, Mead, 1970), p. 418.
7. Townsend Hoopes, *The Limits of Intervention* (New York: David McKay, 1969), p. 32.
8. Arthur M. Schlesinger, Jr., *The Bitter Heritage* (Boston: Houghton Mifflin, 1966), p. 48.
9. Ibid.
10. David Halberstam, *The Best and the Brightest* (New York: Random House, 1972), p. 414.
11. Leslie Gelb with Richard K. Betts, *The Irony of Vietnam: The System Worked* (Washington, D.C.: Brookings Institution, 1979), p. 2.
12. Ibid.
13. Ibid., p. 10.
14. Ibid.
15. Ibid., p. 354.
16. Edwin S. Reischauer, "Back to Normalcy," *Foreign Policy*, Fall 1975, p. 200.
17. Charles Kadushin, *The American Intellectual Elite* (Boston: Little, Brown, 1974), p. 164.
18. Ibid., pp. 164–165.
19. Richard A. Gabriel and Paul L. Savage, *Crisis in Command* (New York: Hill and Wang, 1978), p. 4.
20. Ibid., p. 10.
21. Douglas Kinnard, *The War Managers* (Hanover, Mass.: University Press of New England, 1977), pp. 24, 45, 54, 75, 111.
22. Lieutenant General W. R. Peers, *The My Lai Inquiry* (New York: W. W. Norton, 1979), pp. 212–213.
23. Ibid., pp. 84–85.
24. Lewis Sorley, "Prevailing Criteria: A Critique," in *Combat Effectiveness: Cohesion, Stress, and the Volunteer Military*, edited by Sam C. Sarkesian, Sage Research Progress Series on War, Revolution, and Peacekeeping, vol. 9 (Beverly Hills, Calif.: Sage Publications, 1980), p. 68.
25. Gabriel and Savage, *Crisis in Command*, P. 89.
26. Sorley, "Prevailing Criteria: A Critique," in Sarkesian, *Combat Effectiveness*, pp. 68–73.
27. David R. Segal, "Leadership and Management: Organization Theory," in *Military Leadership*, edited by James H. Buck and Lawrence J. Knob, Sage Research Progress Series on War, Revolution, and Peacekeeping, vol. 10 (Beverly Hills, Calif.: Sage Publications, 1981), p. 44.
28. Ibid., p. 53.

29. Stephen D. Wesbrook, "The Potential for Military Disintegration," in Sarkesian, *Combat Effectiveness*, p. 274.
30. Ibid., p. 271.
31. Stephen D. Wesbrook, "The Alienated Soldier: Legacy of Our Time," *Army*, December 1979, p. 21.
32. Wesbrook, "The Potential for Military Disintegration," in Sarkesian, *Combat Effectiveness*, pp. 274–275.
33. Stephen D. Wesbrook, *Political Training in the United States Army: A Reconsideration* (Columbus, Ohio: Mershor Center of the Ohio State University, 1979).
34. Wesbrook, "The Potential for Military Disintegration," in Sarkesian, *Combat Effectiveness*, pp. 274–275.
35. Jürgen Habermas, *Legitimation Crisis*, translated by Thomas McCarthy (Boston: Beacon Press, 1975), pp. 1–30.
36. Drew Middleton, "Vietnam and the Military Mind," *New York Times Magazine*, January 10, 1982, p. 37.
37. Ibid.
38. Giap was interviewed by Wilfred Burchett; see his *Catapult to Freedom* (London: Quartet Books, 1978), p. 42.
39. Middleton, "Vietnam and the Military Mind," p. 37.
40. W. Scott Thompson and Donaldson D. Frizzell, eds., *The Lessons of Vietnam* (New York: Crane, Russak, 1977), p. 143.
41. Senator Barry Goldwater, *Congressional Record*, vol. 121, part 14 (June 6, 1975), p. 17558.
42. Public Broadcasting Service's "Frontline" documentary series, June 12, 1983.
43. Colonel Harry Summers, Jr., *On Strategy: a Critical Analysis of the Vietnam War* (Novato, Calif.: Presidio Press, 1982), p. 1.
44. Ibid., p. 88. The quoted passage is from Norman B. Hannah, "Now We Know," in *All Quiet on the Eastern Front*, edited by Anthony T. Bouscaren (New York: Devin-Adair, 1977), p. 149.
45. Summers, *On Strategy*, p. 88.
46. Ibid., p. 90.
47. Vo Nguyen Giap, *Selected Writings, 1969–1972* (Hanoi: Foreign Languages Publishing House, 1972). This was also Giap's strategy against the French; see his book *People's War, People's Army* (New York: Frederick A. Praeger, 1962).
48. Summers, *On Strategy*, p. 96.
49. Frank Snepp, *Decent Interval: An Insider's Account of Saigon's Indecent End Told by the CIA's Chief Strategy Analyst in Vietnam* (New York: Random House, 1977), p. 137.
50. Summers, *On Strategy*, pp. 122–123. General Palmer is quoted many times in Summers's analysis. See Palmer's *Summons of the Trumpet: U.S.–Vietnam in Perspective* (San Rafael, Calif.: Presidio Press, 1978).
51. These figures are from Seymour Melman, *The Permanent War Economy: American Capitalism in Decline* (New York: Simon and Schuster, 1974, p. 18, and Robert Warren Stevens, *Vain Hopes, Grim Realities: The Economic Consequences of the Vietnam War* (New York: New Viewpoints / Franklin Watts, 1976), p. 143. Stevens's 1968, 1969, and 1970 figures do not include military retirement pay. The 1950, 1961, 1974, and 1975 figures do include retirement pay.
52. Noam Chomsky, *Towards a New Cold War: Essays on the Current Crisis and How We Got There (New York: Pantheon Books, 1982), p. 189.*
53. *Budget of the United States*, Office of Management and Budget, January 1983.
54. A review of weapons systems commissioned in the 1950s found that final costs averaged 3.2 times initial estimates. See M. J. Peck and F. M. Scherer, *The Weapons Acquisition Process: An Economic Analysis* (Cambridge, Mass.: Harvard University Graduate School of Business, 1962), p. 429. For discussion of the weapoons procurement process, see Melman, *The Permanent War Economy*, and James Fallows, *The National Defense* (New York: Random House, 1981).
55. For a comparison of the two rates see Robert DeGrasse, Jr., with Paul Murphy and William Ragen, *The Costs and Consequences of Reagan's Military Buildup* (New York: Council on Economic Priorities, 1982), p. 5.

56. Taken from Seymour Melman's address to the Socialist Scholars Conference of April 1–2, 1983, in New York City as reproduced by Alexander Cockburn and James Ridgeway, "Annals of the Age of Reagan," *Village Voice,* April 25, 1983, p. 20.
57. Ibid.
58. Ibid.
59. Major General Hoover's testimony before the House Subcommittee on Procurement and Military Nuclear Systems was presented on April 12, 1982. It was reproduced in the "Readings" section of *Harper's,* April 1984, pp. 21–22.
60. Maxwell Taylor, "The Legitimate Claims of National Security," *Foreign Affairs,* April 1974, pp. 586–587.
61. Michael T. Klare, *Beyond the "Vietnam Syndrome": U.S. Interventionism in the 1980s* (Washington, D.C.: Institute for Policy Studies, 1981), p. 77.
62. *Los Angeles Times,* March 5, 1983.
63. Quoted by Lynda Chavez, "Salvador Forces Confronting Morale Problem,'" *New York Times,* February 12, 1983.
64. Quoted by William T. Tuohy, "El Salvador Faces Ghost of Vietnam," *Los Angeles Times,* March 20, 1983.
65. For a good account of the coup see Stephen Schlesinger and Stephen Kinzer, *Bitter Fruit: The Untold Story of the American Coup in Guatemala* (Garden City, N.Y.: Doubleday, 1983).
66. Beatrice Manz, "Vietnam South," *Nation,* July 9–16, 1983, p. 37.
67. For a review of the U.S. Army's Command and General Staff College see Matthew Stevenson, "The Ivied Walls of War," *Progressive,* March 1983, pp. 46–48.
68. Manz, "Vietnam South," p. 37.
69. Philip Taubman and Raymond Bonner, "U.S. Ties to Anti-Sandinistas Are Reported to Be Extensive," *New York Times,* April 3, 1983.
70. "U.S. Installs Radar at Strategic Honduras Site," *Los Angeles Times,* March 20, 1983.
71. Philip Taubman, "Pentagon Seeking a Rise in Advisers to 125," *New York Times,* July 23, 1983.
72. For a discussion of post-Vietnam military failures such as the Iran rescue mission, the explosion of the Marine Corps barracks in Beirut, and the Grenada invasion, and how these failures were covered up by the military bureaucracy, see Richard A. Gabriel, *Military Incompetence: Why the American Military Doesn't Win* (New York: Hill and Wang, 1985).

APPENDIX:   THE WARRIOR'S KNOWLEDGE: SOCIAL STRATIFICATION AND THE BOOK CORPUS OF VIETNAM

1. For a bibliography of novels, poetry, and plays (but excluding memoirs), see John Newman, *Vietnam War Literature: An Annotated Bibliography of Imaginative Works about Americans Fighting in Vietnam* (Metuchen, N.J.: Scarecrow Press, 1982). Newman's work is based upon the collection held by Colorado State University Library at Fort Collins, Colorado. For a more traditional bibliography of historical works and documents, see Christopher L. Sugnet and John T. Hickey with Robert Crispino, *Vietnam War Bibliography: Selected from Cornell University Echols Collection* (Lexington, Mass.: Lexington Books / D. C. Heath, 1983).
2. Stuart A. Herrington, *Silence Was a Weapon: The Vietnam War in the Villages* (Novato, Calif.: Presidio Press, 1982), p. xiii.
3. Michael Foucault, *Power/Knowledge: Selected Interviews and Other Writings,* edited by Colin Gordon (New York: Pantheon Books, 1980), p. 82.
4. Ibid., p. 83.
5. Ibid., pp. 83–84.
6. William R. Corson, *The Betrayal* (New York: W. W. Norton, 1968), p. 256.
7. Guenter Lewy, *America in Vietnam* (New York: Oxford University Press, 1978), p. v.
8. Michael Foucault, "The Discourse on Language," translated by Rupert Swyer; appendix to *The Archeology of Knowledge* (New York: Pantheon Books, 1972), p. 227.
9. Michael Herr, *Dispatches* (New York: Alfred A. Knopf, 1977), pp. 216–217.
10. I know of no combat accounts by senior noncommissioned officers (sergeants). Indeed, the only work by a senior sergeant is Michael A. Kukler's *Operation Baroom* (Gastonia, N.C.: TCP Publishers, 1980).
11. Very few noncombat works have been published. Three that come to mind are: Charles R.

Anderson, *Vietnam: The Other War* (Novato, Calif.: Presidio Press, 1982); Craig Hiler, *Monkey Mountain* (New York: Tower Publications, 1979); Larry Hughes, *You Can See a Lot Standing under a Flare in the Republic of Vietnam* (New York: William Morrow, 1969).

12. The one book-length memoir published by a black soldier is David Parks, *G.I. Diary* (New York: Harper and Row, 1968). Clark Smith, a white oral historian, interviewed Stanley Goff and Robert Sanders for *Brothers: Black Soldiers in the Nam* (Novato, Calif.: Presidio Press, 1982). Clyde Taylor's edited work, *Vietnam and Black America: An Anthology of Protest and Resistance* (Garden City, N.Y.: Anchor Press / Doubleday, 1973), contains poems and one memoir by Vietnam veterans. Wallace Terry's work is the largest collection of oral history interviews with black veterans. See *Bloods: An Oral History of the Vietnam War by Black Veterans* (New York: Random House, 1984). See also John Alfred Williams's novel about black military experiences, *Captain Blackman* (Garden City, N.Y.: Doubleday, 1972).

13. The memoir is by Lynda Van Devanter with Christopher Morgan, *Home before Morning: The Story of an Army Nurse in Vietnam* (New York: Beaufort Books, 1983). Patricia L. Walsh's novel is called *Forever Sad the Hearts* (New York: Avon Books, 1982). There are occasional interviews with nurses in the major oral history collections, such as Al Santoli's *Everything We Had: An Oral History of the Vietnam War by Thirty-three American Soldiers Who Fought It* (New York: Random House, 1981).

14. For a discussion of the relationships between news organizations and bureaucracies see Gaye Tuchman, *Making News: A Study in the Social Construction of Reality* (New York: Free Press, 1978).

15. Herr, *Dispatches,* pp. 216–217.

16. Robert Roth, *Sand in the Wind* (New York: Pinnacle Books, 1974), p. 461.

17. Tim O'Brien, *Going After Cacciato* (New York: Delacorte Press / Seymour Lawrence, 1978), pp. 320–321.

18. Frank A. Cross, Jr., "The Fifty Gunner," in his collection *Reminders* (Big Timber, Mont.: Seven Buffaloes Press, 1986), p. 12.

19. W. D. Ehrhart, "Hunting," in *Carrying the Darkness: America in Indochina — The Poetry of the Vietnam War,* edited by W. D. Ehrhart (New York: Avon, 1985), p. 95.

20. Herr, *Dispatches,* p. 6.

21. Ibid., p. 71.

# Index

The author gratefully acknowledges the following publishers and individuals for permission to quote copyrighted materials from:

*The Betrayal* by William R. Corson. Copyright © 1968 by William R. Corson (New York: W. W. Norton and Company, 1968).

*The Short-Timer's Journal* (Berkeley, California), Clark Smith, oral historian, editor, publisher. Copyright © 1980, 1981 by Clark Smith.

*Soldier* by Anthony B. Herbert, with James T. Wooten. Copyright © 1972 by Anthony B. Herbert (New York: Holt, Rinehart & Winston, 1972).

*Voices from the Plain of Jars* by Fred Branfman. Copyright © 1972 by Fred Branfman (New York: Harper & Row, 1972).

*Self-Destruction* by Cincinnatus. Copyright © 1981 by Cincinnatus (New York: W. W. Norton and Company, 1981).

*Our Own Worst Enemy* by William J. Lederer. Copyright © 1968 by William J. Lederer (New York: W. W. Norton and Company, 1968).

*Nam* by Mark Baker. Copyright © 1981 by Mark Baker (New York: William R. Morrow & Company, Inc., 1981).

*Spoils of War* by Charles J. Levy. Copyright © 1973 by Charles J. Levy (Boston: Houghton Mifflin Company, 1974).

*Conversations with Americans* by Mark Lane. Copyright © 1970 by Mark Lane (New York: Simon & Schuster, 1970).

*Street Without Joy* by Bernard B. Fall. Copyright © 1964 by Bernard B. Fall (Harrisburg, Pa: Stackpole Books, 1964).

*Prevent the Crime of Silence* by Ken Coates, Peter Limqueco, and Peter Weiss. Copyright © 1971 by Ken Coates, Peter Limqueco, and Peter Weiss (New York: Penguin, 1971).

*Everything We Had* by Al Santoli and Vietnam Veterans of America. Copyright © 1981 by Al Santoli and Vietnam Veterans of America (New York: Random House, 1981).

*A Very Personal War* by James Hamilton-Patterson. Copyright © 1971 by James Hamilton-Patterson (London: Hodder and Stoughton, 1971).

*Dispatches* by Michael Herr. Copyright © 1977 by Michael Herr (New York: Alfred A. Knopf, 1977).

*The Military Half* by Jonathan Schell. Copyright © 1968 by Jonathan Schell (New York: Alfred A. Knopf, 1977).

*Decent Interval* by Frank Snepp. Copyright © 1977 by Frank Snepp (New York: Random House, 1977).

*The Lessons of Vietnam,* W. Scott Thompson and D. D. Frizzell, editors. Copyright © 1977 by Crane, Russak.

"Hunting," by W. D. Ehrhart, from *Carrying the Darkness: America in Indochina — The Poetry of the Vietnam War,* edited by W. D. Ehrhart (New York: Avon, 1985).

"The Fifty Gunner" by Frank A. Cross, Jr., from *Reminders* (Seven Buffaloes Press, Box 249, Big Timber, Montana 59011).

Every reasonable effort has been made to trace the ownership of copyrighted materials. Any omissions of acknowledgment are accidental and will be corrected in future editions if the publisher is notified.